THE DYNAMICS OF PERSUASION

THE DYNAMICS OF PERSUASION

Communication and Attitudes in the 21st Century

Second Edition

Richard M. Perloff
Cleveland State University

LEA LAWRENCE ERLBAUM ASSOCIATES, PUBLISHERS
2003 Mahwah, New Jersey   London

Acquisitions Editor: Linda Bathgate
Textbook Marketing Manager: Marisol Kozlovski
Editorial Assistant: Karin Bates
Cover Design: Marino Belich
Textbook Production Manager: Paul Smolenski
Full-Service & Composition: UG / GGS Information Services, Inc.
Text and Cover Printer: Hamilton Printing Company

This book was typeset in 10/12 pt. Palatino, Italic, Bold, and Bold Italic.
The heads were typeset in News Gothic Bold Condensed.

Photographs by William C. Rieter, with assistance provided by: Tanya Brown,
Frank Cucciarre, Stephen E. Cox, Dick Kraus, and Michael Robertson.

Lawrence Erlbaum Associates, Inc., Publishers
10 Industrial Avenue
Mahwah, New Jersey 07430

Visit www.dynamicsofpersuasion.com for additional text materials.

Library of Congress Cataloging-in-Publication Data

Perloff, Richard M.
   The dynamics of persuasion : communication and attitudes in the
21st century / Richard M. Perloff—2nd ed.
      p. cm.
   Includes bibliographical references and index.
   ISBN 0-8058-4087-7 (case alk. paper)—ISBN 0-8058-4088-5 (pbk alk. paper)
      1. Persuasion (Psychology) 2. Mass media—Psychological aspects. 3. Attitude
   change.
   I. Title

BF637.P4 .P39 2002   2002033865

Books published by Lawrence Erlbaum Associates are printed on acid-free paper,
and their bindings are chosen for strength and durability.

Printed in the United States of America
10 9 8 7 6 5 4 3 2

Brief Contents

Contents

Preface

Writing a second edition has different challenges and joys than preparing the first edition of a book. The second time around, one has the benefit of looking over the work one has done; a skeleton is in place. Initially, one also feels like an alter ego to one's self, worrying, wondering, and bemused, curious whether one's voice the second time around has changed, and daunted by the sheer volume of work that must be done.

In the end, though, it turned out to be very rewarding to write this book, as I realized that I had the opportunity to express the ideas that had been percolating in my mind since the first edition came out in 1993. I also had the chance to reflect, as best as I could, on changes that have occurred in the world and the academic study of persuasion since 1993. It was a challenging, stimulating opportunity, and I thank Lawrence Erlbaum Associates for giving me this shot at revising and modernizing *The Dynamics of Persuasion*.

Obviously, a great deal has happened in our world, from the events of September 11, 2001 to Bill Clinton's impeachment to O. J. Simpson. The Internet, not a force to be dealt with (persuasively speaking) in '93, is a major player in the media landscape today, as are multiple cultural and lifestyle changes that have implications for the study of persuasive communication. In academia, the major models that dominated the field in the early '90s are still dominant today. However, much research on attitudes, cognitive processing, fear appeals, advertising, and communication campaigns has been conducted, requiring a new book that incorporates the findings and their practical applications. I suppose I have changed as well. As one gets older, one is more attuned to the ways in which research fits into the giant trajectory of life—the big picture of society and human nature. Thus, the second edition places more emphasis on appreciating the role that theory and research play in persuasion as it occurs in American society, as well as on ethical implications of ideas and research.

The focus on theory, concepts, and basic research remains. The book is organized in generally the same way as the first edition. However, in an effort to modernize, reflect the field, and connect with readers, particularly students, I have done much rewriting—actually new writing. Although the format is similar and the skeleton of the '93 book remains, this is, in many ways, a new book, one that I hope will be useful and stimulating to students, professors, and other interested readers.

In an effort to incorporate the voluminous research on attitudes and persuasion that has been conducted over the past decade, I have expanded discussion of attitude structure, functions, and measurement. A chapter on attitude formation, which focused to a considerable degree on advertising, has been eliminated, and replaced with a chapter on advertising and persuasion (chapter 11). Social judgment theory, formerly discussed in an entire chapter, has been placed (more appropriately, I believe) in an early chapter on attitudes.

One of the most complex, but ultimately gratifying, tasks involved integrating theory with the everyday practice of persuasion. The first is heady, the second down-to-earth. Theory is abstract and full of possibilities; real life is limited, fraught with structures, institutions, and psychological systems that do not easily bend or wither in response to new ideas. Real life, which can be unforgiving, terribly sad, and cruel, can also be exhilarating and full of passion. It is ultimately the arena in which persuasion theories and research play out, and so I moved restlessly back and forth from theoretical abstractions to complex and messy everyday life. The new edition provides numerous examples of persuasion in action, ranging from the Clinton impeachment (chapter 2) to Nike's advertising (chapter 11) to ways to be a more effective persuader (chapters 5–7). It also emphasizes critical persuasion contexts, such as health and politics. As is my style, I discuss these issues in various chapters—not one place—as applications of theory and research.

The book emphasizes the basic simplicity and importance of persuasion, while also detailing its complex effects and multiple processes by which communications influence audiences. Thus, interactions among concepts and explanations as to why communications change attitudes receive a lot of discussion. Perhaps it would be nice if we could come up with simple answers to all persuasion's questions, but we cannot, and thus the job of a book writer is to summarize the complexities in an interesting way that intelligent people can appreciate. I hope I have succeeded in this goal.

Students will notice that I provide a lot of citations of others' research, using the conventional social science method (name, followed by the year the work was published). I have done this to give credit to scholars who pioneered ideas and conducted valuable research, and to provide a place for students to pursue ideas in more detail at a later point in time.

ACKNOWLEDGMENTS

Usually, writing acknowledgments is an entirely positive and pleasant experience. Unfortunately, several sad events occurred as I wrote this book. Two people who helped me over the years passed away. Jack Matthews, a professor of speech communication at the University of Pittsburgh, had faith in me when I entered the Master's program at Pitt in 1973. Jack was a friend who showed me that communication study could be a positive, intellectually interesting way to spend one's professional life. Steve Chaffee, with whom I worked as a graduate student at Wisconsin, was an affirming force, someone who believed in me, showed me that research was an invigorating, curiosity-quenching activity, and who always looked at problems in an interesting way. Their support motivated me, and their presence is missed.

And there were the thousands lost on September 11, as well as the men and women in the U.S. military who died, fighting for their country's beliefs, in Afghanistan, Central Asia, and elsewhere. As I finished the last chapters of the book in 2001 and 2002, I thought of them. News reports tell us that so many of those killed in the September attacks were pursuing individual dreams in their jobs that day, celebrating others' accomplishments, or trying to save somebody else's life. The values that underline their efforts—freedom, compassion, and tolerance—are the best values of persuasion. Thinking about September 11 and the ensuing war reminded me that persuasion, for all its shortcomings, deceptions, and rampant ethical abuses, remains, as Churchill might say, the worst form of social influence, except for all the others.

This having been said, I can now gratefully acknowledge many individuals. Thanks to the library staff at Cleveland State University. I also appreciate assistance provided by the people at John Carroll University's Grasselli Library, as well as employees of the nearby Shaker Heights Arabica Coffee Shop, especially Michael Feher. The latter's solicitude, coffee, and tea provided needed motivation on many mornings and afternoons. I also appreciate the capable and extraordinarily skillful word processing of Sharon J. Muskin, who did yeoman's work in giving the chapters and figures a professional appearance.

I also want to thank Linda Bathgate, my editor from Lawrence Erlbaum Associates, whose faith and many warm comments sustained me throughout the writing of the book.

In addition, I am grateful to the many fine undergraduate and graduate students from my persuasion classes who have provided enjoyable and enriching class discussions.

A number of colleagues read over chapters and offered good ideas. I appreciate comments or assistance offered by Julie Andsager, Mike Allen,

Erica Weintraub Austin, Jack Baseheart, Brant R. Burleson, Shelly Campo, Fiona Chew, Craig A. Dudczak, Russell H. Fazio, Martin Greenberg, Eddie Harmon-Jones, William Harpine, Jenifer Kopfman, Jon A. Krosnick, James C. McCroskey, Michael Pfau, William K. Price, Andrew S. Rancer, David Roskos-Ewoldsen, Mark Snyder, Pradeep Sopory, and Julia A. Spiker. I also appreciated the thoughtful comments of Roknedin Safavi.

Finally, as always, I thank my family for their abiding love and support.

—Richard M. Perloff

PART 1

Foundations

CHAPTER 1

Introduction to Persuasion

When someone mentions persuasion, what comes to mind? Powerful, charismatic leaders? Subliminal ads? News? Lawyers? Presidential campaigns? Or the Internet perhaps, with those innumerable Web sites shamelessly promoting products and companies? That's persuasion, right? Powerful stuff—the kind of thing that has strong effects on society and spells profit for companies. But what about you? What does persuasion mean to you personally? Can you think of times when the media or attractive communicators changed your mind about something? Anything come to mind? Not really, you say. You've got the canny ability to see through what other people are trying to sell you.

Well, that's perhaps what we like to think. It's everyone else who's influenced, not me or my friends—well maybe my friends, but not me. But wait: What about those Tommy Hilfiger jeans, Gap sweaters, or Nike sneakers you bought? Advertising had to play a role in that decision somehow. And if you search your mind, you probably can think of times when you yielded to another's pushy persuasion, only to regret it later—the time you let yourself get talked into doing a car repair that turned out to be unnecessary or agreed to loan a friend some money, only to discover she had no intention of ever paying you back.

But that's all negative. What of the positive side? Have you ever been helped by a persuasive communication—an antismoking ad or a reminder that it's not cool or safe to drink when you drive? Have you ever had a conversation with a friend who opened your eyes to new ways of seeing the world or with a teacher who said you had potential you didn't know you had?

You see, this is persuasion too. Just about anything that involves molding or shaping attitudes involves persuasion. Now there's another term that may seem foreign at first: attitudes. Attitudes? There once was a rock group that called itself that. But we've got attitudes as surely as we

have arms, legs, cell phones, or personal computers. We have attitudes
toward college, and about music, money, sex, race, even God. We don't
all share the same attitudes, and you may not care a whit about issues
that intrigue your acquaintances. But we have attitudes and they shape
our world in ways we don't always recognize. Persuasion is the study of
attitudes and how to change them.

Persuasion calls to mind images of salespeople and con artists—selfish
strategists like Richard Hatch, the guy on *Survivor* everyone loved to
hate. But there is another side too: Persuasive communications have been
used by good people to implement change. Social activists have used
persuasion to change attitudes toward minorities and women. Consumer
advocates have tirelessly warned people about dishonest business practices. Health communicators have launched countless campaigns to
change people's thinking about cigarettes, alcohol, drugs, and unsafe sex.
Politicians (for example, American presidents) have relied on persuasion
when attempting to influence opinions toward policy issues, or when trying to rally the country behind them during national crises. Some of our
greatest leaders have been expert persuaders—Thomas Jefferson, Martin
Luther King, and Franklin D. Roosevelt come immediately to mind—as
do the crop of current political persuaders, working in the thicket of the
media age.

This book is about all these issues. It is about persuasive communication and the dynamics of attitudes communicators hope to change. The
text also examines applications of persuasion theories to a host of contexts, ranging from advertising to politics to physical health. On a more
personal note, I try to show how you can use persuasion insights to
become a more effective persuasive speaker and a more critical judge of
social influence attempts.

PERSUASION: CONSTANCIES AND CHANGES

The study and practice of persuasion are not new. Persuasion can be
found in the Old Testament—for example, in Jeremiah's attempts to convince his people to repent and establish a personal relationship with God.
We come across persuasion when we read about John the Baptist's exhor-
tations for Christ. John traveled the countryside, acting as Christ's advance man, preaching "Christ is coming, wait till you see him, when you
look in his eyes you'll know that you've met Christ the Lord" (Whalen,
1996, p. 110).

Long before professional persuaders hoped to turn a profit from books
on closing a deal, traveling educators known as the Sophists paraded
through ancient Greece, charging money for lectures on public speaking

and the art of political eloquence. Five centuries before political consultants advised presidential candidates how to package themselves on television, the Italian diplomat Niccolo Machiavelli rocked the Renaissance world with his how-to manual for political persuaders, entitled *The Prince*. Machiavelli believed in politics and respected crafty political leaders. He offered a litany of suggestions for how politicians could maintain power through cunning and deception.

In the United States, where persuasion has played such a large role in politics and society as a whole, we find that communication campaigns are as American as media-advertised apple pie. The first crusade to change health behavior did not occur in 1970 or 1870, but in 1820. Nineteenth-century reformers expressed concern about increases in binge drinking and pushed for abstinence from alcohol. A few years later, activists committed to clean living tried to persuade Americans to quit using tobacco, exercise more, and adopt a vegetarian diet that included wheat bread, grains, fruits, and vegetables (Engs, 2000).

As they say in France: Plus ça change, plus c'est la même chose (the more things change, the more they remain the same). And yet, for all the similarities, there are important differences between our era of persuasion and those that preceded it. Each epoch has its own character, feeling, and rhythm. Contemporary persuasion differs from the past in these five ways:

1. *The sheer number of persuasive communications has grown exponentially.* Advertising, public service announcements, Internet banner ads, and those daily interruptions from telephone marketers are among the most salient indicators of this trend. Eons ago, prior to the development of broadcasting and the Internet, you could go through a day with preciously little exposure to impersonal persuasive messages. That is no longer true. And it's not just Americans who are besieged by persuasion. The reach of mass persuasion extends to tiny villages thousands of miles away. A U.S. college student traveling in remote areas of China reported that, while stranded by winter weather, he came across a group of Tibetans. After sharing their food with the student, the Tibetans began to discuss an issue that touched on matters American. "Just how, one of the Tibetans asked the young American, was Michael Jordan doing?" (LaFeber, 1999, p. 14).

2. *Persuasive messages travel faster than ever before.* Advertisements "move blindingly fast," one writer observes (Moore, 1993, p. B1). Ads quickly and seamlessly combine cultural celebrities (Michael Jordan), symbols (success, fame, and athletic prowess), and commodity signs (the Nike swoosh). With a mouse click, political and marketing campaign specialists can send a communique across the world. Case in point: MP3.com. The online music company launched an e-mail campaign to support legislation

that would allow people to store music digitally and access songs on the Internet from any location. Supporters simply had to locate MP3.com's Web site, click onto "Million Email March," type in their name and e-mail address, and punch the "Send" button. This instantly transmitted a message in support of the bill to members of Congress.

3. *Persuasion has become institutionalized.* No longer can a Thomas Jefferson dash off a Declaration of Independence. In the 21st century the Declaration would be edited by committees, test-marketed in typical American communities, and checked with standards departments to make sure it did not offend potential constituents.

Numerous companies are in the persuasion business. Advertising agencies, public relations firms, marketing conglomerates, lobbying groups, social activists, pollsters, speech writers, image consultants—companies big and small—are involved with various facets of persuasion. The list is long and continues to grow.

4. *Persuasive communication has become more subtle and devious.* We are long past the days in which brash salespeople knocked on your door to directly pitch encyclopedias or hawk Avon cosmetics. Nowadays, salespeople know all about flattery, empathy, nonverbal communication, and likability appeals. Walk into a Nordstrom clothing store and you see a fashionably dressed man playing a piano. Nordstrom wants you to feel like you're in a special, elite place, one that not so incidentally sells brands of clothing that jibe with this image.

Advertising no longer relies only on hard-sell, "hammer it home" appeals, but also on soft-sell messages that play on emotions. A few years back, the Benetton clothing company showed attention-grabbing pictures of a dying AIDS patient and a desperately poor Third World girl holding a White doll from a trash can. The pictures appeared with the tag line, "United Colors of Benetton." What do these images have to do with clothing? Nothing—and everything. Benetton was selling an image, not a product. It appealed to consumers' higher sensibilities, inviting them to recognize that "the world we live in is not neatly packaged and cleansed as most ads depict it . . . at Benetton we are not like others, we have vision." (Goldman & Papson, 1996, p. 52).

5. *Persuasive communication is more complex than ever before.* Once upon a time, persuaders knew their clients because everyone lived in the same small communities. When cities developed and industrialization spread, persuaders knew fewer of their customers, but could be reasonably confident they understood their clients because they all shared the same cultural and ethnic background. As the United States has become more culturally and racially diverse, persuaders and consumers frequently come from different sociological places. A marketer can't assume that her client thinks the same way she does or approaches a communication

encounter with the same assumptions. The intermingling of people from different cultural groups is a profoundly positive phenomenon, but it makes for more dicey and difficult interpersonal persuasion.

At the same time, attitudes—the stuff of persuasion—are ever more complex. Living in a media society in a time of globalization, we have attitudes toward more topics than before, including people and places we have never encountered directly. Few people have met Bill Gates, but many people have opinions about him. We may have attitudes toward global warming or capital punishment or how the news media covered these topics. Some of us may have strong opinions about the media itself, or about how the media changed the minds of people we have never met.

FOUNDATIONS OF PERSUASION

Persuasion is celebrated as a quintessential human activity, but here's a subversive thought: Suppose we're not the only ones who do it? What if our friends in the higher animal kingdom also use a little homespun social influence? Frans de Waal (1982) painstakingly observed chimpanzees in a Dutch zoo and chronicled his observations in a book aptly called *Chimpanzee Politics*. His conclusion: Chimps use all sorts of techniques to get their way with peers. They frequently resort to violence, but not always. Chimps form coalitions, bluff each other, and even show some awareness of social reciprocity, as they seem to recognize that favors should be rewarded and disobedience punished.

Does this mean that chimpanzees are capable of persuasion? Some scientists would answer "Yes" and cite as evidence chimps' subtle techniques to secure power. Indeed, there is growing evidence that apes can form images and use symbols (Miles, 1993). To some scientists, the difference between human and animal persuasion is one of degree, not kind.

Wait a minute. Do we really think that chimpanzees *persuade* their peers? Perhaps they persuade in the *Godfather* sense of making people an offer they can't refuse. However, this is not persuasion so much as coercion. As we will see, persuasion involves the persuader's awareness that he or she is trying to influence someone else. It also requires that the persuadee make a conscious or unconscious decision to change his mind about something. With this definition in mind, chimpanzees' behavior is better described as social influence or coercion than persuasion.

Okay, you animal lovers say, but let me tell you about my cat. "She sits sweetly in her favorite spot on my sofa when I return from school," one feline-loving student suggested to me, "then curls up in my arms, and purrs softly until I go to the kitchen and fetch her some milk. Isn't that persuasion?" Well—no. Your cat may be trying to curry your favor, but she has not performed an act of persuasion. The cat is not cognizant that she is trying to "influence" you. What's more, she does not appreciate that you have a mental state—let alone a belief—that she wants to change.

Nonetheless, the fact that we can talk intelligently about feline (and particularly, chimpanzee) social influence points up the complexities of persuasion. Research on chimpanzee politics forces us to recognize that persuasion has probably evolved through natural selection and helped humans solve many practical dilemmas. Persuasion undoubtedly helped early homo sapiens solve adaptive problems such as pacifying potential enemies and enlisting help from friends. In short: Persuasion matters and strikes to the core of our lives as human beings. This means we must define what we mean by persuasion and differentiate it from related terms.

Defining Persuasion

Scholars have defined persuasion in different ways. I list the following major definitions to show you how different researchers approach the topic. Persuasion, according to communication scholars, is:

- a communication process in which the communicator seeks to elicit a desired response from his receiver (Andersen, 1971, p. 6);
- a conscious attempt by one individual to change the attitudes, beliefs, or behavior of another individual or group of individuals through the transmission of some message (Bettinghaus & Cody, 1987, p. 3);
- a symbolic activity whose purpose is to effect the internalization or voluntary acceptance of new cognitive states or patterns of overt behavior through the exchange of messages (Smith, 1982, p. 7);
- a successful intentional effort at influencing another's mental state through communication in a circumstance in which the persuadee has some measure of freedom (O'Keefe, 1990, p. 17).

All of these definitions have strengths. Boiling down the main components into one unified perspective (and adding a little of my own recipe), I define persuasion as **a symbolic process in which communicators try to convince other people to change their attitudes or behavior regarding an issue through the transmission of a message, in an atmosphere of free choice**. There are five components of the definition.

1. *Persuasion is a symbolic process.* Contrary to popular opinion, persuasion does not happen with the flick of a switch. You don't just change people's minds, snap, crackle, and pop. On the contrary, persuasion takes time, consists of a number of steps, and actively involves the recipient of

the message. As Mark Twain quipped, "habit is habit, and not to be flung out of the window, but coaxed downstairs a step at a time" (cited in Prochaska et al., 1994, p. 47).

Many of us view persuasion in John Wayne, macho terms. Persuaders are seen as tough-talking salespeople, strongly stating their position, hitting people over the head with arguments, and pushing the deal to a close. But this oversimplifies matters. It assumes that persuasion is a boxing match, won by the fiercest competitor. In fact persuasion is different. It's more like teaching than boxing. Think of a persuader as a teacher, moving people step by step to a solution, helping them appreciate why the advocated position solves the problem best.

Persuasion also involves the use of symbols, with messages transmitted primarily through language with its rich, cultural meanings. Symbols include words like freedom, justice, and equality; nonverbal signs like the flag, Star of David, or Holy Cross; and images that are instantly recognized and processed like the Nike Swoosh or McDonald's Golden Arches. Symbols are persuaders' tools, harnessed to change attitudes and mold opinions.

2. *Persuasion involves an attempt to influence.* Persuasion does not automatically or inevitably succeed. Like companies that go out of business soon after they open, persuasive communications often fail to reach or influence their targets. However, persuasion does involve a deliberate attempt to influence another person. The persuader must intend to change another individual's attitude or behavior, and must be aware (at least at some level) that she is trying to accomplish this goal.

For this reason it does not make sense to say that chimpanzees persuade each other. As noted earlier, chimps, smart as they are, do not seem to possess high-level awareness that they are trying to change another primate, let alone modify a fellow chimp's mind.

In a similar fashion, it pushes the envelope to say that very young children are capable of persuasion. True, a mother responds to an infant's cry for milk by dashing to the refrigerator (or lending her breast, if that's her feeding preference). Yes, we have all shopped in toy stores and watched as 2-year-olds point to toys seen on television and scream "I want that." And we have been witness to the pitiful sight of parents, who pride themselves on being competent professionals, helplessly yielding to prevent any further embarrassment.

Yet the baby's cry for milk and the toddler's demand for toys do not qualify as persuasion. These youngsters have not reached the point where they are aware that they are trying to change another person's mental state. Their actions are better described as coercive social influence than persuasion. In order for children to practice persuasion, they must understand that other people can have desires and beliefs, recognize that the persuadee has a mental state that is susceptible to change, demonstrate a primitive awareness that they intend to influence another person, and realize that the persuadee has a different perspective than they do, even if they cannot put all this into words (Bartsch & London, 2000). As children grow, they appreciate these things, rely less on coercive social influence attempts than on persuasion, and develop the ability to persuade others more effectively (Kline & Clinton, 1998).

The main point here is that persuasion represents a conscious attempt to influence the other party, along with an accompanying awareness that the persuadee has a mental state that is susceptible to change. It is a type of social influence. Social influence is the broad process in which the behavior of one person alters the thoughts or actions of another. Social influence can occur when receivers act on cues or messages that were not necessarily intended for their consumption (Dudczak, 2001). Persuasion occurs within a context of intentional messages that are initiated by a communicator in hopes of influencing the recipient. This is pretty heady stuff, but it is important because if you include every possible influence attempt under the persuasion heading, you count every communication as persuasion. That would make for a very long book.

3. *People persuade themselves.* One of the great myths of persuasion is that persuaders convince us to do things we really don't want to do. They supposedly overwhelm us with so many arguments or such verbal ammunition that we acquiesce. They force us to give in.

This overlooks an important point: People persuade themselves to change attitudes or behavior. Communicators provide the arguments. They set up the bait. We make the change, or refuse to yield. As D. Joel Whalen (1996) puts it:

> You can't force people to be persuaded—you can only activate their desire and show them the logic behind your ideas. You can't move a string by pushing it, you have to pull it. People are the same. Their devotion and total commitment to an idea come only when they fully understand and buy in with their total being. (p. 5)

You can understand the power of self-persuasion by considering an activity that does not at first blush seem to involve persuasive communication: therapy. Therapists undoubtedly help people make changes in their lives. But have you ever heard someone say, "My therapist persuaded me"? On the contrary, people who seek psychological help look into themselves, consider what ails them, and decide how best to cope. The therapist offers suggestions and provides an environment in which healing can take place (Kassan, 1999). But if progress occurs, it is the client who makes the change—and it is the client who is responsible for making sure that she does not revert back to the old ways of doing things.

Of course, not every self-persuasion is therapeutic. Self-persuasion can be benevolent or malevolent. An ethical communicator will plant the seeds for healthy self-influence. A dishonest, evil persuader convinces a person to change her mind in a way that is personally or socially destructive.

Note also that persuasion typically involves change. It does not focus on forming attitudes, but on inducing people to alter attitudes they already possess. This can involve shaping, molding, or reinforcing attitudes, as is discussed later in the chapter.

4. *Persuasion involves the transmission of a message.* The message may be verbal or nonverbal. It can be relayed interpersonally, through mass media, or via the Internet. It may be reasonable or unreasonable, factual or emotional. The message can consist of arguments or simple cues, like music in an advertisement that brings pleasant memories to mind.

Persuasion is a communicative activity; thus, there must be a message for persuasion, as opposed to other forms of social influence, to occur.

Life is packed with messages that change or influence attitudes. In addition to the usual contexts that come to mind when you think of persuasion—advertising, political campaigns, and interpersonal sales—there are other domains that contain attitude-altering messages. News unquestionably shapes attitudes and beliefs (McCombs and Reynolds, 2002). Talk to older Americans who watched TV coverage of White policemen beating up Blacks in the South or chat with people who viewed television coverage of the Vietnam War, and you will gain firsthand evidence of how television news can shake up people's world views. News of more recent events—the Challenger disaster, the Clinton impeachment, and, of course, September 11—has left indelible impressions on people's views of politics and America.

Art—books, movies, plays, and songs—also has a strong influence on how we think and feel about life. Artistic portrayals can transport people into different realities, changing the way they see life (Green & Brock, 2000). If you think for a moment, I'm sure you can call to mind books, movies, and songs that shook you up and pushed you to rethink your assumptions. Dostoyevsky's discussions of the human condition, a Picasso painting, Spike Lee's portrayals of race in *Do the Right Thing*, *The Simpsons* television show, a folk melody or rap song—these all can influence and change people's worldviews.

Yet although news and art contain messages that change attitudes, they are not pure exemplars of persuasion. Recall that persuasion is defined as an attempt to convince others to change their attitudes or behavior. In many cases, journalists are not trying to *change* people's attitudes toward a topic. They are describing events to provide people with information, to offer new perspectives, or entice viewers to watch their programs. In the same fashion, most artists do not create art to change the world. They write, paint, or compose songs to express important personal concerns, articulate vexing problems of life, or to soothe, uplift, or agitate people. In a sense, it demeans art to claim that artists attempt only to change our attitudes. Thus, art and news are best viewed as borderline cases of persuasion. Their messages can powerfully influence our worldviews, but because the intent of these communicators is broader and more complex than attitude change, news and art are best viewed as lying along the border of persuasion and the large domain of social influence.

5. *Persuasion requires free choice.* If, as noted earlier, self-persuasion is the key to successful influence, then an individual must be free to alter his own behavior or to do what he wishes in a communication setting. But what does it mean to be free? Philosophers have debated this question for centuries, and if you took a philosophy course, you may recall those famous debates about free will verus determinism.

There are more than 200 definitions of freedom, and, as we will see, it's hard to say precisely when coercion ends and persuasion begins. I suggest that a person is free when he has the ability to act otherwise—to do other than what the persuader suggests—or to reflect critically on his choices in a situation (Smythe, 1999).

I have defined persuasion and identified its main features. But this tells us only half the story. To appreciate persuasion, you have to understand what it is not—that is, how it differs from related ideas.

Persuasion Versus Coercion

How does persuasion differ from coercion? The answer may seem simple at first. Persuasion deals with reason and verbal appeals, while coercion employs force, you suggest. It's not a bad start, but there are subtle relationships between the terms—fascinating overlaps—that you might not ordinarily think of. Consider these scenarios:

- Tom works for a social service agency that receives some of its funding from United Way. At the end of each year, United Way asks employees to contribute to the charity. Tom would like to donate, but he needs every penny of his salary to support his family. One year, his boss, Anne, sends out a memo strongly urging employees to give to United Way. Anne doesn't threaten, but the implicit message is: I expect you to donate, and I'll know who did and who didn't. Tom opts to contribute money to United Way. Was he coerced or persuaded?

- Debbie, a college senior, makes an appointment with her favorite English professor, Dr. Stanley Hayes, to get advice on where to apply for graduate school. Hayes compliments Debbie on her writing style, tells her she is one of the best students he has had in 20 years of teaching, and reflects back on his own experiences as a youthful graduate student in American literature. The two chat for a bit, and Hayes asks if she wouldn't mind dropping by his house for dessert and coffee to discuss this further. "Evening's best for me," Hayes adds. Debbie respects Professor Hayes and knows she needs his recommendation for graduate school, but she wonders about his intentions. She accepts the offer. Was she persuaded or coerced?
- Elizabeth, a high school junior, has been a football fan since grade school and throughout middle school. Waiting eagerly for the homecoming game to start, she glances at the field, catching a glimpse of the senior class president as he strides out to the 50-yard line. Much to her surprise, the class president asks the crowd to stand and join him in prayer. Elizabeth is squeamish. She is not religious and suspects she's an atheist. She notices that everyone around her is standing, nodding their heads, and reciting the Lord's Prayer. She glances to her left and sees four popular girls shooting nasty looks at her and shaking their heads. Without thinking, Elizabeth rises and nervously begins to speak the words herself. Was she coerced or persuaded?

Before we can answer these questions, we must know what is meant by coercion. Philosophers define coercion as *a technique for forcing people to act as the coercer wants them to act, and presumably contrary to their preferences. It usually employs a threat of some dire consequence if the actor does not do what the coercer demands* (Feinberg, 1998, p. 387). Tom's boss, Debbie's professor, and Elizabeth's classmates pushed them to act in ways that were contrary to their preferences. The communicators employed a direct or veiled threat. It appears that they employed coercion.

Things get murkier when you look at scholarly definitions that compare coercion with persuasion. Mary J. Smith (1982) takes a relativist perspective, emphasizing the role of perception. According to this view, it's all a matter of how people perceive things. Smith argues that when people believe that they are free to reject the communicator's position, as a practical matter they are free, and the influence attempt falls under the persuasion umbrella. When individuals perceive that they have no choice but to comply, the influence attempt is better viewed as coercive.

Assume now that Tom, Debbie, and Elizabeth are all confident, strongminded individuals. Tom feels that he can say no to his employer. Debbie, undaunted by Professor Hayes's flirtatiousness, believes she is capable of rejecting his overtures. Elizabeth feels she is free to do as she pleases at the football game. In this case, we would say that the influence agents persuaded the students to comply.

On the other hand, suppose Tom, Debbie, and Elizabeth lack confidence in themselves and don't believe that they can resist these communicators. In this case, we might say that these individuals perceived that they had little choice but to comply. We would conclude that coercion, not persuasion, had occurred.

You see how difficult it is to differentiate persuasion and coercion. Scholars differ on where they draw the line between the two terms. Some would say that the three influence agents used a little bit of both. (My own view is that the first case is the clearest instance of coercion. The communicator employed a veiled threat. What's more, Tom's boss wielded power over him, leading to the reasonable perception that Tom had little choice but to comply. The other two scenarios are more ambiguous, arguably more persuasion because most people would probably assume they could resist communicators' appeals; in addition, no direct threats of any kind were employed in these cases.) More generally, the point to remember here is that persuasion and coercion are not polar opposites, but overlapping concepts. (See Fig. 1.1 and Box 1–1: The Cult of Persuasion.)

Underscoring this point, there are instances in which coercive acts have changed attitudes, and persuasive communications have influenced coercive institutions. The terrible—unquestionably coercive—attacks on the World Trade Center and Pentagon in 2001 produced major shifts in public attitudes. Americans suddenly became much more supportive of drastic military action to prevent terrorism, even tolerating restrictions in personal freedoms to keep the country safe from terrorists (Berke & Elder, 2001). The attacks also changed attitudes toward airport safety, induced mistrust of strangers encountered in public places, and led some to reassess their entire perspective on life.

At the same time, persuasive communications—such as radio communications attempting to rally the Afghan people against terrorist Osama bin Laden in 2001 or the old Radio Free Europe anticommunist messages of the 1950s through '80s—can help influence or bring down coercive

Coercion _____ Persuasion

      Nature of Psychological Threat
      Ability to Do Otherwise
      Perception of Free Choice

Coercion and persuasion are not polar opposites. They are better viewed as lying along a continuum of social influence.

FIG. 1.1 Coercion and persuasion.

BOX 1–1
THE CULT OF PERSUASION

The story broke in late March 1997. By then it was too late to save any of the 39 desperate souls who committed suicide. All one could do was to ask why 39 intelligent, committed men and women—stalwart members of the Heaven's Gate cult—willingly took their own lives, joyfully announcing their decision in a farewell videotape and statement on their Web site. The suicide was timed to coincide with the arrival of the Hale–Bopp comet. Believing that a flying saucer was traveling behind the comet, members chose to leave their bodies behind to gain redemption in a Kingdom of Heaven (Robinson, 1998).

To many people, this provided yet another example of the powerful, but mysterious, technique called brainwashing. The cult leader, Marshall Applewhite, known to his followers as "Do," supposedly brainwashed cult members into committing mass suicide in their home in Rancho Santa Fe, California. Although Heaven's Gate was the first Internet cult tragedy, one that drove millions of curiosity seekers to the group's Web site, it was only the most recent in a series of bizarre cult occurrences that observers could describe only as brainwashing. In one of the most famous of these tragic tales, over 900 members of the People's Temple followed leader Jim Jones' directive to drink cyanide-spiked Kool-Aid at the cult's home in Guyana, South America back in 1978. Other cases, including the violent story of David Koresh's Branch Davidians in Waco, Texas (circa 1993), continue to fascinate and disturb. Searching for a simple answer, people assume that charismatic leaders *brainwash* followers into submission.

Famous though it may be, brainwashing is not a satisfactory explanation for what happens in cults. It does not tell us why ordinary people choose to join and actively participate in cults. It does not explain how leaders wield influence or are able to induce followers to engage in self-destructive behavior. Instead, the brainwashing term condemns people and points fingers.

How can we explain the cult phenomenon? First, we need to define a cult. A cult is a group of individuals who are: (a) excessively devoted to a particular leader or system of beliefs, (b) effectively isolated from the rest of the world, and (c) denied access to alternative points of view. To appreciate how cults influence individuals, we need to consider the dynamics of persuasion and coercion. As an example, consider the case of one young person who fell into the Heaven's Gate cult and, by crook or the hook of social influence, could not get out. Her name was Gail Maeder, and she was one of the unlucky 39 who ended her life on that unhappy March day.

Gail, a soft-hearted soul, adored animals. The lanky 27-year-old also loved trees, so much so that she tried not to use much paper. Searching for something—maybe adventure, possibly herself—she left suburban New York for California. Traveling again, this time in the Southwest, she met

Continued

BOX 1–1
CONTINUED

some friendly folks in a van—members of Heaven's Gate, it turns out. Gail joined the group and told her parents not to worry. She was very happy.

If you look at Gail's picture in *People*, taken when she was 14, you see a bubbly All-American girl with braces, smiling as her brother touches her affectionately (Hewitt et al., 1997). Your heart breaks when you see the photo, knowing what will happen when she becomes an adult.

People join cults—or sects, the less pejorative term—for many reasons. They are lonely and confused, and the cult provides a loving home. Simple religious answers beckon and offer a reason for living. Isolated from parents and friends, young people come to depend more on the cult for social rewards. The cult leader is charismatic and claims to have supernatural powers. He gains followers' trust and devotion. Purposelessness is relieved; order replaces chaos. The more people participate in the group's activities, the better they feel; the better they feel, the more committed they become; and the more committed they are, the more difficult it is to leave.

Initially, cult leaders employ persuasive appeals. Over time they rely increasingly on coercive techniques. Heaven's Gate leaders told followers that they must learn to deny their desires and defer to the group. At Heaven's Gate, it was considered an infraction if members put themselves first, expressed too much curiosity, showed sexual attraction, trusted their own judgment, or had private thoughts. Everyone woke at the same time to pray, ate the same food, wore short haircuts and nondescript clothing, and sported identical wedding rings on their fingers to symbolize marriage to each other. Individual identity was replaced by group identity. Autonomy gave way, slowly replaced by the peacefulness of groupthink (Goodstein, 1997).

Once this happens—and it occurs slowly—cult members no longer have free choice; they are psychologically unable to say no to leaders' demands. Coercion replaces persuasion. Conformity overtakes dissent. Persuasion and coercion coexist, shading into one another. Simple demarcations are hard to make.

Gail Maeder wasn't street smart, her father said. "She just got sucked in and couldn't get out" (Hewitt et al., p. 47).

Events like Heaven's Gate are deeply troubling. It is comforting to affix blame on charismatic cult leaders like Applewhite. It is easy to say that they brainwashed people into submission. But this ignores the powerful role that coercive social influence and persuasive communication play in cults. And it tragically underplays the psychological needs of people like Gail, folks who persuaded themselves that a doomsday cult provided the answer to their problems.

It would be a happy ending if Heaven's Gate were the last cult that exploited individuals' vulnerabilities. However, in recent years, we have witnessed the growth of a more violent sect: an international terrorist cult composed of men who are zealous devotees of Osama bin Laden, and are convinced that America is the enemy of Islam and are willing to kill innocent people, particularly Americans and Jews, if directed by bin Laden or their *maulanas*, or masters (Goldberg, 2000). It is tempting to view these individuals as victims of terrorist brainwashing—automatons directed into action by receipt of an e-mail message. Once again, the brainwashing metaphor simplifies and distorts. These individuals have frequently joined Muslim religious schools out of their own volition. Bereft of meaning and purpose in a changing world, unable to see that their own nation-states have failed to provide them with a decent set of values, desperately grasping for a way to find an outlet to express decades-long simmering hate, they join terrorist cells, and are groomed, influenced, even coerced by "teachers" and assorted leaders of an international political-religious cult (Zakaria, 2001).

"These are poor and impressionable boys kept entirely ignorant of the world and, for that matter, largely ignorant of all but one interpretation of Islam," notes reporter Jeffrey Goldberg (2000, p. 71). "They are the perfect jihad machines."

regimes, such as Afghanistan or the old Soviet Union. These examples, emotion-packed as they are, speak to the powerful influences both persuasion and coercion have in everyday life, and the complex relationships between persuasion and coercive social influence (see Fig. 1.2).

The Bad Boy of Persuasion

One other term frequently comes up when persuasion is discussed—propaganda. Propaganda overlaps with persuasion, as both are invoked to describe powerful instances of social influence. However, there are three differences between the terms.

First, propaganda is typically invoked to describe mass influence through mass media. Persuasion, by contrast, occurs in mediated settings, but also in interpersonal and organizational contexts. Second, propaganda refers to instances in which a group has total control over the transmission of information, as with Hitler in Nazi Germany, the Chinese Communists during the Chinese Revolution, Saddam Hussein in Iraq, and in violent religious cults. Persuasion can be slanted and one-sided, but it ordinarily allows for a free flow of information; in persuasion situations, people can ordinarily question the persuader or offer contrasting opinions.

A third difference lies in the connotation or meaning of the terms. Propaganda has a negative connotation; it is associated with bad things or evil forces. Persuasion, by contrast, is viewed as a more positive force, one that can produce beneficial outcomes. Subjectively, we use the term

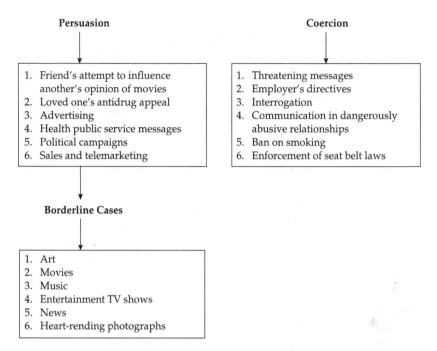

FIG. 1.2. Understanding persuasion, coercion, and borderline cases of persuasion. Note that coercion can be negative or positive (as in smoking bans and enforcement of seat belt laws). Borderline cases focus on persuasion rather than coercion. They lie just outside the boundary of persuasion because the intent of the communicator is not to explicitly change an individual's attitude toward the issue, but is, instead, broader and more complex (see also Gass & Seiter, 1999).

propaganda to refer to *a persuasive communication with which one disagrees and to which the individual attributes hostile intent.* Liberals claim that the news is unadulterated propaganda for Republicans; conservatives contend that the news is propaganda for the Left. Both use the propaganda term to disparage the news.

When you hear people call a persuasive communication *propaganda,* beware. The speakers are using language to denounce a message with which they disagree.

Understanding Persuasive Communication Effects

The discussion thus far has emphasized the differences between persuasion and related terms. However, there are different kinds of persuasive communications, and they have different types of effects. Some messages dramatically influence attitudes; others exert smaller or more subtle impacts. Taking note of this, Miller (1980) proposed that communications exert three different persuasive effects: shaping, reinforcing, and changing responses.

Shaping.   Today everyone has heard of the Nike Swoosh. You've seen it on hundreds of ads and on the clothing of celebrity athletes. It's a symbol that resonates and has helped make Nike a leader in the athletic shoe business. The now-classic ad campaigns featuring Michael Jordan and Bo Jackson helped mold attitudes toward Nike by linking Nike with movement, speed, and superhuman athletic achievement.

A nastier example is cigarette marketing. Tobacco companies spend millions to shape people's attitudes toward cigarettes, hoping they can entice young people to take a pleasurable, but deadly, puff. Marketers shape attitudes by associating cigarettes with beautiful women and virile men. They appeal to teenage girls searching for a way to rebel against boyfriends or parents by suggesting that smoking can make them appear defiant and strong willed. ("I always take the driver's seat. That way I'm never taken for a ride," says one Virginia Slims ad.)

Reinforcing.   Contrary to popular opinion, many persuasive communications are not designed to convert people, but to reinforce a position they already hold. As discussed in chapter 2, people have strong attitudes toward a variety of topics, and these attitudes are hard to change. Thus, persuaders try to join 'em, not beat 'em.

In political campaigns, candidates try to bolster party supporters' commitment to their cause. Democratic standard-bearers like Al Gore have made late-campaign appeals to African American voters, the overwhelming majority of whom are registered Democrats. Messages offer additional reasons why these voters should expend the effort to vote Democratic on Election Day. Republican candidates do the same, using media to remind their key supporters that they should vote Republican on the first Tuesday in November.

In a similar fashion, health education experts attempt to strengthen people's resolve to maintain their decision to quit smoking or to abstain from drinking in excess. Persuaders recognize that people can easily relapse under stress, and they design messages to help individuals maintain their commitment to give up unhealthy substances.

Changing.   This is perhaps the most important persuasive impact and the one that comes most frequently to mind when we think of persuasion. Communications can and do change attitudes. Just think how far this country has come in the last 50 years on the subject of race. In the 1950s and '60s, Blacks were lynched for being in the wrong place at the wrong time, many southerners openly opposed school desegregation, and northern Whites steered clear of socializing with Black friends or colleagues. This changed as civil rights campaigns, heart-rending media stories, and increased dialogue between Blacks and Whites led Whites to rethink their prejudiced attitudes toward African Americans (Thernstrom & Thernstrom, 1997). Attitudes have changed on other topics too—sex roles, the environment, fatty fast food, and exercise. Persuasive communications have had strong and desirable effects. They can influence attitudes and social behavior.

HISTORICAL REVIEW
OF PERSUASION SCHOLARSHIP

It is now time to put persuasion scholarship in perspective. It's not a new field—not by a long shot. The area has a long, distinguished history, dating back to ancient Greece. This section reviews the history of persuasion scholarship, offering an overview of major trends and the distinctive features of contemporary research on persuasion.

You may wonder why I review ancient history. There are many reasons, but here are two. Historical overviews help us appreciate the origins of ideas. They remind us that we are not the first to ponder persuasion, nor the first to wrestle with persuasion dilemmas. Second, an historical approach helps us see continuities from present to past to future. It helps us take note of what is unique about our era—and how today's scholarship builds on the shoulders of giants.

Ancient Greece: "It's All Sophos to Me"

"If any one group of people could be said to have invented rhetoric," James L. Golden and his colleagues note, "it would be the ancient Greeks" (Golden, Berquist, & Coleman, 2000, p. 1). The Greeks loved public speech. Trophies were awarded for skill in oratory. Citizens frequently acted as prosecutor and defense attorney in lawsuits that were daily occurrences in the Athenian city-state (Golden et al., 2000). Before long, citizens expressed interest in obtaining training in rhetoric (the art of public persuasion).

To meet the demand, a group of teachers decided to offer courses in rhetoric, as well as other academic areas. The teachers were called **Sophists**, after the Greek word *sophos* for knowledge. The Sophists traveled from city to city, pedaling their intellectual wares—for a fee.

The Sophists were dedicated to their craft but needed to make a living. Several of the traveling teachers—Gorgias and Isocrates—taught classes on oratory, placing considerable emphasis on style.

The Sophists attracted a following, but not everyone who followed them liked what he saw. **Plato**, the great Greek philosopher, denounced their work in his dialogues. To Plato, truth was a supreme value. Yet the Sophists sacrificed truth at the altar of persuasion, in Plato's view. Thus, he lamented that "he who would be an orator has nothing to do with true justice, but only that which is likely to be approved by the many who sit in judgment" (Golden et al., p. 19). The Sophists, he charged, were not interested in discovering truth or advancing rational, "laborious, painstaking" arguments, but in "the quick, neat, and stylish argument that wins immediate approval—even if this argument has some hidden flaw" (Chappell, 1998, p. 516). To Plato, rhetoric was like cosmetics or flattery— not philosophy and therefore not deserving of respect.

The Sophists, for their part, saw persuasion differently. They surely believed that they were rocking the foundations of the educational establishment by giving people practical knowledge rather than "highfalutin" truth. They also were democrats, willing to teach any citizen who could afford their tuition.

Why do we care about the differences of opinion between Plato and the Sophists some 2,500 years later? We care because the same issues bedevil us today. Plato is the friend of all those who hate advertisements because they "lie" or stretch the truth. He is on the side of everyone who turns off the television during elections to stop the flow of "political-speak," or candidates making any argument they can to win election. The Sophists address those practical persuaders—advertisers, politicians, salespeople—who have to make a living, need practical knowledge to promote their products, and are suspicious of "shadowy" abstract concepts like truth (Kennedy, 1963). The Sophists and Plato offer divergent, dueling perspectives on persuasive communication. Indeed, one of the themes of this book is that there are **dual approaches** to thinking about persuasion: one that emphasizes Platonic thinking and cogent arguments, the other focusing on style, oratory, and simpler persuasive appeals that date back to some of the Sophist writers.

The First Scientist of Persuasion

Plato's greatest contribution to persuasion—or rhetoric as it was then called—may not have been the works he created, but the intellectual offspring he procreated. His best student—a Renaissance person before there was a Renaissance, a theorist before "theories" gained adherents—was **Aristotle**. Aristotle lived in the 4th century B.C. and wrote 170 works, including books on rhetoric. His treatise, *Rhetoric*, is regarded as "the most significant work on persuasion ever written" (Golden et al., p. 2).

Aristotle's great insight was that both Plato and the Sophists had a point. Plato was right about truth being important, and the Sophists were correct that persuasive communication is a very useful tool. Aristotle, to some degree, took the best from both schools of thought, arguing that rhetoric is not designed to persuade people but to *discover* scientific principles of persuasion. Aristotle's great contribution was to recognize that rhetoric could be viewed in scientific terms—as a phenomenon that could be described with precise concepts and by invoking probabilities (Golden et al., 2000; McCroskey, 1997). Drawing on his training in biology, Aristotle developed the first scientific approach to persuasion.

Rather than dismissing persuasion, as did Plato, the more practical Aristotle embraced it. "Aristotle said the goal of rhetoric wasn't so much finding the truth of a matter as convincing an audience to make the best decision about that matter," note Martha D. Cooper and William L. Nothstine (1998, p. 25). Aristotle proceeded to articulate a host of specific concepts on the nature of argumentation and the role of style in persuasion. He proposed methods by which persuasion occurred, described contexts in which it operated, and made ethics a centerpiece of his approach. During an era in which Plato was railing against the Sophists' pseudo-oratory, teachers were running around Greece offering short courses on rhetoric, and great orators made fortunes by serving as ghostwriters for the wealthy, Aristotle toiled tirelessly on the scientific front, developing the first scientific perspective on persuasion.

Aristotle proposed that persuasion had three main ingredients: *ethos* (the nature of the communicator), *pathos* (emotional state of the audience) and *logos* (message arguments). Aristotle was also an early student of psychology, recognizing that speakers had to adapt to their audiences by considering in their speeches those factors that were most persuasive to an audience member.

Aristotle's Greece was a mecca for the study and practice of persuasion. Yet it was not always pretty or just. Women were assumed to be innately unfit for engaging in persuasive public speaking; they were denied citizenship and excluded from the teaching professions (Waggenspack, 2000).

When Greek civilization gave way to Rome, the messengers were lost, but not the message. The practical Romans preserved much of Athenian civilization, adapting classic rhetorical works to Roman culture.

A Breezy Tour of Rome and the Centuries that Followed

Roman rhetorical theorists Cicero and Quintilian wrote treatises on the art of oratory. Cicero refined Greek theories of rhetoric, emphasizing the power of emotional appeals. Quintilian developed recommendations for the ideal orator. Their work reminds us that concerns with public persuasion and inclusion of emotional arguments date back to early Rome, and probably earlier if you consider the Sophists.

With the decline of Roman civilization, rhetoric became a less important feature of European society. Earth-shattering events occurred over the ensuing centuries: growth of Christianity, Italian Renaissance, Black Death, European wars. Nonetheless, Aristotle's and Cicero's works survived, and influenced the thinking of rhetorical theorists of their times. Some of these writers' works made their way west, to the intellectual vineyards of the New World.

Rhetorical Developments in the United States

Like Athens, colonial and 18th-century America were a persuader's paradise, with merchants, lawyers, politicians, and newspaper editors crafting arguments to influence people and mold public opinion. Great rhetorical works emerged in the 18th and 19th centuries, including the Declaration of Independence and Lincoln's Gettysburg Address. Yet like ancient Greece, the public paradise was closed to slaves and women. But, unlike Greece, legal limits did not stifle protest voices. Frederick Douglass and, later, W. E. B. DuBois became eloquent spokesmen for disenfranchised African Americans. Elizabeth Cady Stanton and Susan B. Anthony used rhetorical strategies derived from Cicero in their efforts to gain equality for women (Waggenspack, 2000).

Over the course of the 20th century, numerous rhetoricians have written insightful books. Richard Weaver (1953) argued that all language contains values. Kenneth Burke (1950), calling on philosophy and psychoanalysis, showed how good and evil communicators persuade people by identifying their views with the audience. Marshall McLuhan (1967), using the catchy title "The medium is the message," startled, then captivated people by alerting them to the ways in which the medium—television, radio, print—was more important than the content of a communicator's speech. Subsequently, radical scholars argued that the field of rhetoric could itself be studied and critiqued. Michel Foucault questioned the notion that there is such a thing as true knowledge. Instead, he claimed, knowledge and truth are interwoven with power; those who rule a society define what is true and what counts as knowledge (Golden et al., 2000). Feminist critics like Karlyn Kohrs Campbell (1989) pointed out that rhetorical history has been dominated by men and that women were barred from speaking in many supposedly great eras of rhetorical eloquence.

Rhetorical theorists continue to enlighten us with their work. However, their mission has been supplemented and to some degree replaced by legions of social scientists. The social science approach to persuasion now dominates academia. The history of this perspective is summarized next.

Origins of the Social Scientific Approach

Social scientific studies of persuasion began in the 1930s with research on attitudes (Allport, 1935). Scholarship got a boost in World War II when the U.S. War Department commissioned a group of researchers to explore the effects of a series of documentary films. The movies were designed to educate Allied soldiers on the Nazi threat and to boost morale. The War Department asked Frank Capra, who had previously directed such classics as *Mr. Smith Goes to Washington*, to direct the films. They were called simply *Why We Fight*.

Asked to evaluate the effects of the wartime documentaries, the social scientists got the added benefit of working, albeit indirectly, with Capra. It must have been a heady experience, assessing the effects of a Hollywood director's films on beliefs and attitudes. The studies offered some of the first hard evidence that communications influenced attitudes, albeit complexly (Hovland, Lumsdaine, & Sheffield, 1949). The experiments showed that persuasion research could be harnessed by government for its own ends—in this case, beneficial ones, but certainly not value-neutral objectives.

Several of the researchers working on the *Why We Fight* research went on to do important research in the fields of psychology and communication. One of them, Carl Hovland, seized the moment, brilliantly combining experimental research methodology with the ideas of an old persuasion sage, the first scientist of persuasion, the A-man: Aristotle. Working in a university setting, Hovland painstakingly conducted a series of experiments on persuasive communication effects. He and his colleagues took concepts invented by Aristotle—ethos, pathos, logos—and systematically examined their effects, using newly refined techniques of scientific experimentation (Hovland, Janis, & Kelley, 1953). What the researchers discovered—for example, that credible sources influenced attitudes—was less important than how they went about their investigations. Hovland and colleagues devised hypotheses, developed elaborate procedures to test predictions, employed statistical procedures to determine if predictions held true, and reported findings in scientific journals that could be scrutinized by critical observers.

Hovland died young, but his scientific approach to persuasion survived and proved to be an enduring legacy. A host of other social scientists, armed with theories, predictions, and questionnaires, began to follow suit. These included psychologists William J. McGuire and Milton Rokeach, and communication scholar Gerald R. Miller. The list of persuasion pioneers also includes Gordon Allport, the luminary psychologist who did so much to define and elaborate on the concept of attitude.

From an historical perspective, the distinctive element of the persuasion approach that began in the mid-20th century and continues today is its empirical foundation. Knowledge is gleaned from observation and evidence rather than armchair philosophizing. Researchers devise scientific theories, tease out hypotheses, and dream up ways of testing them in real-world settings. No one—not the Greeks, Romans, or 20th-century Western rhetorical theorists—had taken this approach. Capitalizing on the development of a scientific approach to behavior, new techniques for measuring attitudes, advances in statistics, and American pragmatism, early researchers were able to forge ahead, asking new questions, finding answers.

Scholarly activity continued apace from the 1960s onward, producing a wealth of persuasion concepts, far surpassing those put forth by Aristotle and classical rhetoricians. These terms include attitude, belief, cognitive processing, cognitive dissonance, social judgments, and interpersonal compliance. We also have a body of knowledge—thousands of studies, books, and review pieces on persuasion. More articles and books on persuasion have been published over the past 50 years than in the previous 2,500.

What once was a small field that broke off from philosophy has blossomed into a multidisciplinary field of study. Different scholars carve out different parts of the pie. **Social psychologists** focus on the individual, exploring people's attitudes and susceptibility to persuasion. **Communication scholars** cast a broader net, looking at persuasion in two-person units, called dyads, and examining influences of media on health and politics. **Marketing scholars** examine consumer attitudes and influences of advertising on buying behavior. If you look up persuasion under PsycINFO or in Communication Abstracts, you will find thousands of studies, journal articles, and books.

What's more, research plays a critical role in everyday persuasion activities. Advertising agencies spend millions on research. When Nike plans campaigns geared to young people (with ads resembling music videos), company executives plug in facts gleaned from marketing research. Antismoking campaigns hire academic researchers to probe teenagers' attitudes toward smoking. Campaigners want to understand why kids smoke and which significant others are most apt to endorse smoking in order to design messages that change teens' attitudes. In the political sphere, the White House launched a worldwide marketing campaign after September 11 in an effort to change Muslims' negative perceptions of the United States.

Plato, the purist, would be horrified by these developments. Aristotle, the practical theorist, might worry about ethics, but would be generally pleased. Both would be amazed by the sheer volume of persuasion research and its numerous applications to everyday life. Who knows? Maybe they'll be talking about our age 500 years from now! So, sit back and enjoy. You're about to embark on an exciting intellectual journey.

THE CONTEMPORARY STUDY OF PERSUASION

Contemporary scholars approach persuasion from a social science point of view. This may seem strange. After all, you may think of persuasion as an art. When someone mentions the word "persuasion," you may think of such things as "the gift of gab," "manipulation," or "subliminal seduction." You may feel that by approaching persuasion from the vantage point of contemporary social science, we are reducing the area to something antiseptic. However, this is far from the truth. Social scientists are curious about the same phenomena as everybody else is: for example, what makes a person persuasive, what types of persuasive messages are most effective, and why people go along with the recommendations put forth by powerful persuaders. The difference between the scientist's approach and that of the layperson is that the scientist formulates theories about attitudes and persuasion, derives hypotheses from these theories, and puts the hypotheses to empirical test. By empirical test, I mean that hypotheses are evaluated on the basis of evidence and data collected from the real world.

Theory plays a major role in the social scientific enterprise. A theory is a large, umbrella conceptualization of a phenomenon that contains hypotheses, proposes linkages between variables, explains events, and offers predictions. It may seem strange to study something as dynamic as persuasion by focusing on abstract theories. But theories contain ideas that yield insights about communication effects. These ideas provide the impetus for change. They are the pen that is mightier than the sword.

In fact, we all have theories about human nature and of persuasion (Roskos-Ewoldsen, 1997a; Stiff, 1994). We may believe that people are basically good, parents have a major impact on kids' personalities, or men are more competitive than women. We also have theories about persuasion. Consider these propositions:

1. *Advertising manipulates people.*
2. *You can't persuade people by scaring them.*
3. *The key to being persuasive is physical appeal.*

At some level these are theoretical statements, propositions that contain interesting, testable ideas about persuasive communication. But there are problems with the statements, from a scientific perspective. They are not bona fide theories of persuasion.

The first statement is problematic because it uses a value-laden term, *manipulate*. To most people, *manipulation* evokes negative images. Perhaps advertising doesn't manipulate so much as guide consumers toward outcomes they sincerely want. The first rule of good theorizing is to state propositions in value-free language.

The second statement—you can't persuade people by merely scaring them—sounds reasonable until you start thinking about it from another point of view. One could argue that giving people a jolt of fear is just what is needed to get them to rethink dangerous behaviors like drug abuse or binge drinking. You could suggest that fear appeals motivate people to take steps to protect themselves against dangerous outcomes.

The third statement—physical appeal is the key to persuasion—can also be viewed with a critical eye. Perhaps attractive speakers turn audiences off because people resent their good looks or assume they made it because of their bodies, not their brains. I am sure you can think of communicators who are trustworthy and credible, but aren't so physically attractive.

Yet at first blush, the three statements made sense. They could even be called intuitive "theories" of persuasion. But intuitive theories—our homegrown notions of what makes persuasion tick—are problematic. They lack objectivity. They are inextricably linked with our own biases of human nature (Stiff, 1994). What's more, they can't be scientifically tested or disconfirmed. By contrast, scientific theories are stated with sufficient precision that they can be empirically tested (through real-world research). They also contain formal explanations, hypotheses, and corollaries.

Researchers take formal theories, derive hypotheses, and test them in real-world experiments or surveys. If the hypotheses are supported over and over again, to a point of absolute confidence, we no longer call them theories, but laws of human behavior. We have preciously few of these in social science. (Darwinian evolution counts as a theory whose hypotheses have been proven to the point we can call it a law.) At the same time, there are many useful social science theories that can forecast behavior, shed light on people's actions, and suggest strategies for social change.

The beauty of research is that it provides us with a yardstick for evaluating the truth value of ideas that at first blush seem intuitively correct. It lets us know whether our gut feelings about persuasion—for example, regarding fear or good looks—amount to a hill of beans in the real world. Moreover, research provides a mechanism for determining which notions of persuasion hold water, which ones leak water (are no good), and, in general, which ideas about persuasive communication are most accurate, compelling, and predictive of human action in everyday life.

Researchers study persuasion in primarily two ways. They conduct **experiments**, or controlled studies that take place in artificial settings.

Experiments provide convincing evidence that one variable causes changes in another. Because experiments typically are conducted in university settings and primarily involve college students, they don't tell us about persuasion that occurs in everyday life among diverse population groups. For this reason, researchers conduct **surveys**. Surveys are questionnaire studies that examine the relationship between one factor (for example, exposure to a media antismoking campaign) and another (reduced smoking). Surveys do not provide unequivocal evidence of causation. In the example above, it is possible that people may reduce smoking shortly after a media campaign, but the effects may have nothing to do with the campaign. Smokers may have decided to quit because friends bugged them or they wanted to save money on cigarette costs.

Most studies of persuasive communication effects are experiments. Research on attitudes and applications of persuasion are more likely to be surveys. Both experiments and surveys are useful, although they make different contributions (Hovland, 1959).

Research, the focus of this book, is important because it clarifies concepts, builds knowledge, and helps solve practical problems. One must not lost sight of the big picture—the role persuasion plays in society and the fundamental ethics of persuasive communication. The final section of the chapter, building on the preceding discussion, examines these broader concerns. The next portion provides an overall perspective on the strengths and contributions persuasion makes to contemporary life. The final portion examines ethics.

SEEING THE BIG PICTURE

Persuasion is so pervasive that we often don't ask the question: What sort of world would it be if there were no persuasive communications? It would be a quieter world, that's for sure, one with less buzz, especially around dinnertime when telemarketers phone! But without persuasion, people would have to resort to different ways to get their way. Many would resort to verbal abuse, threats, and coercion to accomplish personal and political goals. Argument would be devalued or nonexistent. Force—either physical or psychological—would carry the day.

Persuasion, by contrast, is a profoundly civilizing influence. It says that disagreements between people can be resolved through logical arguments, emotional appeals, and faith placed in the speaker's credibility. Persuasion provides us with a constructive mechanism for advancing our claims and trying to change institutions. It offers a way for disgruntled and disenfranchised people to influence society. Persuasion provides a mechanism for everybody—from kids trading Pokemon cards to Wall Street brokers selling stocks—to advance in life and achieve their goals.

Persuasion is not always pretty. It can be mean, vociferous, and ugly. Persuasion, as Winston Churchill might say, is the worst way to exert influence—except for all the others. (Were there no persuasion, George W. Bush and Al Gore would not have settled their dispute about the 2000 election vote in the courtroom, but on the battlefield.)

Persuasion is not analogous to truth. As Aristotle recognized, persuasive communications are designed to influence, not uncover universal truths (Cooper & Nothstine, 1998). In fact, persuaders sometimes hide truth, mislead, or lie outright in the service of their aims or clients. The field of ethics is concerned with determining when it is morally appropriate to deviate from truth and when such deviations are ethically indefensible. Persuasion researchers do not pretend to know the answers to these questions. Instead, like everyone else, we do the best we can, seeking guidance from philosophers, wise people, and theologians. Hopefully, reading this book will give you insight into your own values, and will help you develop rules of thumb for what constitute ethical, and unethical, social influence attempts.

Persuasion assumes without question that people have free choice—that they can do other than what the persuader suggests. This has an important consequence. It means that people are responsible for the decisions they make in response to persuasive messages. Naturally, people can't foresee every possible consequence of choices that they make. They cannot be held accountable for outcomes that could not reasonably have been foreseen. But one of the essential aspects of life is choice—necessarily based on incomplete, and sometimes inaccurate, information.

Persuaders also make choices. They must decide how best to appeal to audiences. They necessarily must choose between ethical and unethical modes of persuasion. Persuaders who advance their claims in ethical ways deserve our respect. Those who employ unethical persuasion ploys should be held accountable for their choices. This raises an important question: Just what do we mean by ethical and unethical persuasion? The final portion of the chapter addresses this issue.

Persuasion and Ethics

Is persuasion ethical? This simple question has engaged scholars and practitioners alike. Aristotle and Plato discussed it. Machiavelli touched on it. So have contemporary communication scholars and social psychologists. And you can bet that practitioners—Tommy Hilfiger, Phil Knight, Donna Karan, even Michael Jordan—have given it a passing thought, no doubt on the way to the bank.

Yet persuasion ethics demand consideration. As human beings we want to be treated with respect, and we value communications that treat others as an ends, not a means, to use Immanuel Kant's famous phrase. At the same time, we are practical creatures, who want to achieve our goals, whether they be financial, social, emotional, or spiritual. The attainment of goals—money, prestige, love, or religious fulfillment—requires that we influence others in some fashion somewhere along the way. Is the need to influence *incompatible* with the ethical treatment of human beings?

Some scholars would say it invariably is. Plato, who regarded truth as "the only reality in life," was offended by persuasive communication (Golden et al., 2000, p. 17). As noted earlier, he regarded rhetoric as a form of flattery that appealed to people's worst instincts. Although Plato did believe in an ideal rhetoric admirably composed of truth and morality, he did not think that ordinary persuasion measured up to this standard.

The German philosopher Immanuel Kant would view persuasion as immoral for a different reason: In his view, it *uses* people, treating them as means to the persuader's end, not as valued ends in themselves (Borchert & Stewart, 1986). This violates Kant's ethical principles. In a similar fashion, Thomas Nilsen (1974) has argued that persuasion is immoral because a communicator is trying to induce someone to do something that is in the communicator's best interest, but not necessarily in the best interest of the individual receiving the message.

As thoughtful as these perspectives are, they set up a rather high bar for human communication to reach. What's more, these authors tend to lump all persuasive communication together. Some communications are indeed false, designed to manipulate people by appealing to base emotions, or are in the interest of the sender and not the receiver. But others are not. Some messages make very intelligent appeals, based on logic and evidence. In addition, not all persuaders treat people as a means. Therapists and health professionals ordinarily accord clients a great deal of respect. The best counselors treat each person as unique, a mysterious treasure to be deciphered and understood. Many people who do volunteer work—such as those who counsel teens in trouble or AIDS victims—do not receive great financial benefit from their work. Their communications can be very much in the best interest of those receiving the message.

On the other extreme are philosophers who argue that persuasion is fundamentally moral. Noting that people are free to accept or reject a communicator's message, conservative thinkers tend to embrace persuasion. Believing that people are sufficiently rational to distinguish between truth and falsehood, libertarian scholars argue that society is best served by diverse persuasive communications that run the gamut from entirely truthful to totally fallacious (Siebert, Peterson, & Schramm,

1956). Persuasion, they say, is better than coercion, and people are in any event free to accept or reject the communicator's message.

There is some wisdom in this perspective. However, to say that persuasion is inherently moral is an extreme, absolute statement. To assume that people are capable of maturely rejecting manipulative communicators' messages naively neglects cases in which trusted but evil people exploit others' vulnerability. What of men who trick or seduce women and then take advantage of their dependence to demand additional sexual and emotional favors? Perhaps we would argue that the women chose to get involved with the men—they're persuaded, not coerced—but it would be heartless to suggest that such persuasion is moral.

Consider also those nasty car salespeople who stretch the truth or lie outright to make a sale (Robin Williams skillfully played one of these some years back in the movie *Cadillac Man*). Throw in the tobacco companies, which waged campaigns to hook people into smoking even though they knew that smoking was addictive. Don't forget history's legions of con men—the snake oil salesmen of the 19th century who promised that new nutritional cures would work magic on those who purchased them, and their modern counterparts, the hosts of infomercials who tell you that vitamin supplements will boost sales and sex.

It defies credulity to argue that persuasion is inherently ethical.

That brings up a third viewpoint, which comes closest to truth. This approach emphasizes that persuasion is amoral—neither inherently good nor bad, but ethically neutral. Aristotle endorsed this view. He argued that persuasion could be used by anyone: "by a good person or a bad person, by a person seeking worthy ends or unworthy ends" (McCroskey, 1997, p. 9). Thus, charisma can be employed by a Hitler or a Martin Luther King, by a Stalin or Ghandi. Step-by-step persuasion techniques that begin with a small request and hook the person into larger and larger commitments have been used by North Korean captors of American soldiers during the Korean War and by religious cult leaders—but also by Alcoholics Anonymous.

Persuasion does have an amoral quality. There is scholarly consensus on this point. This book endorses the view that *persuasive communication strategies are not inherently moral or immoral, but good or bad, depending on other factors.* Useful as this approach is, it leaves questions unanswered. What determines whether a particular persuasive act is ethical or unethical? How do we decide if a communicator has behaved in a moral or immoral fashion? In order to answer these questions, we must turn to moral philosophy. Philosophers have offered many perspectives on these issues, beginning with Plato and continuing to the present day.

One prominent view emphasizes the consequences of an action. Called **utilitarianism**, it suggests that actions should be judged based on whether they produce more good than evil. If a message leads to positive ends, helping more people than it hurts, it is good; if it produces primarily negative consequences, it is bad. For example, an antismoking campaign is good if it convinces many young people to quit. It is bad if it boomerangs, leading more people to take up the habit.

Deontological philosophers, who emphasize duty and obligation, object to this view. They argue that a successful antismoking campaign sponsored by the tobacco industry is not as morally good as an equally successful program produced by activists committed to helping young people preserve their health (Frankena, 1963). These philosophers frequently emphasize intentions, or the motives of the persuader. James C. McCroskey (1972) is a proponent of intention-based morality. He argues that:

> If the communicator seeks to improve the well-being of his audience through his act of communication, he is committing a moral act. If he seeks to produce harm for his audience, the communicator is guilty of an immoral act. (p. 270)

Yet even those who agree that morality should be based on intentions acknowledge that it is difficult to arrive at objective criteria for judging another's intention.

Still other approaches to ethics have been proposed. Feminist theorists advocate an ethics of caring, empathy, and mutual respect (Jaggar, 2000). Persuasion is viewed not as something one does *to* another, but *with* another (Reardon, 1991). Another useful approach is existentialism, which emphasizes freedom and responsibility. People are free to choose what they want in life, but are responsible for their choices. "There are no excuses, for there is no one to blame for our actions but ourselves," existentialists argue (Fox & DeMarco, 1990, p. 159).

One choice people have is not to be ethical at all, to pursue self-interest at any cost. Philosophers cannot persuade people to make ethical judgments; they cannot convince unsavory characters to behave in humane ways or to use morally acceptable strategies to influence others. One can give many arguments in behalf of ethical persuasion, from the Golden Rule to moral duty to "You'll be more effective if you're honest," which originated with Aristotle. The best argument is that ethical persuasion is one of the requirements of being a decent and beneficent human being. Perhaps as you read this book and think about persuasion ethics, you will discover more reasons to practice ethical persuasive communication.

THE PRESENT APPROACH

There are thousands of books on persuasion, hundreds of thousands of articles, probably more. "How to persuade" books, audios, and Web sites proliferate. No surprise here: A search for the keys to persuasion is surely among the most basic of human desires. Who among us has not entertained the thought that somewhere out there lies the secret to persuasion? Who has not dreamed that he or she might, with luck or perseverance, find the simple trick or magic elixir that contains the formula for social influence?

We may yet find the secret to persuasion or, failing that, we may someday understand perfectly why people need to believe that simple solutions exist. But you won't find a simple formula here. Instead, you will discover intriguing theories, bundles of evidence, creative methodologies, and rich applications of research to everyday life. This book, focusing on academic scholarship on persuasion, attempts to increase your knowledge of attitudes and persuasion. Specifically, I hope that the book will provide you with:

1. greater understanding of persuasion theory and research;
2. increased insight into your own persuasion styles, strengths, and biases;
3. more tolerance of others' attitudes and persuasive techniques;
4. greater skill in resisting unwanted influence attempts;
5. deeper insight into persuasion as it occurs in 21st-century society; and
6. new insights on how to be a more effective and ethical persuader.

The book is divided into three sections. The first part examines the foundations of persuasion: basic terminology, attitude definitions and structure, attitude functions, consistency, and measurement (chapters 1, 2, 3, and 4). The second portion focuses on persuasion theory and communication effects, beginning with an exploration of contemporary cognitive approaches in chapter 5. Chapter 6 examines the communicator in persuasion, discussing such factors as credibility and attractiveness. Chapter 7 focuses on the message, particularly emotional appeals and language. Chapter 8 explores personality and whether certain people are more susceptible to persuasion than others. Chapter 9 discusses the granddaddy of attitude and persuasion approaches: cognitive dissonance theory. Chapter 10 explores interpersonal persuasion and compliance. The third section, focusing on persuasion in American society, examines advertising (chapter 11) and communication campaigns (chapter 12).

Certain themes predominate and run through the book—the central role persuasion plays in contemporary life (from mass marketing to interpersonal politicking); the need to dissect persuasive communication effects carefully; the critical role that people's thinking and cognitive processing play in persuasion effects; the ability of persuasion to manipulate but also soothe and comfort people; the fact that we persuade ourselves and are responsible for outcomes that occur; and the incredible complexity of human behavior, a fact that makes the study of persuasion fascinating, and never ending.

CONCLUSIONS

Persuasion is a ubiquitous part of contemporary life. If you search the term on the Web, you find hundreds of topics, ranging from "Brainwashing Controversies" to "Marketing" to "How to Get People to Like You." The Internet is a persuader's paradise, with Web sites promoting millions of products and services. However, persuasion has more personal components. We can all think of times when we yielded to other people's influence attempts, tried to persuade friends to go along with us, or scratched our heads to figure out ways we could have done a better job of getting a colleague to buy our plan.

Persuasion is an ancient art. It dates back to the Bible and ancient Greece. Yet there are important aspects of contemporary persuasion that are unique to this era. They include the volume, speed, subtlety, and complexity of modern messages.

Persuasion is defined as *a symbolic process in which communicators try to convince other people to change their attitudes or behavior regarding an issue through the transmission of a message, in an atmosphere of free choice.* A key aspect of persuasion is self-persuasion. Communicators do not *change* people's minds; people decide to alter their own attitudes or to resist persuasion. There is something liberating about self-persuasion. It says that we are free to change our lives in any way that we wish. We have the power to become what we want to become—to stop smoking, lose weight, modify dysfunctional behavior patterns, change career paths, or discover how to become a dynamic public speaker. Obviously, we can't do everything: There are limits set by both our cognitive skills and society. But in saying that people ultimately persuade themselves, I suggest that we are partly responsible if we let ourselves get connived by dishonest persuaders. I argue that people are capable of throwing off the shackles of dangerous messages and finding positive ways to live their lives.

Of course, this is not always easy. The tools of self-persuasion can be harnessed by both beneficent and malevolent communicators. It is not always easy for people to tell the difference.

Social influence can be viewed as a continuum, with coercion lying on one end and persuasion at the other. There are not always black-and-white differences between persuasion and coercion. They can overlap, as in religious cults.

Persuasion, so much a part of everyday life, has been studied for thousands of years, beginning with the early Greeks. Plato criticized the Sophists' rhetoric, and Aristotle developed the first scientific approach to persuasion. Since then, numerous rhetorical books have been written, spanning oratory, language, identification, and mass media.

A persistent theme in persuasion scholarship—from Plato to the present era—is ethics. The rub is that persuasive communication can be used by both moral and immoral persuaders, and unfortunately has been successfully exploited by fascist dictators. What makes a particular persuasive encounter ethical or unethical? Philosophers emphasize the consequences of the communication and the communicator's intentions. They have also identified many reasons why individuals should engage in ethical persuasive activities. Persuasion in and of itself is neither all good nor all bad. As students and practitioners of persuasion, we can study its use and become more sensitive to the techniques persuaders employ, as well as the impact they have on individuals and society. By gaining a greater appreciation for persuasion processes and effects, as well as its ethical foundations, we can hopefully wield this powerful instrument in more influential and beneficent ways.

CHAPTER 2

Attitudes: Definition and Structure

Click onto a Web site for, say, religion, capital punishment, animal rights, poverty, or crime. Or if you prefer cultural venues, check out sites for hip hop music, body piercing, tattoos, sports, or cars. If you prefer the older, traditional media, you can peruse books or letters to the editor, or you can tune into a radio talk show. You will find them there.

What you will locate are attitudes—strong, deeply felt attitudes, as well as ambivalent, complex ones. You see, even today, when we communicate through cell phones, laptops, and palm pilots, attitudes are ubiquitous. To appreciate the pervasiveness, depth, and strength of attitudes, I invite you to read over these comments written in the wake of the traumatic events of September 11:

- It is time for America to abandon its candy-colored views of what is right and what is wrong. We are dealing with extremists who recognize no restraints, and we as a country should deal with them at their own level to destroy them. . . . Morality is not the question here. This is war, and who will win it is now the question. If the terrorists want to play on their own terms, then we should play at their level. That is the only way in which they will be defeated. (David Richmond, *The New York Times*, September 17, 2001)
- We hate the people who did this, and we want to torture them for what they've done. But that is wrong. Similar feelings of hatred resulted in these devastating attacks. When does the circle of violence stop? We react. Terrorists then respond to our reaction, and we react again. Rather than hatred, this situation should be about change—a new direction that promotes love for your fellow man. . . . As a nation, let's say a prayer and bond together to get through this. (Clifford J. Fazzolari, *USA Today*, September 12, 2001)
- I would like to take this time to ask all Americans to embrace the Arab-American communities in this country and not blame them for last

Tuesday's terrorist attacks. We all need to pull together to get through this trying time, and it would be a shame to hold a large group of decent, law-abiding citizens responsible for the actions of a few ignorant radicals. If we blame the Arab-American community for being responsible for the actions of terrorists, then we are no better than the people who are attacking us simply because we are Americans. (Jack Norton, *USA Today*, September 18, 2001)

- It would be easier to grasp if there were a shred of reason behind it—reason in the sense of logic, rationality, coherence. But this was just about hate. There are people who hate us. . . . What we have here is an unfortunate fact of our planet: Its dominant species combines extreme cleverness with an unreliable morality and a persistent streak of insanity. Thus, it has ever been; thus it shall ever be. (Joel Achenbach, *The Washington Post Weekly Edition*, September 17–23, 2001)
- The act of war against select targets throughout this country happened because we *are* America. . . . I am proud at this moment to be an American because the very fiber of our nation's principles is such an affront to our enemies that they attempted to break our foundation and failed. It is because of what we are and what we represent that we suffered this tragedy. . . . America cannot be contained within the boundary of 50 states and a few frail buildings. Rather, America is a spirit that inspires the repressed of the world over. In the coming days, let us continue to live, walk and be Americans. (Kristian Dyer, *USA Today*, September 19, 2001)

Attitudes—not always this strong or vitriolic, but an indispensable part of our psychological makeup—are the subject of this chapter and the one that follows. Attitudes, and their close cousins (beliefs and values), have been the focus of much research over the past 50 years. They are the stuff of persuasion—materials persuaders try to change, possessions we cling to tenaciously, badges that define us, categories that organize us, constructs that marketers want to measure and manipulate, and in the final analysis rich textured pieces of our personae that we call on to give life its meaning and depth. The first portion of the chapter defines attitude and discusses its main components. The second section focuses on the structure of attitude, ambivalence, and how people cope with inconsistency. The third portion of the chapter examines the psychology of strong, deeply held attitudes.

THE CONCEPT OF ATTITUDE

"She's got an attitude problem," someone says, telegraphing familiarity with the term, *attitude*. But being familiar with a term does not mean one can necessarily articulate a clear, comprehensive definition. This is a task that we look to scholars to perform, and social scientists have offered a litany of definitions of attitude, dating back to the 19th century. Darwin regarded attitude as a motor concept (a scowling face signifies a "hostile attitude") (see Petty, Ostrom, & Brock, 1981a). Freud, by contrast, "endowed (attitudes) with vitality, identifying them with longing, hatred and love, with passion and prejudice" (Allport, 1935, p. 801). Early 20th-century sociologists Thomas and Znaniecki placed attitude in a social context, defining it as a "state of mind of the individual toward a value" (Allport, 1935).

Their view resonated with a growing belief that the social environment influenced individuals, but then-contemporary terms like *custom* and *social force* were too vague and impersonal to capture the complex dynamics by which this occurred. *Attitude*, which referred to a force or quality of mind, seemed much more appropriate. By the 1930s, as researchers began to study the development of racial stereotypes, Gordon Allport (1935) declared that attitude was the most indispensable concept in contemporary social psychology.

Attitude is a psychological construct. It is a mental and emotional entity that inheres in, or characterizes, the person. It has also been called a "hypothetical construct," a concept that cannot be observed directly but can only be inferred from people's actions. An exemplar of this approach is the Michigan psychology professor who ran through the halls of his department shouting (in jest) that "I found it. I found it. I found the attitude." His comment illustrates that attitudes are different from the raw materials that other scientific disciplines examine—materials that can be touched or clearly seen, such as a rock, plant cell, or an organ in the human body.

Although in some sense we do infer a person's attitude from what he or she says or does, it would be a mistake to assume that for this reason attitudes are not real or are "mere mental constructs." This is a fallacy of behaviorism, the scientific theory that argues that all human activity can be reduced to behavioral units. Contemporary scholars reject this notion. They note that people have thoughts, cognitive structures, and a variety of emotions, all of which lose their essential qualities when viewed exclusively as behaviors. Moreover, they argue that an entity that is mental or emotional is no less real than a physical behavior. As Allport (1935) noted perceptively:

> Attitudes are never directly observed, but, unless, they are admitted, through inference, as real and substantial ingredients in human nature, it becomes impossible to account satisfactorily either for the consistency of any individual's behavior, or for the stability of any society (p. 839).

Over the past century, numerous definitions of attitude have been proposed. The following views of attitude are representative of the population of definitions. According to scholars, an attitude is:

- an association between a given object and a given evaluation (Fazio, 1989, p. 155);
- a learned predisposition to respond in a consistently favorable or unfavorable manner with respect to a given object (Fishbein & Ajzen, 1975, p. 6);
- enduring systems of positive or negative evaluations, emotional feelings, and pro or con action tendencies with respect to social objects (Krech, Crutchfield, & Ballachey, 1962, p. 139);
- a more or less permanently enduring state of readiness of mental organization which predisposes an individual to react in a characteristic way to any object or situation with which it is related (Cantril, quoted in Allport, 1935, p. 804).

Combining these definitions and emphasizing commonalities, one arrives at the following definition of attitude: **a learned, global evaluation of an object (person, place, or issue) that influences thought and action**. I review the components of the definition below.

Characteristics of Attitudes

1. *Attitudes are learned.* People are not born with attitudes. They acquire attitudes over the course of socialization in childhood and adolescence. This has important implications. It means, first, that no one is born prejudiced. Children don't naturally discriminate against kids with different skin color or religious preferences. Over time, kids acquire prejudiced attitudes. Or to be more blunt, they learn to hate.

Fortunately, not all attitudes are so negative. Think about the rush you get when "The Star-Spangled Banner" is played after a U.S. victory at the Olympics. People have positive sentiments toward all sorts of things—hometown sports teams, teachers who lift our spirits, children, pets, cool cars; you get the drift.

Given the powerful role attitudes play in our lives, some researchers have speculated that attitudes contain a genetic component. Tesser (1993) acknowledged that there is not "a gene for attitudes toward jazz in the same way as there is a gene for eye color" (p. 139). But he argued that inherited physical differences in taste and hearing might influence attitudes toward food and loud rock music. Perhaps those who are born with higher activity levels gravitate to vigorous exercise or sports.

These are reasonable, very interesting, claims. In light of growing evidence that genes can influence behavior, it is certainly possible that we may someday discover that people's genetic makeup predisposes them to approach certain activities and avoid others. At present, though, there is little evidence that attitudes have a genetic foundation. Moreover, even if Tesser's claims turned out to be true, it would not mean that genes *cause* certain attitudes to develop. The environment will always have a large impact in shaping our responses and modes of seeing the world. For example, a person might be genetically predisposed to like pineapple, but if pineapple is not available (or affordable), she cannot develop a positive attitude toward the fruit. In addition, if the first time she tastes pineapple she develops a rash or gets bitten by a dog, she is bound to evaluate pineapple negatively.

Thus, even if attitudes have genetic antecedents, these inherited preferences are not equivalent to attitudes. Attitudes develop through encounters with social objects. "Individuals do not have an attitude until they first encounter the attitude object (or information about it) and respond evaluatively to it," Alice H. Eagly and Shelly Chaiken (1998, p. 270) declare.

2. *Attitudes are global, typically emotional, evaluations.* Attitudes are, first and foremost, evaluations. Having an attitude means that you have categorized something and made a judgment of its net value or worth. It means that you are no longer neutral about the topic. That doesn't mean you can't have mixed feelings, but your view on the issue is no longer bland or without color.

Attitudes invariably involve affect and emotions. "Attitudes express passions and hates, attractions and repulsions, likes and dislikes," note Eagly and Chaiken (1998, p. 269).

Affect usually plays an important part in how attitudes are formed or experienced. I say "usually" because some attitudes may develop more intellectually, by absorbing information, while others are acquired through reward and punishment of previous behavior (Dillard, 1993; Zanna & Rempel, 1988). Attitudes are complex. They have different components and are formed in different ways. A classic tripartite model emphasizes that attitudes can be expressed through thoughts, feelings, and behavior (Breckler, 1984). Our attitudes are not always internally consistent, and you may have contradictory attitudes toward the same issue.

Attitudes can be regarded as large summary evaluations of issues and people. (They are global or macro, not micro.) Your attitude toward men's and women's roles is a large, complex entity composed of beliefs, affect, and perhaps intentions to behave one way or another. For this reason, researchers speak of "attitude systems" that consist of several subcomponents. Attitudes encompass beliefs, feelings, intentions to behave, and behavior itself.

3. *Attitudes influence thought and action.* Attitudes (and values) organize our social world. They allow us to quickly categorize people, places, and events and to figure out what's going on. They're like notebook dividers or labels you use to categorize your CD collection. Attitudes shape perceptions and influence judgments. If you're a Republican, you probably evaluate Republican presidents like Ronald Reagan favorably, and have a negative, gut-level reaction to Democratic leaders like former president Clinton. And vice versa if you're a Democrat. On the other hand, if you hate politics and distrust politicians, you filter the political world through this skeptical set of lenses.

Attitudes also influence behavior. They guide our actions and steer us in the direction of doing what we believe. In our society, consistency between attitude and behavior is valued, so people try hard to "practice what they preach." As will be discussed, people usually translate attitudes into behavior, but not always.

Attitudes come in different shapes and sizes. Some attitudes are strong, others are weaker and susceptible to influence. Still others contain inconsistent elements. Some attitudes exert a stronger impact on thought and behavior than others.

In sum: Attitudes are complex, dynamic entities—like people. Persuasion scholar Muzafer Sherif put it best:

> When we talk about attitudes, we are talking about what a person has *learned* in the process of becoming a member of a family, a member of a group, and of society that makes him react to his social world in a *consistent* and *characteristic* way, instead of a transitory and haphazard way. We are talking about the fact that he is no longer neutral in sizing up the world around him; he is *attracted* or *repelled*, *for* or *against*, *favorable* or *unfavorable*. (Sherif, 1967, p. 2)

Values and Beliefs

What do you value? What do you believe about life and society? To answer these questions, it helps to clearly define value and belief. Both concepts play an important role in persuasion. Like attitudes, values and beliefs are learned and shape the ways we interpret information.

Values are ideals, "guiding principles in one's life," or overarching goals that people strive to obtain (Maio & Olson, 1998). They are our "conceptions of the desirable means and ends of action" (Kluckhohn, 1951). Values can either transcend or celebrate selfish concerns. Freedom, equality, and a world of beauty are universal values that extend beyond individual interests (Rokeach, 1973; Schwartz, 1996). Self-fulfillment, excitement, and recognition express strong desires to enrich our own lives. Warm relationships with others and a sense of belonging emphasize love and security (Kahle, 1996).

Values conflict and collide. "Difficult choices are unavoidable," observe Philip E. Tetlock and his colleagues (Tetlock, Peterson, & Lerner, 1996, p. 25; see Box 2–1).

BOX 2–1
VALUE COMPLEXITIES

The following is a list of things that some people look for or want out of life. Please study the list carefully and then rate each thing on how important it is in your daily life, where 1 = important to me, and 9 = extremely important to me.

Important to Me   *Most Important to Me*

---

1. Sense of belonging (to be accepted and needed by our family, friends, and community)
   1 2 3 4 5 6 7 8 9
2. Excitement (to experience stimulation and thrills)
   1 2 3 4 5 6 7 8 9
3. Warm relationships with others (to have close companionships and intimate friendships)
   1 2 3 4 5 6 7 8 9
4. Self-fulfillment (to find peace of mind and to make the best use of your talents)
   1 2 3 4 5 6 7 8 9
5. Being well respected (to be admired by others and to receive recognition)
   1 2 3 4 5 6 7 8 9

Adapted from Kahle (1996)

This is one way that psychologists measure people's values. Lynn Kahle (1996), who developed the above scale, has found that there are countless individual differences in values. For example, fashion leaders value fun and enjoyment in life more than other people. Women favor a sense of belonging and warm relationships with others more than men.

Values may also predict whether people stay together. Perhaps couples who share values when they are forging a relationship, as when both want stimulation and excitement, break up when their values diverge. Having satiated the need for excitement, one partner wants self-fulfillment, while the other still craves ever-more exciting encounters.

People face intrapersonal, as well as interpersonal, value conflicts. When a choice pits two cherished, universal values against one another, individuals weigh each option carefully, realizing that neither alternative will make them totally happy. Such gut-wrenching decisions are common in government, where policymakers must adjudicate between values of diverse constituent groups. Tetlock discusses this in his value–pluralism model, which looks at how people wrestle with difficult ideological choices (Tetlock et al., 1996).

Consider, for example, that a decision to regulate Internet pornography upholds the value of preventing harm to others, but undermines freedom of choice. Former New York Mayor Rudolph Giuliani's policy of stopping and frisking suspicious people violated civil liberties, but reduced crime. Affirmative action presents a choice between two "good" values: promoting diversity and allocating rewards based on merit. The issue is so complicated that philosophers do not agree on what constitutes a fair or just policy.

Abortion is even more daunting. It pits the value of sanctity of life against freedom of choice. Partisans see these issues very differently. Conservative opponents of abortion cannot comprehend how liberals, who are pro-choice, can at the same time oppose capital punishment. In the conservative's view, liberals favor murder of a fetus but oppose execution of a hardened criminal. Liberals wonder how people who oppose abortion can favor capital punishment. How, they wonder, could someone who views abortion as killing babies favor the death penalty (Seligman & Katz, 1996, p. 53)?

George Lakoff, a cognitive linguist sensitive to the meaning of words and power of conceptual systems, wrote a book that explores such apparent contradictions in belief systems. To Lakoff (1996), a liberal does not experience a contradiction in taking a pro-choice position and opposing capital punishment, and a conservative is equally comfortable opposing abortion but favoring the death penalty. Here's why:

A strict conservative has an absolute view of right and wrong. Aborting a baby is morally wrong (of course, the choice of the word "baby" to describe abortion is critical, an issue taken up in chapter 7). A conservative, adhering to a value of self-discipline and responsibility, puts the onus on (for example) the unmarried teenage girl who consented to sex in the first place. She engaged in immoral behavior and should at least have the guts to take responsibility for her actions. Capital punishment fits into a somewhat different cognitive category. Believing that morality involves retribution (punishment for sins committed), conservatives feel strongly that capital punishment is an acceptable method to punish crime.

A pure liberal, by contrast, puts considerable value on protecting rights, and extending compassion to those in need. Arguing that abortion does not involve a human life, but destruction of an embryo or fetus, liberals

Continued

BOX 2–1
(CONTINUED)

gravitate to protecting the freedom of the pregnant woman to choose whether or not to have a baby. In addition, guided by values of compassion and nurturance, liberals look with empathy at the teenage girl's predicament. She made a mistake, they acknowledge, but is not old enough to be a mother; forcing her to have a child when she is not psychologically ready to be a mom will only hurt her child in the long run. When it comes to capital punishment, liberals note that "nurturance itself implies a reverence for life," but "the death penalty denies such a reverence for life" and so is inconsistent with liberal values (Lakoff, pp. 208–209).

There is merit in both liberal and conservative values. Both are grounded in deep commitments to morality, yet liberals and conservatives view morality in different ways. Unfortunately, many people react to labels in knee-jerk ways when someone from the other camp discusses an issue. "You're just a bleeding heart liberal," a conservative shrieks. "He's a real conservative," a liberal moans as if "conservative" were an obscenity.

Values are more global and abstract than attitudes. For example, the value of freedom encompasses attitudes toward censorship, entrepreneurship, political correctness, and smoking in public. People have hundreds of attitudes, but dozens of values (e.g., Rokeach, 1973). Values, even more than attitudes, strike to the core of our self-concepts.

In contrast, **beliefs** are more specific and cognitive. Beliefs number in the hundreds, perhaps thousands. These are typical:

Girls talk more about relationships than do guys.
Maintaining a vegetarian diet improves your state of mind.
Rap has transformed music.
College students drink too much.
Global warming threatens the planet.

Beliefs are more cognitive than values or attitudes. Beliefs are cognitions about the world—subjective probabilities that an object has a particular attribute, or an action will lead to a particular outcome (Fishbein & Ajzen, 1975).

People frequently confuse beliefs with facts. Just because we fervently believe something to be true does not make it so. Stereotypes can contain kernels of truth about ethnic groups, but are typically gross generalizations that are filled with inaccurate perceptions. (Archie Bunker comes to mind here!) Beliefs can be patently and unequivocally false. A Taliban leader from Afghanistan believes that in America, parents do not show love to their children and the only good thing to come out of the United States is candy (Goldberg, 2000). Unfortunately, beliefs like these are tenaciously held and highly resistant to change.

On a more general level, beliefs can be viewed as core components of attitudes. Attitudes are complex components of beliefs and affect.

Beliefs can also be categorized into different subtypes. *Descriptive beliefs*, such as those previously discussed, are perceptions or hypotheses about the world that people carry around in their heads. *Prescriptive beliefs* are "ought" or "should" statements that express conceptions of preferred end-states. Prescriptive beliefs, such as "People should vote in every election" or "The minimum wage should be increased," cannot be tested by empirical research. They are part of people's worldviews. Some scholars regard prescriptive beliefs as components of values.

Beliefs and values are fascinating, yet have received less scholarly attention than attitudes. This is because the attitude concept helped bridge behaviorist and cognitive approaches to psychology. It explained how people could be influenced by society, yet also internalize what they learned. It articulated a process by which social forces could affect behavior, and not merely stamp their response on the organism.

STRUCTURE OF ATTITUDES

Suppose we could glimpse an attitude up close. Let's say we could handle it, feel its shape and texture, and then inspect it carefully. What would we see?

We cannot observe attitudes with the same exactitude that scientists employ when examining molecules under electron microscopes. We lack the attitudinal equivalent to the human genome, the long strand of DNA that contains our 23 critical chromosome pairs. Instead, we infer attitudes from what people do or say, and what they report on carefully constructed survey instruments. This does not make attitudes any less real than chemicals on the Periodic Table, the 30,000 human genes, rocks, plants, or any other material that scientists scrutinize. It simply makes our job of uncovering their basic content more challenging and perhaps more subject to human fallibility.

Just as the human genome and physical substances have structure, attitudes also possess a certain organization. How are attitudes organized? What are their major components? Social scientists have proposed several models to help answer these questions.

Expectancy–Value Approach

The expectancy–value perspective asserts that attitudes have two components: cognition and affect, (or head and heart). Your attitude is a combination what you *believe* or expect of a certain object, and how you *feel* about (evaluate) these expectations. The theory was developed by Martin Fishbein and Icek Ajzen in 1975 and is still going strong today! According to Fishbein and Ajzen, attitude is a multiplicative combination of: (a) strength of beliefs that an object has certain attributes and (b) evaluations of these attributes (see Fig. 2.1). The prediction is represented by the following mathematical formula:

$$A = \text{Sum } b(i) \times e(i)$$

where $b(i)$ = each belief and $e(i)$ = each evaluation.

Formulas like these are helpful because they allow for more precise tests of hypotheses. There is abundant evidence that attitudes can be accurately estimated by combining beliefs and evaluations. Fishbein and Ajzen (1975) showed that beliefs (particularly personally important ones) and evaluations accurately estimate attitudes toward a host of topics, ranging from politics to sex roles. Beliefs are the centerpiece of attitude, and have provided researchers with rich insights into the dynamics of attitudes and behaviors.

Diane M. Morrison and her colleagues (1996) systematically examined beliefs about smoking in an elaborate study of elementary school children's decisions to smoke cigarettes. They measured **beliefs** about smoking by asking kids whether they thought that smoking cigarettes will:

* hurt your lungs
* give you bad breath

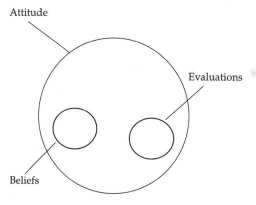

FIG. 2.1   Expectancy–value approach to attitudes.

- make your friends like you better
- make you feel more grown up
- taste good

The researchers assessed **evaluations** by asking children if they felt that these attributes (e.g., hurting your lungs, making your friends like you better) were good or bad. An evaluation was measured in this general fashion:

Do you think that making your friends like you better is:
very good, good, not good or *bad, bad,* or *very bad?*

Morrison and her colleagues gained rich insights into the dynamics of children's attitudes toward smoking. Had they just measured attitude, they would have only discovered how kids evaluated cigarette smoking. By focusing on beliefs, they identified specific reasons why some children felt positively toward smoking. By assessing evaluations, the researchers tapped into the affect associated with these attributes. Their analysis indicated that two children could hold different attitudes about smoking because they had different beliefs about smoking's consequences or because they held the same beliefs but evaluated the consequences differently.

Morrison et al.'s findings shed light on the underpinnings of attitudes toward smoking. Some children evaluate smoking favorably because they believe that their friends will like them better if they smoke, or that smoking makes them feel grown up. Kids who value these outcomes may be particularly inclined to start smoking before they hit adolescence. This information is clearly useful to health educators who design anti-smoking information campaigns.

Affect, Symbols, and Ideologies

A second perspective on attitude structure places emotion and symbols at center stage. According to the symbolic approach, attitudes—particularly political ones—are characterized by emotional reactions, sweeping sentiments, and powerful prejudices. These, rather than molecular beliefs, are believed to lie at the core of people's evaluations of social issues.

Consider racism, sexism, or attitudes toward abortion. These evaluations are rife with symbols and charged with affect. According to David O. Sears, people acquire affective responses to symbols early in life from parents, peers, and mass media (Sears & Funk, 1991). Symbols include the flag, religious ornaments, and code words associated with minority groups. As a result of early learning experiences, people develop strong attitudes toward their country, as well as religious values, ethnic loyalties, and racial prejudices. These "symbolic predispositions," as they are called, lie at the core of people's attitudes toward social issues. Two examples may be helpful here.

During the 1970s, many Whites opposed school busing to achieve racial integration. Some observers suggested that one reason Whites reacted this way was because they were personally affected by busing. Their kids would have to be bused, perhaps taking the bus for a considerable distance. But this turned out not to be the case. In fact, the best predictor of Whites' opposition to busing was racial prejudice, a symbolic predisposition (Sears et al., 1980; Sears, Henry, & Kosterman, 2000).

A more recent example involves AIDS. Although Americans have become more empathic toward the plight of AIDS victims in recent years, many still harbor prejudice toward those who have contracted the AIDS virus. John Pryor and Glenn Reeder (1993) offer the following explanation:

> HIV/AIDS may have acquired a symbolic meaning in our culture. As a symbol or a metaphor, it represents things like homosexual promiscuity, moral decadence, and the wrath of God for moral transgressions. . . . So, when people react negatively to someone with AIDS (or HIV), they may be expressing their feelings about the symbol. This analysis could explain why those strongly opposed to homosexuality react negatively to nonhomosexuals with HIV. Even the infected child bears the symbol of homosexual promiscuity. (p. 279)

Pryor and Reeder argue that we cognitively represent people and ideas in certain ways. A person with AIDS (called a person node) is not a neutral entity, but is connected with all sorts of other ideas and emotions that come to mind when we think about AIDS. AIDS (or HIV) may be associated in an individual's mind with homosexuals, drug users, minorities, promiscuous sex, even death. All of these entities are charged with emotion or affect. These emotions become powerfully associated with a person with AIDS (see Fig. 2.2).

The symbolic attitude perspective goes a long way toward helping us deconstruct people's views on contemporary issues. It calls attention to the role that associations play in attitude structure (as well as the effect of more elaborated beliefs; Sears et al., 2000). In fairness, although the model has done much to clarify the dynamics of racially prejudiced and homophobic attitudes, it has not been applied to the study of other equally strong attitudes, such as those held by militant minority group activists or religious extremists. Presumably, symbolic predispositions are at the foundation of a variety of affect-based social and political attitudes that we encounter in everyday life.

The Role of Ideology.   A third view of attitude organization emphasizes ideology, or worldview. Some people's attitudes are guided by broad

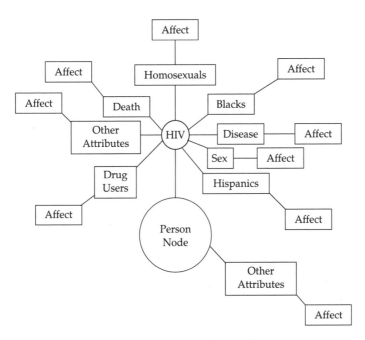

FIG. 2.2 A symbolic view of attitudes toward HIV/AIDS (from Pryor & Reeder, 1993, p. 271).

ideological principles. These individuals typically forge stronger connections among diverse political attitudes than those who don't think much about ideology. For example, conservatives, whose worldviews emphasize self-reliance, responsibility, and reward for hard work, typically oppose welfare because it gives money to those who don't hold down jobs. Conservatives support across-the-board tax cuts because they reward with tax refunds those who have earned the most money (Lakoff, 1996). Attitudes toward welfare and taxes, flowing from a conservative ideology, are therefore interrelated.

By contrast, liberals—who value nurturance, fairness, and compassion for the disadvantaged—favor welfare because it helps indigent individuals who have been left behind by society. Liberal thinkers also oppose across-the-board tax cuts because (in their view) they favor the rich; liberals prefer targeted tax cuts that redistribute money to low- and middle-income people. Attitude toward welfare and tax cuts go together—are correlated—in liberals' minds (see Fig. 2.3).

As a general rule, ideologues view social and political issues differently than ordinary citizens. Unlike many people, who respond to issues primarily on the basis of simple symbolic predispositions, ideologues'

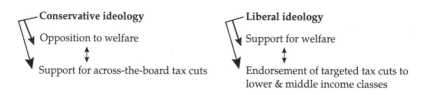

FIG. 2.3 Heavy arrows depict influence of ideology on attitudes. Lighter, smaller arrows denote association between two attitudes.

begin with an ideology, and their attitudes flow from this (see Lavine, Thomsen, & Gonzales, 1997).

The ideological approach to attitudes asserts that attitudes are organized "top-down." That is, attitudes flow from the hierarchy of principles (or predispositions) that individuals have acquired and developed.

A shortcoming with this approach is that it assumes people operate on the basis of one set of ideological beliefs. In fact, individuals frequently call on a variety of prescriptive beliefs when thinking about social issues (Conover & Feldman, 1984). For instance, a student might be a social liberal, believing affirmative action is needed to redress societal wrongs. She could also be an economic conservative, believing that government should not excessively regulate private companies. The student might also have strong religious convictions and a deep belief in a Supreme Being. Her social attitudes are thus structured by a variety of belief systems, sometimes called schema, rather than by one singular ideological set of principles.

ARE ATTITUDES INTERNALLY CONSISTENT?

Expectations, affect, symbolic predispositions, and ideology all influence the nature of attitudes. This raises a new question. Given that attitudes are complex macromolecules with so many different components, one wonders whether they are in harmony or in disarray. Are attitudes at peace or ready to ignite due to the combustible combination of cognitions, affect, and behavior? In other words, when we have an attitude toward an issue, are we all of one mind, consistent in our thoughts and feelings, or are we divided and ambivalent? These are questions that many of us have probably asked in one way or another. We have heard people say, "Intellectually, I agree, but emotionally I don't," or "You're a hypocrite; you say one thing and do another."

Social scientists have explored these issues, guided by theories and empirical methods. This section examines internal consistency of attitudes, and the next chapter focuses on the larger issue of attitude and behavior congruency.

Intra-Attitudinal Consistency

It's pleasant when we are all of one mind on an issue—when our general attitude is in sync with specific beliefs about the topic, or has the same "electrical charge" as our feelings. However, life does not always grant us this pleasure. We are *ambivalent* about many issues. Ambivalence occurs when we feel both positively and negatively about a person or issue (Thompson, Zanna, & Griffin, 1995). Ambivalence is characterized by uncertainty or conflict between attitude elements.

One type of ambivalence occurs when we hold seemingly incompatible beliefs. Many people evaluate their own doctor positively, but view the health system negatively. They believe their family is healthy, but American families are in trouble. And they frequently have kind things to say about their own representative to Congress, but disparage "the bums in Washington" (Perloff, 1996). One source for this discrepancy is mass media, which typically focus on the seamy side of political life. An effect is an ambivalence about the issue in question.

People are also ambivalent when they have strikingly different feelings about an issue. Some (though not all) Americans experienced this after the O. J. Simpson verdict. They were elated that Simpson had been acquitted, noting that "the court system has been biased against Blacks for years; justice was done, this is a victory for Black people." At the same time, they felt very sad, believing that "the victims and their families must have suffered a lot" (Mendoza-Denton et al., 1997, p. 577).

Perhaps the most common type of ambivalence is the head versus heart variety—our cognitions take us one way, but our feelings pull us somewhere else. Expectancy–value theory deals with this when it stipulates that people can have strong beliefs about two or more outcomes, but evaluate the outcomes very differently. For example, a student may believe that her professor taught her a lot about physiology, but at the same time kept her waiting in his office. She evaluates knowledge gain positively, but time misspent negatively. A more dramatic example involves the ambivalent attitudes many young women harbor toward safer sex. For example, many women (correctly) believe that using condoms can prevent AIDS, and they evaluate AIDS prevention positively. They also believe that requesting condoms will upset their boyfriends, and place a negative value on this outcome. "My boyfriend hates them," one young woman said, adding, "Frankly, I can't blame him. For me it certainly puts a crimp on what I would like to do to satisfy him," she noted (Perloff, 2001, p. 13). Persuaders face a challenge in cases like this one. To change this woman's attitude toward safer sex, they must help her rethink her fear of offending her boyfriend.

Sex roles is unquestionably an area in which many people feel a great deal of ambivalence. Some of this stems from conflict between early socialization and later experiences, in which individuals realize that some of the attitudes learned as children don't fit reality. As children, girls traditionally learn that they should get married, have children, and center their lives around caring for others. Boys develop an orientation toward careers, viewing women as trophies to acquire along the way. When girls grow up and come to value independence of mind, and boys view women in a more egalitarian light, they realize that their symbolic upbringing is at odds with their newly acquired beliefs. But old ideas die hard, and the result is conflict between childhood affect and grown-up cognition.

Ambivalence can frequently be found among young women who love the power and responsibility that comes with high-powered corporate jobs, yet also worry that their commitment to career will compromise their chances of raising a family when they reach their 30s. Writer Peggy Orenstein (2000) documented this, interviewing scores of women across the country, asking them to share their feelings about careers, relationships, and future plans to become a mom and raise a family. Some of the 20-something women Orenstein interviewed worried that "having a child 'too soon' would be a disaster: it would cut short their quest for identity and destroy their career prospects" (pp. 33–34). At the same time, these women felt pressure not to have kids too late, noting that women have more difficulty conceiving a child when they reach their late 30s. On the other side of the career track, educated women who "mommy-tracked" their aspirations to raise families also experienced mixed feelings. These women found enormous gratification in being a mom, yet at the same time lamented, as one woman put it, that "I don't really have a career and I feel crummy about that" (p. 224). "Ambivalence may be the only sane response to motherhood at this juncture in history, to the schism it creates in women's lives," Orenstein concluded (p. 141).

Two researchers, finding themselves fascinated by sex-role ambivalence, approached the issue from a different vantage point. Noting that contemporary society could be described as a patriarchy, yet at the same time reveres women as wives and mothers, Peter Glick and Susan T. Fiske (1996) argued that people can have hostile *and* benevolent beliefs about women. They called this mixture ambivalent sexism, and developed a scale to measure it. Their instrument has two components. The first, *hostile sexism*, is characterized by agreement with statements like "Women exaggerate problems at work" and "When women lose fairly, they claim discrimination." The second component, more positive to women, is called *benevolent sexism*. It reflects agreement with statements like "Women should be cherished and protected by men," "Women have a superior moral sensibility," and "Every man ought to have a woman he adores." Although some readers may reasonably wonder why the latter three statements are sexist, Glick and Fiske argue that they demean women and make stereotyped, frequently inaccurate assumptions about them.

The investigators reported that numerous men and women could be characterized as ambivalent sexists. These individuals harbored both hostile and benevolent beliefs about women. Sex role attitudes, like men and women themselves, are complex and not always in harmony.

Balancing Things Out

Ambivalence drives some people crazy. They will do anything to resolve it. More generally, psychologists argue that individuals dislike inconsistency among cognitive elements and are motivated to reconfigure things mentally so as to achieve a harmonious state of mind. Fritz Heider (1958) proposed an algebraic model of attitudes, called **balance theory**. Heider's model involves a triad of relationships: a person or perceiver (P), another person (O), and an issue (X). Heider argued that people prefer a balanced relationship among P, O, and X.

Borrowing from chemistry, Heider suggested that cognitive elements have a positive or negative valence (or charge). A positive relationship, in which P likes O or X, is symbolized with a plus sign. A negative relationship, in which P dislikes O or X, is assigned a minus sign. A visual thinker, Heider diagrammed his model with a series of triangles. Each of the three relationships (P,O, P,X, and O,X) is assigned a plus or minus. Attitudes are in harmony when the signs multiplied together yield a plus. If you remember your elementary arithmetic, you recall that a plus times a plus is a plus, a minus times a minus is a plus, and a plus times a minus yields a minus. Let's see how this works in real life to understand how people cope with inconsistency among attitudinal elements.

Consider for a moment the quandary of a liberal Democrat who learned in 1998 that President Bill Clinton had an adulterous affair with Monica Lewinsky. Let's say the Democrat liked Clinton (this relation is symbolized by a + in the model). Our Democrat also perceived that Clinton approved of his relationship with Lewinsky (+), but disapproved of the Lewinsky affair herself (−). Multiplying the three terms, one gets a minus, suggesting the person's attitude is imbalanced, or not entirely consistent (see Fig. 2.4a).

Presumably, the Democrat would find the inconsistency uncomfortable and would feel impelled to restore mental harmony. Balance theory says she has several options. She could change her attitude toward Clinton, deciding that she really does not think highly of him anymore. This would yield a positive relationship (Fig. 2.4b). Or she could change her mind about Clinton's adultery and decide it was not so bad. This would also produce cognitive balance (Fig. 2.4c).

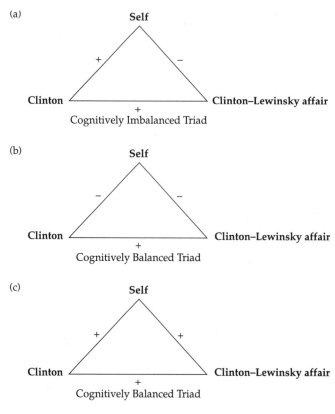

FIG. 2.4 Balance theory analysis of a Democrat's attitudes toward Bill Clinton during 1998 impeachment (+s indicate positive sentiments; −s show negative ones).

Balance theory helps us understand many situations in which people face cognitive inconsistency. For example, one antiabortion activist told a researcher that she could not be a friend with somebody who disagreed with her on abortion (Granberg, 1993). Unfortunately, balance theory does not describe many subtleties in people's judgments. It also fails to describe those situations in which people manage to like people with whom they disagree (Milburn, 1991). For example, during the Clinton impeachment, many Democrats did not reduce their liking of Clinton after they found out about his affair. Nor did they change their negative attitude toward his relationship with Lewinsky. Most Democrats continued to give high marks to Clinton's performance as president, while disapproving of his liaison with Lewinsky. This is not entirely consistent with balance theory. Thus, we need another approach to explain how people grapple with inconsistency. A model proposed by Robert P. Abelson

(1959) is more helpful. Abelson suggested people resolve cognitive conflict in four ways: (a) denial, (b) bolstering, (c) differentiation, and (d) transcendence. Consider how this worked for dissonant Democrats:

Denial. Democrats could try to forget about Clinton's affair or otherwise deny it. Denial is a weak way to resolve inconsistencies, and in this case it was high-nigh impossible because of all the media coverage.

Bolstering. Democrats could add mental elements to their attitude toward Clinton, hoping to overpower knowledge of the affair and (later) Clinton's lying under oath. They could emphasize Clinton's success in improving the economy, his achievements in globalization, and his commitment to diversity. Thus, they could strengthen their positive beliefs about Clinton, hoping it would override the negative information.

Differentiation. Supporters could differentiate Clinton the person from Clinton the leader. They could acknowledge his errors, but point out that great leaders have moral flaws. Defenders frequently noted that other revered presidents, like Franklin Delano Roosevelt and John F. Kennedy, had cheated on their wives. Leadership, Democrats observed, was not about private morality, but public virtue.

Transcendence. Democrats could transcend the situation, creating a new mental structure. They might claim that Clinton was a victim of the vicious, argumentative political culture in which one side (the Republicans and Special Prosecutor Kenneth Starr) stopped at nothing to destroy its political opponents. Democrats transcended the situation by concluding that Clinton was a victim, not a perpetrator.

THE PSYCHOLOGY OF STRONG ATTITUDES

Drugs. Abortion. Teen pregnancy. Gun control. These are what typically come to mind when we think of attitudes. As suggested earlier, not all attitudes are this strong, nor based as exclusively in affect. However, strong attitudes like these seem to have profound influences on thoughts and behavior. From the French Revolution to violence perpetrated against doctors who perform abortion, "the incidents that attract our attention are often those associated with strong sentiments," Jon A. Krosnick and Richard E. Petty (1995) note (p. 1). Intrigued by the dynamics of such attitudes, social psychologists have embarked on a series of studies exploring strong attitude characteristics and effects (see Fig. 2.5).

This might all seem obvious at first blush. People with strong attitudes have lots of passion and care a lot; isn't that what one would expect?

FIG. 2.5 People frequently display strong political attitudes in public. These attitudes are involving, emotional, and invariably complex. (Photograph by William C. Rieter.)

Yes—but remember persuasion scholars take a scientific approach. They want to understand what a strong attitude looks like, what it means psychologically to feel deeply about an issue, how strong attitudes differ from weaker or more ambivalent ones, and the effects of such attitudes on behavior. Remember also that people have done terrible things in the name of strong attitudes. They have killed innocent people and destroyed themselves. The more we can understand such attitudes, the more likely it is that we can devise ways to convince troubled or violent people to rethink their approaches to life.

Attitudes by definition influence thought and action. But strong attitudes are particularly likely to: (a) persist over time, (b) affect judgments, (c) guide behavior, and (d) prove resistant to change (Krosnick & Petty, 1995). Why is this so? Why are strong attitudes stable? According to Maureen Wang Erber and her colleagues (1995):

> First, strong attitudes are probably anchored by other beliefs and values, making them more resistant to change. If people were to change their basic religious beliefs, for example, many other attitudes and values linked to these beliefs would have to be changed as well. Second, people are likely to know more about issues they feel strongly about, making them more resistant to

counterarguments. Third, people are likely to associate with others who feel similarly on important issues, and these people help maintain and support these attitudes. Fourth, strong attitudes are often more elaborated and accessible, making it more likely that they will be at the tip of the tongue when people are asked how they feel on different occasions. Fifth, people with strong attitudes are likely to attend to and seek out information relevant to the topic, arming them with still more arguments with which to resist attempts to change their minds. (Wang Erber, Hodges, & Wilson, pp. 437–438)

Think for a moment about something you feel strongly about. Your attitude might be one of those we have discussed in the book—politics, race, sex roles, abortion. Or it could be something quite different—a vegetarian diet, jogging, cigarette smoking, or downloading music. Now think of something you feel less strongly or personally about. How does the first attitude differ from the second?

Social psychologists who have pondered this issue note that there is not just one way that a strong attitude differs from a weaker one. Attitude strength is a multifaceted concept. Thus, there are a variety of elements that differentiate strong from weak attitudes (Krosnick et al., 1993). Strong attitudes are characterized by:

- importance (we care deeply about the issue);
- ego-involvement (the attitude is linked to core values or the self);
- extremity (the attitude deviates significantly from neutrality);
- certainty (we are convinced that our attitude is correct);
- accessibility (the attitude comes quickly to mind);
- knowledge (we are highly informed about the topic); and
- hierarchical organization (the attitude is internally consistent and embedded in an elaborate attitudinal structure).

Note that a particular strong attitude may not possess all of these characteristics. You could regard an attitude as important, but not link it up to your self-concept (Boninger et al., 1995). You could know a lot about an issue, but not be certain that your knowledge is correct. An attitude could come quickly to mind, but it might not be embedded in an extensive internal structure. The upshot of all this is that certain attitudes may be strong, but they are not likely to be simple.

ATTITUDES AND INFORMATION PROCESSING

Strong attitudes influence message evaluations and judgments of communications. Two theories shed light on how this occurs. They are social judgment theory and the attitude accessibility approach.

Social Judgment Theory

- On the eve of a Subway Series between the New York Yankees and New York Mets a few years back, a reporter filed this tongue-in-cheek report on how Yankee and Met fans saw each other, based on interviews with New York baseball fans:
  "Yankee fans are much more highly educated (Allen Sherman, a Yankee fan) said. . . . " We have to be. It's harder to spell Yankees than Mets. And we can curse in so many different languages. We earn more, so when we throw a beer can it's those high-priced beer cans. . . . " Fred Sayed, 26, a technical support manager from Queens and a Met fan, was able to be pretty explicit himself in defining Yankee fans: "All Yankee fans are just flat-out stupid." (Kleinfield, October 19, 2000, p. 1)
- Ask a baseball pitcher why so many home runs are hit these days and you will hear an impassioned speech from a member of an oppressed minority. You will hear how umpires are calling a fist-size strike zone (*They're sticking it to us!*), . . . the mounds are lower (*They won't give us any edge!*) and, of course, the baseball is different . . . (*We're throwing golf balls out there!*). Ask an infielder, an outfielder or any player *except* a pitcher about the inordinate increase in home runs and a royal smirk often precedes the response. (*The answers are pretty obvious, aren't they?*) You are informed the hitters are stronger than they used to be . . . , train daily (*I am a machine!*) and capitalize on modern technology (*We study videotape between at-bats and recognize the weaknesses in all pitchers*). (Olney, 2000, p. 38)

These anecdotes show that some people have very strong attitudes toward baseball. But they tell more than that. They speak to the biases individuals have when they harbor strong feelings about a topic, and in this way illustrate the social judgment approach to attitudes. Pioneered by Muzafer Sherif and Carolyn Sherif (1967), social judgment theory emphasizes that people evaluate issues based on where they stand on the topic. As Sherif and Sherif noted:

> The basic information for predicting a person's reaction to a communication is *where* he places its position and the communicator relative to himself. The way that a person appraises a communication and perceives its position relative to his own stand affects his reaction to it and what he will do as a result. (p. 129)

Thus, social judgment theory emphasizes that receivers do not evaluate a message purely on the merits of the arguments. Instead, the theory stipulates that people compare the advocated position with their attitude and then determine whether they should accept the position advocated in the message. Like Narcissus preoccupied with his reflection in the water, receivers are consumed with their own attitudes toward the topic. They can never escape their own points of view (see Fig. 2.6).

FIG. 2.6 This painting, "Hand with Reflecting Globe," by the artist Maurits Escher illustrates a central principle of social judgment theory. It highlights the notion that people are consumed by their own attitudes toward a topic. They cannot escape their own perspectives on the issue.

Social judgment theory, so named because it emphasizes people's subjective judgments about social issues, articulates several core concepts. These are: (a) latitudes of acceptance, rejection, and noncommitment; (b) assimilation and contrast; and (c) ego-involvement.

Latitudes. Attitudes consist of a continuum of evaluations—a range of acceptable and unacceptable positions, as well as positions toward which the individual has no strong commitment. The *latitude of acceptance* consists of all those positions on an issue that an individual finds acceptable, including the most acceptable position. The *latitude of rejection* includes those positions that the individual finds objectionable, including the most objectionable position. Lying between these two regions is the *latitude of noncommitment*, which consists of those positions on which the individual has preferred to remain noncommital. This is the arena of the "don't know," "not sure," and "haven't made up my mind" responses (see Fig. 2.7).

Early research focused on the relationship between extreme attitudes and size of the latitudes. Studies indicated that extremity of position influenced the size of the latitudes of rejection and acceptance (Sherif, Sherif, & Nebergall, 1965). Individuals with strong—in particular, extreme—views on a topic have large latitudes of rejection. They reject nearly all opposing arguments and accept only statements that are adjacent to their own stands on the issue. This is one reason why it is hard to change these folks' minds.

Assimilation/Contrast. One way to appreciate these terms is to focus on an entirely different issue for a moment: the weather. For example, if the weather is unseasonably warm in Chicago one December (say, 60 degrees), people will yak on and on about how hot it is. Expecting the temperature to register 30 degrees, they are pleasantly surprised. This is a

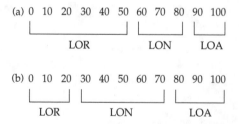

FIG. 2.7 Latitude of rejection (LOR), latitude of noncommitment (LON), and latitude of acceptance (LOA) of individuals with strong and moderate attitudes on an issue. Panel *a* illustrates latitudes of individual with a strong attitude. Panel *b* shows latitudes of individual with a moderate attitude. Hypothetical scale goes from 0 to 100, where 100 indicates a position in total agreement with persuasive message and 0 a position in total disagreement.

contrast effect, in which we focus on how different reality is from expectation. On the other hand, if the thermometer reads 38 in December, people think nothing of it. Expecting the temperature to be in the 30s, they are hardly surprised. They **assimilate** the temperature to what they expected, neglecting the fact that 38 degrees is somewhat warmer than average.

Assimilation and contrast are perceptual mistakes, distortions that result from the tendency to perceive phenomena from the standpoint of a personal reference point or *anchor*. People judge message positions not objectively, but subjectively. Their initial attitude serves as the reference point. In assimilation, people pull a somewhat congenial message toward their own attitude, assuming the message is more similar to their attitude than it really is. They overestimate the similarity between a speaker's attitude and their own. In the case of contrast, individuals push a somewhat disagreeable message away from their attitude, assuming it is more different than it really is. They overestimate the difference between the communicator's attitude and their own (Granberg, 1993).

Assimilation and contrast are part of everyday life. We assimilate our friends' attitudes toward our own, assuming their views are more similar to ours than they really are. This is one reason why people who fall in love are so shocked at their first disagreement. At the same time, we contrast our foes, exaggerating the degree to which their attitudes are different from ours. "You mean, we actually agree," we jokingly say to an opponent at the office.

Assimilation and contrast effects show up frequently in politics. This makes sense when you consider two important facts: (a) politicians frequently make ambiguous statements so that they will not offend key constituents, and (b) social judgment theory says that assimilation/contrast will only occur when communications are ambiguous (Granberg, 1993). (When a message is clear cut, no one has any doubt as to where the communicator stands on the issue.) Thus, American voters end up doing a lot of assimilating and contrasting in presidential elections. Not being that interested in politics to begin with, many just *assume* that their favored candidate shares their position on education or health care, and tell themselves that the person they're not voting for takes *sharply* different positions from their own. After the election, voters are sometimes surprised to discover that the candidate for whom they voted does not share all their viewpoints, and that the opposing candidate was not as different as they feared.

Ego-Involvement. If you had to say which concept from social judgment theory exerted the greatest influence on research, it would be involvement. Social scientists have found involvement fascinating because it seems to have such a strong impact on latitudes and assimilation/contrast.

Practitioners have been intrigued because of its many implications for intractable conflict on social and political issues.

Ego-involvement is "the arousal, singly or in combination, of the individual's commitments or stands in the context of appropriate situations" (Sherif et al., 1965, p. 65). People are ego-involved when they perceive that the issue touches on their self-concepts or core values. Highly involved individuals differ from less involved persons in three ways. First, when people are involved in, or care deeply about, a social issue, they have larger latitudes of rejection relative to their latitudes of acceptance and noncommitment. This means they reject just about any position that is not in sync with their own. Second, and in a related vein, they contrast mildly disagreeable messages from their attitudes more frequently than folks who aren't as invested in the issue. Third, when concerned deeply about an issue, people are apt to assimilate ambiguous messages only when the arguments are generally consistent with their preconceived attitudes (Sherif et al., 1965). Individuals with ego-involved stands are hard to persuade: They are stubborn or resilient, depending on your point of view (see Fig. 2.7).

There has been much research exploring the psychology of ego-involved attitudes. Studies have shown that when individuals are ego-involved in an issue (as people frequently are with the environment, religion, or animal rights), they engage in what is known as **selective perception**. They perceive events so that they fit their preconceived beliefs and attitudes. Two 1950s-era studies documented this tendency. The research was distinctive because the investigators tested hypotheses by locating people with strong views on an issue and then asking them to indicate their perceptions of a message.

Hovland, Harvey, and Sherif (1957), focusing on repeal of a law prohibiting sale of alcoholic beverages in Oklahoma, found that both those opposed to alcoholic beverages and those in favor of drinking thought that a message that by and large agreed with their point of view was fair, but one that disputed it was biased. Hastorf and Cantril (1954) asked Princeton and Dartmouth students to view a film of a football game between their colleges that featured lots of rough play and rule infractions. Students interpreted the game in light of their biases: Princeton and Dartmouth students each saw a game in which their squad was "the good guys" and the other team the "bad guys."

Thus, where we "stand" on an issue depends on where we "sit" psychologically. Flashback to the baseball examples that introduced this section. Yankee and Met fans' strong attitudes colored their views of the other team. Ball players' explanations of increases in home runs differed, depending on whether they were pitchers or hitters.

Recent research, flowing out of the "oldy but goody" tradition of Sherif and Hastorf, has documented that people with strong, ego-involved attitudes still perceive messages in biased ways (Edwards & Smith, 1996; Miller et al., 1993; Newman et al., 1997; Thompson, 1995; see Box 2–2). An intriguing study by Charles Lord and his colleagues (1979) provides a snapshot on current thinking on this issue. The study was conducted over two decades ago, but is regarded as a classic in the field.

BOX 2–2
WHAT'S THE RIGHT THING?

You may have heard of Spike Lee's movie *Do the Right Thing*. It's a disturbing, controversial portrait of relationships among Blacks, Whites, and Hispanics in the New York City neighborhood of Bedford–Stuyvesant. But did you know that Black and White viewers sometimes react to the movie in diametrically opposite ways? That, at least, is the conclusion reached by Brenda Cooper (1998), who studied the ways that White and African American students interpreted the film. Her study provides additional evidence that ego-involvement influences social judgments. Psychologists have made this point for years, but now comes evidence that the same processes operate when people watch blockbuster movies.

The film is set in New York City on a hot summer day. The movie examines the experiences of Black and Hispanic residents and their tense relationship with Sal, an Italian American owner of the neighborhood pizza joint. Mookie, the main Black character, earns $250 a week delivering Sal's pizzas to neighborhood residents. The film edges toward the climax when:

> Buggin' Out, one of Mookie's friends, complains to Sal that all of the pictures on the pizzeria's "Wall of Fame" are of Italian Americans, yet most of his customers are Blacks . . . Buggin' Out enlists another Black man, Radio Raheem, in his boycott of Sal's pizzeria to protest the absence of pictures of African Americans on the "Wall of Fame." The two men confront Sal, and when Radio Raheem refuses to lower the volume of his boom box, Sal smashes his radio with a baseball bat, calls his customers "niggers," and a brawl begins. (Cooper, pp. 205–206)

Subsequently, the police arrive, Radio Raheem is killed, Mookie hurls a garbage can through the window, and the pizzeria goes up in flames. Researcher Cooper, noting that people interpret mass media differently depending on their cultural experiences, predicted that Blacks and Whites would experience the film in dramatically different ways. She asked a group of predominately White and Black students to describe their reactions to the movie. As social judgment theory would predict, the perceptions of Whites differed considerably from those of Blacks. Here is how Whites perceived the film:

> "Sal's character was a loving, hardworking man and he treated Mookie like one of his own sons. . . . Sal was not racist and I believe he tried to do what

Continued

BOX 2–2
(CONTINUED)

was right. . . . Sal, despite his hard-hitting attitude, genuinely cared for the people of the community. . . . If a Black man would have owned that pizzeria, and had pictures of just Black men, none of this would have started. I also don't think that a White man would ever ask a Black person who owned something, to put up pictures of some White guy who Blacks neither like nor know what that person did. . . . The guys who came in breaking Sal's rules incited Sal to react negatively. . . . Even though the Black boy with the radio was killed by the White cops, I do not believe that justifies the cruel act of destroying a man's business." (pp. 212, 214)

African American respondents saw things differently:

"Sal's interactions with the different characters were strictly business. He considered himself to be king of the block and the African Americans were his servants. . . . I saw his (Buggin' Out's) point when he made the statement that if 99% of your business comes from Blacks, then why aren't there any Blacks on the wall? . . . In my community I see exactly what Spike filmed—Whites operate their businesses in Black neighborhoods and yet they do not live in that neighborhood. . . . Sal destroyed his radio—which meant that Sal destroyed a part of Raheem. . . . We received a clear picture of brutality when one of Mookie's friends is killed by the White police. This incident showed us that a Black man was convicted before he was tried. . . . Mookie did the right thing by throwing the garbage can through Sal's window . . . It helped everyone to channel their anger on Sal's property rather than to allow the crowd to continue to attack Sal in revenge for Radio's death." (pp. 212, 215)

Social judgment theorists could find plenty of examples in these comments of assimilation, contrast, and selective perception. On a general level, there is a similarity between predictions made by social judgment theory, a social psychological account, and qualitative, "postmodern" perspectives cited by Cooper. If there is a moral in these approaches and Cooper's findings, it is that we should appreciate that what we "see" in messages reflects our own cultural perspective. Someday historians may discover that our "view" was indeed correct. But until that time, tolerance and understanding seem like useful prescriptions to follow.

Focusing on attitudes toward capital punishment, the investigators followed the Sherif and Hastorf tradition of locating individuals with strong views on an issue. They focused on two groups of students. One group favored the death penalty, believing it to be an effective deterrent against crime. The second group opposed it, maintaining that capital punishment was inhumane or an ineffective deterrent. Individuals from each group read brief descriptions of two purported investigations of the death penalty's deterrent effects. One study always reported evidence that the death penalty was effective (e.g., "in 11 of the 14 states, murder rates were *lower after* adoption of the death penalty"). The other study used similar statistics to make the opposite point—that the death penalty was an ineffective deterrent against crime (in 8 of the 10 states, "murder rates were *higher* in the state *with* capital punishment").

Students evaluated the studies and indicated whether they had changed their attitude toward capital punishment. Thus, students read one study that supported, and one study that opposed, their position on the death penalty. The evidence in support of the death penalty's deterrent effect was virtually the same as the evidence that questioned its impact. Now if people were objective and fair, they would acknowledge that the evidence for both sides was equally strong. But that is not how these ego-involved partisans responded.

Proponents of capital punishment found the pro-death-penalty study more convincing, and opponents found the anti-death-penalty study more persuasive. For example, a supporter of capital punishment said this about a study favoring the death penalty:

> The experiment was well thought out, the data collected was valid, and they were able to come up with responses to all criticisms.

The same person reacted to the anti-capital-punishment study by remarking that:

> There were too many flaws in the picking of the states and too many variables involved in the experiment as a whole to change my opinion.

An opponent of capital punishment said this of a study opposing capital punishment:

> The states were chosen at random, so the results show the average effect capital punishment has across the nation. The fact that 8 out of 10 states show a rise in murders stands as good evidence.

The opponent reacted in this way to the pro-capital-punishment study:

> The study was taken only 1 year before and 1 year after capital punishment was reinstated. To be a more effective study they should have taken data from at least 10 years before and as many years as possible after. (Lord et al., 1979, p. 2103)

Individuals processed information very selectively, exhibiting what the authors called *biased assimilation*. They assimilated ambiguous information to their point of view, believing that it was consistent with their position on capital punishment. What's more, proponents and opponents managed to feel even more strongly about the issue by the study's conclusion. Proponents reported that they were more in favor of the death penalty than they had been at the study's start. Opponents indicated that they were more opposed than they had been at the beginning of the experiment. Reading the arguments did not reduce biased perceptions; it caused partisans to become even more polarized, more convinced that they were right.

Fascinated by the cognitive underpinnings of such perceptions, social psychologists have tried to piece together what happens inside an individual's mind when he or she is faced with conflicting evidence on an issue. They have suggested that people with strong attitudes have no intention of mentally searching for information that might prove their position wrong. On the contrary, they engage in a "biased memory search" at the get-go; convinced that their position is correct, they search memory for facts that support their view of the world, conveniently overlooking or rejecting evidence on the other side that might call their ideas into question (Edwards & Smith, 1996).

Another factor that plays into all this is the way that involved observers visualize the problem. When thinking about welfare, conservatives see a lazy, fat mother thumbing her nose at those who want her to work. Liberals envision a needy, frail person, marginalized by society, doing her best to raise her kids on her own. On the issue of capital punishment, those who favor the death penalty think first about the victims of the murderer's horrific act. Or, when thinking of the killer, they call to mind a depraved, sadistic person who kills for sheer pleasure. Death penalty opponents visualize the sadistic execution of a human being, turned from a person to charred human remains. These cognitive representations powerfully influence thinking, and help explain why involved individuals on different sides of the political fence process the same information so differently (Lord et al., 1994).

Interestingly, ego-involved partisans are not necessarily uninformed about the positions advocated by their opponents. In some cases they know their foes' arguments excruciatingly well, probably better than neutral observers (Pratkanis, 1989). Early social judgment research probably oversimplified the dynamics of social attitudes, suggesting that people shun or quickly forget information that disputes their point of view. Recent studies show that people do not deliberately avoid information that is inconsistent with their viewpoint. Nor do they remember facts congenial with their point of view better than those that are inconsistent with their preexisting attitude (Eagly et al., 1999). On the contrary, when people are ego-involved in an issue, they sometimes scrutinize facts from the other side carefully, and remember them remarkably well, even though they are not persuaded in the least by the position advocated in the message (Eagly et al., 2001). Individuals with strong viewpoints may find it useful to know arguments from the other side, perhaps to develop stronger counterarguments, or they may be intrigued by the entire issue and therefore motivated to find out as much as they can about both sides. Whatever the reasons, it is fair to say that ego-involved partisans have more complex attitude structures than nonpartisans. Unfortunately, this does not make them more objective or open to considering alternative points of view.

Attitude Accessibility

On September 11, 2001, Americans received a massive, tragic jolt from their quiescence. The terrorist attacks on the World Trade Center and Pentagon had an enormous impact on the country. A particularly noteworthy, and surprising, effect was the outpouring of patriotism that the events unleashed. Flags flew everywhere. They could be seen on houses, cars, clothing, book bags, even tattoos. People sang the national anthem and "America the Beautiful" proudly and with feeling, not mumbling the words in private embarrassment. Feelings of patriotism, long moribund, came out in waves, as Americans came to appreciate how deeply they felt about the nation's basic values—independence, freedom, liberty, and equality—and how much they loved their country.

Tragically, the events of September 11 accessed attitudes toward America. They thus provide a poignant introduction to the concept of attitude accessibility, a second approach to attitude dynamics developed by Russell H. Fazio. Fazio (1995) views attitude as an association between an object (person, place, or issue) and an evaluation. It's a linkage between a country (U.S.A.) and a great feeling; an ethnic identity (Black, Hispanic, Asian) and feelings of pride; or a product (Nike tennis shoes) and exhilaration. Prejudiced attitudes, by contrast, are associations between the object and feelings of disgust or hatred.

Attitudes vary along a continuum of strength. Weak attitudes are characterized by a familiarity with the object, but a lukewarm evaluation of its net worth. Your attitudes toward Denmark, Eskimos, and an infrequently advertised brand of sneakers probably fall under the weak label. You have heard of the entities, but don't have particularly positive or negative feelings toward them. You can retrieve your attitude toward these objects, but not automatically or without effort. Strong attitudes— toward country, an ethnic group, a celebrity, or favorite product—are characterized by well-learned associations between the object and your evaluation. These attitudes are so strong and enduring that we can activate them automatically from memory. Simply reading the name of the object in print will trigger the association and call the attitude to mind. (Thought experiment: Look at the word Denmark and observe what comes to mind. Now try U.S.A. What thoughts leap to mind? What emotions do you feel? According to accessibility theory, a global feeling about America should come to mind when you see the word on the page; see Fig. 2.8).

The key constructs of the theory are accessibility and association. *Accessibility* means the degree to which attitude is automatically activated from memory. If you want a simple colloquial phrase, think of accessibility as "getting in touch with your feelings." *Associations* are links among different components of the attitude. The stronger the linkages, the stronger the attitude. Accessibility theory calls on a cognitive model of associative networks to explain attitude strength. It's a complex model, so an example may help you appreciate the associative notion.

Consider attitude toward America, mentioned above. Imagine the attitude is located somewhere in your mind, with "pathways" or "roads" connecting different components of the attitude. Each component is linked with a positive or negative evaluation. Fourth of July is associated with positive affect, which radiates out (in red, white, and blue) to fireworks and hot dogs, also evaluated positively. Other components of the America concept could be freedom of speech, Thomas Jefferson, "the Star-Spangled Banner," baseball, land of opportunity, and rock 'n' roll. Many people have good feelings about these concepts. The stronger the association between the overall concept, America, and a positive evaluation, the more likely it is that a strong favorable attitude will come quickly to mind when people see the word *America*.

Needless to say, not everyone loves America. Some Americans have a negative attitude toward their country. Racial prejudice, school violence, and poverty might be images of the U.S.A. that these individuals have conjured up many times. Having learned to strongly associate America with negative feelings, they have a strong unfavorable attitude that would come automatically to mind when they encounter the name of their country (see Fig. 2.9).

You see how powerful accessing can be. Associations among ideas and feelings, learned early in childhood, can form the bulwark of our attitudes. Strong attitudes can be accessed at the drop of a hat—or powerful symbol, triggering a variety of mental and behavioral reactions. (In this sense, accessibility theory resembles the symbolic attitude approach discussed on pp. 47–48.)

Stimulated by the accessibility notion, researchers have conducted numerous experiments over the past decade. They have examined factors that make it more likely that we are "in touch with" our attitudes. They also have explored the influence of accessibility on processing information

FIG. 2.8 The American flag evokes strong sentiments, typically pride and reverence for country. What comes to mind when you see these flags? (Photograph by William C. Rieter.)

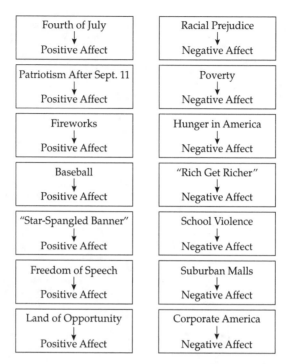

FIG. 2.9 Associations and accessibility. An associative network for individual with positive attitude (left) and negative attitude (right) toward America. When attitudes are strong, they can be accessed immediately—in this case, as soon as individuals see the word *America*.

(Fazio, 1990, 2000; Roskos-Ewoldsen, 1997b; Roskos-Ewoldsen et al., 2002). In order to measure this deep-seated construct, researchers have used reaction time procedures. Participants in the study view the name or picture of an attitude object (e.g., O. J. Simpson) on a computer screen and indicate whether they like or dislike the object. The speed with which they push a button on the computer indexes accessibility. The quicker their response time, the more accessible the attitude. Guided by this and related procedures, psychologists have learned a great deal about attitude accessibility. Key findings include:

1. *The more frequently people mentally rehearse the association between an object and evaluation, the stronger the connection.* Thus, prejudice, on the negative side, and love, on the positive side, are strong attitudes. People have come over time to associate the object of prejudice or love with bad or good feelings. These attitudes come quickly to mind and can influence our behavior, sometimes without our being aware of it. The same

processes occur with attitudes toward country, as in the example of America previously discussed.

2. *Objects toward which we have accessible attitudes are more likely to capture attention* (Roskos-Ewoldsen & Fazio, 1992). Objects that are strongly associated in memory with good or bad feelings are more likely to get noticed. This has interesting implications for advertising, as is discussed in chapter 11.

3. *Accessible attitudes serve as filters for processing information.* People are more likely to process issues in a biased manner if they can access their attitudes from memory (or call them to mind in a situation). An attitude cannot influence thinking if people cannot call it to mind, and attitudes based on strong linkages between the issue and feelings are more apt to be activated when people encounter the issue in real life. An individual may have an extreme position on an issue, but unless he is in touch with his feelings on the topic, it will not influence his judgments.

Attitude accessibility, pioneered over 20 years ago, has become such a popular staple in social psychology that it has generated criticism, as well as praise. Although intrigued by the concept, some researchers question whether accessibility has the strong effects Fazio attributes to it (Doll & Ajzen, 1992). Others have suggested that accessibility is less important than other aspects of attitude strength, such as the ways in which attitudes are mentally structured (Eagly & Chaiken, 1995). These are complex issues. Some researchers, like Fazio, believe that accessibility is the key aspect of attitude strength. Other researchers maintain that personal importance of the attitude is what differentiates strong from weak attitudes, while still other scholars believe that ego-involvement is critical. (And you thought strong attitudes were simple!) Despite their differences, social psychologists agree that accessibility is an intriguing construct, with fascinating implications for information processing and persuasion. We access more of these applications in chapter 3.

CONCLUSIONS

Attitudes, fascinating and controversial parts of the human psyche, have been the focus of much research over the past century. They continue to intrigue scholars. Attitudes are centerpieces of persuasion, for they are the entities that communicators wish to shape, mold, or reinforce. An attitude is defined as a learned, global evaluation of an object (person, place, or issue) that influences thought and action.

Attitudes dovetail with values, defined as conceptions of desirable means and ends, and beliefs, which are defined as cognitions about the world. Beliefs can theoretically be tested to determine if they are true, although people frequently assume their beliefs are equivalent to facts. (They're not.)

One of the interesting questions about attitudes concerns their structure or organization. Expectancy–value theory says that attitudes are composed of expectations (beliefs) and evaluations of these beliefs. It emphasizes the role that salient, or psychologically relevant, beliefs play in shaping attitudes. Expectancy–value theory helps break down the macro concept of attitude into component parts, yielding rich information about the human mind. The symbolic attitude approach argues that symbolic predispositions, like prejudice and deep-seated values, lie at the heart of attitudes. It calls attention to the many affective attributes that are associated with the attitude object. An ideological perspective contends that attitudes are organized around ideological principles, like liberalism–conservatism.

People being complex, attitudes are not always internally consistent. Individuals frequently experience ambivalence, feeling both positively and negatively about a person or issue. Preferring harmony to discord, people strive to reduce inconsistency among cognitive elements. Balance theory and other cognitive consistency models describe ways that individuals can restore mental harmony. We don't always succeed in this endeavor, and inconsistency is inevitably a fact of life.

A particularly noteworthy aspect of attitudes is their strength. Strong attitudes are characterized by personal importance, accessibility, and hierarchical organization. Social judgment theory provides many insights into the nature of strong attitudes, calling attention to ways that ego-involved partisans assimilate and contrast messages so as to maintain their original perspective on the issue.

Another factor that influences message processing is attitude accessibility. Strong attitudes are typically more accessible than weaker ones, characterized as they are by strong associations between feelings and the object (person, place, or political issue). Attitudes that come readily to mind—and are steeped in powerful emotional associations—are likely to lead to biased thinking about persuasive messages.

Theory and research on strong attitudes help us understand why partisans disagree so vehemently about social problems. They size up the problem differently, perceive matters in a biased manner, and tend to be resistant to persuasive communication. Ethicists suggest that if we could just supply people with the facts, they would put aside opinions and act rationally (Frankena, 1963). Unfortunately, there are no such things as pure facts. Partisans come to the table with different interpretations of the facts. Just bringing people from different sides together cannot guarantee that they will reach agreement. This is why negotiations—on issues ranging from labor-management disputes to the Middle East—frequently fail.

CHAPTER 3

Attitudes: Functions and Consequences

Leslie Maltz regards herself as a California housewife, "virtually a by-word for conventionality," as a magazine reporter put it (Adler, 1999, p. 76). But she recently did something a little different. She had her navel pierced and put "a diamond-studded horseshoe through it." As a result, she no longer regards herself as a housewife. "I feel like a sex symbol," she says (Adler, p. 76).

Leslie's bodacious decision illustrates a theme of this chapter: Attitudes serve functions for people, and people must decide whether and how to translate attitudes into behavior. As we will see, the issues of attitude functions and attitude–behavior consistency are intricate, complicated, and filled with implications for persuasion. This chapter continues the exploration of attitudes launched in chapter 2, focusing first on attitude function theory and research. The second section examines the venerable issue of attitude–behavior consistency, more colloquially expressed as: Do people practice what they preach?

FUNCTIONS OF ATTITUDES

Overview

Functional theories of attitude examine why people hold the attitudes they do. These approaches explore the needs attitudes fulfill and motives they serve. Functional approaches turn attitudes on their head. Instead of taking attitudes as a given and looking at their structure, they ask: Just what benefits do attitudes provide? What if people did not have attitudes? What then? Bombarded by numerous stimuli and faced with countless choices about issues and products, individuals would be forced to painstakingly assess the costs and benefits of each particular choice in each of hundreds of daily decisions (Fazio, 2000). Deprived of general attitudes to help structure the environment and position individuals in certain directions, human beings would find daily life arduous. Noting that this is not the case, theorists conclude that attitudes help people manage and cope with life. In a word, attitudes are functional.

The beauty of functional theory is that it helps us understand why people hold attitudes. This is not only interesting to theorists, but appeals to the people watcher in us all. Ever wonder why certain people are driven to dedicate their lives to helping others, why other individuals buy fancy sports cars at the zenith of their midlives, or why younger folks, in a carefree moment, decide to get themselves tattooed? Attitude function theories shed light on these decisions.

Researchers have catalogued the main functions of attitudes or the primary *benefits* that attitudes provide (Katz, 1960; Maio & Olson, 2000a; Smith, Bruner, & White, 1956). These include:

Knowledge.   Attitudes help people make sense of the world and explain baffling events. They provide an overarching framework, one that assists individuals in cognitively coming to terms with the array of ambiguous and sometimes scary stimuli they face in everyday life. Religious attitudes fulfill this function for many people, particularly those who have experienced personal tragedies. For example, relatives of people who were killed in the September 11 attacks found comfort in "religious certainty of a hereafter. 'A plan of exultation, a plan of salvation: they both are in a better place,'" said Margaret Wahlstrom, whose mother-in-law died at the World Trade Center (Clines, 2001, p. B8). In a similar fashion, the Kennedy family, which has experienced great highs but also crushing lows, has found solace in the Catholic religion. Religion seems to offer comfort to family members who experienced inexplicably tragic events, ranging from the assassinations of John and Bobby to the deaths of John Jr. in a plane crash and Michael in a skiing accident.

Utilitarian.   On a more material level, attitudes help people obtain rewards and avoid punishments. Smart, but mathematically challenged, students say that it is functional to develop a positive attitude toward statistics courses. They figure that if they show enthusiasm, the professor will like them more. They also recognize that if they look on the bright side of the course, they can more easily muster the motivation to study. On the other hand, if they decide at the outset to blow off the course because it's too hard, they will deprive themselves of the chance to prove themselves up to the task. In a similar vein, athletes find it functional to develop a positive—rather than hostile—attitude toward a tough coach. A positive attitude can help them get along with the "drill sergeant type," thereby minimizing the chances they will earn the coach's wrath.

Social Adjustive. We all like to be accepted by others. Attitudes help us "adjust to" reference groups. People sometimes adopt attitudes not because they truly agree with the advocated position, but because they believe they will be more accepted by others if they take this side. For example, a student who wants to get along with a musically hip group of friends may find it functional to adopt a more favorable attitude toward new hip-hop bands.

During the 1960s and early '70s, political attitudes served a social adjustive function for some students. Although many young people marched in rallies to express strong attitudes (e.g., opposition to the Vietnam War), not all participated for this reason. Some students attended rallies for social adjustive purposes—to prove to others or themselves that they were "with it," or meshed with the prevailing groove of the time. One 1970 rally in Michigan seemed to have served this function for students, as the following account from a student newspaper of the era suggests:

> Grab your coat, you'll need it tonight. Get your gloves, find a hat; take out the contacts—tear gas can be dangerous. All right, it's 8:30, let's go. All these people, are they headed for (campus)? They are. They're laughing, chanting. . . . Can't miss any of the action. . . . What are we fighting? The system, I suppose, yeah, we're battling the system. . . . The march is a free for all, it doesn't matter what you protest, just as long as you're here. Got to protest, just got to protest. Gotta be here, man, gotta be here. . . . We're at the dorms now. "Join us, join us," someone's got music, let's dance, in the streets. What'd he say? "Everybody must get stoned." Yeah, march and get stoned. Outtasight! (Perloff, 1971, p. 24)

Although the pressures of the protest years may have pushed some students into adopting attitudes for social adjustive reasons, there is no reason to believe that the need to belong does not operate equally strongly in today's era, with its own tensions and undercurrents.

Social Identity. People hold attitudes to communicate who they are and what that they aspire to be (Shavitt & Nelson, 2000). This is one reason people buy certain products; they hope that by displaying the product in their homes (or on their bodies), they will communicate something special about themselves. Women wear perfumes like Obsession, and men don Polo cologne to communicate that they have money and brains (Twitchell, 1999). Others buy T-shirts with the names of brand name stores (Hard Rock Café) or dates of rock band tours to tell passersby something of their identity ("I'm not just an ordinary student; I'm with the band. See my shirt?").

Products other than perfumes, colognes, and T-shirts can fulfill psychological functions. High-tech gadgets can do this too. One study found that men use cell phones "to advertise to females their worth, status and desirability" (Angier, 2000a, p. D5). On our campus I have observed women holding cell phones like they are prized possessions, objects that lift these students from the pedestrian realm of test taking to the lofty arena of transacting deals or settling interpersonal dilemmas. For some men and women, attitudes toward cell phones serve a social identity function.

Value-Expressive.   An important reason people hold attitudes is to express core values and cherished beliefs. Some individuals "claim that they favor capital punishment because they value law and order; they support affirmative action programs as a means of promoting equality; they support recycling programs because they value the environment . . . and they frown on cheating because it is dishonest" (Maio & Olson, 2000b, p. 249).

The value-expressive function is pervasive. Some young people pierce their nose, tongue, belly button . . . or, well, other body parts to express a variety of values, including autonomy and independence from parents. Parents might have merely pierced a left earlobe in an age when *that* showcased rebelliousness. Today, ear pierces are viewed as sooo . . . boring by some avant-garde teens (see Fig. 3.1).

Ego-Defensive.   Attitudes can serve as a "defense" against unpleasant emotions people do not want to consciously acknowledge. People adopt attitudes to shield them from psychologically uncomfortable truths. Let's say a young woman decides to break up with her boyfriend, deciding that the relationship is not going anywhere and fearing he will dump her when they go their separate ways after college. She still has feelings for her soon-to-be-ex, but to defend against these feelings and to make her position known to him clearly and with conviction, she declares in no uncertain terms that their relationship is over, kaput. Adopting a hostile attitude toward her boyfriend is functional because it helps her muster the strength she needs to call off the romance.

Attitudes and Persuasion

A central principle of functional theory is that the same attitudes can serve different functions for different people. In other words, different people can hold the same attitude toward a person, product, or issue; however, they may harbor this view for very different reasons.

Consider attitudes toward shopping. Some people shop for utilitarian reasons. They trek to the mall to happily purchase presents for loved

FIG. 3.1 Body piercing is popular among young people. It does different things for different people, or fulfills diverse psychological functions. (Photograph by William C. Rieter.)

ones and go home once the presents are paid for. Others shop for ego-defensive reasons, to help them forget about their problems or relieve stress. Recent immigrants to America sometimes shop to satisfy value-expressive needs. To these folks, America symbolizes the freedom to do as you wish. For those who grew up in economically and socially impoverished dictatorships, the notion that you can "buy what you want when and where you want it" is one of the great appeals of the United States (Twitchell, 1999, p. 23).

For native-born American teenagers, shopping fulfills entirely different functions. Some teens shop to reinforce a social identity. Stores like Gap, Limited, and Record Town are like "countries for the young." They offer teens a territory in which they are king and queen and can rule the roost. Malls provide adolescents with space to strut about and to shop for products that define them as distinctive and important. (Of course, critics view this somewhat differently. James B. Twitchell says that "the mall approaches a totalitarian Eden into which the innocent and the oppressed enter eagerly, lured by the dream of riches"; p. 299.)

It's not just attitudes toward products that serve diverse psychological functions. People can be deeply religious for different reasons, become active in politics to satisfy different needs, even pursue identical career paths for vastly different motivations. It's fascinating to discover just how different individuals can be once you peel away the superficial attribute of attitude similarity. Such an insight emerges with particular clarity in Mark Snyder's research on the psychology of volunteerism.

Millions of Americans—as many as 89 million—annually volunteer their time and services to help sick, needy, homeless, and psychologically troubled individuals (Snyder, Clary, & Stukas, 2000). They work in soup kitchens on weekends, participate in AIDS walkathons, offer counseling to depressed youth, aid victims of disasters, and try mightily to cheer the spirits of kids who have incurable cancer. A functional theorist, moved by people's willingness to help others in need, asks why. Why do people give so generously of themselves? Do different people have different motives? Snyder and his colleagues found that people volunteer for very different reasons. Their reasons include:

1. expressing values related to altruistic and humanitarian concern for others;
2. satisfying intellectual curiosity about the world, learning about people different from oneself;
3. coping with inner conflicts (reducing guilt about being more fortunate than other people);
4. providing opportunities to participate in activities valued by important others; and

5. providing career-related benefits, such as new skills and professional contacts. (Snyder et al., 2000, pp. 370–371)

These functions are intriguing. They also suggest ideas for how to promote pro-volunteering attitudes and behavior. Functional theory suggests that *a persuasive message is most likely to change an individual's attitude when the message is directed at the underlying function the attitude serves. Messages that match the function served by an attitude should be more compelling than those that are not relevant to the function addressed by the attitude.* The more that a persuasive appeal can explain how the advocated position satisfies needs important to the individual, the greater its impact.

Thus, if you want to recruit volunteers or persuade people to continue engaging in volunteer activities, you must appreciate why individuals chose to volunteer in the first place. One message will not fit all. The message must match the motivational function served by volunteering.

E. Gil Clary, Mark Snyder, and their colleagues (1994) dreamed up a study to test this hypothesis. They asked students to rate the importance of a series of reasons for volunteering. Reasons or functions included knowledge ("I can learn useful skills"), utilitarian ("I can gain prestige at school or work"), value expressive ("I believe someone would help me if I were ever in a similar situation"), and ego-defensive ("Good things happen to people who do good deeds") (Clary et al., p. 1133). The researchers then computed each student's responses to identify the volunteering function that was most and least important to him or her. Armed with this information, Clary and colleagues assigned individuals to watch a videotaped message that recommended involvement in volunteer activities. The message targeted a student's most important volunteer function (*matched* condition) or his or her least important function (*mismatched* condition). Each student watched either a matched or mismatched videotape.

For example, if a student said that volunteering mostly served a utilitarian function, he would watch a matched videotape that contained a utilitarian appeal: "You know, what I really like about all this is that I can make myself more marketable to employers and be a volunteer at the same time." If another student indicated that volunteering primarily fulfilled a value-expressive need, she would view a matched value-expressive video that noted that: "By volunteering I get to turn my concerns into actions and make a difference in someone else's life" (Clary et al., pp. 1147–1148). Other students received *mismatched* videos (e.g., a student who volunteered for value-expressive reasons watched the utilitarian video).

Students then rated the effectiveness of the videotape. The results showed that matched messages were more persuasive than mismatched ones. Videotapes that targeted students' most important volunteering functions were more appealing than those that were directed at less important

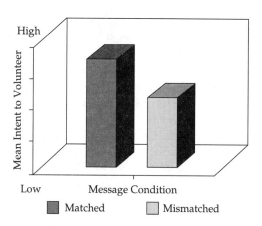

FIG. 3.2 Mean intent to volunteer as a function of match of message with personal motivations (Reprinted with permission from *Journal of Applied Social Psychology*, Vol. 13, No. 13, pp. 1129–1150, © V. H. Winston & Son, Inc., 360 South Ocean Boulevard, Palm Beach, FL 33480. All rights reserved).

functions (see Fig. 3.2). The implications are intriguing: They suggest that if we know the motives volunteering fulfills, we can promote positive attitudes toward helping others. For example, if a person volunteers to reduce guilt or escape her problems, it will do no good to appeal to knowledge or utilitarian needs. Instead, the message should explain how volunteering can alleviate personal problems and help people feel good about themselves.

Attitude Dysfunctions.   There is, unfortunately, a dark side to attitude functions. An attitude that helps an individual satisfy certain needs can be detrimental in another respect. An attitude can assist the person in coping with one problem, while exerting a more harmful or dysfunctional effect in another area of the person's life.

Consider, for example, the teenager who "hangs" at the mall, shops constantly with friends, and gains self-identity from shopping. Nothing wrong with shopping—it's an American pastime. But if the teen neglects studying or athletics, we could say that shopping is dysfunctional, producing negative effects on grades or performance in sports.

Consider attitudes toward body piercing. *The New York Times* reported the story of a 15-year-old named David, who had his tongue pierced over the objections of his father (Brody, 2000). The tongue pierce may have fulfilled a value-expressive function for David, a way to stake out his autonomy from his dad. But the stud in the tongue quickly became dysfunctional when David found that "for more than a week, he could hardly talk and could eat little other than mush." David now warns: "Think of the consequences and things that might happen afterward. When one says that the first five or six days is close to hell, you won't fully understand it until you get a tongue-pierce" (Brody, p. D8).

Complicating matters, attitudes can be functional for one individual, but dysfunctional for others. Talking on a cell phone can serve social identity needs for a phone buff, but try listening to someone rant and rave over the phone while you wait in line at the drugstore! Harboring prejudiced attitudes may serve an ego-defensive function for a bigot ("It's not my fault. It's them—those blankety blank others"). However, prejudice is not exactly functional for those at the other end of the hate monger's stick.

The foregoing discussion alerts us to several problems with the functional approach. It is hard to know whether an attitude is primarily functional or dysfunctional. If it helps the individual satisfy a need, do we call it functional, even if it leads to negative consequences? How do we weigh the benefits the attitude provides the individual with negative consequences on others? It can also be difficult to clearly identify the function an attitude serves. People may not know why they hold an attitude or may not want to admit the truth. However, no theory is perfect, and on balance the functional approach is more functional than dysfunctional for persuasion scholarship! It contains hypotheses for study and generates useful insights for everyday life. These include the following nuggets:

- People are deep and complicated creatures. We often do things that appear inexplicable or strange, until you probe deeper and understand the needs they satisfy.
- We should extend tolerance to others. People have many reasons for holding an attitude. These may not be our motivations, but they can be subjectively important to the person him- or herself.
- Persuaders must be acutely sensitive to the functions attitude serve. "What warms one ego, chills another," Gordon Allport (1945) observed (p. 127). A message can only change attitudes if it connects with people's needs. One may totally disagree with a person's attitude, believing it to be immoral. However, condemning the other may be less useful than probing why the individual feels the way he or she does and gently nudging the individual toward change.

ATTITUDES AND BEHAVIOR

- Kelly has strong values, but you wouldn't guess this by observing her in everyday situations. She is charming, likable, and adept at getting along with different kinds of people. Her friends sometimes call her a chameleon. Yet Kelly has strong views on certain issues, notably the environment and protecting endangered species. At a party, conversation turns to politics and several people advocate drilling for oil in the Arctic National Wildlife Refuge. Will Kelly take issue with their position?

• Susan is an agnostic, a skeptic who has doubts about the existence of God, and believes religion is of little use in today's society. She is a strong believer in Darwinian evolution, a forceful critic of creationist philosophy. At the same time, Susan has a soft spot for religion because it means a lot to her dad. An old friend of her dad calls one day. He's been teaching Sunday school, but will be out of town next week when the class is scheduled to discuss the beauty of God's creation of the universe. Would Susan mind filling in for him just this once, he asks? Will Susan agree?

What's your best guess? Do these anecdotes remind you of people you know or conflicts you've experienced? The two examples above are fictitious, but are based on factors studied in actual psychological experiments. They also focus on a central issue in attitude research—the connection between attitudes and behavior. The question is of theoretical and practical importance.

Theoretically, attitudes are assumed to predispose people to behave in certain ways. For example, suppose we found that attitudes had no impact on behavior. There would be less reason to study attitudes in depth. We would be better advised to spend our time exploring behavior. From a practitioner's perspective, attitudes are important only if they predict behavior. Who cares what consumers think about fast food or fast cars if their attitudes don't forecast what they buy? On the other hand, if attitudes do forecast behavior, it becomes useful for marketers to understand people's attitudes toward commercial products. Then there's us. The people watcher—intuitive psychologist—in us all is intrigued by the attitude–behavior relationship. We can all think of times when we didn't quite practice what we preached. You probably know people who frequently say one thing and do another. The research discussed in this section sheds light on these issues.

The discussion that follows examines conditions under which people are likely to display attitude–behavior consistency. A subsequent section introduces theories of the attitude–behavior relationship. The final part of the chapter views consistency in a larger perspective.

Historical Background

It's morning in America, 1933. President Roosevelt is hard at work in Washington, DC, trying to harness the forces of government to get the country moving again. It's a daunting task. Depression and frustration are adrift in the land. People are unemployed, and some take out their anger on minorities. A psychologist, Richard LaPiere, is aware of the prejudice that one ethnic group, located in his home state of California, faces. He decides to examine the relationship between behavior and attitudes toward the Chinese.

Accompanied by a personable Chinese couple, LaPiere stops at restaurants and hotels across America. Much to his surprise, the group is served at all but one of the restaurants or hotels. But when they send out questionnaires asking if owners would accept members of the Chinese race as guests in their establishments, over 91% of those surveyed reply "No" (LaPiere, 1934).

The findings surprise LaPiere and attract the attention of scholars. It appears as if behavior (serving the Chinese) is out of whack with attitude (questionnaire responses). For years, LaPiere's findings dominate the field. Researchers conclude that attitudes do not predict behavior, and some researchers recommend that we discard the term attitude entirely (Wicker, 1969).

But hold the cell phone! It turns out that LaPiere's study had a number of problems. First, different people waited on the Chinese couple than filled out the questionnaires. Second, the survey probed intention to serve a Chinese couple, but the behavioral measure involved serving a personable Chinese couple accompanied by an educated Caucasian man. What is more, when researchers systematically examined the relationship between attitude and behavior over the ensuring decades, they found that LaPiere's study was an anomaly. Most surveys reported significant correlations between attitudes and behavior (Fishbein & Ajzen, 1975; Kim & Hunter, 1993).

But give the early scholars their due. They correctly observed that attitudes do not *always* predict behavior. They called attention to the fact that attitudes do not forecast action nearly as well as one might assume on the basis of common sense. But they threw out the attitudinal baby with the dirty behavioral bath water! Sure, attitudes don't always predict what we will do. But that doesn't mean they aren't useful guides or aren't reasonable predictors, given the incredible complexity of everyday life. The consensus of opinion today is that attitudes do influence action; they predispose people toward certain behavioral choices, but not all the time. Under some conditions, attitudes forecast behavior; in other circumstances they do not. The relationship between attitude and behavior is exquisitely complex.

Now here's the good news: We can identify the factors that moderate the attitude–behavior relationship. Key variables are (a) aspects of the situation, (b) characteristics of the person, and (c) qualities of the attitude (Fazio & Roskos-Ewoldsen, 1994; Zanna & Fazio, 1982).

Situational Factors

The context—the situation we're in—exerts a powerful impact on behavior. We are not always aware of how our behavior is subtly constrained by norms, roles, and a desire to do the socially correct thing. A norm is an individual's belief about the appropriate behavior in a situation. Roles are parts we perform in everyday life, socially prescribed functions like professor, student, parent, child, and friend.

Norms and Roles.   Individuals may hold an attitude, but choose not to express the attitude because it would violate a social norm. You may not like an acquaintance at work, but realize that it violates conventional norms to criticize the person to his face. Someone may harbor prejudice toward coworkers, but be savvy enough to know that she had better hold her tongue lest she get in trouble on the job (Kiesler, Collins, & Miller, 1969).

Norms vary across cultures. In traditional Middle Eastern societies, friendly, outgoing behavior is held in low repute. Gregarious behavior that is regarded positively in the United States ("Hey, how ya' doin?") is viewed negatively in Middle Eastern countries. Instead, the norm is to be serious, even somber in public (Yousef, 1982). Thus, a person may hide her affection for a colleague when seeing him at work. Attitude fails to predict behavior because the public display of attitude runs counter to cultural norms.

Roles also influence the attitude–behavior relationship. When people take on professional roles, they have to act the part, putting their biases aside. This helps explain why reporters, who have strong political beliefs, rarely display biases in their professional activity at newspapers or television stations. For example, many Washington reporters are liberal Democrats, but their news stories go right down the middle, offering criticism of Democrat and Republican politicians (Perloff, 1998). One of the requirements of news is that it show no favoritism to either side—that it be perceived as fair and objective. Journalists know that if they write biased news stories, they will quickly lose their jobs or will be viewed as unprofessional by colleagues. Thus, liberal political attitudes do not reliably predict reporters' public behavior.

Scripts.   To illustrate the concept of script, I ask that you imagine you face a term paper deadline and are hard at work at your word processor. A phone rings; it's a telemarketer, the 10th to call this week. She's asking for money for injured war veterans, a cause you normally support because a relative got hurt while serving in the Persian Gulf War. Not thinking and mindlessly putting on your "I'm busy, leave me alone" hat, you cut the volunteer off, telling her in no uncertain terms that you have work to do. Trying to be cute, you use the line from a recent TV quiz show: "You're the weakest link; goodbye."

Your attitude obviously didn't come into play here. If it had, you would have promised a donation. Instead, you invoked a script: an "organized bundle of expectations about an event sequence" or an activity (Abelson, 1982, p. 134). Like an actor who has memorized his lines and says them on cue, you call on well-learned rules about how to handle pushy telemarketers interrupting your day. Your expectations of how the transaction with the telemarketer is going to proceed—the overly pleasant intro, follow-up for money, plea to keep you on the phone—set the tone for the conversation, and you mindlessly follow the script rather than taking the time to consult your attitude toward veterans.

Characteristics of the Person

Individuals differ in the extent to which they display consistency between attitudes and behavior. Some people are remarkably consistent, others are more variable. Social psychological research has helped pinpoint the ways in which personal factors moderate the attitude–behavior relationship. Two moderating factors are self-monitoring and direct experience.

Self-Monitoring. Social psychologist Mark Snyder, whose research we glimpsed before, confidently believes people can be divided into two categories. A first group consists of individuals who are concerned with displaying appropriate behavior in social situations. Adept at reading situational cues and figuring out the expected behavior at a given place and time, these individuals adjust their behavior to fit the situation. When filling out Snyder's (1974) scale, they agree that "in different situations and with different people, I often act like very different persons." These individuals are called high self-monitors because they "*monitor* the public appearances of *self* they display in social situations" (Snyder, 1987, pp. 4–5).

A second group is less concerned with fitting into a situation or displaying socially correct behavior. Rather than looking to the situation to figure out how to behave, they consult their inner feelings and attitudes. "My behavior is usually an expression of my true inner feelings, attitudes, and beliefs," they proudly declare, strongly agreeing with this item in the self-monitoring scale. These individuals are called low self-monitors.

High and low self-monitors differ in plenty of ways (see chapter 8). One relevant difference is that high self-monitors exhibit less attitude–behavior consistency than do low self-monitors (Snyder & Kendzierski, 1982; Snyder & Tanke, 1976). High self-monitors look to the situation to decide how to act; as "actor types" who enjoy doing the socially correct thing, they don't view each and every situation in life as a test of character. If a situation requires that they put their attitudes aside for a moment, they happily do so. Low self-monitors strongly disagree. Living by the credo, "To thine own self be true," low self-monitors place value on practicing what they preach and maintaining congruence between attitude and behavior. Not to do so would violate a personal canon for low self-monitors.

In the example given earlier, Kelly—the outgoing, chameleon-like young woman who has strong attitudes toward wildlife preservation— would be in a pickle if acquaintances at a party began taking an antienvironmental stand. Her personality description suggests she is a high self-monitor. If so, she would be unlikely to challenge her acquaintances. Instead, she might smile sweetly, nod her head, and resolve to talk up the environmental issue in situations where she could make a difference. Needless to say, a low self-monitor who shared Kelly's values would be foaming at the mouth when her friends began saying that we should drill for oil in the National Wildlife Refuge. She probably wouldn't hesitate to tell them how she felt.

Direct Experience.   Experience also moderates the attitude–behavior relationship. Some of our attitudes are based on direct experience with an issue; we have encountered the problem in real life, it has evoked strong feelings, or led us to think through the implications of behaving in a certain way. Other attitudes are formed indirectly—from listening to parents or peers, reading books, watching television, or partaking in Internet chat rooms. Attitudes formed through direct experience "are more clearly defined, held with greater certainty, more stable over time, and more resistant to counter influence" than attitudes formed through indirect experience (Fazio & Zanna, 1981, p. 185; see also Millar & Millar, 1996). Attitudes produced by direct experience also come more quickly to mind than attitudes acquired through indirect experiences. For these reasons, people are more apt to translate attitude into behavior when the attitude has been formed through direct experiences in real-world situations (Fazio & Zanna, 1978).

Consider a contemporary issue, but one most people don't like to talk about much: safe sex. Two teenagers may both have positive attitudes toward safer sex practices. However, one may have formed her attitude through unpleasant experiences—trying to convince a boyfriend to put on a condom, only to find him intransigent, getting scared and then resolving to assert herself more forcefully next time around. Another young woman may have read articles about safer sex in *Cosmopolitan*, and heard the condom rap from parents on different occasions. Comes time to decide whether to put the attitude into practice: A relationship blossoms, spring is in the air, passions lead to sex, then the excitement is broken by an awkward silence.

Can you see why the teenager who developed a positive attitude toward safe sex from direct (albeit unpleasant) experience would be more likely to broach the topic of condoms than the second young woman? In the first case, the attitude would be more clearly defined and, therefore, would be easier to call to mind at the moment of decision.

Sex is by no means the only arena in which experience moderates attitude–behavior consistency. Consider any issue about which people feel strongly, but differ in their experience: politics, education, cigarette smoking, drug use. You will invariably find that those with direct experience on an issue will be more likely to behave in accord with their attitudes. Those with less experience are apt to look to other factors to help them decide what to do. They may, therefore, be particularly likely to yield to persuasive communicators, some of whom are adept at manipulating inexperienced young people.

Characteristics of the Attitude

As noted in chapter 2, attitudes differ in their structure and strength. The nature of an attitude moderates the relationship between attitudes and behavior.

General Versus Specific Attitudes. Ajzen and Fishbein (1977) distinguished between *general* and *highly specific* attitudes. A general attitude, the focus of discussion up to this point, is the global evaluation that cuts across different situations. A specific attitude, called *attitude toward a behavior*, is evaluation of a single act, or specific behavior that takes place in a particular context at a particular time. For example, consider the issue of predicting religious behavior from religious attitudes. The general attitude is the individual's attitude toward religion. This is the sum total of the person's evaluations of many religious behaviors, such as praying, attending religious services, partaking in holiday rituals, talking about religion in everyday life, and donating money to religious causes. The specific attitude is the attitude toward one of these behaviors at a particular place and time.

A general attitude, sometimes called attitude toward the object, will not predict each and every religious behavior. A Ph.D. student who is deeply religious may attend only a handful of religious services over the course of 6 months—not because he has abandoned religion, but because he is immersed in doctoral comprehensive exams and realizes he must forsake this part of his religious identity for a time. (To compensate, the student regularly may devote time to reading inspirational portions of the Bible.) The student harbors a favorable attitude toward religion, but rarely, it seems, translates attitude into behavior.

But here's the rub: If you include the dozens of other religious behaviors in which the student could (and does) partake (from praying to Bible reading), and include them in your equation, you will discover that attitude predicts behavior rather handsomely.

This is the conclusion that Fishbein and Ajzen reached in an exhaustive review of this topic. In a 1974 study—old but still good—the investigators asked people to indicate their general religious attitude, as well as how frequently they participated in each of 100 specific religious behaviors (Fishbein & Ajzen, 1974). The correlation, or association, between general attitude toward religion and any specific action was .15. This is a very small correlation; it means that attitude toward religion is not closely related to a particular behavior in a given situation. But when Fishbein and Ajzen looked at the overall behavior pattern, focusing not at one situation but at the sum total, they discovered that the relationship between attitude toward religion and religious behavior was substantial. The correlation was .71, approaching 1 (the latter a perfect correlation).

Other researchers, focusing on different behaviors, have obtained similar findings. For example, Weigel and Newman (1976) found that individuals who had favorable attitudes toward environmental preservation were more likely than those with less positive attitudes to participate in a variety of environmental protection projects. The projects included signing petitions opposing construction of nuclear power plants, distributing petitions to family members and friends, and partaking in a roadside litter pickup. The more positive individuals' environmental attitudes, the more likely they were to engage in a broad range of pro-environmental activities.

However, harboring a positive attitude toward the environment did not lead people to participate in each and every environmental cause. For example, one woman who scored high on the environmental attitude scale declined to participate in a litter pickup project. Her husband asked her not to do so. Apparently, the man was also an environmentalist, and as luck would have it, planned to organize a local Boy Scout troop in a similar project. He feared that his wife's litter pickup project might interfere with his plans. His wife, either because she agreed with him or chose to be deferent, opted not to participate in the recycling project.

Again, it was not that the woman had displayed marked inconsistency between attitude and behavior, for she apparently translated her environmental attitude into action across most other domains (signing petitions, distributing them, and so forth). It was that, as often happens in life, something else came up. If you wished to predict the woman's behavior in particular circumstances, you would be better advised, Fishbein and Ajzen say, to consider her *specific attitude* toward participating in the environmental project in question.

These ideas are an outgrowth of what Ajzen and Fishbein (1977) call **the compatibility principle**. A strong relationship between attitude and behavior is possible only if the attitudinal predictor corresponds with the behavioral criteria. "Corresponds with" means that the attitudinal and behavioral entities are measured at the same level of specificity. Thus, specific attitudes toward a behavior predict highly specific acts. General attitudes predict broad classes of behavior that cut across different situations (see Fig. 3.3).

Attitude Strength. Another moderator of the attitude–behavior relationship is the strength of the individual's attitude. Strong attitudes are particularly likely to forecast behavior (Lord, Lepper, & Mackie, 1984). This makes sense psychologically and resonates with ordinary experience. Those with strong convictions on issues ranging from abortion to gay rights are the ones who are out there on the picket lines or are lobbying Congress to pass legislation favorable to their groups.

It gets more complicated when you consider those instances when we're ambivalent about issues. When people have strong feelings on both sides of an issue or are torn between head and heart, they are less apt to translate attitude into behavior (Armitage & Conner, 2000; Lavine et al., 1998). Different feelings push people in different behavioral directions. Alternatively, the affective aspect of an attitude (feelings) can propel people toward one choice, while the cognitive dimension (beliefs) can push them in a different direction. Faced with these cross-pressures, individuals may behave in accord with their attitude in one situation, but not so much in another.

Consider the case of Susan, the agnostic who believes strongly in evolution, but has a soft spot for religion because it means a lot to her dad. Asked to teach a Sunday school class in which she has to take a creationist position on evolution, Susan is likely to have mixed feelings. Her negative views toward religion should propel her to reject the request. (Fishbein and Ajzen's model suggests that her specific negative evaluation of teaching creationism should also push her in that direction.) However, cognition clashes with affect: Susan's relationship with her dad means a lot, and the call from an old friend of her father evokes fond

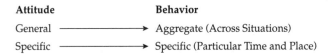

FIG. 3.3   Compatibility principle. Arrows denote strong relationships between attitude and behavior. General attitude will not predict specific behavior, and a specific attitude will not forecast behavior in the aggregate.

memories. If heart governs head, and feelings overpower thoughts, she is likely to agree to teach the class. If she opts to base her decision on logic, she will politely decline. Much depends on what information comes to mind at the moment of decision, and how she goes about deciding which course to take (Wang Erber et al., 1995).

MODELS OF ATTITUDE–BEHAVIOR RELATIONS

People are complex. They can be consistent, practicing what they preach, or they can surprise you, doing things that you would not expect based on their attitudes. Research sheds light on these phenomena. We know that attitudes frequently guide behavior, though under some circumstances, for some individuals, and with some attitudes more than others. The studies offer a patchwork—a pastiche—of conditions under which attitudes are more or less likely to influence action. Social scientists prefer more organized frameworks, such as models that explain and predict behavior. Three models of attitude–behavior relations have been proposed: the theory of reasoned action, the theory of planned behavior, and the accessibility model.

Theory of Reasoned Action

Fishbein and Ajzen, who brought you the precision of the compatibility principle, also formulated a major model of attitude–behavior consistency: the theory of reasoned action (Fishbein & Ajzen, 1975). The model assumes that people rationally calculate the costs and benefits of engaging in a particular action and think carefully about how important others will view the behavior under consideration. The hallmark of the model is its emphasis on conscious deliberation.

There are four components of the theory. The first is *attitude toward the behavior* ("the person's judgment that performing the behavior is good or bad"); the second is *subjective norm* ("the person's perceptions of the social pressures put on him to perform or not perform the behavior in question") (Ajzen & Fishbein, 1980, p. 6). The third component is *behavioral intention*, the intent or plan to perform the behavior. The final aspect is behavior itself—action in a particular situation (see Fig. 3.4). Although the terms in the model are abstract, the theory has many practical applications.

Consider this example: After you graduate, you land a job with the American Cancer Society. Your task is to explore why some young people succeed in quitting smoking and why others fail. You recall that the theory of reasoned action is a major model of attitude–behavior relations and focus your empirical efforts on the reasoned action approach.

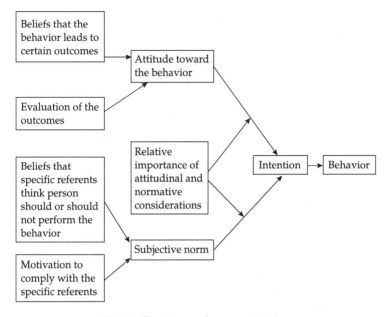

FIG. 3.4 The theory of reasoned action.

It's a smart choice. The theory offers precise strategies for assessing attitudes and has an excellent track record in forecasting actual behavior (Sutton, 1998). Let's examine the model and its applications to smoking in detail below.

Attitude. Attitude toward the behavior is a highly specific attitude. It consists of two subcomponents: behavioral beliefs (beliefs about consequences of the behavior) and outcome evaluations (evaluations of the consequences). These two elements are combined, as they were in the simple expectancy–value model described in chapter 2. Each behavioral belief is multiplied by the corresponding evaluation, and results are summed across items. Beliefs and evaluations regarding quitting smoking could be measured in the following way:

Behavioral Beliefs

1. Quitting smoking will increase my physical endurance.
   Likely 1 2 3 4 5 6 7 Unlikely
2. Quitting smoking will cause me to gain weight.
   Likely 1 2 3 4 5 6 7 Unlikely

Outcome Evaluations

1. Increasing my physical endurance is:
   Good   1   2   3   4   5   6   7   Bad
2. Gaining weight is:
   Good   1   2   3   4   5   6   7   Bad

Subjective Norm.   This factor also consists of two components: normative beliefs ("the person's beliefs that specific individuals or groups think he should or should not perform the behavior") and motivation to comply (the individual's motivation to go along with these significant others) (Ajzen & Fishbein, 1980). Subjective norms are calculated by multiplying the normative belief score by the corresponding motivation to comply and then summing across all items.

Normative Beliefs

1. My mom thinks that I:
   Definitely should   1   2   3   4   5   6   7   Definitely should not
   quit smoking   quit smoking
2. My girlfriend/boyfriend thinks that I:
   Definitely should   1   2   3   4   5   6   7   Definitely should not
   quit smoking   quit smoking

Motivation to Comply

In general, how much do you care about what each of the following thinks you should do:

1. My mom:
   Care very much   1   2   3   4   5   6   7   Do not care at all
2. My girlfriend/boyfriend:
   Care very much   1   2   3   4   5   6   7   Do not care at all

Behavioral Intention.   As the name suggests, behavioral intention is the intention to perform a particular behavior, a plan to put behavior into effect. Intention to quit smoking, measured as specifically as possible, could be assessed in this way:

I intend to quit smoking tomorrow.
Likely   1   2   3   4   5   6   7   Unlikely

Intention is a function of attitude toward the behavior and subjective norm. For example, if I have a strong, favorable attitude toward quitting and everyone around me wants me to quit, I am apt to say that I will give quitting a try. I am likely to formulate a plan to quit smoking cigarettes.

The model uses a mathematical formula to combine attitude and norm. It relies on empirically derived criteria that take into account the particular situation in which the behavior occurs.

Behavior. Fishbein and Ajzen argue that most social behavior is under the individual's control. Thus, intention to perform a particular behavior should predict the actual performance of the act. However, intention is most likely to predict behavior when it corresponds with—is identical to—the behavior in key ways. If you want to predict whether teenagers will quit smoking high-tar cigarettes tomorrow, you should ask them if they intend to quit smoking such cigarettes tomorrow. Asking them if they plan to stop smoking or stop engaging in risky behavior is too general and would not predict this specific behavior.

Predicting Behavior from Attitude. The theory of reasoned action allows us to specify the precise impact that attitudes exert on behavior. In the present case, young people who *strongly* believe that quitting smoking will lead to positive outcomes should be especially likely to intend to quit smoking. In the same fashion, teenagers who find smoking satisfying—those who hold a negative attitude toward quitting—should not plan to quit smoking. These individuals may believe that if they quit smoking, they will gain weight—a highly undesirable outcome. In either case, attitude predicts behavior.

In some cases, though, attitude will not forecast action. An adolescent might positively evaluate smoking, but decide to quit because significant others keep bugging her to give up the habit. In this case, attitude is less important than subjective norm. Social pressures trump attitude.

Thus, the theory offers a framework for predicting behavior from attitudes. While earlier researchers might have thrown up their hands when they discovered attitudes do not always predict action, concluding that behavior is ultimately not predictable, Fishbein and Ajzen offer a calmer, more reasoned approach. They caution that behavior can be predicted, but you need to consider both likes and dislikes (attitudes) and people's natural propensity to want to please others (norms).

The theory has an excellent track record in predicting behavior. Numerous studies have tested its propositions. They have found that attitudes and subjective norms forecast intentions, and intentions help predict behavior (Fishbein & Ajzen, 1975; Hale, Householder, & Greene, 2002; Sheeran, Abraham, & Orbell, 1999; Sutton, 1998). For example, attitudes and subjective norms forecast:

- intentions to eat meals in fast-food restaurants (Brinberg & Durand, 1983);

- women's occupational orientations (Sperber, Fishbein, & Ajzen, 1980);
- condom use among high-risk heterosexual adults (Morrison, Gill-more, & Baker, 1995); and
- breast-feeding or bottle-feeding infants (Manstead, Proffitt, & Smart, 1983).

Shortcomings.   Although it has a good batting average for predicting behavior, and particularly intention, the theory (like all approaches) has limitations. Some scholars protest that attitude and behavioral intention measures are virtually the same, making predictions obvious and not so interesting. Others note that contrary to the assumption that the impact of attitudes on behavior is mediated by intentions, attitudes exert a direct impact on behavior (Bentler & Speckhart, 1979; Fazio, Powell, & Williams, 1989). The main shortcoming of the model, though, is that it assumes that people have control over their behavior—in other words, that they are psychologically capable of acting on their attitude or carrying out their intentions. In some cases, this assumption is not tenable. What happens when people lack control or perceive that they can't control their behavior? For example, what of the person who wants to lose weight, but can't muster the psychological strength; the individual who wants to stop binge drinking but can't; or the woman who wants to say no to unsafe sex, but in the heat of the moment, finds herself psychologically unable to reject her boyfriend's advances? In such cases, the theory of reasoned action breaks down: People don't act on attitude or norm. They do not do what they intend.

Noting the problem, Icek Ajzen, one of the architects of the reasoned action model, proposed an alternative approach. Like a rock star who drops out of a big band to sing songs solo, Ajzen had his own message to impart. While clearly showing respect for the Fishbein–Ajzen model, Ajzen argued that another theory might do a better job of forecasting behavior.

Theory of Planned Behavior

Ajzen (1991) developed a theory of planned behavior that adds another component to the reasoned action model: *perceived behavioral control.* Ajzen argues that behavioral intention is determined by three factors: attitude, subjective norm, and perceptions of behavioral control. Perceived behavioral control is the individual's perception of how much control he or she has over the behavior; it is a subjective estimate of how easy or difficult it will be to perform the behavior. The more I perceive that I can perform the action, the more successful I should be in translating intention into behavior (see Fig. 3.5).

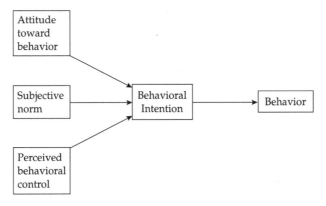

FIG. 3.5 Theory of planned behavior.

Like the reasoned action approach, the theory of planned behavior has an excellent track record in predicting behavior (Conner & Armitage, 1998; Sutton, 1998). If you want to predict whether someone is going to quit smoking, you would definitely want to consider the planned behavior model. If you've smoked and tried unsuccessfully to quit, you can appreciate the important role that personal control plays in your efforts to break the habit. Perceived behavioral control could be measured in the following way:

Now this is just a "what if" question, but if you decided you were going to quit smoking tomorrow, how sure are you that you could?
Extremely sure   1   2   3   4   5   6   7   Extremely sure
I could not   I could

Summary. Despite their differences, planned behavior and reasoned action theories both emphasize that attitudes can predict behavior under certain circumstances. They also acknowledge that attitudes will not predict behavior when subjective norms apply, or when people lack the psychological ability to translate attitude into action.

Accessibility Theory

It's a humid summer day, and you feel like a cold one. Glancing over the usual suspects—Miller Lite, Coors, Michelob, Bud Lite—your mouth watering, you want to make a quick choice of which six-pack to buy at the convenience store. Suddenly, the word "Whazzup" from an advertisement of some years back leaps into your mind. You smile, and reach for the Budweiser.

According to Fazio's accessibility model (see chapter 2), your attitude toward Budweiser is accessible, or capable of being quickly activated from memory. Your favorable attitude toward Bud Lite predicts your purchase behavior. Now if we wanted, we could measure your behavioral beliefs, normative beliefs, perceptions of behavioral control, and other variables from the models previously discussed. However, all this would be beside the point and far too laborious a process, according to accessibility theory. The core notion of accessibility theory is that attitudes will predict behavior if they can be activated from memory at the time of a decision. If a person is in touch with her attitudes, she will act on them. If not, she will be swayed by salient aspects of the situation.

This captures the gist of the model, but the core notions are more complicated. In reality, two things must transpire for an attitude to influence behavior. First, the attitude must come spontaneously to mind in a situation. That is, it must be activated from memory. Second, the attitude must influence perceptions of an issue or person, serving "as a filter through which the object is viewed" (Fazio & Roskos-Ewoldsen, 1994, p. 85). These perceptions should then color the way people define the situation, pushing them to behave in sync with their attitude. (If people do not call up their attitude from memory, they will be susceptible to influence from other factors in the situation, such as norms or eye-catching stimuli; see Fig. 3.6).

In short: You can harbor an attitude toward a person or issue, but unless the attitude comes to mind when you encounter the other person or issue, you cannot act on the attitude in a particular situation. This is one reason why it's good to be in touch with your attitudes: You can act on them when important issues come up in life.

Accessibility theory complements the reasoned action/planned behavior approach. Fazio argues that under some conditions people behave like Fishbein and Ajzen (1975) suggest: They carefully consider the consequences of behaving in a particular fashion and deliberate about pros and cons of doing x or y. But when people lack the *motivation* or *opportunity* to

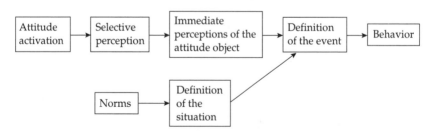

FIG. 3.6 Fazio's attitude-to-behavior process model (Reprinted with permission from Fazio © 1986 p. 212).

deliberate in this fashion, they act more spontaneously. In such situations, attitude can guide behavior if people automatically call up attitudes from memory.

Research supports these propositions (Kraus, 1995). One study found that individuals who were "in touch" with attitudes toward then-President Reagan were more likely to vote for Reagan than those who could not quickly access their favorable assessment of Reagan (Fazio & Williams, 1986; see also Bassili, 1995). In a similar vein, students who could immediately call to mind a favorable attitude toward food products were more inclined to select these products as a free gift than those with less accessible attitudes (Fazio, Powell, & Williams, 1989). Interestingly, two students might have equally favorable attitudes toward Snickers candy bar. The student who was more "in touch" with her feelings about Snickers—could say immediately that she loved Snickers—was more likely to select Snickers than a fellow student who had to think a little before recognizing how much she adored Snickers.

Implications for Persuasion

Research on attitude–behavior consistency tells us a great deal about attitudes. But what does it say about persuasion? Quite a bit, as it turns out. Ultimately, most persuaders want to change behavior, and they hope to do so by influencing attitudes. The more researchers know about when and how attitudes influence behavior, the more useful their recommendations are to real-life persuaders. Imagine that as a follow-up to your work for the American Cancer Society you are asked to devise a media campaign to convince teenagers to quit smoking. The three theories discussed suggest different types of campaign strategies. First, the theory of reasoned action suggests that as a campaign coordinator, you should:

1. Target relevant beliefs. You should probe teens' salient or relevant beliefs to discover what would induce them to give up smoking. Don't assume reasons that apply to you also apply to adolescents. Teenagers might tell you that they are least concerned with dying (they think they will live forever), but believe that smoking causes body odors or leads others to think smokers are uncool. Use this information to devise campaign messages.

2. Locate relevant reference groups. Teens may be more influenced by peers than by the Surgeon General, but the particular peers will differ depending on the subculture.

Planned behavior theory, by contrast, suggests that you:

Convince young people that they are psychologically capable of quitting. Messages could remind young people that *they*, not their parents or friends, are the ones lighting up cigarettes, and that they have the power to quit (Parker, Stradling, & Manstead, 1996).

Accessibility theory takes a different tack. It suggests that campaign planners:

> Put teenagers in touch with their desire to quit smoking. Teens might draw a self-portrait of what they look and feel like when they smoked too many cigarettes. They could carry the picture in their wallets and look at it whenever they are tempted to take a puff. This might remind them of their commitment to give up smoking.

JUDGING CONSISTENCY

Hypocrite.

This term frequently gets bandied about when people observe inconsistencies between attitudes and behavior. It reflects an ethical concern, the belief that an individual is not living up to prescribed standards. Now that you have an appreciation for the complex underpinnings of attitude–behavior consistency, we can proceed to this more controversial aspect of the consistency issue.

Every day, it seems, we hear of famous men or women behaving badly and subsequently earning the wrath of observers, who call them hypocrites. A celebrated case occurred some years back and involved a president of the United States: Bill Clinton. During his first term and while running for reelection in 1996, Clinton championed family values, telegraphing what appeared to be a positive attitude toward marriage and monogamy. Yet he behaved quite differently, cheating on his wife and engaging in a long, sordid affair with Monica Lewinsky. Critics pointed to the blatant contradictions between Clinton's words and actions (Bennett, 1998).

Others viewed the situation differently. We should be wary of "judging a complex being by a simple standard," one psychoanalyst said of the Clinton quandary. "To equate consistency with moral (and political) virtue, and then to demand consistency of people," wrote Adam Phillips (1998), "can only cultivate people's sense of personal failure" (p. A27). In other words, we should not ask people to be consistent. To do so is to set people up for failure, as none of us is perfect in this regard.

Consider the case of Reverend Jesse Jackson, who preached religious values, commitment to Biblical commandments like "Thou shalt not commit adultery," and counseled President Clinton regarding his sexual sins. In early 2001, the public learned that Jackson fathered a child out of wedlock. Was Jackson a hypocrite? He would seem to be, if one consults

Webster's dictionary definition. A hypocrite, the dictionary tells us, is one who pretends to be what he or she is not, or harbors principles or beliefs that he or she does not have. However, critic Michael Eric Dyson, taking a different view of hypocrisy, viewed Jackson differently. Dyson argued that:

> It is not hypocritical to fail to achieve the moral standards that one believes are correct. Hypocrisy comes when leaders conjure moral standards that they refuse to apply to themselves and when they do not accept the same consequences they imagine for others who offend moral standards. (p. A23)

Noting that Jackson accepted responsibility for his behavior, Dyson said he was not a hypocrite.

Thus, the term "hypocrite" is subject to different readings and different points of view. In trying to decide if someone behaved in a hypocritical fashion, a variety of issues emerge. What criteria do we use to say that someone is a hypocrite? Is it enough for the individual to display one inconsistency between attitude and behavior? Or is that too harsh a criterion? How many inconsistencies must the person commit before the hypocrite label fits? Do certain inconsistencies get more weight than others? Does a blatant violation of an individual's deeply held values cut more to the heart of hypocrisy than other inconsistencies? Are certain kinds of attitude–behavior inconsistencies (e.g., violations of marital oaths) more ethically problematic, and therefore more deserving of the hypocrite label than others? Is hypocrisy culturally relative, with certain kinds of inconsistencies more apt to be regarded as hypocritical in one culture than in another? Does application of the label "hypocrite" tell us more about the observer than the person being judged?

There are no absolute answers to these questions. Like other issues in the psychology of persuasion, they are complex, controversial, and shaded in gray rather than black or white.

CONCLUSIONS

Attitude research sheds light on the reasons people hold the attitudes they do and the degree to which attitudes predict behavior.

Functional theory stipulates that people would not hold attitudes unless they satisfied core human needs. Attitudes help people cope, serving knowledge, utilitarian, social adjustive, social identity, value-expressive, and ego-defense functions. Two people can hold the same attitude for different reasons, and an attitude that is functional for one person may be dysfunctional for someone else. An attitude can help a person function

nicely in one part of his or her life, while leading to negative consequences in another domain. Attitude function research also suggests
strategies for attitude change. It emphasizes that persuaders should
probe the function a particular attitude serves for an individual and design the message so it matches this need.

The bottom-line question for attitude researchers is whether attitudes
forecast behavior. Decades of research have made it abundantly clear
that attitudes do not always predict behavior and people are not entirely
consistent. People are especially unlikely to translate attitude into behavior when norms and scripts operate, they are ambivalent about the issue,
or regard themselves as high self-monitors. Under a variety of other conditions, attitudes predict behavior handsomely. When attitudes and
behavior are measured at the same level of specificity, attitudes forecast
behavior. Attitudes guide and influence behavior, just not in every life
situation.

Three models of attitude–behavior consistency—theory of reasoned
action, theory of planned behavior, and accessibility—offer rich insights
into attitude–behavior relations. The models tell us that under some conditions people will deliberate on attitudes, thoughtfully considering their
implications for behavior, while in other circumstances individuals spontaneously use their feelings as a guide for action. These models and empirical research help us understand when and why people are consistent.

A final issue concerns judgments of those who do not translate attitude into behavior. We frequently call such individuals hypocrites.
Sometimes they are. However, it is important to understand that use of
the term "hypocrite" reflects a series of assumptions about what counts
as an inconsistency, the weight attached to the particular inconsistency in
question, and the observer's value judgments.

CHAPTER **4**

Attitude Measurement

Pollsters do it with precision. Theorists do it with conceptual flair. Survey researchers do it for a living. "It," of course, is designing questionnaires to measure attitudes!

Puns and double entendres aside, attitude measurement plays a critical role in the study and practice of persuasion. It is the practical side of the field, the down-to-earth domain that provides the instrumentation to test hypotheses and to track changes in attitudes and beliefs. If there were no reliable scientific techniques to measure attitudes, we would not know how people evaluated social and political issues. We would not know the impact that persuasive communications had on people's feelings and thoughts. Documenting the effects of large-scale media campaigns would permanently elude us.

This chapter explores the main themes in attitude measurement. It describes scales used to tap attitudes, as well as the pitfalls and challenges researchers face when trying to empirically assess attitudes. After reading this chapter, you should know more about how to write good attitude questions and how to locate valid surveys that measure specific attitudes.

OVERVIEW

Attitude questionnaires date back to 1928. It was in this year that psychologist Louis Thurstone published an article titled "Attitudes Can Be Measured." Thurstone proposed an elaborate procedure to assess people's views on social issues. Although measurement techniques have been streamlined over the years, Thurstone "started the fire." We now have established methodologies for assessing attitudes. What's more, thousands of questionnaires have been developed to tap beliefs and attitudes on countless issues.

Are you interested in attitudes toward race or racial issues? You can find dozens of surveys, such as those developed by McConahay (1986) and Sniderman and Piazza (1993). Are you concerned about capital punishment? If so, you can check out surveys described in Ellsworth and Gross (1994)? Does censorship of media unnerve you? If so, you can find a valid measure in Hense and Wright (1992). There are questionnaires tapping attitudes on hundreds of issues, including religion, abortion, environmental pollution, homophobia, prejudice against fat people, adulation of thin models, sex, sex roles, basking in the glory of sports teams, political activism, even cloning human beings.

It is not easy to write good attitude questions. You can appreciate this if you ever tried to dream up questions assessing views on one or another issue. Administering your survey to others, you may have found respondents scratching their heads and asking, "What do you mean by this question?" Devising reliable attitude items is not as easy as it looks. There are people who do this for a living—folks who are so proficient at devising questions that they work for professional research centers or advertising firms. There is a science to writing attitude questions, one that calls on principles of measurement, statistics, and cognitive psychology (Hippler, Schwarz, & Sudman, 1987; Tourangeau & Rasinski, 1988). It all flows from an underlying belief—core assumption—that one can measure phenomena by assigning numbers to objects on the basis of rules or guidelines (Stevens, 1950; see Fig. 4.1).

Perhaps the simplest way to assess attitudes is to ask people if they like or dislike the attitude object. Gallup polls tap Americans' attitudes toward the president by asking if they approve or disapprove of the way the chief executive is handling the job of president. However, there are two problems with this procedure. First, the agree–disagree scale offers people only two choices. It does not allow for shades of gray. Second, it measures attitudes with only one item. This puts all the researcher's eggs in one basket. If the item is ambiguous or the respondent misunderstands the question, then all hope of accurately measuring the attitude goes out the window. In addition, by relying on only one item, the researcher misses the opportunity to tap complex, even contradictory, components of the attitude.

For these reasons, researchers prefer to include many survey items and to assess attitudes along a numerical continuum. Questionnaires that employ these procedures are called **scales**. There are three standard attitude scales: (a) Likert, (b) Guttman, and (c) the semantic differential.

Panel A: Stair-Step Scale

Question: What is your attitude toward the Democratic Party?
Instructions: Place a check mark on the stair step that best describes your attitude.

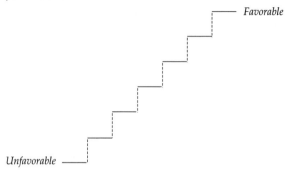

Panel B: Opinion Thermometer

Question: How do you feel about former president Bill Clinton?
Instructions: Circle the number on the thermomenter scale that best describes your feelings.

FIG. 4.1 Two different types of numerical attitude scales (From Sharon Shavitt & Timothy C. Brock, *Persuasion: Psychological Insights and Perspectives*, © 1994 by Allyn & Bacon. Reprinted/adapted by permission).

QUESTIONNAIRE MEASURES OF ATTITUDE

Likert Scale

The nice thing about being the first to do something is they name it after you.

A psychologist named Rensis Likert refined Thurstone's procedures in 1932. Likert recommended that researchers devise a series of opinion statements and ask individuals to indicate their agreement or disagreement with each statement along a numerical scale. A Likert scale assumes that each item taps the same underlying attitude and there are significant interrelationships among items. It also presumes that there are equal intervals between categories. For example, on a 5-point (Strongly Agree, Somewhat Agree, Neutral, Somewhat Disagree, Strongly Disagree) scale, researchers assume that the psychological difference between Strongly Agree and Somewhat Agree is the same as between Strongly Disagree and Somewhat Disagree.

Likert scales are commonplace today. No doubt you've completed dozens of these strongly agree–strongly disagree surveys. An example is the course evaluation questionnaire students complete on the last day of class (you know, the day your professor acts oh-so-nice to you and bakes those fudge brownies!). Students indicate how much they agree or disagree with statements regarding the prof's teaching abilities and the course content.

Likert scales can proceed from 1 to 5, as noted above. They can also go from 1 to 7, 1 to 9, or 1 to 100. Most researchers prefer 5- or 7-point scales because they allow respondents to indicate shades of gray in their opinions, but do not provide so many categories that people feel overwhelmed by choices. A sample Likert scale, measuring attitudes toward sex roles, appears in Table 4.1. You might enjoy completing it to see how you feel about this issue.

Guttman Scale

Sometimes it seems that the person with the strongest attitude toward a topic is the one willing to take the most difficult stands, those that require the greatest gumption. One may not agree with these positions, but one is hard pressed to deny that these are difficult positions to endorse. A Guttman scale (named after Louis Guttman) takes this approach to measuring attitudes (Guttman, 1944).

The scale progresses from items easiest to accept to those most difficult to endorse. Those who get a high score on a Guttman scale agree with all items. Those with moderate attitudes agree with the easy- and moderately difficult-to-endorse questions, and those with mildly positive attitudes agree with only the easy-to-accept items. A Guttman scale for sex roles appears in Table 4.2.

Guttman scales are hard to construct. They are not as easy to administer as Likert scales. However, they can be useful in tapping attitudes on sensitive topics like prejudice. People might be willing to take liberal stands on such easy-to-accept items as favoring enforcement of fair housing laws, supporting school integration, and philosophically backing interracial marriage. However, prejudice might surface on more difficult-to-accept items such as encouraging *one's own* child to date someone from

TABLE 4.1
Likert Scale for Sex Role Attitudes

Please indicate whether you Strongly Agree (SA), Agree (A), are Neutral (N), Disagree (D), or Strongly Disagree (SD) with each of these statements.

	SA	A	N	D	SD
1. Women are more emotional than men.	1	2	3	4	5
2. Swearing and obscenity are more repulsive in the speech of a woman than of a man.	1	2	3	4	5
3. When two people go out on a date, the man should be the one to pay the check.	1	2	3	4	5
4. When a couple is going somewhere by car, it's better for the man to do most of the driving.	1	2	3	4	5
5. If both husband and wife work full time, her career should be just as important as his in determining where the family lives.	1	2	3	4	5
6. Most women interpret innocent remarks or acts as being sexist.	1	2	3	4	5
7. Society has reached the point where women and men have equal opportunities for achievement.	1	2	3	4	5
8. Many women have a quality of purity that few men possess.	1	2	3	4	5
9. Women should be cherished and protected by men.	1	2	3	4	5

Note. Items 1, 2, 6, 7, and 8 can be regarded as descriptive beliefs; Statements 3, 4, 5, and 9 are prescriptive beliefs.

Statement 2 is from Spence, Helmreich, & Stapp (1973); Statements 4 and 5 are from Peplau, Hill, & Rubin (1993); Items 6, 8, and 9 are from Glick and Fiske (1996); and Statement 7 is from Swim et al. (1995).

TABLE 4.2
Guttman Scale for Sex Roles

Least Difficult to Accept	1. Fathers should spend some of their leisure time helping to care for the children.
	2. Fathers should share in infant care responsibilities, such as getting up when the baby cries at night and changing diapers.
	3. If both parents work, the father and mother should divide equally the task of staying at home when children get sick.
Most Difficult to Accept	4. If both parents work, the father and mother should divide equally the task of raising the children.

another race, or supporting without argument *your own child's* decision to marry someone from a different racial or ethnic group.

Semantic Differential

Charles Osgood and his colleagues never got a scale named for them, but they developed one of the most frequently used scales in the attitude business. Osgood, Suci, and Tannenbaum (1957) chose not to assess beliefs or agreement with opinion statements. Instead, they explored the meanings that people attach to social objects, focusing on the emotional aspect of attitude. The term *semantic* is used because their instrument asks people to indicate feelings about an object on a pair of bipolar, adjective scales. The term *differential* comes from the fact that the scale assesses the different meanings people ascribe to a person or issue.

Participants rate a concept using bipolar adjectives: One adjective lies at one end of the scale; its opposite is at the other end. Osgood and his colleagues have discovered that people typically employ three dimensions to rate concepts: *evaluation* (is it good or bad for me?), *potency* (is it strong or weak?), and *activity* (is it active or passive?) (Osgood, 1974). A semantic differential scale for sex roles appears in Table 4.3. You could also use this scale to tap attitudes toward female politicians, corporate leaders, or media stars. Any come to mind?

Pitfalls in Attitude Measurement

There is no perfect attitude scale. Even the best scales can fail to measure attitudes accurately. Inaccuracies result from such factors as: (a) respondent

TABLE 4.3
Semantic Differential for Sex Roles

Feminism
Good - - - - - - - - Bad
Pleasant - - - - - - - - Unpleasant
Strong - - - - - - - - Weak
Heavy - - - - - - - - Light
Active - - - - - - - - Passive
Wholesome - - - - - - - - Unhealthy
Valuable - - - - - - - - Worthless

Note. Numbers do not appear underneath the dashes. For each item, a response is assigned a score from +3 to −3, with a +3 assigned to the blank closest to the positive pole and a −3 to the blank nearest the negative pole.

carelessness in answering the questions, (b) people's desire to say the socially appropriate thing rather than what they truly believe, and (c) a tendency to agree with items regardless of their content (Dawes & Smith, 1985). Although these problems can be reduced through adroit survey measurement techniques (see next section), some inaccuracy in responses to attitude scales is inevitable.

A particularly gnawing problem in survey research involves the format and wording of questions. The way the researcher words the question and designs the questionnaire can elicit from the respondent answers that may not reflect the individual's true attitude (Schuman & Presser, 1981; Schwarz, 1999). The manner in which the question is asked can influence the response that the researcher receives. It reminds one of the statement that writer Gertrude Stein reportedly said on her death bed. With death near, a friend in search of the guiding principle of life asked Stein, "What is the answer?" To which she famously replied, "What is the question?"

Two key survey design factors that can influence—or bias—attitude responses are survey context and wording.

Context. Survey questions appear one after another on a piece of paper, computer screen, or in an interview administered over the telephone. Questions occurring early in the survey can influence responses to later questions. This is because thoughts triggered by earlier questions can shape subsequent responses. The answers that individuals supply may thus be artifacts of the "context" of the survey instrument rather than reflections of their actual attitudes.

For instance, voters asked to evaluate the sexual morality of politicians might respond differently if they heard Bill Clinton's name at the beginning rather than at the end of a list (Schwarz & Bless, 1992). With Clinton as an anchor or standard of comparison, they might give other politicians' high ratings, thinking "none of them was as bad as he was!" But if Clinton's name did not appear until the end, voters would not be so likely to base evaluations of other politicians on opinions of the Clinton-Lewinsky scandal. As a result, other political leaders might not look so good by comparison.

Howard Schuman and Stanley Presser (1981) documented question order effects in a classic study of Americans' attitudes toward abortion. Naturally, abortion attitudes were complex, but a majority supported legalized abortion. When asked, "Do **you** think it should be possible for a pregnant woman to obtain a **legal** abortion if she is married and does not want any more children?" over 60% said "Yes." However, support dropped when the following question was asked first:

*Do **you** think it should be possible for a pregnant woman to obtain a **legal** abortion if there is a strong chance of serious defect in the baby?*

In this case, only 48% agreed that a married woman should be able to obtain a legal abortion if she did not want any more children. To be sure, these attitudes are controversial and would outrage those who oppose abortion in all instances. But the point here is methodological, not ideological. The order of questions influenced evaluations of abortion. Something of a contrast effect appears to have emerged.

When asked to consider the question of legal abortion for married women, pro-choice respondents had no anchor other than their support for a woman's right to choose. A substantial majority came out in favor of abortion in this case. But after considering the gut-wrenching issue of aborting a fetus with a medical defect and deciding in favor of this option, a second group of respondents now mulled over the question of abortion for married women who did not want any more children. In comparison to the birth defect choice, this seemed relatively unsubstantial, perhaps trivial. Using the birth defect case as the standard for comparison, the idea that a woman should get a legal abortion if she did not want any more children seemed not to measure up to these individuals' moral criterion for abortion. Not surprisingly, fewer individuals supported abortion in this case.

It is also possible that, in light of the ambivalence many pro-choice supporters feel toward abortion, those who supported abortion in the case of a serious defect in the baby felt guilty. To reduce guilt, some may have shifted their position on abortion for married women, saying they opposed abortion in this less taxing situation. Whatever the explanation, it seems clear that the order in which the questions appeared influenced respondents' reports of their attitudes.

Wording.   As writers have long known, language is full of meaning, capable of conveying powerful sentiments. It should, therefore, come as no surprise that the way a question is worded can influence respondents' evaluations of the issue.

This has become abundantly clear on the topic of affirmative action (Kinder & Sanders, 1990). A New York Times/CBS News poll probed Americans' attitudes toward racial diversity, using a variety of questions to tap beliefs. When asked their opinion of programs that "*give preferential treatment to racial minorities,*" just 26% of respondents indicated they would favor such programs. But when asked their views of programs that "*make special efforts to help minorities get ahead,*" significantly more Americans (55%) expressed approval of such programs (Verhovek, 1997).

Perhaps the most striking example of wording effects came from polls probing an even more emotional issue: Americans' belief that the Holocaust actually occurred.

With some anti-Semitic groups arguing that the Holocaust had never happened and was a figment of Jews' imagination, the Roper polling organization launched a national survey to see how many Americans actually bought into this false belief. In 1992, Roper probed Americans' attitudes toward the Holocaust, tapping beliefs with this key question:

The term Holocaust usually refers to the killing of millions of Jews in Nazi death camps during World War II. Does it seem possible or does it seem impossible to you that the Nazi extermination of the Jews never happened?

Amazingly, 22% of respondents said it was "possible" that the mass executions never happened, about 12% claimed they "didn't know," while 65% said it was "impossible" that the event had not happened. "The fact that nearly one fourth of U.S. adults denied that the Holocaust had happened . . . raised serious questions about the quality of knowledge about recent history," observed Carroll J. Glynn and her colleagues (1999, p. 76). It also raised the possibility that large numbers of Americans consciously or unconsciously subscribed to an anti-Semitic ideology.

Public opinion researchers suspected the problem, once again, was not ideological, but methodological. They suggested that the Roper question was misleading and the double negative had confused people. Several polling organizations, including Roper, conducted new surveys, this time with clearer questions like:

Does it seem possible to you that the Nazi extermination of the Jews never happened, or do you feel certain that it happened?

This time, 91% said they were certain it happened. Just 1% of the public said it was possible the Holocaust never happened, and 8% did not know (Smith, 1995).

The results restored faith in the public's knowledge and good sense. It also revealed the strong effect that question wording has on reports of attitudes.

Implications. Wording and context effects have aroused much concern among survey researchers. Some scholars have gone so far as to argue that the reason that questionnaire format exerts such strong effects is that people don't have full-blown attitudes at all. Instead, these researchers suggest, individuals construct their attitudes on the spot, based on what happens to be on their minds at the time, or on thoughts triggered by survey questions (Wilson, LaFleur, & Anderson, 1996; Zaller, 1992). In support of this position, research has found that large numbers of people volunteer opinions on fictitious issues, those that the pollster has invented for purposes of the survey. For example, over 50% of respondents gave their opinion of the Monetary Control Bill, legislation dreamed up by survey researchers (Bishop, Tuchfarber, & Oldendick, 1986)!

People *do* construct attitudes on the spot, in response to pollsters' questions. We should not assume that this is the norm, however. It probably pushes the envelope to argue that people lack attitudes on many topics, particularly those that hit close to home, are the product of socialization, or touch on values. Still, there is no denying that weakly held attitudes can be susceptible to influence by pollsters' questions, a fact that has not been lost on savvy practitioners hoping to manipulate public opinion (see Box 4–1).

BOX 4–1
SKEWING THE SURVEY RESULTS

You've probably heard television advertisements that claim that "a majority of people interviewed in a major survey" said such-and-such about the product. The results make it sound like a scientific study proved that people prefer Crest to Colgate, Coke to Pepsi, Burger King to McDonald's, or Yahoo! to every other search engine. As you listened, you no doubt thought to yourself, Is this research real, or what?

"Or what" is the appropriate answer. Some of the research that companies cite in their behalf is based on questionable methods. It is a powerful example of how marketing researchers can cook the data to fit the client, or design surveys that assure that companies will receive the answers they desire. Reporter Cynthia Crossen (1991) discussed this trend in *The Wall Street Journal*. She reported that:

- When Levi Strauss & Co. asked students which clothes would be most popular this year, 90% said Levi's 501 jeans. They were the only jeans on the list.
- A survey for Black Flag said: "A roach disk ... poisons a roach slowly. The dying roach returns to the nest and after it dies is eaten by other roaches. In turn these roaches become poisoned and die. How effective do you think this type of product would be in killing roaches?" Not surprisingly, 79% said effective.
- (A) Chrysler study showing its cars were preferred to Toyota's included just 100 people in each of two tests. But more important, none of the people surveyed owned a foreign car, so they may well have been predisposed to U.S.-made vehicles. (pp. A1, A7)

> Summarizing her report on the use of marketing research, Crossen acknowledged that some studies use valid measurement techniques. But many surveys are filled with loaded questions and are designed to prove a point rather than investigate one. "There's been a slow sliding in ethics," said Eric Miller, who reviewed thousands of marketing studies as editor of a research newsletter. "The scary part is, people make decisions based on this stuff. It may be an invisible crime, but it's not a victimless one" (Crossen, p. A1).

ASKING GOOD QUESTIONS

As long as surveys are constructed by human beings and administered to human beings, we will never totally eliminate order or wording effects. You have to put your questions in a certain order and use particular words to communicate meaning. These are bound to influence respondents. Nonetheless, we can minimize the impact of context factors by taking precautions when designing the survey. More generally, there are many things researchers can do to improve the quality of attitude questions (Sudman & Bradburn, 1982). Next time you are asked to develop a self-report survey, you might consider these suggestions:

1. Use words that all respondents can comprehend.
2. Write specific and unambiguous items.
3. Avoid double negatives.
4. Pretest items to make sure people understand your questions.
5. If you think order of questions will influence respondents, ask questions in different sequences to check out order effects.
6. Avoid politically correct phrases that encourage socially desirable responses.
7. Write items so they take both the positive and negative sides of an issue (to reduce respondents' tendency to always agree).
8. Consider whether your questions deal with sensitive, threatening issues (sex, drugs, antisocial behavior). If so, ask these questions at the end of the survey, once trust has been established.
9. Allow people to say "I don't know." This will eliminate responses based on guesses or desire to please the interviewer.
10. Include many questions to tap different aspects of the attitude.

You can also save yourself some time—and improve the quality of your questionnaire—by turning to established attitude scales. You don't have to reinvent the wheel if someone else has developed a scale on the topic you're researching. To paraphrase the lyrics of an old folk song, "You can get anything you want at Alice's Restaurant," you can get pretty much any scale you want, if you do a thorough search! There are many standardized scales out there that tap attitudes very effectively. The advantage of using someone else's scale (other than that it frees you up to relax!) is that the scale has passed scientific muster—it is reliable, valid, and is comprehensible to respondents. You can find scales from computerized databases, such as PsycINFO, Health and Psychosocial Instruments, and Communication Abstracts, or in specialized books (for example, Robinson, Shaver, & Wrightsman, 1999; Rubin, Palmgreen, & Sypher, 1994). Of course, if you're researching a new issue or want to cook up your own questions, you will have to devise your own questionnaire. Just remember as you construct your survey that people are complex, and you will need good questions to tap their attitudes.

Open-Ended Measures

The main advantage of attitude scales—they offer an efficient way to accurately measure social attitudes—is their main drawback. Scales do not always shed light on the underlying dynamics of attitudes—the rich underbelly of cognitions and emotions. These components can be measured through more open-ended, free-form techniques. Open-ended measures complement the structured attitude scales that have been discussed thus far. They are like essay questions.

One open-ended technique involves assessing **cognitive responses** to communications (Petty, Ostrom, & Brock, 1981b). Individuals typically read or view a message and list their cognitive reactions (i.e., thoughts). For example, if you wanted to measure people's cognitive responses regarding sex roles, you might have them view a sexist advertisement and ask them to write down the first ideas that come to mind. These responses could be subsequently categorized by researchers according to specific criteria (Cacioppo, Harkins, & Petty, 1981).

Affect can also be assessed in an open-ended way. People can be asked to write down 10 emotions that they ordinarily feel toward members of a group, organization, or nation (Eagly, Mladinic, & Otto, 1994; see also Crites, Fabrigar, & Petty, 1994).

Combining open-ended measures with traditional attitude scales increases the odds that researchers will tap attitudes accurately and completely. Of course, this does not guarantee success. Even the best survey researchers err. Some years ago pollster Richard Morin (1997) listed "the worst of the worst"—the most terrible questions ever asked in a poll.

One of them appeared in a 1953 Gallup Poll and is listed below:

If you were taking a new job and had your choice of a boss, would you prefer to work under a man or a woman? (Morin, 1997, p. 35)

INDIRECT METHODS TO MEASURE ATTITUDES

In light of such doozies (the question just cited) and the methodological problems noted earlier, some researchers recommend measuring attitude through ways other than questionnaires. They advocate the use of a variety of indirect techniques to assess attitudes, such as the following:

Unobtrusive Measures. Researchers can observe individuals unobtrusively or without their knowledge. Behavior is used as a surrogate for attitude. Unobtrusive measures can be useful in cases where it is not possible to administer self-report scales or one fears individuals will not accurately report attitudes (Webb et al., 1966). For example, if investigators wanted to assess attitudes toward American music in a dictatorship like Iraq, they might examine the amount of wear and tear on rock and roll CDs or check out the number of hits on hip-hop musicians' Web sites. Useful as these techniques could be, the obvious problem is that they might not tap liking of the music so much as interest or idle curiosity.

Physiological Measurements. Did you ever sweat a little when you asked someone out for a date? Do you know anyone whose pupils seem to get bigger when they are talking about something they really care about? Have you ever noticed how some people's facial muscles—eyebrows and cheeks—can telegraph what they are feeling? If so, you are intimately aware of the physiology of attitudes. Physiological measures can provide useful indirect assessments of attitudes.

A physiological approach to attitudes has gained adherents in recent years as researchers have recognized that attitudes have a motor or bodily component (Cacioppo, Priester, & Berntson, 1993). There are a host of ways of tapping attitudes through physiological techniques. These include (a) *galvanic skin response*, a change in the electrical resistance of the skin (e.g., measurements of sweating); (b) *pupil dilation* (precise assessments of expansion of the pupils); and (c) *facial electromyographic (EMG) techniques* that tap movements of facial muscles, particularly in the brow, cheek, and eye regions. The latter can provide a particularly sensitive reading of attitudes. In one study, students imagined they were reading an editorial with which they agreed or disagreed. Findings showed that students displayed more EMG activity over the brow region when imagining they were reading an article they disliked than one they liked (Cacioppo, Petty, & Marshall-Goodell, 1984).

Physiological measures can be useful in tapping feelings people are not aware they have, or which they might choose to disguise on a questionnaire. Marketing firms have used galvanic skin response measures to test advertising copy (LaBarbera & Tucciarone, 1995). Advertising researchers have found that facial electromyographic techniques can provide a more sensitive measure of emotional responses to ads than self-reports (Hazlett & Hazlett, 1999). Pupil dilation measures can shed light on abnormal sexual attitudes (Atwood & Howell, 1971).

Useful as these devices are, they can unfortunately tap responses other than attitudes. Sweating, pupil dilation, and facial muscle activity can occur because people are interested in, or perplexed about, the attitude object. Physiological reactions do not always provide a sensitive indication of the directionality (pro vs. con) of people's feelings. It is also frequently impractical or expensive to use physiological techniques. In addition, wide use of physiological measurements has been hampered by the jargon-based language that is frequently used to communicate physiological findings.

Response Time. These measures assess the latency or length of time it takes people to indicate if they agree or disagree with a statement. For example, individuals may sit before a computer screen and read a question (e.g., "Do you favor capital punishment?"). They are instructed to hit a button to indicate whether they do or don't favor capital punishment. Researchers do not focus on whether individuals are pro or con, or favorable or unfavorable to the attitude object. Their primary interest is in how long it takes individuals to make their selection (Fazio, 1995). The assumption is that the longer it takes people to access their attitude, the less well developed or strong the attitude is. Conversely, the quicker people punch a button to indicate their attitude, the stronger the attitude is presumed to be.

Response time measures can provide an indication of the accessibility of attitudes. Such measures can be useful in tapping a variety of attitudes, including prejudices that people might not care to admit (Dovidio & Fazio, 1992). They also provide a more honest way to assess bigoted attitudes than earlier techniques, some of which duped individuals into thinking that a machine shed true light on their prejudices (Jones & Sigall, 1971).

An advantage of response time is that it can be readily assessed through new technologies, such as laptop computers. However, it too is susceptible to human error, as when people become careless, tired, or annoyed with the research procedure.

CONCLUSIONS

Attitude measurement plays a critical role in persuasion research. Persuasion is a science, as well as an art, and we need valid instruments to assess attitudes. Three venerable scales are typically employed: Likert, Guttman, and the semantic differential. Likert is used most frequently because it taps beliefs and can be constructed easily. Open-ended measures, such as cognitive responses, can supplement closed-ended, structured scales.

There are a variety of problems in measuring attitudes through self-reports, including survey context and wording effects. To minimize these problems, researchers have devised strategies to improve questionnaire quality that focus on asking questions clearly and thoughtfully. Supplementing self-report surveys are several indirect techniques to assess attitudes, such as unobtrusive, physiological, and response time measures. Indirect techniques do not yield as sensitive information about the directionality and complexity of attitudes, which is why self-report measures, for all their shortcomings, will probably continue to dominate the field.

PART 2

Changing Attitudes and Behavior

CHAPTER 5

Processing Persuasive Communications

Kate and Ben, recently married, delightfully employed, and happy to be on their own after four long years of college, are embarking on a major decision—a happy one, but an important one. They're buying a car. They have some money saved up from the wedding and have decided that, the way the stock market has been going, they'd be better off spending it than losing cash on some risky Internet investment.

Sitting in their living room one Thursday night watching TV, they find that they are tuning in more closely to the car commercials than the sitcoms. "That's a sign we're an old married couple," Kate jokes. Ben nods in agreement.

The next day after work, at Kate's request they click onto the *Consumer Reports* Web site and print out information about compact cars. On Saturday they brave the car dealerships, get the lowdown from car salesmen, and take spins in the cars. Kate, armed with her incredible memory for detail and ten 3 × 5 cards, hurls questions at the car salesmen, while Ben, shirt hanging out, eyes glazed, looks dreamily at the sports cars he knows he can't afford.

By early the next week, they have narrowed down the choices to a Honda Civic and a Saturn SC. Her desk covered with papers, printouts, and stacks of warranties and brochures from the dealerships, Kate is thinking at a feverish pace; she pauses, then shares her conclusions with her husband.

"Okay, this is it. The Honda gets more miles per gallon and handles great on the highway. But *Consumer Reports* gives the new Saturn better ratings on safety on account of their four-wheel antilock brakes, and traction control, which is important. The Saturn also has a better repair record than the Civic. But the big thing is we get a stronger warranty with the Saturn dealer and, Ben—the Saturn is a thousand bucks cheaper. Soooo . . . what do you think?"

Ben looks up. "Well, you know, I'm not into all this technical stuff like you are. I say if the Saturn gets better ratings from *Consumer Reports*, go for it. I also think the Saturn salesman made a lot of good points—real nice guy. The Honda guy basically blew us off when he found out we couldn't get an Accord."

"There's also the other thing," says Kate, sporting a grin.

"What?"

"The name."

"It's true," says Ben a bit sheepishly. "The name Saturn is cool. I like it."

"What am I going to do with you?" Kate asks, with a smile and a deliberately exaggerated sigh.

"How about, take me to the Saturn dealer, so we can buy our new car?" Ben says, gently running his hands through the 3×5 cards as he walks out the front door.

The story is fiction—but perhaps not too far from everyday experience. It is based on interviews with consumers and observations of people buying cars. The example illustrates two very different styles of processing information: careful consideration of message arguments (Kate), and superficial examination of information and a focus on simple cues (Ben). These two ways of processing information are the main elements of contemporary theories of persuasion and form the centerpiece of the present chapter.

This chapter launches the second part of the book, which examines theory and research on the effects of persuasive communication. The chapter describes guiding models of attitude and behavior change—approaches that underlie much of the research and applications that follow. The cornerstone of these theoretical approaches is a focus on *process*. Scholars believe that if they can understand *how* people cognitively process messages, they can better explicate the impact that communications have on attitudes. They believe that the better they comprehend individuals' modes of processing information, the more accurately they can explain the diverse effects messages have on attitudes. This is what scholars mean when they say you cannot understand the effects of communications on people without knowing how people process the message.

Contemporary models evolved from earlier perspectives on persuasion—notably Hovland's pathbreaking work, and research conducted in the 1960s. It is important to describe these programs of research because they contributed helpful insights and also laid the groundwork for current theorizing. The first section of the chapter provides an overview of these approaches. The second portion of the chapter describes a major cognitive processing model of persuasion, the Elaboration Likelihood Model, along with evidence that backs it up. Subsequent sections focus on real-life applications, fine points of the model, intellectual criticisms, and the model's contributions to persuasion.

HISTORICAL FOUNDATIONS

As noted in chapter 1, Carl Hovland and his colleagues at Yale University conducted the first detailed, empirical research on the effects of persuasive communications. The **Yale Attitude Change Approach** was distinctive because it provided facts about the effects on attitudes of the communicator's credibility, message appeals, and audience members' personality traits. Convinced by theory and their generation's experience with World War II persuasion campaigns that communications had strong effects on attitudes, the researchers set out to examine *who* says *what* to *whom* with *what effect* (Hovland, Janis, & Kelley, 1953; Smith, Lasswell, & Casey, 1946).

Although Hovland and his colleagues' findings were interesting, it was their theory-driven approach and commitment to testing hypotheses that proved enduring. The Yale researchers were also interested in understanding why messages changed attitudes. Working in an era dominated by reward-based learning theories and research on rats' mastery of mazes, Hovland naturally gravitated to explanations that focused on learning and motivation. Hovland emphasized that persuasion entailed learning message arguments and noted that attitude change occurred in a series of steps. To be persuaded, individuals had to attend to, comprehend, learn, accept, and retain the message (see Fig. 5.1).

It sounds logical enough. Indeed there is considerable evidence that learning is a component of persuasion—the more people learn and comprehend message arguments, the more likely they are to accept the advocated positions (Chaiken, Wood, & Eagly, 1996). However, the thesis misses

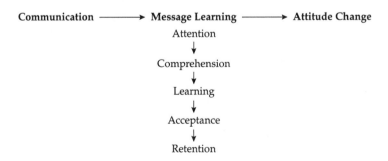

FIG. 5.1   The Hovland/Yale Model of Persuasion.

the mark in an important respect. It assumes that people are spongelike creatures who passively take in information they receive. In fact, as Leon Festinger and Nathan Maccoby (1964) noted, an audience member

> does not sit there listening and absorbing what is said without any counter-action on his part. Indeed, it is more likely that under such circumstances, while he is listening to the persuasive communication, he is very actively, inside his own mind, counterarguing, derogating the points the communicator makes and derogating the communicator himself. (p. 360)

Think of how you react to a persuasive message. Do you sit there, taking in everything the speaker says? Are you so mesmerized by the communicator that you stifle any thoughts or mental arguments? Hardly. You actively think about the speaker, message, or persuasion context. You may remember message arguments, yet probably recall with greater accuracy your own criticisms of the speaker's point of view. This view of persuasion developed in the years that followed the publication of Hovland's research and is known as the **Cognitive Response Approach to Persuasion**. The approach asserts that people's own mental reactions to a message play a critical role in the persuasion process, typically a more important role than the message itself (Brock, 1967; Greenwald, 1968; Petty, Ostrom, & Brock, 1981b). Cognitive responses include thoughts that are favorable to the position advocated in the message (*proarguments*) and those that criticize the message (*counterarguments*). Persuasion occurs if the communicator induces the audience member to generate favorable cognitive responses regarding the communicator or message.

The cognitive response view says that people play an active role in the persuasion process. It emphasizes that people's *own* thoughts about a message are more important factors in persuasion than memory of message arguments (Perloff & Brock, 1980; see Fig. 5.2). There is a good deal of evidence to substantiate this view. In fact, it may seem *obvious* that thoughts matter in persuasion. But remember that what is obvious at one

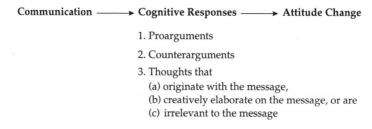

Communication ⟶ Cognitive Responses ⟶ Attitude Change

1. Proarguments

2. Counterarguments

3. Thoughts that
   (a) originate with the message,
   (b) creatively elaborate on the message, or are
   (c) irrelevant to the message

FIG. 5.2   The Cognitive Response Model of Persuasion.

point in time is not always apparent in an earlier era. During the 1950s and early '60s, animal learning models of human behavior dominated psychology, and, on a broader level, Americans were assumed to follow lock, stock, and barrel the dictates of government and free enterprise capitalism. It only seemed natural to theorize that persuasion was primarily a passive process of learning and reinforcement.

With the advent of the 1960s, all this changed. Cognitive models emphasizing active thought processes gained adherents. It became clear that older views, while useful, needed to be supplemented by approaches that afforded more respect to the individual and assigned more emphasis to dynamics of the gray matter inside the brain.

"Feed your head," the rock group Jefferson Airplane belted out during this decade. The cognitive response approach echoed the refrain. It stimulated research, bottled old scholarly wine in new explanations, and helped pave the way for new theories of attitude change. By calling attention to the role thoughts play in persuasion, the cognitive response approach illuminated scholarly understanding of persuasion. Consider these examples.

The first involves **forewarning**. Forewarning occurs when a persuader warns people that they will soon be exposed to a persuasive communication. This is a common occurrence in life, and research has explored what happens when people are warned that they are going to receive a message with which they staunchly disagree. Cognitive response studies have clarified just what happens inside people's minds when this occurs. Individuals generate a large number of counterarguments, strengthening their opposition to the advocated position (Petty & Cacioppo, 1977). An old expression, "Forewarned is forearmed," describes this phenomena, but sheds no light on why it occurs. Cognitive response analysis helps us understand it better. When a close friend marches out of the house in the middle of an argument, vowing "We'll talk about this when I get home," you are likely to intensify your resolve not to give in. Generating arguments in your behalf and persuading yourself that you are right, you arm yourself with a battering ram of justifications that you invoke when your friend returns. In fact, as cognitive response research predicts, forewarning someone in this general fashion significantly reduces the likelihood that a subsequent persuasive communication will succeed. "Forewarning an audience to expert a persuasive message tends to make that message less persuasive," William L. Benoit (1998) concludes after studying this issue (p. 146).

Cognitive responses also help explain an off-beat persuasion effect called **distraction**. Sometimes people are distracted from paying attention to a communication with which they disagree. Other people may be talking, or music may be blaring at a party at precisely the moment when someone chooses to explain why she disagrees with a position one holds on an issue. In other cases, communicators intentionally distract receivers from paying attention to a message. Advertisers do this all the time, using humor, music, and sex to take people's attention away from the message. In such circumstances, people can be highly susceptible to persuasion.

The distraction hypothesis holds that distraction facilitates persuasion by blocking the dominant cognitive response to a message (Petty, Wells, & Brock, 1976). If I listen to a message with which I disagree, my normal response is probably to counterargue with the communicator in my head. But if my mind is elsewhere—I'm grooving to the music or am laughing at a joke—I am not able to formulate arguments against the message. I, therefore, have fewer mental objections to the advocated position. As a result, I end up moving somewhat closer to the communicator's point of view than I would have, had I not been distracted in this way.

Notice what is going on here. It's not the distraction from the message that counts, it's the distraction from our own arguments regarding the message (Osterhouse & Brock, 1970). Recognizing that people are primed to contest advertisements in their own minds, advertisers resort to all sorts of clever distractions (see chapter 11). Sometimes they even seem to be aware that we mentally take issue with ads that appear on television, as they try to tease us into not taking the ad so seriously. This too can be distracting and can facilitate persuasion. Mind you—distraction does not always succeed, and it does not always work by inhibiting counterargument production. Indeed, David B. Buller and John R. Hall (1998) present an array of evidence that challenges the counterargument disruption thesis. However, the distraction research caught researchers' eye by raising the possibility that cognitive responses could influence attitude change. This in turn stimulated scholarship and suggested new ideas for everyday persuasion (see, for example, Boxes 5–1 and 5–2).

BOX 5–1
INOCULATION THEORY

Persuasion not only involves changing attitudes. It also centers on convincing people *not* to fall prey to unethical or undesirable influence attempts. Communicators frequently attempt to persuade individuals to resist social and political messages that are regarded as unhealthy or unwise. For example, health campaigns urge young people to "say no" to drugs, smoking, drinking when driving, and unsafe sex. In the political domain, candidates attempt to persuade wavering voters to resist the temptation to bolt their party and vote for the opposing party candidate or a third-party contender.

A variety of techniques have been developed to strengthen resistance to persuasion. The techniques work by triggering counterarguments which, along with other factors, help individuals resist persuasive appeals. One of the most famous strategies evolved from a biological analogy and is known as inoculation theory. The theory is an ingenious effort to draw a comparison between the body's mechanisms to ward off disease and the mind's ways of defending itself against verbal onslaughts. In his statement of the theory, William McGuire noted that doctors increase resistance to disease by injecting the person with a small dose of the attacking virus, as in a flu shot (McGuire & Papageorgis, 1961). Preexposure to the virus in a weakened form stimulates the body's defenses: It leads to production of antibodies, which help the body fight off disease. In the same fashion, exposure to a weak dose of opposition arguments, "strong enough to stimulate his defenses, but not strong enough to overwhelm him," should produce the mental equivalent of antibodies—counterarguments (McGuire, 1970, p. 37). Counterarguing the oppositional message in one's own mind should lead to strengthening of initial attitude and increased resistance to persuasion.

One of the hallmarks of inoculation research is the creativity with which it has been tested. McGuire and his colleagues chose to expose people to attacks against attitudes that had been rarely if ever criticized: cultural truisms, or beliefs individuals learn through socialization. Cultural truisms include: "You should brush your teeth three times a day" and "People should get a yearly checkup." In essence, participants in the experiments received either a supportive defense—arguments defending the truism—or an inoculation defense (for example, arguments against the notion that you should brush your teeth three times a day, along with refutation of these arguments). Individuals who received the inoculation defense were more likely to resist subsequent attacks on a brush-your-teeth-three-times-a-day type truism than those who just received supportive arguments (McGuire & Papageorgis, 1961). Presumably, the attack and refutation stimulated individuals to formulate arguments why the truism was indeed correct. They were apparently more motivated than those who heard the usual "rah-rah, it's true" supportive arguments.

These findings provided the first support for inoculation theory. The theory fundamentally stipulates that resistance to persuasion can be induced by exposing individuals to a small dose of arguments against a particular idea, coupled with appropriate criticism of these arguments. In essence, inoculation works by introducing a threat to a person's belief system and then providing a way for individuals to cope with the threat (that is, by refuting the counterattitudinal message). As Michael Pfau (1997) points out, "by motivating receivers, and then preemptively refuting one or more potential counterarguments, inoculation spreads a broad blanket of protection both against specific counterarguments raised in refutational preemption and against those counterarguments not raised" (pp. 137–138).

Continued

BOX 5-1
(CONTINUED)

Other research suggests that inoculation enhances persuasion by providing the persuader with an opportunity to reframe the arguments before the opposition gets to them (Williams & Dolnik, 2001). Although there is healthy debate about just which processes account best for inoculation effects, there is little doubt that inoculation provides a useful way to encourage resistance to persuasive communications (Benoit, 1991; Pfau, 1997; Szabo & Pfau, 2002).

Indeed, inoculation theory has stimulated considerable research over the years, usefully transcending its initial focus on cultural truisms, explored in exclusively laboratory settings. Communication scholars have taken the concept to the real world, examining its applications to commercial advertising, political campaigns, and health (Pfau, Van Bockern, & Kang, 1992; see chapter 12). A number of practical conclusions have emerged from this research. They include the following:

1. *Inoculation can be a potent weapon in politics.* Politicians can anticipate the opposition's attacks, and preempt them by using inoculation techniques (Pfau & Kenski, 1990; Pfau & Burgoon, 1988). Bill Clinton used the technique in 1992 when accepting his party's nomination for president. Anticipating that Republicans would attack his record as governor of Arkansas, he sought to preempt the attack at the outset by acknowledging that "there is no Arkansas miracle." He then deflected the criticism by explaining his achievements as governor. Eight years later, Democratic nominee Al Gore borrowed the strategy from Clinton's playbook. Acknowledging criticism that he was not the most exciting politician in America, Gore told a cheering crowd of Democrats that he was nonetheless dedicated and would work hard every day for Americans if elected president. Although Gore lost the election, he won the popular vote, perhaps in part due to strategies like this.

2. *In a world filled with unethical persuaders, inoculation offers a helpful technique to help people resist unwanted influence attempts.* The theory says that the best way to induce resistance to unethical persuasion is to provide people with a small dose of the dangerous information and then help them refute it. This offers a useful counterpoint to those who say that parents should shield children from the world's evils or shelter them from unpleasant realities. As Pratkanis and Aronson (1992) note, "we cannot resist propaganda by burying our heads in the sand. The person who is easiest to persuade is the person whose beliefs are based on slogans that have never been seriously challenged" (p. 215).

BOX 5−2
THE POWER OF THOUGHT

"There is nothing either good or bad, but thinking makes it so."
—Shakespeare, *Hamlet*

Shakespeare may have been one of the earliest proponents of the cognitive response approach. Quite possibly, the London bard would also have endorsed the idea that thinking plays a critical role in mental and physical problems. There is much evidence to support the notion that thinking plays an important role in the self-persuasion process. Christopher D. Ratcliff and his colleagues (1999) demonstrated this in an intriguing study.

Noting that "the majority of couch potatoes admit that their health would benefit from greater exercise (and) the majority of students recognize that their grades and career chances would be enhanced if they spent more time studying," Ratcliff and his associates argued that one way to help these individuals achieve their goals is to encourage them to think about the positive results of these activities (p. 994). Ratcliff and his colleagues asked students to think about actions that might make studying enjoyable. They found that compared to students in other experimental conditions, these students reported more positive intentions to spend time studying. Thinking of the benefits of studying may have strengthened attitudes toward studying, as well as perceptions that one could actually achieve this goal.

Thinking and positive cognitive responses also play a part in the well-known placebo effect—the tendency of patients to get better not because of the actual effects of a medical treatment, but due to a belief that the treatment will cure them. There is evidence from pain studies that placebos (dummy pills that do not actually control pain) are about 60% as effective as active medications like aspirin and codeine (Blakeslee, 1998). Patients suffering pain after getting a wisdom tooth extracted feel just as much relief from a fake ultrasound application as from a real one, provided both patient and doctor believe the ultrasound machine is on. Researchers have reported that they could successfully dilate asthmatics' airways by simply telling them they were inhaling a bronchodilator, even though they actually were not (Talbot, 2000).

Naturally there are many reasons why placebos work, and of course they don't work in each and every circumstance (Kolata, 2001). However, thinking you are going to get better and rehearsing these thoughts to yourself as the doctor gives you the treatment may actually help you to achieve the desired result.

ELABORATION LIKELIHOOD MODEL

These is little doubt that the cognitive response approach advanced knowledge of persuasion. It also provided a method to creatively measure cognitive aspects of attitudes. After a time, though, researchers realized that the approach had two limitations. First, it assumed that people think carefully about messages. Yet there are many times when people turn their minds off to persuasive communications, making decisions based on mental shortcuts. Second, the cognitive response approach failed to shed much light on the ways that messages influence people. It did not explain how we can utilize cognitive responses to devise messages to change attitudes or behavior. In order to rectify these problems, scholars proceeded to develop process-based models of persuasion.

Two models currently dominate the field. The first, devised by Shelly Chaiken and Alice H. Eagly, is called the **Heuristic–Systematic Model** (Chaiken, 2002; Chaiken, Liberman, & Eagly, 1989; Chen & Chaiken, 1999). The second, formulated by Richard E. Petty and John T. Cacioppo, is the **Elaboration Likelihood Model** (Petty & Cacioppo, 1986; Petty & Wegener, 1999). Both approaches emphasize that you cannot understand communication effects without appreciating the underlying processes by which messages influence attitudes. Both are **dual-process** models in that they claim that there are two different mechanisms by which communications affect attitudes. This chapter focuses on the Elaboration Likelihood Model (ELM) because it has generated more research on persuasive communication and offers a more comprehensive framework for understanding communication effects.

Main Principles

The first question students may have when reading about an elaboration likelihood model of persuasion is: "Just what does the term *elaboration likelihood* mean?" This is a reasonable question. *Elaboration* refers to the extent to which the individual thinks about or mentally modifies arguments contained in the communication. *Likelihood*, referring to the probability that an event will occur, is used to point up the fact that elaboration can be either likely or unlikely. Elaboration is assumed to fall along a continuum, with one end characterized by considerable rumination on the central merits of an issue, and the other by relatively little mental activity. The model tells us when people should be particularly likely to elaborate, or not elaborate, on persuasive messages.

The ELM stipulates that there are two distinct ways people process communications. These are called routes, suggesting that two different highways crisscross the mind, transporting thoughts and reactions to messages. The term *route* is a metaphor: We do not know for sure that these routes exist (anymore than we know with absolute certainty that any mental construct exists in precisely the way theorists use it). Social scientists employ terms like processing route (or attitude) to describe complex cognitive and behavioral phenomena. As with attitude, the term *processing route* makes eminent sense and is supported by a great deal of empirical evidence. The ELM refers to the two routes to persuasion as the **central and peripheral routes**, or central and peripheral processes.

The central route is characterized by considerable cognitive elaboration. It occurs when individuals focus in depth on the central features of the issue, person, or message. When people process information centrally, they carefully evaluate message arguments, ponder implications of the communicator's ideas, and relate information to their own knowledge and values. This is the thinking person's route to persuasion.

The peripheral route is entirely different. Rather than examining issue-relevant arguments, people examine the message quickly or focus on simple cues to help them decide whether to accept the position advocated in the message. Factors that are peripheral to message arguments carry the day. These can include a communicator's physical appeal, glib speaking style, or pleasant association between the message and music playing in the background. When processing peripherally, people invariably rely on simple decision-making rules or *heuristics*. For example, an individual may invoke the heuristic that "Experts are to be believed," and for this reason (and this reason only) accept the speaker's recommendation.

Thus, the ELM says that people can be simple information processors— "cognitive misers" as they are sometimes called (Taylor, 1981)—or deep, detailed thinkers. Under some conditions (when processing superperipherally), they are susceptible to slick persuaders—and can be thus characterized by the saying attributed to P. T. Barnum: "There's a sucker born every minute!" In other circumstances (when processing centrally), individuals are akin to Plato's ideal students—seeking truth and dutifully considering logical arguments—or to Aristotlean thinkers, persuaded only by cogent arguments (logos). The model says people are neither suckers nor deep thinkers. Complex creatures that we are, we are both peripheral *and* central, heuristic *and* systematic, processors. The critical questions are when people process centrally, when they prefer the peripheral pathway, and the implications for persuasion. The nifty thing about the ELM is that it answers these questions, laying out conditions under which central or peripheral processing is most likely, and the effects of such processing on attitude change.

The key factors that determine processing strategy are **motivation** and **ability**. When people are *motivated* to seriously consider the message, they process centrally. They also pursue the central route when they are cognitively *able* to ponder message arguments. Situations can limit or enhance people's ability to process centrally; so too can personal characteristics. On the other hand, when people lack the motivation or ability to carefully process a message, they opt for a simpler strategy. They process superficially.

It is frequently neither possible nor functional to process every message carefully. "Just imagine if you thought carefully about *every* television or radio commercial you heard or ad you came across in newspapers or magazines," note Richard Petty and his colleagues (1994). "If you ever made it out of the house in the morning, you probably would be too mentally exhausted to do anything else!" (p. 118). Contemporary society, with its multiple stimuli, unfathomably complex issues, and relentless social change, makes it inevitable that people will rely on mental shortcuts much of the time.

In addition to spelling out factors that make peripheral processing most likely, the ELM contains hypotheses about the impact that such processing exerts on persuasion. Different persuasive appeals are effective, depending on the processing route. These appeals also differ in their long-term effects on attitudes (see Fig. 5.3).

Motivation to Process

Involvement.   Can you think of an issue that has important implications for your own life? Perhaps it is a university proposal to raise tuition, a plan to change requirements in your major, or even a proposal to ban drinking in fraternities and sororities. Now think of an issue that has little impact on your day-to-day routines. This could be a proposal to strengthen the graduation requirements at local high schools or a plan to use a different weed spray in farming communities. You will certainly process the first issues differently than the second. Different persuasive appeals are likely to be effective in these two circumstances as well.

The topics just cited differ in their level of personal involvement, or the degree to which they are perceived to be personally relevant to individuals. *Individuals are high in involvement when they perceive that an issue is personally relevant or bears directly on their own lives. They are low in involvement when they believe that an issue has little or no impact on their own lives.*

The ELM stipulates that when individuals are high in involvement, they will be motivated to engage in issue-relevant thinking. They will recognize that it is in their best interest to carefully consider the arguments in the message. Even if they oppose the position advocated in the message, they may change their attitudes if the arguments are sufficiently compelling to persuade them that they will benefit by adopting the advocated position. Under high involvement, people should process messages through the central route, systematically scrutinizing message arguments.

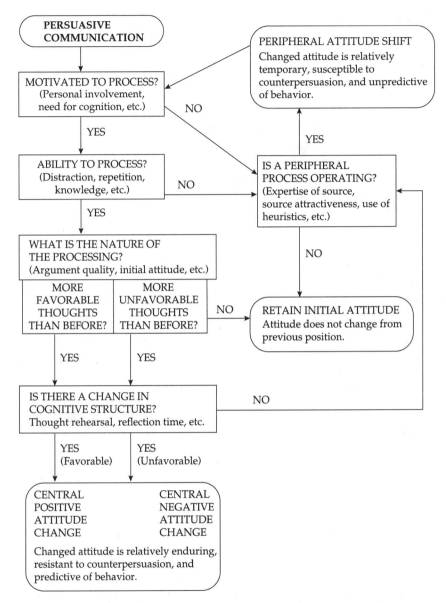

FIG. 5.3 The Elaboration Likelihood Model of Persuasion (Reprinted and adapted with permission from Petty and Wegener, 1999).

By contrast, under low involvement, people have little motivation to focus on message arguments. The issue is of little personal consequence; consequently, it doesn't pay to spend much time thinking about the message. As a result, people look for mental shortcuts to help them decide whether to accept the communicator's position. They process the message peripherally, unconcerned with the substance of the communication.

These predictions are intriguing, but how do we know if they hold water in the real world? In order to discover if hypotheses are correct, researchers test them empirically. Petty, Cacioppo, and Goldman (1981) examined these hypotheses in a now-classic study. To help you appreciate the procedures, I ask that you imagine that the experiment was being conducted again today using equivalent methods and materials. Here is how it would work:

You first enter a small room in a university building, take a seat, and wait for the experimenter. When the experimenter arrives, she tells you that the university is currently reevaluating its academic programs and is soliciting feedback about possible changes in policy. One proposal concerns a requirement that seniors take a comprehensive exam in their major area of study.

If randomly assigned to the high-involvement condition, you would be told that the comprehensive exam requirement could begin next year. That's clearly involving as it bears directly on your educational plans. How would you feel if you learned that you might have to take a big exam in your major—communication, psychology, marketing, or whatever it happened to be? You would probably feel nervous, angry, worried, or curious. Whichever emotion you felt, you clearly would be concerned about the issue.

If, on the other hand, you had been assigned to the low-involvement condition, you would be told that the exam requirement would not take effect for 10 years. That clearly is low involvement. Even if you're on the laid-back, two-classes-a-semester plan, you do not envision being in college 10 years from now! Realizing the message is of little personal consequence, you would gently switch gears from high energy to autopilot.

Regardless of involvement level, you would be asked now to listen to one of two messages delivered by one of two communicators. The particular message and source would be determined by lot, or random assignment.

You would listen to either strong or weak arguments on behalf of the exam. Strong arguments employ statistics and evidence ("Institution of the exams had led to a reversal in the declining scores on standardized achievement tests at other universities"). They offer cogent arguments in behalf of the exam requirement. Weak arguments are shoddy and unpersuasive (for example, "A friend of the author's had to take a comprehensive exam and now has a prestigious academic position").

Lastly, you would be led to believe that the comprehensive exam proposal had been prepared by either a communicator high or low in expertise. If assigned to the high-expertise group, you would be told that the report had been developed by the Carnegie Commission on Higher Education, which had been chaired by an education professor at Princeton University. If randomly assigned to the low-expertise communicator, you would be informed that the proposal had been prepared by a class at a local high school. You would then indicate your overall evaluation of the exam.

This constituted the basic design of the study. In formal terms, there were three conditions: involvement (high or low), argument quality (strong or weak), and expertise (high or low). Petty and his colleagues found that the impact of arguments and expertise depended to a considerable degree on level of involvement.

Under high involvement, argument quality exerted a significant impact on attitudes toward the comprehensive exam. Regardless of whether a high school class or Princeton professor was the source of the message, strong arguments led to more attitude change than did weak arguments. Under low involvement, the opposite pattern of results emerged. A highly expert source induced more attitude change than did a low-expert source, regardless of whether the arguments were strong or weak (see Fig. 5.4).

The ELM provides a parsimonious explanation of the findings. Under high involvement, students believed that the senior exam would affect them directly. This heightened motivation to pay careful attention to the quality of the arguments. Processing the arguments carefully through the central route, students naturally were more swayed by strong than by weak arguments. Imagine how you would react if you had been in this condition. Although you would hardly be overjoyed at the prospect of an exam in your major area of study, the idea would grab your attention, and you would think carefully about the arguments. After reading them, you would not be 100% in favor of the comprehensive exam—but having thought through the ideas and noted the benefits the exam provided, you might be more sympathetic to the idea than you would have been at the outset, and certainly more favorable than if you had listened to weak arguments in behalf of the exam.

Now imagine you had been assigned to the low-involvement–high-expertise group. You'd be on autopilot because the exam would not take place until long after you graduated. Blasé about the whole thing, feeling little motivation to think carefully about the issue, you would understandably have little incentive to pay close attention to the quality of arguments. You would focus on one salient cue—a factor that might help you decide what to do about this issue so you could complete the assignment and get on with your day. The fact that the communicator was from Princeton might capture your attention and offer a compelling reason to go along with the message. "If this Princeton prof thinks it's a good idea,

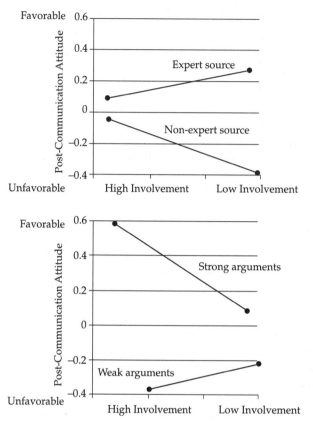

Top panel: Effects of involvement and source expertise on attitudes.
Bottom panel: Effects of involvement and argument quality on attitudes.

FIG. 5.4 Effects of involvement, source expertise, and argument quality on attitudes (From Petty, Cacioppo, & Goldman, *Journal of Personality and Social Psychology*, 41, pp. 847–855. © 1981 by the American Psychological Association. Reprinted with permission).

it's fine with me," you might think. Click-whirr, just like that, you would go along with the message (Cialdini, 2001).

As we will see, these findings have intriguing implications for everyday persuasion.

Looking back on the study findings, it may seem as if the main principle is that under high involvement, "what is said" is most important, and under low involvement, "who says it" is the key. There is some truth to this, but it greatly oversimplifies matters. The key point is *not* that message appeals are more effective under high involvement and communicator appeals are more compelling under low involvement. Instead, the core issue is that people engage in issue-relevant thinking under high involvement, but under low involvement focus on simple cues that are peripheral to the main issues. In fact, there are times when a peripheral aspect of the *message* can carry the day under low involvement.

Case in point: Number of message arguments. This attribute is absolutely irrelevant, or peripheral, to the quality of the message. A speaker can have nine shoddy arguments or one extremely cogent appeal. However, number of arguments can signify quality of argumentation in the minds of perceivers. If people would rather not think too deeply about an issue, they may fall into the trap of assuming that the more arguments a message has, the more convincing it is. This is exactly what Petty and Cacioppo (1984) discovered. When students were evaluating a proposal to institute senior comprehensive exams at their own school 10 years in the future, they were more influenced by a message that had nine arguments. It didn't matter if all of them were weak. However, when contemplating a senior exam policy that would take place next year, they were naturally more motivated to devote energy to thinking about the issue. They processed arguments centrally, seeing through the shoddy ones and accepting the message only if arguments were strong.

Other Motivational Factors. Critical as it is, personal involvement is not the only factor that influences message processing. If you expect to deliver a message to an audience, you should be highly motivated to expend cognitive effort processing the message (Boninger et al., 1990). If you are concerned with making a good impression on others when giving your pitch, you should also be motivated to systematically scrutinize the arguments you are going to discuss (see Leippe & Elkin, 1987; Nienhuis, Manstead, & Spears, 2001).

There is one other motivational factor that influences processing, and it is a particularly interesting one. It is a personality characteristic: **the need for cognition**. The need for cognition is a need to understand the world and to employ thinking to accomplish this goal. People who score high in need for cognition "prefer complex to simple problems" and "enjoy a task that involves coming up with new solutions to problems" (Cacioppo & Petty, 1982, pp. 120–121). These individuals tend to prefer central to peripheral processing. Different types of persuasive appeals work on people high in need for cognition than on those low in cognitive needs. These issues are taken up in chapter 8.

Ability

A second determinant of processing strategy (besides motivation) is the person's ability to process the message. Situations can enhance or hamper individuals' ability to process a message. For example, people are less able to process a message when they are distracted, resulting in persuasive effects discussed earlier. More interestingly, we centrally or peripherally process messages depending on our cognitive ability, or knowledge.

Knowledge is a particularly important factor. When people know a lot about an issue, they process information carefully and skillfully. They are better able to separate the rhetorical wheat from the chaff than those with little knowledge of the issue. They are more capable of evaluating the cogency of information and are adept at identifying shortcomings in message arguments (Wood, Rhodes, & Biek, 1995). It doesn't matter what the issue is: It could be nuclear physics, baseball, or roof repair. Knowledgeable people process information centrally and are ordinarily tough nuts for persuaders to crack (Wood et al., 1995). By contrast, people with minimal knowledge on a topic lack the background to differentiate strong from weak arguments. They also may lack confidence in their opinions. They are the peripheral processors, more susceptible to persuasion in most situations.

As an example, think of an issue you know a lot about—let's say, contemporary movies. Now conjure up a topic about which you know little—let's say, computer scanners. The ELM says that you will process persuasive messages on these topics very differently, and that persuaders should use different techniques to change your mind on these topics. Given your expertise on modern films (you know all about different film techniques and the strengths and weaknesses of famous directors), there is every reason to believe you would centrally process a message that claims 1960s movies are superior to those of today. The message would grab your attention and could change your attitudes—provided it contained strong, compelling arguments.

A "rational" approach like this would be stunningly ineffective on the subject of scanners that digitize photos and convert words on a printed page into word-processing files. Given your ignorance of scanners, you would have difficulty processing technical arguments about optical character recognition, driver software, or high-resolution scans. On the other hand, the salesperson who used a peripheral approach might be highly effective. A salesperson who said she had been in the business 10 years or who furnished 10 arguments why Canon was superior to Epson might easily connect with you, perhaps changing your attitude or inducing you to buy a Canon scanner. Consistent with this logic, Wood and her colleagues (1985) found that argument quality had a stronger impact on attitudes among individuals with a great deal of knowledge on an issue, but message length exerted a stronger influence on those with little knowledge of the issue.

PERIPHERAL PROCESSING IN REAL LIFE

There is nothing as practical as a good theory, Kurt Lewin famously said. This is abundantly apparent in the case of the ELM. Once you appreciate the model, you begin to find all sorts of examples of how it is employed in everyday life. Three examples of peripheral processing follow, and in the next section implications of central processes are discussed.

1. The Oprah Book Club Effect

Some 13 million Americans watch Oprah's Book Club, a monthly segment of *The Oprah Winfrey Show* that features engaging discussions of recently published novels. Book Club shows involve a discussion among Winfrey, the author, and several viewers, who discuss the book and its relationship to their own lives. "The show receives as many as 10,000 letters each month from people eager to participate," a reporter relates. "By the time the segment appears, 500,000 viewers have read at least part of the novel. Nearly as many buy the book in the weeks that follow. . . . Oprah's Book Club has been responsible for 28 consecutive best sellers. It has sold more than 20 million books and made many of its authors millionaires" (Max, 1999, pp. 36–37).

The Book Club is a great thing for books and publishing. It is also an example of peripheral processing in action. What convinces hundreds of thousands of people to buy these novels? What persuades them to purchase Wally Lamb's *She's Come Undone*, the story of an intelligent—overweight—woman who overcomes problems stemming from sexual abuse, rather than an equally compelling novel about abuse and redemption? The answer, in a word, is Oprah. Her credibility, warmth, and celebrity status suggest to viewers that the book is worth a try. It's not that audience members are meticulously comparing one book to another and integrate Oprah's advice with their literary assessments of the plot and character development. They lack motivation and perhaps ability. So, they rely on Oprah's advice and purchase the book, much to the delight of the publishing house and struggling novelist.

2. The Electoral Road Show

To many Americans, politics is like a traveling road show, a circus that the media cover every four years, complete with clowns, midgets, and daredevils who will do just about anything to win the crowd's approval. Politics does not affect them personally—or so many believe. About half of the electorate votes in presidential elections, and many are cynical about the political process (Doppelt & Shearer, 1999). "We have no control over what's going on," one disconnected citizen told researchers Jack Doppelt and Ellen Shearer (1999). Another said that "I don't really think any of the candidates are interested in the issues that I am" (p. 16).

Feeling cynical about politics and blasé about their participation, large numbers of voters put little mental energy into the vote decision.

Instead, they process politics peripherally, if at all. When it comes time to cast their vote, low-involved voters consider such peripheral cues as:

- *Candidate appearance.* Although people hate to admit it, they are influenced by candidates' physical appeal (Budesheim & DePaola, 1994; Rosenberg & McCafferty, 1987). Voters look at a physically attractive candidate, feel positively, and connect their positive affect with the candidate when it comes time to cast their vote.
- *Endorsements.* Political ads frequently contain long lists of endorsements. Names of well-known groups—for example, the American Bar Association, Fraternal Order of Police, and National Organization for Women—as well as not-so-famous organizations, appear on a television screen, while the voice-over praises the candidate. The list serves as a peripheral cue, inviting the inference that "If all these groups endorse that candidate, he's got to be qualified."
- *Names.* In low-involving elections, the name of the candidate can make a difference. Voters prefer candidates whose names they have heard many times, in part because such names have positive associations (Grush, McKeough, & Ahlering, 1978). In an Illinois primary election, two candidates with relatively smooth-sounding names (Fairchild and Hart) defeated candidates with less euphonious names (Sangmeister and Pucinksi). Many voters were probably shocked to discover that Mark Fairchild and Janice Hart were followers of the extremist and unconventional political candidate, Lyndon LaRouche (O'Sullivan et al., 1988)!

Candidates are not exactly oblivious to these points. They appreciate the psychology of low-involvement voting, and they develop persuasive messages to reach these voters. They hire image consultants, who advise them on what to wear and how to present themselves positively in public. Some years back, during the 2000 election, Al Gore was counseled to take on a more macho appearance by releasing his "inner-alpha-male" (Bellafante, 2000). In one political debate, he showed up wearing a three-button suit, a French blue shirt, and a horizontally striped tie. Although he looked more like a movie producer than a candidate, he hoped this would resonate with Democrats dissatisfied with his personae.

At other times, candidates rely on slogans. Candidates who use catchwords that resonate with voters—"social justice" for Democrats, "family values" for Republicans—can elicit positive perceptions from individuals who lack motivation to consider issue positions (Garst & Bodenhausen, 1996). Hearing the "right" words may be all it takes to convince these individuals to cast their vote for the candidate.

What do attractiveness, slogans, endorsements, and name sound have to do with a candidate's qualifications for office? Not too much: They are peripheral to the main issues of the campaign. Yet low-involved voters often rely on these cues and can be swayed by superficial appeals.

3. Jargon

Has this ever happened to you? Your car engine is on the blink; you take the auto to the mechanic; he (they're usually guys) looks at you with an expression that says "You're clueless about cars, aren't you?" then puts his hands to his hips and begins to talk in tongues—invoking the most complicated car jargon you have ever heard. Impressed by the verbiage and afraid to admit you don't know much about cars, you acquiesce to his appeal.

Tom and Ray Magliozzi, hosts of the National Public Radio show *Car Talk*, echoed this point in a humorous, but telling, article. Asked by an interviewer how someone could fake being a car mechanic, they recommend a heavy use of jargon (Nitze, 2001). Use words like "the torque wrench and torquing," Tom says. Ray replies, "Torquing always sounds good." Tom adds:

> I'll bet you, you could walk into some party and mention the expression "negative torque," there would be nobody who would have the guts to ask you what that meant. A pro included. (p. 38)

This fits right in with the ELM. Individuals with little knowledge about car mechanics have trouble following explanations involving torque or car computer systems. When a mechanic begins using the jargon, they invoke the heuristic, "Mechanics who talk this way know their stuff; if they say this, it must be so." And, just like that, the mechanic persuades these customers to make the purchase. (A similar example comes from the movie *My Cousin Vinny*, when the character played by Marisa Tomei wows a judge and jury, using jargon comprehensible only to car experts to prove that a getaway car could not possibly have been driven by the two men accused of the crime.)

CENTRAL PROCESSING

Peripheral processing is a persuader's paradise. It allows communicators to devise simplistic—sometimes deceptive—appeals to influence individuals. Tempting as it is to conclude that this is the basis to all contemporary persuasion, the fact is that much persuasion also involves careful, thoughtful consideration of message arguments. As discussed earlier, when people are motivated or able to process messages, they don't rely exclusively on peripheral cues, nor necessarily fall for persuader's ploys. Instead, they attend closely to the communicator's arguments. In these situations, persuasion flows through the central route, and appeals are necessarily crafted at a higher intellectual level.

Thus, when people typically buy big-ticket items like stereo systems, computers, and, of course, houses, they respond to cogent arguments in support of the particular product in question. In politics, when voters are out of work or concerned about the economy, they listen closely to candidates' plans to revitalize the nation's finances. For example, in 1980, with the country reeling from double-digit inflation, Ronald Reagan made the economy a centerpiece of his campaign against then-president Jimmy Carter. "Are you better off than you were four years ago?" he asked Americans in a presidential debate. Reagan went on to suggest that many folks were worse off than they had been prior to Carter taking office. In posing the question this way, Reagan induced people to think seriously about their own economic situations and at the same time to give his challenge to an incumbent president dutiful consideration. His appeals apparently worked, for Reagan handily defeated Carter in the November election (Ritter & Henry, 1994).

Arguments, however, do not always carry the day in persuasion. Cogent arguments can fall on deaf ears when they run counter to an individual's strong attitudes or values. Recall the discussion in chapter 2 of how passionate supporters and opponents of the death penalty reacted to evidence that questioned their position. They did not alter their attitudes. On the contrary, they criticized data that disputed their point of view, praised evidence that supported their position, and emerged with renewed confidence that their view on capital punishment was correct. How could this be, one wonders, if people are supposed to rationally consider arguments when they are interested in the issue in question?

The answer points to a complexity in the ELM. All central-route processing is not rational and free of bias. Human beings are not objective thinkers. The key is the degree to which the issue touches on an individual's strong attitudes, values, or ego-entrenched positions. It is useful to distinguish between issues that are of interest because they bear on important *outcomes* in the individual's life—comprehensive exams, tuition increases, the economy—and those that bear on *values* or deep-seated attitudes. When the message focuses on a personally relevant outcome, people process information in a relatively unbiased way, focusing on the merits of issue arguments. However, when the issue touches on core values or *ego-involved* schemas, individuals can be highly biased and selective in how they think about the entire matter. Make no mistake: In both cases, they process centrally, engaging in considerable thinking and evaluating the basic ideas contained in the message. However, when thinking about outcomes (a comprehensive exam) they are open to cogent arguments. When considering a message that touches on core values (capital punishment, abortion), they attend to the opponent's arguments, but usually reject them (Johnson & Eagly, 1989; Wood, Rhodes, & Biek, 1995). Highly knowledgeable people with strong attitudes will muster all sorts of sophisticated reasons why the opponent's plan is a bad one. They will impress you with their ability to remember the other side's arguments, but in the end they will prove to be just as biased as anyone else.

In these situations, people behave like ostriches, stubbornly rejecting ideas that are inconsistent with their attitude, and sticking only with communications that fall into the latitude of acceptance. How do communicators persuade people in such situations? With great difficulty and care, to be sure. Social judgment theory (see chapter 2) suggests that when trying to persuade people about issues that touch on core values, persuaders must strive to do two things. First, they should encourage individuals to *assimilate* the issue, or candidate, to their position. That is, they want people—or voters, applying this to a political context—to perceive that the candidate shares their position on the issue. The goal is not to change the voter's position on abortion, defense spending, the environment, or affirmative action. Instead, the idea is to convince voters that the candidate shares their positions on the issue and is sympathetic with their concerns (Schwartz, 1973).

At the same time, a communicator wants to make sure that people do not come away from the persuasive encounter perceiving that they are in sharp disagreement with the communicator on the issue (Kaplowitz & Fink, 1997). If voters *contrast* their position from a politician's, and assume that the politician takes a very different position on a key issue, the candidate is in deep do-do, as former president George Bush liked to say. For these reasons, candidates are frequently careful not to take strong positions on hot-button issues like abortion, gun control, capital punishment, and racial quotas. They are fearful of alienating undecided voters—of pushing voters' contrast effect buttons. If this happens, these folks may vote for the opposing candidate or stay home. Thus, there is a practical reason why candidates take "fuzzy" positions on hot-button issues. Yet this points up a troubling ethical issue. Candidates must camouflage or moderate their positions to get elected (Granberg & Seidel, 1976). However, in so doing they risk compromising their integrity or turning off voters who suspect the worst in politicians. Yet if they admirably stick to their guns and take strong positions, they alienate middle-of-the-roaders, and end up being right—not president.

Central processing frequently leads to reinforcement, or strengthening of attitudes. (There are times when this is a good thing—for example, in the case of solidifying a negative attitude toward cigarette smoking or drugs.) Nonetheless, there are cases in which central processing has produced profound changes in attitude—not just reinforcement. Americans radically changed their attitudes toward smoking, health, and exercise, in part due to central processes emphasized by the ELM. The ELM, in this way, explains how people modify their attitudes under high-involvement conditions. Individuals reconsider earlier positions, gradually alter their assessments of the issue, think deeply about the matter (sometimes through painful reassessment of themselves and their values), and over time link up the new attitude with other aspects of themselves. This leads to the attitude becoming a more permanent fixture of individuals' self-systems. Attitudes changed through deep, central route thinking are more likely to persist over time than those formed through short-circuited thinking or peripheral cues (Petty, Haugtvedt, & Smith, 1995). The hopeful side of this is that prejudice and dysfunctional attitudes *can* be changed. Once modified, such changes can also persist and lead to improvements in the person's overall mental state.

COMPLICATIONS AND CRITICISMS

In the many years that have elapsed since the Elaboration Likelihood Model was first introduced, the theory has been discussed, criticized, clarified, extended, and, yes, elaborated on in a variety of ways. In this section, I review these intellectual developments, hoping to illuminate the fine points of cognitive theorizing about persuasion.

A key issue involves the ability of a particular variable to do different things or serve diverse functions. Consider physical attractiveness. If you had to describe the role physical attractiveness plays in persuasion based on the earlier discussion, you might suggest that it serves as a peripheral cue. You might speculate that when people do not care much about an issue or lack ability to process the message, they fall back on the physical appeal of the speaker. Opting not to process the message carefully, they let themselves get carried away a bit by the speaker's good looks. The pleasant association of the communicator with the communication pushes individuals toward accepting the message. This analysis of attractiveness is indeed in sync with the ELM, as it has been discussed thus far. Attractiveness frequently has just this effect, serving as a cue for peripheral processing.

Unfortunately, matters become more complicated when we examine other persuasion settings. For example, suppose a young woman is looking for a beauty product, flips through the pages of *Glamour* magazine, and sees models promoting L'Oreal and Cover Girl lipcolors. The models' good looks represent key selling points for the products. Isn't a model's attractiveness central to the decision regarding the product, not peripheral? Couldn't the physical appeal of the model—the fact that she is beautiful and uses this product—serve as a compelling reason to purchase the particular facial cream, lipcolor, or makeup? The answer is "Yes."

The ELM argues that theoretically a particular variable can serve in one of three capacities. It can function as: (a) *a persuasive argument*, (b) *peripheral cue*, or (c) *factor that influences thinking about the person or issue*. Thus, for someone trying to decide whether to purchase a beauty product or shampoo, the communicator's attractiveness can serve as an *argument* for the product (Kahle & Homer, 1985). In another context—electoral politics—attractiveness can function as a *peripheral cue*, as when people decide to vote for candidates because they think they're cute.

Now consider a third situation, this involving a different aspect of politics. Let's say a person has mixed feelings on environmental and energy issues. She believes that the United States needs to locate alternative sources of fuel, but also feels it is important to preserve breathtakingly beautiful wildlife refuges. When an attractive source like actor Robert Redford (2001) criticizes policies to drill for oil in the Arctic National Wildlife Refuge, she may find herself *devoting more cognitive energy* to the communicator's arguments. She may picture Redford in her mind, link up his attractive appearance with the beauty of the wilderness, and therefore give his arguments more thought than if a less attractive communicator had advanced these positions.

Or consider the complex question of cutting taxes. Liberals oppose massive tax cuts, saying they favor the rich or that money collected from taxes is needed to cover Social Security and Medicare. Conservatives disagree. They argue that the government has (or had!) a surplus and owes it to citizens to refund their money; besides, they say, tax cuts will stimulate the economy. Enter the chairman of the Federal Reserve. He enthusiastically endorses tax cuts, providing sound arguments. The Federal Reserve chairman is a very credible source. His opinion and arguments can influence people. What does the ELM say about the role played by credibility (peripheral cue) and arguments?

The model offers up a complicated prediction (Petty & Wegener, 1999). It says that the Fed chairman's expertise *can* serve as a peripheral cue for people low in political involvement or economic knowledge. These folks may say to themselves, "Who knows what's the right policy here? It's beyond me. I'll go with what the Fed chairman says. If he says this, it must be right."

For those with a great deal of political motivation and economic knowledge, the chairman's endorsement may actually function as an argument. They may think, "I know he has been cautious about cutting taxes in the past. If he favors tax cuts now, it probably has some grounding in economic theory. Besides, given his power, the very fact that he endorses tax cuts may act as a stimulant to the economy."

To other individuals, with moderate knowledge or involvement, the chairman's endorsement of tax cuts may stimulate issue-relevant thinking. They may consider the issue more carefully now that a high-credibility-source has endorsed tax cuts. They may not change their minds, especially if they have strong views on the issue. However, the high-credible-source endorsement might catalyze their thinking, leading them to develop more detailed arguments on the issue.

In this way, a particular variable can serve multiple functions. Just as an attitude can serve different functions for different people, so too a persuasion factor can play different roles in different situations.

Criticisms and Reconciliations

Any persuasion model that stimulates research will generate criticism. This is as it should be: Theories are meant to be criticized and subjected to empirical scrutiny. Knowledge advances from the dueling of conflicting scholarly guns. New ideas emerge from the critical exchange of points of view.

The ELM has elicited its share of criticism, with bullets targeted at the multiple functions notion previously discussed. Critics have lamented the lack of clarity of this notion. They have argued that the ELM position permits it "to explain all possible outcomes," making it impossible in principle to prove the model wrong (Stiff & Boster, 1987, p. 251). "A persuader can conduct a post mortem to find out what happened but cannot forecast the impact of a particular message," Allen and Preiss (1997a) contend (pp. 117–118).

ELM proponents have thundered back, arguing that critics fail to appreciate the model's strengths (Petty et al., 1987; Petty, Wegener et al., 1993). As a general rule, proponents note, individuals will be more likely to elaborate on messages when they are high in motivation or ability, and more inclined to focus on peripheral cues when they are lower in ability or motivation. What's more, they say, if you understand the particular variable under investigation and the situation in which it operates, you can make clear predictions about the influences of persuasion factors on attitudes (Haugtvedt & Wegener, 1994; Petty & Wegener, 1998). Persuasion and human behavior are so complex, ELM proponents assert, that it is not possible to make precise predictions for every variable in each and every situation. On balance, they maintain, the ELM offers a highly useful framework for understanding how persuasion works in the panoply of situations in which it occurs in everyday life.

Both sides have a point. The multiple functions notion discussed earlier is intriguing, but it points to a problematic ambiguity in the model, making it so all-inclusive it is difficult to prove incorrect. At the same time, the ELM has many compensating virtues, as both critics and proponents acknowledge. It offers a comprehensive theory of cognitive processing. This is an important contribution, one that should not be minimized. Before the ELM (and Heuristic–Systematic Model: see Box 5–3) was invented, there were few in-depth approaches to understanding cognition and persuasive communication. There was a hodgepodge of results—findings about this type of communicator, that type of message, and this kind of message recipient. It was like a jigsaw puzzle that didn't quite fit together. The ELM has helped provide us with a unified framework to understand the blooming, buzzing confusion of persuasion. For example, it helps explain why certain attitudes persist longer and predict behavior better than others (the former are elaborated on, accessed more, and linked up to a greater degree with other mental elements). To be sure, the model has imperfections (e.g., it can be difficult to derive message appeals for some real-world persuasion situations). However, it takes us from processes to effects and sheds enormous light on the variety of ways that persuasive communications achieve their effects. In the end, as several scholarly critics note, it would be difficult to overstate the model's contribution to our knowledge of persuasive communication (Kruglanski, Thompson, & Spiegel, 1999, p. 294; see also Booth-Butterfield & Welbourne, 2002, and Slater, 2002).

BOX 5–3
HEURISTIC AND SYSTEMATIC THINKING

The Heuristic–Systematic Model (HSM) complements the ELM. It too has generated a great deal of research. No discussion on persuasion would be complete without discussing its main features.

Like the Elaboration Likelihood Model, the HSM emphasizes that there are two processes by which persuasion occurs. Instead of calling the routes central and peripheral, it speaks of systematic and heuristic processing. Systematic processing entails comprehensive examination of issue-relevant arguments. Heuristic processing, discussed earlier in this chapter, involves the use of cognitive shortcuts. People invoke heuristics, or simple rules of thumb that enable them to evaluate message arguments without much cognitive effort. For example, the notion that "Experts are always right" is a cognitive heuristic.

Continued

BOX 5–3
(CONTINUED)

There are subtle differences between central and systematic, and peripheral and heuristic, processing. However, they are by and large the same.

Like the ELM, the Heuristic–Systematic Model says that motivation and ability determine processing strategy. It emphasizes that people can be motivated by a need to hold accurate attitudes, defensive needs to maintain attitudes that bear on the self-concept, or desire to make a positive impression on others (Chen & Chaiken, 1999).

The HSM interestingly emphasizes that heuristic and systematic processes are not mutually exclusive. Instead, it says that, under certain circumstances, people could rely on heuristics *and* systematically process a message.

More than the ELM, the model says that people often prefer the short-circuited heuristic route than the detailed, systematic path. People are viewed as "'minimalist information processors" who are unwilling to devote much effort to processing persuasive arguments (Stiff, 1994). They like their shortcuts and they use them frequently in everyday life.

CONCLUSIONS

We can trace dual-process models to ancient Greece. Plato's ideal thinkers epitomized systematic, deep processing of persuasive messages; some of the Sophist writers (at least as depicted by Plato) embodied the colorful, stylistic appeals we associate with the peripheral route. Contemporary models, attempting to explain a very different world of persuasion than that which bedeviled the Greeks, hark back to the duality that preoccupied Plato in the 4th century B.C.

Contemporary models stipulate that there are two routes to persuasion—one thoughtful, focusing on the main arguments in the message, the other superficial and short-circuited, characterized by an attempt to make a quick choice, an easy fix. The ELM and Heuristic–Systematic Model, building on the Yale Attitude Change and Cognitive Response Approaches, offer insights about how people process messages in many situations. Motivation and ability determine processing strategy. Processing route, in turn, determines the type of message appeal that is maximally effective in a particular context, as well as the long-term effects of the message on attitudes. In other words, if you understand the factors impinging on someone and how he or she thinks about a persuasive message, you have a good chance of devising a message that will target the individual's attitudes.

Complications arise when we consider that persuasion factors perform multiple functions. A given factor can serve as a cue, an argument, or catalyst to thought, depending on the person and situation. The multiple functions notion helps explain a variety of persuasion effects; however, its ambiguity can frustrate attempts to derive clear applications of the ELM to real-life situations. Taken as a whole, however, the model offers scholars a framework for understanding persuasion and provides practitioners with ideas for designing effective appeals (see Box 5–4). In essence, the model tells persuaders—in areas ranging from politics to health—to understand how their audiences approach and process messages. The ELM cautions against confrontation. Instead, it instructs communicators to build audience orientations into persuasive campaigns.

BOX 5–4
PERSUASION TIPS

One of the nifty things about the ELM is it contains practical, as well as theoretical, suggestions. Here are several suggestions for everyday persuasion, gleaned from the model:

1. Next time you are trying to convince someone of something, ask yourself: What is central, or most critical, to my attempt to change the other's mind? What type of appeal will serve my goal best? For example, people are frequently scared of giving a public speech and assume that the most important thing is to look nice—buy fancy clothes, put on lots of makeup, and so forth. This can be an important aspect of persuasion, but it may be peripheral to the task. If you are trying to make a sale, you need compelling arguments that the purchase is in the client's interest. If you are trying to convince people to get more exercise, you must show them that exercise can help them achieve their goals.

2. By the same token, remember that something that appears peripheral to you may be of considerable importance to the person you are trying to convince (Soldat, Sinclair, & Mark, 1997). You may spend a lot of time coming up with great arguments to convince neighbors to sign a petition against McDonalds' building a new franchise near a beautiful park located down the block. But if your memo has a couple typos or your Web site containing the message is overloaded with information, people may think a little less of you. They may jump to the conclusion that your arguments are flawed. To you, the typos or abundance of information is of much less consequence than the cogency of your arguments. And you may be right. But what is peripheral to you can be central to someone else. Put yourself in the minds of those receiving your message, and consider how they will react to what you say and how you package your message.

Continued

**BOX 5–4
(CONTINUED)**

3. When you are on the other end of the persuasion stick and are receiving the message, ask a couple of questions. First, is this something I really care about, or is it a low-involvement issue to me? Second, can I figure out what the persuader is promoting, or is this beyond me? If it is a high-involvement issue or you can understand where the persuader is coming from, you will probably scrutinize the message carefully and make a good decision. If you decide it's a low-involvement issue or you lack knowledge on the topic, you may find yourself turning to peripheral cues or relying on mental shortcuts. You may search for the easy way to make up your mind. There is nothing wrong with this, but it can lead you to place more trust in a persuader than perhaps you should. You could get snookered as a result!

To protect yourself, always ask yourself if you're trying to go for the quick fix, either because you don't care or don't know much about the issue. If you recognize that you are relying on mental shortcuts, take the opposite tack. Spend more time than you ordinarily would on the decision. Think about the issue. You may find it's more interesting or less difficult than you thought. The extra few minutes you spend thinking may help prevent you from making a costly or embarrassing mistake.

Ethically speaking, the model is value neutral. Reliance on peripheral or central cues can be functional or dysfunctional. Messages containing peripheral cues can take advantage of audiences' lack of motivation to consider issues under low involvement; centrally processed arguments can be cogent, but deceptive. As a psychological theory of persuasion, the model is silent as to whether people's motivation to carefully process issues under high involvement balances out their susceptibility to manipulation under low involvement. The most reasonable answer to these conundrums is that individuals are responsible for the persuasive decisions they make. It is our responsibility to recognize that we like to take mental shortcuts when we care or know little about an issue and that persuaders will try to take advantage of this tendency. In the short and long run, it is our responsibility to protect ourselves from being taken in by the peripheral persuaders of the world.

CHAPTER 6

"Who Says It": Source Factors in Persuasion

Charisma. It's a word that comes to mind frequently when people speak of persuasion. You probably think of great speakers, a certain magnetic quality, or perhaps people you know who seem to embody this trait. Charisma is also one of those "god-terms" in persuasion (Weaver, 1953)—concepts that have positive connotations, but have been used for good and evil purposes. We can glimpse this in the tumultuous events of the 20th century, events that were shaped in no small measure by the power of charismatic leaders. Consider the following examples:

On August 28, 1963, hundreds of thousands of people converged on Washington, DC, protesting racial prejudice and trying to put pressure on Congress to pass a Civil Rights Bill. Their inspirational leader was Reverend Martin Luther King, Jr., the apostle of nonviolence and eloquent spokesman for equality and social justice. The protesters marched from the Washington Monument to the Lincoln Memorial, listening to a litany of distinguished speakers, but waiting patiently for King to address the crowd. King had worked all night on his speech, a sermonic address that would prove to be among the most moving of all delivered on American soil. He alluded to Abraham Lincoln, called on Old Testament prophets, and presented "an entire inventory of patriotic themes and images typical of Fourth of July oratory," captivating the audience with his exclamation, repeated time and again, that "I Have a Dream" (Miller, 1992, p. 143). King's wife, Coretta Scott King, recalls the pantheon:

> Two hundred and fifty thousand people applauded thunderously, and voiced in a sort of chant, *Martin Luther King.* . . . He started out with the written speech, delivering it with great eloquence. . . . When he got to the rhythmic part of demanding freedom *now*, and wanting jobs *now*, the crowd caught the timing and shouted *now* in a cadence. Their response lifted Martin in a surge of emotion to new heights of inspiration. Abandoning his

written speech, forgetting time, he spoke from his heart, his voice soaring magnificently out over that great crowd and over to all the world. It seemed to all of us there that day that his words flowed from some higher place, through Martin, to the weary people before him. Yea—Heaven itself opened up and we all seemed transformed. (King, 1969, pp. 238–239)

Charisma also was in force some 60 years earlier, at a different place, during a different time. In cities like Nuremberg and Berlin, to audiences of Germans—young, old, educated, uneducated, cultured, and uncultured— Adolf Hitler spoke, using words and exploiting symbols, bringing audiences to their feet "with his overwhelming, hysterical passion, shouting the same message they had heard over and over again, that they had been done in by traitors, by conspirators . . . , by Communists, plutocrats, and Jews" (Davidson, 1977, p. 183). Like King, Hitler's oratory moved people and appealed to their hopes and dreams. But his speeches malevolently twisted hope into some gnarled ghastly entity and appealed to Germans' latent, darkest prejudices. Here is how a journalist, who carefully observed Hitler, described the Fuhrer's charismatic skill:

With unerring sureness, Hitler expressed the speechless panic of the masses faced by an invisible enemy and gave the nameless specter a name. He was a pure fragment of the modern mass soul, unclouded by any personal qualities. One scarcely need ask with what arts he conquered the masses; he did not conquer them, he portrayed and represented them. His speeches are day-dreams of this mass soul; they are chaotic, full of contradictions, if their words are taken literally, often senseless as dreams are, and yet charged with deeper meaning. . . . The speeches always begin with deep pessimism, and end in overjoyed redemption, a triumphant, happy ending, often they can be refuted by reason, but they follow the far mightier logic of the subconscious, which no refutation can touch. Hitler has given speech to the speechless terror of the modern mass, and to the nameless fear he has given a name. That makes him the greatest mass orator of the mass age. (quoted in Burleigh, 2000, pp. 100–101)

Charisma—exploited for evil purposes by Hitler, used to lift human spirits by Martin Luther King—describes the power of so many forceful speakers, including (in the political realm) Franklin Delano Roosevelt, John F. Kennedy, Ronald Reagan, and Bill Clinton; Jesse Jackson and Louis Farrakhan in the domain of race and civil rights; Bella Abzug and Gloria Steinem in the arena of women's equality; and Nelson Mandela and Mahatma Ghandi in the international domain of human rights. Regrettably, it also describes a legion of cult leaders, who enchanted, then deceived, dozens, even hundreds of starry-eyed followers. The list of charismatic cult leaders includes Charles Manson; Jim Jones, who induced 900 people to commit suicide in Guyana; David Koresh, leader of the ill-fated Branch Davidians in Waco, Texas; Marshall Applewhite, who led 38 members of the Heaven's Gate cult to commit suicide in 1997; and most recently Osama bin Laden, who masterminded the September 11 attacks and, to many, is the personification of evil.

What is charisma? Coined over a century ago by German sociologist Max Weber (1968), charisma is "a certain quality of the individual personality by virtue of which he is set apart from ordinary men and treated as endowed with supernatural, superhuman, or at least exceptional powers and qualities" (p. 241). Scholars who have studied charisma acknowledge the powerful influence it can have over ordinary people Yet they also are quick to identify its limits. Charismatic individuals, after all, are not superhuman, but are seen in this light by their followers. Followers, for their part, influence the self-perception of leaders. As Ronald E. Riggio (1987) notes, "the charismatic leader inspires the crowd, but he also becomes charged by the emotions of the followers. Thus, there is an interplay between leader and followers that helps to build a strong union between them" (p. 76).

Charisma is also bound and bracketed by history. A person who has charisma in one era might not wield the same influences on audiences in another historical period. The chemistry between speaker and audience is a product of a particular set of circumstances, psychological needs, and social conditions. Martin Luther King might not be charismatic in today's more complex multicultural era, which involves increased tolerance for racial diversity but also wariness of the costs of worthy social experiments like affirmative action. Franklin Delano Roosevelt, a grand and majestic speaker on radio, might not move millions of television viewers, who would view a crippled president clutch his wheelchair for support.

Charisma, a powerful force in the 20th century, is not likely to disappear. People need to believe in the power of myth, and charismatic leaders feed—and can exploit—this motivation. Twenty-first-century charismatic leaders will exude different qualities than orators of previous eras. They will adapt their styles to the conditions and media of their times.

What more can be said of charisma? What role does it play in everyday persuasion? These questions are more difficult to answer. Charisma is an intriguing factor in persuasion, but an elusive one, to be sure. Granted, charisma involves a persuader's ability to command and compel an audience, but what specific traits are involved? The communicator's sociability? Attractiveness? Power? Or is it an attribute of the message: the words, metaphors, or nonverbal communication (hand motions and eye contact, for example)? Or does charisma have more to do with the audience—individuals' own vulnerability and need to believe that a communicator has certain qualities they yearn for in life? These questions point to the difficulty of defining charisma with sufficient precision that it can be studied in social scientific settings. There is no question that charisma exists and has been a powerful force in persuasion. On a practical level, it is difficult to study the concept and to determine just how it works and why.

Thus, those who wish to understand why the Martin Luther Kings and Hitlers of the world have profoundly affected audiences must take a different tack. They must either study political history or take a more finely tuned, social scientific approach to examining communicator effects. More generally, those of us who want to comprehend how persuaders persuade are advised to chip away at the question by examining the different pieces of the puzzle. A key piece of the puzzle—a core aspect of charisma—is the communicator. His or her qualities, and the ways in which these characteristics interact with the audience, can strongly influence attitudes. The chapters that follow explore other noteworthy aspects of this jigsaw puzzle of persuasive communication effects: the message (chapter 7) and the psychology of the audience (chapters 8 and 9).

The present chapter begins with an overview of communicator (or source) factors. It then discusses key factors in depth, applying them to contemporary life.

UNDERSTANDING THE COMMUNICATOR

Just as there is not one type of charismatic leader (Ronald Reagan differed vastly from Jesse Jackson), there is not one defining characteristic of effective communicators. Communicators have different attributes and influence audiences through different processes. There are three fundamental communicator characteristics: **authority**, **credibility**, and **social attractiveness**. Authorities, credible communicators, and attractive ones produce attitude change through different mechanisms (Kelman, 1958).

Authorities frequently influence others through *compliance*. Individuals adopt a particular behavior not because they agree with its content, but because they expect "to gain specific rewards or approval and avoid specific punishments or disapproval by conforming" (Kelman, 1958, p. 53). In other words, people go along with authority figures because they hope to obtain rewards or avoid punishment.

Credible communicators, by contrast, influence attitudes through *internalization*. We accept recommendations advanced by credible communicators because they are congruent with our values or attitudes.

Attractive communicators—likable and physically appealing ones— seem to achieve influence through more affective processes, such as *identification*. People go along with attractive speakers because they identify with them, or want to establish a positive relationship with the communicators (Kelman, 1958).

Although Kelman's analysis oversimplifies matters to some degree, it provides a useful framework for understanding communicator effects. The next sections examine the impact of authority, credibility, and attractiveness on persuasion.

AUTHORITY

It was an amazing study—unique in its time, bold, yet controversial, an attempt to create a laboratory analogue for the worst conformity in 20th-century history and one of the most graphic cases of criminal obedience in the history of humankind. Legendary psychologist Gordon W. Allport called the program of research "the Eichmann experiment" because it attempted to explain the subhuman behavior of Nazis like Adolf Eichmann, who after ordering the slaughter of 6 million Jews said "it was unthinkable that I would not follow orders" (Cohen, 1999, p. A1). More generally, the research was designed to shed light on the power that authorities hold over ordinary people, and how they are able to induce individuals to obey their directives, sometimes in ways that violate human decency.

You may have heard of the research program, called the Milgram experiments after psychologist Stanley Milgram who conceptualized and directed them. They are described in social psychology and social influence texts. A documentary film depicting the studies has been shown in thousands of college classrooms (you may have seen it). Milgram's (1974) book, *Obedience to Authority*, has been translated into 11 languages. A rock musician of the 1980s, Peter Gabriel, called on the research in his song, "We Do What We're Told—Milgram's 37."

Experimental Procedures and Results

Milgram conducted his research—it was actually not one study, but a series of experiments—from 1960 to 1963 at Yale University and nearby Bridgeport, Connecticut. The basic procedure follows:

Each individual receives $4.50 for participating in the experiment, billed as a study of memory and learning. At the laboratory, participants are joined by a man introduced as a fellow subject in the study, but who is actually working for the researcher.

At this point the participants are told that they will draw slips of paper to determine who will serve as the "teacher" and who will take the "learner" role. The drawing is rigged so that the naive subject is always selected to be the teacher.

The experimenter tells teacher and learner that the study concerns the effects of punishment on learning. The teacher watches as an experimenter escorts the learner to a room, seats him in a chair, straps his arms to prevent too much movement, and attaches an electrode to his wrist. The learner is told that he must learn a list of word pairs. When he makes a mistake, he will receive electric shocks, the intensity increasing with each error committed.

The teacher then is seated before a shock generator that contains a horizontal line of 30 switches varying from 15 to 450 volts and descriptions ranging from SLIGHT SHOCK to DANGER—SEVERE SHOCK. The experimenter instructs the teacher to read the word pairs to the learner, located in the next room. When the learner responds incorrectly, the teacher is to administer an electric shock, starting at the mildest level (15 volts) and increasing in 15-volt increments. After a series of shocks have been administered, the learner begins to express pain, grunting, complaining, screaming at 285 volts, and then remaining silent. Each time the teacher expresses misgivings about administering a shock, the experimenter orders him or her to continue, saying "it is absolutely essential that you continue."

In reality, of course, the learner is not getting shocked. The experiment does not concern the effect of punishment on learning, but instead is designed to determine how far people will go in obeying an authority's directives to inflict harm on a protesting victim (Milgram, 1974). Although the shocks are not real, they seem quite authentic to individuals participating in the study. Participants frequently experience considerable tension, torn between sympathy for a suffering compatriot and perceived duty to comply with authority. As Milgram (1963) notes:

> I observed a mature and initially poised businessman enter the laboratory smiling and confident. Within 20 minutes he was reduced to a twitching, stuttering wreck, who was rapidly approaching a point of nervous collapse. . . . At one point he pushed his fist into his forehead and muttered: "Oh God, let's stop it." And yet he continued to respond to every word of the experimenter, and obeyed to the end. (p. 377)

The businessman was the norm, not the exception. Although a group of psychiatrists predicted that only 1 in 1,000 individuals would administer the highest shock on the shock generator, as many as 65% went this far. Large numbers of individuals were perfectly content to go along with the experimenter's orders.

The Milgram studies are one of many investigations of the effects of authority on behavior. There is an entire research literature on this topic (Kelman & Hamilton, 1989). The Milgram research provides a useful framework for understanding these effects—it is a window on the role authority plays in persuading individuals to comply with diverse requests.

Milgram's interest was in obedience, but not typical obedience in everyday life, like obeying traffic signs or laws prohibiting shoplifting. This obedience is not objectionable. Milgram's focus was obedience to malevolent authority, obedience that violates moral judgments, what Kelman and Hamilton call "crimes of obedience." Authority—the concept that preoccupied Milgram—is assumed to emanate not from personal qualities, *"but from (the person's) perceived position in a social structure"* (Milgram, 1974, p. 139). A legitimate authority is someone who is presumed to have "the right to prescribe behavior" for others (Milgram, pp. 142–143). In the experimental drama of the Milgram studies, the experimenter exploited his authority and led many people to administer shocks to a helpless victim.

Explanations

Why? Why would normal, upstanding human beings ignore their consciences and administer what they thought were electric shocks to a middle-aged learner? The explanation must lie in part with the power that situations can exert on human behavior, particularly the effects of the aura—or trappings—of authority. Interpretations of the Milgram findings include:

1. *Early socialization.* People are socialized to obey authority, and they get rewarded for doing so. Success in school, on sports teams, in corporate organizations, and even in Hollywood movies requires complying with the requests of authorities. "We learn to *value* obedience, even if what ensues in its name is unpleasant," Arthur G. Miller and his colleagues (1995) note. "We also *trust* the legitimacy of the many authorities in our lives," they remark (p. 9).

2. *Trappings of authority.* Various aspects of the experimental situation contributed to its majesty, or "aura of legitimacy" (Kelman and Hamilton, p. 151). These included: (a) status of the institution, Yale University; (b) complex, expensive scientific equipment in the room; (c) the experimenter's clothing (his lab coat served as a symbol of scientific expertise); and (d) the experimenter's gender—men are accorded more prestige "simply by virtue of being male" (Rudman & Kilianski, 2000, p. 1315). These trappings of authority could have served as peripheral cues, calling up the rule of thumb that "you do what authorities ask."

3. *Binding forces.* The experiment set in motion powerful psychological forces that "locked" participants into compliance. Participants did not want to harm the learner, and probably harbored doubts about the necessity of

administering severe electric shocks to advance scientific knowledge of memory. Still, they were reluctant to mention these concerns. Believing they lacked the knowledge or expertise to challenge the experimenter's requests, afraid of what would happen if they confronted the experimenter, concerned that he might implicitly indict them for failing to serve the noble goals of science and Yale University, they knuckled under. "To refuse to go on meant to challenge the experimenter's authority," Kelman and Hamilton note (p. 153). While some people were willing to undertake this challenge, most did not. They did not perceive that they had the right or ability to question the experimenter, and thus opted to accept his view of the situation.

The Milgram experiments illustrate the powerful impact that social influence can exert on behavior. To some degree, the experiments straddle the line between coercion and persuasion. There is a coercive aspect to the studies in that the experimenter was pushing individuals to act contrary to their preferences, and participants may have experienced the authority's directives as a threat. But the bottom line is that no one was holding a gun to participants' heads; they were free to stop the shocks whenever they wanted, and some individuals did. The experimenter set up the bait, but individuals persuaded themselves to go along with his commands.

Additional Issues

Milgram conducted a variety of studies of obedience, varying aspects of the experimental situation. He found that obedience was more likely to occur under certain conditions than others. For example, substantially more individuals obeyed when the experimenter sat a few feet from the teacher than when he left the room and relayed orders by telephone. In one experiment, three individuals served as teachers. Unbeknownst to the subject, two worked for the experimenter. When the two individuals refused to shock the learner, obedience dropped sharply. This is the most hopeful aspect of the research. It suggests that authorities lose their grip if enough people resist.

Over the years, Milgram's studies have generated considerable discussion in the academic community. It would be ironic if academics accepted Milgram's findings lock, stock, and barrel—if they marched to Milgram's music in unison, just as his subjects followed the experimenter's order. I am happy to report that this is not what has occurred. Milgram's studies have been endlessly debated, criticized, and praised (Miller, 1986; Orne & Holland, 1968).

Critics have pointed out that the study involved the use of archaic, physical violence; yet much violence involves verbal or psychological abuse (Meeus & Raaijmakers, 1986). Scholars have also suggested that individuals' obedience was not as nasty as Milgram suggested. "Subjects take it for granted that the experimenter is familiar with the shock generator and that he knows that the shocks are not fatal," two researchers contended (Meeus & Raaijmakers, p. 312). In response, Milgram has noted that research participants—the teachers—perceived that the experimental situation was very real—not a game. They believed that the shocks had inflicted pain.

Others have objected to the experiments on ethical grounds, arguing that Milgram had no right to play God. They suggest that it was immoral to leave participants with knowledge that they could be cruel, slavishly obedient creatures (Baumrind, 1964). The ethical critique has stimulated much discussion, with Milgram (1974) pointing out that participants in his studies had been debriefed, had not suffered harm, and actually viewed the experiment as enlightening. Yet even if one shares Milgram's positive assessment of the research, there is still something unsettling about deceiving people in the name of science.

So where does this leave us? The obedience experiments were conducted about a half century ago, in a profoundly different time. Perhaps, one might suggest, they only describe the behavior of men who served in the military during World War II or individuals reared during the conformist 1950s. Intrigued by this possibility, researchers conducted obedience studies modeled after Milgram's or developed new procedures to tap obedience. These more recent studies also reported disturbing evidence of obedience (Blass, 1992, 1999). For example, over 90% of subjects in one study followed the experimenter's orders to make 15 negative remarks to a test taker, even though they knew it would make the other person tense (Meeus & Raaijmakers, 1986).

Applications

The Milgram experiments have emerged, in the words of one scholar, as "one of the most singular, most penetrating, and most disturbing inquiries into human conduct that modern psychology has produced" (quoted in Blass, 1999, p. 957). They provide an explanation—not the only one, but a powerful one—for the Holocaust of the Jews. They help us understand why American soldiers followed orders to slaughter women, children, and old men in Vietnam. The findings also shed light on phenomena other than wartime massacres.

They help us understand why White House aides have followed presidents' commands to cover up illegal acts, lie about them, or stonewall the press. Events such as these occurred during Watergate (Kelman & Hamilton, 1989), and to some degree during the Clinton–Lewinsky scandal. The

Milgram studies also explain actions taken in health maintenance organizations (HMOs), as when doctors slavishly follow HMO authorities' orders to have special medical procedures performed only at the HMO. Some years back, a physician found that a patient's appendix was inflamed, but told her she would have to wait over a week to have an exam performed by the HMO staff. While waiting for her appointment, the patient's appendix burst, leading to a complicated medical situation (Greenhouse, 1999). Had the physician not followed orders, she might have found a way out of the logjam.

The Milgram study also sheds light on a much different problem: the distress professional secretaries experience when their bosses ask them to commit unethical acts. Eighty-eight percent of administrative professionals admitted they had told a "little white lie" for a supervisor (Romano, 1998). Some have done worse, like the secretary for a school district who routinely complied with her boss' requests to inflate grades of college-bound students. "What am I supposed to do?" the 48-year-old woman, a single mother of two children, said to reporter Lois Romano. "I have to put food on the table. I need the benefits and so I am forced to do things I know are not correct. I have nowhere to go" (Romano, p. 29).

The woman's comments illustrate the tension people feel when faced with having to carry out orders they know are wrong. The secretary is frank about her problem, but mistaken in one respect, I maintain.

She says she has nowhere to go. Yet people always have places to go. There are always choices in life, and people can usually find a way to reconcile conscience with survival needs. The secretary may not have been able to quit her job, but she could have blown the whistle on the boss by asking a newspaper reporter to investigate the issue. Failing that, she could have kept a diary, and at a later time in life—when she could afford to leave the job or had retired—could reveal all. Or, realizing she had to put bread on the table, she might have thought through her predicament, redefined the situation as one in which her compliance was required but did not reflect her true personality, and resolved to do morally upstanding things in other aspects of her life.

The point is: There is always a way to respect conscience and resist exploitive authorities, in some way, shape, or form. If ever you are faced with a situation in which you must choose between your morals and the tempting desire to follow the crowd or a boss, remember the Milgram results. Ask yourself: What do I believe? Is this something I really want to do? How will I feel tomorrow when I realize I could have respected my own beliefs? If you ask these questions, you will be less likely to acquiesce to authority and more inclined to do something that will sit well with your inner convictions.

CREDIBILITY

Take a deep breath. We're about to shift gears now, moving from the transcendental moral issues of authority to everyday questions of credibility. Credibility is one of the "Big 3" communicator factors—along with authority and social attractiveness. It dates back to Aristotle, who coined the term *ethos* to describe qualities of the source that facilitated persuasion. Hovland explored it in his early research, communication researchers deconstructed credibility in the 1960s and '70s, and the concept continues to fascinate scholars today. Of course, corporate managers, salespeople, and politicians are very interested in what makes someone credible. Nowadays, consultants offer pointers to clients who want to improve the credibility of their commercial Web sites. D. Joel Whalen (1996), in a book on persuasive business communication, says that credibility is "the single biggest variable under the speaker's control during the presentation" (p. 97). Jay A. Conger (1998), writing about the role persuasion plays in business, observes that "credibility is the cornerstone of effective persuading; without it, a persuader won't be given the time of day" (p. 90).

So, what is credibility? First, let's say what it is *not*. It is not the same as authority, although the two are frequently confused. Authority emanates from a person's position in a social structure. It involves the ability to dispense rewards and punishments. Credibility is a psychological or interpersonal communication construct. You can be an authority, but lack credibility. Parents can be authority figures to their kids, but have zero credibility in their children's eyes due their hypocrisy or indifference. In politics, a president is the nation's commander-in-chief—the top political authority. However, a president can lack credibility in the nation's eyes if he (or she) ignores the nation's economic problems or gets embroiled in a scandal. Dictators like Saddam Hussein of Iraq can do as they please; they have total, supreme authority. But ask their citizens in private what they think of these men and you will quickly discover that authority does not translate into credibility.

Credibility is defined as **"the attitude toward a source of communication held at a given time by a receiver"** (McCroskey, 1997, p. 87). It is an audience member's perceptions of the communicator's qualities. Although we commonly think of credibility as something a communicator *has*, it is more complex. As Roderick Hart and his colleagues (1983) note:

> Credibility is *not a thing*. It is not some sort of overcoat that we put on and take off at will. Rather, it is a *perception* of us that lies inside of the people to whom we talk. (Hart, Friedrich, & Brummett, p. 204)

Credibility is more than a psychological characteristic. It is also a communication variable. It is part of the two-way interaction between communicator and message recipients—a dynamic entity that emerges from the transaction between source and audience member. This means that communicators are not guaranteed credibility by virtue of who they are, their title, or academic pedigree. As Hart reminds us, credibility "is not something we can be assured of keeping once gotten. Credibility can only be earned by paying the price of effective communication" (pp. 204–205). There is something democratic about credibility. It says that communicators have to enter the rough-and-tumble realm of persuasion. They must meet and greet—either interpersonally or electronically—those they seek to influence. They must earn an audience's respect and win its credibility.

Core Characteristics

What are the main attributes of credibility? What does it mean to be a credible speaker?

Communication researchers have explored these time-honored questions, using empirical methodologies and survey research. Scholars asked people to evaluate the believability of famous people, giving speeches on various topics, and to rate friends or supervisors on semantic differential scales. They found that credibility is not a simple, unitary concept: It has more than one dimension, more than a single layer. Credible communicators are perceived as having expertise, trustworthiness, goodwill, dynamism, extroversion, sociability, and composure (e.g., Berlo, Lemert, & Mertz, 1969; McCroskey & Young, 1981).

By far the most important characteristics—the ones that have emerged in study after study or generated the greatest theoretical interest—are (a) expertise, (b) trustworthiness, and (c) goodwill.

Expertise and trustworthiness have emerged with greatest regularity, and goodwill has been uncovered in systematic research by James McCroskey (McCroskey & Teven, 1999). Based on the studies as a whole, one can say that a credible communicator is one who is seen as an expert, regarded as trustworthy, and displays goodwill toward audience members. Each quality is important and deserves brief discussion.

Expertise is the knowledge or ability ascribed to the communicator. It is the belief that the communicator has special skills or know-how. You see experts used all the time in commercials. Lawyers pay for experts to testify for their side in courtroom trials. There is abundant evidence that experts are perceived as credible and can influence attitudes (Petty & Wegener, 1998). However, expertise has limits. For instance, if you are trying to reach inner city drug abusers, you might think twice about calling on the Surgeon General. True, he is a recognized expert on health, but he also is seen as a member of the ruling class. It would be better to employ a former drug user who has seen the error of his or her ways and can communicate on the same wavelength as the inner city audience (Levine & Valle, 1975). The former drug user also inspires trust, which is an important attribute of credibility.

Trustworthiness, the next core credibility component, refers to the communicator's perceived honesty, character, and safety. A speaker may lack expertise, but can be seen as an individual of integrity and character. This can work wonders in persuasion. Some years ago, Ross Perot, the billionaire businessman-turned-politician, declared on a television talk show that he would be willing to run for president if citizens worked steadfastly in his behalf. His declaration stimulated a flood of support from ordinary Americans who liked his personae and plans to reduce the deficit. Within months he had an army of loyal campaign workers. Legions of reporters trailed him everywhere, and he became a major force in the '92 election campaign. Perot was no political expert; he had never held political office, although he was widely known to the public for his committed political stances. Many Americans perceived Perot as a man of integrity, someone who said what he meant and meant what he said. Finding this refreshing, they supported Perot—and he led the polls for a time, in mid-June (Abramson, Aldrich, & Rohde, 1994).

The final core communicator factor is *goodwill*, or perceived caring. Communicators who display goodwill convey that they have listeners' interests at heart, show understanding of others' ideas, and are empathic toward their audiences' problems (McCroskey & Teven, 1999). You can probably think of a doctor who knows her stuff, is honest, but seems preoccupied or uninterested in you when you complain about medical problems. The physician undoubtedly gets low marks on your credibility scale, and her advice probably has little impact on you.

On the positive side, communicators who show us they care can gain our trust and inspire us. Goodwill is an element of charisma, as embodied by leaders like Ghandi and Martin Luther King. It also is a quality that can help persuaders achieve practical goals. Salespeople who understand their clients' needs can tailor their appeals to suit their clients. This can help them achieve day-to-day success on the job (McBane, 1995).

Role of Context

Expertise, trustworthiness, and goodwill are the primary attributes of credibility. Communicators who are credible have all or at least one of these qualities. There is a complicating factor, however: context. As anyone who has worked in telemarketing, politics, or community organizing can tell you, the situation you are in can potently influence persuasion.

This means that different facets of credibility will be influential in different social situations. This conclusion emerged from early academic studies of credibility, which found that results varied, depending on the ways in which researchers probed credibility and circumstances in which the speeches were delivered (Cronkhite & Liska, 1976). Critical situational factors include audience size, communicator role, and cultural dynamics.

Audience Size. Do you remember those big lecture classes where no one knows anyone else and you have to listen to a professor talk or present material via Power Point for an hour? It's hard to impart information in these contexts, and if I were in charge of American universities, I'd get rid of them immediately! Unfortunately, mass lectures are here to stay because they allow universities to educate thousands of students efficiently and at low cost. And, in fairness, some lecture classes can be pretty interesting, even entertaining. That brings me to the point. If a prof hopes to gain credibility in a large lecture, he or she must be dynamic and extroverted. These qualities are necessary to capture students' attention.

Now consider a small seminar. A professor who is bold and talkative, hams it up, and booms out lecture material in a loud voice may be perceived as insensitive or "in-credible" in a small seminar. In this context, students want a teacher to listen, share information, and help them relate personally to the course. A more empathic, caring style of communicating may be perceived as more credible in this situation.

Communicator Role. In a similar vein, the role a communicator plays— or functions he or she performs for the individual—can determine the particular aspect of credibility that is most important. In the case of a therapist, credibility involves composure, poise, character, and goodwill. Yet if a communicator is addressing cognitive aspects of attitudes—for example, beliefs about a far-reaching issue—he or she is better advised to dramatize a different aspect of credibility. A scientist speaking to an audience about global warming should convey expertise—that is, intelligence and knowledge of the technical aspects of this subject.

Culture. National and political culture can play an important role in credibility judgments. American students evaluate political leaders on the basis of competence and character, while Japanese students sometimes employ two additional attributes: consideration and appearance (King, Minami, & Samovar, 1985). What's more, the particular type of credibility that is important can depend on the particular time and political place. In some national elections, expertise can be the key attribute that Americans value in a president. A long time ago, in 1972, Richard Nixon emphasized his political experience. Realizing that he was not a particularly likable guy but had vastly more expertise than his opponent, his consultants urged Nixon to stress his qualifications and experience. Nixon defeated George McGovern by a landslide in 1972.

What a difference four years makes! After Nixon's blatant lies to the public during the Watergate affair, the nation yearned for a more honest political leader. Along came Jimmy Carter riding on a white horse, and striking many as a "John Boy Walton" character (after the popular television show of the 1970s). Carter promised he would never lie to the American people, thereby stressing trustworthiness and integrity. Carter defeated incumbent Gerald Ford in a close election.

Fast-forward to the 1990s, and you find candidate Bill Clinton exuding compassion and sensitivity, trying to distance himself from the incumbent president, George Bush. Many Americans perceived Bush as out of touch with their problems and insufficiently concerned with the economic recession (Denton, 1994). Showing goodwill and empathy toward the plight of ordinary Americans, Clinton gained in stature and credibility. This helped him defeat Bush in the 1992 election.

Trustworthiness was in vogue again in 2000, especially among voters displeased with Clinton's sexual shenanigans and lies under oath during the Lewinsky scandal. Democratic candidate Al Gore and Republican nominee George W. Bush tripped over themselves to show that they could be trusted not to violate family values Americans held dear. Thus, the lesson for persuasion students is that the particular brand of credibility communicators emphasize depends on the time and political place.

If there is an overarching lesson in this, it is that we need to adopt a flexible approach to credibility. If credibility were a key, it would have to be adapted to fit the particular persuasion door in question. If credibility were a recipe, chefs would have to take the main ingredients and season them to suit the tastes of the folks at the restaurant. Smart persuaders know how to adapt their traits to fit the situation. They apply persuasion knowledge to the context in question, selecting the particular style of expertise, trustworthiness, and goodwill that best suits the audience and circumstances.

A Theoretical Account

As you know, social scientists like to develop theories to account for phenomena. In the case of credibility, researchers have devised a model that assumes people are canny, skeptical observers of persuaders. Eagly, Wood, and Chaiken (1978) argue that people figure persuaders have their own motives for saying what they do. What's more, audience members attribute persuaders' statements to various factors. The attribution individuals make can exert an important influence on credibility judgments and persuasion.

Eagly and her colleagues point out that individuals make predictions—or develop expectations—about what a particular communicator will say, based on what they know about him or her, and the situation. For instance, if you were told that a member of the college track team was going to talk about exercise, you probably would assume he was going to explain why running is healthy. Or, to take a political example, if informed that a candidate was speaking to a pro-environmental group, you might assume he or she was going to sing the praises of conservation.

Expectations can be confirmed—it turns out you are correct—or disconfirmed—you end up being wrong. When a speaker disconfirms your expectation, you scratch your head and want to figure out why this occurred. In such cases, you may (as we will see) conclude that the communicator is a credible source. The underpinnings for this lie in two psychological concepts: *knowledge bias* and *reporting bias*.

Knowledge Bias.   Suppose you were told that a young female professor was scheduled to give a lecture on affirmative action. If you ventured a prediction about what she was going to say, you might guess that, being young and a professor (and, therefore you assume, liberal), she would advocate affirmative action programs for women. If the speaker confirmed your prediction, you might conclude that she possessed what is called a knowledge bias. *A knowledge bias is the presumption that a communicator has a biased view of an issue.* It is an audience member's belief that the speaker's background—gender, ethnicity, religion, or age—has prevented him or her from looking objectively at the various sides of the issue. The audience member concludes that the communicator has a limited base of knowledge, produced by a need to view an issue in accord with the dominant views of her social group. "Oh, she's a modern woman; of course she'd see things that way," you might say, meaning no disrespect. Communicators who are perceived to harbor knowledge biases lack credibility and do not change attitudes (Eagly et al., 1978).

Now suppose that the speaker took the unexpected position and spoke out *against* affirmative action programs for women. The theory says that individuals might be taken aback by this and would feel a need to explain why the communicator defied expectation. Unable to attribute her position to gender or background, they would have to conclude that something else was operating. They might reasonably infer that the arguments against affirmative action were so compelling that they persuaded the young professor to go against the grain and take an unpopular stand. Or they might conclude that the communicator was a bit of an iconoclast, someone who defied the norm. Both these interpretations could enhance the speaker's credibility and increase the odds that she would change

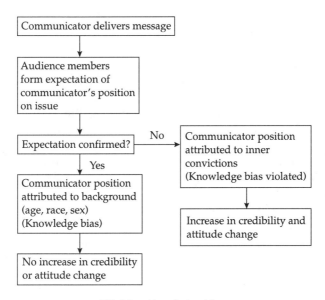

FIG. 6.1a Knowledge bias.

audience attitudes. As a general rule, when communicators are perceived to violate the knowledge bias, they gain in credibility (see Fig. 6.1a).

Knowledge bias is admittedly a different way of looking at communicators and so it takes some getting used to. But once you appreciate the idea, it becomes an appealing way to explain seemingly paradoxical situations in everyday life. Consider the following examples:

- Some years back, the American Civil Liberties Union (ACLU), a group with many Jewish members, spoke out in favor of the right of American Nazis to hold a rally in Skokie, Illinois. Skokie had many Jewish residents, some of whom had survived the Holocaust, and for these individuals the rally was an odious reminder of the horrific past. One might expect that a group with Jewish leaders would oppose the rally. By defying expectation, the ACLU probably enhanced its credibility.
- African American lawyer David P. Baugh defended Barry E. Black, a White member of the Ku Klux Klan accused of burning a cross. The case was intriguing because of "the paradox of an African-American defending a white supremacist, who, if he had his way, would oppress his lawyer because of his race" (Holmes, 1998, p. A14). Arguing that the principle of free speech overwhelmed any discomfort he had about the defendant's actions, the lawyer violated the knowledge bias and may have enhanced his credibility in the case.

- Long-time advocates of capital punishment with law and order credentials have increasingly raised questions about the ethics of the death penalty. For example, an Illinois governor who for years supported capital punishment imposed a moratorium on the death penalty, after discovering that the system was error-ridden and had come close to taking innocent lives (Johnson, 2000). When long-time death penalty proponents support a moratorium, it defies expectation and may therefore carry more weight than when liberals or pacifists take this position.
- Some of the country's wealthiest Americans, including Warren Buffet and David Rockefeller Jr., urged Congress *not* to repeal federal taxes on estates. Although they would benefit from repeal of the tax, since they own lavish estates, Buffet, Rockefeller, and other billionaires said repealing the tax "would enrich the heirs of America's millionaires and billionaires while hurting families who struggle to make ends meet" (Johnston, 2001, p. A1). This is not what you would expect these rich people to say and, for this reason, may enhance their credibility.
- Before Jerry Springer and the current hosts of "shock" TV there was Morton Downey Jr., a pioneer of "in your face" TV talk shows. Downey smoked five packs a day and died of lung cancer some years ago. While still alive and informed he had cancer, Downey changed his tune and became a passionate antismoking advocate. Violating the knowledge bias (you wouldn't expect a chain smoker to become a leading advocate of nonsmoking), Downey attracted a following, gaining credibility for his position. Downey is an example of a *convert communicator*, an individual who has converted from one lifestyle or ideology to a totally opposite set of beliefs. Such communicators can be credible spokespersons for their causes (Levine & Valle, 1975). Other examples include former drug-using rock musicians (like the legendary David Crosby of Crosby, Stills, Nash and Young) who lecture young people about the terrible effects of drugs. Converts are not always persuasive though. If audiences perceive that the convert has not freely changed his or her mind, credibility goes out the window. A Mafia hit man who testifies against the crime syndicate and lectures about the evils of crime may be "incredible" if people believe he is doing these things to get his sentence reduced. An ex-producer of pornographic Web sites who preaches about the healing power of Christ may not be credible if people believe he is doing this to pedal his latest book.

Reporting Bias. When judging communicators, audience members also examine the extent to which speakers are taking the position merely to make points with the audience. If they believe the communicator is brownnosing the group, they assume that the speech reflects a situational pressure to say the socially correct thing. They conclude that the communicator has withheld—or chosen not to report—facts that would upset the group. *This is the reporting bias, the perception that the communicator has opted not to report or disclose certain facts or points of view.* When individuals believe that speakers are guilty of a reporting bias, they downgrade their credibility. For example, consider a political candidate who told an audience that held somewhat favorable attitudes toward the environment that she favored harsh penalties for polluters. "I figured she'd tell them that to get their votes," an audience member might say. The politician would not be seen as particularly credible.

On the other hand, when audience members' expectations are violated— the communicator says something that is inconsistent with group values— the speaker is seen as credible and convincing. Individuals figure that anyone who has the courage to go against the grain must truly believe what he or she is saying. They figure that the position must be so compelling and cogent that it led the speaker to ignore social conventions and adopt the position as her own. A communicator who told a moderately pro-environmental group that the United States needed to worry less about preserving the environment and more about finding alternative sources of energy would be perceived as credible, and (at least in theory) could influence observers' attitudes (Eagly et al., 1978; see Fig. 6.1b).

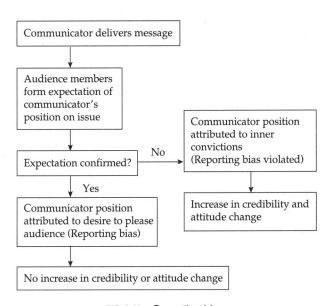

FIG. 6.1b Reporting bias.

The reporting bias helps us understand why voters greet maverick candidates like Ralph Nader, John McCain, and contemporary third-party contenders with enthusiasm. The candidates violate the reporting bias and are seen as having the guts to challenge the status quo. Unfortunately their positions do not resonate with the bulk of the public. Violating the reporting bias will *not* change attitudes if, as discussed in chapter 2, attitudes are deeply felt or strongly held.

SOCIAL ATTRACTIVENESS

Credibility is an important factor in persuasion. But it is not the only communicator characteristic that influences attitudes. Socially attractive communicators—those who are likable, similar to message recipients, and physically appealing—can also induce attitude change. Let's see how.

Likability

Do you know someone who is just so nice and appealing you can't reject what he says? This person may score high on likability. There is evidence that likable communicators can change attitudes (Rhoads & Cialdini, 2002; Sharma, 1999). There are several reasons for this. First, a likable person makes you feel good, and the positive feelings become transferred to the message. Second, a likable persuader puts you in a good mood, which helps you access positive thoughts about the product the persuader is pedaling. Third, a likable speaker may convey that she has your interest at heart, which communicates goodwill.

Sometimes we make persuasion too complicated. Just being likable can help a communicator achieve his or her goals. The likability effect operates in a variety of areas, including one that you might not think of initially: tipping waiters and waitresses.

Restaurant servers who are likable get bigger tips (e.g., Rind & Bordia, 1995). What's more, there are several techniques that waiters and waitresses can use to make themselves more likable, which, in turn, has been found to increase the amount of money customers leave on the table. If anyone reading this book is currently waiting tables, he or she may find these strategies lucrative, or at least useful! Research indicates that the following techniques increase tip size:

1. writing "Thank you" on the back of the check;
2. dawing a happy, smiling face on the back of checks before giving them to customers;
3. squatting down next to tables; and

4. touching the diner's palm or shoulder (waitresses only; sorry, guys) (suggestions culled from Crusco & Wetzel, 1984; Lynn & Mynier, 1993; and Rind & Bordia, 1995, 1996).

Similarity

Is a communicator who shares your values or perspective, or dresses like you do, more apt to change attitudes than one who does not? The answer is yes, but especially under some conditions.

Similarity between source and receiver can facilitate persuasion in business (Brock, 1965), on social issues (Berscheid, 1966), and for health problems. For example, research indicates that African American women are more likely to feel positively toward performing a breast self-exam and to getting tested for HIV when the message is delivered by an African American female (Anderson & McMillion, 1995; Kalichman & Coley, 1995).

Similarity works for some of the same reasons likability succeeds. It induces positive affect and promotes favorable cognitive responses. In addition, people compare themselves to similar others. I may infer that if someone who is similar to me endorses a position, it's a good bet that the proposal will work for me as well.

Similarity is particularly likely to succeed if the similarity is relevant to the message (Berscheid, 1966). People selling DVDs and compact discs are more likely to make a sale if they emphasize that they share the customer's taste in music than if they confess that they too like to play golf on Saturday afternoons. However, similarity may fail if it suggests to the receiver that the persuader is "just like I am" and is therefore no expert. In this case, the persuader is believed to lack expertise and the recommendation is rejected.

This raises the knotty question of when communicators should stress similarity and when they should emphasize expertise. There are no quick and easy answers. Research suggests that similarity is more effective when people must make personal and emotional decisions (Goethals & Nelson, 1973). In these cases we feel a kinship with the similar other and assume that the similar communicator is more apt to empathize with our concerns than a dissimilar speaker. By contrast, when the issue concerns factual matters, experts' intellectual knowledge may carry the day.

The question of whether a communicator should emphasize expertise or similarity comes up in many real-life persuasion situations. Politicians, advertisers, and salespeople are often faced with deciding whether to emphasize their experience or the fact that they are "just plain folks." Increasingly, it seems, companies are putting a premium on similarity, particularly similarity in appearance. Many businesses, finding that formal attire can turn off clients dressed in jeans or simple pants suits, are telling employees to dress like their clients (Puente, 1999).

Steve Constanides, an owner of a computer graphics firm, exemplifies the trend. "When you went on a sales call, you definitely got a cooler reaction if you showed up in a nice suit, because the clients would see you as just a salesman," Constanides related. "If I came in more casual attire, all of a sudden I'm like them. And it's easier to get a project," he said (Puente, p. 2D). However, if his computer graphics sales staff abandoned expertise *entirely* and talked just like the clients—saying "Hey, what's up dude?" or "Man, that's awesome"—they would probably not sell much high-tech equipment!

Physical Attractiveness

Flip through any issue of *GQ* magazine and you will come across advertisements featuring sensationally attractive male models sporting a fashionably tailored suit or sport coat. Turn on the TV and you will see beautiful female models promoting perfume or a new brand of clothing for women. Advertisers obviously believe that attractiveness sells products. So do most of us. We buy new clothes, get our hair done, and buy contact lenses to make a good impression in persuasive presentations.

Does attractiveness change attitudes? You could argue that it does because people are fascinated by beauty. Or you could say that it doesn't because people resent extremely attractive people—or assume they're dumb. To decide which of these is correct and how attractiveness plays out in persuasion, researchers conduct experiments and articulate theories.

Most studies find that attractiveness does change attitudes. In a nifty study, Chaiken (1979) recruited individuals who were high and low in physical appeal and instructed them to approach students on a university campus. Attractive and not-so-attractive communicators gave a spiel, advocating that the university stop serving meat at breakfast and lunch at the campus dining hall. Students who heard the message from the attractive speakers were more inclined to agree that meat should not be served than were students exposed to the less attractive communicators. The arguments that both sets of speakers gave were exactly the same; the only difference was that one group of communicators was nicer looking than the other. Yet this peripheral factor carried the day, inducing students to change their minds on the topic.

Why does attractiveness influence attitudes? First, people are more likely to pay attention to an attractive speaker, and this can increase the odds that they will remember message arguments. Second, attractiveness becomes associated with the message. The pleasant affect one feels when gazing at a pretty woman or handsome guy gets merged with the message, resulting in an overall favorable evaluation of the topic. Third, people like and identify with attractive communicators. At some level, perhaps unconscious, we feel we can improve our own standing in life if we do what attractive people suggest. Fourth, attractive individuals may simply be better public speakers. According to this view, it is not their attractiveness per se that persuades people, but the fact that they are more fluent and confident (Chaiken, 1979).

Contextual Factors. A communicator's physical appeal can add sweetness and value to a product. Attractive communicators seem to be more effective than their less attractive counterparts, everything else being equal. But everything else is never totally equal. Attractiveness influences attitudes more under certain conditions than others.

First, attractiveness can help form attitudes. One reason people begin buying certain perfumes or toothpastes is that they link the product with attractive models, and develop a favorable attitude toward the product. Unfortunately, the same process can work with unhealthy products like cigarettes, which is one reason why cigarette advertisements feature attractive-looking smokers.

Second, attractiveness can be effective when the communicator's goal is to capture attention. This is one reason why advertisers use drop-dead gorgeous models. They want to break through the clutter and get people to notice the product. Once that is accomplished, they rely on other strategies to convince people to purchase the good or service.

Third, attractiveness can be effective under low involvement, as when people are trying to decide which of two advertised convenience store products to buy or for whom to vote in a low-level election. In these cases, physical appeal acts as a peripheral cue.

Fourth, on the other extreme, attractiveness can be a deciding factor when the communicator's physical appeal is relevant to the product. In cases of beauty products or expensive clothing lines, a model's or salesperson's good looks can swing the sale. Physical appeal serves as an argument for the product, as the Elaboration Likelihood Model suggests.

Fifth, attractiveness can influence opinions when it violates expectations. Consider the true story of Rebekka Armstrong, former *Playboy* Playmate who contracted HIV from intercourse with a male model. After years of suffering, denial, and drug abuse, Armstrong went public with her story, trying to teach young people the dangers of unprotected sex. She has spoken to capacity university crowds and has her own Web site (Perloff, 2001). Why might she be effective?

Your image—or schema—of a *Playboy* model does not include contracting HIV. This disconfirms your expectation, and you have to think about it to put things back together mentally. As one listens to an attractive model like Armstrong talk, one discovers that she is arguing for these positions not because of a knowledge or reporting bias—but because she truly believes people must take precautions against AIDS. Thus, when attractive communicators say or do unexpected things that seem out of sync with their good looks, and these events can be attributed to inner convictions, these speakers can influence attitudes.

When doesn't attractiveness make a difference?

Physical appeal cannot change deeply felt attitudes. Listening to an attractive speaker explain why abortion is necessary is not going to change the mind of a staunch pro-life advocate. Attractiveness is rarely enough to close a deal when the issue is personally consequential or stimulates considerable thinking.

Just as attractiveness can work when it positively violates expectations, it can fail when it negatively violates expectations of what is appropriate for a particular job or role (Burgoon, 1989). You would not expect your family doctor to be sensationally attractive; if the doctor is blessed with extremely good looks, the looks could interfere with processing the message or lead you to derogate the doctor (e.g., "I wonder if he hits on female patients when they're in his office").

Finally, attractiveness effects tend to be rather short-lived. As a primarily peripheral cue, it tends not to be integrated with the person's overall attitude. The person may feel positively toward the communicator, but fail to do the cognitive work necessary to develop a strong, lasting attitude toward the issue.

Beauty, in sum, has always fascinated us. It always will. Attractiveness is commonly assumed to weave a magical spell on people. Its effects are more psychological than astrological, and are inevitably due to individuals letting themselves be bowled over by an attractive person or allowing themselves to fantasize about what will happen if they go along with the communicator's recommendations. (See Box 6–1: Physical Attractiveness and Culture.)

BOX 6–1
PHYSICAL ATTRACTIVENESS AND CULTURE

Is attractiveness relative?

Is physical beauty culturally relative, or are standards of beauty universal phenomena? It's an interesting question, with relevance for attractiveness effects in persuasion.

Some scholars argue that signs of youth–such as cleanliness, clear skin, and absence of disease—are universally perceived as attractive. They note that there is consensus across cultures that symmetrical faces are attractive (Buss & Kenrick, 1998). Perhaps—but culture leaves its imprint in a host of other ways.

In the United States, thin is in. Lean, ever-skinnier female models define the culture's standard for beauty in women. There has been a significant reduction in body measurements of *Playboy* centerfolds and beauty pageant contestants in recent years (see Harrison & Cantor, 1997). Yet thinness in women—propelled by the fashion industry, advertising, and young girls' desire to emulate sometimes dangerously thin models—is a relatively new cultural invention. In earlier eras, voluptuous body shapes were regarded as sexy. "The concept of beauty has never been static," researcher April Fallon (1990) reports (p. 84).

Going a long, long way back in time, one finds that between 1400 and 1700, "fat was considered both erotic and fashionable. . . . Women were desired for their procreative value and were often either pregnant or nursing. The beautiful woman was portrayed as a plump matron with full, nurturant breasts" (Fallon, p. 85). The art of Botticelli and Rubens reflected this ideal.

There are also subcultural variations in what is regarded as beautiful in the United States. Research that shows that African American women are less likely than White women to be preoccupied with body weight (Angier, 2000b). "It's a cultural thing," observed Roneice Weaver, a coauthor of *Slim Down Sister*, a weight loss book for Black women. She said that Black men don't judge women's physical appeal by their waist size (Angier, p. D2).

The attractiveness of other body features also varies with culture. In America breast size is linked with beauty, as indicated by the popularity of bras that pad and surgical breast implants. Yet in Brazil, large breasts are viewed as déclassé, "a libido killer," and in Japan bosoms are less enchanting than the nape of the neck, which is seen as an erotic zone (Kaufman, 2000, p. 3). In Peru, big ears are considered beautiful, and Mexican women regard low foreheads as an indication of beauty (de Botton, 2000).

Standards for male attractiveness also vary across cultures and historical periods. Macho guys like Humphrey Bogart and Marlon Brando have been replaced by softer-looking icons of attractiveness, like Leonardo DiCaprio, Ben Affleck, Tiger Woods, and music stars just breaking into the mainstream (Fitzpatrick, 2000).

To be sure, there are some universals in physical appeal. However, as Fallon notes, "culturally bound and consensually validated definitions of what is desirable and attractive play an important part in the development of body image" (p. 80). Our standards for what is beautiful are acquired and molded through culture, with the mass media playing an influential role in transmitting and shaping cultural norms. Over the course of socialization, we have acquired conceptions of a physically attractive communicator, and we apply these—consciously or unconsciously—in evaluating everyday persuaders.

CONCLUSIONS

This chapter has focused on the communicator—a key feature of persuasion. The concept of charisma comes to mind when we think about the communicator, and for good reason: Charismatic speakers have seemed to magnetize audiences, influencing attitudes in benevolent and malevolent ways. Charisma involves a host of characteristics, not well understood, and for this reason scholars have tried to break down the term into constituent parts. Preferring a scientific approach to this topic, researchers have focused painstakingly on three core communicator qualities: authority, credibility, and social attractiveness.

Authority, epitomized by the Milgram study of obedience, can influence behaviors through a process of compliance. Participants in the Milgram study obeyed a legitimate authority significantly more than experts predicted, a testament to the role of early socialization, authority's trappings, and binding psychological forces. Although Milgram's experiments raised serious questions about the ethics of deception in research, they nonetheless shed light on continuing crimes of obedience in society.

Credibility, a distant cousin of authority, is a critical communicator factor, the cornerstone of effective persuasion. Research suggests that expertise, trustworthiness, and goodwill are the three core dimensions of credibility. (Expertise and trustworthiness have emerged with greatest regularity, and goodwill has been uncovered in more recent research.) Each of these factors is important in its own right, and can interact with contextual factors, such as audience size, communicator role, and historical epoch.

Major theoretical approaches to credibility include the ELM and an expectancy–violation model. The latter assumes that communicators gain in credibility to the degree that they take unexpected positions on issues, stands that audiences cannot attribute to their background or situation.

Social attractiveness consists of three elements: likability, similarity, and physical appeal. All three factors can influence attitudes under particular conditions and have intriguing implications for everyday persuasive communication (see Box 6–2: Communicator Tips).

BOX 6–2
COMMUNICATOR TIPS

Can research and theory offer practical suggestions on how to be a more effective communicator? You bet! Here are five ideas, gleaned from persuasion concepts and experiments:

1. If you are delivering a speech and have technical knowledge about the topic, you should let your audience know this at the outset. Don't blow your horn too much or you will come off as obnoxious. Instead, discreetly note your credentials. If, on the other hand, you are new on the job and have not accumulated much technical knowledge, don't mention this before you give the talk. This may needlessly reduce your credibility in the audience's eyes (Greenberg & Miller, 1966). Instead, demonstrate your qualifications as you discuss your ideas (Whalen, 1996).

2. Show your audience you care about both the topic and your role as a persuader. Goodwill counts for a great deal in persuasion, as discussed earlier. People forgive a lot if they believe you have their interests at heart. You should be true to yourself here: Don't fake deep caring if you don't feel it. Instead, identify one or two areas that you are legitimately interested in imparting, and focus on these.

3. Try to get the audience to like you. Likability can enhance persuasion (Sharma, 1999), so you should find a feature of your personality that you are comfortable with and let this shine through during your talk. It may be your serenity, sensitivity, gregariousness, or sense of humor. Use this as a way to connect with the audience.

4. Find out as much as you can about your audience's tastes, attitudes, and familiarity with the issues under discussion. The ELM emphasizes that persuasion works best when it is attuned to the processing style of the audience. If working in an organization, "you should make a concerted effort to meet one-on-one with all the key people you plan to persuade," Conger (1998) advises (p. 89). This will provide you with the range of viewpoints on the issue and help you gear your presentation accordingly.

5. When it comes to attractiveness, keep in mind Aristotle's emphasis on moderation and balance (Golden et al., 2000). You want to look nice because it can enhance persuasion, especially in some situations. What's more, you may develop a positive view of yourself if you are well groomed and well dressed. This positive self-perception can lead you to feel better about yourself, which can increase your persuasive power. But unless you are working in the fashion industry, attractiveness is of limited value. Prior to a presentation, some people spend a lot of time worrying about their wardrobe or trying to make a smashing physical appearance. But what worked for Erin Brockovich or Julia Roberts in the movie of this name may not work for you. What's more, if you look like you're preoccupied with appearance, audience members may conclude you are not concerned with them, which can reduce your credibility. Better to spend that valuable prepresentation time honing your arguments and figuring out ways to present your ideas in a cogent, interesting fashion.

CHAPTER 7

Message Factors

The message has fascinated scholars for centuries. Aristotle emphasized that deductive syllogisms are the bases of rhetorical arguments. Twentieth-century rhetoricians, building on Aristotle's foundations, identified key components of valid, cogent arguments (Toulmin, 1958). Contemporary scholars, taking as a given that messages work in concert with audience members, have explored the influences of different message factors on audiences, trying to understand which components are most impactful and why. This chapter examines the time-honored factor of the persuasive message, a key component of persuasion and a critical consideration for communication practitioners.

UNDERSTANDING THE MESSAGE

It seems pretty obvious.

The message—what you say and how you say it—influences people. Uh-huh, an intelligent person impatient with intellectual theories might think; now can we move on? Persuasion scholars would like to move on too—they have books to write, students to teach, and families to feed. But they—and you too no doubt—recognize that the message construct is so big and unwieldy that it needs to be broken down, decomposed, and analyzed in terms of content and process. Contemporary scholars, taking note of this issue, have seized on a concept that fascinated ancient philosophers and deconstructed it. Their research offers us a wealth of insights about communication effects.

There are three types of message factors. The first concerns the structure of the message—how it is prepared and organized. The second is the content of the communication—its appeals and arguments. The third

TABLE 7.1
Key Message Factors

Message Structure
1. Message sidedness
2. Conclusion drawing
3. Order of presentation (primacy vs. recency)*

Message Content
1. Evidence
2. Fear
3. Framing

Language
1. Speed of speech
2. Powerless versus powerful language
3. Intense language

*Primacy occurs when an argument presented early in a message, or the first of two opposing messages, is most persuasive. Recency occurs when an argument presented later in a message, or the second of two opposing messages, is most compelling. There is no conclusive evidence in favor of either primacy or recency. Effects depend on situational factors, such as amount of time that elapses between messages, and audience involvement.

factor is language—how communicators use words and symbols to persuade an audience (see Table 7.1).

MESSAGE STRUCTURE

How should you package your message? What is the best way to organize your arguments? These are practical questions, ones that have attracted research interest since Hovland's pathbreaking studies of the 1950s. There are two particularly interesting issues here. The first concerns whether communicators should present both sides of the issue or just their own. The second focuses on the most persuasive way to conclude the message.

One or Two Sides?

A *one-sided message* presents one perspective on the issue. A *two-sided communication* offers arguments on behalf of both the persuader's position and the opposition. Which is more persuasive?

You might argue that it is best to ignore the other side and hammer home your perspective. After all, this lets you spend precious time detailing reasons why your side is correct. On the other hand, if you overlook opposition arguments with which everyone is familiar, you look like you have something to hide. For example, let's say you staunchly oppose people talking on cell phones when they drive and have decided, after years of frustration, to take this issue to the city council. Should you present one or both sides of this issue to council members?

A review of message sidedness research provides an answer to this question. Two communication scholars conducted **meta-analyses** of research on one- and two-sided messages. A meta-analysis is a study of other studies. A researcher locates all the investigations of a phenomenon and uses statistical procedures to determine the strength of the findings. After exhaustively reviewing the many studies in this area, researchers Mike Allen (1998) and Daniel J. O'Keefe (1999) reached the same conclusion, something that does not always happen in social science research! Researchers O'Keefe and Allen concluded that **two-sided messages influence attitudes more than one-sided messages, provided one very important condition is met: The message refutes opposition arguments**. When the communication mentions, but not does demolish, an opponent's viewpoint, a two-sided message is actually less compelling than a one-sided message.

Refutational two-sided messages, as they are called, gain their persuasive advantage by (a) enhancing the credibility of the speaker (he or she is perceived as honest enough to discuss both sides of the coin), and (b) providing cogent reasons why opposing arguments are wrong.

This has obvious implications for your speech urging a ban on driving while talking on a cell phone. You should present arguments for your side (talking on a handheld cell phone while driving is a dangerous distractor) and the other position (there are other distractors, like putting a CD in the disc player or applying makeup, that should also be banned if government is going to restrict cell phone use). You should then refute the other side, citing evidence that talking on a cell phone while driving has caused large numbers of automobile accidents; cell phone use results in more serious accidents than other distractors; and talking on a cell phone is a prolonged, not temporary, distraction from the road.

On a more philosophical level, the sidedness research leaves us with a reassuring finding about human nature. It tells us that communicators can change attitudes when they are fair, mention both sides, and offer cogent arguments in support of their position. The results celebrate values most of us would affirm: honesty and intellectual rigor.

Conclusion Drawing

Should persuaders *explicitly* draw the conclusion? Should they wrap things up for listeners in an unambiguous, forceful fashion, making it 100% clear which path they want audience members to pursue? Or should they be more circumspect and indirect, letting audience members put things together for themselves? These questions point to the question of explicit versus implicit conclusion drawing. Arguments can be made for both sides. Perhaps, since audience attention wanders, it is best to present a detailed and forceful conclusion. On the other hand, people might prefer if persuaders don't explicitly tell them what to do, but instead allow them to believe they arrived at the conclusion on their own.

A meta-analysis of research provides us with an answer to this dilemma. O'Keefe (1997) found that messages clearly or explicitly articulating an overall conclusion are more persuasive than those that omit a conclusion. As McGuire (1969) bluntly observed: "In communication, it appears, it is not sufficient to lead the horse to the water; one must also push his head underneath to get him to drink" (p. 209). Making the conclusion explicit minimizes the chances that individuals will be confused about where the communicator stands. It also helps people comprehend the message, which in turn enhances source evaluations and persuasion (Cruz, 1998).

Continuing Issues

There is little doubt that message organization influences attitudes. Certain methods are more effective than others. But message organization does not work in a vacuum. Context and modality matter. For example, in politics, communicators organize messages around negative arguments. Negative advertising spots—featuring criticisms of the other candidate, sometimes with great gusto—are commonplace, and can be remarkably effective (West, 1997). Voters expect politicians to run negative campaigns, and to some degree people want to be told the shortcomings of opposing candidates. Try the same technique in an organizational setting—lambasting your office rival in a group discussion—and see how far it gets you. The requirements and expectations of organizational persuasion are much different than those of politics.

In the same fashion, messages delivered interpersonally should be structured differently than those relayed over television and via the Internet. The Web, with its nonlinear approach to communication, presents persuaders with opportunities and challenges. They can use graphics, links, and navigational aids to help organize message arguments. Advocacy Web pages do this all the time, and persuaders are becoming increasingly adept at effectively structuring Web-based communications (Alexander & Tate, 1999).

The remainder of the chapter focuses on other message factors: the content of the message (evidence, fear appeals, and framing) and language.

EVIDENCE

- Passive smoking is a major cause of lung cancer. A husband or wife who has never smoked has an approximately 16% increased chance of contracting lung cancer if he or she lives with a smoker.
- A United Nations panel of experts on climate change has concluded that global warming is occurring at a faster rate than previously believed. The UN-sponsored panel reported that the bulk of the warming observed over the past half century is attributable to human activities.
- Herbal medicines contain tonics that strengthen the nervous system, making it more resilient to everyday stressors. Studies show that these over-the-counter herbal products offer a regular supply of the neurotransmitters needed to ward off serious physical and mental ailments.
- Ballistic tests conducted by the Prosecutor's Office prove that the bullet that killed Kenneth Lewis could not have been fired from the gun owned by the defendant.

These diverse arguments have one thing in common: They use evidence to substantiate their claims. Evidence is employed by persuaders working in a variety of settings, including advertising, health, and politics. Evidence, John C. Reinard (1991) notes, is a classic "building block of arguments," or "information used as proof" (p. 102). Evidence is a broad term, McCroskey (1969) observes. He defined it as:

"factual statements originating from a source other than the speaker, objects not created by the speaker, and opinions of persons other than the speaker that are offered in support of the speaker's claims" (McCroskey, 1969, p. 170)

Evidence consists of factual assertions, quantitative information (like statistics), eyewitness statements, narrative reports, and testimonials, or opinions advanced by others. We're all familiar with evidence and have witnessed its use many times. Communication researchers, also intrigued by evidence, have conducted numerous studies over a 50-year period, probing the effects of evidence on attitudes. Does evidence change attitudes?

You bet.

"The use of evidence produces more attitude change than the use of no evidence," Rodney A. Reynolds and J. Lynn Reynolds (2002) declare after reviewing the many studies in the area (p. 428). Reinard (1988) goes further, observing that "there actually may be more consistency in evidence research than can be found in almost any other area of persuasion. Evidence appears to produce general persuasive effects that appear surprisingly stable" (p. 46).

Evidence is especially persuasive when attributed to a highly credible source—an outgrowth of principles discussed in the previous two chapters. Evidence is also more apt to change attitudes, the more plausible and novel it is (Morley & Walker, 1987).

Persuaders must do more than simply mention evidence: Audience members must recognize that evidence has been offered in support of a proposition and perceive the evidence to be legitimate (Reynolds & Reynolds, 2002). If individuals are dozing off and don't hear the evidence, or dispute the legitimacy of the factual assertions, the evidence presented has less impact on attitudes.

Evidence, in short, must be processed. The Elaboration Likelihood Model reminds us that the ways in which evidence is elaborated determine its effect on persuasion. When people are highly involved in, or knowledgeable about, the issue, evidence will be processed centrally. Under these circumstances, quality of evidence matters. Cogent evidence can change people's minds. But remember: Even the most compelling evidence is unlikely to change strong attitudes—those that touch on the self-concept or core values.

Evidence can have striking effects under low involvement, but it works through different processes. When people lack motivation or ability to decipher the issue, they rely on peripheral cues. They may go along with arguments that sound impressive because the communicator cites many facts, uses highfalutin statistics, or throws in testimonial statements. The trappings of evidence are more important than the legal or statistical quality of the facts. Evidence operates more as a cue than an argument when people aren't motivated or knowledgeable about the issue. In such cases, communicators can use evidence truthfully, or they can lie with statistics (Huff, 1954).

Persuaders can also err by citing too much evidence. In ELM terms, they can use evidence as an *argument* rather than a *cue*, thereby failing to connect with low- or modestly involved audience members. Presidential candidates who have used too much evidence—trying to bowl over voters with numbers and mastery of facts—have tended to *lose* presidential debates (Levasseur & Dean, 1996). "Instead of appearing as a 'man with the facts,' a candidate is more likely to appear as one who creates confusion," two researchers concluded (Levasseur & Dean, 1996, p. 136).

The winning formula in political debates, and many other contexts in which audiences are modestly interested in the issue, is to use evidence in such a way that it enhances, rather than reduces, credibility. Evidence should be used to buttress arguments rather than distract audiences from the communicator or the message. John F. Kennedy succeeded in using evidence in this manner in the first 1960 debate, linking data with claims and repeating phrases to hammer in his arguments ("I'm not satisfied to have 50 percent of our steel mill capacity unused. I'm not satisfied when the United States had last year the lowest rate of economic growth of any major industrialized society in the world"). By using evidence in this way, Kennedy achieved the goal that all persuaders wish to achieve: He appeared like a "farsighted leader" with vision rather than a boring policy wonk (Levasseur & Dean, 1996).

Types of Evidence: The Case of Case Histories

Has this ever happened to you? You are trying to decide whether to add a course at the beginning of the semester. You're tempted to take the class because a variety of people you spoke with recommended it, and the class received positive ratings in course evaluation data posted on the student government Web site. The day before the drop–add deadline you ask a friend what she thinks and she says in no uncertain terms, without even flinching or hesitating, "The prof sucks. That was the worst class I've ever taken. You don't want to take that course with him." You don't add the course.

This example illustrates the power that vivid case studies or narratives exert on persuasion. Your friend's evidence was attention grabbing and emotional, the information from course evaluations pallid and abstract. Yet the course evaluation data was more representative of student opinion toward the course since it drew on a larger and more diverse cross-section of course enrollees. By contrast, your friend could be an outlier, someone whose views lay outside the distribution of student opinion, shaped perhaps by an idiosyncratic response to the professor.

Social psychologists argue that people are frequently more influenced by concrete, emotionally interesting information than by "dry, statistical data that are dear to the hearts of scientists and policy planners" (Nisbett et al., 1976, p. 132). Vivid case histories—personalized stories or narrative evidence—exert particularly strong effects on attitudes (Taylor & Thompson, 1982). What is meant by "vivid case histories" and "narrative evidence"? These are emotionally engaging stories of one particular person's experiences with a problem in life. They are gripping anecdotes of how one or a handful of individuals have coped with an issue. These cases engage the imagination, but are not necessarily representative of the larger population.

The mass media are filled with stories about how one person battled cancer, another died tragically in a car crash when she was hit by a drunk driver, or others had their lives cut short by AIDS. Persuaders—running the gamut from attorneys to advocacy groups to health practitioners— frequently call on vivid anecdotes, hoping these will tug at our heartstrings and influence beliefs (see Box 7–1).

BOX 7-1
A VIVID NARRATIVE ON DRINKING AND DRIVING

Mothers Against Drunk Driving and Students Against Drug Driving frequently rely on vivid anecdotes—narrative evidence—to convey their arguments. They undoubtedly regard these as more persuasive than gray statistics about the number of deaths caused by drunk drivers. Here is one particularly gripping example, supplied by a student. She read it during high school prom week, the narrative poem made an indelible impression, and she kept it over the years. As you read it over, ask yourself if you find this persuasive—and if so, why?

I went to a party, Mom, I remembered what you said.
You told me not to drink, Mom, so I drank a coke instead . . .
I know I did the right thing, Mom, I know you're always right.
Now the party is finally ending, Mom, as everyone drives out of sight . . .
I started to drive away, Mom, but as I pulled onto the road,
The other car didn't see me, Mom, it hit me like a load.
As I lay here on the pavement, Mom, I hear the policeman say
The other guy is drunk, Mom, and I'm the one who'll pay.
I'm lying here dying, Mom, I wish you'd get here soon.
How come this happened to me, Mom?
My life burst like a balloon . . .
The guy who hit me, Mom, is walking.
I don't think that's fair.
I'm lying here dying, Mom, while all he can do is stare . . .
Someone should have told him, Mom, not to drink and drive.
If only they would have taken the time, Mom, I would still be alive.
My breath is getting shorter, Mom. I'm becoming very scared . . .
Please don't cry for me Mom, because when I needed you, you were
    always there.
I have one last question, Mom, before I say goodbye,
I didn't ever drink, Mom, so why am I to die?

Some scholars argue this is a stunningly effective strategy. They contend that, when it comes to persuasion, narrative evidence is more compelling than statistics. According to this view, vivid case histories evoke stronger mental images than abstractly presented information, are easier to access from memory, and are therefore more likely to influence attitudes when the individual is trying to decide whether to accept message recommendations (Rook, 1987). Narratives, are—let's face it—more interesting than statistical evidence (Green & Brock, 2000). As stories, they engage the imagination and are "intuitively appealing to humans, as we are all essentially storytellers and avid story recipients' (Kopfman et al., 1998, p. 281).

An alternative view, put forth by other scholars, is that vivid evidence can be so distracting that it interferes with reception of the message. When this occurs, people fail to process message arguments or neglect to connect the evidence with the position advocated in the communication (Frey & Eagly, 1993). According to this view, statistical evidence, dull though it may be, has the upper hand in persuasion. Statistics also can evoke heuristics like "An argument backed by numbers is probably correct."

With such strong logic on the sides of both narrative and statistical evidence, it should come as no surprise that both have been found to influence attitudes (Allen et al., 2000; Kazoleas, 1993). Some scholars believe that vivid narratives are more compelling; others contend that statistics are more persuasive than narratives (Allen & Preiss, 1997b; Baesler & Burgoon, 1994). Still other researchers say that it depends on the persuader's purpose: Narratives may be more effective when communicators are trying to shake up people who strongly disagree with the message; statistics carry more weight when persuaders are trying to influence cognitions or beliefs (Slater & Rouner, 1996; Kopfman et al., 1998).

Summary

Simple and prosaic as it sounds, evidence enhances persuasion. If you use evidence in your public or electronic presentations, you are apt to influence attitudes or at least to increase your credibility. Things quickly become more complex when we try to discover why evidence works (central and peripheral processes are important), and the types of evidence that are most influential in particular contexts (the issue of narratives vs. statistics surfaces). Evidence does not stamp its imprint on receivers, but must be recognized and processed to influence attitudes. What's more, evidence does not, as commonly assumed, automatically fall into the category of a *rational* message factor. Contrary to common beliefs, which suggest that certain factors like evidence are rational and others, like fear or guilt, are emotional, evidence can be viewed as rational or emotional. It is rational when people appreciate high-quality evidence in a message and change their attitudes because they recognize that the weight of evidence favors a certain option. But evidence can also be an emotional factor when individuals go along with evidence-based messages for affective reasons (as when they tell themselves that "Any argument with that many numbers has got to be right"), or feel terribly sad after reading statistics about the spread of AIDS in Africa and decide on the spot to donate $50 to AIDS research.

By the same token, factors that seem oh-so-emotional, like fear, have cognitive as well as affective aspects. Classifying message content factors as rational or emotional is a tempting way to differentiate message factors.

It turns out that messages and people are too complex to permit this simple dichotomy. Messages change attitudes because they stimulate thought, arouse affect, and mesh with receivers' motivations and needs. In the next section, I discuss another major message factor—fear, a concept rich in intellectual and practical content.

FEAR APPEALS

Several years back, Maureen Coyne, a college senior enrolled in a persuasion class, ruminated about a question her professor asked: Think of a time when you tried to change someone's attitude about an issue. How did you go about accomplishing this task? After thinking for a few moments, Maureen recalled a series of events from her childhood, salient incidents in which she mightily tried to influence loved ones' attitudes. "My entire life," she related, "I have been trying to persuade my lovely parents to quit smoking. It started with the smell of smoke," she said, recollecting that:

> I would go to school and kids could smell it on me to the extent that they would ask me if my parents smoked. It was humiliating. Then the lessons began from the teachers. They vehemently expressed how unhealthy this habit was through videos, books, and even puppet shows. In my head, the case against smoking was building. From my perspective, smoking was hurting my parents, my younger brothers, and me. With this in mind, it is understandable that a young, energetic, opinionated child would try and do something to rid her life of this nasty habit. Well, try I did. I educated them *constantly* about the dangers of first and second-hand smoke, with help from class assignments. I would tell them about the cancers, carbon monoxide, etc., and remind them every time I saw something on TV or in the paper about smoking statistics. I begged and begged and begged (and then cried a little). I explained how much it hurt my brothers and me. I reminded them that they should practice what they preach (they told us not to smoke). (Coyne, 2000)

Although Maureen's valiant persuasive efforts ultimately failed (her parents disregarded her loving advice), she showed a knack for devising a compelling fear appeal to influence attitudes toward smoking. Maureen is hardly alone in trying to scare people into changing a dysfunctional attitude or behavior. Fear appeals are ubiquitous. Consider the following:

- Hoping to deter juvenile criminals from a life of crime, a New Jersey prison adopted a novel approach in the late 1970s. Teenagers who had been arrested for crimes like robbery were carted off to Rahway

State Prison to participate in a communication experiment. The teens were seated before a group of lifers, men who had been sentenced to life imprisonment for murder and armed robbery. The men, bruising, brawling criminals, intimidated the youngsters, swearing at them and threatening to hurt them. At the same time, they used obscene and intense language to scare the youngsters into changing their ways. The program, *Scared Straight*, was videotaped and broadcast on national television numerous times over the ensuing decades (Finckenauer, 1982).

- Public service announcements (PSAs) in magazines, on television, and on Web sites regularly arouse fear, in hopes of convincing young people to stop smoking, quit popping Ecstasy pills, or avoid binge-drinking episodes. Some PSAs have become world famous, like the Partnership for a Drug-Free America's "brain on drugs" ad ("This is your brain. This is drugs. This is your brain on drugs. Any questions?").

- Advertisers, who exploited fears long before public health specialists devised health PSAs, continue to appeal to consumers' fears in television spots. Toothpaste and deodorant ads suggest if you don't buy their products, you will be shunned by friends who smell your bad breath or body odor. Liquid bleach commercials warn that a baby's clothing can breed germs that cause diaper rash or other skin irritations. To avoid these consequences—and the larger danger of being a bad parent—you only need plunk down some money to buy Clorox or another liquid bleach.

- Parents use fear, from the get-go, to discourage children from approaching dangerous objects and people. They warn toddlers that they can choke and die if they put small parts of toys in their mouths. School-age kids are warned what can happen if they don't buckle up safety belts or wear bicycle helmets, or if they play with firearms. When they reach adolescence, youngsters are told of the dangers of risqué Web sites, promiscuous peers, and unsafe sex.

Fear appeals evoke different reactions in people. They remind some individuals of the worst moments of adolescence, when parents warned them that every pleasurable activity would end up haunting them in later life. Others, noting that life is full of dangers, approve of and appreciate these communications. Still other observers wonder why we must resort to fear; why can't we just give people the facts?

Appealing to people's fears is, to a considerable degree, a negative communication strategy. The communicator must arouse a little pain in the individual, hoping it will produce gain. The persuader may have to go further than the facts of the situation warrant, raising specters and scenarios that may be rather unlikely to occur even if the individual continues to engage in the dysfunctional behavior. In an ideal world, it would not be necessary to arouse fear. Communicators could simply present the facts, and logic would carry the day. But this is not an ideal world; people are emotional, as well as cognitive, creatures, and they do not always do what is best for them. People are tempted by all sorts of demons—objects, choices, and substances that seem appealing but actually can cause quite a bit of harm. Thus, fear appeals are a necessary persuasive strategy, useful in a variety of arenas of life.

The Psychology of Fear

Before discussing the role that fear plays in persuasion, it is instructive to define our terms. What is fear? What is a fear appeal? Social scientists define the terms in the following way:

> Fear: an internal emotional reaction composed of psychological and physiological dimensions that may be aroused when a serious and personally relevant threat is perceived (Witte, Meyer, & Martell, 2001, p. 20)
>
> Fear appeal: a persuasive communication that tries to scare people into changing their attitudes by conjuring up negative consequences that will occur if they do not comply with the message recommendations

Over the past half century, researchers have conducted numerous studies of fear-arousing messages. As a result of this research, we know a great deal about the psychology of fear and the impact of fear appeals on attitudes. The research has also done much to clarify common-sense notions—in some cases misconceptions—of fear message effects.

At first glance, it probably seems like it is very easy to scare people. According to popular belief, all persuaders need do is conjure up really terrible outcomes, get the person feeling jittery and anxious, and wait as fear drives the individual to follow the recommended action. There are two misconceptions here: first, that fear appeals invariably work, and second, that fear acts as a simple drive. Let's see how these notions oversimplify matters.

Contrary to what you may have heard, it is not easy to scare people successfully. Arousing fear does not always produce attitude change. After reviewing the research in this area, Franklin J. Boster and Paul Mongeau (1984) concluded that "manipulating fear does not appear to be an easy task. What appears to be a highly-arousing persuasive message to the experimenter may not induce much fear into the recipient of the persuasive message" (p. 375).

More generally, persuaders frequently assume that a message scares audience members. However, they may be surprised to discover that individuals either are not frightened or did not tune into the message because it was irrelevant to their needs. This has been a recurring problem with automobile safety videos—those designed to persuade people to wear seat belts or not drink when they drive. Message designers undoubtedly have the best of intentions, but their persuasive videos often are seen by audience members as hokey, far-fetched, or just plain silly (Robertson et al., 1974).

Not only can fear appeals fail because they arouse too little fear, they can also backfire if they scare individuals too much (Morris & Swann, 1996). Fear messages invariably suggest that bad things will happen if individuals continue engaging in dangerous behaviors, like smoking or drinking excessively. None of us like to admit that these outcomes will happen to us, so we deny or defensively distort the communicator's message. There is considerable evidence that people perceive that bad things are less likely to happen to them than to others (Weinstein, 1980, 1993). In a classic study, Neil D. Weinstein (1980) asked college students to estimate how much their own chances of experiencing negative life events differed from the chances of their peers. Students perceived that they were significantly less likely than others to experience a host of outcomes, including:

- dropping out of college,
- getting divorced a few years after getting married,
- being fired from a job,
- having a drinking problem,
- getting lung cancer, and
- contracting venereal disease.

The belief that one is less likely to experience negative life events than others is known as **unrealistic optimism** or **the illusion of invulnerability**. People harbor such illusions for several reasons. They do not want to admit that life's misfortunes can befall them. They also carry around in their heads a stereotype of the typical victim of negative events, and blithely maintain that they do not fit the mold. For example, in the case of cigarette smoking, they may assume that the typical smoker who gets lung cancer is a thin, nervous, jittery, middle-aged man who smokes like a chimney. Noting that they smoke but do not fit the prototype, individuals conclude they are not at risk. This overlooks the fact that few of those who get cancer from smoking actually match the stereotype (see Box 7–2).

BOX 7–2
ILLUSIONS OF INVULNERABILITY

"I never thought I needed to worry about AIDS," confessed Jana Brent. "I thought it only happened to big-city people, not people like me who are tucked away in the Midwest. But 18 months ago, I was diagnosed with the virus that causes AIDS. Now I live in fear of this deadly illness every single day of my life," Jana told a writer from *Cosmopolitan* (Ziv, 1998).

Born in Great Bend, Kansas, Jana had an unhappy childhood: broken home, deadbeat dad, life in foster homes. After moving to Kansas City and completing vocational training, Jana met Sean, a good-looking 22-year-old, who flattered her with compliments, told her he loved her, and seemed like the answer to her prayers. They soon became sexually intimate. "We had sex, on average, four times a week," Jana recalled. "We didn't talk about using condoms or getting tested, and I wasn't worried about using protection. We used condoms only when we had any lying around." Fearing Jana might get pregnant, Sean coaxed her into having anal sex, which they performed 10 times, never with a condom.

One day in July, Jana decided to get an AIDS test. The test confirmed her worst fears: She was HIV-positive and had been infected by Sean. He had tested positive years earlier, but never bothered to tell Jana. Although she knew the dangers of unprotected sex, Jana felt invulnerable. "I was one of those girls who thought, *AIDS won't happen to me*," Jana said (p. 241).

What crosses your mind when you read this story? That it's sad and tragic? That Jana took risks, ones your friends or you wouldn't take? That she's not like you, with her checkered past and desperate need for companionship?

Perhaps you didn't have such thoughts at all—but if you did, if you tried to psychologically distance yourself from Jana or told yourself her situation is *much* different from yours or silently whispered "this couldn't happen to me because . . . ," you've revealed something important. You've shown yourself a mite susceptible to what psychologists call the illusion of invulnerability.

How forcefully the illusion of invulnerability operates in the arena of HIV-AIDS! The rate of HIV infection has risen sharply among young people (DiClemente, 1992). Sexually transmitted diseases are common among adolescents (about one in every seven reports an STD), and the presence of STDs increases susceptibility to HIV. Yet college students perceive they are less susceptible to HIV infection than are other persons; they underestimate their own susceptibility to HIV, while overestimating other students' risk. What's more, although students know that condom use helps prevent HIV, they frequently engage in unprotected sex. Sexually active college students report that they used condoms less than 50% of the time when they had sex over the past year (Thompson et al., 1996).

Continued

BOX 7–2
(CONTINUED)

But wait a minute. The overwhelming number of AIDS cases in America are found among gay men and injecting drug users. "Heterosexual AIDS in North America and Europe is, and will remain, rare," Robert Root-Bernstein (1993) notes, observing that "the chances that a healthy, drug-free heterosexual will contract AIDS from another heterosexual are so small they are hardly worth worrying about" (pp. 312–313). Experts across the scientific and political spectrum agree with this analysis.

And yet, bad things do happen to innocent people: Healthy individuals like you and me get cancer or contract viruses we never heard of (the odds of this happening are one in a million, but I bet you can think of someone, one person, you know personally who suddenly got very sick or died young). Although middle-class, heterosexual American high school and college students are not primarily at risk for HIV infection, handfuls of young people from these backgrounds will fall prey to HIV in the coming years. Sexually transmitted diseases like chlamydia and herpes are spreading at alarming rates, particularly among adolescents (Stolberg, 1998). STDs produce lesions, which offer the HIV convenient access to an individual's bloodstream. Although sexually transmitted infections don't cause HIV infection, they can increase the odds that a person will contract the AIDS virus. (Adapted from Perloff, 2001.)

The illusion of invulnerability is a major barrier to fear appeals' success. If I don't believe or don't want to believe that I am susceptible to danger, then I am unlikely to accept the persuader's advice.

The second misconception of fear appeals follows from this tendency. Fear is commonly thought to be a simple *drive* that propels people to do as the persuader requests. According to this notion (popularized by early theorists), fear is an unpleasant psychological state, one that people are motivated to reduce. Supposedly, when the message provides recommendations that alleviate fear, people accept the recommendations and change their behavior (Hovland, Janis, & Kelley, 1953). To be sure, fear is an unpleasant emotional state, but contrary to early theorists, people do not behave in a simple, animal-like manner to rid themselves of painful sensations. Fear is more complicated.

A message can scare someone, but fail to change attitudes because it does not connect with the person's beliefs about the problem, or neglects to provide a solution to the difficulty that ails the individual. The drive model puts a premium on fear. It says that if you scare someone and then reassure them, you can change a dysfunctional behavior. However, we now know that persuaders must do more than arouse fear to change an individual's attitude or behavior. They must convince message recipients that they are susceptible to negative outcomes and that the recommended response will alleviate threat. Messages must work on a cognitive, as well as affective, level. They must help individuals appreciate the problem and, through the power of words and suggestions, encourage people to come to grips with the danger at hand.

A Theory of Fear Appeals

Devising an effective fear appeal is, to some extent, an art, but it's an art that requires a scientist's appreciation for the intricacies of human behavior. For this reason, theoretical approaches to fear messages are particularly important to develop, and there have been no shortage of these over the years (Dillard, 1994; Rogers, 1975). The most comprehensive is Kim Witte's **Extended Parallel Process Model** (EPPM). As the name suggests, the model *extends* previous work on fear appeals, synthesizing different research strands and sharpening predictions. It also emphasizes two *parallel processes*, or two different mechanisms by which fear appeals can influence attitudes. Like the ELM, the EPPM is a process model, one that calls attention to the ways in which people think and feel about persuasive messages. Reasoning that fear is a complex emotion, Witte (1998) invokes specific terms. She talks about fear, but recognizes that we need to consider other subtle aspects of fear-arousing messages if we are to understand their effects on attitudes.

A fear-arousing message contains two basic elements: **threat and efficacy information**, or a problem and solution. A message must first threaten the individual, convincing him or her that dangers lurk in the environment. To do this, a message must contain the following elements:

1. *Severity information:* information about the seriousness or magnitude of the threat ("Consumption of fatty food can lead to heart disease")
2. *Susceptibility information:* information about the likelihood that the threatening outcomes will occur ("People who eat a junk-food diet put themselves at risk for getting a heart attack before the age of 40")

After threatening or scaring the person, the message must provide a recommended response—a way the individual can avert the threat. It must contain efficacy information or facts about effective ways to cope with the danger at hand. Efficacy consists of two components, which result in two additional elements of a fear appeal:

3. *Response efficacy:* information about the effectiveness of the recommended action ("Maintaining a diet high in fruits and vegetables, but low in saturated fat, can reduce the incidence of heart disease")

4. *Self-efficacy information:* arguments that the individual is capable of performing the recommended action ("You can change your diet. Millions have.")

Each of these message components theoretically triggers a cognitive reaction in the person. Severity and susceptibility information should convince the individual that the threat is serious and likely to occur, provided no change is made in the problematic behavior. Response efficacy and self-efficacy information should persuade the individual that these outcomes can be avoided if the recommended actions are taken to heart.

The operative word is *should*. There is no guarantee a fear appeal will work in exactly this way. Much depends on which of the two parallel processes the message unleashes. The two cognitive processes at the core of the model are *danger control* and *fear control* (see Fig. 7.1). Danger control occurs when people perceive that they are capable of averting the threat by undertaking the recommended action. They turn their attention outward, appraise the external danger, and adopt strategies to cope with the problem. Fear control occurs when people face a serious threat, but focus inwardly on the fear, rather than the problem at hand. They concentrate on ways of containing their fear, keeping it at bay, rather than on developing strategies to ward off the danger. Witte, Meyer, and Martell (2001) invite us to consider how the processes might work:

> Think of a situation in which you were faced with a grave threat. Sometimes, you may have tried to control the danger by thinking about your risk of experiencing the threat and ways to avoid it. If you did this, you engaged in the danger control process. Now, think of times when your fear was so overwhelming that you didn't even think of the threat. Instead, you focused on ways to calm down your racing heart, your sweaty palms, and your nervousness. You may have taken some deep breaths, drunk some water, or smoked a cigarette. These all are fear control strategies. You were controlling your fear, but without any thought of the actual danger facing you. (pp. 14–15)

In essence, a fear appeal works if it nudges the person into danger control. It fails if it pushes the individual into fear control. If the message convinces people that they can cope, it can change attitudes. If people are bowled over by their fear and paralyzed by the severity of the threat, the message backfires.

Witte and her colleagues, attempting to develop a more precise formulation to help theorists and practitioners, emphasize that if perceived efficacy exceeds perceived threat, individuals engage in danger control, and adopt recommendations to avert the danger. They feel motivated to

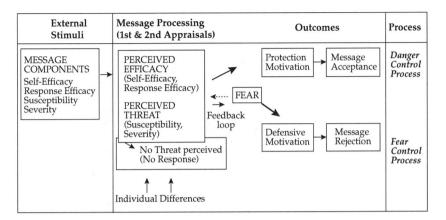

FIG. 7.1   The Extended Parallel Process Model (from Witte, 1998, p. 432).

protect themselves from danger (protection motivation in the model), and take necessary steps to deal with the problem at hand. However, if perceived threat exceeds perceived efficacy, people shift into fear control mode, obsess about the fear, defensively process the message, and do nothing to alter their behavior. For example, an antismoking campaign succeeds if it convinces the person that the risk of cancer can be averted if he quits smoking now and begins chewing Nicorette gum instead of smoking Camels. The campaign fails if it gets the individual so worried he will get cancer that he begins smoking cigarettes just to calm down!

What role does fear play in all this? Fear is probably a necessary condition for messages to succeed. People have to be scared, and messages that arouse high levels of fear can produce significant attitude change (Boster & Mongeau, 1984; Mongeau, 1998). But fear is not enough. In order to change attitudes, a message must harness fear and channel it into a constructive (danger control) direction. This entails "pushing all the right buttons," or more precisely, convincing people that the threat is severe and real, but that there is something they can do to ward off the danger (see Fig. 7.2).

Applying Theory to the Real World

Fear appeal theories like Witte's have generated many studies, mostly experiments. Researchers have randomly assigned one group of subjects to a video that contains a very threatening message. They have exposed an equivalent group to a message that raises milder threats. Experimenters have also varied other aspects of the message, such as the effectiveness of

FIG. 7.2 One way to convince smokers to quit is to scare the heck out of them. However, fear is a dicey weapon in the persuasion arsenal and works only if it is used deftly and sensitively. (Photograph by William C. Rieter.)

the recommended response or self-efficacy. A variety of studies support the thrust of Witte's model. For example, in one study smokers who were led to believe that there was a high probability that smoking causes cancer indicated an intention to quit only if they believed that the recommended practice (quitting smoking) was highly effective (Rogers & Mewborn, 1976).

Naturally, not all the research supports the model to a tee. And there remain questions about precisely what happens psychologically when perceived threat exceeds perceived efficacy. Nonetheless, the model can accommodate a variety of concepts and helps explain diverse findings on fear appeals (Witte & Allen, 2000). It offers a framework for discussing fear appeal effects, an important contribution given the large number of situations in which it is necessary to scare people into making life changes. As human beings, we take risks, underestimate our vulnerability to misfortune, do stupid things, deny we're at risk, and bury our heads in the sand when it comes time to do something to rectify the situation. We need fear appeals. Theories such as the Extended Parallel Process

Model offer general guidelines for designing health risk communications. The following are four practical suggestions that emerge from theory and research:

1. *Communicators must scare the heck out of recipients.* We are frequently tempted to go easy on others, trying not to hurt their feelings. Research suggests that fear enhances persuasion and that high-fear appeals are more effective than low-fear appeals (Boster & Mongeau, 1984). "Adding additional fear-arousing content to a persuasive message is likely to generate greater levels of persuasion," Paul A. Mongeau (1998) concluded after reviewing the research in the area (p. 64). As an example, consider binge drinking, a pervasive problem on college campuses. If you want to convince people to quit abusing alcohol, you should tell them straight out what the dangers are and how susceptible they are to harm. Don't beat around the bush.

2. *Persuaders must discuss solutions, as well as problems.* Communicators must offer hope, telling individuals that they can avert the dangers graphically laid out earlier in the message. Witte (1997) notes that "after you scare someone about terrible outcomes and make them feel vulnerable to negative consequences, you must tell them clearly and explicitly how to prevent this outcome from occurring" (p. 151). Communications must "get 'em well" after they "get 'em sick." They must teach, as well as scare.

3. *Efficacy recommendations should emphasize costs of not taking precautionary actions, as well as benefits of undertaking the activity.* Persuaders frequently must decide how to *frame*, or position, the message. They must decide whether to emphasize benefits of adopting a behavior ("A diet high in fruits and vegetables, but low in fat, can keep you healthy"), or costs of *not* performing the requested action ("A diet low in fruits and vegetables, but high in fat, can lead to cancer") (Salovey & Wegener, 2002). Messages that emphasize benefits of adopting a behavior are *gain-framed*; those that present the costs of not adopting the behavior are *loss-framed*.

Fear messages have usually been couched in terms of gain, but they also can be framed on the basis of losses. It may seem strange to emphasize what people lose from *not* performing a behavior until you consider that negative information—losses linked with inaction—can be more memorable than benefits associated with action. Beth E. Meyerowitz and Shelly Chaiken (1987) demonstrated this in a study of persuasive communication and breast self-examination, a simple behavior that can help diagnose breast cancer but is performed by remarkably few women. Some undergraduate female subjects in the study read *gain-framed* arguments ("By doing breast self-examination now, you can learn what your normal, healthy breasts feel like so that you will be better prepared to no-tice any small, abnormal changes that might occur as you get older"). Others read *loss-oriented* arguments ("By not doing breast self-examination now, you will not learn what your normal, healthy breasts feel like so that you will be ill prepared to notice any small, abnormal changes that might occur as you get older") (Meyerowitz & Chaiken, p. 506). Women who read the loss-framed arguments held more positive attitudes toward breast self-exams and were more likely than gain-oriented subjects to re-port performing this behavior at a 4-month followup.

Behavior being complex, there are also cases in which gain-framed ar-guments are more compelling. Alexander J. Rothman and his colleagues (1993) compared the effects of gain- and loss-framed pamphlets regard-ing skin cancer prevention. The gain-framed message emphasized bene-fits rather than costs, and focused on positive aspects of displaying concern about skin cancer ("Regular use of sunscreen products can pro-tect you against the sun's harmful rays"). The loss-framed message stressed risks, rather than benefits ("If you don't use sunscreen products regularly, you won't be protected against the sun's harmful rays"). Seventy-one percent of those who read the positive, gain-framed message re-quested sunscreen with an appropriate sun protection factor. Only 46% of those who read the loss-framed pamphlet asked for sunscreen with an appropriate sun protection level. Researchers now believe that gain-framed messages are more effective in promoting *prevention behaviors* (sunscreen use, physical exercise, and use of infant car restraints). How-ever, loss-framed messages are more effective in influencing *early detec-tion behaviors*, such as obtaining a mammogram, performing monthly breast self-exams, and getting tested for HIV (Salovey, Schneider, & Apanovitch, 2002).

4. *Threats and recommendations should be salient—or relevant—to the target audience.* You cannot assume that what scares you also terrifies your tar-get audience. Different fears are salient to different groups. If you want to scare middle-class high school girls into practicing safer sex, you should stress that they might get pregnant. These teens don't want to have a baby; pregnancy represents a serious threat. However, if your tar-get audience is poor ethnic women, you should rethink this appeal. To many poor ethnic women, pregnancy is not a negative, but a positive, consequence of sexual intercourse It produces a human being who de-pends on them and loves them to bits; it also, at least in the best of worlds, shows that they have a loving, trusting, relationship with a man, which provides status and emotional fulfillment (Sobo, 1995; Witte et al., 2001).

Surprisingly perhaps, the main drawback of getting pregnant, in the view of inner-city teenage girls, is that you get fat and lose your friends

(Witte et al., 2001). Thus, a campaign to promote abstinence or safer sex among inner-city teenagers should emphasize how much weight you gain when you're pregnant. It should also explain that you can lose your friends if you have to spend time taking care of a baby rather than hanging with them (Witte et al., 2001). As is discussed in chapter 12, campaign specialists must carefully consider the needs and values of the target audience before developing their communications.

Summary

Fear appeals are among the diciest weapons in the persuader's arsenal. This is because they evoke fear, a strong emotion with physiological correlates, touch on ego-involved issues, and attempt to change dysfunctional behaviors that are difficult to extinguish. To succeed, fear-arousing messages must trigger the right emotional reaction, lest they push the message recipient into fear control mode. Kathryn A. Morris and William B. Swann (1996) aptly observed that health risk communications must "walk the whisker-thin line between too little and too much—between making targets of persuasive communications care enough to attend to the message but not dismiss the message through denial processes" (p. 70). The campaign communication floor is littered with examples of fear appeals that failed because they did not maintain the proper balance between fear and danger, or threat and efficacy. Yet for all their problems, fear appeals that take context into account, put theoretical factors into play, and are of high-aesthetic quality can influence attitudes. It's tough to scare people effectively, but it can be done. Although one would rather not resort to fear, given its negative and volatile qualities, it can't be ignored in a risky world where people don't always do as they should and often put themselves and loved ones in harm's way.

LANGUAGE

Great persuaders have long known that how you say it can be as important as what you say. Persuasion scholars and speakers alike recognize that the words persuaders choose can influence attitudes. But just what impact does language have? How can we get beyond the generalities to hone in on the specific features of language that matter most? Can language backfire and cause audience members to reject a communicator's message, possibly because it is too strident or obscene? How can you use language more effectively yourself in your efforts to convince people to go along with what you recommend?

These are social scientific questions—specific inquiries that allow us to explore theories and see how they play out in everyday life. They aren't the big, gigantic questions that people frequently ask about language and persuasion—queries like "What sorts of language make someone charismatic?" and "Do cult leaders like Charles Manson brainwash people with language?" These are difficult questions to answer, in some cases impossible because the terminology (e.g., brainwashing) obfuscates and defies clear explication. However, the queries mentioned in the preceding paragraph have intrigued persuasion scholars and generated interesting insights about language and attitude change.

Speed of Speech

Ever since America mythologized the fast-talking salesman, people have assumed that fast speakers are more compelling than slow ones. The character Harold Hill in the American classic, *The Music Man*, epitomizes our stereotype of the fast-talking peddler of wares. Since then, movies, videos, and songs have rhapsodized about the supposed persuasive effects of fast-talking persuaders. (The '60s song, *Fast-Talking Guy*, comes to mind.)

Leave it to social scientists to study the phenomenon! Does speed of speech enhance persuasion? Early studies suggested it did (Miller et al., 1976; Street & Brady, 1982). However, more recent studies have cast doubt on this glib conclusion. Researchers have discovered that speech rate does not inevitably change attitudes, and under some conditions may not exert a particularly strong impact on attitudes or beliefs (Buller et al., 1992). Just as you can hypothesize that faster speech should be persuasive because it acts as a credibility cue, you can also reason that it should reduce persuasion if it interferes with message processing or annoys the audience ("Don't y'all know we don't speak as fast as you Yankees down here in ol' Alabama?").

Thus, there are both theoretical and practical reasons to argue that speech rate does not have a uniformly positive or negative effect on persuasion. Instead, the most reasonable conclusion is that effects depend on the context. Several contextual factors are important.

Speech rate enhances persuasion when the goal of the persuader is to capture attention or to be perceived as competent. Speaking quickly can suggest that the communicator is credible, knowledgeable, or possesses expertise. Moderately fast and fast speakers are seen as more intelligent, confident, and effective than their slower-speaking counterparts. These effects are particularly likely when audience members are low in involvement (Smith & Shaffer, 1995). Under low involvement, speech rate can serve as a peripheral cue. Invoking the heuristic or cultural stereotype that "fast talkers know their stuff," audience members may go along with fast speakers because they assume they are credible or correct. Fast speech may be a facade, employed to disguise a lack of knowledge, but by the time message recipients discover this, they may have already plunked down their money to purchase the product.

Speech rate can also enhance persuasion when it is relevant to the message topic. A now-famous advertisement for Federal Express depicted a harried businessman, facing an urgent deadline. The man barked out orders to two subordinates and spoke in a staccato voice at lightning-quick speed:

> *Businessman:* You did a bang up job. I'm putting you in charge of Pittsburgh.
> *Employee:* Pittsburgh's perfect.
> *Businessman:* I know it's perfect, Peter. That's why I picked Pittsburgh. Pittsburgh's perfect, Peter. Can I call you Pete?
> *Employee:* Call me Pete.

The ear-catching ad helped make FedEx a household name. Its success was due in part to the nice symmetry between the theme of the ad—speed of speech—and the product being sold, a mail delivery service that promised to be there "absolutely, positively, overnight."

Under other conditions, fast speech is not so likely to enhance credibility or persuasion. When the message concerns sensitive or intimate issues, a faster speaker may communicate insensitivity or coldness (Giles & Street, 1994; Ray, Ray, & Zahn, 1991). When a message focuses on medical problems, safer sex, or a personal dilemma, slow speech may be preferable. In these situations, slow speech may convey communicator concern, empathy, and goodwill.

This plays out on a national political level as well. When citizens are experiencing a national crisis, they may respond more positively to a slower speaker, whose slower pace conveys calm and reassurance. During the 1930s and 1940s, when America faced the Depression and World War II, they found solace in the slow speech—and melodious voice—of President Franklin Delano Roosevelt (Winfield, 1994). Had FDR spoken quickly, he might have made people nervous; his pace might have reminded them of the succession of problems that faced them on a daily basis.

Thus, one of the intriguing lessons of speech rate research is that faster speech is not inherently more effective than slow speech. Instead, persuaders must appreciate context, and the audience's motivation and ability to process the message. It would be nice if we could offer a simple prescription, like one your doctor gives the pharmacist. The reality is that speech rate effects are more complex. This also makes them a lot more interesting and challenging to explore.

Powerless Versus Powerful Speech

Has this ever happened to you? You're sitting in class when a student raises his hand and says, "I know this sounds like a stupid question, but. . . . " and proceeds to ask the professor his question. You cringe as you hear him introduce his query in this manner; you feel embarrassed for your classmate and bothered that someone is about to waste your time with a dumb question. Something interesting has just happened. The student has deliberately undercut his own credibility by suggesting to the class that a query that may be perfectly intelligent is somehow less than adequate. The words preceding the question—not the question itself—have produced these effects, another example of the subtle role language plays in communication.

The linguistic form at work here is **powerless speech**. It is a constellation of characteristics that may suggest to a message receiver that the communicator is less than powerful or is not so confident. In contrast, **powerful speech** is marked by the conspicuous absence of these features. The primary components of powerless speech are:

Hesitation forms. "Uh" and "well, you know" communicate lack of certainty or confidence.

Hedges. "Sort of," "kinda," and "I guess" are phrases that reduce the definitiveness of a persuader's assertion.

Tag questions. The communicator "tags" a declarative statement with a question, as in "That plan will cost us too much, don't you think?" A tag is "a declarative statement without the assumption that the statement will be believed by the receiver" (Bradley, 1981, p. 77).

Disclaimers. "This may sound a little out of the ordinary, but" or "I'm no expert, of course" are introductory expressions that ask the listener to show understanding or to make allowances.

Researchers have examined the effects of powerless and powerful speech on persuasion. Studies overwhelmingly show that powerless speech is perceived as less persuasive and credible than powerful speech (Burrell & Koper, 1998; Hosman, 2002). Communicators who use powerless speech are perceived to be less competent, dynamic, and attractive than those who speak in a powerful fashion (e.g., Adkins & Brashers, 1995; Erickson et al., 1978; Haleta, 1996; Holtgraves & Lasky, 1999; Hosman, 1989). There are several reasons why powerless communicators are downgraded. Their use of hedges, hesitations, and qualifiers communicates uncertainty or lack of confidence. Powerless speech may also serve as a low-credibility cue, a culturally learned heuristic that suggests the speaker is not intelligent or knowledgeable. In addition, powerless speech distracts audience members, which reduces their ability to attend to message arguments.

This research has abundant practical applications. It suggests that, when giving a talk or preparing a written address, you should speak concisely and directly. Avoid qualifiers, hedges, tag questions, and hesitations. If you are nervous or uncertain, think through the reasons why you feel that way and try to enhance your confidence. You may feel better by sharing your uncertainty with your audience, but the powerlessness you convey will reduce your persuasiveness.

Another application of powerless speech research has been to courtroom presentations. Two experts in the psychology of law argue, based on research evidence, that "the attorney should, whenever possible, come directly to the point and not hedge his points with extensive qualifications" (Linz & Penrod, 1984, pp. 44–45). Witnesses, they add, should be encouraged to answer attorneys' questions as directly and with as few hesitations and qualifiers as possible.

In some instances, attorneys or consultants may work with witnesses to help them project confidence. Take Monica Lewinsky, the woman who had "sexual relations" with President Clinton in 1995 and became the focal point of the impeachment scandal of 1998. When she first graced the nation's airwaves, she seemed naive and vulnerable, and in her conversations with people at the Clinton White House, tentative and girlish. But when Lewinsky addressed the Senate impeachment trial of Clinton in 1999, "her appearance, voice and vocabulary said she was all grown up" (Henneberger, 1999, p. 1). "Ms. Lewinsky was well-spoken, used no slang and showed only trace evidence of the Valley Girl of her taped phone conversations with Linda R. Tripp. Even her voice seemed different now, more modulated, less high-pitched and breathy," a reporter noted (Henneberger, p. 1). It is likely that Lewinsky was extensively coached for her Senate performance. Her use of powerful speech seems to have enhanced her credibility, perhaps leading some in the audience to place more trust in her story and others to feel more positively toward her version of events.

Although powerful speech is usually more persuasive than powerless language, there is one context in which powerless speech can be effective. When communicators wish to generate goodwill rather than project expertise, certain types of unassertive speech can work to their advantage. Let's say that an authority figure wants to humanize herself and appear more down-to-earth in message recipients' eyes. She may find it useful to end some statements with a question. Physicians and therapists frequently use tags to gain rapport with clients. Tag questions—such as "You've been here before, haven't you?"; "That's the last straw, isn't it?"; and "That must have made you feel angry, right?"—can show empathy with patients' concerns (Harres, 1998). As researcher Annette Harres observed, after studying physicians' use of language devices, "affective tag questions were a very effective way of showing that the doctor was genuinely concerned about the patient's physical and psychological well-being. . . . They can indicate to patients that their concerns are taken seriously" (pp. 122–123).

Language Intensity

This is the aspect of language that most people think of when they free-associate about language effects. Language intensity includes metaphors, strong and vivid language, and emotionally charged words. It is the province of political rhetoric, social activism, hate speech, and eloquent public address. You can read intense language if you click onto Web sites for pro-life and pro-choice abortion groups, supporters and opponents of cloning human embryos, animal rights activists, environmentalists, and the National Rifle Association, among others. You can hear intense language in the speeches of charismatic leaders, political activists, and presidents of the United States.

One prominent feature of language intensity is **metaphor**. A metaphor is "a linguistic phrase of the form 'A is B,' such that a comparison is suggested between the two terms leading to a transfer of attributes associated with B to A" (Sopory & Dillard, 2002, p. 407). For example, former president Ronald Reagan liked to describe America as "a torch shedding light to all the hopeless of the world." The metaphor consists of two parts: A (America) and B ("torch shedding light to all the hopeless of the world"). It suggests a comparison between A and B, such that the properties associated with a torch shedding light to the world's hopeless are transferred to America. There are many other metaphors. Civil rights activists were fond of using "eyes on the prize" to symbolize Blacks' quest for success in America. Opponents of nuclear weapons use terms like "holocaust," "nuclear winter," and "republic of insects and grass" to describe the consequences of global nuclear war (Schell, 1982). Abortion opponents liken abortion to the bloody killing of innocent human beings. More benignly, political partisans of all stripes and colors are fond of using gridlock on the roadways as a metaphor for political gridlock, or the inability of Congress to bridge differences and pass legislation.

Persuaders in all walks of life employ metaphor as a technique to alter attitudes. Do they have this effect? Researchers Pradeep Sopory and

James P. Dillard (2002) conducted a meta-analytic review of the empirical research on metaphor and persuasion. They concluded that messages containing metaphors produce somewhat greater attitude change than do communications without metaphors. They proposed several explanations for this effect:

> Metaphorical language creates greater interest in a message than does literal language, thereby increasing motivation to more systematically process the message. . . . A metaphor helps to better structure and organize the arguments of a persuasive message relative to literal language. A metaphor evokes a greater number of semantic associations, and the different arguments, when consistent with the metaphor, get connected together more coherently via the many available semantic pathways. In addition, the links to the metaphor "highlight" the arguments making them more salient. (p. 417)

Powerful as metaphors are, they are not the only component of intense language (Bowers, 1964; Hamilton & Hunter, 1998; Hosman, 2002). Intense language includes specific, graphic language. It also encompasses emotion-laden words like "freedom" and "beauty," as well as "suffering" and "death." Intense language can also reflect the extremity of the communicator's issue position. A communicator who describes efforts to clone human beings as "disgusting" is using more intense language than one who calls such research "inappropriate." The first speaker's language also points up a more extreme position on the cloning issue.

What impact does such language have on attitudes? Should persuaders deploy vivid, graphic terms? The answer depends on the persuader's goal, his or her credibility, and the audience's involvement in the issue. If the goal is to enhance your dynamism—to convince the audience you are a dynamic speaker—intense language can help you achieve this goal. But intense language will not change the minds of audience members who oppose your position and are ego-involved in the issue (Hamilton & Hunter, 1998; Hosman, 2002). They are too stuck in their ways, too committed to the position for mere word choice to change their minds. By contrast, if the audience disagrees with your position, but is less personally involved in the issue, it is likely to respond to intense language. The only hitch is that you need to be perceived as credible by those who hear or read your speech. *Intense language can goad an audience into changing its attitude toward an issue, provided it is not terribly ego-involved in the matter and the communicator possesses considerable credibility.* Under these conditions, graphic, emotional language can cause people to pay more attention to the message, which in turn can produce more favorable evaluations of the persuader's position (see also Hamilton & Hunter, 1998, for more complex discussions of these issues).

Unfortunately, this all may seem abstract or removed from everyday life. In fact these research findings have intriguing applications to real-life situations. Social activists are adept at choosing metaphors that can galvanize support for their cause. They recognize that the way they frame the issue—and the linguistic terms they select—can strongly influence attitudes. Language intensity may have particularly strong effects when people do not have well-developed attitudes on the issue, are low in involvement, and are exposed to appeals from credible spokespersons. Case in point: the appeals made by opponents and supporters of abortion.

Abortion foes chose the metaphor "pro-life" to describe their heartfelt opposition to abortion in the United States. Just about everyone loves life. By linking a fetus with life, activists succeeded in making a powerful symbolic statement. It placed those who did not believe that a fetus constituted a full, living human being on the defensive. What's more, pro-life activists deployed vivid visual metaphors to make their case. They developed brochures and movies that depicted powerful images—for example, "a fetus floating in amniotic fluid, tiny fetal feet dangled by a pair of adult hands, (and) a mutilated, bloodied, aborted fetus with a misshapen head and a missing arm" (Lavin, 2001, p. 144). These visual images became the centerpiece of a national antiabortion campaign that began in the 1960s and 1970s. As Celeste Condit (1990) recalled:

> Thousands of picture packets were distributed, and television ads as well as billboards focused on the human-like features of the physical appearance of the fetus. Most Americans had no idea what a fetus looked like at any stage of development. . . . Thus, visual display and supporting scientific argument worked together to characterize the fetus as a human being. (p. 61)

Over the ensuing decades, the language became more intense, the rhetoric fiercer. Pro-life activists spent much linguistic energy condemning a specific late-term abortion procedure, called partial-birth abortion. The procedure is unpleasant and controversial, and pro-life supporters have gained rhetorical punch by promoting the name "partial-birth abortion" rather than employing duller medical terms.

On the other side of the abortion divide, women's groups that favor abortion have also exploited the symbolic power of language and pictures. They used a coat hanger dripping blood as a metaphor for "the horrid means and consequences of the illegal abortions that occur when legal abortion is banned" (Condit, p. 92). They argued that the fetus should be characterized as a lump of tissues rather than a baby. They went to lengths to stress that they did not so much favor abortion as a woman's right to choose. One popular pro-choice pamphlet presented the Statue of Liberty, with the line "There are no pictures in this pamphlet, because you can't take a picture of liberty." Condit notes that "the statue—as a woman, a symbol of the downtrodden, and a symbol of Freedom, Liberty, and home—embodied the ideal American representation of Choice or Reproductive Freedom" (pp. 93–94).

Pro-choice activists' intense language hardly changed the minds of abortion foes. Nor did the strident imagery of pro-life Web sites alter attitudes of women committed to choice. But language intensity research suggests that the language influenced those who were less ego-involved in the issue, particularly when communications were delivered by credible spokespersons. Many citizens fall into this category—they have opinions on abortion, but are not emotionally invested in the issue or are profoundly ambivalent. The ways that pro-life and pro-choice persuaders framed the issue undoubtedly had an impact on these individuals' views on abortion, in some cases producing major shifts in public sentiments (Condit, 1990).

Although pro-choice appeals to values like freedom helped to shift the focus of the abortion debate, it did not eliminate the rhetorical power of visual images, like mangled fetuses. The coat hanger packs less rhetorical punch than a bloody fetus, and the choice metaphor loses out in the language intensity war when pit against graphic images of "aborted babies." As one abortion advocate conceded, "When someone holds up a model of a six-month-old fetus and a pair of surgical scissors, we say 'choice,' and we lose." (Klusendorf, 2001). One can acknowledge that some pro-life activists have nothing but pure motives in using this imagery, while also lamenting that it has led to a "visualization of the abortion debate" that has polarized both sides, made compromise more difficult, and in some cases sparked violent and deadly confrontation (Lavin, 2001).

Intense language has also been a persuasive weapon in the ongoing debates over cloning and embryonic stem cell research. Ever since University of Wisconsin researchers isolated stem cells from human embryos, the stem cell issue has become a scientific and political cause célèbre. Stem cells, once extracted from embryos, have the potential to grow into human tissues, which can be used to replace damaged cells that cause such diseases as Alzheimer's, diabetes, and cancer (Stolberg, 2001). Nothing comes without a price, however. Extracting stem cells results in the destruction of the embryo, a centerpiece of human life. This deeply offends religious conservatives, who have likened embryonic stem cell research to murder. Proponents of stem cell research use different language. They couch the discussion in terms of "the dawning of a medical revolution," and the ability of research to save lives. Borrowing from abortion opponents' strategic playbook, research proponents argue that "there is more than one way to be pro-life" (President Bush Waffles, 2001).

Proponents and opponents are battling for public opinion. They are trying to change people's attitudes. This is a complex issue. There are many facets, angles, scientific layers, and moral perspectives. As you read about this topic over the coming years, you should take note of the ways in which activists frame the issue. Listen to the words they use. Be cognizant of the words you select to describe the issue to others. Words matter. They can subtly influence the way we think about social issues.

CONCLUSIONS

Scholarship on the persuasive message dates back to Aristotle and the early Sophist writers. Contemporary research builds on the shoulders of giants. We ask the same questions as our forefathers and foremothers: Which types of appeals are most effective? Is logic more persuasive than emotion? How far should persuaders go in arousing the audience's emotions before the message backfires, producing effects opposite to those intended? There are no simple answers to these questions. Contemporary scholarship has offered more specific answers than earlier work, yielding more clarity. But it has not eliminated complexity or ambiguity.

We can divide the message into three components: structure, content, and language appeals. With regard to structure, we know that: (a) two-sided messages are more persuasive than one-sided messages, provided they refute the opposing side; and (b) it is typically better to draw the conclusion explicitly than implicitly. The content domain—evidence, fear, and framing—has generated numerous theoretical and practical insights. Evidence enhances persuasion, with different types of evidence effective under different psychological conditions. If you want to persuade someone, you are usually better off citing evidence; in some situations, providing narrative evidence (telling stories, offering gripping anecdotes) can be remarkably effective. (Evidence can also have an increased effect with the passage of time; see Box 7–3 for a discussion.)

BOX 7-3
THE SLEEPER EFFECT

McDonald's hamburgers have ground worms.
Girl Scout cookies have been mixed with hashish.
A subliminal message is embedded on the pack of Camel cigarettes.
AIDS is a conspiracy by the U.S. government to wipe out the African American
population.

These statements have been bandied about for years, and some people (more than you would think) assume they are true (Perloff, 2001; Reinard, 1991). But these assertions are false. How do people come to develop false beliefs? There are many explanations, but one, relevant to this chapter, is this: These messages were relayed by communicators who initially inspired little trust or respect. As time elapsed, people forgot the source of the message, but continued to remember—and believe—the message itself.

This illustrates **the sleeper effect**, the notion that the effects of a persuasive communication increase with the passage of time. As Allen and Stiff (1998) note, "the term *sleeper* derives from an expectation that the long-term effect is larger than the short-term effect in some manner (the effect is asleep but awakes to be effective later)" (p. 176).

The core thesis is that a message initially discounted by message receivers comes to be accepted over time. The message is initially accompanied by a *discounting cue* that leads individuals to question or reject the advocated position. At Time 1, individuals recognize that the message is persuasive, but are bowled over by the discounting cue, such as information that the source is not an expert (Gruder et al., 1978). They, therefore, reject the message. Over time the cue (low-credibility source) becomes disassociated from the message. Individuals forget the source of the message, but remember the message arguments, perhaps because the arguments are more extensively processed and more accessible in memory than the source cue (Hannah & Sternthal, 1984).

A vexing part of the sleeper effect is that a message delivered by a highly credible source becomes less persuasive over time, while the same message, transmitted by a low-credible source, becomes more convincing. How can this be? What may occur is that message recipients agree with the message initially *because* the source is credible. The credibility of the source sells them on the message. Over time, source and message become disassociated, and people forget the key selling proposition—the source's credibility. Because this was what sold them on the message, its disappearance from memory reduces the persuasiveness of the message. By contrast, a message delivered by a low-credible communicator can gain in acceptance over time, having never been accepted exclusively on the basis of the credibility of the source.

Continued

BOX 7-3
(CONTINUED)

Keep in mind that sleeper effects are not the norm in persuasion. Highly credible sources are invariably more effective, particularly in the short term. It is certainly better for persuaders to strive to have high rather than low credibility. Nonetheless, there are cases in which sleeper effects occur, and they have intriguing implications for politics and marketing, applications that have not been lost on unsavory marketing specialists.

False messages disseminated by low-credible communicators can come to be viewed as true over time, particularly if they are memorable. Dishonest and opportunistic political consultants exploit the sleeper effect when they try to implant misleading or negative information about their opponents into the public mind. They attempt to do this through *push-polls*, or telephone surveys in which an interviewer working for a political candidate (Candidate A) slips false and negative information about Candidate B into the poll, and asks respondents whether that would change their opinion of Candidate B. The questions are designed to *push* voters away from one candidate and *pull* them toward the candidate financing the poll (Sabato & Simpson, 1996).

In some cases, pollsters have deliberately exploited voter prejudices, hoping this would push individuals away from their preferred candidates. Interviewers have fabricated information, in one case claiming that an Alaska Democrat supported gay marriage when he had never endorsed marriage between homosexuals. In another case, an unmarried Democratic Congressman from Ohio kept receiving reports about push-polls that would ask his supporters, "Would you still vote for him if you knew he was gay?" The candidate noted that he was not gay, but acknowledged the tactic placed him in a catch-22. "What do you do?" he asked. Do you hold a press conference and say, 'I'm not gay!'?" (Sabato & Simpson, p. 265).

The candidate did not hold a press conference. He also did not get re-elected to Congress.

The sleeper effect provides one explanation for those outcomes. The push-pollsters' negative messages about opposing candidates were persuasive, encouraging cognitive elaboration (Priester et al., 1999). The pollster was a low-credible source, a discounting cue. Over time, the cue became disassociated from the message. The message was deeply processed and memorable. At a later point in time, the message awoke and influenced attitudes toward the candidates.

One of the most intriguing areas of message research has centered on fear—whether you should scare someone and if so, how you should go about it. Fear appeals are common in everyday life, from toothpaste commercials to drunk driving PSAs to warnings about sexual exploitation on the Internet. Social scientists have advanced knowledge of fear messages by devising theories of fear arousal and testing hypotheses. The Extended Parallel Process Model stipulates that fear appeals must contain threat and efficacy components, and are most likely to work if they convince the person that he or she is capable of undertaking a protective action that will avert the threat. The "magic point" at which efficacy exceeds threat is not easy to reach. Consequently, fear appeals can fail to change attitudes. However, sounding a more optimistic note, fear messages derived from theory and research have exerted substantial effects in communication campaigns (see chapter 12).

Language appeals, among the most interesting of all message factors, emphasize speech rate, powerful speech, and language intensity. Speaking quickly, powerfully, and with intensity can increase a communicator's credibility, and this in turn can enhance persuasion. But it is difficult to tick off specific rules that tell you which factor to use in a given situation. This is because context and audience expectations of a speaker exert important effects on persuasion (Burgoon, Denning, & Roberts, 2002; see Box 7–4). Intelligent speakers take the audience's expectations into account—"Do they expect me to wow them with big words? Will they be offended if I throw in a four-letter word?"—when they deliver persuasive messages.

BOX 7–4
LANGUAGE TIPS

How can you use language to spruce up your persuasive communications? Here are several suggestions, based on research and theory:

1. Avoid "uh," "um," and other noninfluences.
2. Don't use disclaimers ("I'm no expert, but. . . . "). Just make your point.
3. Vary your pitch as much as possible. Avoid the boring monotone.
4. Accommodate your speech to listeners' language style. If your audience speaks quickly (and your talk does not concern intimate issues), speak at a faster clip.
5. Accommodate to audience language style, but don't pander. One African American student related a story of a White speaker who addressed her high school class. Trying to be hip, he infused his talk with Black lingo (using phrases of the "yo, what's poppin'?" variety). The students laughed, seeing through his insincere attempt to appeal to them.
6. Be careful about using intense, obscene speech. Intense language can work, particularly when the communicator is credible and the topic

Continued

BOX 7–4
(CONTINUED)

is of low ego-involvement. Obscenities can be effective, if listeners expect the speaker to use four-letter words. Radio DJ Howard Stern's fans expect him to use obscene speech, and when he uses it, he may positively influence attitudes. Obscenity can be the norm in certain neighborhoods; thus, if speakers *don't* swear, they will be disregarded. But in most instances, obscene speech is risky; it violates audience expectations of what is appropriate and can offend key constituents.

7. Be aware of your nonverbal expressions. About 65% of the meaning in an interpersonal interaction is communicated nonverbally (Burgoon, 1994). Thus, you may know your stuff, but if you look like you're not happy to be speaking—because you're frowning or clenching your fists—you can trump the positive effects of expertise. Use facial expressions and a posture that you're comfortable with. And unless you're communicating bad news, smile.

The message is a centerpiece of persuasion, and a complex, fascinating one, to be sure. It revolves around arguments, but arguments are diverse entities. They can be logical, statistical, anecdotal, or highly emotional (as in the case of the fetus-as-baby metaphor). People do respond to emotional arguments, and there is debate about whether these are as legitimate as "purely logical" ones. There is also debate about the time-honored issue of whether you should accommodate or confront your audience. It is frequently best to accommodate your audience—using evidence that audience members find persuasive, devising appeals that mesh with cultural norms, speaking quickly if the audience speaks at a rapid clip (Giles & Street, 1994). On the other hand, if persuaders accommodate their audiences too much, they can be accused of pandering, or being so in need of audience approval that they don't raise ethically important issues. Moreover, in some cases, it is necessary to confront audience members—by scaring them or using intense language—so that they consider problematic personal or social issues.

The message remains a work in progress—a critical persuasion factor, one about which we know a lot, but one that changes as new ideas, technologies, and norms diffuse through society. Next time you hear a persuasive message, you might examine whether it contains the key features discussed in this chapter. And when you are on the other side of the persuasion ledger, you should ask yourself if you have done all you can to build the most compelling aspects of the message into your persuasive communication.

CHAPTER **8**

Personality and Persuasion

Are certain people more gullible than others? What differentiates the gullible from the canny? Should communicators take personality into account when devising messages?

These questions are the ones typically asked when we think about the role personality plays in persuasion. It is commonly believed that certain people are more susceptible to persuaders' wiles than others. When you read about schemes to defraud the elderly, Internet credit card hoaxes, and religious cults' success in attracting new recruits, you may suspect that certain people are more vulnerable to persuasion than others. This issue has intrigued researchers and is the focus of this chapter. As has been true of other topics, the myths surrounding the issue of personality and persuasion are plentiful. The first section of the chapter reviews, then debunks, simplistic notions of personality and susceptibility to persuasion. Subsequent sections focus on personality factors—stable aspects of an individual's character—that influence persuasibility, or susceptibility to persuasive communications.

THE MYTH OF THE VULNERABLE OTHER

We commonly assume there is a certain class of people who is most susceptible to persuasive communications. Researchers have tried mightily to discover just who these people are. Initially, researchers speculated that people low in **self-esteem** might be especially inclined to acquiesce to persuasive communicators. They argued, in essence, that if individuals were "down on themselves" or doubted their abilities, they should be highly likely to yield to others, particularly experts. However, this hypothesis has not received much empirical support. Individuals with low self-esteem are not invariably more suggestible than those high in self-regard

(Petty & Wegener, 1998). At first blush, this seems surprising. Wouldn't individuals with a poor self-image be particularly likely to succumb to others' suggestions? It seems like only common sense, right?

Well, what seems to be "only common sense" has a way of turning out to be far more complicated than initially assumed. After carefully considering the issue, McGuire (1968) concluded that there are good reasons to doubt that low-self-esteem individuals will inevitably follow persuaders' recommendations. McGuire noted that persuasion consists of a series of steps, including attending to a message, comprehending it, and yielding to the communicator. Individuals low in self-esteem are preoccupied with their own problems and worried about themselves. Dwelling on their own predicaments, they do not pay attention to, or *comprehend*, the message. As a result, cogent message arguments never get through; they're not processed by low-self-esteem individuals.

It works just the opposite for individuals who are high in self-esteem, McGuire argued. They tune into the message, directing attention outward (to the communication) rather than inward (toward their own thoughts and feelings). A cogent, well-reasoned series of arguments is processed and comprehended by high-self-esteem individuals. However, precisely because they are high in self-esteem, they are not so easily swayed. They understand the communicator's arguments, but refuse to yield. When low- and high-self-esteem individuals' responses are lumped together, something unusual happens. They cancel each other out. At the low end of the self-esteem scale, individuals do not process the message, so they can't be influenced; at the high end, individuals don't yield, so their attitudes can't change either. The result? Those most susceptible to persuasion are those in the middle—individuals with moderate self-esteem (Rhodes & Wood, 1992). But this is a large, heterogeneous group, so big and diverse that it is difficult to identify a specific type of person who is most vulnerable to persuasion.

Another factor that could help us classify people is **intelligence**. We don't like to say it publicly, but perhaps individuals with less innate cognitive ability are the ones most susceptible to persuasion. Some researchers make precisely this case (Rhodes & Wood, 1992). The problem is that intelligence is not a simple, one-dimensional concept. Gardner (1993) has argued that there are different types of intelligence, including verbal skills, mathematical abilities, body-kinesthetic skills, musical skills, and interpersonal skills. Someone high in verbal intelligence might be more skeptical of written arguments than others. However, this individual might be highly susceptible to interpersonal manipulation. Thus, it is difficult to make blanket statements about the effects of intelligence on persuasion.

A final factor that has been bandied about is **gender**. In bygone eras when sexism reigned and women were relegated to housework, researchers suspected that females would be more susceptible to persuasion than males. Women, 1950s-style scholars gently suspected, were the weaker sex. Others argued that it wasn't nature, but nurture. The female role emphasizes submissiveness and passivity, Middlebrook (1974) observed; thus, girls learn that they are expected to yield to persuaders' requests. However, this hypothesis is not supported by the facts. There are few strong sex differences in persuasibility (Eagly & Carli, 1981). When Eagly and Carli performed a meta-analysis of the gender and persuasion research, they discovered that only 1% of the variability in influenceability was accounted for by gender. There are more differences within the same gender than between men and women.

And yet, one intriguing piece of evidence did emerge that suggested the sex differences idea should not be totally discarded. When the investigators looked at research on group pressure situations—in which people are faced with the task of deciding whether to go along with a position advocated by members of a group—they found that women were more likely than men to yield to the advocated viewpoint. When subjects had to decide whether to yield to the group position, and believed that other group members would see or hear their responses, women were more likely than men to acquiesce. One possibility is that women are more insecure about their opinions in group settings than men. However, it is also possible that women yield not because they are bowled over by group opinion, but because "they are especially concerned with maintaining social harmony and insuring smooth interpersonal relations" (Eagly, 1978, p. 103). Yielding helps the conversation proceed and ensures that the group can continue with its business. Men perhaps are more concerned with showing independence, women with showing that they are helpful (Tannen, 1990).

Thus, although the final chapter on sex differences in persuasion has not been written—and never will be, as gender roles are in a state of flux—the once-common myth that women are more gullible than men is not supported by research. Like most things, gender effects on persuasibility are more complex than commonly assumed.

Summary

Someday perhaps, as psychological studies and genetic research advance, we will discover the prototypical gullible human being. More likely, given the complexity of human behavior, we will continue to discover that no personality trait is reliably associated with susceptibility to persuasion. Individuals may be more open to influence—by benign and (I'm afraid) manipulative persuaders—at certain times in their life, perhaps when they are young and lack experience with the issue (Fazio & Zanna, 1978).

Contemporary scholars emphasize that personality influences persuasibility, but not in the way ordinarily assumed. Individuals with a particular personality trait are not necessarily more gullible than others with a different trait. Instead, individuals with different personal characteristics are apt to be influenced by rather different persuasive appeals. To illustrate, I discuss three intriguing personality characteristics: need for cognition, self-monitoring, and dogmatism.

NEED FOR COGNITION

Do you enjoy thinking? Or do you only think as hard as you have to? Do you prefer complex to simple problems? Or do you gravitate to tasks that are important, but don't require much thought?

These questions focus on the need for cognition, a personality characteristic studied by Cohen et al. (1955) and later by Cacioppo and his associates. Need for cognition (NFC) is "a stable individual difference in people's tendency to engage in and enjoy effortful cognitive activity" (Cacioppo et al., 1996, p. 198). People high in need for cognition enjoy thinking abstractly. Those low in NFC say thinking is not their idea of fun, and they only think as hard as they have to (see Box 8–1).

BOX 8–1
NEED FOR COGNITION SCALE

1. I would prefer complex to simple problems.
2. I like to have the responsibility of handling a situation that requires a lot of thinking.
3. Thinking is not my idea of fun.
4. I would rather do something that requires little thought than something that is sure to challenge my cognitive abilities.
5. I try to anticipate and avoid situations where there is a likely chance I will have to think in depth about something.
6. I find satisfaction in deliberating hard and for long hours.
7. I only think as hard as I have to.
8. I prefer to think about small, daily projects to long-term ones.
9. I like tasks that require little thought once I've learned them.
10. The idea of relying on thought to make my way to the top appeals to me.
11. I really enjoy a task that involves coming up with new solutions to problems.
12. Learning new ways to think doesn't excite me very much.

13. I prefer my life to be filled with puzzles that I must solve.
14. The notion of thinking abstractly is appealing to me.
15. I would prefer a task that is intellectual, difficult, and important to one that is somewhat important but does not require much thought.
16. I feel relief rather than satisfaction after completing a task that required a lot of mental effort.
17. It's enough for me that something gets the job done; I don't care how or why it works.
18. I usually end up deliberating about issues even when they do not affect me personally.

Note. Individuals indicate the extent to which each statement is characteristic of them on a 5-point scale: 1 means the item is extremely uncharacteristic of oneself, 5 that it is extremely characteristic. High-NFC individuals agree with items 1, 2, 6, 10, 11, 13, 14, 15, and 18, but disagree with items 3, 4, 5, 7, 8, 9, 12, 16 and 17.

Short form of the need for cognition scale; see Cacioppo, Petty, & Kao (1984); (see also Cacioppo & Petty, 1982, for a report on the original NFC scale).

Need for cognition is not the same as intelligence. The two are related: You have to be somewhat intelligent to enjoy contemplating issues; thus, there is a modest relationship between verbal intelligence and need for cognition. However, two people could score high on verbal intelligence tests, yet one individual could find abstract thinking appealing, while the other could find it monotonous. Need for cognition is a motive, not an ability.

What does need for cognition have to do with persuasion? Plenty. Individuals high in need for cognition recall more message arguments, generate a greater number of issue-relevant thoughts, and seek more information about complex issues than those low in NFC (Cacioppo et al., 1996). Given that people high in need for cognition like to think, they should be more influenced by quality of message arguments than those low in NFC. And in fact cogent issue arguments do carry more weight with high-NFC individuals. By contrast, those low in NFC are more influenced by cues that save them from effortful thought. They are generally swayed more by such simple cues as source credibility, communicator attractiveness, and celebrity endorsements (Cacioppo et al., 1996; Haugtvedt, Petty, & Cacioppo, 1992). Of course, there are times when individuals who are low in need for cognition *will* pay close attention to the message. For example, when the issue bears on their personal lives, low-NFC folks will process arguments centrally.

These findings have interesting practical implications. They suggest that if persuaders are targeting messages to individuals they know are high in need for cognition, they should make certain they employ strong arguments or make cogent appeals to respondents' values. If, on the other hand, the message is directed at low-NFC respondents, persuaders should develop appeals that don't tax these folks' mental capacities. Simple, clear appeals—the simpler, the better—are probably advisable. For example, Bakker (1999), in a study of AIDS prevention messages geared to low-NFC individuals, found that simple, visual safer sex messages were highly effective.

One cautionary note: It is easy to breeze through this and (on a personal level) conclude that it is better to be high than low in need for cognition. That is not necessarily so. You can be high in NFC, enjoy thinking abstractly, but puzzle so long about a simple issue that you lose the forest for the trees. One could be low in need for cognition and get straight to the heart of the issue, without getting bogged down in excessive detail. The key for persuaders is to accept individuals for what and who they are. Communicators are more apt to be successful if they match messages to individuals' personality styles. Individuals who enjoy thinking are more likely to change their minds when they receive cogent messages that stimulate central processing. By contrast, people who make decisions based on intuition and gut feelings may be more swayed by messages that sketch a vision or tug at the heartstrings (Aune & Reynolds, 1994; Smith, 1993).

SELF-MONITORING

Self-monitoring, a fascinating personality variable discussed in chapter 3, has intriguing implications for persuasion. As noted earlier, high self-monitors put a premium on displaying appropriate behavior in social situations. Adept at reading situational cues and figuring out the expected behavior in a given place and time, they adjust their behavior to fit the situation. By contrast, low self-monitors are less concerned with playing a role or displaying socially appropriate behavior. They prefer to "be themselves," and consequently they look to their inner attitudes and feelings when trying to decide how to behave. Attitudes are more likely to predict behavior for low than for high self-monitors.

What implications does self-monitoring have for persuasion? You might guess that high self-monitors are more susceptible to persuasion because they want to impress people or are nervous about how they come across with others. One might also speculate that low self-monitors are resistant to persuasion because they stubbornly insist on being themselves. It turns out that both high and low self-monitors are susceptible to influence, but are swayed by different psychological appeals.

The core notion is attitude function. Chapter 3 describes the different functions that attitudes perform for people, including helping people fit into social situations (social-adjustive) and aiding them in expressing key values (value-expressive function). Theorists argue that attitudes are more apt to serve a social-adjustive function for high self-monitors, concerned as they are with doing the socially appropriate thing. In the case of low self-monitors, attitudes should serve a value-expressive function, as they help these individuals fulfill the all-important need of being themselves (DeBono, 1987).

Kenneth G. DeBono tested this hypothesis in a study of attitudes toward treating the mentally ill in state hospitals and institutions. Tests conducted prior to the experiment revealed that most students opposed institutionalizing the mentally ill. Thus, the stage was set for determining whether social-adjustive and value-expressive appeals on this issue had different effects on high and low self-monitors.

High and low self-monitors listened to a social-adjustive or value-expressive argument in favor of institutionalizing the mentally ill. The social-adjustive message emphasized that the majority of students polled favored treating the mentally ill in hospitals and institutions, thereby providing information on the "socially correct" thing to do. The value-expressive communication stressed that the values of responsibility and loving (values that most students had previously rated as important) underlined favorable attitudes toward institutionalizing the mentally ill.

High self-monitors became more favorable toward institutionalizing the mentally ill after hearing the social-adjustive message. Low self-monitors were more influenced by the value-expressive appeal. Appeals that matched the individual's personality style—or meshed with the appropriate attitude function—were more likely to influence individuals' attitudes on the topic.

Interesting as these findings are, we need to be careful not to overgeneralize from the results of one study. The topic was modestly involving at best. It did not touch on deep personal concerns; nor did it bear directly on issues in individuals' personal lives. It is likely that if we picked an issue that was deeply important to high self-monitors, they would be influenced by value-based arguments. Similarly, if the issue were one in which even low self-monitors felt concerned about being ostracized, we could sway them by appealing to social norms. Yet there are numerous issues that *are* of only modest or low interest to people, and in these situations, social-conformity appeals are apt to carry greater weight with high self-monitors, while value-expressive messages should exert a greater influence on low self-monitors.

Different sources can also have different effects on high and low self-monitors. High self-monitors, concerned as they are with social appearances, devote a great deal of cognitive energy to processing a message when it is delivered by a prestigious, attractive, and popular source. By contrast, low self-monitors, focused as they are on "bottom-line values," are highly attentive when the message comes from an expert (DeBono & Harnish, 1988).

There is much we need to learn about self-monitoring and persuasion. Self-monitoring is a fascinating concept, a complex one too (see Briggs & Cheek, 1988). Undoubtedly, self-monitoring has different effects on attitudes in different situations, an issue worthy of future research. The self-monitoring scale (see Box 8–2) has been employed in hundreds of communication experiments, and you will glimpse its relevance to the world of advertising in chapter 11.

BOX 8–2
THE SELF-MONITORING SCALE

1. I find it hard to imitate the behavior of other people.
2. My behavior is usually an expression of my true inner feelings, attitudes, and beliefs.
3. At parties and social gatherings, I do not attempt to do or say things that others will like.
4. I can only argue for ideas which I already believe.
5. I can make impromptu speeches even on topics about which I have almost no information.
6. I guess I put on a show to impress or entertain people.
7. When I am uncertain how to act in a social situation, I look to the behavior of others for cues.
8. I would probably make a good actor.
9. I rarely seek advice of my friends to choose movies, books, or music.
10. I sometimes appear to others to be experiencing deeper emotions than I actually am.
11. I laugh more when I watch a comedy with others than when alone.
12. In a group of people I am rarely the center of attention.
13. In different situations and with different people, I often act like very different persons.
14. I am not particularly good at making other people like me.
15. Even if I am not enjoying myself, I often pretend to be having a good time.
16. I'm not always the person I appear to be.
17. I would not change my opinions (or the way I do things) in order to please someone else or win their favor.
18. I have considered being an entertainer.

19. In order to get along and be liked, I tend to be what people expect me to be rather than anything else.
20. I have never been good at games like charades or improvisational acting.
21. I have trouble changing my behavior to suit different people and different situations.
22. At a party I let others keep the jokes and stories going.
23. I feel a bit awkward in company and do not show up quite so well as I should.
24. I can look anyone in the eye and tell a lie with a straight face (if for a right end).
25. I may deceive people by being friendly when I really dislike them.

Note. You answer each question True or False. High self-monitors would answer questions in this way: 1 (F); 2 (F); 3 (F); 4 (F); 5 (T); 6 (T); 7 (T); 8 (T) 9 (F); 10 (T); 11 (T); 12 (F); 13 (T); 14 (F); 15 (T); 16 (T); 17 (F); 18 (T); 19 (T); 20 (F); 21 (F); 22 (F); 23 (F); 24 (T); 25 (T). Low self-monitors would give the opposite response to each question.

From Snyder (1987)

DOGMATISM

A final personality variable that influences persuasion focuses on people's tendency to close off their minds to new ideas and accept only the opinions of conventional, established authorities. Highly dogmatic individuals fit this mold (Rokeach, 1960). Low-dogmatic individuals, by contrast, are open-minded, receptive to new ideas, and willing to consider good arguments on behalf of a position. Highly dogmatic individuals agree with statements like "Of all the different philosophies that exist in the world, there is probably only one which is correct," and "In this complicated world of ours the only way we can know what's going on is to rely on leaders or experts who can be trusted" (Rokeach, 1960). Low-dogmatic individuals naturally disagree with these items.

Individuals high in dogmatism find it difficult to come up with evidence that contradicts their beliefs (Davies, 1998). They also are willing to accept the views of an expert, even when he or she uses weak arguments to support the position (DeBono & Klein, 1993). Highly dogmatic individuals tend to be defensive and insecure; accepting the views of a recognized expert provides them with confidence and a sense of superiority.

Low-dogmatic individuals, feeling more motivated by a need to know than a desire to conform, are more willing to acknowledge shortcomings in their arguments. Strong arguments carry more weight with them than does the status of the communicator (DeBono & Klein, 1993).

It is hard to convince high-dogmatic individuals of anything. But you can make some headway if the communicator is a recognized expert. Low-dogmatic individuals are more open to persuasion, particularly from strong arguments. This points up a point made earlier in the book: There are cases in which receptivity to communication is a good thing, the mark of a healthy, flexible person.

CONCLUSIONS

Most of us assume that there is a type of person who is gullible and susceptible to manipulation. It turns out that the relationship between personality and persuasibility is more complex than this. The usual (and old-fashioned) suspects—low-self-esteem individuals, people low in intelligence, and women—turn out to be innocent of the charge that they are gullible. Adopting a more focused approach to the message and the person, researchers have found that need for cognition and self-monitoring are important personality variables. Appeals that match an individual's cognitive needs and self-monitoring tendency are more apt to be successful than those that are not in sync with the individual's cognitive motivation or self-monitoring orientation. The greater the degree that a communicator can fulfill an individual's psychological needs, the more likely it is that the message will change attitudes (see Fig. 8.1).

We don't know as much about personality traits that stiffen resistance to persuasion, although some speculate that argumentativeness has this effect (Infante & Rancer, 1996). We also lack knowledge about the particular situations in which personality traits such as self-monitoring and

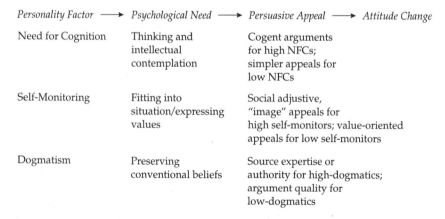

Personality Factor	⟶ Psychological Need	⟶ Persuasive Appeal	⟶ Attitude Change
Need for Cognition	Thinking and intellectual contemplation	Cogent arguments for high NFCs; simpler appeals for low NFCs	
Self-Monitoring	Fitting into situation/expressing values	Social adjustive, "image" appeals for high self-monitors; value-oriented appeals for low self-monitors	
Dogmatism	Preserving conventional beliefs	Source expertise or authority for high-dogmatics; argument quality for low-dogmatics	

FIG. 8.1 Personality, psychology, and attitude change.

need for cognition are most likely to influence persuasibility. Personality traits may have predictable influences on behavior, but they are apt to have stronger effects in certain contexts than others.

Although most research has examined the effect of personality on vulnerability to persuasion, personality can also influence techniques individuals use when they are working the other side of the street—that is, when they are trying to change audience members' minds. People who enjoy arguing and regard it as an intellectual challenge are perceived as credible communicators and experience success in social influence (see Box 8–3). Arguing gets a bad reputation, but in reality this ancient art has personal and professional benefits.

BOX 8–3
PERSONALITY AND ARGUMENTATION

"Early Sophists roamed ancient Greece fulfilling a great need in the city-states and fledgling democracies—they taught citizens how to argue effectively," Dominic A. Infante and Andrew S. Rancer (1996) observe. "Arguing," they note, "was an essential skill for success" (p. 319).

The art of argumentation, long prized in communication, has fallen on hard times. Debate classes are no longer required. Students receive preciously little training in developing cogent, logical arguments. The term "argument" has a negative connotation, calling to mind obstinate, unpleasant, even aggressive individuals. Yet skill in arguing is an important ability to cultivate. It can sharpen the mind and help people appreciate the value of sound, logical thinking. Skill in argumentation can also lead to professional success, as arguments and discussions are a critical aspect of just about any job you can think of. Argumentative skill can also help negotiators defuse interpersonal and ethnic conflicts.

Argumentativeness is defined as "a generally stable trait which predisposes individuals in communication situations to advocate positions on controversial issues and to attack verbally the positions which other people hold on these issues" (Infante & Rancer, 1982, p. 72). Infante and Rancer (1982) developed a reliable, valid 20-item scale to tap argumentativeness. If you are an argumentative person (which can be viewed as a positive trait), you would agree with items like these:

- I enjoy a good argument over a controversial issue.
- I have a pleasant, good feeling when I win a point in an argument.
- I consider an argument an exciting intellectual challenge.
- I enjoy defending my point of view on an issue.

Continued

BOX 8-3
(CONTINUED)

Research shows that contrary to stereotype, argumentativeness confers social benefits. Individuals high in argumentativeness are viewed as more credible persuaders than those low in this trait, and are more inclined to employ a greater range of influence strategies. They also encourage others to give their opinions on controversial matters and are judged as more capable communicators (Infante & Rancer, 1996; Rancer, 1998). Interestingly, argumentative individuals are less apt to use their power to goad others into accepting their positions.

Argumentative individuals are not necessarily verbally aggressive, a point scholars emphasize. "When individuals engage in argumentativeness, they attack the positions that others take or hold on controversial issues," Rancer (1998) notes. "When individuals engage in verbal aggressiveness they attack the self-concept of the other," he adds (p. 152). Verbal aggressiveness includes insults, ridicule, and the universal put-down. It can be the province of the desperate communicator, the one who runs out of arguments and resorts to personal attacks. Do you know people who are verbally aggressive? They would be likely to agree with statements like these:

When individuals are very stubborn, I use insults to soften the stubbornness.

When I am not able to refute others' positions, I try to make them feel defensive in order to weaken their positions.

If individuals I am trying to influence really deserve it, I attack their character.

When people simply will not budge on a matter of importance I lose my temper and say rather strong things to them (Infante & Wigley, 1986).

Verbal aggressiveness reduces the persuader's credibility and overall communication effectiveness (Infante & Rancer, 1996; Wigley, 1998). It produces destructive, rather than constructive, outcomes. Rather than helping or convincing people, one ends up hurting their feelings or feeling guilty oneself.

Scholars are quick to point out that both argumentativeness and verbal aggressiveness are more likely to be activated in certain situations than others, such as when the message concerns ego-involving issues. Noting the negative effects of verbal aggressiveness and the virtues of argumentativeness, researchers have developed training programs to teach individuals to argue constructively and to avoid getting enmeshed in destructive communication spirals (Rancer et al., 1997).

CHAPTER **9**

Cognitive Dissonance Theory

- Edward Yourdon was nothing if not prepared. Fully expecting computers, cash machines, and VCRs to fail on January 1, 2000, the 55-year-old computer programmer took elaborate precautions. He relied on a backup computer to log onto the Internet. He stocked tuna fish and rice in a New Mexico home he built partly due to Y2K concerns, dividing his time between Taos and an apartment in New York. When the much-ballyhooed electronic problems failed to materialize on New Year's Day, few would have been surprised if Mr. Yourdon expressed shame or embarrassment. Instead, the bulky computer programmer stuck by his predictions. "There is going to be another opportunity for bugs (on January 3)," he insisted. "It is possible that bugs will manifest themselves in coming days and weeks," he said, apparently undaunted by reports that Y2K had arrived without serious incident. (Brooke, 2000)
- When Litesa Wallace packed her bags for college at Western Illinois University some years back, she never harbored any doubt that she would pledge a sorority. The initiation rites for Delta Sigma Theta turned out to be a tad more severe than Litesa expected: doing 3,000 sit-ups, drinking hot sauce and vinegar, and swallowing her own vomit. While some might have quit at this point, Litesa endured the hardship. "She wanted to be in the sorority very badly. It's very prestigious, and she believed that it would be beneficial to her life," her attorney explained. Attorney? That's right: Ms. Wallace sued the sorority for hazing after she was hospitalized for injuries sustained during the initiation period. Yet even as she awaited the outcome of her suit, Litesa remained a Delta, apparently feeling considerable loyalty to the sorority. (Pharnor, 1999)
- The following conversation, from the 1982 movie *The Big Chill*, sheds light on a phenomenon with which we are all familiar:

  Sam: Why is it what you just said strikes me as a mass of rationalizations?
  Michael: Don't knock rationalizations. Where would we be without it? I don't know anyone who could get through the day without two or three juicy rationalizations. They're more important than sex.

Sam: Ah, come on. Nothin's more important than sex.
Michael: Oh yeah? You ever gone a week without a rationalization?
(Steele, 1988)

What do these different examples have in common? They illustrate the powerful role that a phenomenon called cognitive dissonance plays in everyday life. You may have heard the term, cognitive dissonance. No surprise: It has become part of the popular lexicon. Writers, politicians, therapists, and ordinary folks use the words to describe conflict or negative feelings about issues. But what exactly does dissonance mean? Why did one psychologist call it the greatest achievement of social psychology (see Aron & Aron, 1989)? What did all those weird, but classic, dissonance experiments actually find? And how can dissonance principles be harnessed in the service of persuasion? This chapter examines these issues.

FOUNDATIONS

Cognitive dissonance is a bona fide theory, one of the oldies but goodies. It contains definitions, hypotheses, explanations, and theoretical statements. It has generated numerous studies, as well as disagreements among scholars as to just why a particular finding has emerged. It is a psychological theory, one of a wave of 1950s-style approaches that assumed people have an overarching need for cognitive consistency or balance. Leon Festinger developed the theory in 1957, conducted some of the major experiments on dissonance effects, and then departed from the social psychology scene to pursue studies of human perception. That was dissonant—or inconsistent—with what you would expect an established, successful theorist to do. But in a way it was typical of dissonance theory—a counterintuitive "reverse psychology" sort of approach that turned ideas on their head, but in a fashion that stimulated and intrigued scholars across the world.

So what do we mean by cognitive dissonance? Dissonance means discord, incongruity, or strife. Thus, cognitive dissonance means incongruity among thoughts or mental elements. Two cognitions are in a dissonant relationship when the opposite of one cognitive element follows from the other. For example, the idea that "eating junk food is bad for your heart" is ordinarily dissonant with the cognition that "I love junk food." The cognition "I just plunked down $20,000 for a car" is dissonant with the observation that "I just found out you can't accelerate past 60 on the highway in this piece of junk." The cognitions, "My boyfriend gets abusive when he's mad" and "I love him and want to stay with him always," are also dissonant. Finally, and most gravely, the cognition "The world is a beautiful and wonderful place" is dissonant with the realization that "evil people can kill thousands of innocent people in a single day."

Dissonance, as these examples suggest, cuts across contexts. It is specifically and formally defined as **a negative, unpleasant state that occurs whenever a person holds two cognitions that are psychologically inconsistent** (Aronson, 1968, p. 6). Notice that I say *psychologically* inconsistent. Two thoughts can be psychologically—but not logically—inconsistent. The cognition "I love junk food" is not logically inconsistent with the belief that "eating junk food is bad for your heart." Knowing that a junk-food diet increases the risk of heart disease does not make it illogical to eat burgers, fries, and nuggets. However, the two cognitions arouse dissonance because psychologically it does not make sense—at least for most people—to engage in a behavior that increases the risk of disease.

Dissonance is a complex theory with many hypotheses. It has been refined many times over the years. Its core components remain the following:

1. Dissonance is psychologically uncomfortable, physiologically arousing, and drives individuals to take steps to reduce it.
2. Dissonance occurs when an individual: (a) holds two clearly incongruent thoughts, (b) freely performs a behavior that is inconsistent with an attitude, (c) makes a decision that rules out a desirable alternative, (d) expends effort to participate in what turns out to be a less-than-ideal activity, or (e) in general is unable to find sufficient psychological justification for an attitude or behavior he or she adopts.
3. The magnitude of dissonance depends on a host of factors, including the number of dissonant elements and the importance of the issue.
4. People are motivated to take steps to reduce dissonance, including changing their attitude in response to a persuasive message.
5. Different people employ different strategies to reduce dissonance. Some people are better at coping with dissonance than others.
6. People may not always succeed in alleviating dissonance, but they are motivated to try.

Dissonance theory is intriguing in an important respect. The theories discussed up to this point have emphasized that changes in attitude lead to changes in behavior. Dissonance theory suggests that the opposite can occur—changes in behavior can produce changes in attitude (Cooper & Scher, 1994). For this to happen, a critical requirement of persuasion must be satisfied: People must persuade themselves to adopt a new attitude on the topic. Dissonance theory, as one would expect from a theory of persuasion, assigns central importance to the power of self-persuasion.

DISSONANCE AND DECISION MAKING

Life is filled with decisions, and decisions (as a general rule) arouse dissonance. For example, suppose you had to decide whether to accept a job in a stunningly beautiful area of the country, or turn down the job so you could be near friends and family. Either way, you would experience dissonance. If you took the job, you would miss loved ones; if you turned down the job, you would pine for the breathtaking mountains, luscious waterfalls, and great evening sunsets. Both alternatives have their good and bad points. The rub is that making a decision cuts off the possibility that you can enjoy the advantages of the unchosen alternative. It also ensures that you must accept the negative elements of the choice you make.

When trying to make up their minds, people frequently experience difficulty, confusion, and conflict. It's only after the decision is made that they experience the particular stress known as dissonance (Aronson, 1968). At this point, they truly are faced with two incompatible cognitions: I chose Alternative A; but this means I must forego the benefits of Alternative B (or C or D, for that matter). We don't experience dissonance after each and every decision. It's the ones that are the most important and least amenable to change that seem to trigger the greatest amount of cognitive dissonance (Simon, Greenberg, & Brehm, 1995; Wicklund & Brehm, 1976). Thus, choosing between two equally desirable paper towels should ordinarily produce less dissonance than selecting between two attractive and similarly priced apartments. In addition, if you can revise your decision—take it back, so to speak—you should have less dissonance than if you have signed the deal on the dotted line and cannot revisit your choice, except with considerable psychological or financial pain. If you suddenly discover, after you signed your lease, that the apartment you're renting is located in a dwelling built with asbestos, you're apt to experience a good deal of cognitive dissonance.

Just how this would feel would depend on you and how you deal with decisional stress. But there is little doubt that it wouldn't feel good! Scholars have actually studied how dissonance "feels," and they conclude it's a complex amalgamation of physiological arousal, negative affect, and mental anguish (Cooper & Fazio, 1984; Elkin & Leippe, 1986; Elliot & Devine, 1994).

So how do people cope with this discomfort we call dissonance? Theorists argue they employ a variety of different techniques. To illustrate, consider this example: You invite a close friend to a movie that has garnered favorable reviews. The movie, obligatory popcorn, and soft drinks are expensive, so you hope the film will pan out. It doesn't; the movie turns out to be a real loser, and you find yourself sitting there, hoping it will get better. Hope springs eternal; the movie stinks.

You're in a state of cognitive dissonance. The cognition "I spent a lot of money on this movie" is dissonant with the knowledge that the movie is no good. Or, the thought that "I'm personally responsible for ruining my friend's evening" is dissonant with your positive self-concept, or your desire to look good in your friend's eyes. How can you reduce dissonance? Research suggests you will try one or several of these techniques:

1. *Change your attitude.* Convince yourself it's a great flick on balance—this may be hard if the movie is really bad.
2. *Add consonant cognitions.* Note how cool the cinematography is or decide that one of the actors delivered an especially convincing portrayal.
3. *Derogate the unchosen alternative.* Tell yourself that going to a movie beats sitting at home listening to CDs.
4. *Spread apart the alternatives.* Let's assume that before you made the choice, you felt just as positively about going to a movie as you did about spending the evening at home. In effect, the two choices were "tied" at 4 on a 5-point scale in your mind. You would spread apart the alternatives by figuratively pushing the movie up to a 4.5 and dropping staying at home to a 3. This would work until it became clear the movie was a disappointment.
5. *Alter the importance of the cognitive elements.* Trivialize the decision by telling yourself it's only a movie, just two hours of your life.
6. *Suppress thoughts.* Deny the problem and just try to get into the movie as much as you can.
7. *Communicate.* Talk up the movie with your friend, using the conversation to convince yourself it was a good decision.
8. *Alter the behavior.* Leave.

It's amazing how few people seem to avail themselves of the last option. Don't we frequently sit through a bad movie, spending our valuable cognitive energy justifying and rationalizing instead of saving ourselves the hardship by walking out? Yet this is consistent with dissonance theory. Dissonance theorists emphasize that people prefer easier to harder ways of changing cognitive elements (Simon et al., 1995). It's hard to alter behavior. Behavior is well learned and can be costly to modify. Walking out could be embarrassing, You might also be wrong; the movie might turn out to be really good at precisely the moment you left. Of course, sticking through a lemon of a movie is not necessarily rational; it's an example of what psychologists call a sunk cost (Garland, 1990). You are not going to get the money back, no matter how much you convince yourself that it was a great film. However, as dissonance theorists are fond of reminding us, human beings are not *rational* animals, but rational*izing* animals, seeking "to appear rational, both to others and (themselves)" (Aronson, 1968, p. 6).

How apt a description of human decision making! Immediately after people make up their minds to embark on one course rather than another, they bear an uncanny resemblance to the proverbial ostrich, sticking their heads in the sand to avoid perspectives that might conflict with the option they chose, doing all they can to reaffirm the wisdom of their decision. If you chose the Saturn instead of the Honda (chapter 5), and suddenly learned that the Saturn's engine is not as well constructed as the Honda's, your first impulse might be to deny this, then perhaps to counterargue it, or to focus on areas in which the Saturn is clearly superior to the Honda. Or, to take another example, let's say a friend of yours smokes a pack a day. If you asked her why she smokes, you would hear a long list of rationalizations speaking to the power of dissonance reduction. Her reasons might include: "I know I should quit, but I've got too much stress right now to go through quitting again"; "I guess I'd rather smoke than pig out and end up looking like a blimp"; and "Hey, we're all going to die anyway. I'd rather do what I enjoy." All these reasons make great sense to your friend; they help restore consonance, but they prevent her from taking the steps needed to preserve her health. Such is the power of cognitive dissonance.

DISSONANCE AND EXPENDITURE OF EFFORT

Have you ever wondered why fraternity pledges come to like a fraternity more after they have undergone a severe initiation procedure? Ever been curious why law students who have survived the torturous experience of being asked to cite legal precedent before a class of hundreds come to think positively of their law school professors? Or why medical interns who work 30-hour shifts, with barely any sleep, vigorously defend the system, sometimes viewing it as a grand way to learn the practice of medicine (Kleinfield, 1999). An explanation of these phenomena can be found in the application of dissonance theory to the expenditure of effort.

The core notion here is quite simple. Aronson and Mills (1959) explained that:

> No matter how attractive a group is to a person it is rarely completely positive; i.e., usually there are some aspects of the group that the individual does not like. If he has undergone an unpleasant initiation to gain admission to the group, his cognition that he has gone through an unpleasant experience for the sake of membership is dissonant with the cognition that there are things about the group that he does not like. (p. 177)

One way to reduce dissonance is to convince oneself that the group has many positive characteristics that justify the expenditure of effort.

Elliot Aronson and Judson Mills tested this hypothesis long ago—in 1959. Yet their findings have been replicated by other experimenters, and continue to shed light on events occurring today. Like many researchers of their era, they preferred to set up a contrived procedure to study dissonance and effort. Believing that they needed to provide a pure test of the hypothesis, they devised an experiment in which female college students were told they would be participating in several group discussions on the psychology of sex. Informed that the group had been meeting for several weeks and they would be replacing a woman who dropped out due to scheduling conflicts, women in the experimental condition were told they would be screened before gaining formal admission to the group. (The experimenters deliberately chose women, perhaps because they felt that the sexual words they would ask women to read would have a stronger effect on these 1950s coeds than on male students. Researchers conducting the study in today's savvy college environment would no doubt employ a different procedure.)

Students assigned to the severe initiation condition read aloud 12 obscene words and 2 graphic descriptions of sexual activity from contemporary novels. Women in the mild initiation condition read 5 sex-related words that were not obscene. Subjects in both conditions were then informed they had performed satisfactorily and had been admitted into the group. All the women subsequently listened to a tape-recorded discussion of a group meeting. The discussion was made to seem dull and banal, with group members speaking dryly and contradicting each other. The discussion was set up this way to arouse dissonance. Female participants in the study had to confront the fact that they had undergone a humiliating experience, reading sexual words in front of some guy they had never met, for the sake of membership in a group that seemed boring and dull.

You might think that women in the severe initiation condition would dislike the group. Indeed, simple learning models would suggest that the unpleasant experience these women underwent would increase antipathy to the group. However, dissonance theory made the opposite prediction. It predicted that women in the severe initiation treatment would evaluate the group most positively. They had the most dissonance, and one way to reduce it would be to rationalize the unpleasant initiation by convincing themselves that the group discussion was not as bad as it seemed and was, in some sense, worth the pain they endured. This is what happened: Women in the severe initiation condition gave the group discussion higher ratings than other subjects.

Although Aronson and Mills' study was intriguing, it did not convince all researchers. Some suggested that perhaps the severe initiation procedure did not embarrass the women at all, but aroused them sexually! If this were true, women in the severe initiation condition would have liked the group more because they associated the pleasant arousal with the group experience (Chapanis & Chapanis, 1964). To rule out this and other alternative explanations, researchers conducted a different test of the effort justification hypothesis, one that involved not a sexual embarrassment test but, rather, different initiation procedures. Using these operationalizations, experimenters found additional support for the Aronson and Mills findings (Cooper & Axsom, 1982; Gerard & Mathewson, 1966).

Applications

We must be careful not to glibly apply these findings to the real world. People do not always rationalize effort by changing their attitude toward the group; they may reduce dissonance in other ways—for example, by trivializing the initiation rite. In some cases, the effort expended is so enormous and the initiation ceremony so humiliating that people cannot convince themselves that the group is worth it. This helps explain why Litesa Wallace, the young woman mentioned at the beginning of the chapter, sued her sorority (while still remaining a Delta). (In response to such egregious cases, antihazing Web sites have cropped up; see www.stop.hazing.org.)

And yet, the effort justification notion sheds light on numerous real-life situations. It helps explain why fraternities and sororities *still* demand that pledges undergo stressful initiation ceremonies. Seniors who underwent the initiation procedure as freshmen rationalize the effort expended, develop a favorable attitude to the group, and derive gratification from passing on this tradition to new recruits (Marklein, 2000; see Fig. 9.1).

Effort justification also can be harnessed for positive purposes. Jewish children spend countless Saturdays and Sundays learning Hebrew and

FIG. 9.1 Why do fraternities like this one frequently require their pledges to undergo challenging—even stressful—initiation ceremonies? Dissonance theory offers a compelling explanation. (Photograph by William C. Rieter.)

reciting the Torah in preparation for their Bar and Bas Mitzvahs. The time spent is dissonant with the knowledge they could be having more fun doing other things, but in the end the need to reduce dissonance pushes them to evaluate the experience positively. This enables the ritual—and religion—to get passed on to future generations.

INDUCED COMPLIANCE

What happens if a person is coaxed to publicly argue for a position he or she does not privately accept? Further, what if the individual is paid a paltry sum to take this position? Suppose you gave a speech that advocated banning cell phone use in cars, although you privately disagreed with this position? Let's say someone paid you a dollar to take this stand. Dissonance theory makes the unusual prediction that under these circumstances, you would actually come to evaluate the proposal favorably.

This prediction is part of a phenomenon known as *induced compliance*. The name comes from the fact that a person has been induced—gently persuaded—to comply with a persuader's request. The person freely chooses to perform an action that is inconsistent with his or her beliefs or attitude. Such actions are called counterattitudinal. When individuals perform a counterattitudinal behavior and cannot rationalize the act—as they could if they had received a large reward—they are in a state of dissonance. One way to reduce dissonance is to change one's attitude so that it is consistent with the behavior—that is, convince oneself that one really agrees with the discrepant message.

This hypothesis was elegantly tested and supported by Leon Festinger and J. Merrill Carlsmith in 1959. Students were asked to perform two tasks that were phenomenally boring: (1) placing spools on a tray, emptying the tray, and refilling it with spools; and (2) turning each of 48 pegs on a peg board a quarter turn clockwise, then another quarter turn, and so on for half an hour. In what could have been an episode from the TV show, *Spy TV*, the experimenter then asked students to do him a favor: to tell the next participant in the study that this monotonous experiment had been enjoyable, exciting, and a lot of fun. You see, the experimenter suggested, the person who usually does this couldn't do it today, and we're looking for someone we could hire to do it for us. The whole thing was a ruse: There was no other person who usually performed the task. The intent was to induce students to say that a boring task was enjoyable—a dissonant act. There was also a twist.

Some students were paid $20 for telling the lie, others were paid $1, and those in a control condition didn't tell a lie at all. Participants then rated the enjoyableness of the tasks. As it turned out, those paid $1 said

TABLE 9.1
Results of Festinger and Carlsmith Study

	Experimental Condition		
Question	$1	$20	Control
1. How enjoyable were tasks? (rated from −5 to +5)	1.35	−.05	−.45
2. Scientific importance of tasks (rated from 0 to 10)	6.45	5.18	5.60
3. Willingness to partake in similar experiments (rated from −5 to +5)	1.20	−.25	−.62

From Festinger and Carlsmith (1959)

they liked the tasks more and displayed greater willingness to participate in similar experiments in the future than did other students (see Table 9.1).

How can we explain the findings? According to theory, the cognition that "the spool-removing and peg-turning tasks were really boring" was dissonant with the cognition that "I just told someone it was lots of fun." The $20 provided students with external justification for telling the lie. It helped them justify why they said one thing (the tasks were exciting), yet believed another (they were really boring). They received $20; that helped them feel good about the whole thing, and they had no need to change their attitude to restore consonance. Like a stiff drink that helps people forget their sorrows, the $20 helped erase the dissonance, or sufficiently so that students didn't feel any need to change their attitude toward the tasks.

For students paid $1, it was a different matter. Lacking a sufficient external justification for the inconsistency, they had to turn inward to get one. They needed to bring their private attitude in line with their public behavior. One way to do this was to change their attitude toward the tasks. By convincing themselves that "the thing with the spools wasn't so bad, it gave me a chance to do something, perfect my hand-eye coordination, yeah, that's the ticket," they could comfortably believe that the statement they made to fellow students ("I had a lot of fun") actually reflected their inner feelings. Dissonance was thus resolved; they had restored cognitive harmony.

Note that these findings are exactly the opposite of what you might expect based on common sense and classic learning theory. Both would suggest that people paid more money would like something more. Reward leads to liking, right? Not according to dissonance theory. Indeed, the negative relationship between reward and liking, consistent with cognitive dissonance theory, has held up in other studies conceptually replicating the Festinger and Carlsmith experiment (Harmon-Jones, 2002; Preiss & Allen, 1998).

The early research had exciting theoretical implications. As researcher Elliot Aronson observed:

> As a community we have yet to recover from the impact of this research—fortunately! . . . Because the finding departed from the general orientation accepted either tacitly or explicitly by most social psychologists in the 1950s: (that) high reward—never *low* reward—is accompanied by greater learning, greater conformity, greater performance, greater satisfaction, greater persuasion. . . . (But in Festinger and Carlsmith,) either reward theory made no prediction at all or the opposite prediction. These results represented a striking and convincing act of liberation from the dominance of a general reward-reinforcement theory. (Aron & Aron, 1989, p. 116)

More generally, the results of this strange—but elegantly conducted—experiment suggested that people could not be counted on to slavishly do as experts predicted. They were not mere automatons whose thoughts could be controlled by behavioral engineering or psychologists' rewards. Like Dostoyevsky's underground man, who celebrated his emotion and spontaneity, dissonance researchers rejoiced in the study's findings, for they spoke to the subjectivity and inner-directedness of human beings.

Applications

The great contribution of induced compliance research is theoretical, in suggesting new ways to think about human attitudes and persuasion. However, the research does have practical applications. The negative incentive effect—paying people less changes their attitudes more—can be applied to the problem of motivating individuals to engage in positive, healthy acts they would rather not perform. For example, consider the case of a parent who wants to convince a couch-potato child to exercise more. Should the parent pay the kid each time she or he jogs, plays tennis, or swims laps? Dissonance theory says no. It stipulates that children frequently face dissonance after engaging in vigorous physical exercise—for example, "*I just ran a mile, but, geez, did that hurt*"; *I just ran five laps, but I could have been watching a DVD.*" By paying sons or daughters money for exercising, parents remove children's motivation to change their attitudes. The money provides strong external justification, erasing the dissonance: The child no longer feels a need to change an antiexercise attitude so that it is compatible with behavior (jogging a mile a day). Instead, the money bridges thought and action, and becomes the main thing the child gets out of the event. Thus, the same old negative attitude toward exercise persists.

By contrast, if parents don't pay their children a hefty sum (or give them only a paltry reward), children must reduce the dissonance on their own.

To be sure, kids may not restore consonance by developing a positive attitude toward exercise (they could blame their parents for "forcing" them to jog, or just complain about how sore their bodies feel). But it is entirely possible—and I've seen examples of this with parents in my neighborhood, to say nothing of research that backs it up (Deci, 1975)— children will change their attitude to fit their behavior. They develop a positive attitude toward exercise to justify their behavior. And once this happens, their attitude "grows legs" (Cialdini, 2001). Exercise becomes a positive, not a negative, force in their lives; it becomes associated with pleasant activities; and the attitude motivates, then triggers behavior. The child begins to exercise spontaneously, on his or her own, without parental prodding.

EXPLANATIONS AND CONTROVERSIES

When a theory is developed, researchers test it to determine if it holds water. If hypotheses generated from the theory are empirically supported, researchers are elated: They have come upon a concept that yields new insights, and they have landed a way to publish studies that enhance their professional reputations. But once all this happens, the question "What have you done for me lately?" comes to mind. The ideas become rather familiar. What's more, scholars begin wondering just why the theory works and come to recognize that it may hold only under particular conditions. These new questions lead to revisions of the theory and advance science. They also help to "keep the theory young" by forcing tests in new eras, with new generations of scholars and different social values.

Dissonance theory fits this trajectory. After the studies of the 1950s and 1960s were completed (yes, they were conducted that long ago!), scholars began asking deeper questions about dissonance theory. They began to wonder just why dissonance leads to attitude change and whether there weren't other reasons why individuals seek to restore dissonance than those Festinger posited. Many theorists proposed alternative accounts of dissonance and tested their ideas. These studies were published from the 1970s through the 1990s, and they continue to fill journals and books today (Harmon-Jones, 2002; Mills, 1999).

The catalyst for this research was the Festinger and Carlsmith boring-task study previously discussed. Like a Rorschach projection test, it has been interpreted in different ways by different scholars. Their research suggests that when people engage in counterattitudinal behavior, there is more going on than you might think. Four explanations of the study have been advanced. Each offers a different perspective on human nature and persuasion. Yet all four agree on one point: Festinger's thesis—people are driven by an overarching need to reduce inconsistency—is **not** the only psychological engine that leads to dissonance reduction. Students in the boring-task study may have been bothered by the inconsistency between attitude toward the task and behavior (telling others it was enjoyable). However, there were other reasons why they changed their attitude than the mere discomfort inconsistency causes. Let's review these four perspectives on cognitive dissonance.

1. Unpleasant Consequences + Responsibility = Dissonance

What really bothered students in Festinger and Carlsmith's experiment, researcher Joel Cooper has suggested, is that they might be personally responsible for having caused unpleasant consequences (Scher & Cooper, 1989). By leading an innocent person to believe that a monotonous study was enjoyable, they had arguably caused a fellow student to develop an expectation that would not be met by reality. This realization caused them discomfort. To alleviate the pain, they convinced themselves that the task was really interesting. Thus, it was not inconsistency per se, but "the desire to avoid feeling personally responsible for producing the aversive consequence of having harmed the other participant" that motivated attitude change (Harmon-Jones & Mills, 1999, p. 14).

2. Dissonance Occurs When You Are Concerned You Look Bad in Front of Others

This view emphasizes people's need to manage impressions or present themselves positively in front of other people (Tedeschi, Schlenker, & Bonoma, 1971). Theorists argue that students in Festinger and Carlsmith's study did not really change their attitudes, but only marked down on the questionnaire that they liked the task to avoid being viewed negatively by the experimenter. Concerned that the experimenter would look down on them for being willing to breach their ethics for the reward of $1, students in the $1 condition strategically changed their attitude so it looked as if they really liked the task. Thus, they could not be accused of selling their souls for a trivial sum of money (Cooper & Fazio, 1984). In addition, students in the $1 condition may not have wanted to appear inconsistent in the experimenter's eyes (i.e., of telling a fellow student the tasks were fun and then marking down on the survey that they were boring). Perceiving that people think more favorably of you when you are consistent, they indicated on the survey that they liked the task, thus giving the impression they exhibited consistency between attitude and behavior.

3. Dissonance Involves a Threat to Self-Esteem

The self-concept is at the center of this interpretation. In Aronson's (1968) view, students in Festinger and Carlsmith's study experienced dissonance between the cognition "I am a good and moral person" and the knowledge that "I just lied to someone, and I won't have a chance to 'set him straight because I probably won't see him again'" (p. 24). Students were not bothered by the mere inconsistency between thoughts, but by the fact that their behavior was inconsistent with—or violated—their positive self-concept. Of course, lying is not dissonant to a pathological liar; yet it was assumed that for most people, telling a fib would be moderately dissonant with their views of themselves as honest individuals. The self-concept is at the center of other contemporary views of dissonance reduction, such as Steele's (1988) theory, which takes a slightly different approach to the issue.

4. It's Not Dissonance, but Self-Perception

Daryl J. Bem (1970) argued that effects observed in experiments like Festinger and Carlsmith's had nothing to do with cognitive dissonance, but were due to an entirely different psychological process. Unlike the three explanations just discussed, Bem dismisses dissonance entirely. Arguing that people aren't so much neurotic rationalizers as dispassionate, cool observers of their own behavior, Bem suggests that people look to their own behavior when they want to understand their attitudes. Behavior leads to attitude, Bem (1972) argues, but not because people want to bring attitude in line with behavior to gain consistency. Instead, behavior causes attitude because people *infer* their attitudes from observing their behavior. For example, according to Bem, a young woman forms her attitude toward vegetarian food by observing her behavior: "I'm always eating noodles and pasta—I never order meat from restaurants anymore. I must really like veggie food." Or a guy decides he likes a girl, not on the basis of his positive thoughts, but because he observes that "I'm always calling her on the phone and am excited when she calls. I must really like her."

Applying this analysis to Festinger and Carlsmith's classic experiment, Bem argued that students paid $20 to say a boring task was interesting quickly looked to the situation, asked themselves why they would do this, and observed that they had just been paid $20 to make the statement. "Oh, I must have done it for the money," they concluded. Having reached this judgment, there was not the slightest reason for them to assume that their behavior reflected an attitude.

Subjects paid $1 looked dispassionately at their behavior to help decide why they told the other student the task was fun. Noting they had received only a buck to lie, they concluded, "I sure didn't do this for the money." Seeking to further understand why they behaved as they did, the $1 subjects then asked themselves, "Now why would I have told the experimenter the tasks were interesting? I didn't get any big external reward for saying this." Then came the explanation, obvious and plausible: "I must have really liked those tasks. Why else would I have agreed to make the statements?" These inferences—rather than rationalizations—led to the $1 students' forming a favorable attitude toward the tasks.

The Dissonance Debate: Intellectual Issues

Who's right? Who's wrong? Which view has the most support or the most adherents? What's the right answer?

These questions probably occur to you as you read the different views of dissonance. However, there is usually not one correct interpretation of a complex phenomenon, but many. Thus, there are various reasons why low rewards or counterattitudinal advocacy leads to attitude change. Inconsistency between cognitions, feeling responsible for producing negative consequences, discomfort at looking bad in front of others, perceiving that one has engaged in behavior that is incongruent with one's sense of self, and subsequent self-perceptions all motivate individuals to change attitudes to fit behavior. Theorists continue to debate which theory does the best job of explaining the research on cognitive dissonance.

There is currently an intellectual tug-of-war going on between those who believe dissonance occurs when one feels responsible for having caused aversive consequences (the first interpretation discussed earlier), and others who believe dissonance is a broader phenomenon, one that occurs even when counterattitudinal behavior does not lead to especially negative outcomes (Harmon-Jones et al., 1996). The second interpretation, impression management, remains viable, but has been undercut to some degree by evidence that dissonance reduction occurs in private settings, in which impressing others is less salient (Harmon-Jones & Mills, 1999). Skipping to the fourth view, self-perception, I note that Bem's theory has stimulated much discussion and has many interesting implications for persuasion (see chapter 10). However, research shows that self-perception can't explain away all dissonance phenomena. Individuals aren't always dispassionate observers of their own behavior, but are motivated to rationalize, justify, and persuade themselves, particularly after they have committed actions that bother them greatly (Elliot & Devine, 1994; Harmon-Jones & Mills, 1999). Contrary to Bem, we don't just sit back and observe our behavior like neutral spectators. We're concerned when our behavior has adverse personal or social consequences, and we are motivated to redress the cognitive dissonance.

The third interpretation, focusing on the self-concept, continues to intrigue researchers, probably because it centers on that quintessential human attribute: the ego (Mailer, 1999).

Researchers disagree on several technical points. For example, some scholars emphasize that people are bothered when they perform an action that is *inconsistent* with their self-concepts (Aronson, 1999). Others from the self-concept school argue that people are less concerned with maintaining consistency between self and behavior than in engaging in actions that affirm their global sense of self (J. Aronson, Cohen, & Nail, 1999; Steele, 1988). According to this view, individuals can reduce dissonance that arises from taking a counterattitudinal position by performing an action that restores global self-integrity, even if it is not related to the issue in question (see Box 9–1). The self-concept approach to the self is intriguing and continues to generate intellectual dialogue among researchers (Stone et al., 1997).

BOX 9–1
DISSONANCE AND MENTAL HEALTH

One of the great things about dissonance theory is that nearly half a century after it was formulated, it continues to contain enlightening ideas about everyday life. Some of these ideas have interesting implications for mental health. Here are five suggestions, culled from theory and research, for how to harness dissonance in the service of a happier, healthier life:

1. *Expect to experience dissonance after a decision.* Don't expect life to be clean and free of stress. If you choose one product or side of the issue instead of another and the selection was difficult, there is bound to be discomfort.

2. *Don't feel you have to eliminate the dissonance immediately.* Some people, uncomfortable with dissonance, mentally decree that no unpleasant thoughts about the decision should enter their mind. But sometimes the more we try to suppress something, the more apt it is to return to consciousness (Wegner et al., 1987). Dissonance can present us with a learning experience; it can help us come to grips with aspects of decisions we didn't like or positions that have more of a gray area than we believed at the outset. The thinking that dissonance stimulates can help us make better decisions, or deliver more compelling persuasive communication next time around. Of course, it is perfectly natural to want to reduce dissonance that follows a decision or performance of a behavior. However, we should also be open to the possibility that dissonance can be a teaching tool, as well as an annoyance—a phenomenon that can deepen our understanding of human experience.

Continued

BOX 9-1
(CONTINUED)

3. *Don't feel bound to each and every commitment you make.* Dissonance research indicates that once people make a public commitment, they are loathe to change their minds, for fear of looking bad or having to confront the fact that they made a mistake, and so on. But there are times—such as undergoing a cruel initiation rite to join a sorority—when backing out of a commitment may be the healthy thing to do. Naturally, we should try to honor our commitments as much as possible, but we also should not feel obligated to do something unhealthy or unethical just because we sunk a lot of time into the project.

4. *Recognize that some people need consistency more than others.* Robert B. Cialdini and his colleagues (1995) report that there are intriguing individual differences in preference for consistency. Some people are more apt than others to agree with statements like: "I get uncomfortable when I find my behavior contradicts my beliefs," "I make an effort to appear consistent to others," and "I'm uncomfortable holding two beliefs that are inconsistent" (p. 328). We're not all cut from the same consistency cloth, and we're apt to have more pleasant interactions with others if we accept that they may need more or less consistency than we do.

5. *Be creative in your attempts to reduce dissonance.* You may not be able to reduce all the dissonance that results from a decision or performance of behavior. A young woman who smokes, quits for a while, and then starts up again is apt to feel dissonance. A deadbeat dad may finally feel guilt or discomfort after years of leaving and neglecting his kids. According to Claude M. Steele and his colleagues, these individuals feel dissonant because they have performed actions that call into question their self-worth or sense of themselves as competent, good people (J. Aronson et al., 1999; Steele, 1988). Given that this is the root of dissonance, these folks can alleviate dissonance by doing things that help them look good in their own eyes, Steele argues. Although the smoker can't reduce all the dissonance aroused by her failure to quit, she might restore a sense of self-competence by completing important projects at work or doing other things that show she can follow up on personal promises she makes. Realistically, the deadbeat dad may have alienated his kids so much he can't do much to regain their trust. However, he might be able to restore a positive sense of self by at least celebrating their major accomplishments, or by taking the radically different step of spending time with other children in need.

The same processes can work at the national level. Millions of Americans felt waves of pain and dissonance after the September 11 attacks. (The dissonance was complex, an outgrowth of a realization that America was now vulnerable, as well as recognition that the belief in a good and just world had been shattered more deeply than before.) Knowing they could not bring these beliefs back to life (anymore than they could bring back the lives of the people killed that September morning), they sought to restore consonance by volunteering—sending money and food to victims, giving blood, even helping rescue workers at the World Trade Center. Collectively, these actions may have restored pride in America and reaffirmed a strong belief in the fundamental decency of human beings.

Summary

If you can think of a time you performed a behavior that caused harm to someone else, violated your self-concept, embarrassed you, or was just plain inconsistent with what you believe, you can appreciate the power of cognitive dissonance. About half a century after Festinger invented the concept, the idea is still going strong; it continues to stimulate dialogue among scholars. There is no question that dissonance produces genuine, abiding changes in attitudes, beliefs, and behavior. It has particularly powerful effects when the issue is important to the individual and touches on the self-concept. What's more, the person must have *freely chosen* to perform the advocated behavior. Dissonance does not produce attitude change when behavior is coerced; in such situations, the person feels no internal need to rationalize the behavior. Dissonance, like persuasion, occurs under situations of free choice.

This brings us to the final issue in this chapter, an important one for this book—implications of dissonance theory for attitude change. The next section explores ways in which communication experts can use dissonance theory to influence attitudes in a variety of real-life settings.

DISSONANCE AND PERSUASION

Dissonance theorists take a decidedly different approach to persuasion than approaches reviewed in earlier chapters. Rather than trying to accommodate the other person's thinking or speech style, like the ELM or speech accommodation, dissonance theory is confrontational. It suggests that persuaders deliberately arouse cognitive dissonance and then let psychology do its work. Once dissonance is evoked, individuals should be motivated to reduce the discomfort. One way they can do this is to change their attitude in the direction the persuader recommends.

Calling on the major implications of the approaches previously discussed, we can suggest several concrete ways that persuaders can use dissonance theory to change attitudes.

1. *Encourage people to publicly advocate a position with which they disagree.* If someone who harbors a prejudiced attitude toward minorities or gays can be coaxed into making a tolerant statement in public, she may feel cognitive dissonance. She privately harbors a negative attitude, but has now made an accepting speech in public. This may heighten the dissonance and, in some instances, motivate the individual to bring her attitude in line with public behavior. In a study that tested this hypothesis, Michael R. Leippe and Donna Eisenstadt (1994) gave White students an opportunity to write essays endorsing a scholarship policy that would significantly increase money available to Blacks, presumably at the expense of Whites. White students who believed their essays could be made public became more favorable toward both the policy and African Americans.

Interestingly, a judge used a variant of this procedure on a bigot who burned a Black doll and a cross in Black residents' yards. In addition to using coercive punishments—such as sentencing him to jail—the judge ordered the man to go to the library to research the impact of cross burnings (Martin, 2001). Studying the issue in a public setting might lead the man to think through and come to grips with his racist attitudes, perhaps inducing attitude change.

2. *Confront people with their own hypocrisy.* Jeff Stone and his colleagues employed this procedure in a 1994 study of safer sex. Recognizing that most students believe they should use condoms to prevent the spread of AIDS, but do not always practice what they preach, Stone et al. reasoned that if they reminded individuals of this fact, "the resulting inconsistency between (students') public commitment and the increased awareness of their current risky sexual behavior should cause dissonance" (p. 117). To alleviate dissonance, students might begin to practice safer sex.

Participants in the study were led to believe they were helping design an AIDS prevention program for use at the high school level. Experimental group subjects wrote a persuasive speech about safer sex and delivered it in front of a video camera. Some students read about circumstances that made it difficult for people to use condoms. They also made a list of reasons why they had not used condoms in the past. This was designed to provoke inconsistency or induce hypocrisy. (Control group subjects did not list these reasons or make the safer sex speech before a video camera.) All students were given an opportunity to buy condoms, using the $4 they had earned for participating in the study.

As predicted, more students in the hypocrisy condition purchased condoms and bought more condoms than students in the control condition. Their behavior was apparently motivated by the discomfort and guilt they experienced when they recognized they did not always practice what they preached (O'Keefe, 2000).

As intriguing as Stone and his colleagues' findings are, we need to be cautious about glibly endorsing hypocrisy induction as a method for safer sex induction. First, making people feel hypocritical may make them angry, and that may cause the treatment to boomerang. Second, safer sex requests in real-world situations meet up against a variety of roadblocks, including the pleasures of sex, reluctance to offend a partner by proposing condom use, and even anxiety about being physically assaulted if one suggests using a condom. Hypocrisy induction may change attitudes in the short term, but may not influence behavior that occurs in such high-pressure sexual situations. Still, it's an important start. More generally, letting people know that a behavior they perform, or position they endorse, is incompatible with an important component of their self-concepts can make them feel uncomfortable. It may provide just the right psychological medicine to goad them into changing their attitudes (see Box 9–2).

BOX 9–2
90210 DISSONANCE

This story is about a father and teenage son who live in the 90210 zip code region of the United States 90210. You know where that is: Beverly Hills. All too ordinary in some respects, the story concerns a high school student who was heavily dependent on drugs, and a dad who found out and tried to do something about it. The story, originally broadcast on the National Public Radio program *This American Life* on January 16, 1998, would not be relevant to this chapter except for one small but important fact: The father used dissonance theory to try to convince his son to quit doing drugs. His dad probably had never heard of cognitive dissonance, but his persuasive effort is a moving testament to the ways that dissonance can be used in family crisis situations. Here is what happened:

Joshua, a student at plush Beverly Hills High School, got involved with drugs in a big way. "I failed English. I failed P.E. even, which is difficult to do, unless, you're, you know, running off getting stoned whenever you're supposed to be running around the track. And I just, you know, I just did whatever I wanted to do whenever I wanted to do it," he told an interviewer. He stole money from his parents regularly to finance his drug habit.

Joshua had no reason to suspect his parents knew. But strange things began to happen. His dad started to punish him, grounding him on the eve of a weekend he planned to do LSD, offering no reason for the punishment. Claiming there was going to be a drug bust at Beverly Hills High, Josh's dad revealed the names of students who were doing drugs. How could his father know this? Josh wondered.

Continued

BOX 9–2
(CONTINUED)

About a month later, Josh and a buddy were hanging out in his back-yard. The night before, there had been a big wind storm. It ripped off a panel from the side of the house. He and his friend were smoking a joint, like they did every day after school, when his buddy, noticing the downed panel, suddenly said, "Dude, what is this? Come here, dude. Come here, dude. Look at this." Josh saw only a strange piece of machinery inside a wall when his buddy shocked him. "Dude, your parents are taping your calls."

Suddenly, Josh understood. That explained his dad's punishments and knowledge of the high school drug group. At this point, the radio program switched to Josh's dad, who revealed what had happened. He said he be-came upset when Josh's grades plunged and his son "started acting like a complete fool." Concerned and noticing that Josh spent a lot of time on the phone, he decided to tape-record Josh's phone calls. The ethical aspects of this appeared not to bother the father.

Aware his dad was taping him, Josh made a decision. He would not quit drugs—that was too great a change—but would tell his friends that he was going straight when they talked on the phone. This worked for a while until Josh felt guilty about lying to his father. He valued his relationship with his dad and decided to talk to him. He cornered his dad at a party and told him that he knew he had been taping his phone calls.

In a dramatic admission, his father conceded he had been tape-recording Josh's conversations and said he was not going to do it anymore. He then told his son that there was something he didn't know yet, and perhaps would not understand. "Josh", he said, "you think that because I'm your father and I am in this role of the disciplinarian, that it's between you and me. What you haven't realized yet is that your actions have far more im-pact on your own life than they will on mine." He told Josh that he was going to take out the tape recorder the following day. At this point, Josh was waiting for a punishment—a severe punitive action, he assumed, per-haps military school. "I'll take the tape recorder out tomorrow," his dad said, "and there is only one thing I want you to do. I have about 40 tapes. I am going to give them to you, and I want you to listen to them, and that's all I ask."

With this statement, Josh's dad hoped to unleash cognitive dissonance in his son. He wanted Josh to hear how he sounded on the tapes—his re-dundant, frequently incoherent conversations, non sequiturs, his treatment of other people. Clearly, his dad wanted to provoke an inconsistency be-tween Josh's self-concept and his behavior on the tapes. And this was exactly what occurred. Josh was embarrassed—appalled—by the conversations that he heard. He listened to a call from his girlfriend, upset that he had ignored her, and that he treated her coldly and with indifference. He showed the same indifference with his friends.

"I had no idea what I sounded like and I didn't like what I sounded like at all," Josh said. "I was very self-centered and egotistical and uncaring of other people. It was about me. I was the star of my own stage and everybody else could basically, you know, go to hell as far as I was concerned. I had never realized that aspect of my personality. I didn't know how mean in that sense I had gotten."

After listening to the tapes over time, Josh changed his attitudes toward drugs, stopped lying, and altered his life's course. His father—who instigated the radical plan—was amazed. "He understood the entire thing that he was doing," he said proudly.

CONCLUSIONS

Cognitive dissonance remains an important, intriguing psychological theory with numerous implications for persuasion. Dissonance is an uncomfortable state that arises when individuals hold psychologically inconsistent cognitions. Dissonance, as revised and reconceptualized over the years, also refers to feeling personally responsible for unpleasant consequences, and experiencing stress over actions that reflect negatively on the self. There are different views of dissonance, and diverse explanations as to why it exerts the impact it does on attitudes.

There is little doubt that dissonance influences attitudes and cognitions. Its effects fan out to influence decision making, justification of effort, compliance under low reward, and advocating a position with which one disagrees. The theory also helps us understand why people commit themselves to causes—both good and bad ones. It offers suggestions for how to help people remain committed to good causes and how to aid individuals in quitting dysfunctional groups. The theory also has intriguing implications for persuasion. Departing from conventional strategies that emphasize accommodating people or meeting them halfway, dissonance theory recommends that persuaders provoke inconsistencies in individuals. Dissonance then serves as the engine that motivates attitude change. In this sense, dissonance is a powerful theory of persuasive communication, emphasizing, as it does, the central role that self-persuasion plays in attitude change.

CHAPTER 10

Interpersonal Persuasion

Bernae Gunderson, a paralegal specialist from St. Paul, has no difficulty deciphering the fine print of legal documents. Still, she was puzzled by materials she received from her mortgage company. They didn't jibe with the home equity loan she and her husband had been promised. Mrs. Gunderson called the company, First Alliance Corporation, asked questions about monthly payments and fees, and was promptly reassured that her understanding of the loan was indeed correct. What Mrs. Gunderson was not told—but soon would discover—was that First Alliance had tacked on $13,000 in fees to the loan, and the interest rate rose a full percentage point every six months. (Henriques & Bergman, 2000)

First Alliance, it turned out, used deceptive sales procedures to promote its services. Sued by regulators in five states, the company recruited unsuspecting borrowers using a high-level con game and elaborate sales pitch that was designed to snooker people into paying higher fees and interest rates than was justified by market factors. The company's loan officers were required to memorize a 27-page selling routine that included the following gambits:

- Establish rapport and a common bond. Initiate a conversation about jobs, children, or pets. Say something funny to get them laughing.
- To soften the financial blow, when talking about dollar amounts, say "merely," "simply," or "only."
- If the customer asks questions about fees, just reply, "May I ignore your concern about the rate and costs if I can show you that these are minor issues in a loan?"
- If all else fails and the sale appears to be lost, say, "I want to apologize for being so inept a loan officer. I want you to know that it's all my fault, and I'm truly sorry. Just so I don't make the same mistake again, would you mind telling me what I did that was wrong? Didn't I cover that? (*And get right back into it.*) (Henriques & Bergman, 2000, p. C12)

There is nothing wrong with using persuasion techniques to make a sale. The problem is that First Alliance trained its loan officers to deceive customers about its services. They lied about the terms of home equity loans and refused to come clean when people like Bernae Gunderson raised questions. They were experts in using strategies of interpersonal persuasion. Unfortunately, they exploited their knowledge, manipulating individuals into signing off on deals that were unduly expensive and unfair.

Interpersonal persuasion, the centerpiece of First Alliance's promotional campaign and subject of this chapter, offers a glimpse into a realm of persuasion that is somewhat different from those discussed so far in the book. Unlike purely psychological approaches, it focuses on the dyad, or two-person unit (persuader and persuadee). In contrast to attitude-based research, it centers on changing behavior—on inducing people to comply with the persuader's requests. Unlike message-oriented persuasion research, which focuses on modifying views about political or social issues, it explores techniques people employ to accomplish interpersonal objectives—for example, how they "sell themselves" to others.

Drawing on the fields of interpersonal communication, social psychology, and marketing, interpersonal persuasion research examines the strategies people use to gain compliance. It looks at how individuals try to get their way with others (something we all want to do). It examines techniques businesses use to convince customers to sign on the dotted line, strategies charities employ to gain donations, and methods that health practitioners use to convince people to take better care of their health. To gain insight into these practical issues, interpersonal persuasion scholars develop theories and conduct empirical studies—both experiments and surveys. In some ways this is the most practical, down-to-earth chapter in the book, in other ways the most complicated because it calls on taxonomies and cognitive concepts applied to the dynamic dance of interpersonal communication.

The first portion of the chapter looks at a variety of techniques that have amusing sales pitch names like foot-in-the-door and door-in-the-face. These persuasive tactics are known as **sequential influence techniques**. Influence in such cases "often proceeds in stages, each of which establishes the foundation for further changes in beliefs or behavior. Individuals slowly come to embrace new opinions, and actors often induce others to gradually comply with target requests" (Seibold, Cantrill, & Meyers, 1994, p. 560). The second section of the chapter focuses more directly on the communication aspect of interpersonal persuasion. It looks at the strategies that people—you, me, our friends, and parents—use to gain compliance, how researchers study this, and the many factors that influence compliance-gaining.

FOOT-IN-THE-DOOR

This classic persuasion strategy dates back to the days when salespeople knocked on doors and plied all tricks of the trade to maneuver their way into residents' homes. If they could just overcome initial resistance—get a "foot in the door" of the domicile—they felt they could surmount subsequent obstacles and make the sale of an Avon perfume, a vacuum cleaner, or a set of encyclopedias. Going door-to-door is out-of-date, but starting small and moving to a larger request is still in vogue. The foot-in-the-door technique stipulates that an individual is more likely to comply with a second, larger request if he or she has agreed to perform a small initial request.

Many studies have found support for the foot-in-the-door (FITD) procedure. Researchers typically ask individuals in an experimental group to perform a small favor, one to which most everyone agrees. Experimenters next ask these folks to comply with a second, larger request, the one in which the experimenter is actually interested. Participants in the control condition receive only the second request. Experimental group participants are typically more likely than control subjects to comply with the second request. For example:

- In a classic study, Freedman and Fraser (1966) arranged for experimenters working for a local traffic safety committee to ask California residents if they would mind putting a 3-inch "Be a safe driver" sign in their cars. Two weeks later, residents were asked if they would place a large, unattractive "Drive Carefully" sign on their front lawns. Homeowners in a control condition were asked only the second request. Seventeen percent of control group residents agreed to put the large sign on their lawns. However, 76% of those who agreed to the initial request or had been approached the first time complied with the second request.
- Participants were more willing to volunteer to construct a hiking trail if they had agreed to address envelopes for an environmental group than if they had not acceded to the initial request (Dillard, 1990a).
- Individuals were more likely to volunteer a large amount of time for a children's social skill project if they had initially assisted a child with a small request—helping an 8-year-old get candy from a candy machine (Rittle, 1981).

Emboldened by results like these, researchers have conducted over 100 studies of the FITD strategy. Meta-analytic, statistically based reviews of the research show that the effect is reliable and occurs more frequently than would be expected by chance (e.g., Dillard, Hunter, & Burgoon, 1984). Given its utility, professional persuaders—ranging from telemarketers to university alumni fund-raisers—frequently employ FITD.

Why Does It Work?

There are several reasons why the foot-in-the-door technique produces compliance (Burger, 1999). The first explanation calls on Bem's self-perception theory, described in chapter 9. According to this view, individuals who perform a small favor for someone look at their behavior and infer that they are helpful, cooperative people. They become, in their own eyes, the kind of people who do these sorts of things, go along with requests made by strangers, and cooperate with worthwhile causes (Freedman & Fraser, 1966, p. 201). Having formed this self-perception, they naturally accede to the second, larger request.

A second interpretation emphasizes consistency needs. Recalling that they agreed to the first request, individuals find it dissonant to reject the second, target request. Perhaps having formed the perception that they are helpful people, they feel motivated to behave in a way that is consistent with their newly formed view of themselves. In a sense, they may feel more committed to the requester or to the goal of helping others.

A third explanation places emphasis on social norms. "Being asked to perform an initial small request makes people more aware of the norm of social responsibility, a norm that prescribes that one should help those who are in need," William DeJong (1979) explains (p. 2236).

When Does It Work?

The FITD technique does not always produce compliance. It is particularly likely to work when the request concerns a pro-social issue, such as asking for a donation to charity or requesting favors from strangers. Self-perceptions, consistency needs, and social norms are likely to kick in under these circumstances. Foot-in-the-door is also more apt to succeed when the second query is "a continuation," or logical outgrowth, of the initial request, and when people actually perform the requested behavior (Burger, 1999; Dillard et al., 1984).

FITD is not so likely to succeed if the same persuader asks for a second favor immediately after having hit up people for a first request. The bang-bang, request-upon-request approach may create resentment, leading people to say "No" just to reassert their independence (Chartrand, Pinckert, & Burger, 1999).

Next time you do a favor for someone and are tempted to accede to a second, larger request, check to see if the facilitating factors operating in the situation match those just described. If they do, you may be more apt to go along with the request, and it may be one that you would rather decline.

DOOR-IN-THE-FACE

This technique undoubtedly gets the award for the most memorable name in the Persuasion Tactics Hall of Fame. It occurs when a persuader makes a large request that is almost certain to be denied. After being turned down, the persuader returns with a smaller request, the target request the communicator had in mind at the beginning. Door-in-the-face (DITF) is exactly the opposite of foot-in-the-door. Foot-in-the-door starts with a small request and moves to a larger one. DITF begins with a large request and scales down to an appropriately modest request. Researchers study the technique by asking experimental group participants to comply with a large request, one certain to be denied. When they refuse, participants are asked if they would mind going along with a smaller, second request. Control group subjects receive only the second request.

The DITF technique has been tested in dozens of studies. It emerges reliably and dependably, meta-analytic studies tell us (O'Keefe & Hale, 1998). Consider the following supportive findings:

- A volunteer, supposedly working for a local blood services organization, asked students if they would donate a unit of blood once every 2 months for a period of at least 3 years. Everyone declined this outlandish request. The volunteer then asked experimental group subjects if they would donate just one unit of blood between 8:00 A.M. and 3:30 P.M. the next day. Control group participants were asked the same question. Forty-nine percent of those who rejected the first request agreed to donate blood, compared with 32% of those in the control group (Cialdini & Ascani, 1976).
- An experimenter working with a boys and girls club asked students if they would mind spending about 15 hours a week tutoring children. When this request was declined, the experimenter asked if students would be willing to spend an afternoon taking kids to a museum or the movies. Students who turned down the initial request were more likely to agree to spend an afternoon with children than those who only heard the second request (O'Keefe & Figgé, 1999).
- An individual claiming to represent a California company asked respondents if they would be willing to spend 2 hours answering survey questions on home or dorm safety. After the request was declined, the experimenter asked if individuals would mind taking 15 minutes to complete a small portion of the survey. Control group participants were asked only the second request. Forty-four percent of those who refused the first request agreed to partake in the shorter survey. By contrast, only 25% of control group subjects complied with the second request (Mowen & Cialdini, 1980).

Why Does It Work?

Several rather interesting explanations for the DITF strategy have been advanced. One view emphasizes a powerful psychological factor akin to dissonance but more emotion-packed: guilt. Individuals feel guilty about turning down the first request. To reduce guilt, an unpleasant feeling, they go along with the second request (O'Keefe & Figgé, 1999). There is some evidence that guilt helps explain DITF effects.

Another view emphasizes reciprocal concessions. As a persuader (deliberately) scales down his request, he is seen as having made a concession. This leads the persuadee to invoke the social rule that "you should make concessions to those who make concessions to you" or "you should meet the other fellow halfway." As a result, the persuadee yields and goes along with the second request (Cialdini et al., 1975; Rhoads & Cialdini, 2002).

It is also possible that social judgment processes operate in the DITF situation. The extreme first request functions as an anchor against which the second request is compared. After having heard the outrageous initial request, the second offer seems less costly and severe. However, control group participants who are asked to comply only with the smaller request do not have this anchor available to them. Thus, experimental group participants are more apt than control group subjects to go along with the target request.

Self-presentation concerns may also intervene. People fear that the persuader will evaluate them negatively for turning down the first request. Not realizing that the whole gambit has been staged, they accede to the second request to make themselves look good in the persuader's eyes.

When Does It Work?

Like other persuasion factors discussed, the door-in-the-face technique is sensitive to contextual factors (Fern, Monroe, & Avila, 1986; O'Keefe & Hale, 1998). DITF works particularly well when the request concerns prosocial issues. People may feel guilty about turning down a charitable organization's request for a large donation or time expenditure. They can make things right by agreeing to the second request.

Door-in-the-face effects also emerge when the same individual makes both requests. People may feel an obligation to reciprocate a concession if they note that the person who asked for too much is scaling down her request. If two different people make the requests, the feeling that "you should make concessions to those who make concessions to you" may not kick in.

The DITF strategy is also more apt to work if there is only a short delay between the first and second requests. If too long a time passes between requests, the persuadee's guilt might possibly dissipate. In addition, the more time that passes between requests, the less salient is the contrast between the extreme first request and the seemingly more reasonable second request.

APPLICATIONS

The foot-in-the-door and door-in-the-face techniques are regularly used by compliance professionals. Noting that you gave $25 to a charity last year, a volunteer asks if you might increase your gift to $50. The local newspaper calls and asks if you would like to take out a daily subscription. When you tell her you don't have time to read the paper every day, she asks, "How about Sunday?" Or the bank loan officer wonders if you can afford a $100 monthly payment on your student loan. When you decline, he asks if you can pay $50 each month, exactly the amount he had in mind from the beginning.

FITD and DITF, like all persuasion techniques, can be used for unethical, as well as morally acceptable, purposes. Unsavory telemarketers or front organizations posing as charities can manipulate people into donating money through adroit use of these tactics. At the same time, prosocial groups can employ these techniques to achieve worthwhile goals. For example, a volunteer from MADD might use foot-in-the-door to induce bar patrons to sign a petition against drunk driving. Sometime later in the evening, the volunteer could ask patrons if they would agree to let a taxi take them home (Taylor & Booth-Butterfield, 1993). In the same fashion, charitable organizations such as the Red Cross or Purple Heart might employ door-in-the-face to gently arouse guilt that inevitably follows refusal of the initial request.

OTHER COMPLIANCE TECHNIQUES

The foot-in-the-door and door-in-the-face strategies have generated the most research, and we know the most about when they work and why. Several other compliance tactics have been explored, and reviewing them offers insights into the canny ways that persuaders use communication to achieve their goals.

The first technique is **low-balling**. This gets its name from the observation that persuaders—typically car salespeople—try to secure compliance by "throwing the customer a low ball." In persuasion scholarship, low-balling has a precise meaning. It occurs when a persuader induces someone to comply with a request and then "ups the ante" by increasing the cost of compliance. Having made the initial decision to comply, individuals experience dissonance at the thought that they may have to back away from their commitment. Once individuals have committed themselves to a decision, they are loathe to change their minds, even when the cost of a decision is raised significantly and unfairly (Cialdini et al., 1978).

Low-balling is similar to foot-in-the-door in that the persuader begins with a small request and follows it up with a more grandiose alternative. In low-balling, though, the action initially requested *is* the target behavior; what changes is the cost associated with performing the target action. In the case of FITD, the behavior that the persuader asks the person to initially perform is a setup to induce the individual to comply with the larger, critical request.

Robert B. Cialdini and his colleagues (1978) have conducted experiments demonstrating that low-balling can increase compliance. Their findings shed light on sales practices in the ever colorful, always controversial business of selling cars. As the authors explain:

> The critical component of the procedure is for the salesperson to induce the customer to make an *active decision* to buy one of the dealership's cars by offering an extremely good price, perhaps as much as $300 below competitors' prices. Once the customer has made the decision for a specific car (and has even begun completing the appropriate forms), the salesperson removes the price advantage in one of a variety of ways. For example, the customer may be told that the originally cited price did not include an expensive option that the customer had assumed was part of the offer. More frequently, however, the initial price offer is rescinded when the salesperson "checks with the boss," who does not allow the deal because "we'd be losing money." . . . In each instance, the result is the same: The reason that the customer made a favorable purchase decision is removed, and the performance of the target behavior (i.e., buying that specific automobile) is rendered more costly. The increased cost is such that the final price is equivalent to, or sometimes slightly above, that of the dealer's competitors. Yet, car dealership lore has it that more customers will remain with their decision to purchase the automobile, even at the adjusted figure, than would have bought it had the full price been revealed before a purchase decision had been obtained. (Cialdini et al., 1978, p. 464; see Fig. 10.1.)

Another tactic that borrows from persuasion practitioners is the **"that's-not-all"** technique. You have probably heard TV announcers make claims like "And that's not all—if you call now and place an order for this one-time only collection of sixties oldies, we'll throw in an extra rock and roll CD—so call right away!" Researcher Jerry M. Burger capitalized on such real-life observations. He conceptualized and tested the

FIG 10.1   Car salesmen have been known to use low-balling and a host of other inter-personal gambits to make a sale. (Photograph by William C. Rieter.)

effectiveness of the that's-not-all technique. In theory, Burger (1986), explained:

> The salesperson presents a product and a price but does not allow the buyer to respond immediately. Instead, after a few seconds of mulling over the price, the buyer is told "that's not all"; that is, there is an additional small product that goes along with the larger item, or that "just for you" or perhaps "today only" the price is lower than that originally cited. The

seller, of course, had planned to sell the items together or at the lower price all along but allows the buyer to think about the possibility of buying the single item or the higher priced item first. Supposedly, this approach is more effective than presenting the eventual deal to the customer in the beginning. (p. 277)

Burger demonstrated that the that's-not-all tactic can influence compliance. In one experiment, two researchers sat at tables that had a sign promoting the university psychology club's bake sale. Cupcakes were featured at the table. Individuals who wandered by sometimes expressed interest in the cupcakes, curious how much they cost. Those assigned to the experimental group were told that cupcakes cost 75¢ each. After listening to a seemingly impromptu conversation between the two experimenters, these individuals were told that the price *included* two medium-sized cookies. By contrast, subjects in the control group were shown the cookies when they inquired about the cost of the cupcakes. They were told that the package cost 75¢. Even though people got the same products for the identical cost in both conditions, more experimental group subjects purchased sweets (73%) than did control group subjects (40%).

Like door-in-the-face, that's-not-all works in part because of the reciprocity norm. We learn from an early age that when someone does a favor for us, we should do one in return. Participants in Burger's experimental group naively assumed the persuader had done them a favor by throwing in two cookies. Not knowing that this was part of the gambit, they acquiesced.

Yet another sequential influence tactic that is sometimes used is called **fear-then-relief**. This is somewhat different from the other techniques in that, in this case, the persuader deliberately places the recipient in a state of fear. Suddenly and abruptly, the persuader eliminates the threat, replaces fear with kind words, and asks the recipient to comply with a request. The ensuing relief pushes the persuadee to acquiesce.

Dolinski and Nawrat (1998) demonstrated fear-then-relief in several clever experiments. In one study, they arranged for jaywalking pedestrians to hear a policeman's whistle (actually produced by an experimenter hidden from view). People glanced nervously and walked quickly, fearing they had done something wrong. Twenty seconds later, they were approached by an experimenter who asked them if they would spend 10 minutes filling out a survey. These individuals were more likely to comply than those who did not hear the whistle. In another experiment, the researchers placed a piece of paper that resembled a parking ticket behind a car's windshield wiper. When drivers arrived at their cars, they experienced that telltale feeling of fear on noticing what looked to be a parking ticket. In fact, the paper was a leaflet that contained an appeal for blood donations. As drivers' anxiety was replaced with reassurance, an experimenter asked them if they would mind taking 15 minutes to complete a questionnaire. Sixty-eight percent of experimental group subjects complied with the request, compared with 36% of control group participants.

Fear-then-relief works for two reasons. First, the relief experienced when the threat is removed is reinforcing. It becomes associated with the second request, leading to more compliance. Second, the ensuing relief places people in a state of "temporary mindlessness." Preoccupied with the danger they nearly fell into and their own supposed carelessness, individuals are distracted. They are less attentive and more susceptible to the persuader's request.

The technique has interesting implications for a powerful domain of persuasion, yet one infrequently discussed—interrogation of prisoners. We often think that compliance with captors results from the induction of terror and fear. Fear-then-relief suggests that a more subtle, self-persuasion dynamic is in operation. Captors initially scream at a prisoner, threaten him or her with torture, and begin to physically hurt the prisoner. Suddenly, the abuse ends and is replaced by a softer tone and a nice voice. In some cases, "the sudden withdrawal of the source of anxiety intensifies compliance" (Dolinski & Nawrat, p. 27; Schein, 1961).

Fear-then-relief is used in peacetime situations too—by parents, teachers, and other authority figures who replace the stick quickly with a carrot. Like other tactics (e.g., Aune & Basil, 1994) it capitalizes on the element of surprise, which succeeds in disrupting people's normal defenses. Surprise is the key in an additional technique that psychologists have studied, one no doubt used by compliance professionals. Known as the **pique technique**, it involves "making the request in an unusual and atypical manner so that the target's interest is piqued, the refusal script is disrupted, and the target is induced to think positively about compliance" (Santos, Leve, & Pratkanis, 1994, p. 756). In an experimental demonstration of the technique, Santos and his colleagues reported that students posing as panhandlers received more money from passersby when they asked "Can you spare 17¢ (or 37¢)?" than when they asked if the people could spare a quarter or any change. When was the last time that a panhandler asked you for 37¢? Never happened, right? Therein lies the ingenuity— and potential lure—of the pique technique.

The pique procedure works because it disrupts our normal routine. It engages and consumes the conscious mind, thereby diverting it from the resistance that typically follows a persuader's request. Disruption of conscious modes of thought plays a critical role in acquiescence to persuasion, in the view of psychologist Eric S. Knowles and his colleagues (2001). Knowles emphasizes that persuaders succeed when they devise clever, subtle ways to break down our resistance (see Box 10–1). He and

---

BOX 10-1
RESISTANCE AND COMPLIANCE

This chapter has focused on how communicators convince other people to comply with their requests. Another way of looking at this is to ask: How can communicators overcome others' resistance to their persuasive requests? Knowles and his colleagues argue that resistance plays a key role in persuasion (Knowles et al., 2001). They point out that most interpersonal persuasion research has focused on devising ways to make a message more appealing rather than on the obverse: figuring out how best to overcome people's resistance to persuasive messages. By understanding why individuals resist messages, researchers can do a better job of formulating strategies to increase compliance.

Scholarly research suggests that persuaders can neutralize resistance in several ways, including: (a) framing the message to minimize resistance, (b) acknowledging and confronting resistance head-on, (c) reframing the message, and (d) disrupting resistance to the message (Knowles & Linn, 2004). These ideas have practical applications. Consider once again the case of an adolescent who wants to practice safer sex, but is afraid to request it, for fear the suggestion will spark resistance from his or her partner. A resistance-based approach suggests the following strategies and appeals:

Strategy	Safer Sex Appeal
Framing the message to minimize resistance	"Please do this for me. I'd feel more comfortable and secure if we'd use condoms tonight."
Acknowledging and confronting resistance	"You say you don't want to talk about condoms. But we've always valued talking and being open about how we feel. Let's talk about this."
Reframing the message	"You say using condoms turns you off. But think how free and unrestrained we'll feel with no worries about sex or pregnancy."
Disrupting and distracting resistance (through humor)	"I have these condoms that a friend of mine sent me from Tijuana that have those Goodyear radial ribs on them that will drive you wild." (Comments adapted from Adelman, 1992, p. 82, and Kelly, 1995, p. 99)

---

his colleagues have shown that persuaders can disrupt resistance by subtly changing the wording of requests. Employing what they call the **disrupt-then-reframe technique**, Knowles and his colleagues have shown that they can dramatically increase compliance by first mildly disrupting "the ongoing script of a persuasive request," and then reframing the request, or encouraging the listener to "understand the issue in a new way" (Knowles, Butler, & Linn, 2001, p. 50).

In the bold tradition of interpersonal persuasion research, the researchers went door-to-door selling Christmas cards. They explained that money from the sales would go—as indeed it did—to a nonprofit center that helps developmentally disabled children and adults. The experimenters told some residents that the price of a Christmas card package was $3. They informed others that the price was $3 and then added, "It's a bargain." In the key disrupt-then-reframe condition, the experimenter stated, "This package of cards sells for 300 pennies" (thereby shaking up the normal script for a door-to-door request). She then added after pausing, "That's $3. It's a bargain" (reframe). Sixty-five percent of respondents purchased cards in the disrupt-then-reframe treatment, compared to 35% in the other groups. Other experiments obtained similar findings, demonstrating that a small, but subtle, variation in a persuasive request can produce dramatic differences in compliance (Davis & Knowles, 1999).

Summary

All the techniques discussed in this section play on what Freedman and Fraser called "compliance without pressure." They are soft-sell, not hardball, tactics that worm their way through consumers' defenses, capitalizing on social norms, emotions, and sly disruption of ordinary routines. Used adroitly by canny professionals, they can be remarkably effective. Just ask anyone who is still kicking him- or herself for yielding to a series of requests that sounded innocent at the time, but ended up costing the person a pretty penny.

COMPLIANCE-GAINING

You want to dine out with someone, but you disagree about which restaurant it is going to be; someone in the department must do an unpleasant job, but you want to make sure that in any case it will not be you; you want to make new work arrangements, but you are afraid your boss will not agree; you want to get your partner to come with you to that tedious family party, but you suspect that he or she does not want to come along. (van Knippenberg et al., 1999, p. 806)

Add to these more serious requests for compliance: an effort to convince a close friend to return to school after having dropped out for a couple of years, a doctor's attempt to persuade a seriously overweight patient to pursue an exercise regimen, a lover's effort to persuade a partner to practice safe sex. Such requests, initiatives, and serious attempts to influence behavior are pervasive in everyday life. They speak to the strong interest human beings have in getting their way—that is, in persuading others to comply with their requests and pleas. This section of the chapter moves from an exploration of how professional persuaders achieve their goals to an examination of us—how we try to gain compliance in everyday life. The area of research is appropriately called compliance-gaining.

Compliance-gaining is defined as a "**communicative behavior in which an agent engages so as to elicit from a target some agent-selected behavior**" (Wheeless, Barraclough, & Stewart, 1983, p. 111). Interpersonal communication scholars, who have pioneered research in this area, have sought to understand how people go about trying to gain compliance in everyday life. What strategies do they use? Can compliance-gaining tactics be categorized in meaningful ways? How do techniques differ as a function of the situation and the person? These are some of the questions scholars pose.

One of the daunting issues researchers face is how to empirically study so broad an area as compliance-gaining. They could devise experiments, of the sort conducted by psychologists researching foot-in-the-door and door-in-the-face. Although these would allow researchers to test hypotheses, they would not tell them how compliance-gaining works in the real world that lies outside the experimenter's laboratory. Scholars could observe people trying to gain compliance—on the job, at school, or in social settings like bars (that might be fun!). However, this would provide an endless amount of data, too much to meaningfully code. Dissatisfied with these methodologies, scholars hit on the idea of conducting surveys that ask people how they would gain compliance, either in situations suggested by the researcher or in an open-ended manner, in the individuals' own words.

The first survey method is **closed-ended** in that it provides individuals with hypothetical situations and asks them to choose among various strategies for compliance. For example, researchers have asked participants to imagine they have been carrying on a close relationship with a person of the opposite sex for two years. Unexpectedly, an old acquaintance happens to be in town one evening. Desirous of getting together with their old friend, but mindful that their current boyfriend or girlfriend is counting on getting together that night, respondents are asked to indicate how they would try to convince their current steady to let them visit their former acquaintance (Miller et al., 1977). Subjects have also been asked to imagine that their neighbors, whom they do not know very well, own a dog, who barks almost all night. This in turn incites the other local canines to do the same. How, students are asked, would they attempt to convince the neighbors to curb their dog's nighttime antics (Cody, McLaughlin, & Jordan, 1980)? Individuals are provided with a list of strategies, such as friendly appeals, moral arguments, manipulative tactics, and threats. They are asked to indicate on a Likert scale how likely they would be to use these techniques.

A second method is **open-ended**. Subjects are asked to write a short essay on how they get their way. Invited to be frank and honest, they describe in their own words how they try to gain compliance from others (Falbo, 1977).

Each technique has benefits and drawbacks. The closed-ended selection technique provides an efficient way to gather information. It also provides insights on how people try to gain compliance in representative life situations. Its drawback is that people frequently give socially desirable responses to closed-ended surveys. They are reluctant to admit that they sometimes use brutish, socially inappropriate tactics to get their way (Burleson et al., 1988).

The strength of the open-ended method is that it allows people to indicate, in their own words, how they get compliance; there is no speculation about hypothetical behavior in artificial situations. A drawback is that researchers must make sense of—and categorize—subjects' responses. This can be difficult and time-consuming. Scholars may not fully capture or appreciate the individuals' thought processes.

Despite their limitations, when taken together, open- and closed-ended questionnaires have provided useful insights about compliance-gaining. Researchers, using both types of procedures, have devised a variety of typologies to map out the techniques people use to gain compliance. These typologies have yielded insights about the major strategies individuals (at least on American college campuses) use to influence others. Strategies can be classified according to whether they are:

1. *Direct versus indirect.* Direct techniques include assertion (voicing one's wishes loudly) and persistence (reiterating one's point). Indirect tactics include "emotion-target" (putting the other person in a good mood) and thought manipulation (trying to get your way by making the other person feel it is his idea) (Falbo, 1977; see also Dillard et al., 1996).
2. *Rational versus nonrational.* Rational techniques include reason (arguing logically) and exchange of favors (for a detailed discussion, see Cialdini, 2001). Nonrational tactics include deceit (fast talking and lying) and threat (telling her I will never speak to her again if she doesn't do what I want) (Falbo, 1977).
3. *Hard versus soft.* Hard tactics include yelling, demanding, and verbal aggression. Soft techniques include kindness, flattery, and flirting (Kipnis & Schmidt, 1996).
4. *External versus internal.* Tactics can be externally focused, such as rewards or punishments. To motivate a child to study, a parent could

use a carrot like promise ("I'll raise your allowance if you study more") or a stick like aversive stimulation ("You're banned from driving until you hit the books"). Techniques can also be internally focused—that is, self-persuasion-type appeals directed at the message recipient's psyche. These include positive self-feeling ("You'll feel good about yourself if you study a lot") and negative self-feeling ("You'll be disappointed with yourself in the long run if you don't study more") (see Marwell & Schmitt, 1967; Miller & Parks, 1982).

Notice that the same techniques can be categorized in several ways. Threat could be direct, nonrational, hard, and external. Positive self-feeling could be indirect, rational, and soft, as well as internal. This cross-categorization occurs because there is not one but a variety of compliance-gaining taxonomies, constructed by different scholars, for different purposes. Nonetheless, these four sets of labels provide a useful way of categorizing compliance-gaining behavior.

Contextual Influences

People are complex creatures. They use different techniques to gain compliance, depending on the situation. In one situation, a person may use reason, in another she may scream and yell, employing verbal aggression. We are, to some extent and in varying degrees, chameleons. Which situations are the most critical determinants of compliance-gaining? Scholars have studied this issue, delineating a host of important contextual influences on strategy selection. The following factors are especially important:

Intimacy. Contexts differ in the degree to which they involve intimate associations between persuader and persuadee. As you move along the continuum from stranger to acquaintance to friend to lover or family member, you find that the same individual can behave very differently, depending on which of these "others" the person is trying to influence. In an old but still engaging study, Fitzpatrick and Winke (1979) reported that level of intimacy predicted use of conflict-reducing strategies. Focusing on people casually involved in romantic relationships, those in serious relationships, and married partners, the investigators found that married persons were especially likely to employ emotional appeals or personal rejections ("withholding affection and acting cold until he or she gives in") to resolve differences.

"You always hurt the one you love," Fitzpatrick and Winke observed. They explained that:

Individuals in a more committed relationship generally have less concern about the strengths of the relational bonds. Consequently, they employ more spontaneous and emotionally toned strategies in their relational conflicts. . . . In the less committed relationships, the cohesiveness of the partners is still being negotiated. . . . Undoubtedly, it would be too risky for them to employ the more open conflict strategies of the firmly committed. (p. 10)

This is not to say that everyone uses more emotional or highly manipulative tactics in intimate settings than in everyday interpersonal encounters. These findings emerged from one study, conducted at one point in time. However, research indicates that intimacy exerts an important impact on compliance-gaining behavior (Cody & McLaughlin, 1980).

Dependency. We use different strategies to gain compliance, depending on whether we are dependent on the person we are trying to influence. People are more reluctant to use hard tactics when the other has control over important outcomes in their lives (van Knippenberg et al., 1999). Graduate teaching assistants who say they "dominate arguments" and "argue insistently" with disgruntled undergraduate students acknowledge that they prefer to use nonconfrontational techniques, even sidestepping disagreements, when discussing job-related conflicts with the professor (Putnam & Wilson, 1982). It is only natural to be more careful when trying to gain compliance from those who have control over important outcomes in your life. Thus, when people lack power, they are more likely to employ rational and indirect tactics "because no other power base is available to them" (Cody & McLaughlin, 1985).

Rights. People employ different tactics to get their way, depending on whether they believe they have the right to pursue a particular option. If they do not feel they have the moral right to make a request, they may use soft tactics. However, if they believe they have the right to make a request, or if they feel they have been treated unfairly, they are more apt to employ hard than soft techniques (van Knippenberg et al., 1999). Consider the marked change in tactics employed by people trying to convince smokers to quit smoking in public places. Decades ago, individuals who objected to smokers polluting public space said little, afraid they would offend smokers. Nowadays, nonsmokers, redefining the meaning of public space and feeling they have the right to insist that smokers not puff in public, frequently use uncompromising, even nonrational, tactics to induce smokers to put out a cigarette. This change in compliance-gaining strategies resulted from years of social protest against smoking. Protests against problematic social norms, and subsequent changes in the law, can empower ordinary people, encouraging them to use feistier techniques to get their way.

Other Situational Factors. Situations also vary in the degree to which (a) the compliance benefits the persuader, (b) the influence attempt has consequences for the relationship between persuader and persuadee, and (c) the target resists the influence attempt (Cody & McLaughlin, 1980). Resistance is particularly important, as people frequently reject persuaders' appeals. Persuaders must adjust their strategy to take resistance into account, although inexperienced communicators are often flummoxed by the recipient's refusal to go along with their request.

Individual Differences

In addition to situations, personality and individual difference factors influence compliance-gaining. Individuals differ dramatically in how they go about trying to get their way. Some people are direct, others are shy. Some individuals worry a great deal about hurting others' feelings; other individuals care not a whit. Some people respect social conventions; other people disregard them. Consider, for example, how sharply people differ on the rather pedestrian matter of inducing someone to repay a loan. Min-Sun Kim and Steven R. Wilson (1994), in a theoretical study of interpersonal persuasion, listed ways that different individuals might formulate this request. They include:

> I have run out of cash.
> I could use the money I loaned you.
> Can I ask you to repay the loan?
> Would you mind repaying the loan?
> You'll repay the loan, won't you?
> I'd like you to repay the loan.
> You must repay the loan.
> Repay the loan. (Kim & Wilson, pp. 214–215)

If individuals differ in their compliance-gaining strategies, can research elucidate or specify the differences? You bet! Scholars have focused on several individual difference factors, including **gender** and a factor familiar to readers of this book: **self-monitoring**.

Largely due to socialization and enculturation, women are more likely than men to use polite tactics and to employ powerless speech (Baxter, 1984; Timmerman, 2002). As noted in chapter 7, these can reduce persuasive effectiveness. What's more, as Linda L. Carli (1999) notes, "female leaders are evaluated more harshly when they exhibit a more directive style of leadership, whereas male leaders have a greater latitude to use a variety of leadership styles" (p. 94). This may be changing, however, as more women assume leadership posts in society and people change their attitudes to fit the new reality. At the same time, men's own socialization can do them a disservice: Trained to emphasize competence rather than likability, male persuaders may get downgraded on the warmth dimension. Socialized to be direct and to-the-point, men may send messages that trample on people's feelings.

Another factor that influences compliance-gaining is the personality factor, self-monitoring. High self-monitors, attuned as they are to the requirements of the situation, tend to adapt their strategy to fit the person they are trying to influence (Caldwell & Burger, 1997). Low self-monitors are more apt to use the same technique with different people. High self-monitors are more likely to develop elaborate strategic plans prior to the actual influence attempt (Jordan & Roloff, 1997). In keeping with their concern with image management, high self-monitors are more apt than low self-monitors to include in their plans a consideration of how they could manipulate their personal impression to achieve their goals.

Complications

The roles that situational and individual difference factors play in compliance-gaining are interesting and complex. People have multiple, sometimes conflicting, goals they want to accomplish in a particular situation (Dillard, 1990b). What's more, people are always balancing various aspects of the intrapersonal and interpersonal context: They want to maintain their autonomy, yet need approval from others (Brown & Levinson, 1987). They want to get their way, but recognize that this can threaten another's image, autonomy, or "face" (Wilson, Aleman, & Leatham, 1998). They don't want to hurt the other's feelings, but recognize that if they are too nice they may kill the clarity of their request with politeness and ambiguity.

Scholars have studied how people process these matters and go about balancing conflicting needs. Their models emphasize that people have elaborate cognitive structures regarding compliance-gaining and ways to achieve their goals (Wilson, 1999). This is fascinating because we all go about the business of trying to get our way, but rarely give any thought to how we think about trying to gain compliance or how we process, in our own minds, "all that stuff going on in the situation." Interpersonal communication models and research shed light on such issues.

For example, researchers find that when people possess incompatible goals—such as trying to convince a target to do something she most definitely does not want to do, while at the same time not hurting her feelings in the slightest—they pause more and don't communicate as effectively (Greene et al., 1993). The incongruity of goals puts stress on the mental system.

Research also suggests ways that we can become more effective interpersonal persuaders. Studies show that successful influence agents are apt to have greater knowledge of the strategies that are most likely to produce compliance, and are also capable of quickly adjusting their behavior to accommodate the changing needs of others (Jordan & Roloff, 1997). They also plan their strategies in advance, consider the obstacles they may face, and figure out how they can overcome them. Taking a chapter from high self-monitors' playbook, they even visualize the personal impressions they want to convey to their audience.

Summary and Applications

Compliance-gaining is a fascinating domain. Research has shed light on the generic strategies people use to get their way, the role situations play, and the individual differences in compliance-gaining. Like any academic area, compliance-gaining studies can be criticized on various grounds. To their credit, interpersonal communication scholars have been particularly assertive in pointing out limitations in this research. They have lamented that compliance-gaining strategies are frequently defined ambiguously, inconsistently, or so specifically that it is difficult to know what the strategies mean (Kellermann & Cole, 1994). In addition, critics have noted that so much of the research is conducted in America, among primarily middle-class young people, that it is inappropriate to generalize findings to different cultures. All true—and yet one would not want to throw out the (maturing) compliance-gaining baby with the dirty methodological bathwater!

This line of research has provided a needed corrective to social psychological experiments that focus on persuasion practitioners. Compliance-gaining studies delightfully and importantly center on how ordinary people gain compliance in everyday life. They also focus on the interpersonal unit rather than solely on the individual or the cognitions of the individual persuader. Compliance-gaining research has also generated insights on a variety of intriguing or socially significant problems. These run the gamut from understanding the amusing ways individuals try to convince police not to give them traffic tickets (see Box 10–2) to helping doctors improve their style of communicating medical information (Burgoon et al., 1989) to assisting young people in securing compliance in the dicey realm of safer sex.

The latter domain is particularly relevant in the wake of evidence that many otherwise cautious young people are reluctant to use condoms (Perloff, 2001). College students admit that once a relationship gets serious, condom use seems to drop off. Young people incorrectly believe that a monogamous relationship is safe, and are concerned that initiating

---

BOX 10–2
COMPLIANCE AND THE COPS

You're driving home one evening, speeding a little because you've got to get ready for a party later that night. The radio's blaring and you're feeling good as you tap your fingers and sing the words of a song you've heard many times before. Out of the corner of your eye you see a couple of lights, but ignore them until you see them again—the telltale flashing light of a police car. Your heart skips a beat as you realize the police car is following you. The siren is sounding now and you get that terrible sinking feeling and agonizing fear that something bad is going to happen.

At this point, many of us faced with the impending possibility of a speeding ticket search our minds ferociously for an excuse, an extenuating reason, a white or black lie, a rhetorical rabbit we can pull out of the hat to convince the officer not to give us a ticket. Of course, in an ideal world, if one ran afoul of the law, he or she would admit it and graciously take responsibility for the mistake. But this is not an ideal world, and most of us are probably more willing to shade the truth a little than to come clean and suffer the indemnity of a fine and points on our record. Thus, many people try to persuade the police officer not to ticket them, relying on a variety of compliance-gaining techniques.

How do people try to secure compliance from a police officer when they are stopped for traffic violations? Jennifer Preisler and Todd Pinetti, students in a communication class some years back, explored this issue by talking with many young people who had found themselves in this predicament. Their research, along with my own explorations, uncovered some interesting findings, including the following responses from young people regarding how they have tried to persuade a police officer not to ticket them:

- "I will be extra nice and respectful to the officer. I will apologize for my negligence and error. I tell them about the police officers I know."
- "I flirt my way out of it, smile a lot. (Or I say,) 'My speedometer is broken. Honestly, it hasn't worked since August.' "
- "When I am stopped for speeding, I usually do *not* try to persuade the officer to *not* give me a ticket. He has the proof that I was speeding, so I don't try to insult his intelligence by making up some stupid excuse. I do try to look very pathetic and innocent, hoping maybe he will feel bad for me and not give me a ticket."
- "I turn on the dome light and turn off the ignition, roll down the window no matter how cold it is outside. I put my keys, driver's license, and proof of insurance on the dashboard, and put my hands at 10 and 2 on the wheel. I do all this before the officer gets to the window. I am honest and hope for the best. I have tried three times and all three were successful."
- "The officer said, 'I've been waiting for an idiot like you (who he could pull over for speeding) all night.' I told him, 'Yeah, I got here as fast as I could.' He laughed for about two minutes straight and let us go."

- "I gain compliance by smiling (big) and saying, 'Officer, what seems to be the problem? I'm on my way to church.' "
- "The line that I have used to get out of a ticket is 'My wife's in labor.' "
- "My technique is when I am getting pulled over, I reach into my glove compartment and spray a dab of hair spray onto my finger. Then I put it in my eyes and I start to cry. I have gotten pulled over about 15 to 20 times and I have only gotten one ticket."

Many people suspect that sex intervenes—that is, male police officers are more forgiving of females than of males who violate a traffic law. Research bears this out. Male police officers issued a greater percentage of citations to male drivers than did female police officers. In a similar fashion, female police officers issued a greater percentage of their traffic citations to female drivers than did male officers (Koehler & Willis, 1994). Police officers may be more lenient with opposite-sex than same-sex offenders; they may find the arguments provided by opposite-sex individuals to be more persuasive because they are attracted sexually to the drivers. Or they may be less apt to believe excuses offered by members of their own gender.

safer sex behavior might threaten trust or intimacy. Women are sometimes reluctant to propose condom use because they fear it will reduce their attractiveness or trigger angry responses from guys. Men fear that broaching the condom topic will make them seem less "macho" in women's eyes or will give women a chance to reject their sexual advances (Bryan, Aiken, & West, 1999).

Research offers some clues about how to help young people better navigate the arousing, yet treacherous, domain of safer sex. One intriguing study of students' condom use concluded that "all one needs to do is to *bring up* the topic of AIDS or condoms in order to get a partner to use a condom" (Reel & Thompson, 1994, p. 137; see also Motley & Reeder, 1995). Other researchers—noting that for many women unsafe sex allows them to enjoy a myth that theirs will always be a faithful, monogamous relationship—suggest that "condoms could be represented as symbolic of the true and loving relationships that many women strive for rather than as necessary armor to protect against partners who will surely cheat" (Sobo, 1995, p. 185).

ETHICAL ISSUES

"Communication is founded on a presumption of truth," two scholars aptly note (Buller & Burgoon, 1996, p. 203). Yet persuasion commonly involves some shading of truth, a tinting that is rationalized by persuaders and lamented by message receivers. Interpersonal persuasion—from the sequential influence techniques discussed earlier in the chapter to the endless variety of compliance-gaining tactics just described—sometimes seems to put a premium on distorting communication in the service of social influence. Distorting communication in the service of social influence? A blunter, more accurate way to describe this is lying.

Lying is remarkably common in everyday life. In two diary studies, college students reported that they told two lies a day. They admitted they lied in one of every three of their social interactions (DePaulo et al., 1996). To be sure, some of these lies were told to protect other people from embarrassment, loss of face, or having their feelings hurt. However, other lies were told to enhance the psychological state of the liars—for example, to make the liars appear better than they were, to protect them from looking bad, or to protect their privacy. Many of these were white lies that we have told ourselves; others were darker distortions, outright falsehoods (DePaulo et al., 1996).

Persuasion—from sequential influence tactics to compliance-gaining—is fraught with lies. Even flattery involves a certain amount of shading of truth, a convention that many people admittedly enjoy and cherish (Stengel, 2000). All this has stimulated considerable debate among philosophers over the years. As discussed in chapter 1, utilitarians argue that a lie must be evaluated in terms of its consequences: Did it produce more negative than positive consequences? Or, more generally, does the institution of lying generate more costs than benefits for society? Deontological thinkers tend to disapprove of lies in principle because they distort truth. Related approaches emphasize that what matters is the motivation of the liar—a lie told for a good, virtuous end may be permissible under some circumstances (Gass & Seiter, 1999).

We cannot resolve this debate. In my view, social discourse—and the warp and woof of social influence—contains much truth, shading of truth, and lies. It also contains certain corrective mechanisms. Those who lie habitually run the risk of earning others' disapproval, or finding that even their truthful statements are disbelieved. Social norms operate to discourage chronic lying. So too do psychodynamic mechanisms that have evolved over human history. Guilt and internalized ethical rules help regulate people's desire to regularly stretch the truth. However, a certain amount of lying is inevitable, indeed permissible in everyday interpersonal communication. Social influence—and persuasive communication—are human endeavors, part of the drama of everyday life, in which people are free to pursue their own ends, restrained by internalized moral values and social conventions (Scheibe, 2000). Democratic, civilized society enshrines people's freedom to pursue their own interests and celebrates those who can exert influence over others. The "downside" of this is that some people will abuse their freedom and seek to manipulate others, distorting truth and using deceitful tactics. Human evolution has not yet evolved to the point that ethics totally trumps (or at least restrains) self-interest, and perhaps it never will. The best hope is education: increased self-understanding, development of humane values, and (trite as it may sound) application of the time-honored, but always relevant, Golden Rule.

CONCLUSIONS

This chapter has examined interpersonal persuasion—the many techniques individuals use to influence one another in dyadic or one-on-one interactions. Social psychological research has documented that gambits like foot-in-the-door and door-in-the-face can be especially effective in securing compliance. Make no mistake: These tactics do not always work, and many consumers have learned to resist them. However, they are used regularly in sales and pro-social charity work, and under certain conditions, for various psychological reasons, they can work handily. Other tactics employed by professional persuaders—low-balling, that's-not-all, fear-then-relief, pique, and disrupt-then-reframe—can also influence compliance.

In everyday life, we employ a variety of tactics to get our way. Interpersonal communication scholars have developed typologies to categorize these techniques. Strategies vary in their directness, rationality, and emphasis on self-persuasion. Different strategies are used in different situations, and the same person may use a direct approach in one setting and a cautious, indirect technique in another. There are also individual differences in compliance-gaining; gender and self-monitoring have emerged as important factors predicting tactics people will use.

Interpersonal persuasion is complex and dynamic. People's cognitions about appropriate and effective compliance-gaining techniques, their goals, and their affect toward the other person influence strategy selection. One-on-one persuasive communication includes many different elements—concern about the relationship, desire to accomplish a goal, and concern about preserving face. These elements intersect and interact complexly and emotionally.

Given the central role interpersonal persuasion plays in everyday life and in socio-economic transactions, it behooves us to understand and master it. One way to do this is to study approaches employed by highly effective persuaders. Successful persuaders recognize that persuasion requires give-and-take, flexibility, and ability to see things from the other party's point of view (Cody & Seiter, 2001; Delia, Kline, & Burleson, 1979; Waldron & Applegate, 1998). "Effective persuaders have a strong and accurate sense of their audience's emotional state, and they adjust the tone of their arguments accordingly," says Jay A. Conger (1998, p. 93). They plan arguments and self-presentational strategies in advance, and "they enter the persuasion process prepared to adjust their viewpoints and incorporate others' ideas. That approach to persuasion is, interestingly, highly persuasive in itself," Conger notes (p. 87).

PART 3

Persuasion in American Society

CHAPTER **11**

Advertising

You've seen it in hundreds of commercials and on all types of clothing—shirts, jackets, and hats. It's an oversized check mark, a smoker's pipe that juts outward, a "curvy, speedy-looking blur" (Hartley, 2000). Take a look below. It's the Nike Swoosh, the symbol of Nike products, promoted by celebrity athletes from Michael Jordan to Tiger Woods, an emblem of Nike's television advertising campaigns, and, to many, the embodiment of speed, grace, mobility, and cool. It's a major reason why Nike is the major player in the sneaker market, and a testament to the success of commercial advertising (Goldman & Papson, 1996).

Advertising. That's a topic we know something about, though if you asked, we would probably politely suggest that it's everyone else who's influenced. Yet if each of us is immune to advertising's impact, how come so many people can correctly match these slogans with the advertised products?

Whassup?
Less filling, tastes great.
Obey your thirst.
Good to the last drop.
We love to see you smile.
Where's the beef?
Like a rock.
Do the Dew.

Answers: Budweiser; Miller Lite; Sprite; Maxwell House coffee; McDonald's; Wendy's; Chevy trucks; Mountain Dew.

Advertising—the genre we love to hate, the ultimate symbol of American society, a representation of some of the best, and most manipulative, aspects of United States culture—is showcased every day on television and each time we log onto Internet Web sites and catch banner spots. It's on buses and billboards, in ballparks and elementary school classrooms. It's the most real of communications, for it promotes tangible objects—things, stuff, and goods. It's also the most surrealistic, most unreal of mass communications. It shows us "a world where normal social and physical arrangements simply do not hold," critic Sut Jhally (1998) observes. "A simple shampoo brings intense sexual pleasure, nerdy young men on the beach, through the wonders of video rewind, can constantly call up beautiful women walking by, old women become magically young offering both sex and beer to young men," he notes.

Advertising has been universally praised and condemned. It has been cheered by those who view it as emblematic of the American Dream—the notion that anyone with money and moxie can promote a product to masses of consumers, along with the promise, cherished by immigrants, that an escape from brutal poverty can be found through purchase of products and services not available in more oppressive economies. Advertising has been roundly condemned by those who despise its attack on our senses, its appropriation of language for use in a misty world located somewhere between truth and falsehood, and its relentless, shameless exploitation of cultural icons and values to sell goods and services (Cross, 1996, p. 2; Schudson, 1986).

Advertising, the focus of this chapter, is a complex, colorful arena that encompasses television commercials, billboards, and posters placed strategically behind home plate in baseball stadiums. It is paid materialist speech—messages for which companies pay to shape, reinforce, and change attitudes. Advertising operates on a micro level, subtly influencing consumer behavior. It also works on the macro level, serving as the vehicle by which capitalist society communicates and promotes goods to masses of consumers. To appreciate advertising's effects, we need to look at both microlevel effects on individuals and macrolevel cultural issues. This chapter and the one that follows build on previous chapters by looking at how commercial and pro-social communication campaigns influence individuals and society.

This chapter covers a lot of territory. I begin by debunking a common myth of advertising; move on to discuss the key psychological effects of advertising on attitudes, applying theories described earlier in the book; and conclude with a look at the complex ethical conundrums of contemporary advertising.

THE SUBLIMINAL MYTH

It began, appropriately enough, in the 1950s, a decade in which post-World War II Americans were bewildered by all manner of things, ranging from reports of flying saucers to the successful Soviet launching of a space satellite. In 1957, the same year the Soviets sent up Sputnik, an enterprising marketer named James Vicary reported an equally jarring set of facts. He arranged for a drive-in movie theater in Fort Lee, New Jersey, a suburb of New York City, to beam the words "Drink Coca-Cola" and "Eat Popcorn" for less than a millisecond during the romantic movie, *Picnic*. Vicary immediately proclaimed success. He claimed an 18% rise in Coke sales and a 58% increase in popcorn purchases, compared to an earlier period.

The nation's media were shocked, *shocked*. Minds have been "broken and entered," *The New Yorker* (September 21, 1957) declared. The National Association of Broadcasters forbade its members from using subliminal ads. One writer, convinced that subliminal messages had dangerous effects, wrote several best-selling books on the subject. Wilson Bryan Key claimed that subliminal stimuli were everywhere! "You cannot pick up a newspaper, magazine, or pamphlet, hear radio, or view television anywhere in North America without being assaulted subliminally," Key (1974) announced (p. 5). He claimed that advertisements for cigarettes, liquor, and perfume contained embedded erotic pictures that caused people to march off and buy these products, like brainwashed automatons from the old film, *Coma*.

You yourself may have heard the term *subliminal* or *subliminal advertising*. It's easy to locate the words on the Web. There are dozens of Web sites with names like "Subliminal Ads—Brainwashing Consumers?" and "The Top 13 Subliminal Messages in Presidential Campaign Ads." Reflecting this belief in the power of subliminal ads, over 70% of respondents in scientific surveys maintain that subliminal advertisements are widely used and are successful in promoting products (Rogers & Smith, 1993; Zanot, Pincus, & Lamp, 1983). In a similar fashion, many people believe that subliminal messages in rock songs manipulate listeners. Some years back, parents of two men who committed suicide charged that the rock group Judas Priest had induced their sons to kill themselves. The parents claimed that Judas Priest had subliminally inserted the words "Do it, Do it" underneath the lyrics in a morbid song called "Beyond the Realms of Death." (The parents lost the case.)

Beliefs are powerful entities. In the case of subliminal advertising, they can drive fears and influence emotions. Researchers, curious about subliminal message effects, have long studied the impact of subliminally embedded words and pictures. Their conclusion: *No credible evidence supports the claim that subliminal ads influence attitudes or behavior*. To appreciate how scholars arrived at this judgment and what it tells us about the psychology of advertising, we need to briefly examine the research on this issue.

Definition

In the popular view, subliminal advertising means powerful advertising that appeals to emotional, even unconscious, needs. Given this broad definition, it is not surprising that many people believe advertising is subliminal. Scholars define subliminal differently—and far more precisely. Subliminal perception refers to an instance in which an individual "responds to stimulation, the energy or duration of which falls below that at which he *ever* reported awareness of the stimulus in some previous threshold determination," or when a person "responds to a stimulus of which he pleads total unawareness" (Dixon, 1971, p. 12). More simply, subliminal perception is perception without awareness of the object being perceived. It is "sub-limen," or below the "limen" or threshold of conscious awareness. Making matters more complicated, the limen is a hypothetical construct, not one that is always easy to pinpoint.

Applying this perceptual concept to advertising is not a simple matter and is far more complicated than glib commentators like Key assume. But if one struggles to apply it to advertising, in order to put popular ideas to the test, we could say that *a subliminal advertisement is one that includes a brief, specific message (picture, words, or sounds) that cannot be perceived at a normal level of conscious awareness.* This definition excludes many appeals commonly associated with subliminal ads. Commercials that contain sexy models, erotic images, vibrant colors, haunting images, or throbbing music are not, in themselves, subliminal. Why? Because the erotic or colorful image appeal is right there—you see it or hear it and if someone asks, you could tell her what you saw or heard. Even product images that have been strategically placed in movies. (e.g., Reese Pieces in *E.T.*, Burger King in *Men in Black II*) are not subliminal because advertisers hope viewers will spot and remember the products (Gass & Seiter, 1999). A subliminal ad—or, more precisely, one that contains a message that eludes conscious awareness—is a very different animal.

Subliminally embedded messages exist though. The key question is: How common are they? A study of advertising executives found that few, if any, advertising agencies strive to develop subliminal ads (Rogers & Seiler, 1994). In view of the powerful impact that ordinary ads exert, it doesn't make much sense for advertisers to rack their brains to embed subliminal messages in commercials. Besides, if the news media ever found out—and in the United States they eventually would—that an agency had slipped a subliminal spot into an ad, the bad press the advertiser would receive would overwhelm any potential benefits of the subliminal message.

Does this mean there are no subliminals *anywhere* in the media? Not quite. In a country as big as the United States with so many creative, ambitious, and slippery characters, it seems likely that a handful of advertising practitioners subliminally embed sexy messages in ads. (They could do this by airbrushing or using high-powered video editing techniques.) What's more, a tiny minority of other communications—rock songs and motivational audiotapes—probably contain brief messages that lie below thresholds of conscious awareness. Thus, the major question is: What impact do subliminal messages have on consumers' attitudes or behavior?

Effects

The first evidence of subliminal advertising effects came in Vicary's report on the effects of we "Drink Coca-Cola" and "Eat Popcorn" messages. At the time, his study seemed to suggest that subliminals could potently shape human behavior. But when scholars peered beneath the surface, they discovered that his research had serious flaws. In the first place, there was no control group, an essential requirement of a scientific experiment. Thus, there is no way of knowing whether moviegoers bought more popcorn and Cokes because they happened to be hungry and thirsty that particular day. It is even possible that the movie itself stimulated sales; it was named "Picnic" and showed scenes of people enjoying food and drinks!

More seriously, Vicary never released his data or published his study. Publication and open inspection of data are basic principles in scientific research, and Vicary's reluctance to do so casts doubt on the validity of his results. Shortly after Vicary's findings were revealed, a respected psychological firm tried to replicate his study under controlled conditions. Using more rigorous procedures, the psychologists reported no increase in purchases of either Coke or popcorn. In 1958, a Canadian broadcast network subliminally transmitted the message "Phone Now" 352 times during a Sunday night TV show. Telephone calls did not rise during this period, and no one called the station (Pratkanis, 1998).

Although these results cast doubt on the subliminal thesis, they do not disprove it. We're talking about only a couple of studies here. A more rigorous test involves dozens of carefully conducted experiments. Researchers have designed and conducted such studies, embedding messages in ads at levels that elude conscious awareness. They have compared the responses of experimental group participants who receive the subliminal stimuli with control group subjects who view a similar message without subliminals. These studies conclusively show that subliminal messages do not influence attitudes or behavior (Theus, 1994; Trappey, 1996). According to one scholar, the impact of subliminal advertising on consumers' decision making is roughly the same as "the relationship between alcohol abuse and a tour of duty in Vietnam"—in other words, negligible or nonexistent (Trappey, p. 517).

Although this may seem surprising in view of what you may have read on this topic over the years, it makes good psychological sense. Indeed, there are several reasons why one should not expect subliminally transmitted messages to influence consumer attitudes or behavior:

1. People have different thresholds for conscious awareness of stimuli. To influence a mass audience, a subliminal message would have to be so discretely beamed that it reached those with normal thresholds of awareness without catching the "attention" of those who are exquisitely sensitive to such stimuli. This would be difficult, perhaps impossible, to achieve using contemporary media.
2. There is no guarantee that consumers "see" or interpret the message in the manner that advertisers intend. (Conceivably, "Drink Coca-Cola" and "Eat Popcorn" moved so quickly across the screen that some moviegoers saw "Stink Coke" or "Beat Popcorn." This could have had the opposite impact on some viewers.)
3. For a subliminal message to influence attitudes, it must, at the very least, command the viewer's absolute attention. Such a situation is possible in the experimenter's laboratory, but not the real world. People are frequently distracted or doing other things when they watch TV or come across magazine advertisements.
4. Even if a subliminal message were embedded in an ad, it might still not get noticed, even at a subconscious level. The faintly detectable words or pictures would probably be overwhelmed by more powerful images or sounds that bombard the senses. Just because a message is "in" an ad does not mean it gets "inside" consumers. If it were that easy, everyone who works for ad agencies would be rich.

Self-Fulfilling Prophecies and Beyond

Research makes abundantly clear that subliminally transmitted messages do not influence consumer attitudes or behavior. But could the *belief* that subliminals are powerful influence one's attitudes toward an issue? Anthony G. Greenwald and his colleagues suspected that it could. As true-blue social scientists, they decided to test their intuition. They focused attention on a different kind of persuasive communication: therapeutic self-help tapes that claim subliminally embedded messages can help listeners solve personal problems.

Greenwald and associates (1991) observed that some self-help tapes promise to enhance self-esteem by subliminally beaming messages like "I have high self-worth and high self-esteem." Others attempt to improve memory skill by subliminally transmitting messages like "My ability to remember and recall is increasing daily." These words might be embedded underneath sounds, like waves lapping against a shore. Knowing the research as they did, Greenwald and his colleagues doubted that such subliminals would have any impact. However, they suspected that consumers' *expectations* that the subliminals were effective might strongly influence beliefs.

In an elaborate study using careful scientific procedures, Greenwald and his associates obtained strong support for their hypothesis. Individuals who heard an audiotape that contained the subliminal message, "I have high self-worth," did not exhibit any increase in self-esteem. In addition, those who listened to the tape that contained the "My ability to remember is increasing" message did not display improvements in memory. But the *belief* in subliminals' impact exerted a significant effect. Subjects who thought they had been listening to a tape designed to improve self-esteem (regardless of whether they actually had) believed their self-esteem had improved. Individuals who thought they had been listening to a memory audiotape (regardless of whether they had) were convinced their memory had gotten better!

The researchers argued that what they had discovered was "an illusory placebo effect—placebo, because it was based on expectations; illusory, because it wasn't real" (Pratkanis, 1998, p. 248). Their findings could also be viewed as another demonstration of the power of self-fulfilling prophecy. This is the idea that if you expect something to occur, sometimes it will, not because of the objective event itself but because you altered your thoughts; the alterations in cognitive structure then lead to changes in behavior.

Notice that a self-fulfilling prophecy operates on the conscious level, not the secretive, subconscious level at which subliminal ads are supposed to work.

This is all interesting, heady stuff. Little wonder that it has intrigued scholars over the course of the past several decades. Even today, about a half century after "Drink Coke, Eat Popcorn," students wonder if those flashy Internet banner ads will subliminally implant themselves into Web users' brains. Once again, it's doubtful. Although people can subliminally perceive information—we're not conscious of everything that slips into our mind 24 hours a day—this does not mean that even the most technologically sophisticated or niftiest subliminal communications can affect consumers' attitudes toward products. On the contrary, the scholarly literature says they can't. (In a similar vein, some people erroneously assume that supposedly subliminally embedded encryptions from terrorist groups will influence computer users. In fact, encryptions, or electronically scrambled information, are unreadable to computer users who come across them, but are decipherable *on a conscious level* to those who possess the private keys to decrypt the messages.)

In view of these bogus notions of subliminal message effects, the interesting question for many researchers is not the objective impact of subliminal stimuli, but the subjective issue. Why are so many people convinced that these short, psychologically vacuous messages have so great an impact on attitudes? Laura A. Brannon and Timothy C. Brock (1994) put forth several explanations for the persistence in belief in subliminal communications, including the assumption that "if something exists it must be having an effect" (p. 289). People also yearn for simple explanations of complex phenomena like advertising, and the subliminal thesis gives them a foolproof, conspiracy-type theory that seems to explain all of advertising's powerful influences on consumers.

With all this in mind, perhaps next time you read that liquor ads contain subliminally embedded faces or bikini-clad women, you might step back a moment and ask yourself a few questions. First, what evidence is there that these faces or scantily dressed women are actually in the ads, rather than a figment of the writer's sexually active imagination? Second, even if they are "there," what evidence exists that they influence perceptions? Third, assuming the stimuli influence perceptions (a large "if"), how realistic is it to assume that they influence consumers' attitudes or behavior? By approaching advertising this way, you will quickly recognize that the mad search for subliminals takes you down the wrong trail in the quest to understand advertising effects. To comprehend the effects of advertising, we need to appreciate the emotional power of ads, but must take a more sophisticated approach.

THE PSYCHOLOGY OF LOW INVOLVEMENT

A good way to appreciate the many effects of advertising is to dust off the Elaboration Likelihood Model discussed in chapter 5 and review its applications to commercial persuasion. Recall that the ELM tells us that people process information differently under high and low involvement, and this has important implications for persuasion strategies. Can you think of products that are personally important, mean a lot to you, and fulfill key psychological functions? These are high-involvement purchases. You are highly involved in the consumption of these products, probably thinking about them a lot, or reckoning that you have something to lose if you make the wrong choice (Mittal, 1995). For most people, these products include cars, computers, CD players, and clothing they wear to work. Now consider the other side of the coin—products that you purchase that are of little personal concern, don't matter much to you, are mundane, and don't stimulate much thought. These are low-involvement purchases. They include soft drinks, countless grocery store products, and convenience goods like paper towels, tissue paper, and toothpaste (see Fig. 11.1).

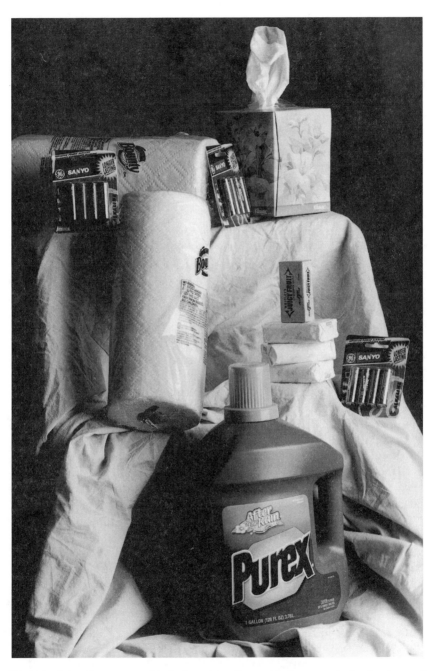

FIG. 11.1 Advertisers use a host of peripheral appeals to promote low-involvement products like these. (Photograph by William C. Rieter.)

The ELM emphasizes that people process messages peripherally under low involvement and are, therefore, susceptible to simple appeals. Under high involvement, individuals think more centrally and deeply, taking into account the merits of the product and values stimulated by the ad. Advertising for high-involvement products cogently describes tangible benefits associated with the products. Ads also attempt to connect products with deep-seated values. The ELM has many interesting implications for advertising effects, suggesting, as it does, that we look separately at low- and high-involving advertising appeals. The next sections explore this approach.

Mere Exposure

According to the mere exposure thesis, simple exposure to communications can influence attitudes. Merely seeing a message repeated over and over again leads to liking (Zajonc, 1968). This is a familiar experience. The longer you gaze at a painting in a museum, the more times you hear a hip-hop song on your CD player, and the more frequently you see an advertisement on TV, the more you come to like these stimuli.

Mere exposure is a strong, robust persuasion phenomenon. It works! Research conducted over the past decades provides strong support for the theory (Bornstein, 1989). Psychologists are not sure exactly why repetition leads to liking, but they believe it has something to do with the reduction of irritation that occurs after seeing or hearing a stimulus many times. The first time television viewers saw the Taco Bell ad in which the little Chihuahua utters, "Yo quiero Taco Bell" ("I want Taco Bell"), they probably were a little confused by the phrase and put off by the presence of a smirking, talking dog in an ad for a fast-food franchise. But with repetition, they got used to the ad, adjusted to the smug little dog, and developed a sense of what would occur as the quirky ad unfolded. The more they saw the ad, the more comfortable they felt and the more they liked it.

Mere exposure places more importance on form than content. It is the format—repeated exposure to a neutral stimulus—that matters, not the content of the ad. In early research on the topic, psychologists asked people to pronounce a variety of nonsense words—for example, *afworbu*, *civrada*, and *nansoma*. The words had no inherent meaning or semantic significance. Yet the more frequently individuals were exposed to the words, the more favorably they evaluated them (Zajonc, 1968). In the same fashion, the more we hear advertising slogans like "Whassup?" (Budweiser) or the time-honored "Double your pleasure, double your fun" (Doublemint gum), or see goofy animals (the Energizer Bunny), the more favorably we evaluate these ads and the products. People made fun of the old Charmin toilet paper ads ("Please don't squeeze the Charmin").

However, the ads apparently worked as Charmin, never known to consumers before, captured a significant share of the market after its nonstop
advertising campaigns.

Is repetition a panacea, a factor that always works? No way! Mere
exposure is most effective under certain conditions. First, it works best
for neutral products and issues—those to which we have not yet developed a strong attitude. It explains how advertising *forms* attitudes toward
products, not how it *changes* them. Second, once people have developed
an especially negative attitude toward a product, company, or politician
for that matter, repetition cannot change the attitude. In fact, it may have
the opposite effect, producing more negative affect toward the issue as
people ruminate about how much they hate the fast-food product, big
corporation, or obnoxious politician (Tesser, 1978).

Finally, you can repeat an advertisement too many times. After a certain point, repetition leads to boredom, tedium, and irritation. A phenomenon known as *wear-out* occurs (Bornstein, 1989; Solomon, 1999).
Early in the mere exposure curve, repetition is a positive experience,
reducing uncertainty, inducing calm, and bringing on a certain amount
of pleasure. After a certain point, repetition has the opposite effect, and
people become annoyed with the ad. Repetition ceases to lead to positive
affect and can induce negative feelings toward the ad or product (see
Fig. 11.2). This is one reason why companies like McDonald's and Coke
frequently switch slogans and change advertising agencies. They want to
prevent wear-out and preserve the effect of a novel campaign slogan.

The Magic of Association

There's a marvelous McDonald's ad I have shown in the classroom over
the years. It never fails to bring forth smiles and to elicit positive reactions

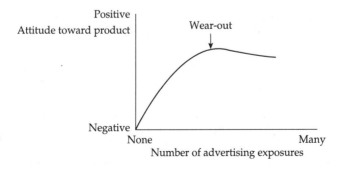

FIG. 11.2 Repetition, advertising, and wear-out. After a certain number of repetitions,
advertising can lead to wear-out.

from students who view it. The ad begins with a football coach lecturing a team of 8-year-old boys. He intones, "A great man once said, 'Winning, gentlemen, isn't everything, it's the only thing.' " Suddenly we hear one of the boys, obviously oblivious to the coach's serious tone, shout, "Look, a grasshopper." All the youngsters jump up to take a look. The coach throws down his hat in mock despair. Another coach, kneeling down, says seriously to one of the boys, "I-formation, 34 sweep, on 2. Got it?" When the boy, doing his best to understand but obviously bewildered, shakes his head, the coach says, "Just give the ball to Matt. Tell him to run for his daddy, okay?" The boy nods happily.

As the camera pans the oh-so-cute boys in their blue uniforms; shows us the misty, but picture-perfect, football day; and lets us watch the players do push-ups while fathers feverishly peer through video cameras to record their sons' every movement, we hear the narrator say, "It starts every September with teams like the Turkey Creek Hawks and the Bronx Eagles." Alas, these September days are about more than just winning football games, the narrator goes on to suggest; they're about dads and sons, good times, and—now the pitch—where you go after the game. Soft, sentimental music builds as the scene slowly shifts to what must be a later point in time—the boys smiling and enjoying themselves at McDonald's, no doubt chomping down burgers and fries. And so, the narrator intones, the scene moving back to football, McDonald's would like to salute the players, coaches, and team spirit that are part of these fall September days. The visual then profiles a boy, looking up at the "winning-isn't-everything" coach. "Can we go to McDonald's now, Coach?" he asks. Patiently, kindly, but firmly, the coach notes, "Sit down, Lenny. It's only halftime." The music, playing softly in the background, trails off and fades, as the ad gently comes to a close.

The advertisement illustrates the principle of association. It associates the good feelings produced by football, boys playing pigskin on weekend afternoons, and autumn with the fast-food franchise, McDonald's. It has linked these images seamlessly, though obviously, using an indirect strategy to promote McDonald's. McDonald's has not told us the reasons why its hamburgers are tasty (that might be a hard sell, given what we know about fast-food diets!). It has not provided cogent arguments that dining at McDonald's is a healthy, useful activity for budding athletes. In fact the ad has provided neither argument nor logic. Instead it has employed the rich language of emotion, telling us a story, associating McDonald's with positive, pleasant images that are peripheral to the purchase decision. If you tried the same technique in a job that required you to provide arguments why clients should purchase your product, trying to associate your product with good times, all the while humming a sentimental tune, you would be fired! Yet McDonald's succeeds because the world of advertising is not purely or primarily rational. It invariably prefers emotion to syllogistic logic. It frequently favors Aristotle's pathos to his deductive logos.

There are countless examples of the use of association in advertising, ranging from perfume and cologne ads that link their products with sex appeal to cigarette ads that associate their brands with relaxation, good times, and virile masculinity (see Box 11–1). Association is perhaps the most important reason why advertising succeeds. It explains why *things*—material objects with no inherent value—acquire powerful meanings (near-magical auras) in consumers' eyes. Scholars have advanced several theories to explain how association works. They include **classical conditioning** and **semiotics**.

BOX 11–1
CIGARETTE ADVERTISING

An antismoking videotape shown in college classrooms offers an intriguing insight into the strategies tobacco companies use to market cigarettes. The video begins as magazine ads and billboards depict attractive young people smiling and relaxing while smoking a Kool or Virginia Slims. Smoke wafts up from a lit cigarette, as a guitar plays and a gentle male voice sings:

If you want some real contentment to live life at its best,
You can buy these dried tobacco leaves to breathe into your chest.
And then look up at the billboard while all the promises come true . . . for you.
You'll feel alive with pleasure, playful as a child
You've come to where the freedom is.
You're cool and mild . . .
So look up at the billboard, see her smile and sexy intent
But the only one who's laughing is the advertising man. (Kilbourne & Pollay, 1992)

Cigarette advertising, a multibillion dollar business around the globe, exploits psychological strategies to hook young people into smoking or to convince satisfied customers to stick with their brands. Ads have associated cigarettes with the pristine outdoors, sexuality, and rugged independence (as in the American icon, the Marlboro Man). Appeals geared to young women play on the psychological functions cigarettes serve, like independence and autonomy. The copy in a Virginia Slims ad says, "I always take the driver's seat. That way I'm never taken for a ride." Because cigarettes cannot be advertised on radio or TV in the United States, advertisers have relied on a variety of other techniques to promote their product, including billboards, magazine ads, event sponsorship, and linking their logos with athletic contests and rock concerts, a practice known as brand-stretching
Continued

BOX 11–1
(CONTINUED)

(Campbell, Martin, & Fabos, 2002). Movies like *Basic Instinct*, *Pulp Fiction*, *My Best Friend's Wedding*, and *Titanic* depicted characters smoking, with apparent enjoyment. In some cases tobacco companies paid movie producers to place cigarettes in their films (Basil, 1997). In an effort to reach the burgeoning youth market, multinational cigarette companies have distributed tobacco-branded clothing abroad, and in the United States have plastered cigarette logos on candy and children's toys.

Perhaps the most famous mass-marketing technique is Old Joe, the cigarette-puffing cartoon character promoting Camels. Several studies reported that Old Joe is recognized by more than 91% of children (e.g., Fischer et al., 1991; Horovitz & Wells, 1997). However, now that cigarette advertising cannot be displayed on large billboards, in sports arenas, or other public places, tobacco companies have taken their graphic, hedonistic images to another venue: the World Wide Web. The Web is a potential gold mine for cigarette advertising. Marketers can deliver moving images and interactive features to a captive audience of kids who love to surf the Net and delight in playing "grown-up" by revealing consumer information to companies. One study found that cigarettes are a "pervasive presence" on the Web, especially on sites that sell products or feature hobbies and recreation. Sites associate smoking with glamorous lifestyles and with thin, physically appealing women (Hong & Cody, 2001).

In light of increases in teen smoking, evidence that more than one third of high school students smoke, and statistics showing that 90% of smokers begin during adolescence, there has been much concern about the effects of such marketing on children (Brown & Walsh-Childers, 2002). Yet so many factors influence smoking behavior—including parental smoking and having siblings who smoke—that it is difficult to parcel out the unique contribution advertising makes. Researchers are not of one mind on this subject. Some scholars are quick to point out that kids may recognize Joe Camel, but have no intention of lighting up a Camel or any other cigarette for that matter (McDonald, 1993).

Even so, the scholarly consensus is that cigarette advertising predicts increased consumption of cigarettes, and that ads increase the symbolic attractiveness of cigarettes, particularly among young people (Andrews & Franke, 1991; Pierce et al., 1998; Schooler et al., 1996). Teenagers are by nature triers and product experimenters. Searching for ways to gain belonging and independence, some adolescents are attracted to cigarettes, and advertising enhances their appeal as badges of youthful identity—products some teens "wear," along with clothing, earrings, and tattoos (Pollay, 1997, p. 62).

What's more, a related marketing strategy—point-of-purchase cigarette marketing—appears to be highly effective. With mass-media advertising being phased out, in the wake of the legal agreement between the state attorneys general and the tobacco industry, the tobacco industry is spending close to $3 billion on aggressively marketing cigarettes in retail establishments like convenience stores. Convenience stores are a prime location, as many young people frequently shop there. In some stores, more than 20 tobacco ads greet customers. The ads, positioned so they catch young people's attention, have marked effects on adolescents' perceptions of tobacco. One study found that in-store promotions significantly enhanced eighth- and ninth-graders' perceptions of the accessibility and popularity of cigarettes, factors that increase the chances young people will begin smoking (Henriksen et al., 2002).

All of this raises important ethical questions. Cigarette marketing unquestionably pushes the ethical envelope of persuasion to its limits. Yet even its fiercest critics acknowledge that tobacco marketing—and advertising in particular—is not *coercive*. People are free to accept or reject advertising's deceptive appeals. Ads are not threatening individuals with sanctions if they don't light up. More broadly, cigarette consumption is legal, and companies have a right to promote their products through the mass media. And yet advertisers associate cigarettes with benefits (sex appeal, ruggedness, independence) that are unlikely to materialize in reality, while saying nothing about the dirty, addictive aspects of the product. Such ads surely must be criticized by those who value honesty and truth telling, particularly to young, vulnerable members of the audience. Legal scholars have noted that cigarette advertising is protected under the First Amendment; yet this does not make it ethically permissible or worthy of endorsement on moral grounds.

It is a complex debate, the question of cigarette advertising—and tobacco marketing more generally. Defenders point to the value of individual liberty and need to preserve a society in which media can promote any product that consumers desire, even those that can kill them. Critics point to the sham of advertisers spending millions of dollars to come up with ever more clever ways to hook young people into depending psychologically on a life-threatening product. Is this the kind of society we want, they retort?

Particularly problematic are tobacco companies' blatant attempts to hook young people into smoking. "The clearest statement (of this)," reporter Philip J. Hilts (1996) discovered, after extensively studying cigarette marketing, "came in a question and answer period at a regional (R. J. Reynolds Company) sales meeting. Someone asked exactly who the young people were that were being targeted, junior high school kids, or even younger?"

The reply came back "They got lips? We want 'em." (Hilts, p. 98).

Classical Conditioning. The granddaddy of association concepts, conditioning dates back to Pavlov. "Does the name Pavlov ring a bell?" Cialdini (2001) asks humorously, reminding us of the Russian psychologist's century-old study that paired an unconditioned stimulus (food) with a conditioned stimulus (bell) to produce a conditioned response (salivation to the bell). Psychologists have applied classical conditioning to social learning, particularly attitude acquisition. In a study conducted in a post-World War II era preoccupied with understanding how Nazi-type prejudice could have developed, Staats and Staats (1958) showed that individuals could acquire negative attitudes toward the word "Dutch" simply by hearing it paired with words that had negative connotations ("ugly," "failure"). In a similar fashion, consumer behavior scholars have shown that attitudes toward products can be classically conditioned through association with pleasant images (Grossman & Till, 1998; Stuart, Shimp, & Engle, 1987).

Classical conditioning processes help us understand how people develop favorable attitudes toward products. However, conditioning is a rather primitive model that does not take into account: (a) people's symbolic representations of objects in their minds, and (b) how they mentally link images with products. Consequently, we need to examine another view of association in advertising.

Semiotics. Semiotics is the study of signs and symbols. It helps us understand how *signs*—visual objects or geometric shapes with no inherent meaning—take on a rich tapestry of social and cultural meaning. A *symbol* is a sign with substance—a sign that bursts with value and emotional signification. Viewed as it might have been prior to Nazi Germany, the swastika is merely a strange, twisted shape. Yet, merged with Hitler's rhetoric and German atrocities, it becomes a symbol of hate, anti-Semitism, and crimes against humanity. The Cross and Star of David are shapes, but as symbols they are much more. The Cross symbolizes Jesus' crucifixion and redemption—an emblem of Christian Love. The Star of David, a six-pointed star formed by superimposing two equilateral triangles, is a symbol of Judaism, Jewish culture, and the State of Israel.

Advertising—like religion and politics—thrives on signs. It transforms signs into symbols that give a product its meaning or "zip" (Goldman & Papson, 1996). Take a look at the signs in Fig. 11.3. Glance first at Coca-Cola, closing your eyes to gain a clearer fix on the image. Do the same for the Nike Swoosh and McDonald's. What comes to mind? Images, feelings, pictures, people? I'd be willing to bet they did, even if you don't like the products or purchase them. Such is the power of advertising. It attempts to fill commodity signs with meaning, to give value to brands, and to stamp imagery onto products that differ only trivially from their

FIG. 11.3   Well-known signs and symbols in American advertising (see also Goldman & Papson, 1996).

competitors. Consider that classic entry in the sneaker wars, the Nike Swoosh. As Robert Goldman and Stephen Papson (1996) observe:

> Once upon a time, the Nike swoosh symbol possessed no intrinsic value as a sign, but value was added to the sign by drawing on the name and image value of celebrity superstars like Michael Jordan. Michael Jordan possesses value in his own right—the better his performances, the higher his value. The sign of Nike acquired additional value when it joined itself to the image of Jordan. Similarly, when Nike introduced a new shoe line named "Air Huarache" and wanted to distinguish its sign from those of other shoe lines, Nike adopted John Lennon's song "Instant Karma," as a starting point for the shoe's sign value. Nike justified drawing on Lennon's classic song by insisting that it was chosen because it dovetailed with Nike's own message of "self-improvement: making yourself better." (p. 10)

This was the Nike "advertising sign machine" of the late 1980s and '90s, featuring associations between its Swoosh and Jordan, Bo ("Bo Knows") Jackson, and Spike Lee. Since then, Nike has embarked on numerous ad campaigns, including ones that feature commercials resembling MTV videos—brilliant, but blatant, attempts to associate the Swoosh with images resonant with a younger market. Nike, like other advertisers, strives constantly to redefine its image in the eyes of a new market niche through ever-inventive ways of combining signs with in-vogue celebrities, trends, and images.

Yet for all of its insights, semiotics does not explain how advertising creeps into the minds of consumers. It is a theory of message content, not message effects. To understand associative advertising impact, we must turn to cognitive psychological concepts. Consider that advertising shapes attitudes toward products by helping forge an association between the product and a pleasant, memorable image. Once the attitude is formed, it must be retrieved or accessed, particularly at the moment when consumers are making a product decision. **Accessibility,** the extent to which people can "call up" an attitude from memory, comes to the fore when discussing advertising's effects on attitudes. Research discussed in chapter 2 suggests that the more exposure consumers have to advertisements that plant the association between a product and image, the more they can quickly get in touch with their attitude when they are trying to decide which soft drink, fast food, or sneaker to purchase. Advertisers recognize this and try to influence the extent to which people can activate product attitudes from memory.

Thus, McDonald's ads try to induce consumers who are in the mood for fast food to call up the feelings they had when they watched an ad like the one described earlier. Coke tries to access years of internalized associations between its product and positive images. These include mid-20th-century linkages between Coca-Cola and patriotic appeals that call to mind artist Norman Rockwell; the classic 1971 song that associated Coke with global, ethnic diversity ("I'd like to buy the world a Coke and keep it company. It's the real thing"); and current multicultural campaigns that span Egypt, Saudi Arabia, and South Africa (see Box 11–2). In the view of some observers, Coke may have even built and activated associations between its soft drink and the Christian religion! A minister once told a Coca-Cola bottler, "I see a strange connection between your slogan, 'The pause that refreshes,' and Christ's own words, 'Come unto me all ye that travail, and I will refresh you' " (Martin, 2000). In these ways, Coke ads give powerful meanings to a "mixture of water, carbon dioxide, sugar, flavorings, and colorings" (Myers, 1999, p. 7).

BOX 11–2
SELLING GOD, COUNTRY, AND COKE

How did a drink composed of sugar, caramel, caffeine, lime juice, and kola nuts become a multibillion dollar seller? How, in short, did Coke become "the real thing"? In two words: "advertising" and "marketing," conclude authors like Mark Pendergrast, who wrote the book, *For God, Country and Coca-Cola*. Based on his research, Pendergrast offers a number of suggestions on how to market products like Coke through mass media. They include the following:

1. **Sell a good product.** And if it contains a small dose of an addictive drug or two, all the better.
2. **Develop a mystique.** An air of mystery, with a touch of sin, sells.
3. **Sell a cheaply produced item.** Coca-Cola has always cost only a fraction of a cent per drink to produce.
4. **Make your product widely available.**

5. **Use celebrity endorsements wisely—but sparingly.**
6. **Get 'em young.** Obviously, if you can achieve loyalty among youthful consumers, you've possibly fostered lifelong consumption.
7. **Develop cultural sensitivity.** If you intend to sell your product around the world, do not trap yourself in an "Ugly American" image.
8. **Be flexible enough to change.**
9. **Pay attention to the bottom line.**
10. **Advertise an image, not a product.** As one Coke advertiser liked to remind his creative staff, "We're selling smoke. They're drinking the image, not the product" (Pendergrast, 2000, pp. 461–465).

Other advertisements employ similar strategies. Ads for Levi's 501 jeans, particularly outside the United States, attempt to call up connections between jeans and such positive values as youth, rebelliousness, and the U.S.A. The American commercial icon, Campbell's Soup, spent much of the 20th century building powerful linkages between its product and down-home days with Mom and Dad (albeit of the White variety). Campbell's ads seemingly left an imprint, as one consumer acknowledged:

> Campbell's tomato soup is the only one that will do. It's like a cozy, comforting thing. It tastes good mainly because you associate it with what it did for you when you were a kid. Maybe it doesn't even taste that good, but somehow it works on a level beyond just your taste buds. (Langer, 1997, p. 61)

In these ways advertisers subtly build associations into signs, products, and brands, transforming things into symbols of desire, warmth, and hope, and making objects the stuff of dreams (Langrehr & Caywood, 1995; McCracken, 1986). Although ads do not always exert this impact—the floors in advertising agencies are littered with footage from unsuccessful meaning-making campaigns—ads can potently influence affect toward products. In light of advertising's widely recognized ability to shape product attitudes, it is little wonder that people unschooled in advertising effects leapt onto the subliminal seduction bandwagon.

Peripheral Processing

The ELM's emphasis on peripheral processes complements discussion of association and mere exposure. When consumers are in a low-involvement mode—as most are when they encounter ads for soft drink, lip balm, paper towel, and toothpaste products—they process ads through the peripheral route. Repeated exposure and associations serve as peripheral cues; so do source factors, like celebrity endorsements and use of sexually attractive product endorsers.

Celebrities are particularly interesting and potentially powerful source factors. Celebrities transfer meanings from their cultural identity to the product. As researcher Grant McCracken (1989) observed:

> No mere model could bring to Baly-Matrix the properties that Cher delivers, nor could any model have summoned the impatient, time-tested integrity, John Houseman gave the Smith-Barney line "We make money the old-fashioned way, we earn it." Only a man playing Houseman's roles in the way Houseman played them could empower the slogan as Houseman did. Celebrities have particular configurations of meaning that cannot be found elsewhere. (p. 315)

Celebrities are particularly apt to enhance consumer attitudes when their characteristics "match up with," or are relevant to, the product being promoted (Chew et al., 1994; Lynch & Schuler, 1994). For example, when Michael Jordan and soccer star Mia Hamm promoted Nike, their athletic expertise was salient. It served as a simple "click-whirr" reason to prefer Nike sneakers (Cialdini, 2001). Ditto for Bob Dole, the former senator who product-endorsed Viagra after running unsuccessfully for president at the age of 73.

Celebrity characteristics do not always match product attributes, however. Former professional football quarterback Joe Montana promoted Diet Pepsi. So did Ray Charles, in an amusing skit that played on his knowledge of his blindness. Pop singers Britney Spears and Shakira celebrity-endorsed Pepsi. In these cases, their fame bonded to the product, enhancing its sign value.

Celebrities' physical attractiveness can also serve as a peripheral cue. Attractiveness can influence attitudes by blending, association-style, with the product, or it can work by stimulating identification processes ("I want to 'be like Mike' "). (Celebrity endorsers can net advertisers millions, but they also can be persuasive liabilities, as Pepsi discovered years ago when Madonna created controversy for her "Like a Prayer" video. Pepsi pulled the ad. And then there's the case of once-in-demand, now-taboo, O. J. Simpson.)

Ads can also work peripherally simply by putting low-involved consumers in a good mood. Just being in a good mood can influence positive affect toward products, without impacting beliefs in the slightest (see Petty et al., 1993). Pleasant music, goofy gimmicks (Budweiser's frogs), and incongruous, humorous situations can put people in a good mood.

This can increase memory and liking of the ad, which can influence brand attitudes (Muehling & McCann, 1993).

The same consumer psychology applies when people process Internet advertising under low-involvement conditions. When cruising the Net in a low-involved state or glancing over banner ads for products that don't touch on important needs, consumers are apt to be swayed by attention-grabbing cues, like the size, color, and dynamic animation of banner ads (Cho, 1999).

HIGH INVOLVEMENT

Another category of advertising concerns high-involvement products—those that are important to us personally, touch on our self-concepts, or are big-ticket, expensive items (see Fig. 11.4). When consumers are in the market for an ordinarily high-involvement product, like a car, jewelry, computer, or even clothing, they process ads centrally. The Elaboration Likelihood Model emphasizes that under high-involvement conditions, people consider the merits of the product, connect the product to core values, and systematically process product commercials (Andrews & Shimp, 1990; Roehm & Haugtvedt, 1999). They carefully process factual information like price and consider the material benefits of the purchase (see Fig. 11.5). When they are on-line and come across banner ads for high-involvement products like cars, consumers may be uninfluenced by the ads' size or color. Instead, they may be especially likely to click the ads to request more information about the product (Cho, 1999). As a general rule, strong, cogent arguments on behalf of the product should carry the day.

But what constitutes a strong, cogent argument on behalf of a product? On this point, our ordinarily useful Elaboration Likelihood Model lets us down. It doesn't tell us the specific arguments that are likely to be most compelling under high consumer involvement. To identify the types of messages that are apt to resonate with people purchasing personally important products, we need to turn to another persuasion theory. Functional theory, discussed in chapter 3, helps bridge consumer attitudes and persuasion. You may recall that the functional approach says that attitudes serve specific psychological functions or needs for individuals. Messages are most likely to influence attitudes if they target the function the attitude serves. Let's see how this works in the case of advertising.

Some attitudes serve a **utilitarian** function. People purchase products to gain specific, tangible rewards (Shavitt & Nelson, 2000). Parents who need a minivan to transport their kids, pets, or groceries have utilitarian

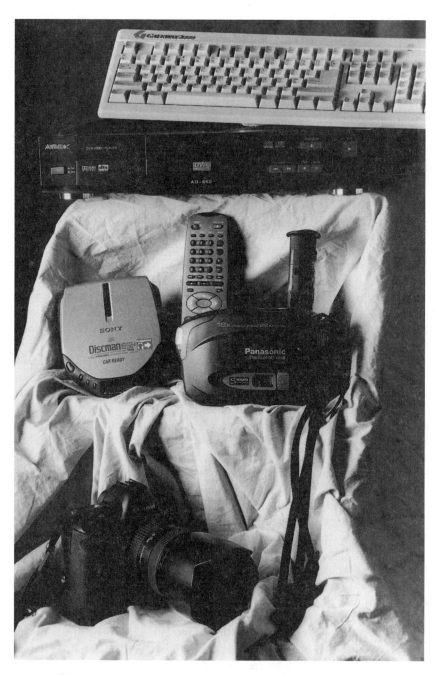

FIG. 11.4 To many consumers, computer, photographic, and electronic products are highly involving. Advertisers use factual, social, and value-based appeals to promote these products. (Photograph by William C. Rieter.)

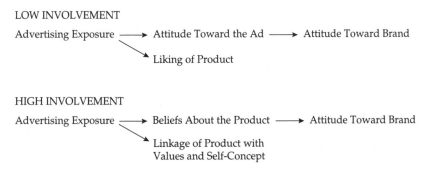

LOW INVOLVEMENT

Advertising Exposure ———➤ Attitude Toward the Ad ———➤ Attitude Toward Brand

➤ Liking of Product

HIGH INVOLVEMENT

Advertising Exposure ———➤ Beliefs About the Product ———➤ Attitude Toward Brand

➤ Linkage of Product with
Values and Self-Concept

FIG. 11.5 Involvement and brand attitudes (From Mitchell, "Effects of Visual and Verbal Components of Advertisements on Brand Attitudes," JOURNAL OF CONSUMER RESEARCH 13 (1986), pp. 12–24).

reasons for purchasing a car. Ads targeted at these parents commonly emphasize the passenger space and roominess of, say, a Chevy Suburban or Honda Odyssey.

People buy products for reasons other than tangible benefits. They buy to fulfill ambitions, dreams, and fantasies. Thus, product attitudes serve symbolic, as well as material, functions.

For example, some attitudes serve a **social-adjustive** function. People purchase products to gain acceptance from peers. One mother confessed that "in my neighborhood, if you don't have a brand name bicycle, the kids rib you. We had to go out and buy (my son) a $300 bike so the kids would leave him alone. He was getting harassed because he had a cheaper bike" (Langer, 1997, p. 64). Although the mother's comment may seem silly or petty or worse, it does reflect a common perspective toward products. Advertising designed to reach this mom might hype the brand name of the bike or suggest that the advertised bike is a best-seller among kids.

Product attitudes also serve a **social identity** function. Consumers purchase cars, jewelry, and other highly involving goods to enhance their identities—to set them apart from others. People buy big-ticket items to gain status, look cool, show off an identity to others, or express love. Ads appeal to these needs, using pictures, images, and the syntax of advertising to suggest that owning products makes you happy. "May promote feelings of superiority," a tag line for a Nissan car unabashedly stated.

Advertisements for highly involving products also employ associational appeals, but they invite deeper processing than do association-based appeals for low-involving products. As Paul Messaris (1997) notes:

> In the single category of automotive ads, one can encounter analogies to lions (Toyota), tigers (Exxon), cheetahs (BMW), military aircraft (Dodge, Honda, Jaguar, etc.), and Fabergé eggs (Lincoln). . . . If the creator of an ad

wants to make the point that a certain car is powerful, the verbal text can convey this message explicitly, through such words as "dynamic," "breath-taking," "supercharged," or, indeed, "powerful." When it comes to the ad's pictorial content, though, this aspect of verbal syntax, the adjective–noun relationship, has no direct visual counterpart. One alternative, then, is simply to show an image of the car accelerating rapidly and trust the viewer to make the appropriate inference. . . . Showing the car next to some other object or entity that also possesses power increases the likelihood that the viewer will get the point, not so much because of the doubling of powerful objects as because the juxtaposition should lead the viewer to intuit what it is that they have in common. (pp. 191,193)

Consumer attitudes also serve a **value-expressive** function. Individuals purchase products to express deep-seated values. People with strong environmental attitudes steer clear of things that damage the environment and seek out products that are environmentally friendly. Advertisers target environmentally conscious consumers by playing up concern for ecology in their ads. The Body Shop plays up its opposition to scientific testing of animals. L. L. Bean advertises its "durable, practical products for men and women who love the outdoors" (Goldman & Papson, p. 194). Advertisers take code words like *recycling* and *green* and cleverly associate them with their products. In these ways they try to convince middle-class Baby Boomers and Gen Xers that they can shop til they drop, while at the same time purchasing products that are oh-so environmentally correct.

Value-based appeals have long been a staple of advertising. In fact, advertising agencies have developed elaborate strategies to measure consumers' values and lifestyle choices, hoping to tailor ads to match the values of particular audience segments. Automobile companies, hoping to solidify their niche in the competitive car market, have been particularly concerned with tapping into consumers' values. Some years back they discovered that minivan buyers sought out cars for different reasons than sport-utility customers. Summarizing market research on the topic, a reporter noted that "minivan buyers tend to be more comfortable than sport utility buyers with being married; sport utility buyers are more commonly concerned with still feeling sexy, and like the idea that they could use their vehicles to start dating again" (Bradsher, 2000, p. A1). Minivan buyers are more apt to participate in family gatherings and in conversations with friends. The more restless, self-focused sport-utility owners prefer to dine at fine restaurants, go to sporting events, or physically work out.

Advertisers have exploited these findings. Ads for Ford's Windstar minivan feature a dozen mothers and their kids arrayed around a Windstar. The ads note that the moms are all Ford employees who worked together to redesign the van. In contrast, a TV ad for Jeep Grand Cherokee Limited depicts a driver who had to climb a pile of rocks that blocked access to his mansion. Automobile designers also take advantage of value-based marketing studies. They design SUVs so that they are masculine and aggressive, "often with hoods that resemble those on 18-wheel trucks (and) vertical metal slats across the grilles to give the appearance of a jungle cat's teeth. . . . By contrast . . . sedans and station wagons have open grilles that look toothless" (Bradsher, p. A16).

Summary

Advertisers centrally process high-involved consumers, just as highly involved viewers centrally scrutinize ads. Advertising executives like to stay one step ahead of the consumer, using market research to devise ads that match the functions products serve for individuals in a given culture (Han & Shavitt, 1994).

In addition to functional theory, the Elaboration Likelihood Model helps us understand the effects of advertising. Involvement, the centerpiece of the discussion, has complex influences. A particular product (for example, shampoo) can be low involving for one consumer and highly involving to another. As noted in chapter 5, a particular factor (a model's attractiveness) can function as a peripheral cue, argument, or catalyst for additional thought. Complicating matters even further, involvement is not a static variable in the world of advertising. Advertisers frequently try to convince people that a low-involving product (sneakers) is of deep, personal importance. Global events also shake up consumers' involvement with goods and services. Airline advertising used to be a low-involvement game. After September 11, airline safety became an issue of paramount importance, necessitating a change in airlines' TV appeals.

THE ROLE OF PERSONALITY

Another factor that enters into the psychology of advertising is personality. Individuals differ in their evaluations of advertising. Advertisers take this into account when they devise ads that appeal to different personality types or audience niches. The personality factor that has generated the most attention is one discussed earlier in this book—self-monitoring. You may recall that image-conscious high self-monitors differ in a variety of ways from the relentlessly "Be yourself" low self-monitors. High self-monitors adopt attitudes for social-adjustive purposes, to help them fit into social situations. Low self-monitors hold attitudes for value-expressive reasons, to assist them in expressing their core views toward life.

Psychologist Kenneth G. DeBono argued that these differences in the functional basis of attitudes have interesting implications for advertising. High self-monitors, he suspected, should be especially responsive to advertising messages that help one adjust one's image to fit a particular situation. Low self-monitors, by contrast, should be more influenced by ads that call attention to the intrinsic value or performance of the product.

DeBono tested his ideas in a series of intriguing experiments. As he suspected, high self-monitors were especially influenced by "soft-sell" appeals that called attention to the image one could project by purchasing the product. Low self-monitors were swayed more by "hard-sell" ads that highlighted the quality or durability of the product (DeBono, 2000; Snyder & DeBono, 1985). These findings can be easily applied to advertising campaigns. Advertisements frequently highlight the image associated with owning a product. Such ads should be more effective with high- than low self-monitors. For example, this classic, savvy Sprite ad of a few years back geared to a female market should be particularly influential with high self-monitoring women:

> You're a woman
> of the 90's.
> Bold, self-assured and empowered.
> Climbing the ladder of success at work
> and the Stairmaster at the gym.
> You're socially aware and politically correct.
> But you probably know all this already
> because every ad and magazine
> has told you a zillion times.
> No wonder you're thirsty. (Goldman & Papson, p. 264)

On the other hand, this MasterCard ad, exploiting the desire for authenticity, should appeal more to low self-monitors. The ad shows a guy sitting on top of a hill overlooking a lovely Mediterranean town. As he gazes into the distance, the narrator remarks:

> Alright, brace yourselves. Your credit line has nothing to do with your value as a person, OK? You could have a shiny Gold MasterCard with a credit line of at least $5000, I don't care. It doesn't make you a better person. (He pauses, and shifting his tone of voice he wonders aloud:) Well, I don't know, maybe it does? I mean if knowing that the Master Assist Plan can refer you to a good doctor or lawyer anywhere in the world, let you relax and stop being so uptight and just have fun and be yourself—then, yeah, I suppose a Gold MasterCard could have some effect. (Goldman & Papson, pp. 143–144)

Keep in mind that these are general predictions. There is not one type of low-self-monitoring consumer, nor one kind of high-self-monitoring buyer (Slama & Singley, 1996). Low self-monitors like jazzy products, and high self-monitors don't want products that will break once they buy them. Nonetheless, research on self-monitoring reminds us that one size does not fit all when it comes to advertising, and that advertising is more apt to be effective when it targets the needs that products fulfill.

ADVERTISING ETHICS

It is a lot easier to document advertising effects than to arrive at universally accepted conclusions about its ethics. Long before the arrival of Old Joe Camel and the Budweiser frogs, critics debated the ethics of advertising. Adopting a deontological approach (see chapter 1), critics have argued that the test of ethical communication is whether it treats people as an end, not a means—or, more practically, whether the communicators' motives are honorable or decent. Viewed in this way, advertising can fall drastically short of an ethical ideal. Advertisers develop ads that make promises they know products can't deliver. Cigarettes don't offer hedonistic pleasure; cars don't make you rich or famous; and making pancakes for your kids on Saturday won't assuage your guilt about neglecting them all week, despite the plaintive plea of a Bisquik pancake commercial.

Advertisers want consumers to project fantasies onto products in order to hook individuals on the image of the brand. Viewed from a deontological perspective, advertising is not ethical because advertisers are not truthful. If the decency of the communicators' motives is the criterion for ethical communication, advertising fails. Advertisers deliberately construct fantasies to serve their clients' needs, not to aid the customer in living a healthier, happier life.

Responding to these criticisms, defenders of advertising note that consumers recognize that advertising creates untruths. They do not expect ads to tell them "the way things really are in society," Messaris (1997) notes. "Almost by definition," he says, "the portrayals of the good life presented in ads carry with them the implicit understanding that they are idealizations, not documentary reports" (p. 268). In effect, advertising defenders say, "Don't worry; be happy." Advertising is capitalism's playful communication, an effort to give people an outlet for universal human fantasies.

In the end, the verdict on advertising depends on the criteria we use to judge it. Judged in terms of consequences on society, advertising's effects are ambiguous. Exposure to beautiful people or unimaginable wealth may cause dissatisfaction in some consumers (Richins, 1991), but can lead others to reach for loftier goals. Judged strictly on truth-telling criteria, advertising rarely makes product claims that are demonstrably false.

However, it almost always exaggerates, puffs up products, and links products with intangible rewards. "All advertising tells lies," Leslie Savan (1994) says. However, she notes that "there are little lies and there are big lies. Little lie: This beer tastes great. Big lie: This beer makes *you* great" (p. 7).

In the final analysis, advertising will remain an ethically problematic, but necessary, part of capitalist society. Needed to differentiate and promote products that (truth be told) differ only trivially from one another, advertising keeps the engines of the free market economy rolling. It increases demand and allows companies to sell products, prosper, and employ managers and workers. On the macroeconomic level, advertising plays an essential, critical role in contemporary capitalism. From an ethical perspective, advertising remains, as Schudson (1986) put it, an "uneasy persuasion."

CONCLUSIONS

Advertising is such a pervasive part of American culture that is difficult to conjure up images of products that are not influenced by what we have seen in commercials. If you were asked to free-associate about Coca-Cola, Budweiser, Nike, Herbal Essence, or cars running the gamut from Mustangs to minivans, your mental images would undoubtedly contain ideas and pictures gleaned from commercials. It is physically difficult, if not impossible, to call to mind an advertising-free image of products. This is because advertising plays a critical role in shaping, reinforcing, even changing attitudes toward products.

Little wonder that critics have charged that advertising's power comes from subliminally embedded messages that elude conscious awareness. Research finds that subliminal communications exert virtually no impact on attitudes. However, the conscious belief that a message contains a subliminal message can influence attitudes. The subliminal notion is more hoax than reality, but it persists because people cling to simplistic ideas about how advertising works.

As suggested by the ELM, advertising works through different pathways under low and high involvement. When viewing ads for low-involvement products, consumers process information peripherally. Repetition, associational appeals, and celebrity source endorsements are influential. Association, whose theoretical foundations run the gamut from classical conditioning to accessibility, is a potent weapon in advertising campaigns.

When thinking about more personally consequential purchases, consumers process ads centrally, taking into account the benefits products offer and the psychological functions that products serve. When directing ads at highly involved consumers, advertisers use factual messages and symbolic appeals targeted to particular attitude functions.

Although advertising is pervasive, it does not magically alter attitudes. As social judgment theory reminds us, advertising will not mold deep-seated attitudes toward products. It is not apt to change attitudes on the spot. Instead, it works gradually, influencing cognitions, enhancing positive affect, and meshing with consumers' values, lifestyles, and even fantasies about products.

Ever controversial, advertising has been condemned by those who see in it a ready way to manipulate Americans into buying products they don't need. Critics argue that advertising inculcates a strange philosophy of life that puts great faith in the ability of products to satisfy universal human desires. Yet even those who criticize advertising ethics acknowledge that people seem to have a need for the "things" advertisers promote. Whether due to human nature, contemporary capitalism, or a complex combination of both, "things are in the saddle," critic Twitchell (1999) notes. But he adds, "we put them there. If some of us want to think that things are riding us, that's fine. The rest of us know better" (p. 19).

CHAPTER 12

Communication Campaigns

Bill Alcott and Sy Graham were horrified. They were aghast at what people did to their bodies, day after day shoveling unhealthy, even dangerous, food into their mouths. Didn't people know the damage that meat, fried foods, and butter did to the stomach and heart? Convinced that Americans needed to change their diets, Alcott and Graham organized a health food store that supplied fresh fruits and vegetables. A proper diet, in their view, consisted of wheat bread, grains, vegetables, fruits, and nuts. By eating healthy food and avoiding anything that harmed the body, Graham and Alcott emphasized, people could live longer, healthier lives.

Sound familiar? Another example of contemporary activists trying to convince consumers to give up junk food? Well—not exactly. Alcott and Graham were committed health reformers, but they communicated their message some time ago. More than 150 years ago, to be precise! William Alcott and Sylvester Graham, born in the late 1700s, promoted their nutrition reform campaign in the 1830s. They were early advocates of health education, pioneers in a clean-living movement that began in the United States in the 1800s and continues to this day. Alcott's writings can be found in scattered libraries across the country. Graham—or at least his name—is known worldwide through his Graham cracker (Engs, 2000).

Long before it became fashionable to tout one's opposition to smoking or drugs, activists were pounding the pavement, preaching and proselytizing. Campaigns to improve the public health date back to the early 1800s, with Alcott and Graham's vegetarianism, health reformers' condemnation of the "evil, deadly" tobacco, and the Temperance Movement's efforts to promote abstinence from alcohol. Clean-living movements, as Ruth Clifford Engs (2000) calls them, took on special urgency during the 1830s and 1840s, with the outbreak of cholera, an infectious disease that spread through filthy water, a common problem during a time when drainage systems were poor if nonexistent and pigs roamed the streets feeding on uncollected garbage. Although the causes of cholera could be traced to the social environment, cholera (like AIDS a century and a half later) was viewed as "God's punishment for vice, sin, and moral flaws" (Rushing, 1995, p. 168).

The cholera epidemic led to massive changes in sanitation. It also catalyzed the public health movement in the United States. Over the course of the 19th and 20th centuries, in response to infectious diseases and public health problems, reformers launched campaign after campaign. These included promotion of "do-it-yourself," herb-based cures for disease, religious revivalist efforts in the 1880s that linked physical fitness to moral fitness, and venereal disease education movements that began in the early 20th century and continue apace in the 21st.

Public campaigns have not focused exclusively on health. Some of the most potent campaigns in the United States have centered on political issues. The Revolutionary Generation—Washington, Jefferson, Adams, and Revere—used newspapers and symbolic protests like the Boston Tea Party to convince their peers to revolt against England. The 19th century witnessed the growth of antislavery abolitionists, the Women's Suffrage (Right to Vote) Movement, and—unfortunately—crusades to prevent "undesirable" people (such as Irish Catholics) from emigrating to the United States (Engs, 2000; Pfau & Parrott, 1993).

Political and health campaigns flourished in the 20th century, with the proliferation of television and realization that activists could change institutions through a combination of persuasion and protest. In the public health arena, we have continuing campaigns to convince people to quit smoking, stop boozing, reject drugs, and practice safer sex. In the political arena, campaigns are ubiquitous. Presidential elections, local elections, crime prevention, gun control, abortion, stem cell research, the war on terrorism—these are all arenas that have witnessed intensive communication campaigns.

Campaigns reflect this nation's cultivation of the art of persuasion. They rely on argumentation, sloganeering, and emotional appeals in an effort to mold public attitudes. They are not always pretty or logical. They can cross into coercion, as when antismoking groups push for bans on smoking in the workplace. They are conducted to shape public policy, as well as attitudes.

Campaigns—colorful, vibrant, controversial, and American in their smell and taste—are the focus of this final chapter. The chapter is organized into several sections. The first describes the nature of campaigns. The second reviews major theories of campaign effects. In the third section, I summarize knowledge of key campaign effects. The fourth section touches on ethical issues surrounding campaigns, and the final portion looks briefly at campaigns waged in the political arena.

THINKING ABOUT CAMPAIGNS

Just say no to drugs. . . . This is your brain on drugs. . . . Welcome to Loserville. Population: You. . . . Friends don't let friends drive drunk. . . . Only you can prevent forest fires.

These are some of the most famous emblems of public information campaigns in the United States. However, campaigns involve more than clever slogans. They are systematic, organized efforts to mold health or social attitudes through the use of communication. Or, to be more specific, campaigns can be defined broadly as:

> (a) purposive attempts; (b) to inform, persuade, or motivate behavior changes; (c) in a relatively well-defined and large audience; (d) generally for noncommercial benefits to the individuals and/or society at large; (e) typically within a given time period; (f) by means of organized communication activities involving mass media; and (g) often complemented by interpersonal support. (Rice & Atkin, 2002, p. 427)

People don't devise campaigns with the flick of a wrist. They require time and effort. Typically, activists or professional organizations hatch a campaign concept. They sculpt the idea, working with marketing and communication specialists, pretest messages, and take their communications to the real world in the hope they will influence behavior.

Like advertising, information campaigns apply theories to practical problems. However, advertising campaigns differ from their public information counterparts in a variety of ways:

1. Commercial advertising is designed to make profit for companies. Information campaigns are not purely capitalistic undertakings. They are designed to promote social ideas or improve public health. Typically, prosocial projects have smaller budgets than advertising campaigns. This can limit their effectiveness.

2. News plays a greater role in information campaigns than it does in advertising. Advertising involves paid commercial messages. Campaigns utilize ads, but they also attempt to relay messages through the "nonpaid media": news. For example, health education planners have worked with journalists to produce stories that discuss dangers of cigarette smoking and a high-cholesterol diet (Flora, 2001).

3. Interpersonal and organizational communication plays a more important role in campaigns than in advertising. The McGruff "Take a Bite Out of Crime" campaign supplemented media messages with supportive communication from community groups, businesses, and local police forces (O'Keefe et al., 1996). The Stanford cardiovascular risk reduction project involved multiple communication efforts, including hundreds of

educational sessions and distribution of thousands of nutrition tip sheets to grocery stores. The D.A.R.E. (Drug Abuse Resistance Education) campaign developed an elaborate school curriculum, with police officers teaching children ways to say no to drugs.

4. Ad campaigns try to induce people to *do* something, like buying a six-pack of beer or soft drinks. Information campaigns often try to convince consumers *not* to perform a particular activity (not to smoke, litter, or drive after imbibing).

5. Information campaigns invariably face more daunting obstacles than commercial efforts. It is usually easier to convince someone to buy a commercial product than to "buy into" the idea that she should quit smoking or drinking alcohol.

6. Campaigns frequently target their messages at the 15% of the population that is *least* likely to change its behavior (Harris, 1999). These may be the poorest, least educated members of society, or the most down-and-out intravenous drug users who continue to share HIV-infected needles. By contrast, commercial campaigns focus on the mainstream—on those who are shopping for a product or a dream.

7. Information campaigns involve more highly charged political issues than do commercial efforts. Campaigns frequently encounter strong opposition from powerful industries, such as tobacco companies, beer distributors, oil companies, or gun manufacturers. Antitobacco campaigns, for example, have become embroiled in the politics and economics of tobacco production.

8. Campaigns are more controversial than ads. Even critics acknowledge that advertising is humorous, fun, and clever. Campaigns touch more directly on values, prejudices, or self-interested positions. They can elicit strong sentiments. For example, gun control campaigns pit the value of social responsibility (gun companies should not sell products that endanger citizens) against the equally important value of individual liberty (people have a right to arm themselves to protect their property and families).

Locating Effects

What impact do campaigns and media have on public health? That's a big question; thus, you need big ideas to help you grapple with it. Communication scholars Jane D. Brown and Kim Walsh-Childers (2002) developed a framework to help explain media influences on personal and public health. They proposed that mass media effects fall into three categories: (a) intention of the message producer (intended/unintended), (b) level of influence (personal/public), and (c) outcome (positive/negative). An effect can be intended, as when health communicators develop campaigns to reduce binge drinking, or unintended, as when teenagers conclude from watching music videos that drinking is cool. The bulk of effects discussed in this chapter are intended, since they emanate from campaigns designed to influence attitudes.

A campaign effect can occur at the personal level (a public service ad convinces parents to buy a new child safety seat to protect their infant) or at the public level (Americans learn from news stories that properly installed child seats can reduce the risk of injury to young kids, or a legislator decides, after watching campaign ads, to introduce a bill requiring that all new cars have a special anchoring device to keep the safety seat in place). Finally, effects can be positive or negative.

Viewed in this way, campaigns are multifaceted phenomena. They are complex events that can be examined from different points of view. A good way to begin this examination is to look at theories articulated to explain campaign effects.

THEORETICAL PERSPECTIVES

Three major models of campaigns have been developed. The first is a psychological, individual-level perspective. The other two approaches focus on the bigger picture, viewing campaigns from a macro, community-level orientation.

The **psychological approach** emphasizes that you can't expect a campaign to change behavior instantly, lickety-split. Instead, change occurs gradually, in stages, in line with the ancient Chinese proverb that "a journey of a thousand miles begins with a single step." For example, J. O. Prochaska and his colleagues note that people progress through different stages of change, including precontemplation, during which they are not aware they have a psychological problem, to contemplation, in which they begin considering how to make a change in behavior, to action, in which they actually modify risky behaviors (Prochaska, DiClemente, & Norcross, 1992). Persuasive communications are tailored to the needs of people at a particular stage. Messages directed at precontemplators try to convince them that their behaviors (chain-smoking) put them and loved ones at risk, while communications geared to contemplators encourage them to consider substituting a new behavior for the risky behavior (chewing Nicorette gum instead of smoking Newports).

A second approach combines stages of change with persuasive communication theory. According to McGuire (1989), persuasion can be viewed as a series of input and output steps. In Fig. 12.1, the input column labels refer to standard persuasion variables out of which messages can be constructed.

INPUT: Independent (Communication) Variables / OUTPUT: Dependent Variables (Response Steps Mediating Persuasion)	SOURCE						MESSAGE						CHANNEL				RECEIVER					DESTINATION			
	number	unanimity	demographics	attractiveness	credibility	••	type appeal	type information	inclusion/omission	organization	repetitiveness	••	modality	directness	context	••	demographics	ability	personality	lifestyle	••	immediacy/delay	prevention/cessation	direct/immunization	••
1. Exposure to the communication																									
2. Attending to it																									
3. Liking, becoming interested in it																									
4. Comprehending it (learning what)																									
5. Skill acquisition (learning how)																									
6. Yielding to it (attitude change)																									
7. Memory storage of content and/or agreement																									
8. Information search and retrieval																									
9. Deciding on basis of retrieval																									
10. Behaving in accord with decision																									
11. Reinforcement of desired acts																									
12. Post-behavioral consolidating																									

FIG. 12.1 Persuasion and campaign stages (From Rice, Public (2nd E.), COMM CAMPAIGNS (CLOTH), p. 45, copyright © 1989. Reprinted by permission of Sage Publications, Inc.).

The output row headings correspond to the steps that individuals must be persuaded to take if the message is to have its intended impact.

As the figure shows, a message must clear many hurdles if it is to successfully influence attitudes and behavior. An antidrug campaign may not clear the first hurdle—exposure—because it never reaches the target audience, or alternatively because receivers, finding the message threatening, tune it out as soon as they view it. Or the message may pass the first few steps, but get knocked out of the box when it threatens deeper values or psychological needs.

The input–output matrix has an optimistic side. It says that campaigns can succeed even if they don't lead to major changes in behavior. Indeed, such changes aren't always reasonable to expect, based only on short-term exposure to communications. Campaigns can be regarded as successful if they get people to remember an antidrug ad (Step 4) or if they teach them how to say no to attractive drug-using peers (Step 5). Over time, through subsequent interventions, people can be persuaded to make long-term behavioral changes (Steps 10–12).

Stage-based psychological models are useful. However, they ignore the larger context—the community and society in which campaigns take place. The next two theories address these issues.

Diffusion Theory

Developed by Everett Rogers (1995), this approach examines the processes by which innovations diffuse, or spread through, society. Campaigns are viewed as large-scale attempts to communicate innovative ideas and practices through mass media and interpersonal communication. The following can be regarded as innovations:

- seat belts
- child safety seats
- bicycle helmets
- designated drivers
- jogging
- low-cholesterol diets
- sun tan lotion
- latex condom use
- pooper scoopers

Diffusion theory identifies a number of factors that influence the adoption of innovations. An important variable is the *characteristic of the innovation*. The more compatible an innovation is with people's values and cultural norms, the more likely it is to diffuse rapidly in society. Conversely, the less congruent an innovation is with prevailing values, the less rapidly it is accepted. Environmental recycling and dropping litter in trash cans did not take hold in the 1960s because they diverged from the dominant ideologies: "Bigger is better", "Commercial growth trumps all". Two decades later, when environmental preservation had emerged as a major cultural value, these practices were more widely adopted.

Another attribute of an innovation is the degree to which it promises a clear, salient reward to the individual. A barrier to condom use is that condoms do not offer an immediate reward. The advantage condoms offer—preventing pregnancy or HIV infection—is not visible immediately after the consummation of sex. As Rogers notes, "the unwanted event that is avoided . . . is difficult to perceive because it is a non-event, the absence of something that otherwise might have happened" (p. 217). Partly because the benefits of condom use are not readily apparent, safer sex practices have not always been a quick, easy sell. By contrast, in a different behavioral domain, adoption of a low-cholesterol diet brings immediate, observable changes in weight and blood pressure. It thus has been successfully promoted in a variety of campaigns.

Communication plays a critical role in the spread of innovations. Diffusion theory asserts that mass media are most influential in enhancing knowledge of the innovation, while interpersonal communication is more effective in changing attitudes toward the innovation. Newspapers, television, and the Internet have played a major role in informing people of unhealthy lifestyles. Why do you think so many people know that smoking causes cancer, buckling up can save your life, or unprotected, risky sex can lead to AIDS? Why do so many of us know you can reduce your cancer risk by quitting smoking, that physical exercise can promote longevity, or condoms can prevent HIV? The media have told us these things. Although the media are frequently criticized, they deserve credit for providing information about unhealthy lifestyles and ways to live a healthier life.

Such information comes from both news and entertainment media. News stories frequently *set the agenda*, or influence people's beliefs about what constitute the most important problems facing society (McCombs & Reynolds, 2002). Entertainment programming can also have an innovation-diffusing or agenda-setting impact. Spurred by activist groups, television producers have increasingly included discussion of such innovations as designated drivers, rape hotlines, and birth control pills in their programs. One study reported a 17% increase in viewers' knowledge of emergency contraception after *ER* showed a victim of date rape being treated with a morning-after pill (Brown & Walsh-Childers, 2002).

It is not all blue skies and rosy fields, however, when it comes to media and campaigns. Consider that poor people or those with little education frequently know less about health issues than people who are wealthier or have more education under their belts (Freimuth, 1990). One objective of campaigns is to narrow the gap between the advantaged and disadvantaged members of society. Unfortunately, just the opposite can occur. Campaigns can widen the disparity, so that by the end of the campaign, the rich and better educated people are even more

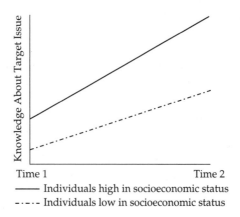

FIG. 12.2   Schematic diagram of the knowledge gap. Communication campaign occurs between Times 1 and 2.

knowledgeable of the problem than their poorer, less-educated counterparts (Gaziano, 1983; Viswanath & Finnegan, 1996). (This is known as *the knowledge gap*; see Fig. 12.2.) There are a number of reasons why such knowledge gaps occur. One key reason is that the health information is less likely to reach, or be mentally accepted by, disadvantaged individuals. Those who have been disadvantaged by society may be so preoccupied with tangible, survival needs that they neglect to focus on health issues that are of long-term personal importance.

Diffusion research suggests ways to reach low-income, low-educated individuals. The news media can publicize health innovations through special programming (Chew & Palmer, 1994). They can also supplement media coverage with intensive interpersonal efforts in the community. The similarity principle comes into play here (see chapter 6). Individuals are typically more receptive to communications delivered by those who are perceived as sharing their values and background. As a staff member in an AIDS prevention program geared to gay Native Americans remarked, "I think this is pretty basic for us, the philosophy of Natives helping Natives, and we got 100% Native staff, 100% Native board, most of our volunteers are Native, and it's really about hearing the information coming from another Native gay man" (Dearing et al., 1996, p. 357). Of course, in an ideal world it wouldn't matter a whit whether the communicator was Native or gay—just whether the individual knew his stuff and cared about those he sought to influence (the basics of credibility). However, this is a real world, and people are frequently more apt to listen to someone who they perceive to be similar to themselves, particularly when the topic is a stressful one.

Diffusion theory, in sum, tells us a great deal about how communications can publicize and promote innovations. However, it neglects the hard-nosed, savvy world of media marketing, a key element in today's campaigns. This is the focus of a second, macro approach to campaigns that applies marketing principles to health.

Social Marketing

Social marketing is defined as **"a process of designing, implementing, and controlling programs to increase the acceptability of a prosocial idea among population segments of consumers"** (Dearing et al., 1996, p. 345). Social marketing is an intriguing concept. It says, in effect: "You know all those great ideas developed to sell products? You can use them to sell people on taking better care of their health. But to do that, you must understand marketing principles." There are five strategic steps in a social marketing campaign: (a) planning, (b) theory, (c) communication analysis, (d) implementation, and (e) evaluation (Maibach, Kreps, & Bonaguro, 1993; see Fig. 12.3).

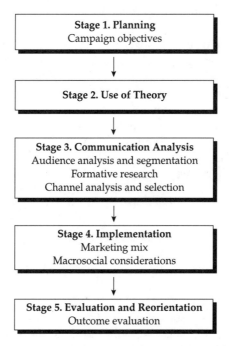

FIG. 12.3 A strategic health communication campaign model (Copyright 1993 from AIDS: Effective Health Communication for the 90's by Maibach, Kreps, & Bonaguro. Reproduced by permission of Taylor & Francis, Inc., http://www.routledge-ny.com).

Planning. During this first phase, campaigners make the tough choices. They select campaign goals. They decide whether to focus on creating cognitions or changing existing ones. They deliberate about whether to target attitudes or behavior.

Theory. Models, concepts, and theories are the backbone of campaigns. You cannot wage a campaign without some idea of what you want to achieve and how best to attain your objectives. The central issue is whether your idea is sound, based on concepts, and of sufficient breadth so as to suggest specific hypotheses. Ideas may be cheap, but good ideas are invaluable. One thing that differentiates effective and ineffective campaigns is that the former reflect painstaking application of theoretical principles; the latter are based on "seat of the pants" intuitions. Theories suggest a host of specific campaign strategies, appeals, and ways to modify projects that aren't meeting stated objectives. Campaigns have employed behavioral theories, affective approaches, and cognitive models (Cappella et al., 2001; Witte et al., 1993). We see how these work in actual situations later in the chapter.

Communication Analysis. After a guiding theory is selected, it must be applied to the context. This occurs during the down-to-earth communication analysis phase of the campaign. Early on, campaign specialists conduct *formative research* to probe audience perceptions (Atkin & Freimuth, 2001). If you were devising a campaign to persuade children not to try cigarettes, you would want to know the negative consequences that kids associate with cigarettes (Bauman et al., 1988; Morrison et al., 1996). You would discover that children don't worry about dying from smoking; they're more concerned about bad breath or becoming unpopular. Armed with these facts, you would develop messages that creatively played up these negative consequences. You would pretest your advertising spots to see which ones worked best, edit them, and ship them to local media for airing at appropriate times of the day.

Implementation. During this phase, the campaign is designed, finalized, and launched. Marketing principles play a critical role here. Of particular importance are the four Ps of marketing: product, price, placement, and promotion.

Product? Most of us do not associate products with health campaigns. Yet products can be prosocial, as well as commercial. Products marketed in health campaigns include Neighborhood Crime Watch posters, child safety seats, gun trigger locks, and Don't Drink and Drive pledge cards.

Products come with a price. The price can be monetary or psychological. In the AIDS context, planners debate whether to charge a price for condoms (dispensing them free of charge saves people money, but it also can make the product seem "cheap" or "unworthy"). Psychologically, the price of using condoms may be less-pleasurable sex or fear of offending a partner. Campaigns devise messages to convince people that these costs are more than offset by the benefits safer sex provides.

Placement involves deciding where to transmit the message. This is critically important, as correct placement can ensure reaching the target audience; incorrect placement can mean that a good message misses its target. The favorite weapon in communication campaigns is the public service advertisement (PSA), a promotional message placed in news, entertainment, or interactive media. Once novel, PSAs are now part of the media landscape, informational sound bites that savvy young people have come to enjoy or ignore. Clever, informative PSAs get noticed and can shatter illusions of invulnerability; dull—or obnoxious—ones are mentally discarded. Thus, market research and creative concept development play important roles in sculpting effective PSAs.

The channel—TV, print, or Internet—is a key factor in placement decisions. Television allows campaigners to reach lots of people and to arouse emotions through evocative messages. However, it is very expensive. Print reaches fewer people but can more effectively impart specific, complex information (Schooler et al., 1998). Interactive media—CD-ROMs, video games, Web sites, the Internet—usually reach fewer people than conventional mass media. However, they offer several advantages. They are usually cheaper than other media, permit upgrading of messages, and allow campaigns to tailor messages to audience subgroups (Kreuter et al., 2000).

There are numerous Web sites and CD-ROMs that impart health information, making them theoretically useful as modes of reaching target audiences, particularly young people. Researchers, who have pondered ways of most effectively using interactive media to influence young audiences, have noted that interactive media are likely to be especially effective when they use age-appropriate role models, promote on-line discussion, and involve learning by doing (Lieberman, 2001). Engaging, interactive techniques are especially appropriate in campaigns that revolve around video games. For example, one game, *Packy & Marlon* (www.clickhealth.com), teaches diabetic children self-management skills by simulating a diabetic character's blood sugar levels. Players can win the game if the food and insulin choices they make for the character allow his blood sugar to stay at normal, healthy levels. They lose if they make choices that push the character's blood sugar to such low or high levels that he cannot function. The game has produced improvements in diabetic children's self-management behaviors. Kids who regularly played the game experienced a 77% reduction in emergency room visits (Lieberman, 2001).

Promotion, the final marketing P, flows out of the planning process. Promotion involves persuasion—application of theories discussed in this book and implemented in a campaign setting.

Evaluation.   This is the final phase of the campaign—the point at which planners discover if the campaign worked. Unlike campaigns of the 19th and early 20th centuries, today's projects can be empirically assessed. Effects can be studied at the *individual level*, as when researchers compare those who saw many campaign messages with those who did not. If the campaign worked, individuals who saw many PSAs should change their attitude more in the intended direction than those who saw relatively few.

Researchers also evaluate campaigns at the *community level*. One town is randomly assigned to be the treatment group; its citizens receive promotional materials, for example, on seat belt use. An equivalent community serves as the control—its residents are not exposed to campaign messages. Researchers then compare the communities, for instance by having police officers stand on street corners counting the number of drivers wearing safety belts. If a higher proportion of drivers in the treatment community wears safety belts than in the control town, the campaign is declared a success (Roberts & Geller, 1994).

Evaluation is critical because it indicates whether campaign objectives have been met. It's not a perfect science. In surveys, one never knows for sure whether those who saw campaign messages were the same in all other ways as those who did not happen to view the campaign. In community evaluations, researchers can never be 100% certain that the treatment and control towns are exactly alike. If the treatment community in the safety belt study had more drivers who were older (and therefore more safety-conscious) than the control community, the older age of drivers, rather than the campaign, could have produced the observed effects. Researchers take precautions to factor in these extraneous variables, quantifying their contributions in statistical tests.

Evaluation is a valuable way to assess campaign impact. It gives campaigners useful feedback for future campaigns. It also serves an important political function. Private and public groups spend hundreds of thousands of dollars on campaigns. They are entitled to know if they have gotten their money's worth. When government spends taxpayer money on antismoking or antidrug campaigns, the public has a right to know if socially valuable goals—reducing smoking or drug use—have actually been achieved.

There is one last point to be made about social marketing. Campaigns may be based on theory, planned according to marketing principles, and evaluated through high-powered statistics. However, they take place in the real world, with its rough edges, cultural norms, and political constraints.

Societal norms and macrosocial factors influence campaigns in a variety of ways. Antismoking campaigns had little chance of changing attitudes so long as most Americans trusted the tobacco companies or doubted that smoking caused cancer. As Americans learned that tobacco companies withheld knowledge that smoking was addictive and accepted as fact evidence of the causal impact of smoking on cancer, antismoking campaigns faced a more receptive audience to their messages. Even so (and not surprisingly), antismoking campaigns attempting to increase public support for regulation of the tobacco industry have faced daunting opposition from the tobacco industry, as the gripping, factually based movie *The Insider* documented.

In a similar vein, AIDS prevention campaigns have been influenced by macrosocial and cultural factors. Americans' discomfort with homosexuality has impeded—indeed, doomed to failure—activists' efforts to persuade television networks to broadcast PSAs that talk frankly about safer sex among gay men (Perloff, 2001). On the other side of the cultural divide, gay political leaders in cities like San Francisco have sometimes stridently opposed public health campaigns to clean up or close city bathhouses. Their resistance has stemmed from a strong libertarian desire to pursue private (but sometimes dangerous) pleasures and activities, as well as more understandable fears of being stigmatized by social institutions (Rotello 1997). Thousands of miles away, in AIDS-infected Africa where tens of millions are expected to die in the first decade of the 21st century, campaigns are hampered by pro-sex cultural norms. In many African societies, sex is viewed 100% positively, as an essential form of recreation between lovers, casual friends, and even adulterers. Polygamy is widespread and sanctioned (Rushing, 1995). In addition, African prostitutes, who would like their clients to use condoms, are hindered by cultural norms that put sex in men's control. "We are women, we are weak and shy, we cannot ask them to use condoms," one prostitute acknowledged (Cameron, Witte, & Nzyuko, 1999, p. 153).

All these factors affect the design and implementation of social marketing campaigns. When we take theory into the real world, with all its politics, values, and emotional messiness, we find that life is more complex and campaigns are inseparable from the culture in which they take place.

CAMPAIGN EFFECTS

Do campaigns work? Do they influence targeted attitudes and behaviors? What do *you* think? What's your best guess?

There is little question that campaigns face an up-hill battle. As McGuire's input/output matrix notes, interventions must first attract the target audience and capture its attention. This can be difficult. For a variety of psychological reasons, Caroline Schooler and her colleagues (1998) note, "those whom a campaign most seeks to reach with health information are the least motivated to pay attention to it" (p. 414). The last thing addicted smokers, drug users, or gamblers want to do is pay attention to moralistic messages that tell them to stop doing what makes them happy.

Not only don't campaigns always succeed in reaching difficult-to-influence audiences, they turn them off with preachy messages or communications that aren't in sync with audience needs. Even campaigns with creative messages may fail because planners lack money to repeat the message enough times to guarantee an effect. Effects produced by a campaign also may not persist over time. Knowledge of emergency contraception obtained from watching the *ER* episode mentioned earlier dropped significantly at a follow-up measurement (Brown & Walsh-Childers, 2002). Thus, there is no guarantee a campaign will work. It may fail, and many do.

Okay—but I wouldn't be devoting an entire chapter to this topic if campaigns failed consistently and repeatedly! In fact, a half century of research indicates that if practitioners know their stuff, apply theory deftly, and utilize principles of social marketing, they can wage effective campaigns. Campaigns will succeed when practitioners:

1. Understand the audience and tailor messages to fit its needs and preexisting attitudes.
2. Segment the audience into different subgroups, fitting messages ever more exquisitely to the orientations of specialized groups.
3. Refine messages so that they are relevant, cogent (based on principles discussed in this book), and of high production value.
4. Coordinate efforts across media, and repeat messages over time and in different media and interpersonal channels.
5. Choose media channels (PSAs, news, entertainment TV, Internet) that are viewed by members of the target audience.
6. Use entertaining characters, visuals, and themes that weave together different messages (O'Keefe et al., 1996; Parrott, 1995).
7. Supplement media materials as much as possible with community contacts (McAlister & Fernandez, 2002; Rice & Atkin, 2002).
8. Appreciate that it is frequently easier to promote a new behavior (fruit and vegetable consumption) than to convince people to stop a dysfunctional behavior (unsafe sex) (Snyder, 2001).
9. Try, whenever possible, to build enforcement into the campaign (Snyder & Hamilton, 2002). Seat belt campaigns that have emphasized that police will be enforcing seat belt laws have been especially effective in promoting seat belt use.

10. Be realistic. Keep in mind how difficult it is to change deep-seated attitudes and well-learned behaviors. "Set realistic expectations of success . . . , be prepared for a long haul . . . , (and) give more emphasis to relatively attainable impacts, by aiming at more receptive segments of the audience and by creating or promoting more palatable positive products" (Atkin, 2002, p. 37).

With these factors in mind, it is time to turn to specific applications of campaign principles. The next sections review communication campaigns in context.

THE McGRUFF CRIME PREVENTION PROJECT

Some years back, there was considerable concern about rising crime rates and rampant drug abuse. During the 1980s and '90s, many people worried they would be mugged if they walked outside at night; inner-city neighborhoods were like war zones, terrorized by drug dealers; and there was little cooperation between neighborhood residents and police. In hopes of changing things for the better, the National Crime Prevention Council sponsored a public communication campaign designed to teach crime and drug prevention behaviors and to encourage citizens to take steps to protect themselves, their families, and neighborhoods (O'Keefe et al., 1996).

The campaign, produced by the Advertising Council and widely disseminated in the media, centered on a series of entertaining public service announcements. The PSAs attempted to arouse fear about crime, while also generating anger at drug dealers and criminals. The centerpiece of the media campaign was an animated trench-coated dog named McGruff who urged viewers to take concrete steps "to take a bite out of crime," such as by locking doors and windows and participating in neighborhood crime watch programs (see Fig. 12.4). Over time, the campaign branched out. Children and teens became a target audience, with PSAs focusing on missing children, drug abuse, and resisting peer pressure to take drugs.

McGruff, as the campaign is sometimes called, is generally regarded as a classic, textbook case of how to run an effective communication campaign. The project was well funded, repeated messages in different media using different motifs (thereby capitalizing on *mere exposure* principles), and promoted cognitive learning by employing an entertaining character (the McGruff dog). It also supplemented media by employing extensive community activities.

Here are six things vandalism is **not**:

1. Not cool.

2. Not a game.

3. Not lawful.

4. Not smart.

5. Not pretty.

6. Not cheap.

What vandalism is, is "WRECK-CREATION". It's not something to be proud of. So if you know a group of vandals, don't treat 'em like stars—let 'em know it's not cool. Let's face it, when they bust a window, it's got to be fixed. And that same money could've bought your class a field trip instead. So talk to your principal, and find out what you can do to stop vandalism. Help me, McGruff.®

TAKE A BITE OUT OF

CRIME.

McGruff,
The
Crime Dog ®

FIG. 12.4   A McGruff "Take a bite out of crime" ad. (Reprinted with permission of the National Crime Prevention Council.)

Garrett J. O'Keefe and his colleagues systematically evaluated the project. Their findings:

- Eighty percent of a sample of U.S. adults recalled having seen or heard McGruff PSAs.
- Nearly 9 in 10 respondents said they believed the ads had increased children's awareness of neighborhood drug abuse. About a quarter of individuals exposed to the campaign said they had taken specific crime prevention precautions as a result of having viewed the PSAs.
- The decade-long campaign coincided with sharp increases in the number of people who used outdoor security lights and special locks on doors or windows.
- Exposure to the campaign led to significant increases in crime prevention behaviors, including reporting suspicious activities to the police and joining with others to prevent crime (O'Keefe, 1985).

Successful as the campaign was, it is possible that it exerted several unanticipated negative effects. It might have led to increases in accidents by stimulating people untrained in gun use to purchase guns for self-protection. By encouraging people to report suspicious activities to the police, it may have unwittingly increased mistrust or suspicion of unorthodox, but hardly criminal, individuals. Campaigns frequently have unintended effects, and campaigners must hope that the benefits (crime reduction and increased citizen participation in community policing) exceed the costs. In the case of McGruff, the pluses far exceeded the minuses.

ANTISMOKING AND CARDIOVASCULAR RISK REDUCTION CAMPAIGNS

These are probably the most famous public information campaigns in America. Many of us recall seeing PSAs that associate cigarettes with ugly, despicable images or suggest that no one cool smokes anymore ("Welcome to Loserville. Population: You"). Where do the ideas for these campaigns come from?

In a word, theory! Antismoking campaigns have been among the most theory driven of all public communication interventions. Campaigns have applied **cognitive**, **affective**, and **behavioral** concepts to the development of campaigns (Ohme, 2000).

Cognitively based campaigns have targeted children's beliefs about smoking and the types of people who smoke. Guided by the theory of reasoned action (see chapter 3), researchers identify perceived drawbacks of smoking. "It's a gross habit, it smells, ... Even just being around people who smoke, you know, my eyes start to water and burn," children told researchers Laura A. Peracchio and David Luna (1998), who used this information to devise antismoking messages (p. 51). Based on findings that short-term negative consequences of smoking (bad smell and harm to eyes) are of central importance to kids, the researchers developed print ads that played on these themes:

> One of the ads, "Sock", depicts a dirty, grimy sweatsock with the caption, "Gross," next to an ashtray full of cigarette butts with the caption, "Really gross" . . . . (A second) ad, "Tailpipe", reads, "Inhale a lethal dose of carbon monoxide and it's called suicide. Inhale a smaller amount and it's called smoking. Believe it or not, cigarette smoke contains the same poisonous gas as automobile exhaust. So if you wouldn't consider sucking on a tailpipe, why would you want to smoke?" (Peracchio & Luna, p. 53)

The first ad was simple and concrete; it worked well with 7- and 8-year-olds. The second was more complex and resonated more with 11-year-olds.

A more elaborate intervention, devised by Michael Pfau and his associates, succeeded in stiffening adolescents' resistance to experimenting with cigarettes. Pfau drew on inoculation theory, a cognitive approach discussed in chapter 5. Persuaders employing inoculation deliberately expose people to a message they want them to reject, then follow up this initial treatment with a dose of powerful arguments refuting the message. Applying inoculation to antismoking, Pfau and Van Bockern (1994) told seventh-grade students that peer pressure would cause some of them to modify their opposition to smoking and begin to smoke. This was subsequently followed by statements that smoking was cool or won't affect "me," coupled with *refutations* of these arguments. The inoculation treatment intensified negative attitudes toward smoking.

A cautionary note: Cognitive campaigns directed at young people should start before high school. Around the end of middle school, as pressures to be popular mount and self-esteem frequently plummets, teenagers look to smoking as a way to be cool or to enhance their identities (e.g., Pfau & Van Bockern, 1994). Researchers recommend that inoculation campaigns commence in seventh grade—or before.

Affectively oriented campaigns focus on feelings associated with smoking. Tobacco advertising has succeeded in linking smoking with relaxation, pleasant affect, and popularity (Romer & Jamieson, 2001). To counter this, campaigns apply classical conditioning and associative network ideas discussed earlier in this book. They explicitly associate ads with negative images. For example:

> In one ad . . . a young male is chewing tobacco and spitting it from time to time into a soft drink paper cup. His female friend, whose attention is

absorbed by the movie they are watching, mechanically grabs the cup and reaches it to her mouth without looking inside. A scream is then heard, suggesting that the friend was horrified and disgusted when she tasted the liquid and, by extension, was also horrified and disgusted by her friend's behavior. . . . (In another ad), a beautiful girl is smoking a cigarette, but each time she inhales her face is covered with more and more nicotine and tar. This ad creates a huge aesthetic dissonance and shows that, regardless of how attractive you are, smoking makes you repulsive. (Ohme, 2000, p. 315)

Other affectively oriented ads play cleverly on fear appeals, walking the razor-thin line between not scaring teens enough and scaring them too much. One TV spot developed by the American Legacy Foundation parodies a soft-drink ad. Three young people bungee jump off a bridge to save cans of fictional Splode soda. Two of the jumpers grab a can and are yanked back to the safety of the bridge. The third jumper's can explodes as he opens it, and he disappears in a burst of flames. On the screen appear the words, "Only one product actually kills a third of the people who use it. Tobacco."

The third category of antismoking campaigns—behavioral interventions—draws on social learning theory, a model developed by Albert Bandura. Noting that people do not have to be rewarded, like rats or pigeons, to learn new behaviors, Bandura (1977) has called attention to the powerful role that observing role models plays in social influence. Theorists have adapted his ideas to public health. Using mass media, interpersonal instruction, and behavior modification techniques, they have detailed the dangers of smoking and of maintaining a high-cholesterol diet. At the same time, campaigns have taught people the cognitive skills necessary to quit smoking and adopt a healthier lifestyle.

The classic and most elaborate of these interventions were developed at Stanford University. The campaigns included TV spots, radio PSAs, and a weekly doctor's column that appeared in Spanish language newspapers. School curricula, workplace classes, and intensive interpersonal instruction supplemented the media messages. During interpersonal sessions, counselors used behavior modification techniques, encouraging smokers to substitute sugar-free lozenges and asking others to keep track of the healthy food they ate each week.

Researchers dreamed up a nifty way to evaluate the campaigns. They chose several small California cities with comparable demographic characteristics. Certain cities were assigned to the media treatments, others served as controls. Researchers then compared respondents in the treatment and control cities on several indices, including health knowledge, smoking reduction, and decreases in cholesterol level.

The campaigns had modest effects, smaller than some anticipated, but practically significant (Hornik, 2002). The Stanford communications increased knowledge of healthy eating, diet, and exercise. What's more, communities that received the campaign displayed significant decreases in cholesterol level and blood pressure. At-risk individuals who received interpersonal instruction dramatically reduced the number of cigarettes they smoked a day (Farquhar et al., 1990; Maccoby & Farquhar, 1975).

State Antismoking Campaigns

Emboldened by Stanford's efforts but determined to do better, campaign planners in several states have mounted impressive antismoking interventions. Using state funds and monies available from the legal settlement with the tobacco companies, states have blitzed the airwaves with antismoking messages. Armed with as much as $90 million, campaigners have enlisted help from creative advertising agencies, developing ads like one aired in California. The advertisement "used actual footage from a congressional hearing, during which the chief executives of each of the major tobacco companies denied, under oath, that nicotine was addictive. The advertisement culminated with the question, 'Do they think we're stupid?'" (Pierce, Emery, & Gilpin, 2002, p. 100).

Campaigns in California, Arizona, Massachusetts, and elsewhere in the United States have significantly influenced smoking attitudes and behavior (Burgoon, Hendriks, & Alvaro, 2001; Pierce et al., 2002; Siegel & Biener, 2002). A multimillion dollar, decade-long campaign seems to have produced a sharp decline in cigarette consumption in California (see Fig. 12.5). An Arizona media campaign that endlessly repeated the hip phrase, *"Tobacco: Tumor-causing, teeth-staining, smelly, puking habit,"* pushed young people to evaluate smoking more negatively. In addition, media PSAs, coupled with school-based smoking prevention programs, reduced smoking by 35% in portions of the U.S. Northeast and Northwest (Worden & Flynn, 2002).

Macrosocial Picture

One of the critical hard-fact realities of antismoking campaigns is that they take place in a heavily politicized environment, in which well-funded public health groups battle billion-dollar tobacco companies, who in turn heavily lobby state legislators who control the purse strings for these campaigns. In California, the fighting has been particularly vicious. When the campaign aired its "Do they think we're stupid?" spot, the tobacco industry issued a legal threat to the network TV stations in California. Under political pressure, state campaign planners dumped the ad (Pierce et al., 2002).

In spite of these obstacles, the California campaign succeeded. It did so because the tobacco control program had significant grassroots support; its messages also contained emotional arguments that smokers

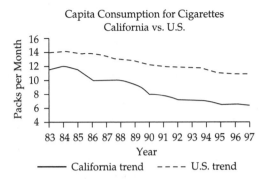

Capita Consumption for Cigarettes
California vs. U.S.

FIG. 12.5 Seasonally adjusted trend of per capita cigarette consumption, California versus the United States (from Pierce et al., 2002). *Note:* Smoking dropped in the United States and California from 1983 to 1997, but the rate of decline increased dramatically in California after the state's smoking campaign began in 1989. In the rest of the United States it did not. Smoking consumption in California was also below that of the rest of the United States.

found persuasive. Antismoking campaigns have had similar success elsewhere in the country (and abroad as well). Yet at the outset few believed that tobacco education stood much of a chance, in light of the political and economic power wielded by cigarette companies. However, media campaigns have succeeded in changing attitudes toward smoking, promoting bans on secondhand smoke, and creating a public opinion climate that has made it easier for attorneys to successfully sue tobacco companies for damages. By riding the wave of a contemporary public health movement, seizing on antipathy to Big Tobacco, appealing to American values of self-improvement, and controversially working with coercive bans on smoking in public places, the David of anticigarette marketing has successfully battled the Goliath of American tobacco companies. While many Americans smoke—and they always will, as long as cigarettes are legal—the contemporary antismoking movement will long be remembered for helping create a cleaner, smoke-free environment in the United States.

ANTIDRINKING CAMPAIGNS

The school year over, Carla Wagner and her friend Claudia Valdes enjoyed a leisurely lunch at the Green Street Café in Miami's Coconut Grove. After Wagner, then 17, paid the tab with her credit card, the two hopped into her 2000 Audi A4 and headed to a girlfriend's house, stopping en route to pick up a $25 bottle of tequila using a bogus ID. There Wagner and Valdes drank several shots, passed around two pipefuls of pot and watched

TV. . . . Wagner jumped back into her car with Valdes, then 18, taking the passenger seat. . . . Racing home, Wagner rounded one curve at more than 50 mph. . . . A few moments afterward, as Wagner tried to dial a cell phone, the car hit gravel and fishtailed out of control. Valdes, who sustained a broken pelvis and lacerated liver, recalled later, "I think I saw an image walking or Rollerblading or whatever she was doing."

That shadow was Helen Marie Witty, 16, out for an early-evening skate. But the Audi, doing 60 mph in a 30-mph zone, had left the northbound lane and veered onto the bike path, hitting Witty and tossing her 30 ft. before the car wrapped itself, like a giant C, around a tree. . . .

As for Witty, "She still looked like an angel, her eyes open" (says a motorist who saw the crash and realized she was dead). "She looked peaceful and angelic." (Charles, Trischitta, & Morrissey, 2001, pp. 67–68).

Stories like these are all too common. Some 16,000 Americans are killed in alcohol-related car crashes each year, accounting for 40% of all traffic deaths (Webb, 2001). Excessive drinking has other negative consequences. It can cause liver disease and cancer, and induce severe memory loss. Given the gravity of these effects, social activists have launched a variety of antialcohol campaigns.

The public service advertisement has been a major weapon in media campaigns. PSAs run the gamut from the famous "Friends don't let friends drive drunk" to ads that question the popular image that drinking equals fun by depicting a young woman vomiting after drinking beer (Andsager, Austin, & Pinkleton, 2001). It is tempting to assume that these campaigns work; after all, they are produced by advertising specialists and appear on national television. However, as noted throughout this chapter, such an assumption is unwarranted. Young people frequently complain that popular antidrinking PSAs are corny, cheesy, and preachy (Andsager et al., 2001; see also Slater et al., 1998). Some PSAs fail to provide a realistic discussion of drinking. By focusing on "generic peers," they neglect to consider the important role that same-sex friends and parents play in decisions about whether to drink (Austin & Meili, 1994; Trost et al., 1999). Still other campaigns fail to create messages powerful enough to undo the effects of sexy, slick pro-drinking commercial spots.

The news is not all bad. Two campaign interventions, with solid foundations in social marketing principles, have helped to reduce alcohol abuse.

The Designated Driver Campaign

The designated driver is such a simple, potentially effective innovation you would think it would have been invented soon after the first reports of traffic fatalities surfaced. The notion that a group of friends selects one person to abstain from drinking that evening is intuitive and appealing. However, social change takes time, and it took years for the innovation to diffuse. Now, it is commonly accepted, thanks to campaigns organized by activist groups, including the Harvard School of Public Health (Winsten & DeJong, 2001).

Working with Hollywood production studios and TV networks, campaigners succeeded in placing dialogue or messages in 160 entertainment programs, including such classics as *Beverly Hills 90210*, *Growing Pains*, and *Cheers*. PSAs have appeared widely, with some featuring appearances from U.S. presidents.

The campaigns seemed to have influenced beliefs and behaviors. Years ago people used to joke about drinking when under the influence. In 1964, President Lyndon B. Johnson gave reporters a tour of his Texas ranch, driving 90 miles per hour and sipping a cup of beer. As late as 1988, two months before the campaign began, just 62% of respondents said they and their friends designated a driver all or most of the time. Following the campaign, the proportion shot up significantly to 72% and is undoubtedly higher today.

The belief that people should not be allowed to drink when they drive has reached such high levels it can be regarded as a social norm. Although the campaign cannot take credit for all this success, it certainly has helped to legitimize the use of designated drivers in the United States.

Public health experts Jay A. Winsten and William DeJong argue that the campaign succeeded because: (a) it had support from powerful Hollywood insiders; (b) the designated driver message (which places responsibility on the individual, not beer companies) allows the networks to do something positive about drinking, while not alienating the alcohol industry, on whom they depend for much of their advertising; and (c) the message could be easily sandwiched into programs (all a character need ask is, "Who's the designated driver tonight?"). In contrast, teen pregnancy and AIDS prevention appeals are more controversial and more difficult to incorporate into program scripts.

Social Norms Marketing

It isn't clear whether Leslie Baltz, who was in her fourth year (at the University of Virginia), wanted to drink that much. The 21-year-old honor student, who had a double major in art history and studio art, liked to paint and sketch. Once, at the age of 11, she wrote 31 poems for her mother, one for each day of the month, about love, dreams, and impermanence.

At a party that Saturday, Ms. Baltz drank enough booze-spiked punch that she decided to lie down at a friend's house while her buddies went out. When they returned that night after U. Va.'s 34–20 upset of Virginia Tech, they found her unconscious at the foot of a stairway.

Ms. Baltz's blood-alcohol level was 0.27%, more than triple the state's legal limit for drivers, but probably survivable if not for her fall. . . . She was declared dead of head injuries.

Thus, Ms. Baltz became the fifth Virginia college student to die of alcohol-related causes that autumn, and the 18th at U. Va. since 1990. (Murray & Gruley, 2000, p. A10)

Unfortunately, Leslie is not the only student to die as a result of alcohol abuse. Accidents due to drinking claim too many students' lives each year. Drinking, of course, is common on campus. Over 90% of students have tried alcohol, close to 25% display symptoms of problem drinkers, and others report experiences such as these over the course of a year:

Had a hangover	62.8%
Got nauseated or vomited	53.8%
Drove a car while under the influence	31.3%
Were taken advantage of sexually	12.2%
Took advantage of someone else sexually	5.1%
(Murray & Gruley, 2000)	

Still others can be defined as "binge drinkers"—men who consume at least five, and women who drink four or more, drinks in one sitting (see Fig. 12.6)

For years, universities used a pastiche of antidrinking appeals, ranging from scare tactics to pictures of cars destroyed by drunk drivers. Convinced that these did not work and searching for something new, they recently perfected a technique based on communication and social marketing. Called social norms marketing, it targets students' perception that other people drink a lot. The idea is that students overestimate how much alcohol their peers consume. Believing that everyone else drinks a lot and wanting to fit into the dominant college culture, they drink more than they would like. The solution follows logically: "*If students' drinking practices are fostered, or at least maintained, by the erroneous perception that other students feel more positively toward these practices than they do,*" two scholars noted, "*then correcting this misperception should lower their alcohol consumption*" (Schroeder & Prentice, 1998, p. 2153).

A number of universities have adopted this approach in an effort to curb alcohol abuse. The University of Virginia placed posters in the blue and orange school colors in freshman dorms. "Most U. Va. 1st years have 0 to 4 drinks per week," posters declared. "Zero to 3," stated frisbees distributed at Cornell University, making reference to the number of drinks most students consume when at a party. A Rutgers University "RU SURE?" campaign devised messages listing the top 10 misperceptions on campus, ranging from the humorous ("It's easy to find a parking place on campus") to the critical ("Everyone who parties gets wasted"). The latter

FIG. 12.6 Binge drinking is a major problem on college campuses. Universities have employed a variety of strategies to curb binge drinking, with varying success. (Photograph by William C. Rieter.)

was followed with the answer that two thirds of Rutgers students stop at three or fewer drinks (Lederman et al., 2001). At Washington State University, Project Culture Change blanketed the campus with posters that said, "Heavy drinking at WSU has decreased every year for the past five years" (see Box 12–1).

BOX 12–1
PROBING PERCEPTIONS OF AN ANTIDRINKING CAMPAIGN

How do researchers conduct formative research and probe audience perceptions of campaign messages? How do planners of a social norm antidrinking campaign adjust their strategies to fit students' points of view? These questions were on the minds of a group of Washington State University communication researchers when they evaluated a campus social norming project (Hansen, Kossman, Wilbrecht, & Andsager, 2000). The researchers conducted in-depth interviews with a variety of Washington State University (WSU) freshmen, asking them pointed questions about binge drinking and campaign messages. Here is some of what they found:

Moderator: Some of you say that 16 to 17 drinks is binge drinking. Do you think, on average, that's what a lot of people do?

A.C. (a student): Well, for guys and girls, it's, like, different.

Kelly (a student): It depends on the girl.

Moderator: On average, how many drinks do you think the average person has when they go out?

A.C.: It depends on what you do.

Zach (a student): Yeah, it depends on what kind of party you go to.

A.C.: If you're drinking to get drunk, then you will have a lot, but if you're drinking to socialize and, like, meet some girls or something like that, then you just want to be buzzed so you're just like sort of loose, and you don't have inhibitions or anything like that.

Moderator: Do you think drinking is a problem on the WSU campus?

A.C.: We drink a lot more than some of the other college campuses I have been on.

Lisa (a student): I think everybody knows about it because Pullman is out in the middle of nowhere. What else is there to do but go out and party.

A.C.: We should form a drinking team (laughter from the group).

Moderator: So at what point do you think that drinking is out of control?

A.C.: I think if you're passing out every time you drink.

Kelly: I think puking. If you pass out or, like, puke and pass out, that's bad. You shouldn't drink that much to puke.

Lisa: I think it's either passing out or just blacking out. If you do that every single time you drink, then maybe that's out of control.

Moderator: Okay, we're going to show you some ads that have been developed to kind of dispel any misconceptions about how much drinking there is, and then we're going to talk about them a little bit. (Moderator presents an ad with a picture of three students smiling and standing arm in arm. The tag line is: "Most WSU students drink moderately. 65% of WSU students have 4 or fewer drinks when they socialize.")

Zach: It doesn't look like they're drinking. I don't think they were drinking at all. I think he just randomly got some picture. If they had like keg cups and stuff, that would be a rocking picture. (Later.) See, there's, like, a number of people on campus who just don't drink at all and they bring down that mark by a whole lot.

Moderator: So you should separate them out into those who drink on campus (and those who don't)?

Kelly: It could be true for girls to have four drinks and be buzzed and good to go. But for guys, I think it's totally different. I think there should be a difference for guys and girls.

Moderator: (Presents an ad with students rock climbing. The copy reads: "Most WSU students drink moderately. Heavy drinking at WSU has decreased every year for the past five years.") Okay, what do you guys think of this one?

Zach: What's with the people climbing?

A.C.: Most people don't drink when they're rock climbing. As that would be very dangerous.

Moderator: Do you think the ad would be more effective if there were people with alcohol in the pictures? Basically, are you saying that the message in the ad just isn't believable?

Kelly: Well, the message is maybe okay, but the pictures just really don't go.

Zach: That's a believable message though.

Kelly: It's very believable—but just different pictures.

(Excerpts adapted from Hansen et al., 2000)

Note. The interviewers' questions were folksy and tapped into students' beliefs. To their credit, students responded openly and genuinely. Based on the interviews, the researchers concluded that university freshmen were not educated about binge drinking (they defined binge drinking as having 16 drinks or puking, when in fact binging involves having 4 to 5 drinks on a single occasion). Researchers concluded that messages should emphasize the impact of drinking on students' lives. Ads, they suggested, should contain pictures that relate more to the message. This type of formative research provides useful insights into students' perceptions, suggesting more effective ways to appeal to the target audience.

What's the verdict? Does social norming work? Empirical studies offer some—but not total—support. Northern Illinois University implemented a social norms campaign, which used communications to decrease the number of students who thought binge drinking was the campus norm.

Prior to the campaign, 70% of the students believed binge drinking was common practice. By the campaign's conclusion, the percentage had dropped to 51%. Self-reported binge drinking decreased by nearly 9% during this period (Haines & Spear, 1996).

Other studies, using more fine-tuned scientific methods, have reported similar findings (Godbold & Pfau, 2000; Schroeder & Prentice, 1998).

These results have intrigued scholars, but raised questions. Some wonder whether students genuinely changed their views or were just saying they had, in order to comply with the norm of pleasing the faculty investigator. Other scholars doubt that simply providing correct information is sufficient to overcome more emotional reasons people choose to drink (Austin & Chen, 1999). Still others fear that social norming encourages drinking. "Are you saying that four drinks a week is a healthy choice?" one student asked campaign coordinators. "I mean, maybe it is, maybe it isn't. It's definitely illegal for the first-years (at U. Va.)" (Murray & Gruley, 2000, p. A10).

One other potential dilemma of social norms marketing has also surfaced, pointing to the role social context plays in communication campaigns. Which industry do you think might like the idea of encouraging students to drink, if only modestly? That's right: The beer industry! Anheuser-Busch Brewers funded the University of Virginia social norms campaign to the tune of $150,000. Coors and Miller gave the University of Wyoming and Georgetown University thousands of dollars for similar campaigns. Anheuser made certain that the ads displayed its corporate logo. This raises ethical questions. Did beer industry sponsorship inhibit campaigners, causing them to shy away from developing hard-hitting antidrinking ads? Did the association of moderate drinking and the beer company logo actually strengthen pro-boozing attitudes?

Thus we glimpse the complex issues surrounding social norms marketing. It is an engaging idea, one that creatively plays on young people's desire to fit in with the majority. However, it probably works best when implemented in conjunction with other persuasion principles.

DRUG PREVENTION CAMPAIGNS

"The facts are these," researchers Jason T. Siegel and Judee K. Burgoon (2002) observe. "Almost half of all high school students surveyed used marijuana on at least one occasion, and more than 25% of high school students who were questioned reported using marijuana 30 days prior to being surveyed. Illicit drug use costs taxpayers upward of $110 billion a year. In addition to impairing cognitive functioning, marijuana use is associated with increased risk of dropping out of high school, driving under the influence, engaging in crime, and destroying property. . . . The goal is simple: Persuade people not to do drugs. Seems easy enough in principle. Unfortunately, even with $3 billion being spent by the Partnership for a Drug-Free America on media time alone, the amount of people who use illegal substances is not decreasing" (p. 163).

Modern antidrug campaigns date back to First Lady Nancy Reagan, who famously urged a generation of young people tempted by crack-cocaine and other '80s-style substances to "just say no to drugs." Her advice got a lot of bad press at the time. However, it had a simplicity to it, based, as it appeared to be, on Nike's Zen-oriented "Just do it" advertising of the era. The 1980s campaign and a more recent project launched by the U.S. government's Office of National Drug Control Policy have centered on PSAs. These have included the world-famous "This is your brain on drugs" and a host of recent spots, including ones in which teens criticize their parents for controlling their behavior when they were younger, but at the end, each says "thanks" to their parents for keeping them drug free.

Judging by the number of people who can remember these ads, you might think the campaigns were phenomenal successes. However, recall does not equal attitude change, nor does it signal a motivation to alter an intention to experiment with drugs. The campaigns raised awareness, a necessary step in motivating people to change problematic behaviors. However, some ads came off as controlling or condescending, a kiss of death in campaigns directed at naturally rebellious adolescents (see Burgoon, Alvaro et al., 2002). In order to change young people's attitudes toward drugs, campaigns must consider communication principles, such as these:

1. *Pretest, target, and tailor.* Antidrug campaigns are more apt to succeed if they identify young people's salient beliefs and target them in compelling messages (Fishbein et al., 2002). Formative research tells us that teenagers, who believe they will live forever, are not particularly impressed by the argument that drugs can kill you. More intimidating is the prospect that drugs will ruin a relationship. One successful antidrug campaign put this insight to use in message design, featuring an ad in which a teenage girl complains that since her boyfriend started smoking marijuana, "he just lays around and is forgetting things. . . . She complains he avoids her like he avoids all his other 'problems,' and she walks out, slamming the door. A message board reads, 'Marijuana: it's messed up a lot of relationships' " (Palmgreen et al., 2002, p. 40).

2. *Segment the audience.* Social marketing emphasizes that campaigns should devise different appeals to fit different subgroups. A key factor that has emerged in drug prevention research is the personality variable, sensation seeking. People who are high in sensation seeking (you may be

one or know someone who is) enjoy thrills and adventures, like bungee jumping and parachuting. They prefer a nonconformist lifestyle (characterized by unconventional music and art), and seek out a variety of stimulating social and sexual experiences (Zuckerman, 1979). They also derive psychological and physical gratification from drugs and are more apt to use drugs than people who are low in sensation seeking (Donohew, Palmgreen, & Lorch, 1994). Given the many ways that high sensation seekers differ from low sensation seekers, it makes sense that drug prevention communications targeting highs should employ different appeals than those geared to lows. This viewpoint has been articulated and elaborately tested by Lewis Donohew, Philip Palmgreen, and their associates (Donohew et al., 2002; Palmgreen et al., 2002). Far from arguing that the same message fits all potential drug users, Palmgreen and Donohew suggest that communications should be tailored to fit high and low sensation seekers' different needs. In order to reach high sensation seekers, messages should be novel, exciting, graphic, and emotionally strong. Communications targeted at low sensation seekers should be familiar, easygoing, and less intense. However, as a general rule, given that so many drug users are high in sensation seeking, campaigners with a fixed budget are advised to develop PSAs that point out exciting alternatives to drug dependence.

3. *Use multiple formats and channels*. Media PSAs can create awareness and help people recognize they have a drug problem. To help people move from mental to behavioral change, PSAs must be supplemented by news stories mentioning celebrities who have maintained a drug-free lifestyle, as well as by extensive community activities to help people talk with counselors or stay in treatment programs.

VALUES AND ETHICS

You know the old game "Where's Waldo?" that you played when you were a kid? You would try to spot the cagey character, Waldo, who was hiding somewhere in the house or outdoors. He was always there, you just had to locate his whereabouts. So it is with values and ethical aspects of campaigns, an issue touched on but not directly broached in this chapter. Noted one ethicist, "They are always there, the value judgments: the choices in policy decisions. There are always choices made" (Guttman, 2000, p. 70).

It's nice to think of campaigns as these objective entities, planned by scientifically minded behavioral engineers, implemented by marketing specialists, and evaluated by statisticians. Although campaigns have measurable effects to be sure, they take place in real-world contexts

Social–structural factors, political complexities, and value judgments necessarily intervene. You can appreciate this by considering the following questions. They appear simple at first blush but are actually tinged with value issues:

1. *What is the problem the campaign hopes to solve?* A healthy-eating campaign may be designed to change attitudes toward eating high-cholesterol food, or to slowly put pressure on fast-food restaurants to offer healthy food choices. A gun control campaign may focus on teaching gun owners to take safety precautions when loading a gun, or on intensifying public opinion pressure on legislators to support legal suits against the gun industry like those brought against Big Tobacco.

2. *What is the locus of the dilemma?* Campaigners may perceive that the roots of a health problem are psychological—for example, personal shortcomings of drug abusers. Alternatively, they may take a more macro view, arguing that the problem is rooted in social conditions: a billion-dollar global drug industry, indirectly backed by the U.S. government, that preys on vulnerable youth. The perceived locus of the problem will influence campaign strategies and choice of social marketing techniques.

3. *If the goal is to benefit the public good, is the campaign designed to do more good for certain members of the public than others?* There is no absolute definition of "public good." Instead, the definition inevitably reflects value judgments. Should good be defined in utilitarian terms—a cardiovascular risk reduction campaign designed to reach the greatest number of people? Or should it be viewed in a more deontological fashion, emphasizing values like justice—as when planners of a blood pressure screening campaign, acknowledging that poverty produces great psychological stress, choose to focus only on poor people? Similarly, as Nurit Guttman (1997) puts it, "should campaign resources be devoted to target populations believed to be particularly needy or those who are more likely to adopt its recommendations?" (p. 181). It is more difficult to reach needy individuals, as well as the hard core that is at greatest risk for disease. By opting for reachable goals—trying to do the greatest good for the greatest number—are campaigns copping out at the get-go, favoring the advantaged over the disenfranchised?

4. *How are values implicated in the solutions campaigners recommend?* An AIDS prevention campaign that urges people to practice safer sex has opted not to communicate the values of abstinence or waiting to have sex until you are married. Social norm-based antidrinking campaigns advocate moderate drinking, an option that some parents oppose.

5. *How do values influence criteria used to proclaim success?* Evaluators must devise benchmarks that can be used to determine if a campaign has succeeded. Values come into play here. For example, an intervention to

promote breast cancer screening could be deemed successful if it increased the number of women who had mammograms yearly. However, given that those most likely to get mammograms are women with insurance that covers the procedure, the criteria for success excludes poor women (Guttman, 2000). The evaluator may reason that a campaign cannot do everything, and note that increases in mammography even among those with insurance policies is an achievement. That may be a reasonable call, but it reflects a certain set of value judgments.

6. Finally, although different values shape campaigns, all campaigns are based on a core assumption: *The world will be a better place if social interventions effortfully try to change individual behavior.* Campaigns assume that social marketing interventions to change individual behavior and improve the public health are worthwhile ventures. This puts communication campaigns at odds with a strict libertarianism that regards individual liberty as an unshakable first principle. Libertarians would question why we need campaigns since people know that smoking causes cancer but choose to smoke, or know all about the risks of HIV but prefer to practice unsafe sex because it's fun. Don't people have a right to make their own choices and live life according to their own rules, even those that strike others as self-destructive?

It is a good question, one that philosophers have been asking in one fashion or another for centuries. Campaigns must necessarily balance individual liberties and the public good. Both are important values. Clearly, when your liberty (to smoke) threatens my good health by exposing me to secondhand smoke, it's a no-brainer for many people. But how far should you go in taking away liberties for the sake of the larger whole? Is it right to ban smoking in *every* public place, as the more coercive of antismoking activists would recommend? Where do you draw the line?

AND NOW PLEASE—A WORD FROM OUR POLITICAL SPONSOR

It happens every four years. Not that most American voters are enormously invested in presidential election campaigns. About half of the electorate votes, and young people are particularly unlikely to cast their ballots (Doppelt & Shearer, 1999). Nevertheless, politics (a topic not much discussed in this chapter) matters. Political decisions—on such issues as education, tax cuts, Social Security, and crime—have an enormous impact on our lives.

Electoral campaigns determine who will represent us in national and local government. They also shape public policy. Nowadays, political campaigns are not limited to electoral matters. We live in the era of the "permanent campaign," in which political marketers (a late-20th-century innovation) wage campaigns to influence public opinion on all manner of issues, including health care reform, stem cell research, the death penalty, and the U.S. war on terrorism.

No persuasion book could possibly be complete without a discussion of politics. Although persuasion theories have been applied to politics elsewhere in the book, thus far there has been no description of political communication campaigns. The topic is so big and interdisciplinary it cannot be discussed in detail in a general book like this one. However, it is possible to venture several main pointers about the role persuasive communications play in political campaigns. Thus, the next section switches from the health to the political and international campaign contexts. I draw on research and theory to briefly outline strategies that candidates and issue proponents can employ to attain their objectives. To win contemporary campaigns, research suggests that candidates deploy the following persuasive strategies:

1. **Develop a core set of positions that spring from a political philosophy**. Harking back to the ancient era of the 1980s, one notes that Ronald Reagan ran as a conservative opposed to big government and in support of a bolder U.S. foreign policy. His platform appealed to voters looking for leadership and tired of the Democrats' big-government policies. He won the 1980 election handily.

2. **Communicate a vision through strategic use of media**. The message, a centerpiece of persuasive communication, is of central importance in politics. The still-classic example is Bill Clinton's 1992 campaign, in which he focused relentlessly on the nation's economic woes, offering specific proposals. Guided by the slogan, "It's the Economy, Stupid," Clinton's campaign succeeded in setting the agenda—that is, in convincing people that the economy was the most important issue facing the country, and also in suggesting that Clinton was the most qualified candidate to take on this challenge.

3. **Market an image**. In an age of mass media, few voters meet the candidates. They must, therefore, rely on the image communicated through TV and other media. Campaigns manufacture images through marketing, polling, and positioning the candidate in appealing ways. Images are never entirely accurate: John F. Kennedy loved his family, but he also loved cavorting with women, an image Americans did not acquire until much later.

4. **Make a personal, emotional connection with people**. The ability to connect with people still counts, even in a media age (Newman & Perloff, in press). The reason George W. Bush, a newcomer to national politics in

2000, fared so well is that he forged strong emotional connections with sympathetic voters, implicitly taking a chapter from the source attractiveness playbook. Forging a personal connection is as important a factor in political success in the early 21st century as it was in the early 20th.

5. **Appeal persuasively to undecided voters.** In recent elections, undecided voters have played a key role in determining the outcome of the race. To reach these voters, candidates must poll incessantly, tailor different messages to diverse audience subgroups, avoid political gaffes, and take ambiguous positions on hot-button issues like abortion and gun control. It's the latter ambiguity—skeptics call it dishonesty—that turns off some people to politics and gives third-party candidates their charm.

The Campaign Like No Other

It's been called a hinge moment in history, one of those "pivots on which our lives move from one world to another" (Garreau, 2001, p. 6). The events of September 11 had a shattering impact on people's psyches. We all remember the destruction of the World Trade Center—even today. The attacks transformed America's military and political priorities, causing its leaders and citizens to recognize that we had to fight and win a new kind of war, a war like no other, as was frequently said in the immediate aftermath of 9/11.

Few doubted the need for military action; indeed, nearly 90% of Americans supported military action in retaliation for the terrorist attacks (Drinkard, 2001). More surprising to many, perhaps, was the call for a campaign to influence opinion in the United States and abroad. Americans were accustomed to campaigns waged to win elections, influence opinion on political matters, and, of course, to change unhealthy behaviors. However, George W. Bush's decision to mount a full-scale domestic and international campaign to influence opinions toward the war and the United States came as a surprise to some Americans, particularly when they learned that Bush had appointed a former advertising executive, dubbed the "Queen of Madison Avenue," to serve as campaign director (McCarthy, 2001).

A persuasion campaign made eminent sense, however, when one considered the critical role that public opinion played in democracy. Health campaigners recognized the need to influence public opinion when they waged antismoking and antidrinking campaigns. They not only sought to change individuals' attitudes toward cigarettes and booze, but also to apply indirect pressure on the tobacco and alcohol industries to change their policies toward advertising directed at young people. In a similar fashion, the Bush administration recognized it could not mount a successful war effort without strong support from the American people.

It also realized that if it was to gain support from foreign governments and influential Arab leaders, it would have to combat the images of America held by so many Arabs and Muslims across the world.

The campaign would be fought on two fronts: domestic and international. The domestic campaign centered on rallying the American public behind the president and his war policies. This required a keen appreciation of persuasion principles. One of the most critical was **language** and the use of what Theodore Roosevelt called "the bully pulpit." As "the symbolic embodiment of the nation," the president's words and expressions can sway emotions and influence policy (Euchner, 1990). Although not known for his glib rhetoric, Bush used language skillfully in the months that followed the terrorist attack. Adapting the words of the great British prime minister, Winston Churchill, to the present moment, Bush told the nation, "We will not tire. We will not falter. And we will not fail." Nonverbally, he projected calm and strength—not easy qualities to muster when your nation is attacked and all eyes are fixated on you, but precisely the qualities a leader needs to convey during times of crisis.

Bush appealed to American values—faith in God, tolerance for people of diverse faiths (notably, Muslims and Arab Americans), and optimism for the future. In this way he hoped to say things that resonated with people, and were **cognitively consistent**—not dissonant—with their core values. Recognizing the power of organizing principles, what social scientists call frames, Bush **framed** terrorism as an attack on freedom and civilization itself. Liberal scholars thought the frame understated the extent to which terror is rooted in socioeconomic conditions (Rothstein, 2001). Yet the overwhelming number of Americans shared Bush's belief that it was really quite simple—a battle of good versus evil, the legitimate need of a country to defend itself against unspeakable attack. His poll numbers in the fall of 2001 reflected Americans' support of his policies and frame: Over 85% of the public approved of the job he was doing as president. While some of his war policies troubled civil libertarians, he used rhetoric and public relations effectively in 2001, rallying the public around the flag and war effort.

As Bush worked the airwaves, his aides worked the street: Rodeo Drive, Beverly Hills, to be specific. White House aides met with Hollywood executives to enlist their help in promoting the war on terrorism. Celebrity actors and actresses—Julia Roberts, Jennifer Lopez, Tom Cruise, Robert DeNiro—willingly did promos for the war effort or entertained the troops in well-publicized media tours.

The International Campaign. The battle for world public opinion shaped up as a far more difficult contest, one that took place on a larger, more complex, and volatile playing field. How do you influence millions of Muslims and Arabs who have come to love America's commercial products (from Levi's jeans to Michael Jordan), but despise the U.S. government, and misunderstand America herself (Burns, 2001)? How do you influence Arab young people, who cannot find meaningful employment in their own countries, are provided no legitimate outlet for expressing political grievances, and, "with one foot in the old world and another in the new," find Islamic fundamentalism a simple, tempting alternative (Zakaria, 2001, pp. 30, 32)? How can you realistically hope to change these folks' attitudes toward America or succeed in making "American values as much a brand name as McDonald's hamburgers or Ivory soap" (Becker, 2001, p. A1)?

The campaign, launched in the fall of 2001, faced an additional problem— the terrorists' ability to manipulate modern media to their own ends. Osama bin Laden, like other evil charismatic leaders, displayed a canny knowledge of media and symbols. Within hours after the United States bombed Afghanistan in October 2001, the terrorist appeared in a videotape, "citing Islamic scripture, his rifle leaning against a rock beside him," celebrating the September 11 attacks (Kifner, 2001, p. 5). To be sure, his rhetoric turned off those Muslims who recognized his exploitation of their religious doctrine for his purposes. Yet it resonated to some degree with hopeless men and women on the Arab street or with those who had internalized years of anti-Western education. For still others—who planned to join the jihad and deluded themselves into thinking that Jews flew the planes into the World Trade Center—his speech was pure political poetry (Bragg, 2001).

Under such circumstances (facing fanatics and daunting odds), how do you conduct a campaign to influence worldwide opinion? For starters, one must recognize that it is essential to carefully apply communication campaign principles to the problem at hand. The U.S. government did this, attempting in its communication to do the following:

1. *Capture audience attention.* After a faulty start, the administration realized that to reach the Arab world, it had to beam its message to Arab media. U.S. military leaders did interviews with Al Jazeera, the Arab satellite television channel. Experts argued that it needed to supplement this by communicating messages on TV channels that showed the popular Arabic version of "Who Wants to Be a Millionaire"(Fandy, 2001).

2. *Appeal to the undecideds.* One scholar estimated that 40% of Arab public opinion agreed with the United States and not the terrorists, another 10% supported bin Laden, while the remaining 50% disliked bin Laden's band of thugs, but distrusted the U.S. approach to the Middle East (Fandy, 2001). Trying to appeal to the latter Arab men and women,

the United States released a videotape that showed bin Laden smiling and boasting of attacks that killed over 3,000 people.

3. *Display goodwill.* In early speeches, George W. Bush took pains to show that he respected the religious faith of the world's Muslims. "The enemy of America is not our many Muslim friends," he said. "We respect your faith. . . . Its teaching are good and peaceful, and those who commit evil in the name of Allah blaspheme the name of Allah" (McQuillan, 2001, p. 3A).

4. *Use credible communicators.* There is only so much that an American president can do to appeal to Arabs and Muslims worldwide. Experts argued that moderate Arab opinion leaders, or celebrities like Muhammad Ali, who condemned terrorism, were more credible sources. (Ali, perhaps the most celebrated individual of Muslim faith in the world, did a one-minute spot designed for broadcast over Arab television networks in which he stressed that the war was not directed at Islam, but against terrorists who murdered innocent people.) Communicators like Ali violate the knowledge bias and can enhance trustworthiness.

5. *Understand your audience's beliefs—the logic behind their dislike of America—and target beliefs that are most susceptible to change.* It doesn't help to talk about enduring freedom to people who have no freedom. Instead, it is better to frame arguments about America's democratic values in terms that those in Arab countries can appreciate.

Needless to say, these weren't easy tasks. A campaign could do only so much. Nonetheless, the U.S. campaign appeared to have made inroads into anti-American attitudes held by some of the world's Muslims. Naturally, the campaign planners and the U.S. president made their share of mistakes (like Bush's early calling for a "crusade" on terrorism, a term that evoked images of Western attacks a thousand years ago). The communication campaign also changed directions in response to changing military and political events. The campaign was neither static nor perfect. Yet in one sense it reflected the best of American society: appeals to reason and respect for freedom to make up one's mind—values terrorists abhor.

CONCLUSIONS

Communication campaigns are vital activities, focused on using media and persuasion to improve social conditions. They have a long, proud history in this country. Contemporary campaigns are creatures of the current era, with its technological marvels and cultural diversity. Campaigns are guided by psychological, diffusion, and social marketing approaches. They can't save the world or change the political structure, but, executed effectively, they can influence individual behaviors and public policies. We have seen how campaigns can have significant, positive effects in the health and political arenas.

This chapter and the book as a whole have argued that if we understand how people think and feel about communication, we have a pretty good chance of changing their views in socially constructive ways. That is a foundation of persuasion scholarship. It seems to have a great deal of empirical support. Yet it is always worth playing devil's advocate with oneself and noting that there are people whose attitudes you can't change. There are people who will smoke no matter how many times they are exposed to an antismoking message, and others who will abuse drugs even after you tell them they can get busted precisely because they enjoy the thrill of testing the law. Still others will practice unsafe sex, knowing full well they are HIV-positive.

Persuasive communication, like all forces in life, has limits, a point emphasized at various times in this text. The fact that communication has limits does not mean it is powerless or ineffectual or always plays into the hands of the rich or corrupt. Persuasion can have these effects, of course, but it can also be an instrument of self-insight, healing, and social change. Whether it is a force for good or bad depends on us and our values—on how we go about trying to change people's minds at work and at home, on how we approach the practice of persuasion with strangers and those we love.

References

Abelson, R. P. (1959). Modes of resolution of belief dilemmas. *Journal of Conflict Resolution, 3*, 343–352.

Abelson, R. P. (1982). Three modes of attitude–behavior consistency. In M. P. Zanna, E. T. Higgins, & C. P. Herman (Eds.), *Consistency in social behavior: The Ontario symposium* (Vol. 2, pp. 131–146). Hillsdale, NJ: Lawrence Erlbaum Associates.

Abramson, P. R., Aldrich, J. H., & Rohde, D. W. (1994). *Change and continuity in the 1992 elections*. Washington, DC: CQ Press.

Achenbach, J. (2001, September 17–23). The terrible mornings after. *Washington Post National Weekly Edition, 31*.

Adelman, M. B. (1992). Healthy passions: Safer sex as play. In T. Edgar, M. A. Fitzpatrick, & V. S. Freimuth (Eds.), *AIDS: A communication perspective* (pp. 69–89). Hillsdale, NJ: Lawrence Erlbaum Associates.

Adkins, M., & Brashers, D. E. (1995). The power of language in computer-mediated groups. *Management Communication Quarterly, 8*, 289–322.

Adler, J. (1999, November 29). Living canvass. *Newsweek*, pp. 75–76.

Ajzen, I. (1991). The theory of planned behavior. *Organizational Behavior and Human Decision Processes, 50*, 179–211.

Ajzen, I., & Fishbein, M. (1977). Attitude–behavior relations: A theoretical analysis and review of empirical research. *Psychological Bulletin, 84*, 888–918.

Ajzen, I., & Fishbein, M. (1980). *Understanding attitudes and predicting social behavior*. Englewood Cliffs, NJ: Prentice-Hall.

Alexander, J. E., & Tate, M. A. (1999). *Web wisdom: How to evaluate and create information quality on the Web*. Mahwah, NJ: Lawrence Erlbaum Associates.

Allen, M. (1998). Comparing the persuasive effectiveness one- and two-sided message. In M. Allen & R. W. Preiss (Eds.), *Persuasion: Advances through meta-analysis* (pp. 87–98). Cresskill, NJ: Hampton Press.

Allen, M., Bruflat, R., Fucilla, R., Kramer, M., McKellips, S., Ryan, D. J., & Spiegelhoff, M. (2000). Testing the persuasiveness of evidence: Combining narrative and statistical forms. *Communication Research Reports, 17*, 331–336.

Allen, M., & Preiss, R. (1997a). Persuasion, public address, and progression in the sciences: Where we are at what we do. In G. A. Barnett & F. J. Boster (Eds.), *Progress in communication sciences* (Vol. 13, pp. 107–131). Greenwich, CT: Ablex.

Allen, M., & Preiss, R. W. (1997b). Comparing the persuasiveness of narrative and statistical evidence using meta-analysis. *Communication Research Reports, 14,* 125–131.

Allen, M., & Stiff, J. B. (1998). An analysis of the sleeper effect. In M. Allen & R. W. Preiss (Eds.), *Persuasion: Advances through meta-analysis* (pp. 175–188). Cresskill, NJ: Hampton Press.

Allport, G. W. (1935). Attitudes. In C. Murchison (Ed.), *A handbook of social psychology* (Vol. 2, pp. 798–844). Worcester, MA: Clark University Press.

Allport, G. W. (1945). The psychology of participation. *Psychological Review, 53,* 117–132.

Andersen, K. (1971). *Persuasion: Theory and practice.* Boston: Allyn & Bacon.

Anderson, R. B., & McMillion, P. Y. (1995). Effects of similar and diversified modeling on African American women's efficacy expectations and intentions to perform breast self-examination. *Health Communication, 7,* 324–343.

Andrews, J. C., & Shimp, T. A. (1990). Effects of involvement, argument strength, and source characteristics on central and peripheral processing in advertising. *Psychology & Marketing, 7,* 195–214.

Andrews, R. L., & Franke, G. R. (1991). The determinants of cigarette consumption: A meta-analysis. *Journal of Public Policy & Marketing, 10,* 81–100.

Andsager, J. L., Austin, E. W., & Pinkleton, B. E. (2001). Questioning the value of realism: Young adults' processing of messages in alcohol-related public service announcements and advertising. *Journal of Communication, 51(1),* 121–142.

Angier, N. (2000a, November 7). Cell phone or pheromone? New props for the mating game. *New York Times,* D5.

Angier, N. (2000b, November 7). Who is fat? It depends on culture. *New York Times,* D1–D2.

Armitage, C. J., & Conner, M. (2000). Attitudinal ambivalence: A test of three key hypotheses. *Personality and Social Psychology Bulletin, 26,* 1421–1432.

Aron, A., & Aron, E. N. (1989). *The heart of social psychology: A backstage view of a passionate science* (2nd ed.) Lexington, MA: Lexington Books.

Aronson, E. (1968). Dissonance theory: Progress and problems. In R. P. Abelson, E. Aronson, W. J. McGuire, T. M. Newcomb, M. J. Rosenberg, & P. H. Tannenbaum (Eds.), *Theories of cognitive consistency: A sourcebook* (pp. 5–27). Chicago: Rand McNally.

Aronson, E. (1999). Dissonance, hypocrisy, and the self-concept. In E. Harmon-Jones & J. Mills (Eds.), *Cognitive dissonance: Progress on a pivotal theory in social psychology* (pp. 103–126). Washington, DC: American Psychological Association.

Aronson, E., & Mills, J. (1959). The effect of severity of initiation on liking for a group. *Journal of Abnormal and Social Psychology, 59,* 177–181.

Aronson, J., Cohen, G., & Nail, P. R. (1999). Self-affirmation theory: An update and appraisal. In E. Harmon-Jones & J. Mills (Eds.), *Cognitive dissonance: Progress on a pivotal theory in social psychology* (pp. 127–147). Washington, DC: American Psychological Association.

Atkin, C. (2002). Promising strategies for media health campaigns. In W. D. Crano & M. Burgoon (Eds.), *Mass media and drug prevention: Classic and contemporary theories and research* (pp. 35–64). Mahwah, NJ: Lawrence Erlbaum Associates.

Atkin, C. K., & Freimuth, V. S. (2001). Formative evaluation research in campaign design. In R. E. Rice & C. K. Atkin (Eds.), *Public communication campaigns* (3rd ed., pp. 125–145). Thousand Oaks, CA: Sage.

Atwood, R. W., & Howell, R. J. (1971). Pupilometric and personality test score differences of female aggressing pedophiliacs and normals. *Psychonomic Science, 22*, 115–116.

Aune, R. K., & Basil, M. D. (1994). A relational obligations approach to the foot-in-the-mouth effect. *Journal of Applied Social Psychology, 24*, 546–556.

Aune, R. K., & Reynolds, R. A. (1994). The empirical development of the normative message processing scale. *Communication Monographs, 61*, 135–160.

Austin, E. W., & Chen, Y. J. (1999, August). *The relationship of parental reinforcement of media messages to college students' alcohol-related behaviors.* Paper presented to the annual convention of the Association for Education in Journalism and Mass Communication, New Orleans.

Austin, E. W., & Meili, H. K. (1994). Effects of interpretation of televised alcohol portrayals on children's alcohol beliefs. *Journal of Broadcasting & Electronic Media, 38*, 417–435.

Baesler, E. J., & Burgoon, J. K. (1994). The temporal effects of story and statistical evidence on belief change. *Communication Research, 21*, 582–602.

Bakker, A. B. (1999). Persuasive communication about AIDS prevention: Need for cognition determines the impact of message format. *AIDS Education and Prevention, 11*, 150–162.

Bandura, A. (1977). *Social learning theory.* Englewood Cliffs, NJ: Prentice Hall.

Bartsch, K., & London, K. (2000). Children's use of mental state information in selecting persuasive arguments. *Developmental Psychology, 36*, 352–365.

Basil, M. D. (1997). The danger of cigarette "special placements" in film and television. *Health Communication, 9*, 191–198.

Bassili, J. N. (1995). Response latency and the accessibility of voting intentions: What contributes to accessibility and how it affects vote choice. *Personality and Social Psychology Bulletin, 21*, 686–695.

Bauman, K. E., Brown, J. D., Bryan, E. S., Fisher, L. A., Padgett, C. A., & Sweeney, J. M. (1988). Three mass media campaigns to prevent adolescent cigarette smoking. *Preventive Medicine, 17*, 510–530.

Baumrind, D. (1964). Some thoughts on ethics of research: After reading Milgram's "Behavioral study of obedience." *American Psychologist, 19*, 421–423.

Baxter, L. A. (1984). An investigation of compliance-gaining as politeness. *Human Communication Research, 10*, 427–456.

Becker, E. (2001, November 11). In the war on terrorism, a battle to shape opinion. *New York Times*, A1, B4, B5.

Bellafante, G. (2000, October 8). Read my tie: No more scandals. *New York Times*, 9-1, 9-9.

Bem, D. J. (1970). *Beliefs, attitudes, and human affairs.* Belmont, CA: Brooks/Cole.

Bem, D. J. (1972). Self-perception theory. In L. Berkowitz (Ed.), *Advances in experimental social psychology* (Vol. 6, pp. 1–62). New York: Academic Press.

Bennett, W. J. (1998). *The death of outrage: Bill Clinton and the assault on American ideals.* New York: Free Press.

Benoit, W. L. (1991). Two tests of the mechanism of inoculation theory. *Southern Communication Journal, 56*, 219–229.

Benoit, W. L. (1998). Forewarning and persuasion. In M. Allen & R. W. Preiss (Eds.), *Persuasion: Advances through meta-analysis* (pp. 139–154). Cresskill, NJ: Hampton Press.

Bentler, P. M., & Speckhart, G. (1979). Models of attitude–behavior relations. *Psychological Review, 86*, 452–464.

Berke, R. L., & Elder, J. (2001, September 16). Strong backing for using force is found in poll. *New York Times*, 1, 4.

Berlo, D. K., Lemert, J. B., & Mertz, R. J. (1969). Dimensions for evaluating the acceptability of message sources. *Public Opinion Quarterly, 33*, 563–576.

Berscheid, E. (1966). Opinion change and communicator–communicatee similarity and dissimilarity. *Journal of Personality and Social Psychology, 4*, 670–680.

Bettinghaus, E. P., & Cody, M. J. (1987). *Persuasive communication* (4th ed.) New York: Holt, Rinehart & Winston.

Bishop, G. F., Tuchfarber, A. J., & Oldendick, R. W. (1986). Opinions on fictitious issues: The pressure to answer survey questions. *Public Opinion Quarterly, 50*, 240–250.

Blakeslee, S. (1998, October 13). Placebos prove so powerful even experts are surprised. *New York Times*, D1, D4.

Blass, T. (1992). The social psychology of Stanley Milgram. In M. P. Zanna (Ed.) *Advances in experimental social psychology* (Vol. 25, pp. 277–329). San Diego: Academic Press.

Blass, T. (1999). The Milgram paradigm after 35 years: Some things we now know about obedience to authority. *Journal of Applied Social Psychology, 29*, 955–978.

Boninger, D. S., Brock, T. C., Cook, T. D., Gruder, C. L., & Romer, D. (1990). Discovery of a reliable attitude change persistence resulting from a transmitter tuning set. *Psychological Science, 1*, 268–271.

Boninger, D. S., Krosnick, J. A., Berent, M. K., & Fabrigar, L. R. (1995). The causes and consequences of attitude importance. In R. E. Petty & J. A. Krosnick (Eds.), *Attitude strength: Antecedents and consequences* (pp. 159–189). Hillsdale, NJ: Lawrence Erlbaum Associates.

Booth-Butterfield, S., & Welbourne, J. (2002). The elaboration likelihood model: Its impact on persuasion theory and research. In J. P. Dillard & M. Pfau (Eds.), *The persuasion handbook: Developments in theory and practice* (pp. 155–173). Thousand Oaks, CA: Sage.

Borchert, D. M., & Stewart, D. (1986). *Exploring ethics*. New York: Macmillan.

Bornstein, R. F. (1989). Exposure and affect: Overview and meta-analysis of research, 1968–1987. *Psychological Bulletin, 106*, 265–289.

Boster, F. J., & Mongeau, P. (1984). Fear-arousing persuasive messages. In R. N. Bostrom (Ed.), *Communication Yearbook 8* (pp. 330–375). Beverly Hills: Sage.

Bowers, J. W. (1964). Some correlates of language intensity. *Quarterly Journal of Speech, 50*, 415–420.

Bradley, P. H. (1981). The folk-linguistics of women's speech: An empirical examination. *Communication Monographs, 48*, 73–90.

Bradsher, K. (2000, July 17). Was Freud a minivan or S.U.V. kind of guy? *New York Times*, A1, A16.

Bragg, R. (2001, October 14). Nurturing young Islamic hearts and hatreds. *New York Times*, A1, B5.

Brannon, L. A., & Brock, T. C. (1994). The subliminal persuasion controversy: Reality, enduring fable, and Polonius's weasel. In S. Shavitt & T. C. Brock (Eds.), *Persuasion: Psychological insights and perspectives* (pp. 279–293). Needham Heights, MA: Allyn & Bacon.

Breckler, S. J. (1984). Empirical validation of affect, behavior, and cognition as distinct components of attitude. *Journal of Personality and Social Psychology, 47*, 1191–1205.

Briggs, S. R., & Cheek, J. M. (1988). On the nature of self-monitoring: Problems with assessment, problems with validity. *Journal of Personality and Social Psychology, 54*, 663–678.

Brinberg, D., & Durand, J. (1983). Eating at fast-food restaurants: An analysis using two behavioral intention models. *Journal of Applied Social Psychology, 13*, 459–472.

Brock, T. C. (1965). Communicator–recipient similarity and decision change. *Journal of Personality and Social Psychology, 1*, 650–654.

Brock, T. C. (1967). Communication discrepancy and intent to persuade as determinants of counterargument production. *Journal of Experimental Social Psychology, 3*, 296–309.

Brody, J. E. (2000, April 4). Fresh warnings on the perils of piercing. *New York Times*, D8.

Brooke, J. (2000, January 3). A Cassandra with no regrets, and besides, it is not over yet. *New York Times*, A16.

Brown, J. D., & Walsh-Childers, K. (2002). Effects of media on personal and public health. In J. Bryant & D. Zillmann (Eds.), *Media effects: Advances in theory and research* (2nd ed., pp. 453–488). Mahwah, NJ: Lawrence Erlbaum Associates.

Brown, P., & Levinson, S. C. (1987). *Politeness: Some universals in language usage.* Cambridge, UK: Cambridge University Press.

Bryan, A. D., Aiken, L. S., & West, S. G. (1999). The impact of males proposing condom use on perceptions of an initial sexual encounter. *Personality and Social Psychology Bulletin, 25*, 275–286.

Budesheim, T. L., & DePaola, S. J. (1994). Beauty or the beast?: The effects of appearance, personality, and issue information on evaluations of political candidates. *Personality and Social Psychology Bulletin, 20*, 339–348.

Buller, D. B., & Burgoon, J. K. (1996). Interpersonal deception theory. *Communication Theory, 6*, 203–242.

Buller, D. B., & Hall, J. R. (1998). The effects of distraction during persuasion. In M. Allen & R. W. Preiss (Eds.), *Persuasion: Advances through meta-analysis* (pp. 155–173). Cresskill, NJ: Hampton Press.

Buller, D. B., LePoire, B. A., Aune, R. K., & Eloy, S. V. (1992). Social perceptions as mediators of the effect of speech rate similarity on compliance. *Human Communication Research, 19*, 286–311.

Burger, J. M. (1986). Increasing compliance by improving the deal: The that's-not-all technique. *Journal of Personality and Social Psychology, 51*, 277–283.

Burger, J. M. (1999). The foot-in-the-door compliance procedure: A multiple-process analysis and review. *Personality and Social Psychology Review, 3*, 303–325.

Burgoon, J. K. (1994). Nonverbal signals. In M. L. Knapp & G. R. Miller (Eds.), *Handbook of interpersonal communication* (2nd ed., pp. 229–285). Thousand Oaks, CA: Sage.

Burgoon, M. (1989). Messages and persuasive effects. In J. J. Bradac (Ed.), *Message effects in communication science* (pp. 129–164). Newbury Park, CA: Sage.

Burgoon, M., Alvaro, E., Grandpre, J., & Voulodakis, M. (2002). Revisiting the theory of psychological reactance: Communicating threats to attitudinal freedom. In J. P. Dillard & M. Pfau (Eds.), *The persuasion handbook: Developments in theory and practice* (pp. 213–232). Thousand Oaks, CA: Sage.

Burgoon, M., Denning, V. P., & Roberts, L. (2002). Language expectancy theory. In J. P. Dillard and M. Pfau (Eds.), *The persuasion handbook: Developments in theory and practice* (pp. 117–136). Thousand Oaks, CA: Sage.

Burgoon, M., Hendriks, A., & Alvaro, E. (2001, May). *Tobacco prevention and cessation: Effectiveness of the Arizona Tobacco Education and Prevention Media Campaign.* Paper presented to the annual convention of the International Communication Association, Washington, DC.

Burgoon, M., Parrott, R., Burgoon, J., Birk, T., Pfau, M., & Coker, R. (1989). Primary care physicians' selection of verbal compliance-gaining strategies. *Health Communication, 2*, 13–27.

Burke, K. (1950). *A rhetoric of motives.* New York: Prentice Hall.

Burleigh, M. (2000). *The Third Reich: A new history.* New York: Hill and Wang.

Burleson, B. R., Wilson, S. R., Waltman, M. S., Goering, E. M., Ely, T. K., & Whaley, B. B. (1988). Item desirability effects in compliance-gaining research: Seven studies documenting artifacts in the strategy selection procedure. *Human Communication Research, 14*, 429–486.

Burns, J. F. (2001, September 16). America inspires both longing and loathing in Arab world. *New York Times*, 17.

Burrell, N. A., & Koper, R. J. (1998). The efficacy of powerful/powerless language on attitudes and source credibility. In M. Allen & R. W. Preiss (Eds.), *Persuasion: Advances through meta-analysis* (pp. 203–215). Cresskill, NJ: Hampton Press.

Buss, D. M., & Kenrick, D. T. (1998). Evolutionary social psychology. In D. T. Gilbert, S. T. Fiske, & G. Lindzey (Eds.), *The handbook of social psychology* (4th ed., Vol. 2, pp. 982–1026). Boston: McGraw-Hill.

Cacioppo, J. T., Harkins, S. G., & Petty, R. E. (1981). The nature of attitudes and cognitive responses and their relationships to behavior. In R. E. Petty, T. M. Ostrom, & T. C. Brock (Eds.), *Cognitive responses in persuasion* (pp. 31–54). Hillsdale, NJ: Lawrence Erlbaum Associates.

Cacioppo, J. T., & Petty, R. E. (1982). The need for cognition. *Journal of Personality and Social Psychology, 42*, 116–131.

Cacioppo, J. T., Petty, R. E., Feinstein, J. A., & Jarvis, W. B. G. (1996). Dispositional differences in cognitive motivation: The life and times of individuals varying in need for cognition. *Psychological Bulletin, 119*, 197–253.

Cacioppo, J. T., Petty, R. E., & Kao, C. F. (1984). The efficient assessment of need for cognition. *Journal of Personality Assessment, 48*, 306–307.

Cacioppo, J. T., Petty, R. E., & Marshall-Goodell, B. (1984). Electromyographic specificity during simple physical and attitudinal tasks: Location and topographical features of integrated EMG responses. *Biological Psychology, 18*, 85–121.

Cacioppo, J. T., Priester, J. R., & Berntson, G. G. (1993). Rudimentary determinants of attitudes. II: Arm flexion and extension have differential effects on attitudes. *Journal of Personality and Social Psychology, 65*, 5–17.

Caldwell, D. F., & Burger, J. M. (1997). Personality and social influence strategies in the workplace. *Personality and Social Psychology Bulletin, 23*, 1003–1012.

Cameron, K. A., Witte, K., & Nzyuko, S. (1999). Perceptions of condoms and barriers to condom use along the Trans-Africa Highway in Kenya. In W. N. Elwood (Ed.), *Power in the blood: A handbook on AIDS, politics, and communication* (pp. 149–163). Mahwah, NJ: Lawrence Erlbaum Associates.

Campbell, K. K. (1989). *Man cannot speak for her: A critical study of early feminist rhetoric* (Vol. 1). New York: Greenwood.

Campbell, R., Martin, C. R., & Fabos, B. (2002). *Media & culture: An introduction to mass communication* (3rd. ed.). Boston: Bedford/St. Martin's.

Cappella, J. N., Fishbein, M., Hornik, R., Ahern, R. K., & Sayeed, S. (2001). Using theory to select messages in antidrug media campaigns: Reasoned action and media priming. In R. E. Rice & C. K. Atkin (Eds.), *Public communication campaigns* (3rd ed., pp. 214–230). Thousand Oaks, CA: Sage.

Carli, L. L. (1999). Gender, interpersonal power, and social influence. *Journal of Social Issues, 55*, 81–99.

Chaiken, S. (1979). Communicator's physical attractiveness and persuasion. *Journal of Personality and Social Psychology, 37*, 1387–1397.

Chaiken, S., Liberman, A., & Eagly, A. H. (1989). Heuristic and systematic information processing within and beyond the persuasion context. In J. S. Uleman & J. A. Bargh (Eds.), *Unintended thought: Limits of awareness, intention, and control* (pp. 212–252). New York: Guilford.

Chaiken, S., Wood, W., & Eagly, A. H. (1996). Principles of persuasion. In E. T. Higgins & A. W. Kruglanski (Eds.), *Social psychology: Handbook of basic principles* (pp. 702–742). New York: Guilford Press.

Chapanis, N. P., & Chapanis, A. C. (1964). Cognitive dissonance: Five years later. *Psychological Bulletin, 61*, 1–22.

Chappell, T. (1998). Platonism. In R. Chadwick (Ed.), *Encyclopedia of applied ethics* (Vol. 3, pp. 511–523). San Diego: Academic Press.

Charles, N., Trischitta, L., & Morrissey, S. (2001, August 13). End of the party. *People*, pp. 67–68, 70.

Chartrand, T., Pinckert, S., & Burger, J. M. (1999). When manipulation backfires: The effects of time delay and requester on the foot-in-the-door technique. *Journal of Applied Social Psychology, 29*, 211–221.

Chen, S., & Chaiken, S. (1999). The heuristic–systematic model in its broader context. In S. Chaiken & Y. Trope (Eds.), *Dual-process theories in social psychology* (pp. 73–96). New York: Guilford.

Chew, F., Mehta, A., & Oldfather, A. (1994). Applying concept mapping to assess the influence of celebrity-message dynamics on communication effectiveness. In K. W. King (Ed.), *Proceedings of the 1994 Conference of the American Academy of Advertising* (pp. 26–39). New York: American Academy of Advertising.

Chew, F., & Palmer, S. (1994). Interest, the knowledge gap, and television programming. *Journal of Broadcasting & Electronic Media, 38,* 271–287.

Cho, C-H. (1999). How advertising works on the WWW: Modified elaboration likelihood model. *Journal of Current Issues and Research in Advertising, 21,* 33–50.

Cialdini, R. B. (2001). *Influence: Science and practice* (4th ed.). Boston: Allyn & Bacon.

Cialdini, R. B., & Ascani, K. (1976). Test of a concession procedure for inducing verbal, behavioral, and further compliance with a request to give blood. *Journal of Applied Psychology, 61,* 295–300.

Cialdini, R. B., Cacioppo, J. T., Bassett, R., & Miller, J. A. (1978). Low-ball procedure for producing compliance: Commitment then cost. *Journal of Personality and Social Psychology, 36,* 463–476.

Cialdini, R. B., Trost, M. R., & Newsom, J. T. (1995). Preference for consistency: The development of a valid measure and the discovery of surprising behavioral implications. *Journal of Personality and Social Psychology, 69,* 318–328.

Cialdini, R. B., Vincent, J. E., Lewis, S. K., Catalan, J., Wheeler, D., & Darby B. L. (1975). Reciprocal concessions procedure for inducing compliance: The door-in-the-face technique. *Journal of Personality and Social Psychology, 31,* 206–215.

Clary, E. G., Snyder, M., Ridge, R. D., Miene, P. K., & Haugen, J. A. (1994). Matching messages to motives in persuasion: A functional approach to promoting volunteerism. *Journal of Applied Social Psychology, 24,* 1129–1149.

Clines, F. X. (2001, October 21). In uneasy time, seeking comfort in the familiar frights of Halloween. *New York Times,* B8.

Cody, M. J., & McLaughlin, M. L. (1980). Perceptions of compliance-gaining situations: A dimensional analysis. *Communication Monographs, 47,* 132–148.

Cody, M. J., & McLaughlin, M. L. (1985). The situation as a construct in interpersonal communication research. In M. L. Knapp & G. R. Miller (Eds.), *Handbook of interpersonal communication* (pp. 263–312). Beverly Hills, CA: Sage.

Cody, M. J., McLaughlin, M. L., & Jordan, W. J. (1980). A multidimensional scaling of three sets of compliance-gaining strategies. *Communication Quarterly, 28,* 34–46.

Cody, M. J., & Seiter, J. S. (2001). Compliance principles in retail sales in the United States. In W. Wosinska, R. B. Cialdini, D. W. Barrett, & J. Reykowski (Eds.), *The practice of social influence in multiple cultures* (pp. 325–341). Mahwah, NJ: Lawrence Erlbaum Associates.

Cohen, A. R., Stotland, E., & Wolfe, D. M. (1955). An experimental investigation of need for cognition. *Journal of Abnormal and Social Psychology, 51,* 291–294.

Cohen, R. (1999, August 13). Why? New Eichmann notes try to explain. *New York Times,* A1, A3.

Condit, C. M. (1990). *Decoding abortion rhetoric: Communicating social change.* Urbana: University of Illinois Press.

Conger, J. A. (1998, May–June). The necessary art of persuasion. *Harvard Business Review, 76,* 84–95.

Conner, M., & Armitage, C. J. (1998). Extending the theory of planned behavior: A review and avenues for further research. *Journal of Applied Social Psychology, 28,* 1429–1464.

Conover, P. J., & Feldman, S. (1984). How people organize the political world: A schematic model. *American Journal of Political Science, 28,* 95–126.

Cooper, B. (1998). "The White–Black fault line": Relevancy of race and racism in spectators' experiences of Spike Lee's *Do the Right Thing. Howard Journal of Communications, 9,* 205–228.

Cooper, J., & Axsom, D. (1982). Effort justification in psychotherapy. In G. Weary & H. L. Mirels (Eds.), *Integrations of clinical and social psychology* (pp. 214–230). New York: Oxford Press.

Cooper, J., & Fazio, R. H. (1984). A new look at dissonance theory. In L. Berkowitz (Ed.), *Advances in experimental social psychology* (Vol. 17, pp. 229–266). Orlando, FL: Academic Press.

Cooper, J., & Scher, S. J. (1994). When do our actions affect our attitudes? In S. Shavitt & T. C. Brock (Eds.), *Persuasion: Psychological insights and perspectives* (pp. 95–111). Boston: Allyn and Bacon.

Cooper, M. D., & Nothstine, W. L. (1998). *Power persuasion: Moving an ancient art into the media age.* (2nd ed.). Greenwood, IN: Educational Video Group.

Coyne, M. (2000). Paper prepared for course on persuasion and attitude change, Cleveland State University.

Crites, S. L., Jr., Fabrigar, L. R., & Petty, R. E. (1994). Measuring the affective and cognitive properties of attitudes: Conceptual and methodological issues. *Personality and Social Psychological Bulletin, 20,* 619–634.

Cronkhite, G., & Liska, J. (1976). A critique of factor analytic approaches to the study of credibility. *Communication Monographs, 43,* 91–107.

Cross, M. (1996). Reading television texts: The postmodern language of advertising. In M. Cross (Ed.), *Advertising and culture: Theoretical perspectives* (pp. 1–10). Westport, CT: Praeger.

Crossen, C. (1991, November 14). Studies galore support products and positions, but are they reliable? *Wall Street Journal,* A1, A7.

Crusco, A. H., & Wetzel, C. G. (1984). The Midas touch: The effects of interpersonal touch on restaurant tipping. *Personality and Social Psychology Bulletin, 10,* 512–517.

Cruz, M. G. (1998). Explicit and implicit conclusions in persuasive messages. In M. Allen & R. W. Preiss (Eds.), *Persuasion: Advances through meta-analysis* (pp. 217–230). Cresskill, NJ: Hampton Press.

Davidson, E. (1977). *The making of Adolf Hitler.* New York: Macmillan.

Davies, M. F. (1998). Dogmatism and belief formation: Output interference in the processing of supporting and contradictory cognitions. *Journal of Personality and Social Psychology, 75,* 456–466.

Davis, B. P., & Knowles, E. S. (1999). A disrupt-then-reframe technique of social influence. *Journal of Personality and Social Psychology, 76,* 192–199.

Dawes, R. M., & Smith, T. L. (1985). Attitude and opinion measurement. In G. L. Lindzey & E. A. Aronson (Eds.), *Handbook of social psychology* (3rd ed., Vol. 1, pp. 509–566). New York: Random House.

Dearing, J. W., Rogers, E. M., Meyer, G., Casey, M. K., Rao, N., Campo, S., & Henderson, G. M. (1996). Social marketing and diffusion-based strategies for communicating with unique populations: HIV prevention in San Francisco. *Journal of Health Communication, 1,* 343–363.

DeBono, K. G., (1987). Investigating the social-adjustive and value-expressive functions of attitudes: Implications for persuasion processes. *Journal of Personality and Social Psychology, 52,* 279–287.

DeBono, K. G. (2000). Attitude functions and consumer psychology: Understanding perceptions of product quality. In G. R. Maio & J. M. Olson (Eds.), *Why we evaluate: Functions of attitudes* (pp. 195–221). Mahwah, NJ: Lawrence Erlbaum Associates.

DeBono, K. G., & Harnish, R. J. (1988). Source expertise, source attractiveness, and the processing of persuasive information: A functional approach. *Journal of Personality and Social Psychology, 55,* 541–546.

DeBono, K. G., & Klein, C. (1993). Source expertise and persuasion: The moderating role of recipient dogmatism. *Personality and Social Psychology Bulletin, 19,* 167–173.

de Botton, A. (2000). *The consolations of philosophy.* New York: Pantheon.

Deci, E. L. (1975). *Intrinsic motivation.* New York: Plenum Press.

DeJong, W. (1979). An examination of self-perception mediation of the foot-in-the-door effect. *Journal of Personality and Social Psychology, 37,* 2221–2239.

Delia, J. G., Kline, S. L., & Burleson, B. R. (1979). The development of persuasive communication strategies in kindergartners through twelfth-graders. *Communication Monographs, 46,* 241–256.

Denton, R. E., Jr. (Ed.) (1994). *The 1992 presidential campaign: A communication perspective.* Westport, CT: Praeger.

DePaulo, B. M., Kashy, D. A., Kirkendol, S. E., Wyer, M. M., & Epstein, J. A. (1996). Lying in everyday life. *Journal of Personality and Social Psychology, 70,* 979–995.

de Waal, F. (1982). *Chimpanzee politics: Power and sex among apes.* London: Jonathan Cape Ltd.

DiClemente, R. J. (Ed.) (1992). *Adolescents and AIDS: A generation in jeopardy.* Thousand Oaks, CA: Sage.

Dillard, J. P. (1990a). Self-inference and the foot-in-the-door technique: Quantity of behavior and attitudinal mediation. *Human Communication Research, 16,* 422–447.

Dillard, J. P. (1990b). A goal-driven model of interpersonal influence. In J. P. Dillard (Ed.), *Seeking compliance: The production of interpersonal influence messages* (pp. 41–56). Scottsdale, AZ: Gorsuch-Scarisbrick.

Dillard, J. P. (1993). Persuasion past and present: Attitudes aren't what they used to be. *Communication Monographs, 60,* 90–97.

Dillard, J. P. (1994). Rethinking the study of fear appeals: An emotional perspective. *Communication Theory, 4,* 295–323.

Dillard, J. P., Hunter, J. E., & Burgoon, M. (1984). Sequential-request persuasive strategies: Meta-analysis of foot-in-the-door and door-in-the-face. *Human Communication Research, 10,* 461–488.

Dillard, J. P., Kinney, T. A., & Cruz, M. G. (1996). Influence, appraisals, and emotions in close relationships. *Communication Monographs, 63,* 105–130.

Dixon, N. F. (1971). *Subliminal perception: The nature of a controversy.* London: McGraw Hill.

Dolinski, D., & Nawrat, R. (1998). "Fear-then-relief" procedure for producing compliance: Beware when the danger is over. *Journal of Experimental Social Psychology, 34,* 27–50.

Doll, J., & Ajzen, I. (1992). Accessibility and stability of predictors in the theory of planned behavior. *Journal of Personality and Social Psychology, 63,* 754–765.

Donohew, L., Palmgreen, P., & Lorch, E. P. (1994). Attention, need for sensation, and health communication campaigns. *American Behavioral Scientist, 38,* 310–322.

Donohew, L., Palmgreen, P., Lorch, E., Zimmerman, R., & Harrington, N. (2002). Attention, persuasive communication, and prevention. In W. D. Crano & M. Burgoon (Eds.), *Mass media and drug prevention: Classic and contemporary theories and research* (pp. 119–143). Mahwah, NJ: Lawrence Erlbaum Associates.

Doppelt, J. C., & Shearer, E. (1999). *Nonvoters: America's no-shows.* Thousand Oaks, CA: Sage.

Dovidio, J. F., & Fazio, R. H. (1992). New technologies for the direct and indirect assessment of attitudes. In J. M. Tanur (Ed.), *Questions about questions: Inquiries into the cognitive bases of surveys* (pp. 204–237). New York: Russell Sage Foundation.

Drinkard, J. (2001, September 17). America ready to sacrifice. *USA Today,* 1A.

Dudczak, C. A. (2001, January). Comments on *The Dynamics of Persuasion.* Prepared for Lawrence Erlbaum Associates.

Dyer, K. (2001, September 19). Sept. 11: "Day of pride." *USA Today,* Letter to the Editor, 14A.

Dyson, M. E. (2001, January 22). Moral leaders need not be flawless. *New York Times,* A23.

Eagly, A. H. (1978). Sex differences in influenceability. *Psychological Bulletin, 85,* 86–116.

Eagly, A. H., & Carli, L. L. (1981). Sex of researchers and sex-typed communications as determinants of sex differences in influenceability: A meta-analysis of social influence studies. *Psychological Bulletin, 90,* 1–20.

Eagly, A. H., & Chaiken, S. (1995). Attitude strength, attitude structure, and resistance to change. In R. E. Petty & J. A. Krosnick (Eds.), *Attitude strength: Antecedents and consequences* (pp. 413–432). Hillsdale, NJ: Lawrence Erlbaum Associates.

Eagly, A. H., & Chaiken, S. (1998). Attitude structure and function. In D. T. Gilbert, S. T. Fiske, & G. Lindzey (Eds.), *Handbook of social psychology* (4th ed., Vol. 1, pp. 269–322). Boston: McGraw-Hill.

Eagly, A. H., Chen, S., Chaiken, S., & Shaw-Barnes, K. (1999). The impact of attitudes on memory: An affair to remember. *Psychological Bulletin, 125,* 64–89.

Eagly, A. H., Kulesa, P., Chen, S., & Chaiken, S. (2001). Do attitudes affect memory?: Tests of the congeniality hypothesis. *Current Directions in Psychological Science, 10,* 5–9.

Eagly, A. H., Mladinic, A., & Otto, S. (1994). Cognitive and affective bases of attitudes toward social groups and social policies. *Journal of Experimental Social Psychology, 30,* 113–137.

Eagly, A. H., Wood, W., & Chaiken, S. (1978). Causal inferences about communicators and their effect on opinion change. *Journal of Personality and Social Psychology, 36,* 424–435.

Edwards, K., & Smith, E. E. (1996). A disconfirmation bias in the evaluation of arguments. *Journal of Personality and Social Psychology, 71,* 5–24.

Elkin, R. A., & Leippe, M. R. (1986). Physiological arousal, dissonance, and attitude change: Evidence for a dissonance–arousal link and a "don't remind me" effect. *Journal of Personality and Social Psychology, 51,* 55–65.

Elliot, A. J., & Devine, P. G. (1994). On the motivational nature of cognitive dissonance: Dissonance as psychological discomfort. *Journal of Personality and Social
Psychology, 67*, 382–394.

Ellsworth, P. C., & Gross, S. R. (1994). Hardening of the attitudes: Americans'
views on the death penalty. *Journal of Social Issues, 50*, 19–52.

Engs, R. C. (2000). *Clean living movements: American cycles of health reform.* Westport,
CT: Praeger.

Erickson, B., Lind, E. A., Johnson, B. C., & O'Barr, W. M. (1978). Speech style and
impression formation in a court setting: The effects of "powerful" and "powerless" speech. *Journal of Experimental Social Psychology, 14*, 266–279.

Euchner, C. C. (1990). Presidential appearances. In M. S. Benjaminson, M. Nelson,
& J. L. Moore (Eds.), *The presidents and the public* (pp. 109–129). Washington,
DC: Congressional Quarterly Press.

Falbo, T. (1977). Multidimensional scaling of power strategies. *Journal of Personality and Social Psychology, 35*, 537–547.

Fallon, A. (1990). Culture in the mirror: Sociocultural determinants of body
image. In T. F. Cash & T. Pruzinsky (Eds.), *Body images: Development, deviance,
and change* (pp. 80–109). New York: Guilford.

Fandy, M. (2001, December 10–16). The proper channels. *Washington Post National
Weekly Edition*, 22.

Farquhar, J. W., Fortmann, S. P., Flora, J. A., Taylor, C. B., Haskell, W. L., Williams,
P. T., Maccoby, N., & Wood, P. D. (1990). Effects of community-wide educa-
tion on cardiovascular disease risk factors: The Stanford Five-City Project.
Journal of the American Medical Association, 264, 359–365.

Fazio, R. H. (1989). On the power and functionality of attitudes: The role of atti-
tude accessibility. In A. R. Pratkanis, S. J. Breckler, & A. G. Greenwald (Eds.),
Attitude structure and function (pp. 153–179). Hillsdale, NJ: Lawrence Erlbaum
Associates.

Fazio, R. H. (1990). Multiple processes by which attitudes guide behavior: The
MODE model as an integrative framework. In M. P. Zanna (Ed.), *Advances in
experimental social psychology* (Vol. 23, pp. 75–109). San Diego: Academic Press.

Fazio, R. H. (1995). Attitudes as object-evaluation associations: Determinants,
consequences, and correlates of attitude accessibility. In R. E. Petty &
J. A. Krosnick (Eds.), *Attitude strength: Antecedents and consequences* (pp. 247–282).
Hillsdale, NJ: Lawrence Erlbaum Associates.

Fazio, R. H. (2000). Accessible attitudes as tools for object appraisal: Their costs
and benefits. In G. R. Maio & J. M. Olson (Eds.), *Why we evaluate: Functions of
attitudes* (pp. 1–36). Mahwah, NJ: Lawrence Erlbaum Associates.

Fazio, R. H., Powell, M. C., & Williams, C. J. (1989). The role of attitude accessibility in the attitude-to-behavior process. *Journal of Consumer Research, 16*, 280–288.

Fazio, R. H., & Roskos-Ewoldsen, D. R. (1994). Acting as we feel: When and how
attitudes guide behavior. In S. Shavitt & T. C. Brock (Eds.), *Persuasion: Psychological insights and perspectives* (pp. 71–93). Boston: Allyn and Bacon.

Fazio, R. H., & Williams, C. J. (1986). Attitude accessibility as a moderator of the
attitude–perception and attitude–behavior relations: An investigation of the
1984 presidential election. *Journal of Personality and Social Psychology, 51*,
505–514.

Fazio, R. H., & Zanna, M. P. (1978). Attitudinal qualities relating to the strength of the attitude–behavior relationship. *Journal of Experimental Social Psychology, 14*, 398–408.

Fazio, R. H., & Zanna, M. P. (1981). Direct experience and attitude–behavior consistency. In L. Berkowitz (Ed.), *Advances in experimental social psychology* (Vol. 14, pp. 162–202). New York: Academic Press.

Fazzolari, C. J. (2001, September 12). Don't return hatred. *USA Today*, Letter to the Editor, 18A.

Feinberg, J. (1998). Coercion. In E. Craig (Ed.), *Routledge encyclopedia of philosophy* (pp. 387–390). London: Routledge.

Fern, E. F., Monroe, K. B., & Avila, R. A. (1986). Effectiveness of multiple request strategies: A synthesis of research results. *Journal of Marketing Research, 23*, 144–152.

Festinger, L. (1957). *A theory of cognitive dissonance*. Stanford, CA: Stanford University Press.

Festinger, L., & Carlsmith, J. M. (1959). Cognitive consequences of forced compliance. *Journal of Abnormal and Social Psychology, 58*, 203–210.

Festinger, L., & Maccoby, N. (1964). On resistance to persuasive communications. *Journal of Abnormal and Social Psychology, 68*, 359–366.

Finckenauer, J. O. (1982). *Scared straight and the panacea phenomenon*. Englewood Cliffs, NJ: Prentice Hall.

Fischer, P. M., Schwartz, M. P., Richards, J. W., Jr., Goldstein, A. O., & Rojas, T. H. (1991). Brand logo recognition by children aged 3 to 6 years. *Journal of American Medical Association, 266*, 3145–3148.

Fishbein, M., & Ajzen, I. (1974). Attitudes toward objects as predictors of single and multiple behavioral criteria. *Psychological Review, 81*, 59–74.

Fishbein, M., & Ajzen, I. (1975). *Belief, attitude, intention and behavior: An introduction to theory and research*. Reading, MA: Addison-Wesley.

Fishbein, M., Cappella, J., Hornik, R., Sayeed, S., Yzer, M., & Ahern, R. K. (2002). The role of theory in developing effective antidrug public service announcements. In W. D. Crano & M. Burgoon (Eds.), *Mass media and drug prevention: Classic and contemporary theories and research* (pp. 89–117). Mahwah, NJ: Lawrence Erlbaum Associates.

Fitzpatrick, C. (2000, May 18). A new era of male attractiveness? *Plain Dealer*, 5-F.

Fitzpatrick, M. A., & Winke, J. (1979). You always hurt the one you love: Strategies and tactics in interpersonal conflict. *Communication Quarterly, 27*, 1–11.

Flora, J. A. (2001). The Stanford community studies: Campaigns to reduce cardiovascular disease. In R. E. Rice & C. K. Atkin (Eds.), *Public communication campaigns* (3rd ed., pp. 193–213). Thousand Oaks, CA: Sage.

Fox, R. M., & DeMarco, J. P. (1990). *Moral reasoning: A philosophic approach to applied ethics*. Ft. Worth, TX: Holt, Rinehart & Winston.

Frankena, W. (1963). *Ethics*. Englewood Cliffs, NJ: Prentice Hall.

Freedman, J. L., & Fraser, S. C. (1966). Compliance without pressure: The foot-in-the-door technique. *Journal of Personality and Social Psychology, 4*, 195–202.

Freimuth, V. (1990). The chronically uninformed: Closing the knowledge gap in health. In E. B. Ray & L. Donohew (Eds.), *Communication and health: Systems and applications* (pp. 171–186). Hillsdale, NJ: Lawrence Erlbaum Associates.

Frey, K. P., & Eagly, A. H. (1993). Vividness can undermine the persuasiveness of messages. *Journal of Personality and Social Psychology, 65*, 32–44.

Gardner, H. (1993). *Multiple intelligences: The theory in practice.* New York: Basic Books.

Garland, H. (1990). Throwing good money after bad: The effect of sunk costs on the decision to escalate commitment to an ongoing project. *Journal of Applied Psychology, 75*, 728–731.

Garreau, J. (2001, October 22–28). Hinge moments in history. *Washington Post National Weekly Edition*, 6–7.

Garst, J., & Bodenhausen, G. V. (1996). "Family values" and political persuasion: Impact of kin-related rhetoric on reactions to political campaigns. *Journal of Applied Social Psychology, 26*, 1119–1137.

Gass, R. H., & Seiter, J. S. (1999). *Persuasion, social influence, and compliance gaining.* Boston: Allyn & Bacon.

Gaziano, C. (1983). The knowledge gap: An analytical review of media effects. *Communication Research, 10*, 447–486.

Gerard, H. B., & Mathewson, G. C. (1966). The effect of severity of initiation on liking for a group: A replication. *Journal of Experimental Social Psychology, 2*, 278–287.

Giles, H., & Street, R. L., Jr. (1994). Communicator characteristics and behavior. In M. L. Knapp & G. R. Miller (Eds.), *Handbook of interpersonal communication* (2nd ed., pp. 103–161). Thousand Oaks, CA: Sage

Glick, P., & Fiske, S. T. (1996). The ambivalent sexism inventory: Differentiating hostile and benevolent sexism. *Journal of Personality and Social Psychology, 70*, 491–512.

Glynn, C. J., Herbst, S., O'Keefe, G. J., & Shapiro, R. Y. (1999). *Public opinion.* Boulder, CO: Westview Press.

Godbold, L. C., & Pfau, M. (2000). Conferring resistance to peer pressure among adolescents: Using inoculation theory to discourage alcohol use. *Communication Research, 27*, 411–437.

Goethals, G. R., & Nelson, R. E. (1973). Similarity in the influence process: The belief–value distinction. *Journal of Personality and Social Psychology, 25*, 117–122.

Goldberg, J. (2000, June 25). The education of a holy warrior. *New York Times Magazine*, 32–37, 53, 63–64, 70–71.

Golden, J. L., Berquist, G. F., & Coleman, W. E. (2000). *The rhetoric of Western thought,* (7th ed.). Dubuque, IA: Kendall/Hunt.

Goldman, R., & Papson, S. (1996). *Sign wars: The cluttered landscape of advertising.* New York: Guilford Press.

Goodstein L. (1997, April 7). No one put a gun to their heads. *The Washington Post National Weekly Edition*, 32.

Granberg, D. (1993). Political perception. In S. Iyengar & W. J. McGuire (Eds.), *Explorations in political psychology* (pp. 70–112). Durham, NC: Duke University Press.

Granberg, D., & Seidel, J. (1976). Social judgments of the urban and Vietnam issues in 1968 and 1972. *Social Forces, 55*, 1–15.

Green, M. C., & Brock, T. C. (2000). The role of transportation in the persuasiveness of public narratives. *Journal of Personality and Social Psychology, 79*, 701–721.

Greenberg, B. S., & Miller, G. R. (1966). The effects of low-credible sources on message acceptance. *Speech Monographs, 33*, 127–136.

Greene, J. O., McDaniel, T. L., Buksa, K., & Ravizza, S. M. (1993). Cognitive processes in the production of multiple-goal messages: Evidence from the temporal characteristics of speech. *Western Journal of Communication, 57*, 65–86.

Greenhouse, L. (1999, September 29). Managed care challenge to be heard by high court. *New York Times*, A22.

Greenwald, A. G. (1968). Cognitive learning, cognitive response to persuasion, and attitude change. In A. G. Greenwald, T. C. Brock. & T. M. Ostrom (Eds.), *Psychological foundations of attitudes* (pp. 147–170). New York: Academic Press.

Greenwald, A. G., Spangenberg, E. R., Pratkanis, A. R., & Eskenazi, J. (1991). Double-blind tests of subliminal self-help audiotapes. *Psychological Science, 2*, 119–122.

Grossman, R. P., & Till, B. D. (1998). The persistence of classically conditioned brand attitudes. *Journal of Advertising, 27*, 23–31.

Gruder, C. L., Cook, T. D., Hennigan, K. M., Flay, B. R., Alessis, C., & Halamaj, J. (1978). Empirical tests of the absolute sleeper effect predicted from the discounting cue hypothesis. *Journal of Personality and Social Psychology, 36*, 1061–1074.

Grush, J. E., McKeough, K. L., & Ahlering, R. F. (1978). Extrapolating laboratory exposure research to actual political elections. *Journal of Personality and Social Psychology, 36*, 257–270.

Guttman, L. (1944). A basis for scaling qualitative data. *American Sociological Review, 9*, 139–150.

Guttman, N. (1997). Ethical dilemmas in health campaigns. *Health Communication, 9*, 155–190.

Guttman, N. (2000). *Public health communication interventions: Values and ethical dilemmas*. Thousand Oaks, CA: Sage

Haines, M., & Spear, S. F. (1996). Changing the perception of the norm: A strategy to decrease binge drinking among college students. *Journal of American College Health, 45*, 134–140.

Hale, J. L., Householder, B. J., & Greene, K. L., (2002). The theory of reasoned action. In J. P. Dillard and M. Pfau (Eds.), *The persuasion handbook: Developments in theory and practice* (pp. 259–286). Thousand Oaks, CA: Sage.

Haleta, L. L. (1996). Student perceptions of teachers' use of language: The effects of powerful and powerless language on impression formation and uncertainty. *Communication Education, 45*, 16–28.

Hamilton, M. A., & Hunter, J. E. (1998). The effect of language intensity on receiver evaluations of message, source, and topic. In M. Allen & R. W. Preiss (Eds.), *Persuasion: Advances through meta-analysis* (pp. 99–138). Cresskill, NJ: Hampton Press.

Han, S-P., & Shavitt, S. (1994). Persuasion and culture: Advertising appeals in individualistic and collectivistic societies. *Journal of Experimental Social Psychology, 30*, 326–350.

Hannah, D. B., & Sternthal, B. (1984). Detecting and explaining the sleeper effect. *Journal of Consumer Research, 11*, 632–642.

Hansen, M., Kossman, C., Wilbrecht, K., & Andsager, J. (2000). *Culture change on campus*. Unpublished paper, Washington State University.

Harmon-Jones, E. (2002). A cognitive dissonance theory perspective on persuasion. In J. P. Dillard & M. Pfau (Eds.), *The persuasion handbook: Developments in theory and practice*. (pp. 99–116) Thousand Oaks, CA: Sage.

Harmon-Jones, E., Brehm, J. W., Greenberg, J., Simon, L., & Nelson, D. E. (1996). Evidence that the production of aversive consequences is not necessary to create cognitive dissonance. *Journal of Personality and Social Psychology, 70*, 5–16.

Harmon-Jones, E., & Mills, J. (1999). An introduction to cognitive dissonance theory and an overview of current perspectives on the theory. In E. Harmon-Jones & J. Mills (Eds.), *Cognitive dissonance: Progress on a pivotal theory in social psychology* (pp. 3–21). Washington, DC: American Psychological Association.

Harres, A. (1998). "But basically you're feeling well, are you?": Tag questions in medical consultations. *Health Communication, 10*, 111–123.

Harris, R. J. (1999). *A cognitive psychology of mass communication* (3rd. ed.). Mahwah, NJ: Lawrence Erlbaum Associates.

Harrison, K., & Cantor, J. (1997). The relationship between media consumption and eating disorders. *Journal of Communication, 47(1)*, 40–67.

Hart, R. P., Friedrich, G. W., & Brummett, B. (1983). *Public communication* (2nd ed.) New York: Harper & Row.

Hartley, R. E. (2000). *Marketing mistakes* (8th ed.). New York: Wiley.

Hastorf, A., & Cantril, H. (1954). They saw a game: A case study. *Journal of Abnormal and Social Psychology, 49*, 129–134.

Haugtvedt, C. P., Petty, R. E., & Cacioppo, J. T. (1992). Need for cognition and advertising: Understanding the role of personality variables in consumer behavior. *Journal of Consumer Psychology, 1*, 239–260.

Haugtvedt, C. P., & Wegener, D. T. (1994). Message order effects in persuasion: An attitude strength perspective. *Journal of Consumer Research, 21*, 205–218.

Hazlett, R. L., & Hazlett, S. Y. (1999). Emotional response to television commercials: Facial EMG vs. self-report. *Journal of Advertising Research, 39(2)*, 7–23.

Heider, F. (1958). *The psychology of interpersonal relations.* New York: Wiley.

Henneberger, M. (1999, February 7). Cool refusal to take on damsel role. *New York Times*, 1, 26.

Henriksen, L., Flora, J. A., Feighery, E., & Fortmann, S. P. (2002). Effects on youth of exposure to retail tobacco advertising. *Journal of Applied Social Psychology*.

Henriques, D. B., & Bergman, L. (2000, March 15). Profiting from fine print with Wall Street's help, *New York Times*, A1, C12–C13.

Hense, R., & Wright, C. (1992). The development of the Attitudes Toward Censorship Questionnaire. *Journal of Applied Social Psychology, 22*, 1666–1675.

Hewitt, B., Fields-Meyer, T., Frankel, B., Jewel, D., Lambert, P., O'Neill, A.M., & Plummer, W. (1997, April 14). Who they were. *People*, pp. 40–56.

Hilts, P. J. (1996). *Smokescreen: The truth behind the tobacco industry cover-up.* Reading, MA: Addison-Wesley.

Hippler, H.-J., Schwarz, N., & Sudman, S. (Eds.) (1987). *Social information processing and survey methodology.* New York: Springer-Verlag.

Holmes, S. A. (1998, November 20). Klan case transcends racial divide. *New York Times*, A14.

Holtgraves, T., & Lasky, B. (1999). Linguistic power and persuasion. *Journal of Language and Social Psychology, 18*, 196–205.

Hong, T., & Cody, M. J. (2001, May). *Presence of pro-tobacco messages on the Web.* Paper presented to the annual convention of the International Communication Association, Washington, DC.

Hornik, R. (2002). Public health communication: Making sense of contradictory evidence. In R. Hornik (Ed.), *Public health communication: Evidence for behavior change* (pp. 1–19). Mahwah, NJ: Lawrence Erlbaum Associates.

Horovitz, B., & Wells, M. (1997, January 31–February 2). How ad images shape habits. *USA Today*, 1A–2A.

Hosman, L. A. (1989). The evaluative consequences of hedges, hesitations, and intensifiers: Powerful and powerless speech styles. *Human Communication Research, 15*, 383–406.

Hosman, L. A. (2002). Language and persuasion. In J. P. Dillard & M. Pfau (Eds.), *The persuasion handbook: Developments in theory and practice.* (pp. 371–390) Thousand Oaks, CA: Sage.

Hovland, C. I. (1959). Reconciling conflicting results derived from experimental and survey studies of attitude change. *American Psychologist, 14*, 8–17.

Hovland, C. I., Harvey, O. J., & Sherif, M. (1957). Assimilation and contrast effects in reactions to communication and attitude change. *Journal of Abnormal and Social Psychology, 55*, 244–252.

Hovland, C. I, Janis, I. L., & Kelley, H. H. (1953). *Communication and persuasion: Psychological studies of opinion change.* New Haven, CT: Yale University Press.

Hovland, C. I., Lumsdaine, A. A., & Sheffield, F. D. (1949). *Experiments on mass communication.* Princeton, NJ: Princeton University Press.

Huff, D. (1954). *How to lie with statistics.* New York: Norton.

Infante, D. A., & Rancer, A. S. (1982). A conceptualization and measure of argumentativeness. *Journal of Personality Assessment, 46*, 72–80.

Infante, D. A., & Rancer, A. S. (1996). Argumentativeness and verbal aggressiveness: A review of recent theory and research. In B. Burleson (Ed.), *Communication yearbook 19* (pp. 319–351). Thousand Oaks, CA: Sage.

Infante, D. A., & Wigley, C. J., III (1986). Verbal aggressiveness: An interpersonal model and measure. *Communication Monographs, 53*, 61–69.

Jaggar, A. M. (2000). Feminist ethics. In H. LaFollette (Ed.), *The Blackwell guide to ethical theory* (pp. 348–374). Malden, MA: Blackwell.

Jhally, S. (1998). *Advertising and the end of the world* (video). Northampton, MA: Media Education Foundation.

Johnson, B. T., & Eagly, A. H. (1989). Effects of involvement on persuasion: A meta-analysis. *Psychological Bulletin, 106*, 290–314.

Johnson, D. (2000, May 21). No executions in Illinois until system is repaired. *New York Times*, 14.

Johnston, D. C. (2001, February 14). Dozens of rich Americans join in fight to retain the estate tax. *New York Times*, A1, A18.

Jones, E. E., & Sigall, H. (1971). The bogus pipeline: A new paradigm for measuring affect and attitude. *Psychological Bulletin, 76*, 349–364.

Jordan, J. M., & Roloff, M. E. (1997). Planning skills and negotiator goal accomplishment: The relationship between self-monitoring and plan generation, plan enactment, and plan consequences. *Communication Research, 24*, 31–63.

Kahle, L. R. (1996). Social values and consumer behavior: Research from the list of values. In C. Seligman, J. M. Olson, & M. P. Zanna (Eds.), *The psychology of values: The Ontario symposium*, (Vol. 8, pp. 135–151). Mahwah, NJ: Lawrence Erlbaum Associates.

Kahle, L. R., & Homer, P. M. (1985). Physical attractiveness of the celebrity endorser: A social adaptation perspective. *Journal of Consumer Research, 11*, 954–961.

Kalichman, S. C., & Coley, B. (1995). Context framing to enhance HIV-antibody-testing messages targeted to African American women. *Health Psychology, 14*, 247–254.

Kaplowitz, S. A., & Fink, E. L. (1997). Message discrepancy and persuasion. In G. A. Barnett & F. J. Boster (Eds.), *Progress in communication sciences* (Vol. 13, pp. 75–106). Greenwich, CT: Ablex.

Kassan, L. D. (1999). *Second opinions: Sixty psychotherapy patients evaluate their therapists*. Northvale, NJ: Jason Aronson Press.

Katz, D. (1960). The functional approach to the study of attitudes. *Public Opinion Quarterly, 24*, 163–204.

Kaufman, L. (2000, September 17). And now, a few more words about breasts. *New York Times*, Week in Review, 3.

Kazoleas, D. C. (1993). A comparison of the persuasive effectiveness of qualitative versus quantitative evidence: A test of explanatory hypotheses. *Communication Quarterly, 41*, 40–50.

Kellermann, K., & Cole, T. (1994). Classifying compliance gaining messages: Taxonomic disorder and strategic confusion. *Communication Theory, 4*, 3–60.

Kelly, J. A. (1995). *Changing HIV risk behavior: Practical strategies*. New York: Guilford.

Kelman, H. C. (1958). Compliance, identification, and internalization: Three processes of attitude change. *Journal of Conflict Resolution, 2*, 51–60.

Kelman, H. C., & Hamilton, V. L. (1989). *Crimes of obedience: Toward a social psychology of authority and responsibility*. New Haven: Yale University Press.

Kennedy, G. (1963). *The art of persuasion in Greece*. Princeton, NJ: Princeton University Press.

Key, W. B. (1974). *Subliminal seduction*. New York: Signet Books.

Kiesler, C. A., Collins, B. E., & Miller, N. (1969). *Attitude change: A critical analysis of theoretical approaches*. New York: Wiley.

Kifner, J. (2001, November 11). The new power of Arab public opinion. *New York Times*, 4-1, 4–5.

Kilbourne, J., & Pollay, R. (1992). *Pack of lies: The advertising of tobacco* (videotape). Northampton, MA: Foundation for Media Education.

Kim, M-S., & Hunter, J. E. (1993). Attitude–behavior relations: A meta-analysis of attitudinal relevance and topic. *Journal of Communication, 43(1)*, 101–142.

Kim, M-S., & Wilson, S. R. (1994). A cross-cultural comparison of implicit theories of requesting. *Communication Monographs, 61*, 210–235.

Kinder, D. R., & Sanders, L. M. (1990). Mimicking political debate with survey questions: The case of White opinion on affirmative action for Blacks. *Social Cognition, 8*, 73–103.

King, C. S. (1969). *My life with Martin Luther King, Jr.* New York: Holt, Rinehart & Winston.

King, S. W., Minami, Y., & Samovar, L. A. (1985). A comparison of Japanese and American perceptions of source credibility. *Communication Research Reports, 2*, 76–79.

Kipnis, D., & Schmidt, S. (1996). The language of persuasion. In E. J. Coats & R. S. Feldman (Eds.), *Classic and contemporary readings in social psychology* (pp. 184–188). Upper Saddle River, NJ: Prentice Hall.

Kleinfield, N. R. (1999, November 15). For three interns, fatigue and healing at top speed. *New York Times*, A1, A28.

Kleinfield, N. R. (2000, October 19). It's root, root, root, but for which team? *New York Times*, A1, C27.

Kline, S. L., & Clinton, B. L. (1998). Developments in children's persuasive message practices. *Communication Education, 47*, 120–136.

Kluckhohn, C. (1951). Values and value-orientations in the theory of action: An exploration in definition and classification. In T. Parsons & E. A. Shils (Eds.), *Toward a general theory of action* (pp. 388–433). Cambridge, MA: Harvard University Press.

Klusendorf, S. (2001). *Why pro-Life advocates should use graphic visual aids.* On-line: http://www.str.org/free/bioethics/visuals.htm

Knowles, E. S., Butler, S., & Linn, J. A. (2001). Increasing compliance by reducing resistance. In J. P. Forgas & K. D. Williams (Eds.), *Social influence: Direct and indirect processes* (pp. 41–60). Philadelphia: Taylor & Francis.

Knowles, E. S., & Linn, J. A. (2004). Omega-based attitude change: Increasing persuasion by decreasing resistance. In E. S. Knowles & J. A. Linn (Eds.), *Resistance and persuasion.* Mahwah, NJ: Lawrence Erlbaum Associates.

Koehler, S. P., & Willis, F. N. (1994). Traffic citations in relation to gender. *Journal of Applied Social Psychology, 24*, 1919–1926.

Kolata, G. (2001, May 24). Placebo effects is more myth than science, a study says. *New York Times*, A1, A19.

Kopfman, J. E., Smith, S. W., Ah Yun, J. K., & Hodges, A. (1998). Affective and cognitive reactions to narrative versus statistical evidence organ donation messages. *Journal of Applied Communication Research, 26*, 279–300.

Kraus, S. J. (1995). Attitudes and the prediction of behavior: A meta-analysis of the empirical literature. *Personality and Social Psychology Bulletin, 21*, 58–75.

Krech, D., Crutchfield, R. S., & Ballachey, E. L. (1962) *Individual in society.* New York: McGraw-Hill.

Kreuter, M., Farrell, D., Olevitch, L., & Brennan, L. (2000). *Tailoring health messages: Customizing communication with computer technology.* Mahwah, NJ: Lawrence Erlbaum Associates.

Krosnick, J. A., Boninger, D. S., Chuang, Y. C., Berent, M. K., & Carnot, C. G. (1993). Attitude strength: One construct or many related constructs? *Journal of Personality and Social Psychology, 65*, 1132–1151.

Krosnick, J. A., & Petty, R. E. (1995). Attitude strength: An overview. In R. E. Petty & J. A. Krosnick (Eds.), *Attitude strength: Antecedents and consequences* (pp. 1–24). Hillsdale, NJ: Lawrence Erlbaum Associates.

Kruglanski, A. W., Thompson, E. P., & Spiegel, S. (1999). Separate or equal?: Bimodal notions of persuasion and a single-process "unimodel." In S. Chaiken & Y. Trope (Eds.), *Dual-process theories in social psychology* (pp. 293–313). New York: Guilford.

LaBarbera, P. A., & Tucciarone, J. D. (1995). GSR reconsidered: A behavior-based approach to evaluating and improving the sales potency of advertising. *Journal of Advertising Research, 35(5)*, 33–53.

LaFeber, W. (1999). *Michael Jordan and the new global capitalism*. New York: Norton.

Lakoff, G. (1996). *Moral politics: What conservatives know that liberals don't*. Chicago: University of Chicago Press.

Langer, J. (1997). What consumers wish brand managers knew. *Journal of Advertising Research, 37(6)*, 60–65.

Langrehr, F. W., & Caywood, C. L. (1995). A semiotic approach to determining the sins and virtues portrayed in advertising. *Journal of Current Issues and Research in Advertising, 17*, 33–47.

LaPiere, R. T. (1934). Attitudes vs. action. *Social forces, 13*, 230–237.

Lavin, M. (2001). *Clean new world: Culture, politics, and graphic design*. Cambridge, MA: MIT Press.

Lavine, H., Thomsen, C. J., & Gonzales, M. T. (1997). The development of interattitudinal consistency: The shared-consequences model. *Journal of Personality and Social Psychology, 72*, 735–749.

Lavine, H., Thomsen, C. J., Zanna, M. P., & Borgida, E. (1998). On the primacy of affect in the determination of attitudes and behavior: The moderating role of affective–cognitive ambivalence. *Journal of Experimental Social Psychology, 34*, 398–421.

Lederman, L. C., Stewart, L. P., Barr, S. L., Powell, R. L., Laitman, L., & Goodhart, F. W. (2001). RU SURE?: Using communication theory to reduce dangerous drinking on a college campus. In R. E. Rice & C. K. Atkin (Eds.), *Public communication campaigns* (3rd ed., pp. 295–299). Thousand Oaks, CA: Sage.

Leippe, M. R., & Eisenstadt, D. (1994). Generalization of dissonance reduction: Decreasing prejudice through induced compliance. *Journal of Personality and Social Psychology, 67*, 395–413.

Leippe, M. R., & Elkin, R. A. (1987). When motives clash: Issue involvement and response involvement as determinants of persuasion. *Journal of Personality and Social Psychology, 52*, 269–278.

Levasseur, D., & Dean, K. W. (1996). The use of evidence in presidential debates: A study of evidence levels and types from 1960 to 1988. *Argumentation and Advocacy, 32*, 129–142.

Levine, J. M., & Valle, R. S. (1975). The convert as a credible communicator. *Social Behavior and Personality, 3*, 81–90.

Lieberman, D. A. (2001). Using interactive media in communication campaigns for children and adolescents. In R. E. Rice & C. K. Atkin (Eds.), *Public communication campaigns* (3rd ed., pp. 373–388). Thousand Oaks, CA: Sage.

Likert, R. (1932). A technique for the measurement of attitudes. *Archives of Psychology, 140*, 1–55.

Linz, D. G., & Penrod, S. (1984). Increasing attorney persuasiveness in the courtroom. *Law and Psychology Review, 8*, 1–47.

London, H. (1973). *Psychology of the persuader*. Morristown, NJ: General Learning Press.

Lord, C. G., Desforges, D. M., Fein, S., Pugh, M. A., & Lepper, M. R. (1994). Typicality effects in attitude toward social policies: A concept-mapping approach. *Journal of Personality and Social Psychology, 66*, 658–673.

Lord, C. G., Lepper, M. R., & Mackie, D. (1984). Attitude prototypes as determinants of attitude–behavior consistency. *Journal of Personality and Social Psychology, 46*, 1254–1266.

Lord, C. G., Ross, L., & Lepper, M. R. (1979). Biased assimilation and attitude polarization: The effects of prior theories on subsequently considered evidence. *Journal of Personality and Social Psychology, 37,* 2098–2109.

Lynch, J., & Schuler, D. (1994). The matchup effect of spokesperson and product congruency: A schema theory interpretation. *Psychology & Marketing, 11,* 417–445.

Lynn, M., & Mynier, K. (1993). Effect of server posture on restaurant tipping. *Journal of Applied Social Psychology, 23,* 678–685.

Maccoby, N., & Farquhar, J. W. (1975). Communication for health: Unselling heart disease. *Journal of Communication, 25,* 114–126.

Maibach, E. W., Kreps, G. L., & Bonaguro, E. W. (1993). Developing strategic communication campaigns for HIV/AIDS prevention. In S. Ratzan (Ed.), *AIDS: Effective health communication for the 90s* (pp. 15–35). Washington, DC: Taylor & Francis.

Mailer, N. (1999). Ego. In D. Halberstam (Ed.), *The best American sports writing of the century* (pp. 713–737). Boston: Houghton Mifflin.

Maio, G. R., & Olson, J. M. (1998). Values as truisms: Evidence and implications. *Journal of Personality and Social Psychology, 74,* 294–311.

Maio, G. R., & Olson, J. M. (Eds.) (2000a). *Why we evaluate: Functions of attitudes.* Mahwah, NJ: Lawrence Erlbaum Associates.

Maio, G. R., & Olson, J. M. (2000b). What *is* a "value-expressive" attitude? In G. R. Maio & J. M. Olson (Eds.), *Why we evaluate: Functions of attitudes* (pp. 249–269). Mahwah, NJ: Lawrence Erlbaum Associates.

Manstead, A. S. R., Proffitt, C., & Smart, J. L. (1983). Predicting and understanding mothers' infant-feeding intentions and behavior: Testing the theory of reasoned action. *Journal of Personality and Social Psychology, 44,* 657–671.

Marklein, M. B. (2000, October 11). Ugly truths about hazing. *USA Today,* 6D.

Martin, D. (2000, January 9). What's in a name: The allure of labels. *New York Times,* 4-2.

Martin, M. (2001, March 30). Man sentenced to educate himself. *Plain Dealer,* 1-B, 5-B.

Marwell, G., & Schmitt, D. R. (1967). Dimensions of compliance-gaining behavior: An empirical analysis. *Sociometry, 30,* 350–364.

Max, D. T. (1999, December 26). The Oprah effect. *New York Times Magazine,* 36–41.

McAlister, A. L., & Fernandez, M. (2002). "Behavioral journalism" accelerates diffusion of healthy innovations. In R. Hornik (Ed.), *Public health communication: Evidence for behavior change* (pp. 315–326). Mahwah, NJ: Lawrence Erlbaum Associates.

McBane, D. A. (1995). Empathy and the salesperson: A multidimensional perspective. *Psychology and Marketing, 12,* 349–369.

McCarthy, M. (2001, November 9). Ad experts take fight to a new front. *USA Today,* 1B.

McCombs, M., & Reynolds, A. (2002). News influence on our pictures of the world. In J. Bryant & D. Zillmann (Eds.), *Media effects: Advances in theory and research* (2nd ed. pp. 1–18). Mahwah, NJ: Lawrence Erlbaum Associates.

McConahay, J. B. (1986). Modern racism, ambivalence, and the Modern Racism scale. In J. F. Dovidio & S. L. Gaertner (Eds.), *Prejudice, discrimination, and racism* (pp. 91–125). Orlando, FL: Academic Press.

McCracken, G. (1986). Culture and consumption: A theoretical account of the structure and movement of the cultural meaning of consumer goods. *Journal of Consumer Research, 13*, 71–84.

McCracken, G. (1989). Who is the celebrity endorser?: Cultural foundations of the endorsement process. *Journal of Consumer Research, 16*, 310–321.

McCroskey, J. C. (1969). A summary of experimental research on the effects of evidence in persuasive communication. *Quarterly Journal of Speech, 55*, 169–176.

McCroskey, J. C. (1972). *An introduction to rhetorical communication.* Englewood Cliffs, NJ: Prentice Hall.

McCroskey, J. C. (1997). *An introduction to rhetorical communication* (7th ed.). Boston: Allyn and Bacon.

McCroskey, J. C., & Teven, J. J. (1999). Goodwill: A reexamination of the construct and its measurement. *Communication Monographs, 66*, 90–103.

McCroskey, J. C., & Young, T. J. (1981). Ethos and credibility: The construct and its measurement after three decades. *Central States Speech Journal, 32*, 24–34.

McDonald, C. (1993). Children, smoking and advertising: What does the research really tell us? *International Journal of Advertising, 12*, 279–287.

McGuire, W. J. (1968). Personality and susceptibility to social influence. In E. F. Borgatta & W. W. Lambert (Eds.), *Handbook of personality theory and research,* (pp. 1130–1187). Chicago: Rand McNally.

McGuire, W. J. (1969). The nature of attitudes and attitude change. In G. Lindzey & E. Aronson (Eds.), *Handbook of social psychology* (2nd ed., Vol. 3, pp. 136–314). Reading, MA: Addison-Wesley.

McGuire, W. J. (1970, February). A vaccine for brainwash. *Psychology Today,* pp. 36–39, 63–64.

McGuire, W. J. (1989). Theoretical foundations of campaigns. In R. E. Rice & C. K. Atkin (Eds.), *Public communication campaigns* (2nd ed., pp. 43–65). Thousand Oaks, CA: Sage.

McGuire, W. J., & Papageorgis, D. (1961). The relative efficacy of various types of prior belief-defense in producing immunity against persuasion. *Journal of Abnormal and Social Psychology, 62*, 327–337.

McLuhan, M. (1967). *The medium is the message.* New York: Random House.

McQuillan, L. (2001, September 21). "Freedom and fear are at war," president says. *USA Today,* 3A.

Meeus, W. H. J., & Raaijmakers, Q. A. W. (1986). Administrative obedience: Carrying out orders to use psychological-administrative violence. *European Journal of Social Psychology, 16*, 311–324.

Mendoza-Denton, R., Ayduk, O. N., Shoda, Y., & Mischel, W. (1997). Cognitive-affective processing system analysis of reactions to the O. J. Simpson criminal trial verdict. *Journal of Social Issues, 53*, 563–581.

Messaris, P. (1997). *Visual persuasion: The role of images in advertising.* Thousand Oaks, CA: Sage.

Meyerowitz, B. E., & Chaiken, S. (1987). The effect of message framing on breast self-examination attitudes, intentions, and behavior. *Journal of Personality and Social Psychology, 52*, 500–510.

Middlebrook, P. N. (1974). *Social psychology and modern life*. New York: Knopf.

Milburn, M. A. (1991). *Persuasion and politics: The social psychology of public opinion*. Pacific Grove, CA: Brooks/Cole.

Miles, H. L. White (1993). Language and the orang-utan: The old "person" of the forest. In P. Cavalieri & P. Singer (Eds.), *The great ape project: Equality beyond humanity* (pp. 42–57). New York: St. Martin's Griffin.

Milgram, S. (1963). Behavioral study of obedience. *Journal of Abnormal and Social Psychology, 67*, 371–378.

Milgram, S. (1974). *Obedience to authority: An experimental view*. New York: Harper & Row.

Millar, M. G., & Millar, K. U. (1996). The effects of direct and indirect experience on affective and cognitive responses and the attitude–behavior relation. *Journal of Experimental Social Psychology, 32*, 561–579.

Miller, A. G. (1986). *The obedience experiments: A case study of controversy in social science*. New York: Praeger.

Miller, A. G., Collins, B. E., & Brief, D. E. (1995). Perspectives on obedience to authority: The legacy of the Milgram experiments. *Journal of Social Issues, 51*, 1–19.

Miller, A. G., McHoskey, J. W., Bane, C. M., & Dowd, T. G. (1993). The attitude polarization phenomenon: Role of response measure, attitude extremity, and behavioral consequences of reported attitude change. *Journal of Personality and Social Psychology, 64*, 561–574.

Miller, G. R. (1980). On being persuaded: Some basic distinctions. In M. E. Roloff & G. R. Miller (Eds.), *Persuasion: New directions in theory and research* (pp. 11–28). Beverly Hills, CA: Sage.

Miller, G. R., Boster, F., Roloff, M., & Seibold, D. (1977). Compliance-gaining message strategies: A typology and some findings concerning effects of situational differences. *Communication Monographs, 44*, 37–51.

Miller, G. R., & Parks, M. R. (1982). Communication in dissolving relationships. In S. Duck (Ed.), *Personal relationships 4: Dissolving relationships* (pp. 127–154). Orlando, FL: Academic Press.

Miller, K. D. (1992). *Voice of deliverance: The language of Martin Luther King, Jr. and its sources*. New York: Free Press.

Miller, N., Maruyama, G., Beaber, R. J., & Valone, K. (1976). Speed of speech and persuasion. *Journal of Personality and Social Psychology, 34*, 615–624.

Mills, J. (1999). Improving the 1957 version of dissonance theory. In E. Harmon-Jones & J. Mills (Eds.), *Cognitive dissonance: Progress on a pivotal theory in social psychology* (pp. 25–42). Washington, DC: American Psychological Association.

Mitchell, A. A. (1986). Effects of visual and verbal components of advertisements on brand attitudes. *Journal of Consumer Research, 13*, 12–24.

Mittal, B. (1995). A comparative analysis of four scales of consumer involvement. *Psychology & Marketing, 12*, 663–682.

Mongeau, P. A. (1998). Another look at fear-arousing persuasive appeals. In M. Allen & R. W. Preiss (Eds.), *Persuasion: Advances through meta-analysis* (pp. 53–68). Cresskill, NJ: Hampton Press.

Moore, M. T. (1993, June 15). Visual overload: Fleeing ad images catch viewers. *USA Today*, B1.

Morin, R. (1997, September 1). The worst of the worst. *Washington Post National Weekly Edition*, 35.

Morley, D. D., & Walker, K. B. (1987). The role of importance, novelty, and plausibility in producing belief change. *Communication Monographs, 54*, 436–442.

Morris, K. A., & Swann, W. B., Jr. (1996). Denial and the AIDS crisis: On wishing away the threat of AIDS. In S. Oskamp & S. C. Thompson (Eds.), *Understanding and preventing HIV risk behavior: Safer sex and drug use* (pp. 57–79). Thousand Oaks, CA: Sage.

Morrison, D. M., Gillmore, M. R., & Baker, S. A. (1995). Determinants of condom use among high-risk heterosexual adults: A test of the theory of reasoned action. *Journal of Applied Social Psychology, 25*, 651–676.

Morrison, D. M., Gillmore, M. R., Simpson, E. E., Wells, E. A., & Hoppe, M. J. (1996). Children's decisions about substance use: An application and extension of the theory of reasoned action. *Journal of Applied Social Psychology, 26*, 1658–1679.

Motley, M. T., & Reeder, H. M. (1995). Unwanted escalation of sexual intimacy: Male and female perceptions of connotations and relational consequences of resistance messages. *Communication Monographs, 62*, 355–379.

Mowen, J. C., & Cialdini, R. B. (1980). On implementing the door-in-the-face compliance technique in a business context. *Journal of Marketing Research, 17*, 253–258.

Muehling, D. D., & McCann, M. (1993). Attitude toward the ad: A review. *Journal of Current Issues and Research in Advertising, 15*, 25–58.

Murray, S., & Gruley, B. (2000, November 2). On many campuses, big brewers play a role in new alcohol policies. *Wall Street Journal*, A1, A10.

Myers, G. (1999). *Ad worlds: Brands, media, audiences.* London: Arnold.

Newman, B. I., & Perloff, R. M. (in Press). Political marketing: Theory, research, and applications. In L. Kaid (Ed.), *Handbook of political communication* (2nd ed.). Mahwah, NJ: Lawrence Erlbaum Associates.

Newman, L. S., Duff, K., Schnopp-Wyatt, N., Brock, B., & Hoffman, Y. (1997). Reactions to the O. J. Simpson verdict: "Mindless tribalism" or motivated inference processes? *Journal of Social Issues, 53*, 547–562.

Nienhuis, A. E., Manstead, A. S. R., & Spears, R. (2001). Multiple motives and persuasive communication: Creating elaboration as a result of impression motivation and accuracy motivation. *Personality and Social Psychology Bulletin, 27*, 118–132.

Nilsen, T. R. (1974). *Ethics of speech communication* (2nd ed.) Indianapolis: Bobbs-Merill.

Nisbett, R. E., Borgida, E., Crandall, R., & Reed, H. (1976). Popular induction: Information is not necessarily informative. In J. S. Carroll & J. W. Payne (Eds.), *Cognition and social behavior* (pp. 113–133). Hillsdale, NJ: Lawrence Erlbaum Associates.

Nitze, S. P. (2001, April 8). How to be an impostor. *New York Times Magazine*, 38–40.

Norton, J. (2001, September 18). "Embrace Arab-American communities." *USA Today*, Letter to the Editor, 23A.

Ohme, R. K. (2000). Social influence in media: Culture and antismoking advertising. In W. Wosinka, R. B. Cialdini, D. W. Barrett, & J. Reykowski (Eds.), *The practice of social influence in multiple cultures* (pp. 309–324). Mahwah, NJ: Lawrence Erlbaum Associates.

O'Keefe, D. J. (1990). *Persuasion: Theory and research.* Newbury Park, CA: Sage.

O'Keefe, D. J. (1997). Standpoint explicitness and persuasive effect: A meta-analytic review of the effects of varying conclusion articulation in persuasive messages. *Argumentation and Advocacy, 34,* 1–12.

O'Keefe, D. J. (1999). How to handle opposing arguments in persuasive messages: A meta-analytic review of the effects of one-sided and two-sided messages. In M. E. Roloff (Ed.), *Communication Yearbook, 22,* 209–249.

O'Keefe, D. J. (2000). Guilt and social influence. In M. E. Roloff (Ed.), *Communication Yearbook 23* (pp. 67–101). Thousand Oaks, CA: Sage.

O'Keefe, D. J., & Figgé, M. (1999). Guilt and expected guilt in the door-in-the-face technique. *Communication Monographs, 66,* 312–324.

O'Keefe, D. J., & Hale, S. L. (1998). The door-in-the-face influence strategy: A random-effects meta-analytic review. In M. E. Roloff (Ed.), *Communication Yearbook 21* (pp. 1–33). Thousand Oaks, CA: Sage.

O'Keefe, G. J. (1985). "Taking a bite out of crime": The impact of a public information campaign. *Communication Research, 12,* 147–178.

O'Keefe, G. J., Rosenbaum, D. P., Lavrakas, P. J., Reid, K., & Botta, R. A. (1996). *Taking a bite out of crime: The impact of the National Citizens' Crime Prevention Media Campaign.* Thousand Oaks, CA: Sage.

Olney, B. (2000, July 9). Hitters vs. pitchers. *New York Times Magazine,* 38–41.

Orenstein, P. (2000). *Flux: Women on sex, work, kids, love, and life in a half-changed world.* New York: Doubleday.

Orne, M. T., & Holland, C. H. (1968). On the ecological validity of laboratory deceptions. *International Journal of Psychiatry, 6,* 282–293.

Osgood, C. E. (1974). Probing subjective culture/Part I: Cross-linguistic tool-making. *Journal of Communication, 24, 1,* 21–35.

Osgood, C. E., Suci, G. J., & Tannenbaum, P. H. (1957). *The measurement of meaning.* Urbana: University of Illinois Press.

Osterhouse, R. A., & Brock, T. C. (1970). Distraction increases yielding to propaganda by inhibiting counterarguing. *Journal of Personality and Social Psychology, 15,* 344–358.

Ostrom, T. M., Bond, C. F., Jr., Krosnick, J. A., & Sedikides, C. (1994). Attitude scales: How we measure the unmeasurable. In S. Shavitt & T. C. Brock (Eds.), *Persuasion: Psychological insights and perspectives* (pp. 15–42). Boston: Allyn and Bacon.

O'Sullivan, C. S., Chen, A., Mohapatra, S., Sigelman, L., & Lewis, E. (1988). Voting in ignorance: The politics of smooth-sounding names. *Journal of Applied Social Psychology, 18,* 1094–1106.

Palmgreen, P., Donohew, L., Lorch, E. P., Hoyle, R. H., & Stephenson, M. T. (2002). Television campaigns and sensation seeking targeting of adolescent marijuana use: A controlled time series approach. In R. Hornik (Ed.), *Public health communication: Evidence for behavior change* (pp. 35–56). Mahwah, NJ: Lawrence Erlbaum Associates.

Parker, D., Stradling, S. G., & Manstead, A. S. R. (1996). Modifying beliefs and attitudes to exceeding the speed limit: An intervention study based on the theory of planned behavior. *Journal of Applied Social Psychology, 26,* 1–19.

Parrott, R. L. (1995). Motivation to attend to health messages: Presentation of content and linguistic considerations. In E. Maibach & R. L. Parrott (Eds.), *Designing health messages: Approaches from communication theory and public health practice* (pp. 7–23). Thousand Oaks, CA: Sage.

Pendergrast, M. (2000). *For God, country and Coca-Cola: The definitive history of the great American soft drink and the company that makes it.* New York: Basic Books.

Peplau, L. A., Hill, C. T., & Rubin, Z. (1993). Sex role attitudes in dating and marriage: A 15-year follow-up of the Boston couples study. *Journal of Social Issues, 49, 3,* 31–52.

Peracchio, L. A., & Luna, D. (1998). The development of an advertising campaign to discourage smoking initiation among children and youth. *Journal of Advertising, 27,* 49–56.

Perloff, R. (1971). Caught up in the dreams of revolution. In C. R. Reaske & R. F. Willson, Jr. (Eds.), *Student voices/one* (pp. 24–25). New York: Random House.

Perloff, R. M. (1996). Perceptions and conceptions of political media impact: The third-person effect and beyond. In A. N. Crigler (Ed.), *The psychology of political communication* (pp. 177–197). Ann Arbor: University of Michigan Press.

Perloff, R. M. (1998). *Political communication: Politics, press, and public in America.* Mahwah, NJ: Lawrence Erlbaum Associates.

Perloff, R. M. (2001). *Persuading people to have safer sex: Applications of social science to the AIDS crisis.* Mahwah, NJ: Lawrence Erlbaum Associates.

Perloff, R. M., & Brock, T. C. (1980). "And thinking makes it so": Cognitive responses to persuasion. In M. E. Roloff & G. R. Miller (Eds.), *Persuasion: New directions in theory and research* (pp. 67–99). Beverly Hills, CA: Sage.

Petty, R. E., & Cacioppo, J. T. (1977). Forewarning, cognitive responding, and resistance to persuasion. *Journal of Personality and Social Psychology, 35,* 645–655.

Petty, R. E., & Cacioppo, J. T. (1984). The effects of involvement on responses to argument quantity and quality: Central and peripheral routes to persuasion. *Journal of Personality and Social Psychology, 46,* 69–81.

Petty, R. E., & Cacioppo, J. T. (1986). The elaboration likelihood model of persuasion. In L. Berkowitz (Ed.), *Advances in experimental social psychology* (Vol. 19, pp. 123–205). New York: Academic Press.

Petty, R. E., Cacioppo, J. T., & Goldman, R. (1981). Personal involvement as a determinant of argument-based persuasion. *Journal of Personality and Social Psychology, 41,* 847–855.

Petty, R. E., Cacioppo, J. T., Kasmer, J. A., & Haugtvedt, C. P. (1987). A reply to Stiff and Boster. *Communication Monographs, 54,* 257–263.

Petty, R. E., Cacioppo, J. T., Strathman, A. J., & Priester, J. R. (1994). To think or not to think: Exploring two routes to persuasion. In S. Shavitt & T. C. Brock (Eds.), *Persuasion: Psychological insights and perspectives* (pp. 113–147). Boston: Allyn and Bacon.

Petty, R. E., Haugtvedt, C. P., & Smith, S. M. (1995). Elaboration as a determinant of attitude strength: Creating attitudes that are persistent, resistant, and predictive of behavior. In R. E. Petty & J. A. Krosnick (Eds.), *Attitude strength: Antecedents and consequences* (pp. 93–130). Hillsdale, NJ: Lawrence Erlbaum Associates.

Petty, R. E., Ostrom, T. M., & Brock, T. C. (1981a). Historical foundations of the cognitive response approach to attitudes and persuasion. In R. E. Petty,

T. M. Ostrom, & T. C. Brock (Eds.), *Cognitive responses in persuasion* (pp. 5–29). Hillsdale, NJ: Lawrence Erlbaum Associates.

Petty, R. E., Ostrom, T. M., & Brock, T. C. (Eds.) (1981b). *Cognitive responses in persuasion.* Hillsdale, NJ: Lawrence Erlbaum Associates.

Petty, R. E., Schumann, D. W., Richman, S. A., & Strathman, A. J. (1993). Positive mood and persuasion: Different roles for affect under high- and low-elaboration conditions. *Journal of Personality and Social Psychology, 64,* 5–20.

Petty, R. E., & Wegener, D. T. (1998). Matching versus mismatching attitude functions: Implications for scrutiny of persuasive messages. *Personality and Social Psychology Bulletin, 24,* 227–240.

Petty, R. E., & Wegener, D. T. (1999). The elaboration likelihood model: Current status and controversies. In S. Chaiken & Y. Trope (Eds.), *Dual-process theories in social psychology* (pp. 41–72). New York: Guilford.

Petty, R. E., Wegener, D. T., Fabrigar, L. R., Priester, J. R., & Cacioppo, J. T. (1993). Conceptual and methodological issues in the elaboration likelihood model of persuasion: A reply to the Michigan State critics. *Communication Theory, 3,* 336–363.

Petty, R. E., Wells, G. L., & Brock, T. C. (1976). Distraction can enhance or reduce yielding to propaganda: Thought disruption versus effort justification. *Journal of Personality and Social Psychology, 34,* 874–884.

Pfau, M. (1997). The inoculation model of resistance to influence. In G. A. Barnett & F. J. Boster (Eds.), *Progress in communication sciences* (Vol. 13, pp. 133–171). Greenwich, CT: Ablex.

Pfau, M., & Burgoon, M. (1988). Inoculation in political campaign communication. *Human Communication Research, 15,* 91–111.

Pfau, M., & Kenski, H. C. (1990). *Attack politics: Strategy and defense.* New York: Praeger.

Pfau, M., & Parrott, R. (1993). *Persuasive communication campaigns.* Boston: Allyn and Bacon.

Pfau, M., & Van Bockern, S. (1994). The persistence of inoculation in conferring resistance to smoking initiation among adolescents: The second year. *Human Communication Research, 20,* 413–430.

Pfau, M., Van Bockern, S., & Kang, J. G. (1992). Use of inoculation to promote resistance to smoking initiation among adolescents. *Communication Monographs, 59,* 213–230.

Pharnor, A. (1999, May). Breaking the code. *The Source,* p. 72.

Phillips, A. (1998, October 2). How much does monogamy tell us? *New York Times,* A27.

Pierce, J. P., Choi, W., Gilpin, E. A., Farkas, A. J., & Berry, C. C. (1998). Tobacco industry promotion of cigarettes and adolescent smoking. *Journal of the American Medical Association, 279,* 511–515.

Pierce, J. P., Emery, S., & Gilpin, E. (2002). The California tobacco control program: A long-term health communication project. In R. Hornik (Ed.), *Public health communication: Evidence for behavior change* (pp. 97–114). Mahwah, NJ: Lawrence Erlbaum Associates.

Pollay, R. W. (1997). Hacks, flacks, and counter-attacks: Cigarette advertising, sponsored research, and controversies. *Journal of Social Issues, 53,* 53–74.

Pratkanis, A. R. (1989). The cognitive representation of attitudes. In A. R. Pratkanis, S. J. Breckler, & A. G. Greenwald (Eds.), *Attitude structure and function* (pp. 71–98). Hillsdale, NJ: Lawrence Erlbaum Associates.

Pratkanis, A. R. (1998). Myths of subliminal persuasion: The cargo-cult science of subliminal persuasion. In K. Frazier (Ed.), *Encounters with the paranormal: Science, knowledge, and belief* (pp. 240–252). Amherst, NY: Prometheus Books.

Pratkanis, A. R., & Aronson, E. (1992). *Age of propaganda: The everyday use and abuse of persuasion.* New York: W. H. Freeman.

Preiss, R. W., & Allen, M. (1998). Performing counterattitudinal advocacy: The persuasive impact of incentives. In M. Allen & R. W. Preiss (Eds.), *Persuasion: Advances through meta-analysis* (pp. 231–242). Cresskill, NJ: Hampton Press.

President Bush waffles (2001, August 10). *New York Times*, A22.

Priester, J., Wegener, D., Petty, R., & Fabrigar, L. (1999). Examining the psychological process underlying the sleeper effect: The elaboration likelihood model explanation. *Media Psychology, 1*, 27–48.

Prochaska, J. O., DiClemente, C. C., & Norcross, J. C. (1992). In search of how people change: Applications to addictive behaviors. *American Psychologist, 47*, 1102–1114.

Prochaska, J. O., Redding, C. A., Harlow, L. L., Rossi, J. S., & Velicer, W. F. (1994). The transtheoretical model of change and HIV prevention: A review. *Health Education Quarterly, 21*, 471–486.

Pryor, J. B., & Reeder, G. D. (1993). Collective and individual representations of HIV/AIDS stigma. In J. B. Pryor & G. D. Reeder (Eds.), *The social psychology of HIV infection* (pp. 263–286). Hillsdale, NJ: Lawrence Erlbaum Associates.

Puente, M. (1999, September 7). Casual clothes hit sour note with some. *USA Today*, 1D–2D.

Putnam, L. L., & Wilson, C. E. (1982). Communicative strategies in organizational conflicts: Reliability and validity of a measurement scale. In M. Burgoon (Ed.), *Communication yearbook 6* (pp. 629–652). Beverly Hills, CA: Sage.

Rancer, A. S. (1998). Argumentativeness. In J. C. McCroskey, J. A. Daly, M. M. Martin, & M. J. Beatty (Eds.), *Communication and personality: Trait perspectives* (pp. 149–170). Cresskill, NJ: Hampton Press.

Rancer, A. S., Whitecap, V. G., Kosberg, R. L., & Avtgis, T. A. (1997). Testing the efficacy of a communication training program to increase argumentativeness and argumentative behavior in adolescents. *Communication Education, 46*, 273–286.

Ratcliff, C. D., Czuchry, M., Scarberry, N. C., Thomas, J. C., Dansereau, D. F., & Lord, C. G. (1999). Effects of directed thinking on intentions to engage in beneficial activity: Actions versus reasons. *Journal of Applied Social Psychology, 29*, 994–1009.

Ray, G. B., Ray, E. B., & Zahn, C. J. (1991). Speech behavior and social evaluation: An examination of medical messages. *Communication Quarterly, 39*, 119–129.

Reardon, K. K. (1991). *Persuasion in practice.* Newbury Park, CA: Sage.

Redford, R. (2001, May 23). Bush vs. the American landscape. *New York Times*, A29.

Reel, B. W., & Thompson, T. L. (1994). A test of the effectiveness of strategies for talking about AIDS and condom use. *Journal of Applied Communication Research, 22*, 127–140.

Reinard, J. C. (1988). The empirical study of the persuasive effects of evidence: The status after fifty years of research. *Human Communication Research, 15*, 3–59.

Reinard, J. C. (1991). *Foundations of argument: Effective communication for critical thinking*. Dubuque, IA: Wm. C. Brown.

Reynolds, R. A., & Reynolds, J. L. (2002). Evidence. In J. E. Dillard & M. Pfau (Eds.), *The persuasion handbook: Developments in theory and practice* (pp. 427–444). Thousand Oaks, CA: Sage.

Rhoads, K. V. L., & Cialdini, R. B. (2002). The business of influence: Principles that lead to success in commercial settings. In J. P. Dillard and M. Pfau (Eds.), *The persuasion handbook: Developments in theory and practice* (pp. 513–542). Thousand Oaks, CA: Sage.

Rhodes, N., & Wood, W. (1992). Self-esteem and intelligence affect influence-ability: The mediating role of message reception. *Psychological Bulletin, 111,* 156–171.

Rice, R. E., & Atkin, C. K. (2002). Communication campaigns: Theory, design, implementation, and evaluation. In J. Bryant & D. Zillmann (Eds.), *Media effects: Advances in theory and research* (2nd ed., pp. 427–451). Mahwah, NJ: Lawrence Erlbaum Associates.

Richins, M. L. (1991). Social comparison and the idealized images of advertising. *Journal of Consumer Research, 18,* 71–83.

Richmond, D. (2001, September 17). The moods of America: Grief, rage, resolve. *New York Times,* Letter to the Editor, A14.

Riggio, R. E. (1987). *The charisma quotient: What it is, how to get it, how to use it*. New York: Dodd, Mead.

Rind, B., & Bordia, P. (1995). Effect of server's "thank you" and personalization on restaurant tipping. *Journal of Applied Social Psychology, 25,* 745–751.

Rind, B., & Bordia, P. (1996). Effect on restaurant tipping of male and female servers drawing a happy, smiling face on the backs of customers' checks. *Journal of Applied Social Psychology, 26,* 218–225.

Ritter, K., & Henry, D. (1994). The 1980 Reagan–Carter presidential debate. In R. V. Friedenberg (Ed.), *Rhetorical studies of national political debates, 1960–1992* (2nd ed., pp. 69–93). Westport, CT: Praeger.

Rittle, R. H. (1981). Changes in helping behavior: Self-versus situational perceptions as mediators of the foot-in-the-door effect. *Personality and Social Psychology Bulletin, 7,* 431–437.

Roberts, D. S., & Geller, E. S. (1994). A statewide intervention to increase safety belt use: Adding to the impact of a belt use law. *American Journal of Health Promotion, 8,* 172–174.

Robertson, L. S., Kelley, A. B., O'Neill, B., Wixom, C. W., Eiswirth, R. S. & Haddon, W., Jr. (1974). A controlled study of the effect of television messages on safety belt use. *American Journal of Public Health, 64,* 1071–1080.

Robinson, J. P., Shaver, P. R., & Wrightsman, L. S. (Eds.) (1999). *Measures of political attitudes*. San Diego: Academic Press.

Robinson, W. G. (1998). Heaven's Gate: The end? *Journal of Computer Mediated Communication*. On-line: http://www.ascusc.org/jcmc/vol3/issue3/robinson.html)

Roehm, H. A., & Haugtvedt, C. P. (1999). Understanding interactivity of cyberspace advertising. In D. W. Schumann & E. Thorson (Eds.), *Advertising and the World Wide Web* (pp. 27–39). Mahwah, NJ: Lawrence Erlbaum Associates.

Rogers, E. M. (1995). *Diffusion of innovations* (4th ed.). New York: Free Press.

Rogers, M., & Seiler, C. A. (1994). The answer is no: A national survey of advertising industry practitioners and their clients about whether they use subliminal advertising. *Journal of Advertising Research, 34, 2*, 36–45.

Rogers, M., & Smith, K. H. (1993, March–April). Public perceptions of subliminal advertising: Why practitioners shouldn't ignore this issue. *Journal of Advertising Research, 33*, 10–18.

Rogers, R. W. (1975). A protection motivation theory of fear appeals and attitude change. *Journal of Psychology, 91*, 93–114.

Rogers, R. W., & Mewborn, C. R. (1976). Fear appeals and attitude change: Effects of a threat's noxiousness, probability of occurrence, and the efficacy of coping responses. *Journal of Personality and Social Psychology, 34*, 54–61.

Rokeach, M. (1960). *The open and closed mind*. New York: Basic Books.

Rokeach, M. (1973). *The nature of human values*. New York: Free Press.

Romano, L. (1998, October 19). Boss, you want me to do WHAT? *Washington Post National Weekly Edition*, 29.

Romer, D., & Jamieson, P. (2001). Advertising, smoker imagery, and the diffusion of smoking behavior. In P. Slovic (Ed.), *Smoking: Risk, perception, & policy* (pp. 127–155). Thousand Oaks, CA: Sage.

Rook, K. S. (1987). Effects of case history versus abstract information on health attitudes and behaviors. *Journal of Applied Social Psychology, 17*, 533–553.

Root-Bernstein, R. S. (1993). *Rethinking AIDS: The tragic cost of premature consensus*. New York: Free Press.

Rosenberg, S. W., & McCafferty, P. (1987). The image and the vote: Manipulating voters' preferences. *Public Opinion Quarterly, 51*, 31–47.

Roskos-Ewoldsen, D. R. (1997a). Implicit theories of persuasion. *Human Communication Research, 24*, 31–63.

Roskos-Ewoldsen, D. R. (1997b). Attitude accessibility and persuasion: Review and a transactive model. In B. R. Burleson (Ed.), *Communication Yearbook, 20*, 185–225.

Roskos-Ewoldsen, D. R., Arpan-Ralstin, L., & St. Pierre, J. (2002). Attitude accessibility and persuasion: The quick and the strong. In J. P. Dillard and M. Pfau (Eds.), *The persuasion handbook: Developments in theory and practice* (pp. 39–61). Sage: Thousand Oaks, CA.

Roskos-Ewoldsen, D. R., & Fazio, R. H. (1992). On the orienting value of attitudes: Attitude accessibility as a determinant of an object's attraction of visual attention. *Journal of Personality and Social Psychology, 63*, 198–211.

Rotello, G. (1997). *Sexual ecology: AIDS and the destiny of gay men*. New York: Dutton.

Rothman, A. J., Salovey, P., Antone, C., Keough, K., & Martin, C. D. (1993). The influence of message framing on intentions to perform health behaviors. *Journal of Experimental Social Psychology, 29*, 408–433.

Rothstein, E. (2001, November 17). Exploring the flaws in the notion of the "root causes" of terror. *New York Times*, A23.

Rubin, R. B., Palmgreen, P., & Sypher, H. E. (Eds.) (1994). *Communication research measures: A sourcebook*. New York: Guilford.

Rudman, L. A., & Kilianski, S. E. (2000). Implicit and explicit attitudes toward female authority. *Personality and Social Psychology Bulletin, 26*, 1315–1328.

Rushing, W. A. (1995). *The AIDS epidemic: Social dimensions of an infectious disease.* Boulder, CO: Westview.

Sabato, L. J., & Simpson, G. R. (1996). *Dirty little secrets: The persistence of corruption in American politics.* New York: Times Books.

Salovey, P., Schneider, T. R., & Apanovitch, A. M. (2002). Message framing in the prevention and early detection of illness. In J. P. Dillard & M. Pfau (Eds.), *The persuasion handbook: Developments in theory and practice* (pp. 391–406). Thousand Oaks, CA: Sage.

Salovey, P., & Wegener, D. T. (2002). Communicating about health: Message framing, persuasion, and health behavior. In J. Suls & K. Wallston (Eds.), *Social psychological foundations of health and illness.* Oxford: Blackwell.

Santos, M. D., Leve, C., & Pratkanis, A. R. (1994). Hey buddy, can you spare seventeen cents?: Mindful persuasion and the pique technique. *Journal of Applied Social Psychology, 24,* 755–764.

Savan, L. (1994). *The sponsored life: Ads, TV, and American culture.* Philadelphia: Temple University Press.

Scheibe, K. E. (2000). *The drama of everyday life.* Cambridge, MA: Harvard University Press.

Schein, E. H. (1961). *Coercive persuasion: A socio-psychological analysis of the "brainwashing" of the American civilian prisoners by the Chinese communists.* New York: W.W. Norton.

Schell, J. (1982). *The fate of the earth.* New York: Knopf.

Scher, S. J., & Cooper, J. (1989). Motivational basis of dissonance: The singular role of behavioral consequences. *Journal of Personality and Social Psychology, 56,* 899–906.

Schooler, C., Chaffee, S. H., Flora, J. A., & Roser, C. (1998). Health campaign channels: Tradeoffs among reach, specificity, and impact. *Human Communication Research, 24,* 410–432.

Schooler, C., Feighery, E., & Flora, J. A. (1996). Seventh graders' self-reported exposure to cigarette marketing and its relationship to their smoking behavior. *American Journal of Public Health, 86,* 1216–1221.

Schroeder, C. M., & Prentice, D. A. (1998). Exposing pluralistic ignorance to reduce alcohol use among college students. *Journal of Applied Social Psychology, 28,* 2150–2180.

Schudson, M. (1986). *Advertising, the uneasy persuasion.* New York: Basic Books.

Schuman, H., & Presser, S. (1981). *Questions and answers in attitude surveys: Experiments on question form, wording, and context.* Orlando, FL: Academic Press.

Schwartz, S. (1996). Value priorities and behavior: Applying a theory of integrated value systems. In C. Seligman, J. M. Olson, & M. P. Zanna (Eds.), *The psychology of values: The Ontario symposium* (Vol. 8, pp. 1–24). Mahwah, NJ: Lawrence Erlbaum Associates.

Schwartz, T. (1973). *The responsive chord.* Garden City, NJ: Anchor Press.

Schwarz, N. (1999). Self-reports: How the questions shape the answers. *American Psychologist, 54,* 93–105.

Schwarz, N., & Bless, H. (1992). Scandals and the public's trust in politicians: Assimilation and contrast effects. *Personality and Social Psychology Bulletin, 18,* 574–579.

Sears, D. O., & Funk, C. L. (1991). The role of self-interest in social and political attitudes. In M. P. Zanna (Ed.), *Advances in experimental social psychology* (Vol. 24, pp. 1–91). San Diego: Academic Press.

Sears, D. O., Henry, P. J., & Kosterman, R. (2000). Egalitarian values and contemporary racial politics. In D. O. Sears, J. Sidanius, & L. Bobo (Eds.), *Racialized politics: The debate about racism in America* (pp. 75–117). Chicago: University of Chicago Press.

Sears, D. O., Lau, R. R., Tyler, T. R., & Allen, H. M., Jr. (1980). The Self-interest vs. symbolic politics in policy attitudes and presidential voting. *American Political Science Review, 74,* 670–684.

Seibold, D. R., Cantrill, J. G., & Meyers, R. A. (1994). Communication and interpersonal influence. In M. L. Knapp & G. R. Miller (Eds.), *Handbook of interpersonal communication* (2nd ed., pp. 542–588). Thousand Oaks, CA: Sage.

Seligman, C., & Katz, A. N. (1996). The dynamics of value systems. In C. Seligman, J. M. Olson, & M. P. Zanna (Eds.), *The psychology of values: The Ontario symposium* (Vol. 8, pp. 53–75). Mahwah, NJ: Lawrence Erlbaum Associates.

Sharma, A. (1999). Does the salesperson like customers? A conceptual and empirical examination of the persuasive effect of perceptions of the salesperson's affect toward customers. *Psychology and Marketing, 16,* 141–162.

Shavitt, S., & Nelson, M. R. (2000). The social-identity function in person perception: Communicated meanings of product preferences. In G. R. Maio & J. M. Olson (Eds.), *Why we evaluate: Functions of attitudes* (pp. 37–57). Mahwah, NJ: Lawrence Erlbaum Associates.

Sheeran, P., Abraham, C., & Orbell, S. (1999). Psychosocial correlates of heterosexual condom use: A meta-analysis. *Psychological Bulletin, 125,* 90–132.

Sherif, C. W., Sherif, M., & Nebergall, R. E. (1965). *Attitude and attitude change: The social judgment-involvement approach.* Philadelphia: W.B. Saunders.

Sherif, M. (1967). Introduction. In C. W. Sherif & M. Sherif (Eds.), *Attitude, ego-involvement, and change* (pp. 1–5). New York: Wiley.

Sherif, M., & Sherif, C. W. (1967). Attitude as the individual's own categories: The social judgment-involvement approach to attitude and attitude change. In C. W. Sherif & M. Sherif (Eds.), *Attitude, ego-involvement, and change* (pp. 105–139). New York: Wiley.

Siebert, F. S., Peterson, T., & Schramm. W. (1956). *Four theories of the press: The authoritarian, libertarian, social responsibility, and Soviet communist concepts of what the press should be and do.* Urbana: University of Illinois Press.

Siegel, J. T., & Burgoon, J. K. (2002). Expectancy theory approaches to prevention: Violating adolescent expectations to increase the effectiveness of public service announcements. In W. D. Crano & M. Burgoon (Eds.), *Mass media and drug prevention: Classic and contemporary theories and research* (pp. 163–186). Mahwah, NJ: Lawrence Erlbaum Associates.

Siegel, M., & Biener, L. (2002). The impact of antismoking media campaigns on progression to established smoking: Results of a longitudinal youth study in Massachusetts. In R. Hornik (Ed.), *Public health communication: Evidence for behavior change* (pp. 115–130). Mahwah, NJ: Lawrence Erlbaum Associates.

Simon, L., Greenberg, J., & Brehm, J. (1995). Trivialization: The forgotten mode of dissonance reduction. *Journal of Personality and Social Psychology, 68,* 247–260.

Slama, M. E., & Singley, R. B. (1996). Self-monitoring and value-expressive vs. utilitarian ad effectiveness: Why the mixed findings? *Journal of Current Issues and Research in Advertising, 18,* 39–52.

Slater, M. (2002). Involvement as goal-directed strategic processing: Extending the elaboration likelihood model. In J. P. Dillard & M. Pfau (Eds.), *The persuasion handbook: Developments in theory and practice* (pp. 175–194). Thousand Oaks, CA: Sage.

Slater, M. D., Karan, D., Rouner, D., Murphy, K., & Beauvais, F. (1998). Developing and assessing alcohol warning content: Responses to quantitative information and behavioral recommendations in warnings with television beer advertisements. *Journal of Public Policy & Marketing, 17,* 48–60.

Slater, M. D., & Rouner, D. (1996). Value-affirmative and value-protective processing of alcohol education messages that include statistical evidence or anecdotes. *Communication Research, 23,* 210–235.

Smith, B. L., Lasswell, H. D., & Casey. R. D. (1946). *Propaganda, communication, and public opinion.* Princeton, NJ: Princeton University Press.

Smith, M. B., Bruner, J. B., & White, R. S. (1956). *Opinions and personality.* New York: Wiley.

Smith, M. J. (1982). *Persuasion and human action: A review and critique of social influence theories.* Belmont, CA: Wadsworth.

Smith, R. D. (1993). Psychological type and public relations: Theory, research, and applications. *Journal of Public Relations Research, 5,* 177–199.

Smith, S. M., & Shaffer, D. R. (1995). Speed of speech and persuasion: Evidence for multiple effects. *Personality and Social Psychology Bulletin, 21,* 1051–1060.

Smith, T. W. (1995). Review: The Holocaust denial controversy. *Public Opinion Quarterly, 59,* 269–295.

Smythe, T. W. (1999). Moral responsibility. *Journal of Value Inquiry, 33,* 493–506.

Sniderman, P. M., & Piazza, T. (1993). *The scar of race.* Cambridge, MA: Belknap Press.

Snyder, L. B. (2001). How effective are mediated health campaigns? In R. E. Rice & C. K. Atkin (Eds.), *Public communication campaigns* (3rd ed., pp. 181–190). Thousand Oaks, CA: Sage.

Snyder, L. B., & Hamilton, M. A. (2002). A meta-analysis of U.S. health campaign effects on behavior: Emphasize enforcement, exposure, and new information, and beware the secular trend. In R. Hornik (Ed.), *Public health communication: Evidence for behavior change* (pp. 357–383). Mahwah, NJ: Lawrence Erlbaum Associates.

Snyder, M. (1974). Self-monitoring of expressive behavior. *Journal of Personality and Social Psychology, 30,* 526–537.

Snyder, M. (1987). *Public appearances/Private realities: The psychology of self-monitoring.* New York: W. H. Freeman.

Snyder, M., Clary, E. G., & Stukas, A. A. (2000). The functional approach to volunteerism. In G. R. Maio & J. M. Olson (Eds.), *Why we evaluate: Functions of attitudes* (pp. 365–393). Mahwah, NJ: Lawrence Erlbaum Associates.

Snyder, M., & DeBono, K. G. (1985). Appeals to image and claims about quality: Understanding the psychology of advertising. *Journal of Personality and Social Psychology, 49,* 586–597.

Snyder, M., & Kendzierski, D. (1982). Acting on one's attitudes: Procedures for linking attitude and behavior. *Journal of Experimental Social Psychology, 18,* 165–183.

Snyder, M., & Tanke, E. D. (1976). Behavior and attitude: Some people are more consistent than others. *Journal of Personality, 44,* 510–517.

Sobo, E. J. (1995). *Choosing unsafe sex: AIDS-risk denial among disadvantaged women.* Philadelphia: University of Pennsylvania Press.

Soldat, A. S., Sinclair, R. C., & Mark, M. M. (1997). Color as an environmental processing cue: External affective cues can directly affect processing strategy without affecting mood. *Social Cognition, 15,* 55–71.

Solomon, M. R. (1999). *Consumer behavior: Buying, having, and being* (4th ed.) Boston: Allyn & Bacon.

Sopory, P., & Dillard, J. P. (2002). Figurative language and persuasion. In J. P. Dillard & M. Pfau (Eds.), *The persuasion handbook: Developments in theory and practice* (pp. 407–426). Thousand Oaks, CA: Sage.

Spence, J. T., Helmreich, R., & Stapp, J. (1973). A short version of the Attitudes Toward Women Scale (AWS). *Bulletin of the Psychonomic Society, 2,* 219–220.

Sperber, B. M., Fishbein, M., & Ajzen, I. (1980). Predicting and understanding women's occupational orientations: Factors underlying choice intentions. In I. Ajzen & M. Fishbein, *Understanding attitudes and predicting social behavior* (pp. 113–129). Englewood Cliffs, NJ: Prentice Hall.

Staats, A. W., & Staats, C. K. (1958). Attitudes established by classical conditioning. *Journal of Abnormal and Social Psychology, 57,* 37–40.

Steele, C. M. (1988). The psychology of self-affirmation: Sustaining the integrity of the self. In L. Berkowtiz (Ed.), *Advances in experimental social psychology* (Vol. 21, pp. 261–302). San Diego: Academic Press.

Stengel, R. (2000). *You're too kind: A brief history of flattery.* New York: Simon & Schuster.

Stevens, S. S. (1950). Mathematics, measurement, and psychophysics. In S. S. Stevens (Ed.), *Handbook of experimental psychology* (pp. 1–49). New York: Wiley.

Stiff, J. B. (1994). *Persuasive communication.* New York: Guilford.

Stiff, J. B., & Boster, F. J. (1987). Cognitive processing: Additional thoughts and a reply to Petty, Kasmer, Haugtvedt, and Cacioppo. *Communication Monographs, 54,* 250–256.

Stolberg, S. G. (1998, March 9). U.S. awakes to epidemic of sexual diseases. *New York Times,* A1, A14.

Stolberg, S. G. (2001, August 10). A science in its infancy, but with great expectations for its adolescence. *New York Times,* A17.

Stone, J., Aronson, E., Crain, A. L., Winslow, M. P., & Fried, C. B. (1994). Inducing hypocrisy as a means of encouraging young adults to use condoms. *Personality and Social Psychology Bulletin, 20,* 116–128.

Stone, J., Wiegand, A. W., Cooper, J., & Aronson, E. (1997). When exemplification fails: Hypocrisy and the motive for self-integrity. *Journal of Personality and Social Psychology, 72,* 54–65.

Street, R. L., Jr. & Brady, R. M. (1982). Speech rate acceptance ranges as a function of evaluative domain, listener speech rate, and communication context. *Communication Monographs, 49,* 290–308.

Stuart, E. W., Shimp, T. A., & Engle, R. W. (1987). Classical conditioning of consumer attitudes: Four experiments in an advertising context. *Journal of Consumer Research, 14*, 334–349.

Sudman, S., & Bradburn, N. M. (1982). *Asking questions.* San Francisco: Jossey-Bass.

Sutton, S. (1998). Predicting and explaining intentions and behavior: How well are we doing? *Journal of Applied Social Psychology, 28*, 1317–1338.

Swim, J. K., Aikin, K. J., Hall, W. S., & Hunter, B. A. (1995). Sexism and racism: Old-fashioned and modern prejudices. *Journal of Personality and Social Psychology, 68*, 199–214.

Szabo, E. A, & Pfau, M. (2002). Nuances in inoculation: Theory and applications. In J. P. Dillard & M. Pfau (Eds.), *The persuasion handbook: Developments in theory and practice* (pp. 233–258). Thousand Oaks, CA: Sage.

Talbot, M. (2000, January 9). The placebo prescription. *New York Times Magazine,* 34–39, 44, 58–60.

Tannen, D. (1990). *You just don't understand: Women and men in conversation.* New York: William Morrow.

Taylor, S. E. (1981). The interface of cognitive and social psychology. In J. H. Harvey (Ed.), *Cognition, social behavior, and the environment* (pp. 189–211). Hillsdale, NJ: Lawrence Erlbaum Associates.

Taylor, S. E., & Thompson, S. C. (1982). Stalking the elusive "vividness" effect. *Psychological Review, 89*, 155–181.

Taylor, T., & Booth-Butterfield, S. (1993). Getting a foot in the door with drinking and driving: A field study of healthy influence. *Communication Research Reports, 10*, 95–101.

Tedeschi, J. T., Schlenker, B. R., & Bonoma, T. V. (1971). Cognitive dissonance: Private ratiocination or public spectacle? *American Psychologist, 26*, 685–695.

Tesser, A. (1978). Self-generated attitude change. In L. Berkowitz (Ed.), *Advances in experimental social psychology* (Vol. 11, pp. 181–227). New York: Academic Press.

Tesser, A. (1993). The importance of heritability in psychological research: The case of attitudes. *Psychological Review, 100*, 129–142.

Tetlock, P. E. (1986). A value pluralism model of ideological reasoning. *Journal of Personality and Social Psychology, 50*, 819–827.

Tetlock, P. E., Peterson, R. S., & Lerner, J. S. (1996). Revising the value pluralism model: Incorporating social content and context postulates. In C. Seligman, J. M. Olson, & M. P. Zanna (Eds.), *The psychology of values: The Ontario symposium* (Vol. 8, pp. 25–51). Mahwah, NJ: Lawrence Erlbaum Associates.

Thernstrom, S., & Thernstrom, A. (1997). *America in black and white: One nation, indivisible.* New York: Simon & Schuster.

Theus, K. T. (1994). Subliminal advertising and the psychology of processing unconscious stimuli: A review of research. *Psychology & Marketing, 11*, 271–290.

Thompson, L. (1995). "They saw a negotiation": Partisanship and involvement. *Journal of Personality and Social Psychology, 68*, 839–853.

Thompson, M. M., Zanna, M. P., Griffin, D. W. (1995). Let's not be indifferent about (attitudinal) ambivalence. In R. E. Petty & J. A. Krosnick (Eds.), *Attitude strength: Antecedents and consequences* (pp. 361–386). Hillsdale, NJ: Lawrence Erlbaum Associates.

Thompson, S. C., Anderson, K., Freedman, D., & Swan, J. (1996). Illusions of safety in a risky world: A study of college students' condom use. *Journal of Applied Social Psychology, 26*, 189–210.

Thurstone, L. L. (1928). Attitudes can be measured. *American Journal of Sociology, 33*, 529–544.

Timmerman, L. M. (2002). Comparing the production of power in language on the basis of sex. In M. Allen, R. W. Preiss, B. M. Gayle, & N. A. Burrell (Eds.), *Interpersonal communication research: Advances through meta-analysis* (pp. 73–87). Mahwah, NJ: Lawrence Erlbaum Associates.

Toulmin, S. (1958). *The uses of argument.* New York: Cambridge University Press.

Tourangeau, R., & Rasinski, K. A. (1988). Cognitive processes underlying context effects in attitude measurement. *Psychological Bulletin, 103*, 299–314.

Trappey, C. (1996). A meta-analysis of consumer choice and subliminal advertising. *Psychology & Marketing, 13*, 517–530.

Trost, M. R., Langan, E. J., & Kellar-Guenther, Y. (1999). Not everyone listens when you "just say no": Drug resistance in relational context. *Journal of Applied Communication Research, 27*, 120–138.

Twitchell, J. B. (1999). *Lead us into temptation: The triumph of American materialism.* New York: Columbia University Press.

van Knippenberg, B., van Knippenberg, D., Blaauw, E., & Vermunt, R. (1999). Relational considerations in the use of influence tactics. *Journal of Applied Social Psychology, 29*, 806–819.

Verhovek, S. H. (1997, December 14). In poll, Americans reject means but not ends of racial diversity. *New York Times*, 1, 18.

Viswanath, K., & Finnegan, J. R., Jr. (1996). The knowledge gap hypothesis: Twenty-five years later. In B. R. Burleson (Ed.), *Communication yearbook 19* (pp. 187–227). Thousand Oaks, CA: Sage.

Waggenspack, B. (2000). Women's role in rhetorical traditions. In J. L. Golden, G. F. Berquist, & W. E. Coleman, *The rhetoric of Western thought* (7th ed., pp. 340–370). Dubuque, IA: Kendall/Hunt.

Waldron, V. R., & Applegate, J. L. (1998). Person-centered tactics during verbal disagreements: Effects on student perceptions of persuasiveness and social attraction. *Communication Education, 47*, 53–66.

Wang Erber, M., Hodges, S. D., & Wilson T. D. (1995). Attitude strength, attitude stability, and the effects of analyzing reasons. In R. E. Petty & J. A. Krosnick (Eds.), *Attitude strength: Antecedents and consequences* (pp. 433–454). Hillsdale, NJ: Lawrence Erlbaum Associates.

Weaver, R. M. (1953). *The ethics of rhetoric.* Chicago: Henry Regnery.

Webb, E. J., Campbell, D. T., Schwartz, R. D., & Sechrest, L. (1966). *Unobtrusive measures: Nonreactive research in the social sciences.* Chicago: Rand McNally.

Webb, M. I. (2001, November 26–December 2). MADD: Strategies for safer streets. Advertisement supplement to the *Washington Post National Weekly Edition*, 1.

Weber, M. (1968). *On charisma and institution building.* Chicago: University of Chicago Press.

Wegner, D. M., Schneider, D. J., Carter, S. R., III, & White, T. L. (1987). Paradoxical effects of thought suppression. *Journal of Personality and Social Psychology, 53*, 5–13.

Weigel, R. H., & Newman, L. S. (1976). Increasing attitude–behavior correspondence by broadening the scope of the behavioral measure. *Journal of Personality and Social Psychology, 33*, 793–802.

Weinstein, N. D. (1980). Unrealistic optimism about future life events. *Journal of Personality and Social Psychology, 39*, 806–820.

Weinstein, N. D. (1993). Testing four competing theories of health-protective behavior. *Health Psychology, 12*, 324–333.

West, D. M. (1997). *Air wars: Television advertising in election campaigns, 1952–1996* (2nd ed.). Washington, DC: Congressional Quarterly Press.

Whalen, D. J. (1996). *I see what you mean: Persuasive business communication.* Thousand Oaks, CA: Sage.

Wheeless, L. R., Barraclough, R., & Stewart, R. (1983). Compliance-gaining and power in persuasion. In R. Bostrom (Ed.), *Communication yearbook 7* (pp. 105–145). Thousand Oaks, CA: Sage.

Wicker, A. W. (1969). Attitudes vs. actions: The relationship of verbal and overt behavioral responses to attitude objects. *Journal of Social Issues, 25*, 41–78.

Wicklund, R. A., & Brehm, J. W. (1976). *Perspectives on cognitive dissonance.* Hillsdale, NJ: Lawrence Erlbaum Associates.

Wigley, C. J., III. (1998). Verbal aggressiveness. In J. C. McCroskey, J. A. Daly, M. M. Martin, & M. J. Beatty (Eds.), *Communication and personality: Trait perspectives* (pp. 191–214). Cresskill, NJ: Hampton Press.

Williams, K. D., & Dolnik, L. (2001). Revealing the worst first: Stealing thunder as a social influence strategy. In J. P. Forgas & K. D. Williams (Eds.), *Social influence: Direct and indirect processes* (pp. 213–231). Philadelphia: Taylor & Francis.

Wilson, S. R. (1999). Developing theories of persuasive message production: The next generation. In J. O. Greene (Ed.), *Message production* (pp. 15–44). Mahwah, NJ: Lawrence Erlbaum Associates.

Wilson, S. R., Aleman, C. G., & Leatham, G. B. (1998). Identity implications of influence goals: A revised analysis of face-threatening acts and application to seeking compliance with same-sex friends. *Human Communication Research, 25*, 64–96.

Wilson, T. D., LaFleur, S. J., & Anderson, D. E. (1996). The validity and consequences of verbal reports about attitudes. In N. Schwarz & S. Sudman (Eds.), *Answering questions: Methodology for determining cognitive and communicative processes in survey research* (pp. 91–114). San Francisco: Jossey-Bass.

Winfield, B. (1994). *FDR and the news media.* New York: Columbia University Press.

Winsten, J. A., & DeJong, W. (2001). The designated driver campaign. In R. E. Rice & C. K. Atkin (Eds.), *Public communication campaigns* (3rd ed., pp. 290–294). Thousand Oaks, CA: Sage.

Witte, K. (1997). Preventing teen pregnancy through persuasive communications: Realities, myths, and the hard-fact truths. *Journal of Community Health, 22*, 137–154.

Witte, K. (1998). Fear as motivator, fear as inhibitor: Using the extended parallel process model to explain fear appeal successes and failures. In P. A. Andersen

& L. K. Guerrero (Eds.), *Handbook of communication and emotion: Research, theory, applications, and contexts* (pp. 423–450). San Diego: Academic Press.

Witte, K., & Allen, M. (2000). A meta-analysis of fear appeals: Implications for effective public health campaigns. *Health Education & Behavior, 27*, 591–615.

Witte, K., Meyer, G., & Martell, D. (2001). *Effective health risk messages: A step-by-step guide.* Thousand Oaks, CA: Sage.

Witte, K, Stokols, D., Ituarte, P., & Schneider, M. (1993). Testing the health belief model in a field study to promote bicycle safety helmets. *Communication Research, 20*, 564–586.

Wood, W., Kallgren, C. A., & Preisler, R. M. (1985). Access to attitude-relevant information in memory as a determinant of persuasion: The role of message attributes. *Journal of Experimental Social Psychology, 21*, 73–85.

Wood, W., Rhodes, N., & Biek, M. (1995). Working knowledge and attitude strength: An information-processing analysis. In R. E. Petty & J. A. Krosnick (Eds.), *Attitude strength: Antecedents and consequences* (pp. 283–313). Hillsdale, NJ: Lawrence Erlbaum Associates.

Worden, J. K., & Flynn, B. S. (2002). Using mass media to prevent cigarette smoking. In R. Hornik (Ed.), *Public health communication: Evidence for behavior change* (pp. 23–33). Mahwah, NJ: Lawrence Erlbaum Associates.

Yousef, F. S. (1982). North Americans in the Middle East: Aspects of the roles of friendliness, religion, and women in cross-cultural relations. In L. A. Samovar & R. E. Porter (Eds.), *Intercultural communication: A reader* (3rd ed., pp. 91–99). Belmont, CA: Wadsworth.

Zajonc, R. B. (1968). Attitudinal effects of mere exposure. *Journal of Personality and Social Psychology Monographs Supplement, 9* (2, Pt. 2), 1–27.

Zakaria, F. (2001, October 15). Why do they hate us? *Newsweek*, pp. 22–30, 32–38, 40.

Zaller, J. R. (1992). *The nature and origins of mass opinion.* New York: Cambridge University Press.

Zanna, M. P., & Fazio, R. H. (1982). The attitude–behavior relation: Moving toward a third generation of research. In M. P. Zanna, E. T. Higgins, & C. P. Herman (Eds.), *Consistency in social behavior: The Ontario symposium* (Vol. 2, pp. 283–301). Hillsdale, NJ: Lawrence Erlbaum Associates.

Zanna, M. P., & Rempel, J. K. (1988). Attitudes: A new look at an old concept. In D. Bar-Tal & A. Kruglanski (Eds.), *The social psychology of knowledge* (pp. 315–334). New York: Cambridge University Press.

Zanot, E. J., Pincus, J. D., & Lamp, E. J. (1983). Public perceptions of subliminal advertising. *Journal of Advertising, 12*, 39–45.

Ziv, L. (1998, February). "I gave him my love, he gave me HIV." *Cosmopolitan*, pp. 240–243.

Zuckerman, M. (1979). *Sensation-seeking: Beyond the optimal level of arousal.* Hillsdale, NJ: Lawrence Erlbaum Associates.

Author Index

Subject Index

HIT THE GROUND
RUNNING

ALISON HUGHES

ORCA BOOK PUBLISHERS

Library and Archives Canada Cataloguing in Publication

Hughes, Alison, 1966-, author
Hit the ground running / Alison Hughes.

Issued also in print and electronic formats.
ISBN 978-1-4598-1544-5 (softcover).—ISBN 978-1-4598-1545-2 (pdf).—
ISBN 978-1-4598-1546-9 (epub)

I. Title.
PS8615.U3165H58.2017   jc813'.6   C2017-900780-7
C2017-900781-5

First published in the United States, 2017
Library of Congress Control Number: 2017932499

Summary: In this novel for teens, Dee and her younger brother, Eddie, make a run for the Canadian border when their father disappears and social workers start snooping around their Arizona home.

Orca Book Publishers is dedicated to preserving the environment and has printed this book on Forest Stewardship Council® certified paper.

Orca Book Publishers gratefully acknowledges the support for its publishing programs provided by the following agencies: the Government of Canada through the Canada Book Fund and the Canada Council for the Arts, and the Province of British Columbia through the BC Arts Council and the Book Publishing Tax Credit.

Edited by Sarah N. Harvey
Cover design by Jenn Playford
Cover image by Creative Market, Dreamstime.com
Author photo by Barbara Heintzman

ORCA BOOK PUBLISHERS
www.orcabook.com

Printed and bound in Canada.

20 19 18 17 • 4 3 2 1

For my mother, Claudette—our family's anchor.

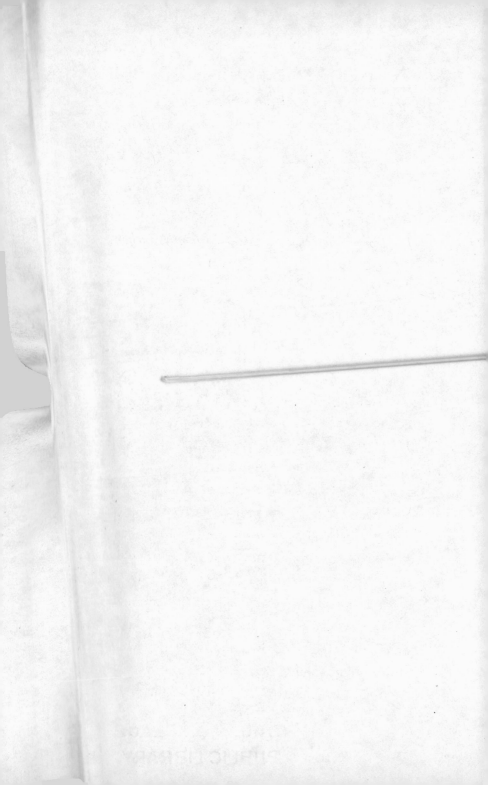

SANTACINO, ARIZONA

WEDNESDAY

Dee stared out the open kitchen window. There wasn't much to see even if she'd really been looking. A stretch of gravel peppered with stalks of scrub grass leading down a hill, past other ramshackle houses, into the endless, barren desert that led all the way to Mexico. Tumbleweed desert. Wile E. Coyote desert. Looming, enormous saguaro cacti stood at meaningless attention. From a distance, they were eerily humanoid, arms raised to the scorching sun, waiting rather than growing.

The early evening was dead still. Silent. No scuttling animals, no traffic. Everything paused, still and mute. Even the crazy acrobatics of the tumbleweeds were stilled by the crippling heat that had already killed the wind. They lay exhausted, inanimate, exposed for what they really were—matted, tangled balls of dead weeds. They were only interesting when they moved, *because* they moved. They briefly enlivened the stillness, the mile after mile of Mars-like sand and burnt-red rock.

Dee's father was drawn to this lonely emptiness that merged into the hazy, blue-brown horizon.

"It's like we're at the edge of the world!" he would marvel, as if that was a good thing, an amazing thing, not something scary or apocalyptic. In the evening, he would sometimes drag a little stool out and sit watching the nothingness, waiting for the sun to sear its horizontal stripes lower and lower, protesting in a scream of red before it bled itself out.

Was the desert big and empty enough to absorb whatever washed over him during his dark, silent times? Dee never knew. She would watch him for a while, then close her eyes, block out the dust and heat, and remember the feel of cool, soft grass on her bare feet and the smell of pine trees on fresh mornings. Although it was all her brother, Eddie, knew, they had not always lived here in the desert at the edge of the world.

Today was one of the heat-wave July days, some of the hottest in the town's history she'd read in the local paper at the gas station. Something non-record-setting, like fourth hottest. But Santacino was a small town, and in small towns the weather always makes the head-lines. Animals too. Whenever a honking, stinking gang of javelinas—wild, ugly creatures that people called desert pigs—snorted through town, it was a sure bet they'd make the front page of the *Santacino Current*. It would be a dark, murky picture, though, with lots of wild, rolling pig eyes. Those pigs were smart; they only ran at night, when it was cooler.

It made no difference at all to Dee that the window was wide open. Furnace-hot inside, furnace-hot out. The three fans that had at least shifted the hot air around had all broken in May, like dominos falling. They probably only had a psychological effect anyway, the movement of air convincing everyone it was marginally cooler. But at least the fans had been activity, noise, movement. Now their poky carcasses were just one more tangled pile of junk in the living room.

"If we lived in, I don't know—Italy? Milan? We'd be artistic prodigies with this sculpture," Dee had said to Eddie one day, idly considering the pile of fans as Eddie burrowed into an old chest, pushing out yellowing sheet music like a mole excavating dirt. "The 'It Kids' of the art world."

They'd tried out various names for their "installation": *Still Life with Three Fans, Death to the Fans, Junk Heap #14*. They'd tried to think of any Italian words they might know, seeing as they were prodigies in Milan, but only the Spanish words they'd learned at school bubbled to the surface. They'd tried out varieties of pasta (*Linguine! Fettuccine!*) and finally came up with *ciao* and *arrivederci*. They were pretty sure those were Italian.

Eddie added *Chow Arivaderchee* to the list of titles in big, scrawling letters, taping the piece of scrap paper to the bottom fan.

But that was then.

Now was the problem.

Dee's hands gripping the edge of the sink were cold. In the stifling heat, she was cold right through, shivery cold down to her feet, paralyzed with it. A trickle of sweat ran down the side of her face.

Fear and panic welled up and smothered everything but the single word blinking in her mind. *Friday.* What was today? What day was it? Her mind was blank and numb.

"Hey, Eddie," she called to the boy in the yard, who crouched as still as the landscape. Her voice was stiff and forced. She licked her lips, straightened a bit and called his name again. "Eddie, what's today? What day is it?" Eddie always knew.

He was squatting on his haunches, chin on his hands, elbows on his knees, carefully observing an insect.

"Wednesday, July 23," he answered automatically, not looking up, not wanting to startle the thing he was watching, not wanting it to take flight. It did anyway, unfurling its wings and swooping away.

"Shoot." He stood and checked his huge watch, twisting it the right way around on his thin wrist. "6:16 PM."

Oh God, Wednesday! That's right—it's already Wednesday. She watched Eddie pick up a rock, look at it, rub it on his shorts, then examine it more closely. He looked very small out there in the field, scuffing along and kicking up dust in his oversized cowboy boots.

Wednesday night, almost Thursday. Dee's heart was pounding, her knuckles whitening as she gripped the sink. *We have a day. One day. Tomorrow. By tomorrow we have to be gone.*

A hot wave of fury bubbled up and momentarily blotted out her panic.

Dad, where the hell are you? One day, Dad. One day...

The visitor at the door an hour ago had been a shock. Dee hadn't known they were under surveillance or being monitored or whatever language social workers used. Probably something nicer, less cop-like, kid-friendlier. Observation?

Anyway, they'd been ratted out, red-flagged by some nosy, disapproving, meddling adult. Dee wondered who. She'd thoroughly covered their tracks at school, signing her father's name convincingly on their report cards, mentioning to one or two teachers that her dad said to say hi. And Mr. Werner, Eddie's school counselor, was such a phenomenal screwup himself that Dee couldn't believe he could have discovered that her father had vanished almost six weeks ago. Mr. Werner, the school joke, who wanted to assess Eddie's "substandard performance," Eddie's "issues." But school had been out for over a month...no, she was pretty sure the betrayal hadn't come from the school.

Dee thought it must have been number 27 down the street. The woman with the frizzy hair, the chain smoker with the mean husband. Dee didn't even know her name, but she'd felt her watching every time she and Eddie walked past her house. Nothing better to do than rat out two innocent kids, the old hag, thought Dee. With other people, like Mr. and Mrs. S. or Theresa's mom, Dee might have understood some well-meaning concern behind their being reported. But not with the hag down the street.

The social worker had been a nice lady, comfortable and practical, with kind eyes, beat-up Birkenstocks, stretch pants and short graying hair. But she was from children's services. Government-land. She may have seemed an unlikely enemy, but Dee knew immediately that she was dangerous.

Why did I open the door? They almost never opened the door. It was never good news. It was either their scrawny, anxious landlord or some utility guy or stony-faced men with trucks and orders to repossess something. Unwritten house rule: let people mill around awkwardly on the front step for long enough, and they will eventually give up and go away. They'll be back, but later.

This time she'd run to the door and flung it open, her face expectant. She'd been sure it was her father, showing up after having lost his key, delighted with some new piece of junk he'd convinced himself was a treasure, some people he'd met, some adventure he'd haplessly lucked into, vaguely unaware that he'd been away so long.

It wasn't him.

"Hello, Dee?" The woman had held up a plastic-covered name tag on a pink string around her neck. "My name is Susan Whitby, and I'm a social worker with the county children's services department. If I could just come in and chat for a few minutes I'd appreciate it." She indicated her clipboard with a grimace, as though she had to tidy up paperwork, had to tick those boxes.

Dee's heart had started hammering at the phrase *children's services*. She knew about these people. In sixth grade a girl in her class had told her about a family called the Johnstons, whose four kids were all picked up one day by children's services. Those kids had been running wild for months, busting windows and stealing bikes, while their mom drank openly on the porch. "Rum," Dee's friend had said, *"and vodka. From the bottle."* She and Dee had shaken their heads knowingly, like: *What can you even do with people like that?*

Their family wasn't like that. Their dad didn't even drink. But these well-meaning children's-services people could pack her and Eddie up just like they had with that family. Nobody ever knew exactly where the

Johnston kids had ended up. One rumor was that some were in Yuma, some as far away as New Mexico. A long way away from Santacino, a long way away from each other. She and Eddie could be like those kids, legally kidnapped and separated and shipped off to different states to live with strangers. And her father would never know, because if Dee couldn't find him, how would children's services?

Where the hell are you, Dad? Dee wondered for the thousandth time.

The nice woman had waited expectantly, sweating on their hot porch. Dee hesitated, on her guard, tense, like a dog making up its mind whether a person was safe or not.

There was really no option.

"Uh, all right. It's...well, come on in..."

She led Susan through to the kitchen, walking her past the living-room mess. The small, stuffy room looked like a flea market, crammed to the ceiling with stacks of books, old vinyl records, boxes and furniture piled high. Couches with end tables and chairs on top, their legs in the air, boxes on top of those. Dad's antique stuff. Some of it might be worth something when it was fixed up, but Dee suspected most of it was complete junk. He was working on it. He was always working on it.

Eddie had a fort in an armchair surrounded by bookcases, covered by an old sheet. He called it "the snake pit," and the book he'd been reading was on the floor, open to a cross section of a snake's fang. *The Path of Venom* was spelled out in oozing green letters.

Two loads of laundry—one dark, one grayish— were dumped in the only small clearing. None of it ever seemed to get folded and put away; they just rummaged and pulled the least wrinkly things off the pile. Eventually the pile got smaller, then got replaced by the same clothes again in a few weeks. It wasn't exactly a system, but it worked. Until you had to bring people into the house, which was never until now.

We live like frigging lunatics. We look like a crazy family. This poor woman's probably wondering how many more scruffy kids will be crawling out from under the junk-shop furniture...

She'd thought the kitchen would be the best place to sit but, taking it in at a glance, she saw it wasn't much better. Dirty dishes were piled on the counter by the filthy stove, dead plants sat desiccating in rock-hard soil on a shelf, and Eddie's collections, neatly labeled, lined the floor and table in old baby-food jars and yogurt containers. A fine layer of desert grit covered the floor, there no matter how much it was swept, which wasn't often. They always kept their shoes on.

Is this normal? Surely at least some of the houses this lady goes into must be kind of messy. Or weird. Not everyone has a perfect, spotless house...

She glanced back at Susan, but the social worker was rummaging in her purse.

Eddie was sitting on the kitchen counter, labeling another set of glass jars. *Insekts. Rocks. Dung. Bonse.* He was interested in every little treasure the dusty desert coughed up.

He was wearing only dirty shorts and his cowboy boots. Like some little psycho hillbilly, Dee thought. But he always ran around that way in the house, and there didn't seem to be any harm in it. Those boots had saved him from a scorpion bite once, and he wore them everywhere.

But seeing things through the social worker's eyes, Dee thought she and Eddie may as well have painted a sign in dripping red letters on the front door: *KIDS IN CRISIS*, with an arrow pointing the way.

"Hey, Eddie, I need to talk to this lady from children's services," Dee said, shooting him a warning glance. *Danger, danger.* It was as clear as if she'd screamed it, and he understood at once. Them against her.

"Okay," he said, sliding off the counter, his face settling into the blank, bland look he reserved for strangers. Dee noticed that his nails were too long and caked with a thin black line of dirt.

"Hey, bud"—Dee couldn't seem to stop her voice from sounding fake—"why don't you go find a shirt?"

"Oh, that's okay, Eddie," said Susan, coming into the kitchen close behind Dee. "Don't mind me."

She called him Eddie! She knows his name! Wait a second, did I just call him Eddie? Maybe she heard me.

No, wait, she called me Dee at the door. She knows who we are. What else does she know?

Eddie glanced at Susan, turned and stomped down the hall to his room, swinging his arms. The boots made him really throw his little hips into the walking.

"Nice pictures," Susan said, indicating Eddie's surreal first-grade artwork that was tacked to the kitchen wall to cover the peeling plaster. Dee liked the bright colors, but the pictures themselves were undeniably odd. A person's head with a snake thing springing out of the top. A dragon-like creature apparently vomiting up a gushing river of blood and people-parts. A fanged humanoid scuttling disturbingly on short, scaly, purple, heavily clawed legs. *Nope, nothing normal here.* Dee's glance slid away from purple reptile-man.

"Eddie's school art," she said. "He's...creative." *And weird. So very weird.*

She walked to the other side of the counter, sliding an empty milk carton in front of an open tin of Alphagetti and shoving some dishes into the sink. She picked up their only apple and set it prominently beside the milk, like props in a presentation on the four food groups. Dairy products. Fruit and vegetables.

"Sorry the place is a bit of a mess," Dee said. "We just got home. I haven't had much of a chance to..." She made vague cleaning motions with her hands.

Susan pulled out a chair, slinging her purse over the back. She glanced around casually, but Dee knew that she was sizing things up, already ticking those boxes.

"Oh, not to worry. You should see *my* house." Susan checked her watch. "Hope you were out somewhere having fun?" She was smiling, and her eyes were kind.

"Just working. I've got a part-time job at the highway gas-station store—you know, with Mr. and Mrs. S.? Just for the summer. Pretty good hours and at least there's air-conditioning. But Dad says school comes first during the year." *Complete lie. When has Dad really given a rat's ass about our schoolwork?* "Eddie comes in sometimes and does homework and reads in the back while I'm working." *And eats Skittles and helps stack cigarette boxes, but I'm not saying that. Stop talking now. Just. Shut. Up.*

"Well, that's a good arrangement, I'd say," Susan said and seemed to mean it. She sighed and glanced down at her clipboard.

"Dee, I'll tell you why I've come. We've had a report that you kids are here on your own, that in fact there's no adult with you at all." She sounded almost apologetic. "Has your dad gone somewhere, honey?"

Dee froze. This was tricky. Technically, it was true. For the last six weeks they had been on their own. No word so far from Dad. But how did you explain to a stranger that he'd always done that, come and gone, an estate sale here, an antique fair there, trolling through huge barns full of crappy old stuff, bringing it back triumphantly to stack in the living room, to work on later to resell for a few more bucks? He always came back, Dee reasoned with herself, like she did late at night when the worry set in.

He always comes back, he loves us, we're his family, this is his home. The last time he'd been away, he'd spent a week in Wickenburg helping a complete stranger, somebody he'd met at an antique barn, build a house.

"I mostly worked on this pretty little porch overlooking the pool," he'd told them when he reappeared. He'd described the design, the landscaping, the view, over burgers paid for from the $100 the grateful temporary friend had paid him for his help. She and Eddie, as usual, got suckered into admiring a house and a view that would never be theirs.

Dee knew things were more serious this time. He'd been away for much longer than he ever had before. *He's such a fool. Hopeless, clueless. He could be anywhere. He could have hitched a ride with anyone, trusted somebody he shouldn't. A child would have more sense. Eddie would have more sense.*

Then she pictured her father, slim and animated, his open, friendly face, his big Eddie-eyes, his unruly hair. Her anger faded.

"A free spirit, a dreamer," was how Auntie Pat described him, with an edge to her voice. "That's what your mom loved about him, his restlessness, his openness, his *plans*. Never mind that she was the one who had to be the adult. The anchor. Every family needs an anchor, Dee."

But what happens when the anchor dies? Then you have an anchorless family, floating wherever the waves take you. And the waves of her mom's death had washed them up here in Santacino, in the middle of the desert, at the end of the world.

Please don't have crossed the border into Mexico, Dad. She'd read the sensational stories that ran in the Phoenix papers. Drug cartels. Shallow graves. Beheadings. *Please, please don't be arrested, don't bring other people's stuff over the border, don't be caught up in some drug war, don't be dead...*

Dee saw Susan looking at her, waiting.

"That's odd," Dee said, doing what she hoped was a good job of sounding genuinely puzzled. "I don't know how you would have heard something like that. He's working. Just working. He's an antique collector. Dealer, actually. So he travels a bit, collecting and selling and stuff." She took a shallow breath and glanced at the kitchen clock.

"He's actually due home any time now." She looked directly at Susan. "You want to wait for him?" It was a lie and a gamble, but the words were out—she couldn't take them back.

"Well, sure, but I can't stay too long..." Susan said.

"Shouldn't be long, but he's not exactly punctual." Dee forced a laugh. "Generally he's home before seven." She eyed Susan. Was this working? No use in bluffing if you're not going to brazen it out, Auntie Pat had once told her.

"Would you like something to drink?" Dee asked, remembering how normal people were supposed to act with visitors. "Lemonade, iced tea?" The words were out before she remembered there was no lemonade or iced tea. Or milk. That left tap water. *Strike one for Little Miss Hostess.*

"Oh, just a glass of water'd hit the spot, thanks," said Susan. Dee turned to the sink with relief. "What a scorcher, hey?"

"Yeah," Dee said, holding out the glass. She felt she should add something more. "Summer," she said with a wry smile, a shake of the head.

Eddie came back down the hall, hesitating in the kitchen doorway. He'd rummaged around to find a cleanish shirt, Dee noticed. Too small for him, and terribly wrinkled, but clean enough.

"Eddie," said Susan quickly, "I'm just waiting to talk to your dad. Do you think he'll be home soon?"

Dee was taken aback by how adeptly Susan had prevented her from tipping off Eddie. The woman was sharper than Dee had given her credit for. Eddie was a smart little guy, but he was only seven years old. She was sixteen and barely handling this interview.

Eddie paused and looked at Susan. He let the pause lengthen in that unnerving way he had, blank blue eyes blinking slowly.

"Guess he'll get here when he gets here," he said, not looking at Dee. He turned back to his labeling.

Susan laughed. "Yep, that's about right, I'd reckon. How old are you now, Eddie?"

Eddie ignored her.

"*Eddie.*" Dee's voice was sharp.

He turned and stared at Susan. Blank. Stupid. Oh, shit, thought Dee, panic flaring up inside her, he's going into his idiot-child routine. He did it to ward off people who asked too many questions—store cashiers, substitute teachers, counselors, librarians. People he was bored of or annoyed with. It worked, mostly, but this was different.

"Eddie, Susan asked you a question," Dee said, her eyes flashing a warning. "He's seven, aren't you, Eddie?" *God, could I sound more fake?* She clenched her teeth. *Act* normal *for once in your life, you little brat. Don't you know what's at stake here?*

Eddie continued to stare as though not understanding the question. *This from the child who just today, just this morning, bored me with a meticulous, technical description of a stingray's anatomy.* She'd been flipping through *People* magazine behind the counter at the gas station, but she'd still listened. Eddie knew if you weren't listening. Cartilaginous, kite-like body, creepy mouth, gill slits, barbed stinger, the whole shebang. *The little brat...*

"Sometimes Eddie just doesn't feel like talking much," she said to Susan with what she hoped was a conspiratorial smile, the kind she'd seen between mothers at the playground near Eddie's school.

Susan smiled and looked at Dee. It was a kind, knowing look. Wait—was there a hint of pity there too?

"You sound like a very good big sister." Susan smiled again. She glanced at her watch. "Darn, I really should get going. Another appointment." She slipped her purse on her shoulder and got up, holding out her hand.

"It's been good to meet you, Dee. I'm sorry I can't stay longer. Could you please tell your father that I'm going to stop back for a chat on Friday morning? Tell him it's important. Here's my card."

"Got it. Friday," Dee said, staring at the card. She looked up, and their eyes met. Dee hesitated.

For a wild, fleeting moment she wanted to explain. To tell this nice woman—who clearly knew there was something fishy about this family—everything. To tell her that their father had never been gone this long, that she should've called the police to report him missing but was scared that if she did they'd take Eddie away, put her and Eddie in separate homes. She wanted to tell her that she'd tried to reach Auntie Pat and Uncle Norm up in Canada, but they were away; that the rent was due in a few days and the money jar was almost empty. She wanted to explain how her dad was kind and generous and harmless and odd and depressed, and how you couldn't hold things against him if you knew him.

It would have been a relief to talk to somebody. But no, not this lady. She was *government*. She was not a friend.

"Okay, so, 'bye," Dee said, lifting her chin. "See you Friday."

She stood on the step and gave Susan a fake-cheerful wave, making sure she drove away. Dee wondered if she'd done all right. On the whole, she thought she had. She'd made children's services go away until Friday.

Friday. They had one day.

One day to get away.

ARIZONA

THURSDAY

Dee lay awake, listening to Eddie reading out loud. It was a strategy they'd started when he was having trouble learning to read, and sometimes he fell back into it, especially when he was really absorbed in what he was reading. He read in a quiet voice, but with emphasis, like he was having a conversation.

"*Imagine having to walk, to move forward constantly because your life depended on it!*" Eddie read, raising his voice a little, part real amazement, part exclamation mark. "*Two dozen of the 400 identified shark species, including the great white shark, the mako shark and the whale shark, must maintain a forward-swimming motion in order to breathe. These obligate ram breathers*"—he sounded it out, liking the scientific phrase, storing it away—"*will actually drown if they stop moving.*" There was a pause, then a rustle of pages. She imagined him flipping to get visuals on all the named sharks.

"Obligate ram breathers," Eddie repeated. He was often up early, reading in bed. Dee had long ago stopped hoping to hear an actual story—Eddie's only interests lay in factual books, usually about animals. He could not even understand the reason behind the creative-writing paragraphs he occasionally was assigned at school.

"But why? What is the point of just making something up?" he would ask at the kitchen table where they both did their homework.

"Just do it, Eddie. Jeez." Dee wrestled with the fact subjects. Math. Chem. What was the point of them? At least you could escape into a story.

Eddie was always up early. Dee would hear him puttering around his side of the room for a while, reading, building with Lego, rattling his collections of rocks and insects and snake skins. Then he'd pull back the sheet curtain and look into Dee's side of the room. They always started their days the same way.

The reading stopped. The book clapped shut. It was time.

Eddie leaned over Dee, peering at her face in the gloom. His curly blond hair, unruly from sleep, framed his face like a halo.

"*Guten Mooorgen,*" he said softly. Dee knew from experience that there was no ignoring him, no putting a pillow over her head—he'd just keep repeating it louder. She'd never figured out where he'd picked up the German.

"*Morgen*, Eddie. What time is it?"

"7:03 AM. Sharp," he announced, pointing to the big watch dangling from his wrist. He always woke her at 7:03.

"What day is it?" she asked, holding up her end of the exchange. But she already knew. She'd been lying awake for hours knowing it.

"Thursday, July 24. Sharp."

Thursday. Their last day. Her heart started to pound. She'd been up late, planning. *And freaking out and panicking; don't forget the freaking out and panicking.* At one point she'd tried to settle down enough to write a list. It took her ten minutes, her mind whirling. When she looked down, she'd written:

money
passports
food
EVERYTHING ELSE

She'd tried to call Auntie Pat one last time, slipping out of the house after Eddie was asleep to use the ancient, decrepit pay phone down the street. She shouldered the phone, wrinkling her nose at the uriney smell in the booth, and plugged in a fistful of quarters, glad for the first time that their phone had been disconnected several weeks ago. *I am officially completely paranoid. Thinking like a criminal already.* But she couldn't shake the feeling that it was safer to call on an outside line.

It was the fourth time she'd tried calling the greenhouse in the past two weeks, letting the phone ring until she heard Auntie Pat's voice-mail message, unusually subdued and formal. "Thank you for calling Rolling Wood Greenhouse and Gardens. Norman and Patricia are unavailable to take your call at this time..."

Auntie Pat and Uncle Norm always went to Shuswap Lake in British Columbia for a break after the flat-out long hours of bedding-plant season in May and June. They loved their old-fashioned little houseboat with its small boxy cabin and *chug-chug* motor, and shook their heads at the sleek new houseboats equipped with theaters, waterslides and hot tubs.

Dee listened to the phone on the other end of the line ring. *Please, please be back, Auntie Pat. I need to talk to you.*

But the voice that answered was not Auntie Pat's. Or Uncle Norm's.

"Rolling Wood Greenhouse and Gardens," a male voice said. You had to answer the phone like that, Dee remembered—the house line was connected to the greenhouses next door. Auntie Pat's motto was "In a family business, you're never off duty." *Except, apparently, when you go to the frigging lake when your niece desperately needs you.*

"Oh, hi," said Dee uncertainly. "Is Pat or Norm around?"

"Nope," he said, "they're not back yet. Should be soon though. Um, you want to leave a message?"

He sounded distracted, as if he was hunting around for a paper and pencil.

"Could you just tell them that Dee called? That I really need to talk to them?"

"Dee? Uh, is that just, like, the letter *D*?"

"No, *D-E-E*," she said. "Stupid name, I know."

"No, no. It's cool. Different. I like it. Kind of code, like K from *Men in Black*. Or M from Bond."

Dee smiled at the cracked glass of the phone booth.

"Wait! You're Pat's niece, right? She's mentioned a Dee," he said.

"Yeah, that's me. And who—I mean, sorry, but I don't know who you are."

"Oh, I'm Jake. I'm—let's see—Norm's cousin's kid. Hal and Linda? I'm house-sitting for Norm and Pat while they're at the lake, which has been *great*, except for this effing cat that wails all night long..."

Dee laughed. "Scout, the diabolical Siamese," she said, and he laughed. Then she thought, What am I doing, chatting with some strange guy like I've got all the time in the world? I have to organize things, plan, pack. And Eddie's home alone...

"Look, I have to go," she said, "but when Auntie Pat gets back, could you let her know that we'll be coming for a visit this summer?" *Like, sooner than anybody could possibly imagine.*

"Okay, got it. You want to leave your cell?"

If I didn't have to spend my savings fleeing the frigging country, I might have a cell phone. Thanks again, Dad.

"It's okay. I'll call. Well, bye, Jake," said Dee awkwardly.

"See you, Dee," said Jake.

She'd sprinted back to the house, feeling slightly better. *I am truly pathetic. A disembodied voice on the other end of a phone half a continent away thinks my stupid name is cool, and I'm feeling all happy and hopeful, like this nine-thousand-mile drive will be a piece of cake...*

But the short conversation had been reassuring. Normal. Normal life unfolded up there, just a few days' drive away. The big old farmhouse with the beautiful gardens still sat on a hill near the greenhouse up in Rolling Wood, just west of Calgary. Auntie Pat and Uncle Norm were still there, still selling petunias and geraniums and fertilizer, and would be back any day now. And there was Scout, still wailing all night. And Jake.

As she'd let herself back into the house, she'd had a moment of total clarity. It was really very simple. They had to act fast, they had to pack essentials, and they had to go as soon as they could the very next day.

Now, as Dee lay there with Eddie looming over her, she struggled to keep her voice normal, willing herself to stay still. Eddie would be upset and bewildered if they didn't finish the morning routine.

"What kinda day is it out there?" she asked. This was Eddie's favorite part.

"STINKIN' HOT!" he yelled, jumping up and bouncing wildly all over the bed. She smiled, watching his scrawny little body monkey-jump.

That last bit will have to change when we get to Canada.

"What's all this stuff for?" Eddie asked through a mouthful of cornflakes, waving his spoon at the box on the table. Dee looked at the box she had packed the night before. Canned pineapple, granola bars, cereal, two bowls, two spoons. Can opener, she thought suddenly, and tossed it in. Eddie watched, chewing.

Dee looked over at her brother.

How do I do this? Not many options truth-wise. "Well, Eddie, you know how our family is so monumentally, phenomenally screwed up...?" Or "Seeing as how Dad's abandoned us, or is possibly locked up in a Mexican jail, or lying bloodied and dead in some highway ditch..." Or "Well, Eddie, you know that nice lady from yesterday? She's gonna come with some cops and haul us off and force us to live with strangers, sooooo..."

"Know what we're doing today, Eddie?" she asked, forcing a smile. "Starts with *R*, ends with *oad trip*."

Eddie's head snapped up.

"Road trip?" he whispered, hardly daring to believe it was true. Dee knew that Eddie loved road trips. Every once in a while, Dad had taken them out for ice cream and somehow they would just keep driving down the highway, sometimes for days, sleeping at tiny motels that sat just off the highway, and eating at Denny's. When they would talk about it later, Eddie would remember seeing desert foxes, climbing the distant blue hills and eating waffles with whipped cream. Dee remembered navigating dusty, unmarked backroads, worrying about getting lost and missing her chemistry midterm.

"Yep. Road trip! A big one! Guess where we're going. Guess." This was going better than she'd hoped.

"What about Dad?" Eddie asked. "Are we going without Dad?" Eddie was hard to sidetrack. His thoughts had brought him around to Dad, and there would be no moving him. "We've never gone on a road trip without him. Just...you and me."

He was a smart little guy. She would tell him as much of the truth as she could.

"Well, you know how we've always talked about visiting our relatives in Canada? Auntie Pat and Uncle Norm? Remember, we used to live with them before we came here? Okay, you wouldn't remember because you were a baby, but anyway, we did. So I thought, Hey, summer vacation; we're not doing much—why not go now?"

Eddie started to say something, but Dee talked over him.

"I know Dad's not around right now—he's doing his antiques stuff—but he's the one who's always suggesting we go. I'll leave a note. He'll follow us up there when he gets back." She tried to sound matter-of-fact, confident. *Like, hell yeah, just following this iron-clad master plan we have going here. Not at all making it up as I go along.*

Eddie considered this.

"But we'll take the car," he said slowly, trying to figure out how it would all work.

"We'll take the car," Dee said, pushing her chair away from the table and bringing the bowls to the sink. She turned her back to him and looked out the window. The sky was a searing blue, the morning already radiating heat.

*Water. I forgot **water** on my four-thing list. My god, pack lots and lots of water…*

"Dee?" Eddie said as she rummaged in a cupboard for their school water bottles.

"Still here," she said.

"If we have the car, how will Dad get there? Up to Canada."

She closed her eyes, gripping the cupboard door. Then she opened them, turned and said mock seriously, "Well, Eddie, there are these amazing things called buses. Also trains and airplanes, in which many—"

"Shut up," he said, starting to laugh.

She smiled back.

"Don't worry, okay?" she said. "He'll find us."

She turned back to the sink and rinsed out the bowls.

"He'll find us," she repeated, watching the sodden remains slip down the drain.

Dee figured they should leave as soon as they could and get right out of the state that day, if it was possible. It would have to be possible. The urgency to leave was settling somewhere around the base of Dee's throat, making it hard to swallow.

"C'mon, Eddie, we have a couple of things to do before we go."

She and Eddie drove to the gas station on the highway. She owed Mr. and Mrs. S. that much, to quit in person. Mr. S. was on his knees, stocking shelves, but looked around as the door jingled.

"Uh-oh. Here's coming the trouble," he said, smiling and getting stiffly to his feet. He was a stout old man who wore undershirts under his collared shirts and pasted three strands of shiny black hair over his otherwise bald head. His English ("Angleesh," as he said) was not so good. His last name was unpronounceable, with baffling, repeated *s/z* combinations. Dee had seen it on the mail and had recoiled from the lack of vowels. They were just Mr. and Mrs. S. to everyone in town. Mrs. S.—similarly stout, accented and dyed—helped run the store and the station. Dee didn't know where they lived; they always seemed to be here.

"Hey, Mr. S.!" called Eddie. "All down this aisle only on the *right* foot, all back on the *left*! Time me!"

Mr. S. grinned, glancing at his watch. "Okay, so… GO!" Eddie took off at a furious hop. They watched the tousled head bob around the map section, then around back to junk foods.

"Annnd...twenty-two! Not bad. Better from yesterday."

Mr. S. frowned, really looking at the time.

"Dee, it's early for working now." She wasn't supposed to be there until eleven.

"Actually, I came for some gas. I, uh, have to quit my job here—just these last few weeks before school starts up. I'm so sorry I couldn't give you more notice." She really was. She liked Mr. and Mrs. S. They were good people. The job was a breeze, sitting in air-conditioning, flipping through the magazines and ringing through the occasional car that turned off the highway. Most of them drove through. There wasn't much to stop for.

It was a huge step up from last summer's wretched job with A+ Landscaping, hosing down parched perennials and worrying about skin cancer in the blazing heat.

"We, Eddie and me...and Dad...are going away for a while. Family vacation! It was a surprise!" She tried to smile like a normal girl in a normal family looking forward to a normal family trip. She had a feeling she wasn't doing it well. There was a little silence. Mr. S. wasn't much of a talker. Neither was Dee, but somebody had to fill the conversational space.

"Sorry for the short notice, but the trip is kind of spur-of-the-moment. Dad just let us know last night."

"Ah," said Mr. S., nodding. "S'okay, s'A-okay. We manage."

He glanced at her, then away. "Well, lemme fill 'er up." It was a phrase he was proud of, a gas-station phrase, a common American phrase. Except Mr. S. pronounced it "feel 'er up."

He stumped out to the car, conferring briefly with Mrs. S. on her way into the shop. Now *she* was a talker, completely undaunted by her limited English.

"Dee-Dee, no! Say *no* to go way! Whaddaya wanna be leavin' quality places like thees? Sun shine so many days, blue sky, so. We *mees* you, Dee-Dee, and the boy, so talking and so…" She finished with a big wave of her arms. Dee smiled. Full of life, she meant.

"We'll miss you too, Mrs. S.," Dee said, feeling awkward and ashamed. *Dad, this is all your fault. It's not me, Mrs. S., it's my hopeless dad.*

"You be callink when coming back, yes?"

"Oh, yeah, yes, Mrs. S. You bet." Dee smiled. *You miserable liar, Dee.*

Mr. S. gave the car a good inspection, filling it up, showing her how to top up the water in the radiator. He checked the tires, making sure the spare in the trunk had air too. When he straightened up, he turned to her, mechanic to customer, gesturing at the rusty, eighteen-year-old Toyota.

"Goink far in this car is no goot. This not goot car to go so far. This you tellink your dad." He poked a dirty, thick finger at her and repeated, "You tellink your dad. He needs taking care of such goot kids."

They were the most words she'd ever heard Mr. S. say in a row. The air between them thrummed with the hug they'd never give each other. But it was there, shimmering in the heat. A ghost hug.

"Thanks, Mr. S." She turned away, blinking quickly.

He wouldn't allow her to pay for the service or the gas, saying they still owed her for two shifts. He rummaged in his pocket, licked a finger and selected three twenties from an old-fashioned money clip. He held them out gruffly, studying the gas pump.

"There. So, Monday, Chusday."

Dee was appalled. Her pay had always been something private, always cash, always left in a sealed envelope with her name printed on it in square capital letters, discreetly half-tucked under the aged telephone behind the counter.

"Oh, no, no, Mr. S.," said Dee. "*I'm* letting *you* down, and you just filled up the car…"

"No. You take. You, or I geev Eddie." He looked around for Eddie, waving the twenties.

Dee took the money.

"Thanks, Mr. S." She smiled. "You looked like a big spender there, waving cash around." Mr. S. beamed. Dee knew from Mrs. S. how he had grown up "dirt poor. Poor like withouting even the shoes," and how proud he was to have succeeded in America.

"C'mon, Eddie, we better get going."

"Chust a minute, chust a minute," cried Mrs. S. She went into the store and ran out a minute later with a plastic bag of "nice thinks" for the trip, crunching Dee in a powerful hug with the bag in the middle. A non-ghost hug, a real clench, a tight, we'll-miss-you kind of hug. She smelled of makeup and sweat and perfume, and her head came up to Dee's shoulder.

Dee drove off, blinking back tears. Eddie waved his whole arm out the window.

"They're so nice," he said from the backseat. "I wish they were our *relatives*."

Dee nodded, knowing what he meant. Relatives were people you were bound to and who were bound to you, no matter what happened, no matter where you were. People you didn't lose. Lifelong people. She doubted if she would ever see Mr. and Mrs. S. again.

"Soda, chips, Skittles, Twinkies, jerky, nuts…" Eddie was already burrowing into the bag and itemizing the loot.

Dee looked in the rearview mirror and saw a tiny Mr. and Mrs. S. silhouetted against the pumps, waving goodbye from their paradise, their dusty little piece of America.

Dee jumped out at the pay phone at the end of their block and gave Auntie Pat one last call. She was running out of quarters.

"Norman and Patricia are unavailable to take your call at this time…"

Not even Jake was home. Dee slammed down the receiver so hard that Eddie jumped and swung around, startled in the act of hanging over the front seat, fiddling with the controls. He scuttled back into his seat as he saw her face.

"What's wrong?" he asked.

"Nothing."

"Because it *seems* like something—"

"It's nothing, Eddie," she snapped, annoyed by how living with Dad had made both her and Eddie alert to the slightest mood change. She forced another smile.

"Nothing, really. Thanks. Now, we're going to make just a *really* quick stop at Theresa's, then go back home to pack up the car." She couldn't leave without saying goodbye to Theresa.

They drove into the nicer part of town, the air-conditioned, landscaped part. Dee slid to a stop under a tree. She had learned early on how important even a little shade was—it could mean the difference between merely sliding into a stifling-hot car or scorching the backs of your thighs.

"I'm not going in. Just going to say bye, okay? No touching stuff up here, Eddie." She gestured at the dashboard and looked him in the eye. "I mean it." He looked back innocently. He was always fiddling with the knobs and buttons, and the last thing Dee needed right at this moment was to start the car to blaring music and windshield wipers going full tilt.

"I know, I know." Eddie settled into the backseat, ripping into some fruit gummies and opening one of his books.

Dee ran up the walk and rang the bell. There was an immediate deafening chorus of shrill barking. Hercules and Atlas, Theresa's family's Chihuahuas, lived for the excitement of people coming to the door. It never got old.

Theresa opened the door, yelling at the dogs to be quiet, her dark, straight hair swinging. Dee envied Theresa's hair. Even in the heat it grew thick and straight. Dee's was brown and curly, the split ends trimmed occasionally with nail scissors in the bathroom, and usually scraped back into a ponytail.

"Herc, Atlas, DOWN! No, shh..." The dogs barked joyfully, rushing out onto the step and reaching up to scratch Dee's knees.

"These dogs, these *DOGS*!" Theresa said, shooing them back inside. "Come in, if you dare." She laughed as she flung the door open, holding back the dogs with one leg.

Dee smiled. Theresa always made her smile. Theresa, with her loud laugh and too-tight clothes, was relentlessly social without being cool. She was happy. She was unafraid.

"Actually, I can't. Eddie's in the car."

"Hey, Eddie!" yelled Theresa. Eddie looked up and waved.

"So I just wanted to say 'bye. Dad's taking us up to visit relatives in Canada." She couldn't trust anyone with her plans. Theresa's mom worked at Eddie's school.

Theresa slipped on flip-flops, came out and closed the door behind her.

"Wow, shut *up*! *Canada*," Theresa said, her eyes wide.

"North," supplied Dee. "Up past Montana, that way."

"I knew it was *north*, you idiot." Theresa laughed. "I just meant that, wow, that's quite a trip."

They didn't do much geography in school. Much of the US, especially the parts that didn't border Arizona, was still a mystery to Dee. All those cramped, tiny, northeastern states. Too many states. Too many Washingtons. Mexico, just an hour's drive south, was in her mind one enormous, undivided, different-colored land mass, the tail end of North America.

"So are you flying out of Phoenix?" Theresa asked.

"Actually, we're driving," Dee said.

"Man, long drive!"

"Yeah, long and hot."

"You'll still be coming to Nadine's party tomorrow night, right?" Theresa was in the midst of a campaign to, as she put it, "party up" their social lives. She'd dragged Dee to a disastrous party several months back. They'd spent an hour and a half getting ready at Theresa's, and then Dad and Eddie had dropped them off down the block from Shawn's friend's house. Shawn—who'd said, "You guys should come!"—wasn't even there. None of

Shawn's friends were either; it seemed to be an out-of-towners party. Dee and Theresa didn't know anybody except a few popular girls who didn't acknowledge them. They spent half an hour yelling at each other over the music, then gave up and walked home, stopping to kick off their sandals and swing at the playground.

"Sorry, Theresa, but we're leaving soon. Like, today, I think. It was a surprise."

"Shoot." Theresa's wide smile fell. Unsmiling, she was a plain, short, plump girl with great hair. Tall, slim, quiet Dee trailed along after her, her big hazel eyes wary and uncertain. Dee was always being told she looked older than sixteen, that she could pass for eighteen, even twenty. Mrs. S. once said, "Dee-Dee, you have the face like a saint! So *serious*. Like the blessed martyrs in the old paintinks." Great, Dee had thought, just what I'd been hoping for. The totally hot look of a blessed martyr. She'd made a point of smiling more after that, but it didn't come naturally, and it didn't last.

Theresa launched into a complicated story about what Chad had said to Kent, and what Kent had told Nadine about Theresa. Theresa had been reeling Chad in for several months now. Dee had been embarrassed at how open she was about it, how she flirted so obviously with him. She watched her friend's animated face.

Good luck, Theresa. Good luck with Chad. Nadine's nice—you'll still have Nadine. Sorry we won't be going into

Phoenix for our prom dresses like we planned. Sorry I'm lying to you. Sorry.

"He's so into you, Theresa. Look, got to go here," Dee said when Theresa finished the story. She reached out and hugged her friend awkwardly. "Take care of yourself."

"Hey," Theresa protested, bear-hugging her back, "it's not like you're never coming back!" *Oh, that's exactly what it is like, my friend.* Dee looked at the ground. "When *are* you back, anyway?"

"I don't really know. Dad's calling the shots. Well, 'bye!"

"Bye, Dee! Bring me an igloo! Or a snowball! At least bring me back a little snow! Or some sexy French guy!"

As she pulled away, Dee waved. Theresa waved back quickly before opening the door, crouching to shoo the dogs back into the house.

We'll keep in touch, Dee thought. Of course we will. We'll email. Facebook...we'll Facebook. But secretly she was a little afraid. Would she just be remembered as Theresa's friend, that tall girl with a name like a letter? Would she be remembered at all? Karen Mulhauser had moved away in ninth grade, and a year later Dee had wondered aloud to a group of friends what had happened to her. Blank faces. "You know, Karen Mulhauser. Blond, with the teeth"—pointing to her front teeth; Karen's had been prominent—"yearbook committee, with the camera?"

"Oh yeah, Karen," some of them said. But some of them, Dee knew, were only pretending to remember her.

That was how it sometimes went with people who weren't there anymore. People sometimes just vanished, evaporated, like spilled water on the hot pavement.

Dee was relieved that there was no child-removal van waiting outside the house when they got back. She imagined it as a sort of pastel dog-pound truck, with unnaturally silent, anxious children lined up on seats inside, barred back doors snapping shut before they were locked with an oversized padlock.

Anyway, it wasn't there. The coast was clear. *I'm thinking like a criminal and I haven't even done anything wrong. I'm the good guy here. Just think practically, Dee. Essentials. Water, food, money, passports.* She repeated the four words to herself like a mantra. *Water, food, money, passports.* Their passports were still valid, expiring in a few weeks. August 17. She didn't have to check the date—it was burned into her mind from the last time she'd looked at them. One of the only definite, solid things left.

August 17 had loomed as the days rolled on with still no sign of her father. If Dad isn't home by Friday, she'd think, we'll leave for Canada. And when Friday rolled around, she'd give it till the Monday, convincing herself that maybe after the weekend sales he'd head home.

And now here they were, with a social worker on their trail. They had to leave for Canada now, today, period.

Months earlier she'd read an article in *Time* magazine at the gas station about Arizona's crackdown on its hundreds of thousands of illegal aliens. Her palms had started to sweat as she read about detentions, deportations, families torn apart. Oh god, are we illegal? she'd wondered in secret panic. Me and Eddie? Are we aliens? Just what the hell are we?

She knew her father was half American. His mom was Canadian, but his dad was from Montana. Her dad was born there. Did that make her and Eddie each a quarter legal American? What about the other three-quarters? She had to know.

She'd gone straight to her father after work that day. "So me and Eddie—what, technically, are we? Nationality-wise."

"Canadian," he said, not looking up from the footstool he was repairing. "I'm American too, right? The old man was good for something. Other than killing innocent animals and expecting us to call him sir. 'Yes, sir!' *God*. My brother and me, *kids*, treated like we were in the frigging military."

"Yeah, but me and Eddie—do we have any official American ID? Anything?"

"Birth certificates. They're here somewhere, right?"

"We were born in Canada, Dad."

"There you go." His voice muffled, from under the stool.

"*Dad!*"

He looked at her for the first time.

"Okay, okay, let me think." He stared off into space. "Passports! Had to get you guys passports before we left Canada, which was a huge hassle—"

"Those would be *Canadian*." She raised her voice. "Are we American too because *you* are? Well, half? Or at least are we permanent residents or *something*?"

He screwed up his eyes, trying to remember. "We're *something*. I'm sure I filled out some forms years ago...Why are you worrying about all this? I'll look into it, okay?" He brushed the hair out of his eyes, waving a screwdriver at her. "But ultimately, Dee, all this nationalist stuff is crap. We're all citizens of the *world*. Remember that."

Yeah, I'll remember that supremely useless thing, Dad. Yes, sir, I'll store that one away to shout at an immigration official. It was exactly the sort of crap Charlie Rivera, the antique dealer, would have called him on ("Pull your head out of your *ass*, Donnelley. There's something called a Real World out here.")

But Dee wasn't like Charlie. She'd said nothing, turned away and walked straight down the hall. She'd dug out the only official documents in their house from the dusty shoe box at the back of the closet. Three birth certificates, three passports. Her dad's passport: American. She didn't even open it. Hers and Eddie's: Canadian. She opened them to look at the five-years-younger versions of her and Eddie, Eddie only two, herself a startled, serious eleven. *We had no clue that we were going anywhere. No clue about any of it. Nationality: Canadian.* Just about to slap the passports shut, she'd noticed the expiry date. August 17 of that year. This summer. One of their only pieces of identification, and if she hadn't happened to look in that box on that day, she wouldn't have known that August 17 was the day. The day she and Eddie would be officially—what? Stateless? She stored the date away, circling it in red on a mental calendar.

What her father had loved about Santacino was that, initially, it really did feel like a place removed from the rest of the world. A small town on the edge of nowhere. She and Eddie just went to school—they never got asked who they were, where they came from. People paid cash for work done; many still did. *But look around, Dad. Santacino's changed—it's grown. Everyone at school knows the Mexican kids who are illegal. We must be illegal like them. We haven't had problems yet, but clearly, after five years you haven't got things figured out. We might right now be on some immigration official's radar.*

The memories took only seconds to flit through Dee's mind as she carefully backed the car along the house, right up to the back door. But they made the urgency to leave feel like a live thing, growing and swelling in her until she had trouble breathing.

Water, food, money, passports. Thank God we at least have the passports. One thing Dad did right. One less hassle as we scramble to get the hell out of here.

Eddie rocketed out of the car into the field to "check something important." *One of his pointless experiments or some stupid bug that doesn't have the sense to fly away somewhere better. I'll tell you what's important, Eddie: getting us on that highway out of town NOW...*

"Okay, but *quick*, all right? *Really* quick. Got to hit the road!" Her voice was higher than usual with the strain of flogging this fun road-trip lie. But she didn't want Eddie spooked.

She surveyed the hot, cluttered little house. So much stuff, so much useless junk.

Eddie banged the door, carrying a jar. She turned to him.

"Hey, so we're only going to pack *essentials*, Eddie, things you really need, right? Toothbrush, pajamas, stuff like that. Nothing alive..." She eyed the dusty jar.

Dee grabbed Eddie's school backpack from where he'd thrown it in the hall on the last day of school. She dumped it out behind the fan "art," shaking out loose paper, stubby pencil crayons, rocks, sand and some reeking lunch remains in a crumpled paper bag.

"*God,* that's disgusting. I wondered what smelled. Whatever. Here—use this." She turned to hand it to him. He was crawling into his fort, reaching for a book.

"*Eddie*! We have to get *going*!" She saw him register her tension, took a deep breath and explained. "Look, it's supposed to be a really hot day. We don't want to be driving in the blazing sun. We've got to leave before it gets *stinking* hot. Before we're *frying* on the seats."

Eddie's face cleared. This was normal. Planning around the heat was what you did in Santacino.

"Oh. Okay," he said, grabbing the bag and trotting down the hallway to his side of their room. Dee turned back to the kitchen, relieved. She'd stooped to pick up a box from the floor when a slight rumbling sound made her freeze. A car. She strained to hear it, to locate which way it was going. It was coming from town, down their street, toward the house.

Oh, shit, we should have left, we should have gone…

Heart hammering, Dee straightened, listening. Yes, it was definitely a car coming this way. She reached out and locked the kitchen door, pulled down the blind on the window and slipped into the living room. Using the piled-up furniture as cover, she inched forward, peering out the window. A car slid to a stop in front of the house. She held her breath as the driver, a woman who was not Susan, looked over at the house, checking the number.

Who the hell are you? She'd never seen this person before. She was younger than Susan, slimmer, dark hair pulled back in a ponytail.

I don't even know you, Dee said silently to the woman in the car, *but right now you get the prize for scariest frigging person in the whole world.*

The woman shifted and looked down at some papers in her hand. Dee took advantage of her momentary distraction and leaped to the front door. She locked it, then ran quickly down the hall to their room.

"I'm almost done, Dee, but—" Eddie began before she could shush him.

"There's another lady outside, Eddie, and I don't want to talk to her, okay?" Dee whispered. "Probably just about another boring bill. We need to be quiet until she goes away, then we're *pffft*"—she jabbed her thumb over her shoulder—"out of here."

He nodded, smiling. It wasn't the first time they had played this game with people at the door. He mimed locking his mouth and throwing an imaginary key over his shoulder.

Footsteps. Heels clicking up the front walk. *Click, click, click.* Stop.

The doorbell rang. She was expecting it, but in the quiet of the house it was so loud that they both jumped.

Dee sat on Eddie's bed with an arm around his shoulders. They waited, completely silent. Eddie kept catching her eye and covering his mouth with his hand, shaking with suppressed giggles. Dee could hear the clock in the hall ticking. She strained to hear what the woman on the other side of the wall would do.

The clock ticked. Another shrill ring from the doorbell. More waiting, then some movement outside on the front step. Footsteps. Clicking footsteps, ordinary footsteps, not stealthy ones, coming past their curtained bedroom window, pausing at the corner of the house. Dee imagined the woman looking down the side of the house into the backyard.

She picked the wrong side, Dee realized, sitting very still. *If she goes the other way, she'll see the car—she'll know somebody's here.*

The woman walked back to the front door and hesitated, as if making up her mind.

"Dee—" Eddie whispered.

"Shh."

Yes, the woman was leaving, going back down the front walk to her car. The door opened, then slammed shut. *Start the car, start the car. Go away, go away...*

"I just wanted to know if I could bring my collections on the road trip," mouthed Eddie, close to her ear.

The car's engine started.

"Mmm. Whatever," said Dee, listening to the sound of the car U-turning, then driving away. She counted off thirty one-thousands, then sprang into action.

"Let's go. Quick."

Dee checked the front window to make sure the woman had really gone. Then she started loading up the car with the boxes she'd packed the night before. She filled old soda bottles and jam jars with water. She ran down the hallway to the closet. Two pillows, two blankets. The trunk filled up quickly.

Dee was ruthless with her stuff. *One small bag. That's it, that's all I'm taking.* Most of her clothes fit anyway, the small stuffed elephant she'd had since she was two, the photo albums, the yearbooks. All her other books would have to stay. She scooped up a bottle of shampoo, a hairbrush and her makeup (a crumbly blush, a gunky mascara and a tube of lip gloss) and shoved them into a side pocket with her toothbrush.

Then Dee reached under her mattress, lifting the corner up as high as she could, bracing it with her shoulder. She grabbed the passports and gathered up the money, pressed flat from the hiding spot.

Her stash. Her hoard. Since they had gotten here that January five years ago, after her mom died, Dee had been saving. She remembered her mom once winking at her and saying, "It's always good to have some cash on hand, Dee" when Dee saw her slipping a twenty out of a coffee tin, then pushing the tin to the back of the cupboard. "You never know what's going to happen." That had been the mantra of her life with Dad, an unpredictable life, but a life she'd loved because she loved him.

True, you don't know what's going to happen. I person-ally couldn't have predicted that I'd be kidnapping my little brother and fleeing the authorities across the country to a border where we might be arrested. Life's kind of funny like that.

Dee's saving had grown into an obsession. She began thinking of the stash as "emergency funds"—a phrase she'd seen in a paper at the gas station. Not money to be frittered away on clothes or outstanding bills, but a safety net for a someday emergency. She collected the spare change rattling around the inside of the washing machine at the Laundromat, and in couches and pay phones. Birthday money from Auntie Pat and Uncle Norm went straight to the stash, as did the landscape money, the gas-station money. The stash grew.

She counted. There was $408—$468 with the $60 from Mr. S. *How much gas does 468 bucks buy you? Enough to get to Canada? It's got to be enough to get to Canada…* She wished she had had a little time, time to plan, time to map it all out.

Dee went into her father's room, veering around the floor-to-ceiling junk, straight to the dresser. There might possibly be some money lying around. She remembered Mr. S.'s tidy money roll with the silver clip, so different from Dad's crumpled bills, jammed into pockets, going through the wash. She rifled through the drawers, then the closet, and found a ten-dollar bill scrunched up in the pocket of his one suit jacket, which he never wore.

She didn't hesitate for a second. That made $478.

As she turned to leave, she saw the wedding picture on the bedside table. Mom and Dad, smiling, young and happy. It wasn't a formal picture, just a snapshot taken by someone at the wedding who had probably called out, "Hey, Sandy, Jamie!" and taken the picture as they glanced over. They were holding hands, not for the cameras, but quietly, privately, because they wanted to. Their faces were lit with a shared laugh. Two people in love, two people who, in a perfect world, should have grown old together.

They were almost the same height, Dee thought suddenly, fighting back tears. *I never noticed that. Five eight, five nine. Mom was tallish like me, Dad shortish.* Somehow, that small fact seemed significant.

She grabbed the picture and wrapped it in one of her dad's old T-shirts. As she walked by the bed, she rumpled the blankets, punching an indent into the pillow. A pretend body, a pretend head.

Dee wrote a note to her father on the back of a blue flyer. She had to stop, take a deep breath and think before she did it. It had to be in a sort of code, in case people like Susan or the other woman read it.

But if Dad reads it— She stopped herself. *Not* if. When. *When Dad reads it, he has to know where we are, how to find us.*

She finally wrote the date, then:

Hey, Dad.

We've just gone to visit Auntie Pat like we planned. Looking forward to it! We'll see you there soon!

Love,

Dee and Eddie

PS. There are veggie burgers in the freezer.

Reading it over, it didn't sound at all like her. Too many perky exclamation marks. But she thought the PS was a nice touch. It was the sort of thing people put in notes.

Normal people who see each other regularly every day and leave casual notes.

Nobody would ever guess that it might be a goodbye.

"Dee? You got a box?" Eddie wandered down the hallway.

Dee straightened from the kitchen table.

"Just leaving a note for Dad," she said.

"Oh, good. Yeah, good idea. So he knows how to find us." He made it all sound so simple and logical. That's the trouble with weird families, Dee thought. You get used to the weirdness.

She walked toward the living-room mess. "There's got to be a box in here somewhere…"

"There's *lots* of stuff in here," said Eddie. The mess was his private playground. His latest fort was inside the space formed by two couches stacked on top of each other, arms to arms. He would lie in there, stretched flat, thinking and reading books with a flashlight. Dee called it his "couch coffin."

"Found twenty bucks in that chair." Eddie pointed at an overstuffed brocade chair that smelled of mold and generations of old people.

Dee looked up.

"Hey, better bring it on the trip." All right, $498. Almost five hundred bucks. The longer they stayed, the more money they made.

She suddenly felt so tired.

"Yeah, maybe we'll stop for some burgers or something," Eddie said happily, "and *I'll* pay!"

"Deal." Dee emptied a box, and they went to their room.

Unbelievable. Just unbelievable. I hand him a backpack, one backpack, and he thinks he's taking his entire room.

Eddie had packed everything. Shoved a few clothes into the backpack, stacked books into boxes and used green garbage bags for stuffed animals. There was, apparently, almost nothing he could leave. He agonized about his specimens in the kitchen, rows and rows of baby-food jars full of dead insects, small bones and cactus bristles. A dead scorpion. Some snake skin that even the frigging *snake* didn't want. Pebbles.

"Rocks, Eddie? Really? Rocks?" Dee said.

"They're *significant*," Eddie pleaded. "Some of them, actually, might have fossil—"

"Okay, okay," she interrupted. "Fine. The rocks, the significant rocks, can come," she said, desperate to get them out the door. "Let's just get all this"—*all this shit*—"all this stuff out to the car."

Not an inch to spare in the trunk, so they shoved bags and boxes in the footwells of the backseat and the front passenger seat. Eddie climbed into the backseat, onto the towel she'd spread out.

Dee ran back for one last scan of the house, wiping her sweaty face on a tea towel. *If I never come back here again, is there anything I'll wish I'd taken?* She hesitated at

Eddie's drawings, the strange, brightly colored ones tacked to the kitchen wall. Kindergarten and first-grade drawings. A little kid's dreams, his imaginings. It seemed awful to leave them there to be stared at or junked by strangers.

But I can't take them. Susan saw them. People don't take pictures off the walls when they go on a vacation. I'm very, very certain people don't generally strip the walls when they go to visit relatives.

She closed her eyes, rubbing them with the palms of both hands, like a tired child. *Oh, God, please let me be doing the right thing. Not just about the pictures, but about this whole thing...*

Dee paused at Vera, the ratty aloe vera plant she had won in an essay competition in fifth grade ("Spectacular Succulents and Their Many Uses!"). Vera was a less-than-spectacular succulent whose dusty, straggly limbs occupied a faded clay pot on the shelf. Dee had managed to keep the plant alive for six years, occasionally cupping water in her hand and letting it drip down her fingers into the heat-hardened soil, or snapping off small pieces of fleshy arm to soothe burns and bug bites.

Could she trust the good folks at children's services to take care of Vera? To not kill her? No, she decided, she could not. You can never know what's important to other people. She grabbed a shoe box and stuffed a tea towel around the pot. *One more passenger. Let's see— a plant, lots of dead bugs, rocks, snake skin...yeah, I think we've got it all. We're all good for this psycho-family road trip.*

She felt a sudden, crushing wave of panic. Eddie was in the car alone. The scary woman, the children's services follow-up, might still be prowling the neighborhood.

She bolted out the back door.

Eddie had already seat-belted himself into the laden backseat. He was sorting through a mound of stuffed animals, his feet resting on an enormous pile of books. Mrs. S.'s goodie bag was open beside him.

He caught her eye.

"Looks *fun* back here, hey?" he said, excitement lighting up his face.

Dee looked at the lively little face, the tangled hair, the happy blue eyes. Her face softened, and she leaned in through the open window for his tight, quick hug, his skinny arm snaking briefly around her neck.

"Sure does, Eddie."

Her fog of panic and fear cleared. She had to get him out of this, had to get him safely up to Auntie Pat's. It was the only thing to do. There were no other options.

They had to go.

They were going.

Together.

Dee started the car, and they crept to the front of the house. At the corner she looked left, right. All clear.

They slid off the gravel driveway and onto the road, turning away from town. It was longer to the highway this way, but at least it circled the town. The other way, they'd have to drive straight down Main Street.

She didn't have a driver's license. Not technically. She'd studied the materials and gone out driving with her dad and assumed she'd eventually get one. But she didn't have the proper ID. The woman had looked blankly at her Canadian birth certificate, turned it over and said, "You got anything American, honey?" Dad, waiting in the car, had said he'd fix it, make some calls, straighten it all out. But the bureaucracy had defeated him, and finally he had slammed the phone down and tossed her the keys.

"*I* know you can drive. *You* know you can drive. Why in hell the government needs all this crap for you to drive to the frigging gas station and back in a small town is beyond me."

"But we'll still figure out how I can get an official license soon, right?" Dee asked anxiously. *I'm not like you. I can't just float, wander, make my own rules.*

She'd started driving anyway—she had to get to and from her job. And she felt better when she found out Mrs. S. didn't have a license either.

"No, I don't got no license," she had said, waving that technicality away with a contemptuous flick of her hand. "But sure I drive, no problem. A-okay. Some cop gonna pull me over? No way. Not *one* time these seven years!

They do, I tell you, Dee, I got plan. I make *beeeg* deal of huntink in my bag. I drop things, take out everythink, songlasses, makeup, okay? I get more and more upsets. Then I say, 'So sorry, Mr. Poleese, I change the purses! The license at home!' He shrug, tell me not do again, and away I go." She'd cackled and squeezed Dee's arm, like they were both in on the joke, both pulling one over on the cops.

Dee had practiced a few slow rounds of the school parking lot on weekends and then inched her way around residential streets. Driving in Santacino was easy, as slow as riding a bike. She'd diligently practiced parallel parking, so that when the time came to get her real license, she'd be ready. Perfect preparation for the interstates, she thought now, her hands slick with sweat on the wheel.

They rolled down all the windows. It was choking hot in the car, the towels she'd laid on the seats to prevent scalding doubling as sweat absorbers. A hot breeze wafted in as they slid down the street. The merciless sun bleached the sky from a clear, cloudless pale blue into white.

"What time is it, Eddie?"

"9:36 AM. Thursday, July 24."

Before they'd even turned off their street onto the lonely road that skirted the town, Eddie started singing "Down by the Bay." It was their road-trip song, usually belted out by Dad and Eddie while she read, ignored them and hoped nobody she knew saw them. Things were different now.

"Did you ever see a whale with a polka-dot tail? Down by the bay, down by the baaaay," they sang as they crossed the old bridge. The river that had at one time flowed under the bridge and through town was gone, leaving behind a smooth trail of cracked earth, a long, snaking water-print of where it had once moved and danced in the sun. It was locally known as *El Fantasma,* the ghost. The memory of a river.

"Did you ever see a bear with a fish in its hair? Down by the bay..."

Left at the street where you'd go right to get to the grocery store, and up the rise to the T intersection. Almost officially out of town. *'Bye, Theresa. 'Bye, Mr. and Mrs. S. 'Bye, Mrs. Turner, nice English teacher. 'Bye, Jarrett, boy I never really got to know but secretly liked. 'Bye, everyone. 'Bye, Dad.*

"Did you ever see a skunk packing a trunk? Down by the bay..."

They turned left, gliding slowly out of town, and exited onto the highway. In the rearview mirror she had a last glimpse of Santacino, their home for five long years. The town sprawled on either side of the dry river, getting smaller and smaller before it shimmered into a haze, then disappeared behind a hill, swallowed up by the unforgiving desert.

The 86 was a small highway that led to the 85, which led to Phoenix, then to the real highway, the big interstate. Two minutes of driving and they were in open desert, as flat and featureless as a calm ocean. They could have been miles from anywhere.

North. North to Phoenix, and then north and north and north. It's pretty simple, Dee. Just head north. Through almost the whole of Arizona and into Utah. Or where did the highway come out? Colorado? Wyoming? Her mind was blank. Did Idaho kind of jut in there? Montana was right on the Canadian border. She was pretty sure of Montana.

"*Did you ever see a snake biting a rake? Down by the bay...*"

Map. We seriously need a map. We need to drive as far north as we can, we need to cross into whatever the hell the state is on the north side of the Arizona border, we need to find a spot to sleep tonight, and we need to get a map. Her mind hopped and raced as Eddie came up with the rhymes.

"*Did you ever see a cat with a baseball bat?*"

She joined in on the next verse:

"*Down by the bay, down by the baaay, where the watermelons grow, back to my home, I dare not go...*"

Dee drove through the scorching desert, keeping one eye on the temperature gauge, which climbed steadily to the top of the red end, then fell dead right down to the bottom and never moved again. There wasn't another car in sight. They were the only thing moving in the red-brown, lunar landscape. It was like they were the last people left on earth.

It reminded her of their first road trip five years ago, the very first one, this exact trip, only in reverse.

"C'mon, Dee." Her father had whispered her awake. "Road trip!"

She had sat up in bed, rubbing her eyes, and watched her father scoop her clothes into a suitcase. He didn't even put on the big light, just shoveled things in by the glow of her night-light.

"Where're we going, Dad?" she'd asked quietly as he carried Eddie, still sleeping heavily, out to the car and strapped him in. She knew this was not a road trip; she knew they were leaving. She just didn't know where they were going.

"Somewhere we can get warm," he'd said, his face set. He had seemed like a stranger, that serious man who had packed them into the freezing car, their parkas over their pajamas, their bare feet shoved into snow boots. She knew now that he couldn't face his sister-in-law Pat, not even to say goodbye. He had thought it was better to leave and call from wherever they settled. A clean break he called it.

Dee had watched him in the rearview mirror in the light of the passing streetlights, his haunted, sad eyes. She saw him take first one hand, then the other, and blow into it. The wheel must have been frozen—they could see their breath in the car. Dee's face was pale in her pink, hooded parka, her hair dark and rumpled, her eyes still puffy from sleep. She willed the anxious eyes in the rear-view mirror to look at her.

"Road trip, Dee!" he'd murmured, trying to smile. "Somewhere we can get warm. A warm place…" Since it all happened, since her mother's death, he had told her he'd been so cold, cold to the bone, cold right through. The whole world had dimmed for all of them. "We need to find the sun again, hey?" He had looked at her briefly in the mirror, and she'd nodded and smiled uncertainly.

Dee had heard Auntie Pat and her dad in the hall days before, Auntie Pat's voice low and insistent.

"Jamie, you have to get some help. You *have* to. For the kids if not for yourself."

Help with what? thought Dee.

"I'm fine. I'm okay, Pat. Just so tired." She could barely hear her dad's voice.

"Then sleep! Take some time. Leave things to me. Just don't make any big decisions right now." Good old Auntie Pat. Grieving quietly for her only sister, her baby sister, and shouldering everyone else's grief as well.

The midnight trip south was her father's doomed big decision. The one he shouldn't have made right then. Dee remembered that night clearly, the quiet darkness sliding by. It was never completely dark when there was snow on the ground. She remembered that was one of the things she loved about snow. You never had to be afraid of the dark because it was never entirely dark. The darkest night became a silvery wonderland of shadows and reflected, pale light.

The whole world was asleep, people hunkering in their houses like animals hibernating in snowdrifts. They were the only thing moving in the frozen white world.

Dee had carved designs on the frosty window with her fingernail, feeling the painful cold as the ice gathered and packed under her nail. She always carved the same thing, an elaborate, ornate "frame" with a picture of a Christmas tree inside it. She stopped occasionally to warm her finger in the fist of her other hand.

When she was done the Christmas picture, she made footprints. She'd press the side of her fist against the window until it was so cold it ached, making a wet imprint like a little baby-Eddie foot. Then the toeprints with her little finger—one big one, four small. It looked almost exactly like Eddie's foot. She scratched *The Foot of Eddie* in the frost below the footprint. She blew holes in the frost with her hot breath, little windows through which she could see nothing but endless fields of snow.

They drove for days. Their world was the inside of the car, relieved only by stops at highway motels, roadside restaurants and gas stations. Dee read and sang to Eddie and rocked his car seat to get him to stop crying and fall asleep. She played peekaboo behind stuffies and blankets, books and hands, fed him arrowroot biscuits and made faces to get him belly-laughing. She drew faces on his fingertips—two dot eyes, dot nose, always a big smile. While he slept, she read and reread the three Little House on the Prairie books that she'd brought with her.

They drove south and south and south, almost in a straight line. They drove for so long she began to worry about the land running out. She wondered if her dad would stop even then. This quiet man with the desperate rearview-mirror eyes might just plow on into the ocean. On to the end of the world.

They did stop, eventually, in a dusty town deep in Arizona.

The old antique barn appeared just after the crumbling sign announcing the town. *Welcome to Santacino, Hidden Gem of the Desert.* The sign at Charlie Rivera's Antique Emporium was yellow, with changeable, imperfect black lettering. Clearly trying to tap into the neighboring Final Rest Funeral Parlor's guaranteed clientele, Charlie's sign read *Check out our GrEat Antique URNs!* Dad had pulled over, stopped the car and laughed until tears rolled down his face. Dee had laughed too, not understanding, not even knowing what urns were. It was a relief to hear her dad laugh again.

"Well, seeing as we're at Urns R Us, we better check them out," he said finally, wiping his eyes and getting stiffly out of the car. The parkas had been stowed in the trunk days ago. They got out of the car, the sun warm on their heads.

"See, Dee?" said Dad, smiling at her, opening his arms wide at the barren desert around them. "Someplace warm."

The desert had been a novelty when they'd arrived, the endless barren vistas, the cartoon cacti, the dancing tumbleweeds, the quail, the lizards. It was as uniform a landscape as they'd left, only instead of glaring white, there was rusty brown as far as you could see. Instead of mountains in the distance, there were small blue hills, lurking low on the horizon, hunkering in the heat.

Why here? she had thought then. She'd wondered that for five years. Because of a stupid sign that made Dad laugh? Because Charlie Rivera had been "a real character," as her dad put it? A glib talker, a storyteller, a suspender-wearing salesman/philosopher, an expert in southwestern junk. A man who showed all his teeth when he smiled and twisted a pinky ring. He kept a stash of lollipops for the bored children obliged to trail after their antique-hunting parents. He'd given lollipops to Dee and Eddie, and they had sucked them down to the sticks before they'd even wandered half of the huge place. Dad took them up and down aisles of saddles and ranch tack, metalwork, Mexican knick-knacks, furniture and jewelry, everything smelling of must and dust. When her father finally put Eddie down and leaned against the counter to talk with Charlie, Dee made sure Eddie didn't put anything in his mouth or break anything.

Dad and Charlie had talked for a long time. When there was nothing more to look at inside, Dee followed Eddie outside. He was a fearless toddler with more enthusiasm than expertise, running, then lurching and crashing. Dee was used to catching him, quickly sliding her arms under his outstretched ones, hauling him back up onto his feet.

It was while they were wandering in the scrub by the parking lot that the antiques man came running out.

"Hey, kids, y'all better just keep a watch out for rattle-snakes, okay?"

It was the beginning of Dee's fear of the desert. She'd hauled Eddie into the car, and they'd sat there, sweltering in the heat, waiting for their father to rescue them.

Driving north out of the desert now, Dee fought to keep calm, to relax her clenched shoulders and back. The car was unbelievably hot, relieved only by the wind roaring in her ears. Driving on even this small highway was stressful, as random cars swooped up behind her only to swerve around and roar past. She passed nobody.

The thought of slipping, however temporarily, into the lane of oncoming traffic terrified her. Besides, nobody was going slower than they were.

Dee slowly, carefully, removed one slick hand from the wheel, wiped it on the seat towel, then did the same with the other. Worries bit away at her like insects.

Dad. She'd worried about him for so long, it felt as natural as loving him. He was so clueless, so completely and totally hopeless. She tried to probe this new worry she felt, feeling her way around it like a tongue on a canker sore. This worry felt different, maybe because he'd seemed depressed the weeks before he left. She went over her facts. He had jumped at the chance to go away for a couple of days. He had gotten into Jim Dunford's truck and waved, his face relaxed and happy for the first time in ages. They were heading to Tucson to antique-hunt. Dad also wanted to see a man about some wood. Teak. Jim Dunford came back without Dad and days later seemed surprised that she was asking about him.

"Told me he'd hop a bus home," Jim said, "seeing as his stuff was small. You know, medals, buttons, old coins." Jim was big and slow and sold hardware at his ancient father's store.

"Yeah, that's what he told me too," Dee had lied, seeing worry cloud Jim's face. "But you know Dad," she said with a laugh, trying to throw him off. "He'll have hitched a trailer onto the next bus with all his junk."

But Dad wasn't on the next bus. Or the next. She started avoiding Jim Dunford and the hardware store. It was easier than lying.

The worry had grown in her until it became a cold, tight knot of dread. *Just stop it*, she would snap at herself late at night. *He's been away before; he'll be back. You can stop being such a drama queen...*

She forced herself to concentrate on the pressing, immediate worries of this trip up to Canada.

The car. Now *there* was a huge, immediate worry. It was old. Ancient. The dents and scratches she could live with. More worrying were the unpredictable, thudding, grinding noises. It labored whenever there was even the slightest rise in the road. She kept hearing Mr. S. in her head: "This not goot car to go so far." You weren't kidding, Mr. S., she thought as they strained up an unexpected hill. She glanced at the speedometer, which was sunk, exhausted, permanently at zero mph. Flying down the highway, with other cars long-honking at her as they passed, the dial still registered zero. The fuel gauge was overly optimistic, showing a tank three-quarters full until it sheepishly sank to a quarter full a couple of minutes later.

Dee didn't even care about the malfunctioning air-conditioning. It hadn't worked for as long as she could remember, and they were used to baking heat. The car was stifling, but they were managing, and they were, she hoped, pointed in a direction that would take them away from the heat, out of the desert. But if they got to Canada alive, in a few months they'd sure need some heat. She stifled a hysterical giggle. *I'm driving a decrepit, crumbling furnace on wheels through a desert where people literally die of the heat, and I'm worrying about having heat in the winter. Can I find anything else to worry about? How about world peace? Disease? Plenty of worries right here and now…*

What if they broke down, here in the baking desert, in this killer landscape? Her mind rolled through a series of scenarios—she and Eddie, dangerously dehydrated, being dive-bombed by impatient vultures, knifed by escaped convicts or deranged child killers. *Got to get through the desert. Got to get out of Arizona today.*

Sleeping. Sleeping was a huge worry. To make the money last as long as it could, Dee thought they should camp in the car most nights. But how safe was that? Carjackers jimmied locks way more sophisticated than these. Where should they park to sleep? Farm fields or Walmart parking lots? She tossed the alternatives around in her mind.

Money. Money was another worry. She had no idea how far $498 would take them. It sounded like a lot. It was a lot. It was her life savings. *But things are always more expensive than you think. Nothing but essentials. Gas. Food. Water.*

The Border. *Oh, shit, the Border.* The Border (always capitalized in her imagination) was the mother of all worries. The longest unprotected border in the world, between friendly countries, trusted neighbors. *Sounds lovely until you're face-to-face with a suspicious border guard with a gun (are they armed now?) who's late for his coffee break and has a dangerous computer at his disposal.*

We're Canadian, she reminded herself. We've got passports, so we're totally legally entitled to enter Canada. We've done nothing wrong. Nothing wrong. She fumbled for the passports in the backpack beside her. They were still there.

On the other hand, she thought, we may possibly have been living illegally in the United States for five years. And we're traveling without a parent. And Susan and the child-protection people will for sure have reported us missing by tomorrow. Would there be some sort of dangerous red flag that appeared on the computer? She pictured her cranky border guard straightening up, a serious look on his face, sliding the window shut and reaching for the phone...

So the Border loomed, a huge, impenetrable red line on the northern horizon, the ultimate worry, the problem that had to be dealt with when they got there. It's just an imaginary line, she reminded herself, totally imaginary. But she didn't believe it. That was like some crap her dad would say: "It's governments that have put up borders. It's really all one land, one people."

Yeah right. Tell that to the border guards, Dad.

"Hey, Dee?" Eddie called from the backseat, over the roar of the open windows. She met his eyes in the rearview mirror and wondered if hers looked like bleak, worried stranger's eyes to him. She tried to soften her gaze, raised her eyebrows, smiled a little.

"Oh, you're still there, hey?" she called back. "How's it going?"

"Dee, I was wondering..." Eddie looked pensive.

She braced herself, fingers tightening on the steering wheel. *Please, Eddie, please don't go asking a million questions. I can't do this right now...*

"You know our names?" he said.

She relaxed. "I *think* so," she said. "Wait, what was yours again?"

He ignored her, tracking this new idea.

"Well, both of 'em have *dee* in them! *Dee*, Ed*dee*. Ever noticed that?" He was craning to look at her triumphantly in the rearview mirror.

Dee laughed, part relief, part just laugh.

"Believe it or not, I have never noticed that. Wow, you're right. Spooky."

Eddie nodded, satisfied. "I wonder if Mom and Dad did that on purpose or whether it was an accident."

"Mmm. I'm thinking accident."

"Yeah, probably," he said, "but you never know."

Dee glanced at him in the rearview mirror, anxious to steer away from the topic of their parents.

"No, you never know. Could've been...something like Cin*dee* and Fred*dee*," she said.

He sat up, excited, his brain working furiously.

"Or San*dee* and Geor*gee*," he shouted, "only that's a *gee*..."

"An*dee*, Ran*dee*..."

"Med*dee*, Ged*dee*, Hea*dee*..." Eddie randomly leaped through the alphabet until the conversation trickled off into silence. He looked out the window, his eyes narrowed against the wind, his hair tangling crazily.

"I guess we could have been anyone, hey? Any *dee*. Or really anything," he said.

This was true. Her parents had been capable of anything.

"Well, at least we're not Dea*dee*," he yelled, grinning at her in the mirror.

Dee laughed helplessly. It was so stupid.

Nope, they weren't dead.

Let's just keep it that way.

Eddie had got her thinking about her name. Dee. What kind of a name was Dee? Just a letter, really, not a proper name. She was always having to spell it out, although, when you thought about it, how else could you spell it?

She'd asked her parents once, before Eddie was born, why they'd named her Dee. What it was short for. Loretta

Lubbuk, a pushy girl in her second-grade class, had confronted her that day.

"It has to be short for *something*," Loretta said with authority. "It can't just be Dee. *Nobody's* just named Dee."

"Loretta Lubbuk" wasn't exactly a jackpot name either, but Loretta had been loud and popular. Nobody had questioned Loretta. Today, Dee would advise Eddie to tell someone like that to shut up, to walk away from them. They don't matter, she'd say.

But at the time it had mattered.

She'd asked her parents about her name, where it came from. They looked up from their books absently, unaware of the intensity of her interest.

"Oh no, it's not short for anything. You're just Dee," her dad had said.

"I think there was an old lady at Grandma's nursing home named Dee," her mother reflected. "Remember, she shared the room with Dorothy?" she said to Dee's father. "We called them Dot and Dee."

"We just thought it was a pretty name. Kind of different." They smiled at each other, looking over at her as if to say, *Is that what you wanted? Have we been helpful?*

Dee remembered hating them both at that moment. For giving her a stupid, old-lady name, for being so clueless, for not understanding the Loretta Lubbuks of the world, for sending her out there to fend for herself. For not even giving her a middle name she could hide behind.

Now, driving down an endless, scorching highway, possibly with a children's-services van on their tail, it seemed silly, all that wasted intensity, all that agonizing and embarrassment over a name. But, she thought, everything has a time and place. It had been the end of the world. The end of her seven-year-old world.

Eddie was reading out loud, shouting against the wind that was screaming in through the open windows.

"*The thorny devil is a ferocious-looking creature no bigger than a man's hand. But despite its fearsome appearance, its main interest is in eating ants and termites, up to 1,000 in a single meal!*" He stared down at the flapping book in his lap, one arm resting along the top, bracing the pages against the wind.

"The size of your *hand*!" he repeated in a loud voice, his face alight, holding the book up and backwards so Dee could see the illustration in the rearview mirror. "Your HAND!"

"Wow. Cool lizard. Reptile. Whatever." Dee hadn't really been listening. She wondered where Eddie got the energy to keep reading when it was such an effort—the yelling, the clamping of the flapping pages…everything. Her left arm was sunburned and starting to ache. Her back was sore from driving so long, her right leg numb. She didn't want to think about the dry, barren place they were leaving, or the scaly creatures that scrabbled out an existence there.

"Hey, Eddie?" she called over her shoulder. "You got any *stories* back there? You know, with characters? A plot? Anything like that?"

"Stories?" He reached out with his left hand and scuffled halfheartedly through a pile of books.

"Nnnnnnope," he said. "But listen to this! *The thorns and spikes on the thorny devil provide protection from predators and help the creature get water. Dewdrops settle on the thorns and trickle into the lizard's mouth!* Imagine that!"

Dee glanced at him in the rearview mirror, ready to say, *Enough with the reptiles.* But then her face softened. Eddie's eyes were closed, and he was smiling to himself, his mouth open slightly.

She knew him well enough to guess that he was imagining how it felt to be a thorny devil tasting the dew.

They finally stopped to get gas just outside of Phoenix after three hours of driving. *Normal people take two hours to get to Phoenix. Everyone in Santacino always says Phoenix is just two hours away. How could it take us so long?* Traffic. Navigating multiple-lane freeways without a map while Eddie called out helpful reptile facts. At one point they had been pelting along the highway to California. It took a *Los Angeles 365* sign to turn them north.

Eddie looked up from his book as they pulled over.

"Are we having lunch here?" he asked.

"Nope. Quick stop. We've got lots of food, so I think we'll eat on the way, okay? Car picnic."

It felt good to get out of the car, even if it was only to top up the gas and use the putrid washroom. Eddie ran up and down the hot asphalt beside the station like a puppy while she paid for the gas (forty dollars gone) and bought a map to study that night: *The Western States*. The attendant gave her directions to the interstate highway that would lead north to Flagstaff. The I-17, the first interstate she would ever drive, not counting that mistake out to California. A serious highway, a fast one.

A few minutes after a scary merge, she decided that she hated the I-17. Within half an hour she loathed it. She concentrated on trying to unclench her back muscles. She straightened up, arching slightly, but within a few minutes was hunched again, aching hands in a death grip on the wheel. She carefully lifted each hand from the wheel, one at a time, doing a few quick flexes.

Eddie was, unbelievably, asleep, lulled by the wind and the sun's pulsing heat. He looks so young, Dee thought, glancing at his flushed face framed by damp hair, his slightly open mouth.

The heat in the car was almost unbearable. Trickles of sweat ran down the sides of Dee's face. She felt sweat slip down the side of her leg into her sandals. *My legs are sweating. Right now, at this very moment, my shins are sweating. I am utterly, completely disgusting.*

She reached carefully for her water bottle and froze as she saw flashing lights in the rearview mirror. *Oh, shit.* Her heart started to hammer. *Shit, shit, shit!*

The police car was behind her, closing in rapidly. She checked her speed. Still zero. She had a wild moment of hope that maybe this wasn't about her—lots of cars had been whipping past her. She hovered uncertainly, watching the cruiser in the mirror, until it signaled her to pull over with a sharp, impatient *blurp* on the siren.

Dee pulled onto the shoulder of the highway, sliding the car to a stop. Without the wind the quiet was broken only by random bursts of noise as other cars sped past. Without the slight breeze it was baking hot.

Dee took a swig from her water bottle, eyes on the car in the mirror. A scary car, she noted, with flashing lights and a grate separating the driver from possible criminals in the back. She had never been pulled over by police, but she remembered her father being stopped once. He'd rummaged in the glove compartment for some papers, looked out with a rueful smile and said, "What seems to be the trouble, officer?" He had the officer laughing within about ten seconds. *But that was Dad.*

She swallowed, ran a hand over her hair and glanced uneasily back at the cruiser in her side-view mirror. *Calm. Gotta be calm. Matter-of-fact. Hyper-polite. Cops like polite.*

Let him talk first. She glanced over her shoulder into the backseat. *Eddie, please stay asleep, please don't wake up.* A massive state trooper took his time finishing up on his radio, then struggled out of his cruiser, which bounced up a couple of inches as he left it. In her side mirror Dee saw him walk toward her, hitching up his belt. A bulky man in a sweat-stained uniform, with a round, flushed face under his hat.

As soon as she saw him looming at the window, she blurted out, "Hi, officer, what seems to be the problem?"

His calm gaze swept over Eddie and the car mess.

"Well," he said, "y'all were going forty, forty-five tops."

"Ah," Dee said. *What the hell? Other cars had been flying past her.* Her face must have mirrored her confusion, because he continued.

"The speed limit on the interstate is seventy miles per hour," he said. "Just as dangerous to go too slow as to speed. Makes people swerve around you. Makes people angry." He pronounced it "*an*gruh," which sounded worse.

"Oh. Sorry," she said, apologizing to the hypothetical angry people.

"It's mostly *old* ladies we pull over for this kind of thing," he said, smiling.

Not a bad enormous old cop after all. She smiled back, hoping it looked kind of natural.

"Well, we're heading to visit relatives," she said with a slight grimace, hoping Eddie wasn't awake. "Not in any hurry to get there." *Sorry, Auntie Pat.*

"Gotcha." He chuckled. "Well, better have a look-see at your license and registration."

"Of course, of course." Dee opened the glove compartment, grabbing the little plastic folder and handing it to him. "Here's the registration. I just have to find my wallet." She grabbed her backpack. *For my nonexistent license. Oh, God.* She put her head down, pawing through the backpack. *Time for makink the beeg show, Dee, findink the license...*

"Now where..." She pulled out a sweatshirt, a pair of shorts, a book. She fished around inside the bag with her arm. "Sorry, sorry," she said. She opened a side zipper, hunted, zipped it back.

Incredibly, her dad had kept the car's registration current, and the insurance was paid until August. That in itself was a miracle. *How long can I pretend to look for my wallet? Two minutes? Then what? Please don't call us in, please don't call us in...*

"You sure got a lot of stuff in that backp—" He stopped, interrupted by an urgent beeping from his cruiser radio.

"Whoops, 'scuse me. *That* one can't wait. Hold on, hold on," he muttered as he shambled back to the cruiser. There was a curt exchange, and then he was striding back to her window, sweat streaming down his face.

"I got to get somewhere ASAP, preferably *yesterday*," he said, "so anyway, remember, keep up with the traffic. Even sixty, sixty-five miles an hour'd be good. Just get *in* there," he said, making a swooping underarm motion with his arm, like he was throwing an imaginary softball.

He looked more like a Little League coach than an enforcer of the law.

Dee nodded.

"Okay, sir, thanks a lot," she said, but he was already heading back to his car.

"You have yourself a nice day," he called over his shoulder, giving the trunk of the car a friendly thump.

Dee watched him lever his bulk into his car, flick on the lights and sirens and accelerate past her. She was trembling with reaction, relief. Saved by some horrible accident or violent crime, she thought. Eddie was still asleep, his head lolling forward over the seat belt. *He'll be so disappointed to have missed the action. The lights, the sirens. He'll be devastated.*

She pulled back onto the highway, brought the car up to what she estimated was the speed limit judging by the other cars, and glared at the useless speedometer that still had them going zero. The wind roared deafeningly in the windows. The engine juddered, rattling the car. Dee gripped the wheel tightly, feeling unsafe and out of control.

But legal, she reminded herself grimly. The speed limit. Completely legal.

"Hey! Dee!" Eddie shouted, his eager face making eye contact in the mirror. "I just saw a sign for the *Grand Canyon*!" He twisted in his seat, gesturing at the back of the sign they had flown by. "Are we going there? We're stopping there, aren't we?" He made it sound as if she was trying to keep this a wonderful secret from him.

Lost in a robotic driver trance, Dee hadn't seen the sign. *Unbelievable. I am so incredibly stupid. I forgot all about that ancient, 1,000-mile-long canyon right in our way.* Laughter bubbled up in her throat. Not fun laughter. Panic laughter, hysterical stress laughter. The kind of laughter people in movies got slapped for.

How could this canyon happen? She had imagined them driving in a straight line up from the bottom of Arizona into Utah. Looked as if they had a slight detour in front of them.

She had to have a serious look at a map. She glanced at Eddie's thrilled, expectant face.

She swallowed.

"Yep, we're stopping there, Eddie. You got it," she said. "Surprise! Grand Canyon, here we come!"

How much does it cost to look at the Grand Canyon? And how long will it take?

"I always *wanted* to go to the Grand Canyon!" Eddie said, resting his head on the back of his seat. "Remember, we almost went there once, but then Dad had to help Mr. Blair move? I *think* we almost went another time, but we never did."

No, they never did, Dee remembered. Something always came up. *But when Dad was feeling restless or freaked or whatever the hell his problem was, we'd take off at a moment's notice. Never to the Grand Canyon or Disneyland though. Always to some other dusty little town baking in the desert.* In her mind she saw the two of them, paid off in candy, trailing their dad through some estate sale, antique auction or barn full of trash.

Screw the cost, she thought angrily, we're going to the Grand Canyon. Who lives in the Grand Canyon State and never sees the Grand Canyon?

"Well, we're going there now," she said firmly, like it had been part of her plan all along. That intricate, well-crafted master plan of hers. "We finally made it." She reached back for Eddie's stinging high five.

"We'll tell Dad *all* about it," he said happily, sitting on his hands.

They sat on a bench right near the rim of the Grand Canyon. It fell away before them in folds of red and bronze and blue-gray, sweeping into the distance, the tiny Colorado River winding away far below like a worm at the bottom of a pail. Dee didn't know what she had expected. Nothing. She had expected nothing. She hadn't thought of the canyon at all, other than as a stop they needed to make before they could move on. She was startled by this calm and infinite majesty. This sense of peace. It was like watching the ocean or the stars. It seemed limitless.

The air was fresher here, much cooler than the desert they had escaped from. The twenty-five-dollars-per-vehicle entrance fee to the park, which had seemed exorbitant when she paid it, now seemed like the bargain of a lifetime.

Whatever happens, wherever we end up, we'll both have this memory.

Eddie was hopping in excitement, trotting back and forth to read the informative signs, storing away the facts.

"It is 277 miles long and 18 miles wide! It took three to six million years to form! Wow."

"Cool. Look, don't go so close to that rope thing, Eddie. Just stay back from the edge."

"The rock at the bottom is *two billion* years old!" He sat down with her on the bench, digesting the information. "We finally made it, Dee! The *GRAND CANYON!*" He said it in a booming, exaggerated monster-truck voice, spreading out his arms like a circus ringmaster.

She smiled. They'd finally hit a landmark, something acknowledged by normal people to be a destination for a family holiday. Something people came from all over the world to see. And they'd done it without their dad.

"Someday I'm going to walk all around it and then down *through* it, and take a boat and float down that river," said Eddie, making it sound simple, inevitable, a piece of cake. "Want to come? Just *some*day," he said.

"Someday, sure. It'd take a long time. Weeks and weeks."

Eddie considered this silently. She knew that in his head he was already paddling down that river.

A family settled on a bench nearby. Mother, father, a boy, a girl. A nice family, thought Dee, watching them covertly. They all had different ice-cream flavors and were offering each other sample licks. The boy was about fourteen, uncertain voice, looking as if he was self-conscious of his height and hair. The girl was maybe twelve. She had a perfect swath of straight, golden hair and a braces-flashing smile. She swung her pristine white flip-flops as she sat, and Dee stared, mesmerized, at the girl's toenails. They were all painted sky blue with a tiny pink flower dotting the center of each one. Theresa would totally approve, thought Dee.

Dee crossed her ankles, shoving her grubby feet in her old sandals under the bench. She looked down at her red left arm, her sweat-stained T-shirt, her crumpled shorts. Eddie was a mess too—Dorito smears on his T-shirt, dirty fingernails, hair a knotted mass from the wind.

Staring over the canyon, hearing the chatter of the happy family, Dee felt loneliness sweep over her. She felt cut off from the crowds, from the ice-cream family beside them, even from Eddie. Because she couldn't really talk to Eddie—she couldn't confide in him. He was too young; it wouldn't be fair. She was alone.

She was very, very tired. Dog tired. She felt old.

"Do you want an ice cream, Eddie?" Dee asked suddenly, her voice louder than she had intended.

"Yesss!" he cried, as though he'd noticed the ice cream but didn't want to ask. The friendly mother caught Dee's eye and smiled.

"Beautiful view," she said.

"Gorgeous," agreed Dee. Unused to making small talk, she hesitated, not knowing whether the woman was going to say anything else.

"Is there any chance you could get a picture of us with the canyon in the background?" the woman asked. "We never get a picture where we're all together, you know?"

Dee knew. She took the camera, and the mom cajoled the kids to stand between her and her husband, with their backs to the canyon. Dee focused the camera on the family, waited until they were all looking at her, and clicked. Then once more, just to make sure. A mother, a sister, a brother, a father, smiling and happy, silhouetted by trees and canyon, frozen in time.

"Thanks a lot," said the dad as Dee handed back the camera. He had friendly, crinkly eyes. "How's about I take one of you two with *your* camera," he offered.

"Oh, that's okay, thanks," Dee said quickly. "We've already got lots of pictures."

Not entirely a lie, she thought, as she joined Eddie on the path leading to the ice-cream store.

The pictures you take in your mind count too.

Dee checked her watch. Almost four o'clock.

The magic of the canyon was gone. She couldn't lose herself in its wild beauty anymore. Now it was just an impediment, a time-wasting, money-sucking detour, a roadblock. We have to get going, we have to get out of Arizona, she thought in rising panic, her footsteps quickening.

On the trail leading to the parking lot, Eddie forced her to turn for "one last look." The canyon, framed by pine trees, looked exactly like the two postcards she had bought, one for her, one for Eddie. *Nice. Let's go already.*

A bird soared over the canyon from the cliffs off to the right.

"Condor. Definitely a condor," said Eddie, pointing. Dee hadn't read the information plaques dotting the trail like Eddie had. All she saw was the breathtaking confidence of the creature, launching out over that endless, cavernous vista. Its calm mastery of height. Its complete lack of fear.

Dee gnawed at her ratty left thumbnail as she watched.

That bird, with a brain probably the size of a peanut, is exactly, precisely everything I'm not. I'm incompetent. I'm afraid. I'm scared to get back in that car, scared of the highway, scared of the coming night...

Eddie turned to her.

"Want a lick, Dee?" he asked, holding out his cone. "What's the matter?" he said when he saw her face.

"Oh, nothing. Just thinking." She bent and took a swipe of his cone with her tongue.

"Wishing you got a cone?" he asked sympathetically.

Eddie, if only it were that simple. And by the way, I just saved us $5.50.

"Nah, not hungry," she said. When did it get dark up here? How far was Utah? The thought of highway driving at night terrified her. She looked back at the canyon, but the bird had gone.

"We better hit the road. Race you to the car."

It was getting dark by the time their headlights flashed on the sign. *Welcome to Utah—The Beehive State.*

"Welcome to *Utah*!" cried Eddie, looking out his window into the gloom. "Wow, *Utah*," he said, as though it was a foreign country, as though he'd see all kinds of wonders outside the smudgy glass. "First other state I've been in. That I remember, I mean. Wonder what it's like. The *Beehive* State. Wonder why it's called that. Other than there must be lots of beehives, but *why* are there?"

Dee didn't care about Utah, anyone who lived there or their puzzling beehives. She had no more energy, even for relief. She couldn't even bring herself to say, *Well, we'll find out tomorrow.* She existed only to stop this car safely, take her clenched claws from the wheel, topple sideways and go to sleep. She hadn't slept for...since...when?

A couple of fitful hours last night in her bed at home, which seemed like years ago and a world away. She'd had Skittles for lunch and beef jerky and Cheetos for dinner.

The Grand Canyon is behind us now. No more detours. Utah. Out of Arizona. Sort-of safety. Next sign of civilization, we are stopping this frigging car.

A sign told her that a town called Kanab was coming up. Dee slowed and took a side road veering off to the right, away from the faint town lights. It was a gravel road, and they bumped and jolted along, peering left and right into the gloom.

"What are we looking for, Dee?" asked Eddie.

"Somewhere to camp for the night. Keep your eyes peeled."

There was a small clearing off to the left, not too far from the gravel road but sheltered from it by some trees and bushes. Dee pulled up and backed the car slowly into the spot under the trees, swinging a little to the left so that the car was hidden from the road and poised for a quick escape if necessary. A branch scraped down the right side of the car, but she didn't care.

She turned off the ignition, and they sat in what she thought was pure silence—until it filled up with night sounds. Crickets, a breeze blowing through leaves, the distant, sporadic rumble of trucks on the main highway. Eddie scrambled out.

"Not far, okay, Eddie?" Dee called.

She sat there, her body aching, her mind blank, feeling nothing, empty.

"Hey, Dee, you got a flashlight?" Eddie called. She fished around in her backpack, found the flashlight and got out of the car, stretching and yawning. The cool air felt wonderful after the stuffy, Cheetos smell of the car.

"Eddie?"

"Here," he said, like it was attendance call in class. He appeared at her side, his face a pale circle hovering beside her.

"It's pretty dark, hey, Dee?" he said, slipping his hand into hers.

"Yeah. Here." She handed him the flashlight.

Reluctant to get back in the car yet, they wandered a little under the trees. Eddie kept stooping to pick up twigs.

"What are you doing?" Dee asked.

"Firewood," he replied, shuffling the twigs in his grubby hands. "You know, camping out—a fire."

"Ummm…"

"Only pretend," Eddie said. "I'm not *stupid*. You can't really make a fire in a car. Well, you *can*, but it's probably not a good idea."

"Yeah, no kidding," said Dee. She delighted Eddie by contributing a few "marshmallows" for the campfire—white mushrooms hiding under a shrub.

There was a sudden scuffling in the bushes, and something darted past them into the trees. Dee jumped and flailed. She grabbed for Eddie's hand.

"Back to the car, back to the car!"

"It was just a *rabbit*, Dee," Eddie said, laughing. "I saw its ears."

Something barked in the distance. *Dog? Coyote? Wolf?*

"Still. We should head back. Got to get that campfire going."

Eddie swung the flashlight back and forth across their path, leading them to their car. Even the dismal messiness of the old car was a haven from the unfamiliar velvet blackness outside.

Doors locked against wildlife and ax murderers, windows open just a crack, they had their pretend campfire in the backseat. Eddie carefully stacked his twigs and energetically pantomimed rubbing two sticks together. Dee gave Vera a few drops of water and snapped off one of her arms, rubbing the soothing, gluey innards across her burned, aching left arm. Good old Vera, thought Dee, wrapping the old T-shirt more firmly around the plant pot. *I'm glad you came.*

"Well," she said, looking at the tiny pile of sticks, "this is definitely the most roaring campfire we ever made."

"Hey!" said Eddie. "How about a ghost story? Not too spooky maybe."

"I hate it when you ask me to tell stories. I'm no good at them," she said, trying to think of something thrilling yet not terrifying. She thought of her dad. Now *he* was a wonderful storyteller. He seemed to have elaborate stories, fully formed, stored in his head, just waiting to be told.

"The Race to the Day Before Yesterday." "The Nine Gates to Freedom." "The Blue Dog's Terrible Fortune."

Dee searched the tired blankness of her mind and came up with nothing. Nothing she could say out loud. *Well, Eddie, once upon a time outside a small border town in Utah, there were two clued-out kids who were lost and on their own. The big kid, the one who had kidnapped and duped the little one, had to be the grown-up, even though she was really scared. The little one was weird, but not in a bad way...*

"How about you tell me one?" she said.

"Nah," Eddie said through a yawn, then sat up. "Hey! How about we switch seats for the night, Dee? How about *I* sleep up front, and *you* sleep in the back? Just for a change."

*Always, always trying to get into the front seat. Such a magical place...*He'd sit in the front of the parked car at home, asking endless questions. "What does that button do? How about this one?" He'd point out things he knew with elaborate nonchalance ("Gas. Brake. Lighter. Innicator.")

"Sure, whatever," she said. "Happy to cuddle up to your collection of reptile claws." She could have slept standing up—her scratchy eyes were already having trouble focusing. "Hey, smell that," she said suddenly. She put her nose to the crack in the window and took a deep breath.

"What?" Eddie asked, stilling and then sniffing the air like a pointer. A sweet evergreen smell wafted in on the night breeze.

"Pine," she said, the smile coming through her voice in the darkness. "Pine trees. You know, Christmas-type trees? Not the fake ones like we have in Arizona. I love that smell. I haven't smelled pine trees since, well, for years and years. Not since we came down here."

"Well, we're not in the desert anymore," murmured Eddie.

"Yeah, you're right," said Dee. "No more desert."

They made two beds in the car, fumbling around in the glow of the one interior light that worked. They slid a pillow over the gearshift in the front. Eddie considered the bump a very small price to pay for being up front. He snuggled down as Dee clambered over the seat to her nest in the back, kicking stuffies and books into the footwell.

It was cold, but Dee left the back window open a crack. Just a crack. Not enough for a hand to get through. Or an ax. She didn't want them to suffocate from breathing in each other's old air all night long.

Eddie took a few swings and finally connected with the button switching off the overhead light. The darkness settled in.

"Wow." Eddie's disembodied voice was loud in the stillness. "*Fun* in here! Sleeping under the stars—if there was no car roof and no clouds, which there *are*. Anyway, a star is dead by the time its light hits Earth."

"Night, Eddie," Dee said, heading off more conversation. She was already half asleep.

"Night, Dee," said Eddie. "Love ya."

"Love you too."

Dee curled over on her side, her knees knocking jars of dead insects and pebbles.

"Dee?" Eddie whispered. A scrabbling sound, and then a black head bobbed above the gray of the seat back.

"Mmm."

"If you open your eyes in the dark, then squeeze them shut *tight*, count to twenty or forty even, then open them again, you can sometimes see more than before. Just a leeetle bit more. Did you know that?"

"Eddie, go to sleep."

"One one thousand, two one thousand—"

"No, no. *Please.*"

"—three one thousand—"

"Shut *up!*" She groped around for a stuffie to throw at him.

"Okay, okay." He laughed. "No more talking. None. I'm taking this key and locking this *mouth*."

She heard him bump around, shift and turn. He sighed. There was a little silence, and then she heard a faint hum, which turned into a droning buzz. What was he doing up there?

Oh, God. She put her pillow over her head as she figured it out. *He's being a Utah bee.*

UTAH

FRIDAY

Dee woke to two long blasts of a horn. Not their horn, but a horn close by. She flinched and cracked her head on the car door handle.

"Shit." She rubbed her head hard, sat up and looked out the window.

A rusted blue pickup truck had pulled over beside them. A grim-faced old woman in curlers and a checkered flannel coat sat at the wheel. She saw Dee and gave her the jerky, sideways-thumb sign, the get-the-hell-off-my-property sign. Dee raised her hand in a confused, conciliatory wave.

She probably thinks we're criminals or perverts. I hope she hasn't called the police. The old woman blasted the horn again.

Dee scrambled over the seat, pushing Eddie into the passenger seat.

"Hey," he mumbled, pulling his blanket closer.

Another long honk.

"Okay, okay," Dee muttered. "Sorry, Eddie. Gotta go. Buckle up," she said, shaking his shoulder. He groggily reached for the seat belt.

Dee pulled the keys from her shorts pocket and started the car. The windshield wipers started up full steam, and a burst of laughter from a morning radio show hit them full blast.

"God damn it, Eddie," she muttered, fumbling to switch them both off. She slammed the car into Drive and hit the gas, and they shot out from their sheltered spot, passing the truck. They made a bumping right turn onto the track leading to the road, spitting up loose gravel as they went.

Right again on the gravel road, toward the interstate.

"Keep an eye on what that truck does, Eddie, okay?" said Dee.

Eddie, fully awake now and thrilled to be riding shotgun, stuck his head out the window, craning to see through the dust.

"Nah, it's not following us," he said. "But you know where we parked, Dee? It was that lady's *yard*! I saw the house back there when we were driving away, now that it's light!" He started laughing and bouncing on the seat, elated by the ludicrous spectacle of them parking right on somebody's front lawn.

Dee started to laugh too. *What kind of crazy people camp in their car on somebody's front lawn? Our kind of crazy people, apparently.*

They drove down the gravel road for a few minutes and then merged onto the quiet highway.

"What time is it anyway, Eddie?"

"6:11 AM. Friday, July 25," he said, consulting his big watch. "Bright and early! Oh—*guten Morgen.*"

"*Morgen.* Not a bad thing to have an early wake-up call," Dee murmured.

She thought they'd better not stop. They needed to get away from whatever the hell town it was back there (Kellam? Kebab?) just in case that old woman had called the police. Without any other cars around and with the speedometer stuck obstinately at zero, Dee tried to remember and approximate the previous day's speed.

An hour later they came to the I-15 and headed north to Salt Lake City. One more hour's driving, peppered with Eddie's estimates of how long he could last before he really, *really* had to pee, and Dee felt that they'd truly left the blue pickup and its angry driver behind for good.

She pulled off the interstate at a gas station.

"*Lots* of soap when you wash your hands after, okay?" she said, glancing down at his dirty fingernails.

"And your face. Wash your face too, Eddie. I'm right outside if you need me."

"I'm not two years old," Eddie muttered, smacking the washroom door open with both hands.

Breakfast smells wafted down the hallway leading into the station's attached restaurant. Coffee. Pancakes.

Eddie came out.

"I'll just be a sec," Dee said. "Stay right here, okay? Don't move."

"I know."

"Right here." She hesitated.

"*Okay.*"

Dee washed her face and hands, scrubbed a wet finger over her teeth and did a quick finger-comb of her long, curly, dusty hair. How did all this grit get in there? she wondered, shaking it out before scraping her hair back into a ponytail again.

"Dee-ee," Eddie said, looking toward the restaurant as she came out.

"Yeah, I know. It smells *wonderful*. Let's go look at the menu." *Let's look at the prices.*

"I'm *starving*," Eddie said. "Probably I'll need the *grown-ups'* menu."

"You're a kids'-menu kid until you're twelve, Eddie," Dee said, scanning the menu posted outside the restaurant. She could just see Eddie ordering the Big Wrangler steak-and-eggs combo for eleven bucks. She tapped the menu. "See here? Says *twelve*. Anyway, the kids' menu is way funner. Pancakes, waffles, lots of stuff." The kids' selections were $2.99, and they came with milk. Dee's stomach rumbled. They had to eat.

They went into the restaurant, waiting to be seated like the sign told them to. An uninterested, tired-looking older waitress showed them to a booth with a view of the gas pumps and the highway. She poured Dee coffee, then drifted away. Dee had never had a cup of coffee in her life but thought it might keep her alert on the drive. She sipped and winced; straight up, it was putrid. She reached for the sugar and cream.

"Booth!" said Eddie, sliding his hands along the padded vinyl. He lay down, crossing his cowboy boots. "Now *this* is more comfortable than the car."

Dee saw the truckers in the next booth look over.

"Eddie, sit up." She shoved the paper place mat and cup of crayons over at him. "Color like a normal kid, okay?"

"You be normal. You color. I hate coloring—it's stupid," he said. "I'm sleeping. I'm a sleepy old rattler, sunning himself on a rock."

One of the truckers lingering over his coffee caught Dee's eye and winked.

"Your boy there looks tuckered out, and it's only eight o'clock!" He chuckled. "Been driving a while?"

"Early-morning start," said Dee. Then she turned and pretended to rummage in her backpack for something.

She kept her face turned to the window as she heard the truckers leave, lame-joking with the waitress before heading over to haul themselves up into their steel monsters.

"Have a nice nap, little buddy!" one of them called. As they stood at the front counter, she heard one of them say to the other, "Jeez, they're having them young these days, hey?"

Dee was stunned. *Seriously? They seriously think I'm Eddie's* mother? Did she really look that old, or were they just phenomenally stupid? Either way...

Dee glared at the trucker's back. She knew she looked older than her age. She was tall, for one thing. She'd hit five foot eight in sixth grade, leaving most of the girls and every single boy at least six inches shorter than her for a couple of years. It wasn't just height though. She was reserved, serious, watchful. *Very mature for her age*, was a standard comment on report cards. She would have preferred Theresa's *A ton of fun to have in class!*

They wolfed down their breakfasts. Dee got the two-egg special for the price ($3.25) and the protein. Eddie immediately tore the bacon smile off his Kiddie Waffle-D-Light and rolled its two strawberry eyes to the side, hacking into the plain waffle with exaggerated dignity.

A missing child stared up at Dee from Eddie's milk carton. *If you have any information as to the whereabouts of this child...* Dee looked at the two pictures: on the left, the image of the child when she went missing (four years old, innocent, big school-picture smile, dimple in her pudgy left cheek, tiny baby teeth); on the right, an artist's reconstruction of what she might look like today, as a still-missing, less-happy twelve-year-old. Dee wondered what the whole story was, then got scared and stopped wondering. She looked away, hoping that the girl was safe.

Did they do that for missing fathers too? Dee imagined her dad's face on the side of a milk carton. *If you have any information about this hopeless, clueless man, please contact his wandering children...*

"C'mon, Eddie. We should get going. Got to get some gas."

Dee filled the tank, leaning on the pump, anxiously imagining money clicking rhythmically out of her stash.

She sniffed an acrid burning smell and prayed it wasn't their car. It had been making a distinct, unusual sound ever since the Grand Canyon. An intermittent *grrrrgrrr-grrr* sound, like the grinding of automotive teeth.

Dee saw a pay phone and scrabbled in the bottom of her backpack, where she'd dumped a jam jar full of coins.

"Okay, Eddie, you can run from here to that post thing and back," she said, pointing to a scrubby field off to the right. "But you gotta stay where I can see you, okay?"

"Time me," he shouted, taking off in a boots-clattering run.

"You're the one with the watch, Eddie." She plugged quarters into the phone and tried to avoid touching the dirty walls of the booth. It smelled of urine, despite the prominent *Restrooms* sign ten feet away. Were these things just made smelling of pee? Because they always did. She was mentally preparing a message for Auntie Pat's answering machine when a voice answered, slurred with sleep. "Rolling Wood Greengardens…"

"Auntie Pat?" Dee asked automatically, stupidly, because she knew it wasn't her.

"What? No, no, it's Jake."

"Oh, sorry, Jake. Did I wake you up? I woke you up. It's Dee."

"No, no. S'okay. I'm up."

"Pat and Norm still not back?" *Is every frigging adult I know out in the frigging wilderness?*

"Nah. Tried to call them"—he stifled a yawn— "yesterday, but they must still be out on the boat. Not much reception out there. The one time of the year they don't mind not being contacted."

A big truck roared out of the gas station, and Jake asked, "Where the hell are you calling from, an airport runway?"

"Just on the road. Interstate." She smiled through the grubby glass, watching Eddie pull at some twisted steel rods protruding from a cement block. Then she blurted, "I'm kind of worried about our car. Do you know what a sort of *grrrrgrrrgrrr* sound means?"

"No clue. Sorry. Not much of a car guy. Probably not good though. You should get somebody to look at it. You know. Car-repair place."

Only problem is, Jake, those places charge money. What I wanted you to say was, "It's probably nothing. Better just drive the hell out of it until you get here. It should last for another three days or so."

"Yeah. Anyway, I better go here. Last quarter. Sorry for waking you up."

"No problem. Gotta feed the cat anyway, or he starts pissing on the rug. Can you believe that? Just because he's mad for some reason. He's got the run of the place, I pet him when he seems to want it, but still with the pissing. Any suggestions for getting that smell out of a couch?"

"Hmmm, hose the thing down? Let the cushions dry in the sun? I don't know."

"Good idea." He sounded relieved. "To be honest, I don't even feel like touching the thing."

Dee laughed. "Good luck with that." She glanced across the field where Eddie was. Where Eddie should have been.

He wasn't there.

Dee's mouth went dry.

"Jake, I gotta go find my brother."

"Okay, see you—" Dee slammed the phone down.

She ran out to the field, scanning left and right. No Eddie. Eddie wasn't there.

Oh my god, it was that truck that pulled out when I was on the phone with Jake. That truck took Eddie! She stood frozen, terrified. *No, it couldn't be. I saw him. He was right there a second ago, a minute ago. How long ago? He has to be here somewhere.*

"Eddie!" she called in a husky, croaking sob. Not loud enough.

"EDDIE!" she screamed. Way too loud. Eddie's head popped up from behind the concrete stump with its Medusa head of warped steel rods at the same time as the waitress and one of the customers ran out of the diner, their eyes wide and alarmed.

"I'm here, Dee. Just here. There's a huge bug on the side of this thing..."

"Sorry," Dee apologized to the diner people, "thought I lost him." She smiled at them tightly. "Slight overreaction maybe." *Move along, folks, hysterical girl's under control.* They smiled sympathetically, turning back to the restaurant.

Dee rounded on Eddie. The sick relief she'd felt when she saw him was ebbing away, swamped by a white-hot fury. *You little brat, you stupid little brat...you and your stupid, stupid frigging bugs...*

Eddie saw her face.

"I was *right here*, Dee," he said, crossing his arms. "I didn't *go* anywhere. I didn't."

Dee wanted to shake him or grab his arm hard and haul him into the car. Exactly the sort of things she hated to see parents doing to their kids in parks or grocery stores. A father hauling a yelling toddler off by one arm, yanking her along, her feet scrabbling at the ground. A mother's angry face pushed close to her little son's, snarling out some warning or ultimatum. She and Eddie were not like that; their family was not like that.

Dee closed her eyes and took a deep breath.

He's right. It's not his fault. He stayed where I told him to. He doesn't know why I'm so tense and tightly wound and paranoid right now.

"Sorry, Eddie. I couldn't see you. I thought you got lost." *Actually, I thought you got taken.*

They turned and started walking toward the car. Eddie gestured to the empty field and the gas station.

"How could I even *get* lost, Dee? Where would I get lost?"

"Nowhere. Forget it. I was just being a panic-face. I did actually say 'stay where I can see you' though," she pointed out.

"I just bent down for a minute. It was a very interesting bug. A beetle with a huge—"

"Later, Eddie. In the car. Now."

Dee drove, wondering what their lives would be like if they ever got to Auntie Pat's. Rolling Wood had probably changed and grown, but she'd gone to school there for five and a bit years, so Eddie would for sure have somewhere to go in September. *And I'll be the weird kid who nobody knows who parachutes in for twelfth grade. They'll point to me in the yearbook years later and say, "Who's that?"* But secretly she hoped it could be a new beginning, one where she wasn't already pegged as the quiet, boring, awkward girl who tagged along after Theresa. Does Jake still go to high school? she wondered.

She hoped Eddie got a teacher who understood him. Just a few weeks before school had ended this past June, Eddie had brought home a note from the school counselor, asking Eddie's parent/guardian to contact him to arrange a meeting about Eddie's "worrisome lack of progress."

"What crap," her dad had said, crumpling the note. "Anybody who's spent ten minutes with Eddie could figure out he's a smart kid. *Really* smart."

"Well, maybe it's not just about him being smart," Dee said. "Maybe it's sort of...social or something. Friends."

"Eddie's got lots of friends," her father said. *Name two, Dad. Name even one.* "Anyway, that counselor's a *joke*. He's totally clueless. I wish he would just leave Eddie alone." He'd chucked the note behind the fans.

When Dad left for an auction outside of Phoenix that week, Dee went to see the counselor. She thought somebody should.

He was a heavy man named Mr. Werner, wearing what he probably thought was a fun tie. A conversation opener with yellow rubber ducks on a blue background.

He was clearly taken aback by Dee's visit but tried to mask it by excessive casualness. He gestured her to a seat.

"Mr. Werner..." she began.

"Oh, *Greg*, please," he interrupted with a small smile, sitting back, hands linked over his paunch.

"Uh, okay, Greg. Well, my father's away at the moment, so I've come in his place. I'm Dee, Eddie Donnelley's sister. We got your note." Dee looked him straight in the eye. *And I'm not saying a word about being sixteen.*

"Well, uh, Dee, very nice to meet you. And might I say that it was very mature of you to come *in loco parentis*, as it were." He looked down at the sheet of paper he'd isolated on his messy desk. Dee could see it was a test, Eddie's test. It was covered in red marks—long, angry red marks.

"Now," began Greg, leaning back, eyes raised to the ceiling, "when I look at a test result like this, only one of many, many samples of Eddie's work that Mrs. Bonner has forwarded to me, I think to myself, I think, Greg, what is causing this child to behave in this way?"

Dee waited. *And how does Greg answer himself?* she wanted to ask.

"Because this child is clearly calling out for help. *Shouting*, in point of fact," he continued.

Dee cleared her throat. "Could I please see that test?"

It was a math test. Basic second-grade addition and subtraction. Dee ran through it, her heart sinking. It was Eddie the idiot-child on paper. For 9-3, he'd answered *S*. For 2+3, he'd written *tar*, though there was an initial squiggle that might have been an *s*. On several of the answer lines he'd written the word *blank*. He had ended the test with a flourish. On the bonus question, 20+5+5, he'd written 230-200 *(Ask the Apes in Africa!)*.

Ask the Apes in Africa? God dammit, Eddie. Dee looked up to find Greg watching her.

"Okay, I see what you mean," she said, sliding the sheet back to him. "He's actually right on the bonus question, though, other than the apes-in-Africa bit, but it's marked wrong." A big ugly red *X*. Mrs. Bonner's patience was thin at the best of times. She and Eddie did not get along.

"Yes, well, not quite the *form* Mrs. Bonner was looking for, I'm sure. I myself don't find her the most patient of individuals," he confided. "My *professional* opinion," he continued, smoothing his duck tie and leaning forward, "is that Eddie should be assessed first thing when school starts up again. I suspect perhaps a borderline learning disability might be holding him back."

Dee stared at him. He really was clued out—her dad was actually right on this one. Eddie would have a field day with this guy.

"Go for it, Greg," she said.

She'd confronted Eddie that afternoon after school. They were at the highway gas-station store, Dee stacking magazines, Eddie playing with her calculator.

"Apes in Africa? *Ask the Apes in Africa*. That's what you wrote for the answer of a math question, Eddie. A *math* question. Jeez. You know how that looks? Makes you look like a total idiot. And you're *not*."

Eddie, his mouth full of chocolate, said, "Was the answer thirty?"

Dee straightened. "Yeah, it *should* have been. Actually, you sort of got it right by saying something like 330-300. Just write the *answer* next time, okay? Don't be cute."

He shrugged. "Okay. Apes in Africa sometimes travel in groups of up to thirty, just so you know."

She slapped down the pile of magazines she'd been holding.

"So what about *S* as an answer? Or *tar*, Eddie? *TAR*?? Any code breaker for those?"

"Hmmm, usually *S* is six, but I don't remember *tar*. Oh, *star*! Five points on a star, so five." Eddie stooped down to start stacking.

Dee stared at the back of his head. "How about the *blank*s, Eddie? The places you wrote *blank*?"

"Oh, I don't know, just bored, I guess. Thinking of something else. School is so *boring*."

"Yeah, well, Mr. Werner's going to have you in for an assessment," Dee warned, "so try to act normal, please. Just *normal*, okay?"

Eddie looked up. "Greg? Oh, good. I hope he wears the gorilla tie."

Neither of them really noticed Utah. People on vacation notice scenery. Sixteen-year-olds who are clenching the wheel, listening intently to the increasingly scary sounds their car is making, don't marvel at mountains. Eddie, torqued up on junk food, was sick of reading and desperate to run around. He rocked in his seat, looking out the window, reading out the signs. Whenever a huge truck flashed past, he would excitedly mime at the driver to honk, using the pulling-on-an-invisible-chain sign. The good-natured ones obliged. The crabbier ones honked at Dee for reasons that had nothing to do with Eddie's back-window gymnastics.

"Eddie, I need *less* honking, not more," Dee said.

They had been down to one lane for miles, striped orange-and-white construction pylons blocking off the left lane, and there was a line of impatient traffic right behind them, just waiting to floor it when the construction zone ended. Dee was trying simultaneously to avoid hitting the pylons on the left and the rumble strips of the shoulder on the right. When the car veered slightly, the strips made an unnerving, loud *vrrrrip, vrrrrip* sound. It was like trying to thread an endless needle at fifty-five miles per hour.

Eddie had been silent for the last ten minutes, only because he was making pinhole patterns on the vinyl seat with a safety pin he had found.

"Can I poke a few holes in the seat with this?" he had asked, holding it up to show her in the rear-view mirror.

"Sure, whatever."

"Twenty-seven holes for a fish," he announced. "Thirty-three for my initials, *E* dot *J* dot *D*."

He was at fifty-two holes and counting for an octopus.

"Getting pretty holey back here. It's okay, though, right?"

Eddie, if it keeps you quiet and happy, I would just suggest more intricate, time-wasting patterns. Scenery. An aquarium. Frigging Disneyland. She wouldn't have cared if he slashed up the whole backseat. She glanced over her shoulder at his bent head. *I am going to be one slack-ass mother someday.*

Dee recalled the map in her head. The I-15 would lead them north into Idaho, an odd, irregularly shaped state. They would pass through the rectangular boxy bit in the south of the state, then head into Montana. *Then, please, God, into Canada. No glitches, no arrests at the border, no breakdowns (automotive or otherwise), just smooth, smooth sailing up to their home and native land. The true north, strong and free.*

Their country, even though it didn't feel like it.

But they had the passports to prove it.

IDAHO

FRIDAY

"No beehives. Not one," Eddie said, looking over his shoulder as they neared the Idaho border.

"Anyway," Dee said, "you got your salt." Eddie smiled as he picked up and tilted a baby-food jar he had in his lap. The crumbly white sludge inside lurched from side to side. Somehow neither of them had made the connection that Salt Lake City was a city by a really salty lake. It had been just a name, like Great Falls or Red Deer. They'd been amazed to see actual salt lying in shallow drifts like snow by the side of the highway.

Dee had pulled over onto the shoulder of the highway, and Eddie had quickly dumped out a jar of his precious Arizona gravel and filled it up with Utah salt. Interesting salt. Salt you don't see every day, lying by the side of the road like that. They only glimpsed the lake between houses and hills as they sped by. Eddie would have liked to have stopped at the lake, but Dee needed to get them into Idaho.

You don't know it, but we're on a tight schedule, buddy—a state a day.

Even with construction and Eddie's salt collecting slowing them down, their early-morning wake-up call had them crossing into Idaho in the late afternoon.

"*Welcome to Idaho. The Gem State*," read Eddie. "Wow. *Gems.*" He straightened up and looked out the window as if expecting to see gems lying in mounds like the salt. But Idaho looked very similar to Utah.

"Mmm. Piles and piles of them just scattered around, I bet," said Dee.

She jumped as another car honked and screamed past her. *That makes three angry honkers in the last hour. I think I'm officially a menace on the roads.* She tried to increase her speed, but the car's growling worsened.

"I have to get out of this *car*," Eddie said in a loud voice, squirming in his seat and tossing his head from side to side.

"I know, I know." Dee was barely listening to him.

"I really need to, Dee. I'm..." He strained hard against his seat belt, his face reddening and his eyes bugging out. "But we just keep driving and driving! We don't do anything fun or have lunch or even *walk around* like when we go on road trips with Dad."

"Yeah, but I haven't dragged you through some barn full of horse-smelling junk," Dee pointed out.

"I'd *love* to be in a barn right now! I need to get out… of…this…seat belt."

"Look, stop it, Eddie!" Dee snapped. "We're on a highway here. Not a spot for freaking out. Hey, if you had to pick a perfect spot for freaking out, where would it be?"

Eddie, his seat belt clutched in both hands, paused. "You mean on this earth?"

"Uh, sure, okay. On this earth."

"Because it's not obvious. Space would be a good place for freaking out because you'd just *float*."

"Good point." Dee could hear the engine making a high-pitched whine.

"So here on Earth…well, somewhere soft…" Eddie looked out the window and began listing soft places. "Beds, pillows, *marshmallows*…"

The engine was definitely screaming, drowning out Eddie's list.

We need to stop. We need to get out of this damn car and let it rest or recharge or whatever. We need to find a town big enough that we won't be noticed, but not so huge that we'll never find our way back to the I-15.

Dee scanned the signs that had begun to dot the side of the highway. Motels ahead, not that they could afford to waste money on those. Restaurants. Idaho State University. A sign welcoming them to *Pocatello, "Smile Capital" U.S.A.*

Hello, Pocatello. We need all the smiles we can get. You might be the answer to my prayers.

A sign for the community recreation center (*Just Minutes Away to Play*) decided her. *Oh, please be open, please be open.*

"Time check, Eddie?" she asked.

"5:47 PM, Friday, July 25," he said.

It will be just my luck if it closes at five. Exactly my luck. She saw the building, pulled into the parking lot and swung by the hours-of-operation sign at the front door. *M-F: 6 AM-10 PM.*

"Grab your stuff, Eddie," Dee called, swinging into a parking spot. "We're going swimming!"

"Oh, no, Dee!" Eddie's face was tragic as he looked up from rifling through his backpack. "I forgot to pack my bathing suit!"

"Let me check." Dee emptied the backpack out on the hood of the car. Eddie had underestimated. He had forgotten to pack almost everything. An old Lakers hoodie, a men's size XL that Theresa's brother had given him, took up most of the space. There was a T-shirt with a prominent hole in the front, a pair of sweats that Dee knew for a fact were about four inches too short, a dress shirt he'd worn in the Christmas play and three socks.

No underwear.

No pajamas.

No shoes.

No bathing suit.

She looked over at Eddie, and the sarcastic comment died on her lips. He had his face turned away like he was studying a bush in the parking lot. His mouth was tight, his arms crossed, and he was blinking hard.

"Do you have any scissors, Eddie? Anything scissorlike?"

"Scissors?" He frowned, his swimming eyes gratefully focused on the problem of scissors. "Well, there's a little pair on my Swiss Army knife." He scrabbled in a box in the backseat. "Here. Why?"

Dee picked up the too-short sweats.

"*You* may see before you some average sweatpants, Eddie," she said. "*I* see a bathing suit just waiting to happen." Eddie laughed delightedly as Dee snipped at a seam, then carefully ripped and hacked each leg off. Finally she held up the uneven legs.

"Not exactly a professional job. But you figure that'll do?" she asked.

"Perfect," said Eddie. "Let's go."

When they'd paid the admission (only six bucks total) and come out of the change rooms, Dee caught a glimpse of their reflection in a mirror as they hung up their stinking seat towels. Eddie's skinny little torso emerged from his "bathing suit," which looked exactly like a pair of sawn-off sweats, the pockets inside hanging visibly lower than the shorts. Dee's bathing suit was a supremely ugly yellow one-piece that was so old it was practically see-through. She wore a baggy gray T-shirt over top.

We are quite a pair, she thought. Quite an awesomely neglected-looking pair of kids. Thankfully there weren't a lot of people to notice them. The place was very quiet. A new mom and her tiny baby, completely absorbed in each other. A few boisterous kids doing cannonballs into the deep end. An old guy doing methodical lengths in the roped-off lane. A teenage lifeguard slumped against the wall, texting on his phone. Dee smoothed her hair and pulled down her T-shirt.

She made Eddie scrub down in the shower by the pool's edge.

"Sign says we have to shower before we go in," she pointed out, as if it was only polite that they follow the rules in this foreign place. We're so disgusting, she thought, pumping the dispenser for a handful of soap to dump on his hair. May as well get this grubby little boy as clean as I can. Border tomorrow if the car doesn't die first, and we probably shouldn't arrive looking homeless.

When Eddie escaped, slipping into the shallow end and hopping up and down to get warm, Dee took her turn in the shower. It was wonderful to feel the warm water rinsing the grit and sweat out of her hair, to soap her blackened feet into normal foot color, to really scrub her face.

"Dee, it's *fun* in here!" Eddie called. She slid into the cool water, hopping and bicycling her legs to keep warm.

They took turns diving underwater, one being the predatory shark, the other the unsuspecting, doomed ocean swimmer. Eddie was better at being the shark than the swimmer. He panicked easily, kicking frantically with his bony legs as if she really were some cartilaginous ocean monster.

"Hey, this *pool* would be a great place for freaking out!" He thrashed around in demonstration, slapping the water.

"*Down*, boy," she said, laughing. "Want to try that slide over there?" Of course he wanted to try it. A million times. As he clambered out of the water and rocketed down the small slide again and again in an obsessive loop, Dee floated on her back, her T-shirt billowing up in odd balloon air lumps.

"Did ya see *that* one, Dee?" Eddie's running commentary was muted by the water. She smiled over at him, raising a thumb. She stretched her arms and legs wide, like a starfish, stared up at the peeling turquoise metal ceiling beams and rocked gently on the waves of Eddie's splash-entries. She forgot the highway, the trucks and the noise, the border, the breaking-down car. She felt weightless, timeless, absolved from thought and worry.

For the first time in as long as she could remember, she felt free.

Hours later, when they were, as Eddie put it, "all swum out," they soaked in the hot tub for the last time, idly reading the *Rules and Regulations of Hot Tub Use* affixed to the wall.

"I've been in here for way longer than it says," said Eddie. "*Way* longer."

"Yeah, but at least we refrained from use while intoxicated, pregnant or with rashes, open sores or communicable diseases," Dee said. She centered a jet on her back, feeling the driving-clenched muscles soften and relax. The clock on the wall read 9:35 PM.

I wonder if we could just stay here, she thought sleepily, just hide out here in old Pocatello, Idaho, smile capital of the world. Maybe we could become smiley Pocatellans? Idahoans? And we could come to this pool every day. Or maybe just live our lives hiding out in the locker rooms...

"I'm starving," Eddie said and yawned.

"Yeah, me too," said Dee. "Let's go see what we have to eat in the car."

"And I guess we have to find somebody's yard to park in for the night!" Eddie said.

Dee laughed, but the worries came slithering back in a rush.

Because when you really thought about it, the night was always scarier than the day.

They ate tinned pineapple, granola bars and fruit gummies in the car, shivering in the cool evening air after the warmth of the hot tub. They both reeked of chlorine, and their fingertips were bleached and puckered. Eddie nestled inside the huge Lakers hoodie like it was a tent, draping it over his whole body and tucking it under his crossed legs. The only visible Eddie parts were his face and a small hand that snaked up through the face hole to ferry gummies to his mouth from a stash inside the hoodie. Dee dug out sweats and a sweater.

"We should stop on our way out of town and buy you some underwear and a T-shirt."

"Nah, I'm good." Eddie gestured to his one T-shirt and pair of shorts.

As Dee shoved garbage into a receptacle, she scanned the parking lot. Too exposed, she decided, noting the lack of trees and the bright lighting. But she was reluctant to leave. This place felt safe, and who knew what the rest of this town was like.

Only two other cars were left in the lot, probably the lifeguard's and the receptionist's, neither of whom had paid them much attention.

"Okay, keep still and low," she said to Eddie in a dramatic whisper. "We have to wait. Let me know when the parking lot is clear." It was their old game of Spy-Guys. Eddie scrambled to the backseat, crouched low and peered out. A reliable sentry, a dependable, sneaky little spy.

Ten minutes passed. Eddie didn't move a muscle. Then he tensed.

"Psst. Here they come. *Together*," he whispered, as if that fact was crucial. Sure enough, shortly after ten the stout receptionist and the teenage lifeguard walked out to their cars. Dee and Eddie heard them talking, saw them wave, heard car doors slam, engines start. The teenager sped off in a loud blast of music. *Friday night. Heading off to a party maybe. Or watching movies with friends, getting pizza. Hanging out with his girlfriend.* Dee thought of all the things normal teenagers did. She was thankful they had parked across the parking lot so he didn't see her crouched in a beat-up car with her little brother. The older woman took longer to leave, and when she did, she turned her head and stared in their direction. The overhead lights glinted off her glasses, making them opaque and giving the woman an oddly creepy, robotic appearance.

"Aaaaand, they're gone!" said Eddie triumphantly, climbing back into the front seat. "What do we do now?"

Pal, if you're looking for answers to almost anything, you got the wrong person. I wonder if this is how parents sometimes feel—like they should have a plan but are mostly making it up as they go along.

She considered the options.

"Well, may as well just drive around back and see if there's anywhere to park that's less public," Dee said.

The car started well enough. It was when she put it into gear that the engine died. Dee froze. She waited a minute, then started it again, slipping it quickly into Drive, flooring the gas and lurching forward. It seemed to be all right, other than the *grrrrgrrrgrrr* sound.

They skirted the building, going the wrong way on an Employees Only road. Dee backed in beside a dumpster that hid them from the main road. A few bushes shielded them from the playground behind the rec center. It was as good as it was going to get.

They spread out their blankets and used their damp towels on top for extra warmth. Dee crammed garbage bags of stuffed animals on the front and back dashes, blocking the windshields, and mostly covered the side windows with pillowcases. She didn't know which made her feel safer, the fact that nobody could look in or that the black night was blocked out.

Eddie fell asleep in his bed up front as Dee settled into the backseat, ears alert for any strange noises. Nothing. Just the distant sound of a car or two, the rustle of the wind in the playground trees, the slight, rhythmic creak of the swings.

She was beyond tired, curled up, half-asleep, the day seeping away from her. *Up at six, drive for twelve hours, swim for three and a half...long day. A long day ending here in...*For a minute she couldn't even remember where they were. Nothing. They were beside a dumpster, she knew that. But where was the dumpster?

She couldn't place the town or state, not anything about where they were.

Where in the world *were* they? She lay rigid in the dark in a fog of worry and fatigue, trying to figure it out, trying to retrace the path that had led them to this moment. And just when she was starting to grope over the seat to make sure Eddie was still there, she thought of her mother. She was laughing, looking right at Dee, her brown eyes crinkled up, her long, dark hair rumpled.

A tear slipped out of Dee's eye, sliding a warm path down her cheek onto the pin-pricked vinyl seat.

Home.

The word slipped into her mind, clear and clean.

Home. We're going home.

Dee woke to a rhythmic, distant beeping. In a haze of sleep confusion, she turned onto her back, knees bent, listening. It was a truck-backing-up sound, she decided. Nobody honks like that other than backer-uppers.

Won't it be nice, if we ever get out of this car, to wake up to some other sound? Something other than honking, beeping traffic sounds? Anything else.

A loud crash had Dee jackknifing bolt upright, straining to pinpoint just how close it was. She ripped the pillowcase from the window and looked out. A garbage truck across the playground was lowering a recently emptied dumpster. It turned and moved slowly in their direction. *It's coming here. To this dumpster,* she thought wildly. *Our dumpster, the one directly beside us.*

Dee scrambled into the front seat, shoved Eddie over and ripped the garbage bag full of stuffies from the front dash. She turned the ignition. It made an unfamiliar *whirwhir* sound and would have died had Dee not hit the gas pedal—hard. She slammed the car into Drive, and they shot out of their spot by the dumpster and screeched left just as the garbage truck turned into the back lot.

Dee gritted her teeth as the car lunged and bumped off a curb. *Wouldn't it be nice, if we ever get out of this car, to not have to flee like escaped convicts every single frigging morning?*

Eddie was still cocooned in his blankets, half on the seat, half in the footwell.

"What the *hell?*" he said as he struggled onto the seat.

"Don't say *hell,*" Dee said automatically.

"*You* do," he snapped, huddling deeper into his blankets.

I thought I only thought it.

She pulled the car over in a spot at the far end of the rec-center parking lot. She put the car in Park but didn't shut off the engine.

"Sorry about that, Eddie. But there was a garbage truck coming to empty that dumpster we parked beside. Didn't want him to miss and shake us into his truck." She held her hands like the prongs of the truck, raising their car and shaking it. "Whole new meaning to the phrase 'dumpster-diving.'"

Eddie laughed, delighted with the image of them falling through the air into a pile of garbage. He sat up and looked around. The garbage truck was disappearing down a residential street.

"We sure will have some funny stories to tell Dad, hey, Dee?"

"Yeah. Auntie Pat and Uncle Norm too." If the car lasted, they could make the Canadian border today. *And then what?* She took a few deep breaths.

"So…breakfast?" Eddie shivered and checked his watch. "6:07 AM. Saturday, July 26."

"We really are getting some good early starts here, hey?" Dee muttered. "I figure we should drive a while, then stop to get something to eat, okay?"

She didn't want to turn off the engine, and there was nobody else around, so Eddie peed on the grass outside the car while Dee looked away and held up the open map like a curtain. He climbed into the backseat, and then they headed out into the misty Pocatello morning, back to the I-15.

"Still north, hey?" said Eddie as they swung onto the ramp.

"Always."

"Someday want to drive west? Or east? Just to see what those directions look like?"

"You bet. I hear southwest rocks."

"Probably northeast as well. Or northwest or southeast. All of 'em. Once we finish this trip north, we can maybe try out some other way."

"Deal," said Dee, happy to promise anything for the future.

They split their last granola bar for breakfast.

MONTANA

SATURDAY

Blackfoot, Idaho Falls, Roberts and Dubois, and that's all there was of Idaho.

"Aaaand *adios* Idaho," Dee murmured as the border sign came up on their right. One more state to go.

Eddie sat up eagerly.

"*Welcome to Montana. The Treasure State!*" he read.

"Don't get your hopes up, Eddie." Was it her imagination, or was every day repeating itself? She looked around at the mountains in the distance. At least Montana looked kind of interesting.

Dee had been so afraid to stop the car that she thought they must be dangerously low on gas. On the outskirts of Butte she pulled into the next station she saw. Eddie was desperate to get out of the car. He was finding it increasingly hard to sit for so long. Dee glanced at him in the rearview mirror every so often to find his eyes fixed intently on her, willing her to pull over. Or she'd notice him rocking rhythmically from side to side. Like a caged animal. Panicky.

Dee anxiously watched the meter as the gas burbled into the car. She tallied her stash as she stood there. They had less than two hundred and fifty dollars left.

Eddie ran around the deserted lot.

"Hmmm, looks like a gas station, another building and a *restaurant!*" he called. He trotted back, his face intent. "Dee, how about getting a burger?" he asked. "With fries?" He linked his thin hands together tightly, as if in prayer.

She hesitated. We have zero car food left. So if we eat a big meal now, we won't need a real dinner. Maybe we could buy a few apples and granola bars. In a few quick calculations, lunch and dinner were solved.

"Hey, good idea," she said, turning back to the pump. Forty-two more dollars gone. "Just let me pay for the gas."

The diner was tiny, with only a few tables and four stools at a counter. Someone had put in a lot of work to make the place homey. One wall was covered in framed sayings. *Bless this Mess. Home is Where the Heart is.* Fake window frames had been painted on the dark paneling; beyond the windows brilliant white sheep grazed in fields of fluorescent green at the foot of craggy mountains. Bizarre Switzerland theme we got going here, Dee thought.

A shelf about three feet from the ceiling ran all around the restaurant. Dolls, tons of them, sat splay-legged in varying states of stiff vacancy, staring sight-lessly down. Old dolls, the kind that weren't smiling and pink-lipped. Grim, watchful, dusty, pioneer-style dolls. Dolls for unsmiling girls in black-and-white pictures.

Eddie looked at the doll collection and shivered.

"Creepy," he whispered. "Imagine when it's *dark* in here. When it's night."

"I know. *There's* your ghost story, Eddie."

The place was empty, and they hesitated in the doorway.

"Counter seats!" Eddie pointed at the stools.

A thin, small woman bustled in from behind the Swiss mountains, wiping her hands on a tea towel.

"Sorry, sorry, heard you come in, but I had potatoes on the boil. Is it just the two of yas?" She grabbed two menus and gestured widely. "Looks like you got your pick."

They settled at the counter, and the woman disap-peared again.

"No spinning, Eddie," Dee said, noting the revolving seats. "Absolutely *no* on the spinning, okay? At least while she's around."

Eddie, who was gripping the edge of the counter with both hands, ready to launch, stopped and pretended he was getting in a good stretch. They had a minor scuffle over the menu.

"You should have *milk*, Eddie," Dee said. "For your bones. Okay? Do it for your bones. I'm not even *mentioning* vegetables." *This must be how mothers sometimes feel, hating having to nag, hating the sound of their own nagging voices...*

Eddie had his heart set on the burger platter, which seemed to come only with soda. They compromised eventually. Dee got a salad and milk with her burger, Eddie got fries and coke with his, and they shared, switching beverages. Better than the handfuls of Corn Pops he's been living off, she thought. Mental note: toothbrushes. And fruit. She watched Eddie smear ketchup meticulously down the length of each fry. He had dark smudges under his eyes. He was very, very thin. How had she not noticed how thin he'd gotten? *Oh God, he's a little bag of bones. Has he got scurvy or something?* She made him eat a cherry tomato.

"Heading through Butte?" asked the waitress. She sounded almost envious. "Nice day for driving."

"Sure is," agreed Dee. *What I mean is, if I never drive another day in my life, it will be too soon.* "We're not going far. Our relatives are just past Butte." *A looong way past Butte.* She shot Eddie a warning look. He rolled his eyes. The waitress wasn't really interested—she was just passing the time.

They were all done except for the milk. Eddie was fake gulping, overdoing it as usual with very obvious *glug, glug, glug* sounds.

"Eddie, if you don't actually drink that milk," Dee warned...*what? What can I threaten? We're not getting back in that car? We're not driving endlessly anymore? We'll turn that car right back to Arizona, mister?*

He ignored her, grinning, twirling on the stool. *Frigging little grinning skeleton.*

"You know what, Eddie? Forget it. I don't care if you drink the milk. Your bones can crumble to little bits for all I care."

Eddie caught at the counter, shot her a worried look, grabbed the glass and drank it back, real swallows convulsing his thin throat. He finished, grimaced and wiped his mouth with his sleeve, like he could wipe away the taste.

"My bones feel better already," he said, trying to catch Dee's eye. She ignored him, stood up, grabbed the check and rummaged in her bag.

"WAIT!" Eddie said, jumping out of the seat and shoving an arm down into his pocket. "Remember, Dee? I'm paying." He slapped the crumpled couch-twenty down on the counter. "*My* treat!"

"Oh yeah, forgot about that," she said. "Well, thanks, Mr. Moneybags. It was a great burger."

"I'm going to tell her to keep the change," he said.

"What? No way—"

"Dad always says that. 'Keep the change.' Why can't I?"

Because we may really need that ten bucks.

"Well, it's too much for a tip. It's a nice idea, Eddie, but it's *way* too much for a tip. How about *I* leave the tip, and *you* keep the ten bucks? You know, to buy something..."

"Yeah, okay," he said, warming to the idea. "A souvenir of our vacation."

"You kids drive safe, hey?" said the waitress, turning to two other diners coming into the restaurant. Rumpled, stiff-legged highway people, smoothing their hair, pulling up a chair in Switzerland to eat burgers under the watchful dolls. Dee and Eddie walked into the small store to buy two apples and two granola bars.

Coming out of the washroom, Dee saw a sign that said *Parts and Service*. A man in coveralls was bending over the open hood of a car. Dee hesitated.

"Just a sec, Eddie," she said and ran over to the man.

"Excuse me, sir, but I'm just wondering if you could take a quick look at our car. The engine's making a funny noise. It's probably nothing serious, but if you have a minute, just a second, I'd appreciate it—" Dee stopped. *And I'm being all casual because I can't afford to pay you almost anything or actually get you to fix the car if it is wrecked. So basically, Mr. Official-Looking Mechanic, I just want you to glance at it, laugh and say, "Oh, that. You've been worrying about* that? *That's nothing. Get out of here, you crazy kids."*

The mechanic straightened and nodded in the direction of their car.

"That yours? Heard it come in. Probably transmission."

"Is that bad? Is transmission bad?" Dee babbled as she and Eddie trailed after him. He was a tubby, grubby man who walked purposefully, short arms pumping, leading with his stomach.

He reached in through the window with an oil-blackened hand, popped the hood and disappeared behind it.

"Start 'er up," he said.

Surprisingly, the car started easily, as if taken unawares. Dee left it running and motioned Eddie into the backseat.

The man straightened and banged the hood shut.

"Yeah, transmission's probably shot," he said with finality, wiping his filthy hands on a filthy rag.

"So…" Dee said, "is that a fixable thing or what?"

"Gotta replace it. Can't do it here."

"Why not?" asked Dee with a sinking feeling.

"Big job. Old car like this, might not be worth it. Yer lookin' at five, six hunnerd dollars," he said. Dee felt sweat start to bead on her upper lip. Eddie was sitting very still and silent.

"How far do you think we can get with the car as it is?" she asked.

"I don't know. Thirty, forty miles? Maybe less. Maybe a lot less. Just going to get worse. Where you headin'?"

"Great Falls," she said, the last city she could remember before the border.

He shrugged.

"Good luck," he said over his shoulder as he walked away.

What does he know? Dee floored it out of the gas station. *Small-town hick mechanic. Doesn't even do big jobs.*

"Don't worry," she said out loud to Eddie. "I'm sure it's nothing." She caught his eye in the rearview mirror. "What does he know? Small-town hick mechanic like that? Doesn't even do big jobs, probably doesn't know anything about cars..."

"Yeah," Eddie agreed. "We've had this car *forever*." He nodded, staring out the window. "That town looks a little like *our* town." It came as a shock to remember that Eddie didn't know that Santacino *had been* their town. Past tense.

That mechanic guy reminds me of somebody back in Santacino, Dee thought. Who? Got it. Charlie Rivera, owner (he would say proprietor) of Charlie Rivera's Antique Emporium. Not in the way he looked, but in the way he was. Definite. Sure of his business.

"Sometimes he's a real pain in the butt," her dad once said to her after Charlie had rejected a desk he had thought was valuable, "but Charlie sure knows his stuff. He's always, *always* right."

Dee stared at the highway, tense and listening to the car's every sound.

Maybe Charlie Rivera was always right.

But that guy wasn't Charlie Rivera. Not really.

The car died. It happened while they were twisting their way through the mountains, snaking along the river, after they'd laughed at the sign that said *Got Cows? We Got Bulls!* Dee didn't even realize the car was dead until she felt their speed slackening. She tried accelerating, but there was no response because the alive part of the car wasn't there anymore. It was only a metal box on wheels, like a big wagon or a wheelbarrow. The shell of a dead car.

"Shit! Shit, shit, *shit!*" Dee wrestled the near-dead car over to the right and coasted slowly off the highway onto the gravel shoulder.

"Hey, why are we stopping, Dee? You see a bull?" Eddie strained to look out the windshield. There were no bulls. There was nothing. They were in the middle of nowhere.

"Just...*quiet*, okay?" Dee sat silently, trying to choke back the panic that clawed inside her chest. With clammy hands, she shoved the gearshift into Park, an automatic, useless action. She had an ominous feeling that they were pretty much parked forever.

Breathe. Just take a deep breath.

It was quiet on the highway, quiet in the car, Eddie frozen like prey in the backseat. She could feel his tension spiraling up to meet hers.

She reached out and turned the key. *Click.* An empty little click, a dead click. No meaning to it.

A ride-on-toy-car click. The sound and feel of flicking a dead light switch.

Click. She tried it again. *Click, click, click. Click. Click.* Whatever ghost had animated this beat-up car for almost twenty years had gone. Dee slowly lowered her head to the steering wheel and closed her eyes.

Please, God, please bring this car back to life, just to get us to the border. We need it. Oh, please, oh, please, oh, please…We need to get to Auntie Pat. Help me get Eddie to Auntie Pat.

She tried it again. *Click.* Nothing. *Click. Click. Clickclickclick.* Dee turned the key so hard she thought she'd snap it. It was no use. She stared sightlessly down at her white knuckles gripping the useless steering wheel.

"Dee?" Eddie's voice was very little.

She opened her door, got out, turned and slammed it shut with all her might. Eddie jumped, then scrambled out his side.

Dee swung around, glared up and down the desolate highway, then turned back to the car. She gave her door a vicious kick. Then another and another. She kicked it again and again and again, crying, ranting in between kicks, "You stu-pid, stu-pid car! You shi-tty, fu-cking car!" She stopped when her foot began to throb.

Eddie watched her face, his own worried, uncertain.

Finally, still crying, Dee limped over to the gravel and sat down, right on the ground, her head in her hands.

Her right foot was throbbing with pain, as if the kicking had opened up a separate pulse on her big toe.

Eddie ran around to the backseat, poured water on his still-damp cutoff sweats, then dabbed gingerly at her bleeding big toe. The residual chlorine made it sting.

"It's okay, Dee, it's not cut so bad. I've got a Band-Aid at the bottom of my backpack. Stay here, okay?" Eddie put a hand on her shoulder, as though afraid she might bolt into the woods that lined the highway. She nodded, trying to control herself, not trusting her voice.

When Eddie had bandaged up her toe, Dee poured some of the water from the bottle into her hands and rubbed her face. She couldn't seem to stop crying.

"It's okay, Dee. It'll be okay." Eddie crouched beside her. "Somebody'll help us. You'd help a couple of kids on a highway, right? So would Dad. Somebody'll stop." He was talking quickly, eagerly, trying to convince her, trying to convince both of them.

"Who knows?" he continued. "Maybe even *Dad* will be coming along on one of those buses to meet up with us, and he'll see us and we'll all go to Canada together!" He opened his eyes wide and held out his hands, trying to convince her of this best-case scenario he'd invented on the spot.

Dee shook her head, her face blotched and red with crying. She ground her dirty palms into her eyes.

"Oh, Eddie, you don't understand!" *Stop it, stop right now!* But she couldn't stop. "Dad's not coming, okay?

He's *not*. I don't know where he is. I have *no idea*, okay? It's just *us*, Eddie. Just us." She stared across the highway at the mountains in the distance, gulping and gasping and sobbing. She was appalled that she'd just dumped all this on Eddie.

Eddie froze.

"What do you mean? About Dad."

Dee didn't answer.

"Dee? Do you mean Dad's...dead?" he asked in a small, uncertain voice.

"No! Of course not. Probably not. I don't know."

Eddie sat down on the gravel beside her.

"So we're not going back home," Eddie said. A statement, not a question.

Did he mean *home* as in the hot shack in the desert? Did he mean the life they'd had before? Or Dad?

"Not back to Santacino, Eddie. We go back and those government people might put us with another family, and maybe even in different homes. I don't know for sure, but that's what could happen." Dee pressed her fingers hard to her eyes, trying to stop the tears that just kept coming. She gave a long, shaky, watery sigh. *I shouldn't have done this, I should be the adult, I shouldn't be burdening him with all this, he's just a little kid...*She turned to Eddie and grabbed his hand. She felt it grab back.

"Sorry, Eddie." She managed a wobbly half smile. "Just...sorry. Look, we have each other, right?"

"Right."

They sat in silence.

Finally, when her tears dried up, she glanced at Eddie.

"You okay?" she asked.

"Yeah. Just thinking." Silence.

"Come on, Dee," said Eddie suddenly, hopping to his feet and hauling at her arm.

"What?" she said, scrambling awkwardly to her feet. She gasped as a sharp pain seared through her right foot. *Serves me right if I broke my toe in my little trash-the-car hissy fit.*

"We should get our backpacks out of the car and start walking. We got to be near *someplace*," Eddie said.

"Well, we can't be that far from Great Falls."

"Yeah! A city! Somebody might even give us a *ride* there, and then they could tow our car there and fix it!" Eddie looked around as though an obliging tow truck was just hovering around the bend, waiting to be summoned.

Oh, Eddie, we don't have enough money to tow this piece of junk or to get it fixed. You heard the man, who turned out to know what he was talking about—it's not even worth fixing. We probably don't even have enough money for bus fare for two to the border.

Dee smiled shakily. "Sounds like a plan."

They stuffed their backpacks as tight as they would go. Eddie took the Utah salt and the scorpion shell and walked away from the rest of his collections without a backward glance.

Dee shoved everything she could fit into her back-pack. Water. Money. Passports. Picture of Mom and Dad. She dug the car registration and insurance out of the glove compartment and stuffed them in her pocket. May as well not advertise who they were. She limped around to peer at the license plate. Arizona plate. Unusual up here, and someone could certainly trace the number. She gave it a little pull—bottom, then top. It was welded on solidly by bolts, rust, heat and age. Without tools it would be impossible to get the thing off. The best she could do was scrub some dirt over it so someone would actually have to stop to investigate it.

Dee straightened and saw Vera, the aloe vera plant, on the back-window ledge. She couldn't very well carry Vera with them without looking completely deranged, but somehow the image of the plant getting crushed and junked along with the car was too much for Dee.

"C'mon, Eddie. We have to do something before we start walking."

They took Vera down into the scrubby bushes by the fence lining the highway, Dee picking her way slowly on her throbbing foot. They scraped a shallow hole in the dry, rocky dirt with the dull blade of Eddie's Swiss Army knife, pulled Vera from her pot and planted her, stamping gently around the base of the plant with their feet. Dee showered Vera with the last drops from one of their water bottles. Among the spindly Montana pines, Vera looked squat and exotic.

"Think Vera'll make it, Dee?" Eddie asked.

"Yeah, I do," said Dee, nodding slowly. "She's a little survivor, Eddie. She survived *us*." Baked, cracked soil, dust coating her fleshy limbs, sitting forgotten on that nothing shelf too high above the kitchen table, Vera had, inexplicably, survived.

They climbed back up to the highway, Dee closest to the road, Eddie on the shoulder, and started walking north. Dee's right foot screamed with pain, so she hobbled slowly, relying on the heel of her foot, sparing the toes. Eddie pulled ahead, slowed to let her catch up, then darted forward again, picked up a rock, tossed it aside.

She didn't know if they should hitchhike openly, with their thumbs out like those people in the seventies movies her dad watched, or just hope that somebody who was not a murderous criminal would take pity on them. Dee thought it might be safer to just walk into Great Falls. Longer, more painful, but less dangerous.

Before they rounded a bend, Dee looked over her shoulder and caught a last glimpse of their car, listing at an angle on the side of the road. It felt strange abandoning it, walking away from the bit of security it offered. The car had been more than just transport. It had been protection, safety. It had hard sides and doors that locked. It was shelter.

They kept walking, two small, soft figures out in the wide open.

An hour of walking brought them to a sign: *Great Falls 19.*

Nineteen miles? Nineteen more miles? Dee's foot was throbbing so badly that she felt light-headed with pain. Another nineteen miles on it was completely, totally impossible. It made her sick to her stomach to think of it.

"Eddie, I think we have to try to wave some car down. I can't go much farther. My foot's killing me."

They turned to face the empty highway, raising their thumbs. Eddie had his right arm straight out, straining and extending it as far as it would go at each passing car, like a horizontal version of the eager kid in class who really, really knows the answer. Dee was more self-conscious, lifting an apologetic thumb, slightly shamed by the public appeal. They walked on, turning when they heard the occasional rumble of a car.

People are too scared to pick up hitchhikers, Dee thought, catching the eye of a startled single woman in a red SUV. No normal people hitchhike anymore. Her parents had hitchhiked around Europe after they were first married. But that was back then. That was Europe.

Half an hour passed, and only one car sped past.

"Not too close, Eddie," Dee warned, pulling him back from a feverish appeal. "You're doing great, it's just, you know, we want to be *live* hitchhikers, okay?"

A beat-up gray car slowed as it passed them, then pulled over onto the shoulder. Its indicator stayed on, blinking at them.

"Got one!" Eddie yelled. He grabbed Dee's hand and pulled her forward. "Hurry, before he changes his mind!"

When they got to the car, the man leaned over and popped open the passenger-side door. His eyes slid over both of them. "Hop in, kids," he said with a smile. "Little one in the back. You," he nodded at Dee, "up here." He patted the seat beside him.

Dee hesitated. There was something about this man with the sweaty face and the big smile that made her hesitate. He's giving orders pretty quick here, she thought. But she was light-headed with pain, desperate to sit down, and they couldn't get into Great Falls on their own. They didn't have a lot of options. She reached for the door handle, but Eddie pulled her back, squeezing her hand hard. She felt his sharp nails dig into her palm.

"You know what, Dee?" he said in a loud, fake voice. "We forgot Auntie Pat! Remember, she's coming to get us?" He looked at her intently, his eyes widening in warning. "Sorry, mister, we don't need a ride anymore." He tugged on Dee's arm, walking them away from the car, farther down the highway.

"Sorry," Dee called back, feeling stupid. Why did she feel a sudden wave of relief that they hadn't gotten into that car? When they were out of earshot, Dee said, "I know that guy was weird, Eddie, but we actually really do need a ride."

"Yeah, but we don't need one from just *anybody*. That guy was just...not a good guy. He didn't even ask us where we were going. And he told me to go in the backseat and *you* to go in the front. Why couldn't we *both* go in the back? And why isn't he at his job or something?"

"I don't know. Isn't it Saturday? He might be traveling like us."

"Didn't have any luggage or anything. Anyway, he wasn't...he didn't...he seemed *hungry*." That was true. Dee knew exactly what he meant. She had noticed the man's bitten-down nails and shiny face and felt his intensity.

"Yeah, you're right. We'll wait for someone else."

Dee glanced back over her shoulder. The gray car was still there, the man sitting still, watching them. The highway was deserted.

"Let's get going, Eddie."

Behind them they heard the car door slam and the man call, "Hey!"

Eddie looked back.

"Why has he gotten out of his car, Dee? Why is he calling us?" There was an edge of panic to his voice. Dee turned. The man was staring straight at them, walking toward them.

"Go *away*," shrieked Eddie, his face red, the veins in his neck popping. His whole body went into the yell— he jumped off the ground with it.

"C'mon." Dee grabbed his hand. Eddie's panic had somehow nudged her fear into rage. *You don't care that you're terrifying a little boy, you asshole. You know it and you don't even care. I've never been in a fight in my life, but I will fight you, I swear to God. I will use every single dirty trick Charlie Rivera taught me after his daughter got groped that time. Sharp knee to the groin. Punch to the throat. Keys slashing eyes. Forehead cracking forehead.*

They were trapped between the highway and the train tracks off to the right. Even if they scrambled over the fence and over the train tracks, there were only a few bushes, a few trees in the distance. There was nowhere to hide, no cover at all. *Plus, our chances of getting someone else to help us are zero if we're over in the bush somewhere. It'd be him against us. Stay on the highway, where someone might see us. We have to stay on the highway.* Dee dug in her pocket, threading the car keys through the fingers of her right hand. *We are not getting into that man's car. Never. Eddie was so right...*

The man was still walking toward them, a slight smile on his face now, like he had all the time in the world. Like he was enjoying this.

"Looks like you need a ride after all," he called.

Why is he doing this? Oh, God, what the hell does he want? Dee and Eddie broke into a run, Dee limping painfully. *I'm too slow. This is never going to work. I'm going to have to fight him. What if another car comes by, what if he says, "It's okay, it's my girlfriend and my kid." What then?*

Then he's got us. I have to talk first, scream, call him out for being a psycho. Think, think...

"Eddie," she gasped desperately, "you might have to run for it." *Keep yourself between him and Eddie.*

"No, no, just *c'mon!*"

Eddie grabbed her arm and hauled her along like a little dog straining on a leash. Dee glanced back over her shoulder. The man was jogging after them, closing on them. But behind him, a huge truck had just rounded the bend of the highway. As it barreled toward them, Dee shoved Eddie to the shoulder and ran right onto the highway, blocking its path, waving her arms, yelling, "Stop! Stop!"

This truck will stop for us. It will. It will have to run me down to get by us.

"It's stopping, Dee!" shouted Eddie. "The blinker! The innicator! It's pulling over!" Dee dropped her arms in relief, scuttling back to Eddie.

The truck's right indicator was on, and it puffed and wheezed over to the shoulder of the highway. They heard the man behind them yell something unintelligible over the rumbling of the big truck. He had stopped running.

Dee and Eddie ran toward the truck, Dee gasping at the pain shooting up her leg with each pounding step. When they reached it, the driver was just walking around the front to meet them. A small person, shorter than Dee, hands in sweatpants pockets, wearing a ballcap and enormous wraparound school-bus-driver sunglasses.

"What's up, kids? That guy bugging you? You looked pretty frantic there." The trucker stared over at the man, who had turned and was walking back to his car.

"Yeah," gasped Dee. "He stopped to offer us a ride, but he seemed weird so we didn't want to go with him, and then he started coming after us. Thank you *so* much for stopping."

"That guy's a *creeper*," said Eddie, his face fierce.

"Jee-zus. Asshole."

"Yeah," agreed Eddie.

"Our car broke down," said Dee. "It's back there."

"Sucks. Yeah, saw a broke-down car on the shoulder back there."

The man in the car roared past them. His face was set and hard, and he didn't even glance over at them.

"Mudded-up plates," said the trucker. "Not good. Glad you kids trusted your instincts. Got 'em for a reason."

The trucker held out a small, surprisingly strong hand.

"Name's Murphy. Friends call me Murph." Dee and Eddie both shook the driver's hand. "Okay, better hit the road. I'm guessing you were heading into Great Falls. Glad you stopped me. Bad back. Needed a stretch."

Dee saw that Eddie was relaxed and happy, eager to climb into the big rig. No spidey senses about this driver, although, objectively speaking, Murph was even weirder-looking than the man in the car. But there were lots of different kinds of weird. Scary-weird was a world away from just odd-weird. *Thank you for stopping, Murph, whoever you are.*

Dee grabbed the rail, took a big step with her pulsing foot and pulled herself up awkwardly into the cab after Eddie.

"It's like we're driving a *hill*," Eddie said as they looked down at the winding highway snaking in front of them. It was the first time on the entire trip that Dee had really noticed the scenery. She was so glad to rest her foot, and grateful to be a passenger. Relieved to be relieved of responsibility, if only for a little while.

The cab of the truck smelled of stale coffee and sun on vinyl. A green cardboard car freshener in the shape of a pine tree dangled from the mirror, coughing out the weak remains of its acrid chemical pine smell as it bobbed. A collection of lapel pins, hundreds of them, hung behind the bench seat, affixed to long shoelaces tied down at both ends. They swayed and clicked on bumps and turns. Eddie was mesmerized by the rows of pins: state flags, sports teams, places, festivals, cute sayings. The Denver Broncos logo, the Rolling Stones lips, the Statue of Liberty, Minnie Mouse, *Keep Calm and Carry On*, *Keep On Truckin'*. Eddie contributed a small cactus pin that he had on his backpack.

"We got them free, from school. The saguaro cactus is Arizona's state plant."

"Now that's one I *don't* have. Not one cactus. I know that without even looking. Thank you, little man. Gonna frame all those when I retire and sit still."

Eddie, sitting in between Dee and Murph, listened in fascination as Murph grunted out the names of the controls. He looked at Dee in excitement when the radio crackled. Murph answered it, a quick, gruff, mystifying exchange overriding the wailing country-music CD.

Dee began noticing billboards along the highway, advertising motels in Great Falls. *Free Wi-Fi and Waterslides 10 mins ahead!* Ten minutes...

"So, Murph, where exactly are you headed?" Dee asked, interrupting Eddie's questions about what kind of cargo Murph carried.

"North. Canada. Edmonton, this time. Then out east."

Dee's heart leaped. She turned in her seat to face Murph, her face serious and anxious.

"Murph, can we come with you? To Canada? Just to Calgary. That's really where we're heading. I could pay you something. Gas! I could pay for some gas." How much gas does a monster truck like this gulp? Dee wondered after she said it, her hand absently checking her front pocket.

Murph looked over at Dee and sighed.

"Into Canada? Look, don't want to pry, but you kids just heading on into Canada by yourselves? Where're your folks?"

"Long story," said Dee. "But we've got an aunt near Calgary. We really do. In Rolling Wood. They own Rolling Wood Greenhouse and Gardens. She's expecting us." *Okay, that's stretching the truth a bit. Poor Auntie Pat doesn't know what's coming.*

Murph digested this in silence.

"You runaways?" Murph asked finally.

"No!" She and Eddie said it indignantly at the same time. To them, runaways were kids with mean families, kids living on the streets, kids living rough. Tough kids with the courage or the desperation to leave dismal, dangerous situations.

But an honest little voice inside Dee said, *Actually, runaways exactly describes what we are. We've run away. We got scared and we ran, and we've been living out of our stupid, recently deceased car. But somehow runaway sounds like a word for other kinds of kids from other kinds of families.*

Dee felt an uneasy kinship with the kids she was imagining. It's not their fault, she thought. I'll bet it's almost never the kids' fault. And yet being called a runaway makes it sound like the kid is the problem.

"Honestly, Murph, we're just going up to our aunt's place. Our dad is coming up later." *This story sounds thinner and thinner the more I tell it. I'm guessing that most normal parents don't usually send the kids first.*

"Well, look," Murph said. "Take you to the border crossing. No promises. There's laws. Especially with kids. They'll figure it all out."

"Thanks," said Dee. "Thanks a lot, Murph."

Eddie found her hand and squeezed it. *Things are looking up*, the excited squeeze said.

Dee squeezed his hand back and forced a smile. *There's laws. Especially with kids…*Everything, *everything* hinged on the border crossing.

How long does it take to find and trace a car abandoned on the side of a highway? How quickly will that be done? I should've tried harder to get that license plate off. Please, God, send out some slack-ass state trooper who doesn't get around to it for a few days, the kind of guy who just lets the old paperwork pile up on his desk…

What day is today?

"Eddie, what day is it?"

"Saturday, July 26, 2014."

Murph gave a gruff, snorting laugh at Eddie's precision.

Saturday! That might be good. They won't put out an alert on the car until at least Monday. Nice, scary social worker Susan was supposed to come Friday—was that really only yesterday? So she and her gang of children-rounder-uppers haven't had much time to put out an alert either. And if they did, would it only be in Arizona, or does that immediately go country-wide?

There's laws. Especially with kids…what laws? What laws was Murph talking about? Laws about kids going over the border without their parents, obviously. Laws about kids being taken over the border by other people.

All this elaborate, frigging child protection supposedly for our benefit, so why do I keep feeling so completely unsafe?

Do we get a phone call at the border if they detain us? We must get a phone call. Everyone gets a phone call. I've seen the shows. Even hard-core criminals like murderers get a phone call.

Are Auntie Pat and Uncle Norm back from BC yet? What if they aren't? Who would...what would...

The panicky thoughts whirled through Dee's head behind her blank, impassive face. She stared out the window, chewing the inside of her lip.

She watched a massive American flag on a hill billow and dance outside of a town called Shelby. The mountains had dwindled into the distance now, and up on a ridge to the left a line of wind turbines rotated slowly— arms outstretched to catch the breeze, falling as they caught it. She heard Eddie ask Murph how they turned "ordinary wind" into "actual electricity." The turbines looked so lonely up there on the rise, expectant, dependent on the whim of the wind. Dee had never seen one before, but they reminded her of something.

She puzzled it out, and a few minutes later she had it: they reminded her of the desert, of those lonely, viciously spiked figures with arms raised to the blistering sun.

Wind turbines: the cacti of the north.

THE
BORDER

SATURDAY

Sweetgrass, Montana (USA–Canada border crossing) 7.
The sign made Dee's stomach clench. Only seven miles.
Sweetgrass. A pretty name for a seriously scary place.

Murph made a throat-clearing sound, turned down
the music and looked over at Dee through those impenetrable sunglasses.

"Dee, some advice. Take it or leave it. When we get up
there, best be honest with them. They're trained to sniff
out, you know, when people are hiding stuff. Their job.
Just tell the truth."

"What if the truth is the problem?" Dee asked, trying
to make it sound like she was joking.

Murph considered this. "Well, then you got to lay it
on them. Make it *their* problem."

They drove in silence for a few minutes. Eddie was twisted around, strumming the shoelaces of pins like a harp.

"Hey," Murph said, "you want to stop at a gas station and give that aunt of yours a heads-up call? I gotta pee anyways."

"Yeah, good, that would be great."

Murph geared down, and the big truck juddered to a stop at the next gas station. Dee carefully climbed down, gingerly lowering herself onto her right foot. Still throbbing. Eddie launched himself from the seat and landed beside her in an ungainly, clattering free fall from the cab.

"Need to go, Eddie?" Dee asked.

"Nah," he said, watching Murph walk over to the restrooms. "Hey, Dee, is Murph a girl or a boy? Do you know?"

"I don't know. Girl, I think."

"I think boy," said Eddie.

Dee shrugged.

"Doesn't matter," said Eddie.

"Nope. C'mon, let's find a phone."

She gave Eddie money to buy a slush and watched him agonizing over the choices, levering down thin, precise strips of each bright flavor, which, in a few swishes of spoon-straw, would inevitably turn a deep, murky brown. There was no pay phone, but the woman behind the counter said Dee could make a call and even talked to the operator for her about reversing the charges. She handed the phone over to Dee.

"Just give her the number you want, honey," she said.

The phone rang five times before Jake picked it up.

"Rolling Wood Greenhouse and Gardens," he said. She started to say, "Hi, Jake," when the tinny official voice of the operator cut in.

"I have a Dee Donnelley on the line. Will you accept the charges?"

"Um, who? Oh, Dee! Yeah, okay, yes, I will accept the charges. Charges accepted." Jake was making an effort to sound official.

"Go ahead, please," said the voice. There was a click, and they were alone on the line. Dee pulled the phone cord as far as it would go, her back turned to the lineup of people paying for gas and junk food. She pressed her right hand over her free ear.

"Hi, Jake? It's Dee."

"Yeah, I know. The Donnelley part kind of threw me there. I thought you were McPherson, like Norm and Pat, but obviously not."

"You did great, Jake. Thanks. Look, I'm sorry I keep bugging you. Are they back yet?"

"Not yet..."

"Shit. I really, really need to talk to Auntie Pat. Like, you don't know how much I need to talk to her. We'll be at the border really soon, and I just..." Dee's voice thickened and stopped, and she screwed up her eyes to stop the tears. She's not there, she reminded herself. You can shut up now. And grow up. You can shut up and grow up.

"Dee? You okay? Yeah, Pat would take on those border patrollers. She'd be the one I'd want too," said Jake. "Look, what border crossing are you at?"

"Sweetgrass. That's Montana. It's 'Coots' or something on the Alberta side. At least, that's what Murph said."

"Who's Murph?"

"A trucker who's giving us a ride. Our car died." *I sound like such a case. I don't talk like this to anyone else, just blurting things out. What is it about this guy that makes me keep blurting things out? Maybe it's that he actually listens, poor sucker.*

"Oh, *man*..."

"Yeah, just died. I kicked the hell out of the door, probably broke my toe, we almost got picked up by a total psycho, and now we're heading to the border, where we'll probably get arrested or something. But other than that, everything's fine." She gave a shaky laugh, gripping the phone.

"Okay, that sounds like a trip from *hell*. Look, I'll do what I can, see if I can find Pat. *Someone* must know where they are. I'll talk to my parents and the greenhouse manager right away. We'll find them. Hang in there, okay?"

I think I love you, Jake.

"That's...thanks, Jake." She saw Murph walk up to Eddie outside the store, saw Eddie hold up his slush for admiration. "I gotta go. Thanks for listening to me. I'm such a whiner."

"No, no. All good. It's not like it's random whining. Sounds like you got lots to whine *about*. I'll whine to you sometime about this cat."

Sometime. A future "sometime." I like the sound of that.

Dee scrubbed at her face with her hand, then turned and thanked the woman behind the counter, who smiled absently, pulled the phone back over the counter and turned to a real, paying customer.

In the shade, without the sunglasses, Murph's eyes were a bleary, red-rimmed, pale blue. They looked moist and naked and unprotected, and Dee was relieved when the sunglasses slid back on.

"Well? All set?" Murph asked.

"Yeah. Ready to go," Dee lied.

"Ready, Eddie?" asked Murph. "Ready, steady Eddie?" Eddie, sipping the brown slush, smiled and nodded. They hauled themselves back into the big rig. Twenty thousand pounds of truck, fifty-five thousand pounds of trailer (assorted electronics) and three people hurtled toward the border.

The seven miles passed in a blink. A few gray buildings, five lanes leading up to five booths, and a sweeping arch protecting it all from the weather marked the border crossing. It was like the entrance to a national park, only with more lines, more booths, more Canadian flags.

And more security, Dee noted uneasily, counting five video cameras focused on each lane. Her hand holding their passports was sweating.

"Keep right/*garder la droite*," read Eddie, butchering the French with hard *r*'s, pronouncing *droite* like it rhymed with *Detroit*.

Dee leaned over to Eddie, speaking low enough that Murph couldn't hear.

"This is *really* important, Eddie," she said as they slid into the trucks-only line. "Like, you don't know how important. So when we get up to that little house thing, you have to be very quiet and leave the talking to me and Murph, okay?"

Eddie was sort of listening, but he was preoccupied with chasing the last trails of brown slush around the bottom of the plastic cup with loud, dry sucks on his straw. She gave him a sharp nudge, and he looked up.

"Okay," he said hurriedly, seeing her tense face. "Okay, Dee. Got it." He mimed turning an imaginary key at his mouth, tossing it over his shoulder.

"So, Murph," said Dee, keeping her voice casual, just interested. "What kind of questions do they ask you up there?"

"Oh, the usual stuff. 'Where you from?' 'Where you going?' 'Purpose of your travels?' 'Any fruits and vegetables?'"

Fruits and vegetables? Well, at least I can answer that one without lying.

"Have you been through this particular border crossing before, Murph?"

"Only about once every couple of weeks. On my regular route."

Murph sighed and looked over Eddie's head at Dee. The huge sunglasses made the look impossible to read.

"Look, Dee, I like you guys. But when that border officer's asking questions, I gotta be honest with them."

"I know, Murph."

"Don't know the situation. Can't lie."

"Wouldn't want you to," said Dee. *What a liar I am. Of course I want you to lie, Murph. I'd dearly love you to say, "These here are my sister's kids, just coming along for the ride," and floor it all the way to Calgary.*

They crawled forward steadily. Soon there was just one truck between them and the booth. Dee sat very still, studying the border officer. He didn't look at all like a slack-ass, unfortunately. He was a trim, athletic man of sixty or so in a dark blue uniform with a Canada Border Services crest on his sleeve. *Is that a bullet-proof vest he's wearing? It is. That is a genuine bullet-proof vest. God.* The officer was one of those military-type guys who semi-shouted rather than spoke. Dee could hear him from where she sat. He leaned out to bark a few questions at the driver in front of them. Dee watched him scrutinize a passport, ask some more questions, then wave the truck on.

Murph put the truck in gear and killed the country music mid-wail. Showtime. Dead silence as they slid up to the booth.

"*You* again," the border services officer (name tag: Randell Carmichael) bellowed at Murph, then his eyes slid past to settle on Eddie and Dee. "He-llo, you usually fly solo. Who you got there with you today?"

"Well, sir, this here's Eddie, that's Dee," said Murph. "Their car broke down. Picked them up on the I-15 outside of Great Falls."

The border services officer's white eyebrows rose. He frowned.

"How about I have a look at some passports." Dee handed hers and Eddie's to Murph, who passed them over.

"So we got Dee...aaand Eddie Donnelley," said the officer, comparing the pictures to their anxious real faces. Then he addressed Murph. "So you have no personal relation to these children?"

"No, sir."

"Just being a Good Samaritan, hey?"

"Helping out. They needed a lift." Murph paused and, staring straight ahead, added, "They're good kids."

The officer leaned in Murph's window, his sharp eyes resting on Dee's tense face. "I'm sure they are. You bet. No doubt about that." He said it automatically, his voice providing cover for his busy brain.

"So where did you kids drive up from before you broke down?"

"Arizona." Dee had been wondering how much of the truth she should divulge. But this man was no rookie officer; there was no hiding from those eagle eyes. *Everything but Dad. Tell them everything but that, and we'll get through to Auntie Pat's and then call down a missing person's alert when we're safely in Canada.*

"Arizona!" he barked. "All the way from the Grand Canyon State! Seen the canyon?"

Dee nodded and smiled faintly. Eddie stared straight ahead.

"Quite a trip. Were you living there or just visiting?" The officer's casual, conversational voice didn't fool Dee. Booth-to-truck conversations, where one of the people talking was wearing a bullet-proof vest and could put the other person in jail, were not casual.

Living or visiting? Can a visit last five years? Was it illegal for us to live there for all that time? Truth. Tell as much of the truth as you can.

"Living there."

"Gotcha. Now, Eddie, important question: are you having a fun summer?" the officer asked, turning his attention to Eddie. His voice changed, softened a bit for the young one. Eddie looked over at him blankly.

Dee nudged him. *I said to be quiet, not to go into your idiot-kid routine.* "He asked you a question, Eddie."

"Yup," said Eddie loudly to the dashboard.

Well, what's he supposed to say? "Yeah, super-fun, sir, running for our lives from perverts, sleeping in the car, driving until I go squirrelly in my own head, learning that my dad's gone and we're never going back home, watching my sister have a complete breakdown." Poor Eddie, what have we all done to you?

"Good stuff, good stuff. So why are you heading into Canada?" he persisted. Eddie's eyes snaked over to the officer and back to the dashboard.

"Visiting our Auntie Pat. And Uncle Norm."

"And where do they live?"

"Rolling Wood, Alberta."

"Nice place. I've been there. You can see the mountains clear as day, right from the center of town." Eddie didn't answer, but Dee knew he was intensely interested in the Rocky Mountains. He'd read her facts about them. Mount Robson was the highest peak. Marmots lived above the tree line. Grizzly bears were bigger and less common than black bears. Elk, though herbivores, should not be approached by people.

The officer glanced at Murph.

Here it comes. Here comes the million-dollar question. The question I don't even know the answer to: Where are your parents? "Tell the truth and put it all on them," Murph had said. "Make it their problem." How much truth? She stared fixedly at the officer.

"So where are Mom and Dad, Dee?" the officer asked, looking down and flipping through some papers, keeping up the pretense of casual chitchat.

"Our mom is…she passed away five years ago," said Dee, "and our dad is in Arizona. He'll be following us up here when he finishes his work. But our auntie Pat, my mom's sister, is expecting us. She invited us." Dee wiped her hands surreptitiously down the sides of her shorts.

The officer ignored Auntie Pat, batting her away and zeroing in on the real problem.

"Just so we're all clear, did your dad give you a letter of permission to cross into Canada unaccompanied? Anything like that?" *Well, shit! If I'd known that's what you needed, I could have forged that. Easy.*

"No. Sir. We didn't know we needed one." She tried out a smilingly confused look.

He didn't smile. He looked preoccupied. He was punching something into the computer.

"Granted, most kids don't walk around with permission letters hanging out of their pockets. Specially if they're visiting relatives. But we have to ask."

Murph sat silently during this exchange, looking straight ahead.

The officer wrote something down, gathered his papers and leaned out of his booth again. He handed back Murph's passport.

"So all clear for you, Murph. But if you could just pull the truck over there to let these kids hop out,

I'd appreciate it. Dee, here are your passports and a paper that you'll need to present to another border services officer inside those doors on your left. Don't actually know how long it will take…" He and Murph shared a look. "Have a good day, guys."

Murph pulled the truck over to the side.

So we're not just sailing through. Of course we aren't. How could I ever have been so stupid as to think we could? This is official customs-and-immigration shit. Even Dad couldn't smile and fudge the rules in this situation. Nobody can.

None of the other cars or trucks in the lineups Dee had watched had been pulled over. Nobody else had gone inside. More officers, more questions, computer searches and phone calls. That first border officer was just the beginning. She clutched their passports and the official-looking paper with a shaking hand.

"Sorry about this, Murph," muttered Dee.

"Sorry?" barked Murph. "What you got to be sorry about? Seems like you kids done pretty damn good to have got up here from *Arizona*. Look," said Murph, pulling out a beat-up wallet from a back pocket, "gonna give you my card. Cell's on there. You give me a call if y'ever…you know…well, anyways, here's the card."

"Thanks, Murph." Dee took the warm card and concentrated on it as her eyes blurred with tears. *Murphy J. Wilson Trucking Services* written in blue across a cartoonish red semi.

"C'mon, Eddie, we better get going."

"'Bye, Murph! Thanks!" Eddie turned to Murph, who held up a hand for Eddie's high five.

"See ya, bud. Thanks for the cactus."

They slid down onto the pavement.

"Good luck!" Murph called from the driver's window. They turned, squinting into the sun, and waved back.

That's exactly what we need now. Luck. A little luck.

They walked away from the truck, from the safety of Murph and the big rig, over to the doors of the gray building. *Somehow, opening this door seems like a significant act. Like we're frigging turning ourselves in, like this is the end of the road.* Dee lifted her chin, avoiding the stares of the bored car people waiting in line to whisk through effortlessly into Alberta. People with simple, uncomplicated lives. People who thought a border crossing was a necessary hassle, a mere nuisance that added another fifteen or twenty minutes to a long day's drive.

She caught Eddie's anxious look as they stopped at the doors emblazoned with the Canada Border Services crest.

"*Eddie and Dee Flee to Canada*, take two," she whispered, clapping her forearms together as if she were a director's assistant. Eddie giggled.

"Yeah," he said. "But maybe there's *food* in there. You think?"

"Maybe. Probably. Who knows?"

Who the hell knows what's going to happen in there, Eddie?

"Murph was nice, hey?" Eddie said.

"Yeah, sure was."

They looked back, but the truck was gone.

Dee pulled open the door and followed Eddie into the building.

While she was hovering at the counter, Dee heard a man's aggrieved voice coming from an office down the hall.

"...did *not* expect to have to pay so much duty on a *secondhand* Oldsmobile..."

A uniformed officer came over to them, holding out her hand for the paper Dee offered and looking past them for their nonexistent parents. Her dyed-red hair was pulled back tightly from her hard cop's face, shellacked there by some powerful spray.

She looked down at the paper, then up again quickly. Border officer number one had clearly heads-upped border officer number two.

"Oh. Right. Just have a seat for a sec."

As she turned away, Dee swiped two wrapped candies from a bowl on the counter and handed one to Eddie. On the television in the small waiting room CBC News blared the latest atrocities. Nobody else was in the waiting room, but Dee never even thought of muting it or changing the channel. You don't touch official stuff, even if it's a TV.

"Hey, Eddie, there's a water cooler. You want some water?" Dee asked in that abnormally low voice people use in doctor's offices. He jumped up, and Dee studied the bulletins and notices tacked on the corkboard. The rows of mug shots of Canada's Most Wanted seared into her skittish brain. *Imagine one of them coming at you on a deserted highway.* She looked closer, wondering if the Montana creeper was on the list.

Eddie busied himself pulling out too many cone-shaped paper cups, gulping water, ferrying one to Dee and filling up his again. Dee wandered the waiting room, idly watching footage of some uprising in Venezuela. As she watched the screen, she scanned the crowd footage, viewing it not just as a crowd but as a collection of faces. With a shock, she realized she was searching for a glimpse of her father. *Ridiculous. Ludicrous. What would he be doing in Venezuela? Is this how it's going to be for my whole life? Always thinking I might see him in a crowd? Scanning the faces on the news, always wondering?*

"Hey, easy on the water, Eddie. Bathroom there if you need it."

They waited in the chilly air-conditioning. People came out of offices, walked down the hall, giving them nothing more than curious glances. Dee tried to breathe slowly and control her heart rate. Eddie read lame jokes out loud from a book on the end table, *101 Canuck Yuks.*

"*What do you call a crying deer? A caribou-hoo-hoo.*" He frowned. "That's stupid. A deer isn't exactly the *same* as a caribou, so how would you guess that? Plus, it's not funny."

Finally border officer number two came back. "Okay, kids, if you could come with me, please."

She led them down the corridor, past the old guy still complaining about his Oldsmobile, and around the corner, pulling up at an office with a nameplate: *Officer Wilfred Crow.* She motioned them to sit on the chairs just outside the office, then double-knocked quickly, opened the door and poked her head into the office, murmuring something to the person inside. There was an answering murmur, and the officer glanced back at Dee and Eddie, stepped inside and closed the door.

Dee and Eddie sat looking at a large, slightly askew print of an oil derrick in a field at sunset. It looked like a giant bug, or an alien, with its long neck and metal snout feeding on the earth.

"What *is* that?" whispered Eddie, fascinated.

"Some kind of oil thing. Machine that gets it out of the ground somehow," Dee said absently. She was straining to pick out words from the rumbling exchange in the office. Nothing.

They both jumped as the office door opened suddenly.

"Okay, in you go," said the redheaded officer with a sweeping motion of her arms, shooing them in like cats. "Officer Crow here'll help you out."

An old guy with a short gray brush cut, a lined, fleshy face and thick glasses sat behind a desk, reading a sheaf of papers. His uniform looked like it was barely able to contain the body struggling underneath, his huge stomach rolling over a thick belt.

He glanced up. "Have a seat." They sat.

He flipped through the papers, straightened them and neatly paper-clipped the stack. He capped a pen, set it straight beside the papers and smoothed the computer mouse cord. *Oh, great. A control freak. A details guy.* She glanced around the bare, pristine office, hoping to find pictures of his children, grandchildren, evidence of him being a family man. She saw only a framed photo of an old, red-eyed bloodhound with a brass name plate: Roscoe.

The officer looked up to find Dee staring at him. She shifted her gaze just over his shoulder, but it was a fraction of a second too late.

"Dee and Eddie Donnelley." A statement, not a question. "I'm Officer Wilfred Crow," he said. He neither stood up nor offered to shake hands.

"Anything to drink?" he asked abruptly.

Booze? Is he asking us if we're carrying alcohol?

"Absolutely not, sir," Dee blurted.

The big man stared at her, then leaned back, hands over his paunch.

"No, I mean, would you like anything to drink?" He said it slowly, as if to non-English speakers. "Tea, milk...."

"Oh. No, thanks," Dee said, flushing. *Not for sale.*

"Do you have any hot chocolate?" Eddie asked excitedly. *Completely bought.*

"Could have." Officer Crow pressed a button on his phone and asked someone to "rustle up" a cup of hot chocolate.

He picked up and scanned the paper in front of him, then opened and shut each passport. The silence lengthened. Dee hoped he couldn't hear her heart hammering.

"This," he said, indicating the paper, "is irregular. Unusual." The keen eyes behind the glasses pinned them to their seats. "You two are unusual. Minors traveling without parental consent raise every red flag we got. Especially ones who've traveled all the way across the country. It's not like you're just cross-border shopping."

"Well, you see, our father is following—" Dee began.

"Yes, yes, I have all that. Your father is 'following you into Canada.'" He curled his thick fingers into air quotes. "He might have foreseen that there would be problems for the two of you arriving at the border without him." He sounded impatient. Their negligent father had made his kids a hassle. A problem. A nuisance.

Good—don't be mad at us, be mad at Dad. I'm kind of feeling that way myself.

"Upshot: You guys have to sit tight until I get a hold of him. And I have to make certain inquiries. Standard procedure."

"What kind of inquiries?" Dee asked.

"Well," he said slowly, glancing at Eddie, then back at Dee, "just have to run a check on a few databases." Missing children, Dee thought, and possibly something for criminals.

"We're going to visit my aunt in Rolling Wood, so you probably need her number as well." Dee stood up, fished the crumpled paper out of her crumpled pocket and slid it across the desk. "Her name is Patricia McPherson. My uncle is Norman McPherson. They own Rolling Wood Greenhouse and Gardens in Rolling Wood, Alberta."

She left the paper on the desk, and he made no move to pick it up.

A double knock and another officer, a younger man with short spiky hair, came in and set the hot chocolate and a couple of granola bars on the desk. "There you go, Wilfred," he said. He caught Dee's and Eddie's eyes and smiled. "Get you kids all sugared up."

"Thank you, Kevin," Crow said, without looking up from his writing.

He turned to his computer, one hand holding their open passports, thick fingers of the other hand poking at the keyboard. While he typed, Dee planned out exactly how much she would reveal. Sort of the truth. Their first priority, though, had to be to get hold of Auntie Pat. Focus on Auntie Pat. Once they were safely at her place, they could deal with where their dad was, report him missing, start some kind of search. The minutes ticked away on a military-style twenty-four-hour clock above the door: 15:21 hours—3:21 PM. Dee stared at Roscoe the bloodhound. A sad-looking dog, with his drooping eyes, his bunchy, moist jowls. Eddie blew circles into his hot chocolate and took little sips.

"Databases running," the border officer said, swiveling away from the computer. "Let's attempt to contact your father. Name of James Edward Donnelley, correct? Santacino, Arizona. Any *reason* he's not accompanying you? Any problems? Domestic issues?" His eyes were big, somehow enlarged by his thick glasses. Dee had the feeling of being under a microscope.

"No," said Dee, ignoring Eddie's quick look over at her. "He travels for his work. Antique dealer. He was away, so we decided to come up to visit our aunt, and Dad said he'd meet us up here." She looked him right in the eyes as she lied.

The thick glasses glinted back.

"Work number?"

"He mostly works from his home office." *Our junkyard of a living room. And a phone booth down the street.*

"Okay. Home number?"

"(520) 684-3891."

You'll soon find out that's been disconnected, but that's your problem. One of the first things to go when the money dried up.

"Cell phone?"

"Doesn't believe in them." Which was the truth, although it was also the truth that they cost money. She smiled and looked over at Eddie for confirmation, and he gave a confused, strained smile in return. "What's today? Saturday? Maybe he'd be in Tucson. Or Yuma. Flea markets and estate sales are big weekend things. He's mostly on the road."

"Then this might take some time."

You have no idea.

The real question, the big one, the one she wanted to ask but couldn't, was: *What happens to us when you can't find him?*

Officer Crow enlisted Kevin, the officer who had brought the drinks, to "show these kids around." Translation: get them the hell out of my hair for a while, Dee thought. Dee and Eddie trailed after Kevin through the border services offices while Officer Crow began making the doomed, futile calls to locate their father. Dee let him make them. There was just a chance that her father might have come back. But then, wouldn't he have called Auntie Pat's and talked to Jake?

"Aaand, through there, even *more* offices," said Officer Kevin. "Oh, wait, there's one thing you don't see every day." He led them down another beige hallway, past computers, flags, pictures of the queen and the prime minister, more offices, and finally over a glass-covered pedway.

Straight to a prison cell.

They have a jail in here? Dee started to panic, her eyes widening.

"Cool," breathed Eddie, running in and lying down on the cot.

Kevin saw the look on Dee's face and said quickly, "Rarely used, and we'd never, ever, put a kid in there. Strictly for the bad guys." He smiled.

"Hey, let me out, let me out! I promise I'll be a *good* guy!" Eddie wailed, a big grin on his face as he held the bars and looked out at them.

"Out, Eddie," Dee snapped.

"It was just *fun*," Eddie muttered.

Kevin led them down to a canteen, pointing out amenities along the way. "Lockers, vending machines, and here's where we eat. Hey, Carrie." He nodded to another officer walking toward them. She glanced curiously at Dee and Eddie.

"Kev, you want anything from McDonald's? I'm hitting the drive-through."

"I'm good, but what about you guys? You hungry?"

"Am I *ever*!" Eddie said dramatically, making both officers laugh.

"Thanks," said Dee. "Maybe a couple of Happy Meals or whatever. With milk." She fished in her pocket and held out a crumpled twenty.

"I think we got this one," the female officer said.

They sat on plastic chairs around one of the lunch tables, and Kevin flicked on the TV.

"Any favorites?" he asked, scrolling through the guide. They settled on a National Geographic special about dung beetles in Africa that roll small balls of poop away from the main dung pile by using the stars as guides.

We could've used one of those suckers in the car on the trip up here, thought Dee, remembering the Grand Canyon and her own poor navigational skills. She watched the repellent little insects scrabbling around in the dung. In spite of herself, she was amazed by them, so small and spiky and soulless, relying on the Milky Way to set them straight. Somehow it was calming, even profound. Eddie was enthralled.

When the food arrived, they were, mercifully, on to another program about antelopes on the African savanna, and they had just finished eating when Officer Crow walked into the cafeteria. The British narrator said in hushed tones that there were lions just over the ridge, so Dee was relieved to be spared the death footage. *Run, little antelopes, keep running.* She stood up and joined Crow at a table by the door.

Dee searched his face for clues, but the hard lines gave nothing away. *What did you find out, you old robot? How much do you know?*

He lowered his bulk into a protesting plastic chair and scraped it up to the table.

"So. I have *not* been able to locate your father. Your home number is not in service."

"Yeah, that happens," mumbled Dee. "Dad probably forgot to pay the bill again." She shook her head. "Clueless. He's absolutely clueless."

"Put out some feelers in Tucson and Yuma," he continued as if she hadn't spoken, "but those will take time. I also had a rather confusing conversation with a young man named Jake at your aunt's place. Seemed to think I was a 'cop,' as he so delicately put it. Your aunt is away. The adults in your family seem to be allergic to cell phones." Officer Crow straightened a napkin dispenser and aligned the salt and pepper shakers on the table. He looked up suddenly at Dee. "Want to tell me anything else?"

"Anything else?" Dee repeated in fake bewilderment, buying time. She shook her head. "There's nothing—"

He cut her off. "Okay, upshot is this: we are Border Services." He tapped the table twice with his thick finger at the words, as though the table itself was proof. "We make our best efforts to ascertain things—in this case, try to contact your father and make sure you and your brother, as unaccompanied minors, have some kind of parental permission to leave the US and come to Canada. *But*," he continued, "when we are unable to move forward, we are obliged to refer the file to the RCMP."

"The RCMP?"

"Royal Canadian Mounted Police."

"The *police*?" Dee said, her heart pounding. "But we haven't done anything wrong!"

Eddie, in the midst of watching the kill, glanced back at Dee over his shoulder. Dee lowered her voice.

"Since when is it a crime to visit relatives? We have Canadian passports. They know we're coming. We haven't *done* anything."

"I got all that," Officer Crow said impatiently. "That's not what I'm saying. What I'm saying is that we have to pass your file on to the RCMP until some adult's in the picture. The rules." He said the last two words clearly and finally. He straightened his papers. There would be no debate.

"But what about here? Couldn't we stay here? Just until we can get hold of Auntie Pat?" Dee loathed the pleading note she heard in her voice. But she was desperate. *Here* felt relatively safe. The police were a whole other ball game. Police were linked with crime and criminals and jail and courts and children's services.

Officer Crow had started shaking his head slowly and mechanically before she'd even finished the question.

I'm really starting to hate you, you frigging robot, Dee thought.

"We have no facilities for—"

"We don't need facilities. This room is good."

He was still shaking his ugly head.

"The rules very clearly—"

Dee cut him off. "Fine, whatever." *Asshole. Rules, rules, rules.* She stood up. "When do we go?"

"Officer Burnham should be here in about"—he looked at the watch denting his wrist—"thirty or forty minutes. The detachment is in Lethbridge, about an hour away, but he was on the road when I talked to him." He gathered his papers and stood, neatly pushing his chair back, pushing his glasses up. "I'm sure he'll get to the bottom of this."

What you don't understand, you miserable old jerk, is that there is no bottom of this. There is just a mucky, messy middle, and we're caught in it.

Dee turned away from him and walked back to Eddie, Kevin and the African antelopes, both the ones that lay dying and the ones that had gotten away.

A short time later there was a burst of laughter from the hallway and loud voices, and a group of men came into the cafeteria. Two border services officers with the same uniform as Kevin, and another officer in a different uniform. This tall balding man with the red face, trim mustache and bow legs must be Officer Burnham from the RCMP. He was finishing a story, the other two looking at him, their faces laughing and expectant.

"...so *I* say, very calmly, 'Mister, assisting a muskrat isn't a crime.'" Laughter. "So we got out some ball gloves from my trunk and shooed the little bugger back into the river." He bent over, eyes and hands wide, as if he was corralling the imaginary rodent.

One of the border services guys turned and called, "Hey, Kev, Gord's here. Obviously."

"Hi, Gord. Good to see you."

"Kevin, nice to see your smiling face again!" He looked past Kevin at Dee's and Eddie's wary faces. "Introduce the old man to your young friends here, will you?"

"You bet. Dee and Eddie Donnelley, this is Officer Gord Burnham."

"Gord. Just Gord," he said.

No, no. Let's not play those games. You're a cop. You're not "just Gord," however much you think that'll make us feel less stressed. You're not our friend.

"Hello, Dee. Hiya, Eddie." Their hands were each engulfed in Gord's big dry hand. He glanced at the McDonald's garbage still littering the table. "Glad to see they did the decent thing and fed you. Kev, you're smarter than you look! Okay, kids, I have to talk to Wilfred for *two* minutes. Then I'll be back, okay?"

"Eddie," Dee whispered, "you should use the bathroom now if you have to. We're driving to another town with Officer Burnham soon."

"In a cop car, I hope! Maybe even with the siren? I gotta ask him about that muskrat. He seems nice, hey?" Eddie said, slipping off the couch.

"Sure." She didn't know. All the laughing and joking didn't fool her—this was a man who could send them straight back to Santacino. But good guy or not, they were going with him. There was no choice. *At least we'll physically be in Canada. Actually in the country, not just teetering in limbo on the border.*

Gord came back with a sheaf of papers in his hand and sat down across from Dee.

"So, Dee, just want to make sure you know that even though I'm—" he looked around "—a *cop*," he whispered, "you're not in any trouble. You and Eddie are just not fitting into the usual boxes we put people in. Wilfred told you that, probably in his tactless, finicky way. So we have to check things out."

Dee nodded.

Eddie wandered back from the bathroom.

"Hey, Eddie, got to tell you something," Gord said.

"What?" Eddie whispered, sidling up to him.

"I have permission, not given to just anyone, let me tell you, for you to run a few laps of these hallways before we take off. Blow off some steam. *If* you want to, of course."

Eddie was already kicking off his boots. He handed his watch to Dee so she could time him. Dee and Gord stood and watched as Eddie flew down the corridors.

"Time check?" he panted as he passed Dee.

"Thirty-one seconds."

That would feel so good. Just to forget everything and to run and run and run. To feel nothing but your bare feet pounding the commercial carpet, rounding the corners, burning off the stress and worry. Sucks being sixteen. At sixteen you don't run down hallways unless you know for a fact that the building is completely, totally empty. Or unless you're Theresa. She had a vivid mental image of Theresa laughing and racing after Eddie, her short arms and legs pumping.

Eddie finished his final lap, and soon Dee and Eddie were in the backseat of the cruiser ("not because you *have* to sit there, *obviously*," Gord said, "but because only Dee could legally sit up front, and it's probably nicer to sit together"). They pulled away from the border services building. The I-15 ended at the border, and they were no longer on an interstate but on a smaller, lower-numbered highway.

Not quite the way I imagined we would enter Canada, thought Dee, looking out the police car window.

"*Welcome to Alberta. Wild Rose Country,*" Eddie read out loud. "Look, a yellow field. A purely yellow field! Are those wild roses? Are roses yellow? Wonder what they're growing that's so *yellow.*"

"That would be canola, Eddie. For cooking oil," Gord said.

As they climbed a hill, Dee looked back over her shoulder. The highway was just one long road, stretching all the way into the horizon, across half a continent, into the southern states. The border station and the signs around the border were the only indications that there was a new country at all—the same landscape stretched in all directions, as far as she could see.

If you took down all the signs, Dee thought, we wouldn't know what was Utah, what was Montana or when the USA turned into Canada. It's just one big chunk of land that we've carved up.

It reminded her of sharing a backseat with Eddie on their early, spontaneous, stressful road trips with Dad, the ones before she could sit up front. "Here's the line, Eddie," she'd say, running the side of her hand back and forth down the middle of the seat. "No, *here's* the line," Eddie would counter, moving it an inch toward her, creating a line of small crescent-shaped indentations with his fingernail. Their father, lost in thought, hadn't appeared to notice their bickering. But next road trip they got in the car and a thick line of duct tape bisected the backseat, exactly equally. On it was Sharpied *The Divine Line*.

"I thought *The Dividing Line* would be kind of boringly overly descriptive," he had explained.

The Divine Line lasted a few summers, then curled up in the heat and was gradually peeled and picked off, leaving behind a long, permanently sticky trail on the beige vinyl that darkened with lint and dirt and hair. A mess, like everything else.

Dee turned to look out the front windshield. *I'm tired of looking back. I'm tired of remembering and trying to figure it all out. Look forward. Look forward to Canada.*

Officer Burnham seemed genuinely interested in their trip up from Arizona, piecing together a fairly accurate picture from Eddie's chatter and Dee's guarded responses. When Eddie told him about refusing a lift from the man in the car when they broke down, Gord boomed, "Good for you! Yep, trust your gut. We got those instincts for a reason. Like animals, right? If you guys *thought* he was a bad guy, he probably *was* a bad guy. Or at least not a *good* guy. Not for sure, but probably."

The radio crackled, and Eddie looked at Dee in thrilled anticipation. Gord listened attentively for a second.

"Nah, somebody else's problem," he murmured.

They entered Lethbridge, passing the longest trestle bridge in the world ("Really? In the *world*?" Eddie stored up this fact, looking at the town with new respect). The highway wound down through a velvety, ridged series of hills that Gord called coulees, then climbed again into civilization.

"I'm going to roll down those hills someday," Eddie said, pointing out the window. "Roll right down to the bottom on that soft green grass." Dee smiled. She remembered feeling like that once. Now she knew the up-close realities of razor-sharp scrub grass and hidden rocks.

At the RCMP detachment, Gord introduced them to the people at the reception desk, and Dee and Eddie followed his bow-legged figure down a hall to his office.

"Have a seat, guys." Gord motioned to a few chairs grouped around a coffee table, slapped his papers on his desk and sighed, running a hand through his thinning hair.

It was a comfortable office, filled with books and framed photos. Gord in a ceremonial uniform, standing with other Gord-like officers. Gord with a horse. Family groupings of Gord with children and grandchildren.

A younger officer walked past the door, looking in curiously.

"See you tomorrow, Gord."

"You taking off already? Slacker! Leaving it all to the grown-ups, eh?" The officer laughed good-naturedly, but Dee thought Gord would be exhausting if you worked with him every day. He wasn't bad, but he was already getting on her nerves.

"Know what?" Gord asked them. "You two don't need to sit here. We got a nice lounge where you could hang, as the kids say, while I make a couple of calls. Hold on." He got to his feet and stumped down the hall, yelling, "Gail! *Gail!*"

As soon as he was gone, Dee got up and darted over to Gord's desk.

"Dee," Eddie hissed, staring at her with wide eyes, "what are you *doing?*"

"Shh. I'm looking at these papers. Which are about *us.* Which are practically ours." She leafed quickly through the pile, peeking at them sideways so as not to disturb them too much. Her heart pounding, Dee flipped through photocopies of their passports, partially-filled-out forms, a missing-children's clearance printout, and came to notes in what had to be border officer Wilfred Crow's neat, cramped, neurotic printing.

Home phone not in service. No cell phone.

Query license plate number.

Query school and children's services Santacino, AZ.

Criminal record check and missing person status negative (underlined twice) on James Edward Donnelley.

Query Mexican authorities.

Query antique sellers, hospitals, morgues—Yuma, Tucson, Phoenix.

The word *morgue* made Dee feel cold. Of course they were considering that, but the word, written out like that, hit her like a slap. *Morgue* was an ugly word, with cold, ugly connotations. She had a sudden, vivid mental image of her father laid out in a chilly room, his face waxy white—

"What do they say, Dee?" Eddie whispered.

"Not much. They don't know much. Looking for Dad."

"Good. That's *good*, isn't it?"

"*Finding* him would be even better."

Before they had left, in the weeks after her father had gone missing, Dee had done some detective work of her own from the pay phone down the street, but she hadn't found any answers. Eventually she'd tried the hospitals. She'd gotten nowhere, no leads at all beyond Jim Dunford's saying he was going to see a man about some teak. After Jim and he separated, James Edward "Jamie" Donnelley had apparently vanished. Maybe the police could have some cop-to-cop talks and find a lead that she hadn't.

"Dee," Eddie whispered. He was standing, pointing urgently at the open door. He had heard the footsteps just before she did. She slipped across the room and was safely back in her seat, rummaging in her backpack, when Gord and another officer came into the room.

"...it's not here, Eddie. Must have left it in the car," she said to cover.

"Oops, we missing something?" boomed Gord.

"Just a pack of mints." She turned to Eddie. "I'll get you some more when we see another vending machine, okay?"

"Sure," Eddie whispered, looking nervously at Gord. *Too obvious, Eddie. Must coach the kid on lying.*

"Well, I can *tell* you where another vending machine is, my friends. In our super-luxurious, exclusive lounge. And Gail here will take you on down there."

"Hi, guys," Gail said cheerfully.

"Gail has three little ones of her own, so she knows all the tricks," Gord warned. "How are the little terrors anyway, Gail?"

"Terrible!" She laughed. "All sick. One stops puking, another one starts. I was so glad to be coming in to work tonight. Like a vacation."

Another long beige hallway with industrial carpet and generic framed prints of Alberta-themed things. The bridge. The mountains. Derricks. Big blue skies and green-and-yellow fields. It eerily resembled the border services offices they had just left. Everything is still repeating itself, Dee thought, rubbing her eyes, exhaustion creeping over her. They turned the corner into an empty, not particularly super-luxurious lounge area. But it had couches and a TV. Gail motioned to a small shelf of DVDs.

"Eddie, any of those worth watching? May as well settle in."

Eddie sprang into action, turning his head completely sideways and running a dirty fingernail over the titles.

"Is there a washroom…?" Dee whispered to Gail. *Why am I whispering? Yes, world, I, Dee, must pee.*

"You bet. Women's locker room is right through there. Do you want to freshen up with a shower or anything? You've had a long drive, I understand, and a car breakdown…"

Gail rummaged in a cupboard. Clothes packed in large, sealed ziplock bags were stacked according to size, gender and season. Gail pulled out a *girl* (*teen*) and a *boy* (*size 6-8*) pack from the *summer* pile.

"Here, we have extra stuff for emergencies. Any of this help you out?" she asked.

Dee looked at the packages, flushing. *Girl (teen)* clothing from a police station. Why would girls need clothes from the police? When theirs were ripped during an assault? When the clothes they were wearing had to be taken as evidence? Dee shied away from the scenarios. She would leave the girl (teen) clothing for the girls who had even bigger problems than she had.

"Thanks," she said, "but I've got my own stuff. I'll take this one for Eddie though"—she peered at the new T-shirt, shorts and underwear—"because he seems to have left most of his clothes in the car." Her grubby little brother stank, there was no getting away from it. He'd worn the same underwear for three days, possibly much longer.

She half-turned to the locker rooms, then hesitated. *Eddie should be completely safe. We're in a frigging police station.*

"Eddie, okay if I..."

"*Kung Fu Panda 2*!" Eddie cried triumphantly, waving the DVD at her. "I've been *wanting* to see this!"

"Pop 'er in," said Gail, smiling. "I'm just going to do some work at this table," she said to Dee. "Not going anywhere."

The locker room was, mercifully, empty. The thought of a shower was irresistible, and Dee grabbed a small towel, locked herself in a stall and stripped down. A two-minute shower, she thought. Two minutes. He'll be fine.

It was one of those showers that drills angrily, almost painfully, at shoulder height and doesn't reach anywhere else. But it was private, and the water was hot. It was heaven. Dee washed her hair twice and scrubbed herself wherever she could reach, cupping the bulleting water in both hands and rinsing her legs and feet. She rummaged in her bag and found a pair of clean underwear and a semi-clean blue T-shirt. The crumpled shorts would have to do. She brushed her hair hard, shoved her perfectly clean feet back into her smelly sandals and bundled up the wet towel.

Eddie was eating Goldfish crackers out of the bag and watching the movie when she went back into the lounge.

"Feel more human?" Gail called.

"Yeah." Dee laughed. "Thanks." She was warm and relaxed as she collapsed on the couch beside Eddie. *For the time it takes to watch this movie, for the whole time Po and the Furious Five are kung fu fighting, I'm not going to worry about where Dad is or what Gord is finding out or what's going to happen to us. Not going to worry at all...*

Gord called Dee over during the movie's last scene.

"Sorry, do you want to finish...?" He gestured to the DVD.

"No, no, it's okay," she said. "Back in a sec, Eddie."

Her heart started to pound as she followed Gord to a table by the window. Darkish outside now.

Is this where our cozy little vacation comes to a screeching, messy end? Is this where good old boy Gord drops his gloves and official RCMP Gord takes over?

"So how's it going? Gail taking care of you?" Gord leaned back in his chair.

"Yeah, she's nice," Dee said, swallowing nervously. *Enough with the small talk, Gord, just tell me...*

"Good stuff, good stuff. Yeah, we got a pretty good crew here."

Dee nodded. *How long is the chitchat going to take?*

"Like family, you know?" Gord clasped his hands together to show how close they all were.

Heartwarming. Would you just frigging tell me...

"So, Dee—" he said, clearing his throat.

Here we go...

"—when's the last time you saw your dad? Can you remember the exact date?"

"Not the exact date, no. It was several weeks ago when he went to antique-hunt in Yuma."

"Several weeks. Like, two? Three?"

"Closer to three, maybe four. Can't get a hold of him? Have you tried my aunt here in Canada?"

"Um-hum. Just a voice mail there." Dee felt a small pang. Even Jake was gone. "Now, I don't want you worrying, you hear? We got calls out. Feelers. We'll track these frustrating folks down. Just take a little time, that's all. Anything else you could tell us that might help?"

Dee shook her head slowly, looking, she hoped, helpful and perplexed. Helpfully perplexed.

"Because we got to have all the facts to do our due diligence—" He broke off as a vehicle screeched into the parking lot. "What the hell—pardon my French—is *that*?"

Dee looked out the window to see what appeared to be a van pull in near the entrance and park haphazardly under a tree. *Is that actually a van? It's an odd shape. An odd texture.* She stared out the window. *The whole thing is covered in grass. A grass-covered van.* Huge bunches of artificial flowers bloomed along the roof of the van and trailed down the back, rustling in the evening breeze.

"What on *earth*," murmured Gord.

A door slammed and a tall figure loped around the back of the van to the detachment's front doors.

"Okay, whatever," said Gord, shaking his head and picking up his pen. "We'll let the folks at reception deal with that one. We get all kinds," he explained.

Oh, no, Gord, Dee thought, almost laughing with relief, you're going to have to deal with this one. Because though she'd never seen that van before, she knew it. She remembered a phone conversation with Auntie Pat from about a year ago.

"He's gone and Astroturfed the van," Auntie Pat had said, referring to Uncle Norm. "Glue-gunned flowers everywhere. You oughta see it, Dee. It's tacky as all hell. Ridiculous. But Norm loves it. He calls it the Rolling Garden. Rolling Wood's Rolling Garden. He says the advertising will be good for business, pay for itself. I told him, fine, whatever. But *I* drive the truck."

Dee grinned, looking out at the Rolling Garden. It was a preposterous vehicle, but Uncle Norm had been right about the advertising. It had made the six o'clock news in Calgary and two national magazines. The Rolling Garden had put Rolling Wood on the map.

But the person who had sprung out of the van wasn't Uncle Norm.

"Gord?" An intercom voice came from the speaker in the police lounge.

"Yep, here," said Gord, rubbing the back of his head.

"Got a young fellow here that says he needs to talk to you *asap*. Name's Jake Matheson."

Jake Matheson, I think I love you. You came. You drove that ridiculous Rolling Garden all the way down here to help us out. Dee sat very still, an absurd feeling of pride and relief flooding over her.

Gord sighed, getting to his feet. "Never heard of him," he said to Dee. Then, louder, to the intercom, "Okeydoke! Coming! 'Scuse me for a minute, Dee."

Dee went back to sit with Eddie. He was smiling, holding both fists to his mouth as he watched a gripping action sequence. Dee grabbed her backpack, ran her brush through her hair and surreptitiously squeezed the last bit of lip gloss out of an almost-flat tube.

"Okay, folks, the more the merrier!" Gord marched back into the room, gesturing to his companion. Jake was probably no more than seventeen, but he was as tall as Gord, an almost-man in a T-shirt and board shorts, his large feet shoved into battered flip-flops.

"This is Jake," Gord said, "who says he knows you."

Jake stood calmly, his hands in his pockets, his eyes

coming to rest on Dee. Was that a *zing!* that passed between them? Even a small one? Dee never knew. Her friend Theresa was a firm and vocal believer in *zing!*—an electric moment of instant attraction.

"It's like—*zing!*—a *shock* that zings through your body just by *looking* at each other. Eye electricity," she had explained to Dee. Theresa was always feeling *zing!* with somebody. Also *buzz!* which was similar but involved touching. Dee had never had a *zing!* moment, other than maybe that time in tenth grade with Dylan Larson, but that had fizzled. Maybe it was only a half *zing!* anyway, a partial one. Because how could you ever know if the other person was *zing*ing too?

"Hey," Jake said. "I think I know *you.*"

"Hi, Jake," Dee said, feeling shy. "Thanks for coming."

It was an odd feeling, knowing the voice but not the face. He had a nice face, dominated by a big bony nose and bright brown eyes and framed by rumpled, shaggy brown hair. *Thank God he's not perfect.* Dee smoothed down her crumpled shorts.

"Eddie, this is Jake. Jake is—" She tilted her head at him. "What are you again?"

He laughed. "Norm's cousin's son. Hal's my dad."

"So, Jake," said Gord wearily, "are there any actual *adults* around that I could talk to in this big extended family of yours?"

"Oh yeah," said Jake, turning to Gord. "I called the guy who runs the general store out at Shuswap where Pat and Norm fuel up and buy their groceries. Caroline, the greenhouse manager, told me where they usually dock. *Anyway*, I left a message with this guy for them to call as soon as they could. Told him it was urgent. He knows them and radioed to some of his friends' boats to look out for their boat. Apparently it's kind of distinctive. Old-style."

"Well, if their taste in vehicles is any indication…" Gord laughed. "Okay, thank you for getting this ball rolling, Jake. We'll have to get you in the force one of these days."

"Everything okay, Dee?" Jake came over to her as Gord turned to confer with Gail.

His eyes had flecks of green in them, she noticed. "They treating you guys okay?" he asked with concern. "I mean, *man*, a cop shop. No fun." He looked around the pleasant lounge uneasily. "Actually, this doesn't look too bad."

Dee felt almost guilty that they weren't in a cell or cuffed or in the process of demanding a lawyer or something. No visible marks of oppression.

"No, they're fine. They've actually been nice. The scary part is just that we're sort of stuck here," Dee said. "They can't get a hold of my dad (*I'll tell you all about that later, Jake*), and they don't know what to do with us. Hey, thanks for trying to track down Auntie Pat."

"No problem. You sounded pretty stressed last time we talked, so I just thought, you know, somehow I could help.

I guess I'll just hang here until Pat calls or gets here or whatever. If that's okay with you."

"Absolutely," Dee said. *Was that too quick, too loud, too needy?* She was appalled to find tears stinging her eyes. She turned away, blinking furiously. It was just such a relief to have reinforcements, support, to be cared about, to be cared for.

Eddie had been watching Jake curiously. "Is there grass *inside* that thing too?" he asked, pointing out the window at the van.

"Like wall-to-wall carpet?" Jake laughed. "Not yet, but I wouldn't put it past Norm. Want to have a look at it, Eddie?" He swung around to Gord and Gail. "We can do that, right?"

Gail took them all outside so that Eddie could fully appreciate the craftsmanship of the Rolling Garden up close.

Eddie trotted ahead of Gail, and Dee found herself walking beside Jake.

"How's Scout?" she asked, remembering the Siamese he was supposed to be looking after.

Jake's sunny face darkened. "Howled the whole friggin' way down here. *Rrrrrraaaaaarrrr. Rrrrrraaaaarrr.* Like, eight million times. *God.*"

"You *brought* him?"

Jake shrugged. "Everyone else was away. I didn't know how long I'd be. Couldn't leave him alone. He's sort of the reason I'm staying there..."

"Well, he's in a carrier, right? Some kind of kennel?"

"He *was* in a carrier. I popped the door open when I parked, so he could stretch his legs. Use his litter. Thought it might shut him up. Was that a bad idea?" he asked quickly, seeing her face.

"It's just—Auntie Pat told me he sort of *sprays* when he's mad…"

"Like, what, spits?"

"Like, pisses…"

"*Shit!*" Jake said, breaking into a lanky jog, fumbling in his pocket for the keys.

Eddie turned to Dee, his face alight. "That is the most hilarious car I ever *saw!*" he said, laughing. "It's like a *hill*! Or a yard! A moving *yard*!"

Jake unlocked the Garden and carefully opened the door a crack. The pungent, distinctive smell of cat pee hit them like a physical force.

"Whoa, what's that *smell*?" Eddie recoiled.

"That smell is a nightmare cat from *hell*, Eddie," said Jake, peering cautiously into the van. "Scout! Scout! Get over here, you. Here kitty, kitty, ki—"

Scout bolted out of the Garden like a streak of gray lightning, darting and crouching in the parking lot, eyes huge and wild.

"You effing little…" muttered Jake, lunging after him. Scout scrambled under a car.

"Shoot," Gail said cheerfully, "that's *my* car. Hope the little bugger doesn't crawl up into the engine." They positioned themselves in a square around the car.

Eddie sat right down on the pavement, peering under the car, talking softly. "You're just scared, aren't you, little buddy? It's okay, it's okay...gooood cat, you're a gooood cat."

Jake grinned at Dee over the top of the car. "He's actually *not* a good cat at all," he whispered. "He's a little *shit!*"

Dee laughed. *Chasing Scout is the most fun I've had in a long time. How pathetic is that?*

Eventually, with a low, long *mrrrroow*, Scout wandered out like all this was no big deal, his tail high and twitching. He rubbed his face against Eddie's shoulder and purred as Eddie pulled him gently into his lap.

"All right," Gail said and sighed. "We should probably head back inside. Cat comes too, I guess. This is becoming quite the odd little party. Better bring his food and litter and a kennel if you have one. And"—she smiled at Jake— "I'd leave the doors open and air that weird sucker out. We're pretty safe here."

We're pretty safe here. Dee considered this as she helped Jake gather Scout's stuff and slide both van doors wide open. *Pretty safe. From criminals. We're safe that way. But otherwise, how safe are we really? It's so nice here, it's hard to remember all the rest of it.*

Are we really safe here, Gail?

Promise?

~~∽⌒~~

My first and hopefully only night at a police station is going pretty well. Feels a bit like a sleepover, other than when we heard that drunk guy being brought in.

Gail, Dee and Jake had found blankets and towels, rearranged furniture and raided snack cupboards and vending machines. Dee and Jake got a couch each, Eddie a loveseat.

Gail set up a laptop at one of the tables and settled in to tackle her "mountain, absolute *mountain* of paperwork." Gord headed home after viewing the unconventional sleeping arrangements.

"The kids are taking over the place! Never had a campout here before." He grinned. "Feel like there should be hot dogs and s'mores!" Eddie told him about the pretend campfire they'd had in the car on the old lady's property on the drive up and had Gord laughing about how she had honked them awake the next morning.

"Oh boy, no kidding? Her front *yard*?"

"Yeah." Eddie laughed excitedly. "Was that illegal?"

"Naah. Depends on who does it and for what purpose. I'd classify that as more of a mistake. I think you guys would've been fine."

"Eddie," said Jake, "I promise you the biggest, realest campfire ever when we get to Pat and Norm's. There's a huge fire pit. Don't mean to brag, but I've perfected the über-s'more—*six* layers of chocolate, marshmallow and graham cracker. Barely fits in your mouth and really gums up the old hands. The s'more, but *way* more."

"Okay, Jake, deal! I bet I could eat four of those things. No, *five!*" Eddie held out his hand wide, shaking it for emphasis.

Dee listened to them, smiling down at the couch she was making into a bed. Please let that happen, she thought. Please let Eddie get to have the monster s'more at Auntie Pat's fire pit.

They finally turned off the lights, and Gail shielded her lamp with a towel. Dee was exhausted but restless. She watched Eddie curl around Scout, and then she lay on her back, staring at the ceiling for a long time.

She was remembering summer at Pat and Norm's house overlooking the greenhouse. Relaxed and open, people dropping in, customers who felt like family friends. Enormous pine trees dotting the property. Flowers, flowers, flowers.

Dee remembered running barefoot down that long sweep of soft grass to the greenhouse parking lot. She remembered the smell of sweet peas that grew in a twisting riot of color along the fence. In her head, she mapped the gravel paths branching off to the office, the greenhouse, the barn-turned-garden-shop that smelled of acrid fertilizer. The memories grew more fragmented: Uncle Norm's crooked front tooth and whinnying laugh, Auntie Pat coming home with an alarming perm that she said made her look "like a chrys*ant*hemum," a tree black with caterpillars, the noise of night crickets, Mom trimming her hair with big kitchen scissors, using a kitchen knife to uproot a dandelion with a long root like a pale carrot, Eddie—bright red and angry—home in a basket.

She remembered walking with her dad to one of Pat and Norm's fields down the road, wandering on the cracked, dry dirt and breathing in the dry, weedy summer smell.

"Might have a house of our own here someday, Dee. When Mom's better," Dad had said. "Maybe build it ourselves. Logs. Or stone." He held out his arms, picturing it vividly. "Wouldn't that be something?"

"Maybe," she'd said uncertainly. Ten years old, already wary of believing him.

Eddie made a muffled sound—part gasp, part sigh. He was sitting up on his loveseat across the lounge of the police station.

"Dee?" he said in a loud, thick sleep-voice.

"Shh, right here."

He came to where she was, crouching over her.

"You okay?" she whispered, grabbing his hand.

"That creeper doesn't know where we *live*, right?" he asked in a slurred rush. This one's easy, Eddie, she thought. *We* don't even know where we live.

"Absolutely not. No way. Don't worry about him. He's in a whole different country. That jerk's gone."

God, if you can't feel safe even sleeping in a police station, where can you feel safe? She hated that Montana man with the fake smile and the shiny face, hated him not only for terrifying them at the time, but for scaring them even when they'd gotten away.

"Yeah, a real *jerk*," Eddie repeated. "A *asshole*. Murph said." She wasn't going to argue or tell him not to swear. He kept standing there, and she began to wonder if he was actually still asleep.

"Look, this couch is probably comfier than that loveseat. It's big. You want to—" She turned on her side, held open the blankets, and he slipped inside, squirming onto his side, back against her. She rested her chin on his hair, her left arm tucked all the way around his bony frame.

"You're safe, Eddie," she whispered. "We're safe."

LETHBRIDGE, ALBERTA

SATURDAY

The light was creeping in around the edges of the blinds when Dee woke up. The station hummed with faint early-morning noises: printers, footsteps in the hallways, the crackle of a police radio, cars pulling into the parking lot. She blinked at the unfamiliar room, eased her arm out from under Eddie's head and sat up. Scout turned his narrow-eyed, impassive gaze toward her from the loveseat he'd had all to himself. Jake was sprawled in a tangle of blankets on the other couch. But Gail was gone, laptop, paperwork and all, her chair pushed in.

Dee heard a creak from over near the window. Somebody else was in the room.

Her head whipped around. There was a tall woman lying back in an armchair by the window, her legs extended, arms crossed over her chest. Her head was tilted away from Dee, on the headrest. She was wearing shorts and walking sandals. Not a police officer. Dee crawled off the couch, trying not to wake Eddie.

"Auntie Pat," she whispered, hardly daring to believe it could be her.

The woman stirred, stretched and opened her eyes.

"Dee!" She struggled to extricate herself from the chair, stood and pulled Dee into a tight hug. "Jeez, good to see you. You got big. Tall."

The relief of having her there rushed over Dee, and she was appalled to find herself crying.

"Shh," Auntie Pat said. "It's okay."

"Sorry, Auntie Pat," she whispered into her aunt's shoulder, rubbing her eyes. "It's just, this is all such a *mess...*"

"Hey, you can always clean up a mess. Cleaned up lots of 'em," Auntie Pat said with a smile.

"This is a huge one. The biggest mess you ever saw."

Auntie Pat led her over to the table and pulled out two chairs.

"Look," she said, her voice low, "I don't know what's happened, where the hell your dad is or why you and Eddie had to drive up here by yourselves. I don't know almost anything, other than Jake's message saying you needed me here ASAP. But we'll sort it out. We just have to get you guys out of here, right?" Dee was so grateful Auntie Pat wasn't a freaker-outer, a crier, a ranter.

"Right."

"Better tell me what you can. While we're alone here."

Eddie and Jake were stirring.

"Dad's *gone*, Auntie Pat. Like, *gone*. I'm scared he's...
He left to antique-hunt weeks and weeks ago, like *six weeks ago*, and Jim Dunford came back but not Dad.
And a social worker came around and started asking questions, and I panicked because she knew something was wrong, and the Johnston kids got separated by children's services, and I had to get Eddie away.
Plus, our passports were expiring, and then we would have had *nothing*."

Dee was breathing hard, blurting everything out incoherently, but Auntie Pat was nodding her understanding, her mouth tight. Dee took a shaky breath to continue and then froze. Noises in the hall.

"I told them we were coming to visit you, and you were expecting us," she whispered urgently. "I said Dad was meeting us up at your place. I thought we should be in Rolling Wood before we tell them he's missing. Otherwise..."

Auntie Pat tapped Dee's leg. A silent message: *Don't worry—that's enough to go on with.*

The door to the lounge opened.

"—so we just got our wires crossed, Dee," Auntie Pat said as though they were in the middle of a conversation, loud enough to carry across the room. "Of course we were expecting you to come up. Just weren't sure when."

"Good morning, all." Gord shouldered his way into the room, carrying a big box from Tim Hortons. Gail came in after him, closing the door behind her.

"Gotta keep this door shut, Gord," she said. "That cat's a runner."

"Oh yeah, the cat," he muttered.

Gord set the box on the table. "Got some breakfast sandwiches, donuts, coffee and milk here. Dig in! Mrs. McPherson! Can't tell you how glad I am to see an adult relation. I'm Gord Burnham. Gail tells me you had quite a trip getting here."

Auntie Pat got to her feet unhurriedly. Dee remembered how unflappable she was.

"Officer Burnham," she said, shaking his hand. "Just a bit of a rush. Got flagged down by another boat, headed to dock, borrowed a car, drove to Kamloops and flew here. I got mixed up on the dates they were coming. Anyway. I'm here now. Looking forward to taking these kids of mine off your hands this morning." Auntie Pat regarded him steadily.

Attagirl, Auntie Pat. You're so much better at this than I am. Over to you, Gord, to say why we can't go. Argue, fight, shout the place down if you have to, Auntie Pat! Get us the hell out of here.

"Well, you and me gotta have a chat about that," he said. "Coffee?"

"Absolutely. Thanks."

"Help yourselves. Back in a second."

Eddie and Jake were sitting up blearily, their hair wild.

"Oh, hey, Pat!" said Jake. "Good, you're here." He smothered a yawn. "Join the cop-shop party!"

"Hey, Eddie," said Dee, "look who came last night. Auntie Pat."

Eddie padded over in just his shorts, leaned against Dee and looked at his unfamiliar aunt.

"Hi, Eddie," said Auntie Pat. "It's been a while since I saw you. You probably don't remember."

"Nope. But I like your crazy van."

Auntie Pat let out a snort of laughter. "So Jake drove that beast down here. I'll tell Uncle Norm you're a fan. I drive a nice truck. Show you when we get to Rolling Wood. How's about some breakfast?"

Eddie and Jake were soon wolfing apple fritters and laughing at a SpongeBob rerun.

Gord came to the door. He shook his head. "Looks like my rec room in here. All right, Mrs. McPherson, let's have a chat in that office there, if you've got a sec..."

"You bet." Auntie Pat got up to follow Gord to an office across the hall. She laid her big chapped hand on Dee's shoulder as she passed her. "Better pack up. We'll be heading out soon."

Dee stood at the door, straining to hear what Gord and Auntie Pat were saying. They'd been in there for ten minutes, and the murmurs had been punctuated by Auntie Pat's deep voice, raised several times. Not shouting, but louder than talking. Determined, emphatic. At one point Dee had heard her bark "*Absolutely* not!" Absolutely not what?

"Everything okay, Dee?" Jake called.

"Oh, yeah, yeah. Just thought I heard something."

"Dee, it's the one where Patrick is a real *jerk*," Eddie said, pointing to the television. "'Member? It's *hilarious*."

"Yeah, that's a good one," Dee said, her mind and ears on the office behind her. *But you know what, Eddie? That talking, pants-wearing sponge and his starfish friend are supremely, irritatingly irrelevant at the moment. And frigging loud.*

She made a sudden decision.

"Be right back," she muttered. She was across the hallway and opening the office door before she'd even really figured out what she was doing. Gail called out to her, but she didn't stop.

Gord and Auntie Pat sat facing each other across the desk. Both had looked up in surprised irritation at the interruption, their faces clearing when they saw who it was.

They got to their feet and spoke at the same time.

"Dee..."

"Everything okay, Dee?"

"No, everything is clearly *not* okay," she said, her voice louder and higher than she'd meant it to be.

"This is about me and Eddie, and I think I have a right to know what you're saying."

"I think Dee's right," said Auntie Pat.

Gord looked at Dee steadily, and she held his gaze.

"I'm not a child," she said. "I'm not just a kid you can throw a donut to while you guys make decisions about me and Eddie."

"Fair enough," he said, gesturing to a seat beside Auntie Pat. "It's okay, Gail," he said to the figure hovering in the doorway. "Dee's staying."

When Dee and Auntie Pat came back into the room, Eddie hopped over to Dee, swinging his arms in big circles.

"Patrick is *so funny* in that—what's wrong?"

"Nothing, nothing. Yeah? It was a great episode, hey?"

"Because it seems like something's *wrong*."

"Nah, just official stuff. No problem. We're taking off. Saying *sayonara* to the cop shop, Eddie."

"Good. With Auntie Pat, right? To her house?"

"Right." She met his high five. *For now, anyway.*

"Well, folks, grab your stuff," Auntie Pat announced. "Time to go home." She scooped up Scout and kicked open the door of his carrier. The cat twisted and flailed as she shoved him in, then protested in a keening wail until Eddie crouched beside the carrier, feeding him tiny bits of egg and sausage.

"God, that cat," Jake muttered, folding a blanket. "That was what I listened to the *whole way down here.*"

Auntie Pat smiled, watching Eddie. "Eddie, we also have two dogs, Rocky and Moose. Outdoor dogs. They've got their own house and everything. They are *supposed* to guard the greenhouses, but spend most of their time sleeping in the sun and getting everyone to pat their fat bellies."

Eddie looked up. "That's a pretty good life for a dog," he said.

"Yeah, they sort of think they own the place. Want to come see them?"

"Rocky and Moose," Eddie repeated. "Why *Rocky*? Why *Moose*?"

Dee was turned away, shoving things in her backpack. Auntie Pat had finally got permission to take them all back to Rolling Wood, after Gord had photocopied every piece of ID she owned and written down every address and telephone number. He'd talked about the missing-person search and temporary guardianship and custody orders. That meant lawyers, that meant money. *I'll have to get over feeling guilty about Auntie Pat and Uncle Norm taking us in. We don't mind sharing a room. Maybe there's a summer job I could do at the greenhouse.*

Thoughts scudded through Dee's head. *Guardianship, custody, whatever. The more legal, the better, the more permanent, the better...I'm scared they won't find Dad...I'm scared they* will *find Dad...I desperately need some new clothes—these aren't even worth packing... Auntie Pat looks so tired...she hasn't made me feel guilty; I'm making me feel guilty...I bet she'd let me and Eddie take the Rolling Garden if we really needed it someday, if we had to get out quick...there's also Murph...and that houseboat out in* BC...

Stop. Dee closed her eyes.

Breathe.

Always waiting for the next disaster, always worrying about what's going to happen. I don't want to live like that. I'm not going to live like that. Right now is pretty good. I will think of right now, of just this moment. She opened her eyes and looked around.

Here, right now, is Eddie, crouching over Scout's kennel, crooning him a little song. Here and now is Auntie Pat, slumped in a chair, laughing with Gail. Here is Jake, leaning on the counter, checking his phone, looking up and catching my eye. Was that a little zing! there?

There's still a long road ahead of us. Not just the ride in that crazy, cat-uriney Rolling Garden either. A longer road than that.

But now is enough. Now might just be everything.

Now, right now, we're heading home.

ACKNOWLEDGMENTS

I am indebted to Sarah "Hard-Line" Harvey for pulling no punches and making this a much better book. Her skill, humor, patience and friendship have meant a lot to me over the years. I am also grateful to my husband, Mitchell, for more than I can list, but in this case for driving endlessly through the desert while I scribbled down notes for this book.

ALISON HUGHES writes for children of all ages and for adults. Her books have been nominated for the Silver Birch, Red Cedar, Diamond Willow and Hackmatack Awards, as well as the Sigurd F. Olson Nature Writing Award. When she's not writing, she presents at schools, volunteers with a family literacy organization and bikes in the river valley. She lives in Edmonton, Alberta, with her husband and children, where her three snoring dogs provide the soundtrack for her writing. For more information, visit www.alisonhughesbooks.com

More <u>BOLD</u> YA from ORCA

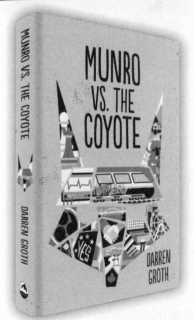